ELIHU ROOT

ELIHU ROOT ON THE DOORSTEP OF HIS HOME IN CLINTON IN 1935

ELIHU ROOT

By

PHILIP C. JESSUP

PROFESSOR OF INTERNATIONAL LAW
COLUMBIA UNIVERSITY

AUTHOR OF
"The Law of Territorial Waters and Maritime Jurisdiction,"
"International Security"
ETC.

VOLUME II
1905—1937

ILLUSTRATED

DODD, MEAD & COMPANY
NEW YORK   MCMXXXVIII

PRINTED IN THE UNITED STATES OF AMERICA
BY THE VAIL-BALLOU PRESS, INC., BINGHAMTON, N. Y.

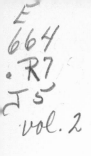
CONTENTS

The chapter titles throughout the book are all quotations from Mr. Root's letters, speeches or conversations.

Volume Two

ILLUSTRATIONS

ELIHU ROOT

PART V—SECTION 2

SECRETARY OF STATE

YEARS 1905–1909
AGE 60–64

CHAPTER XXVII

"The main object of diplomacy"

OF all the important matters which Root handled in the Department of State, those involving the Far East were least distinctively his own. Again it is necessary to say that in many such cases, probably no one can ever know whose ideas first prompted a given line of action. "Probably Roosevelt would have been shocked to discover how little foreign policy he himself created. There was left to him little but to follow the paths which McKinley, Root, and chiefly Hay, had thought out and projected." [1] The biographer of Hay puts his adverb before Hay; biographers of Roosevelt have become dominated by the obtrusive personality and egocentric recollections of their own subject. Yet Roosevelt frequently and generously recognized his debt to Root. One can at least say of Root that he had Roosevelt's ear throughout the presidential period, that he never hesitated to speak into it and that the President was quite ready to listen, perhaps partly because Root never let himself get into the position of a rival for glory. When one reads the sixteen pages on "Roosevelt's Conduct of Foreign Affairs" which Root wrote as a foreword to the eighteenth volume of the memorial edition of Roosevelt's works, one looks in vain for the slightest reference to Root himself or for any indication that Roosevelt had a Secretary of State who assisted him in conducting foreign affairs; even Hay escapes mention. "I never attempted to remember what I had done or what part I had taken in particular things," Root once said. "I considered it of no consequence whatever. I never made notes or kept a diary." [2] Yet much of what Root wrote about Roosevelt is autobiographical: "He did not think of the international situations which demanded action as being mere occasions of the moment, but he treated each situation . . . as an incident to a national course of conduct . . . and he always acted under a strong sense of obligation

[1] Dennett, *John Hay*, p. 349.
[2] Root to the author, November 3, 1934.

3

to make the conduct of America tend toward her own peace and the peace of the world. . . . His kindly consideration for the feelings of other countries was especially marked in his treatment of the questions arising between the United States and Japan."

Root had no particular grandiose schemes which he wanted to put through. For him, "to keep the country out of trouble . . . in the right way, is the main object of diplomacy." [3] There were details, like the new slant given to our relations with Latin America, the reorganization of the State Department's foreign service, the promotion of arbitration and others, but Root does not seem to have considered these as more than means to the general end. Particularly in regard to the Far East, he found a situation in which lines of policy had already been clearly laid out—Hay's reiteration of the open door in China, and Roosevelt's attitude toward Japan. When Root took over Hay's portfolio, Roosevelt had firmly and completely in his own hands the negotiations for terminating the Russo-Japanese War. "He *kept* them in his hands." [4] He talked to Root about some of the details. The Peace of Portsmouth had been signed when Root got back from his fishing trip in Newfoundland in September, 1905, and there remained the problem of sustaining friendly relations with the victorious country which had convinced the world that it could whip a great western power and which felt bitterly cheated by not receiving a large indemnity from Russia. [5] On that point, Roosevelt had talked with Root and Root had "a positive opinion" that Japan was not entitled to one. [6] But apparently neither Roosevelt nor any other western statesman realized at that time that Japan's request to Roosevelt to mediate [7] was inspired by the perilous situation of the Japanese forces in Manchuria. [8]

Roosevelt was personally quite willing to have the United States join the Anglo-Japanese alliance but realized that it was politically impossible. [9] A good deal of fuss has been made about the "unofficial alliance" which Taft was supposed to have arranged with Count Katsura,

[3] Root to St. Loe Strachey, September 9, 1905.
[4] Root to the author, September 13, 1932.
[5] Abbott, *Japanese Expansion and American Policies*, pp. 58 ff.
[6] Root to the author, September 13, 1932.
[7] Dennett, *Roosevelt and the Russo-Japanese War*, pp. 281 ff.
[8] See Kuropatkin, *The Russian Army and the Japanese War*, Vol. I, pp. 230 ff.; Ishii, *Diplomatic Commentaries*, pp. 69 ff.; *Secret Memoirs of Count Hayashi*, p. 230.
[9] Dennett, op. cit., p. 115.

the Japanese Premier, on July 27th, 1905, just eight days after Root took the oath of office as Secretary of State and two weeks before the renewal of the Anglo-Japanese alliance which recognized Japan's special position in Korea. Roosevelt had asked Taft to stop in Japan on his way to the Philippines. His party included Alice Roosevelt and they were given an overwhelming reception in Tokio where the official party was lodged in the Shiba Detached Palace and paid the unprecedented compliment of being the first foreigners ever to be admitted to the Imperial Garden.[10] Taft sent a long cable to Root on July 29th describing in detail his interview with the Japanese Premier. Count Katsura assured him that Japan had no aggressive intentions regarding the Philippine Islands. He recognized the impossibility of securing Senatorial consent to a treaty of alliance with Japan but Taft assured him that the United States agreed in policy with Japan and Great Britain. On the subject of Korea, Count Katsura insisted that Japan must have a free hand. Taft agreed that the establishment of Japanese suzerainty over that country was the logical result of the war and that, while of course he spoke only for himself, he was sure that President Roosevelt shared this view. The substance of the text of Taft's telegram was first made known in an article by Tyler Dennett in *Current History*, October, 1924. Taft's name was not mentioned and the whole transaction was clothed in an air of exciting mystery. Roosevelt's latest biographer, Pringle, asserts, "This was not a casual interview arranged on the spur of the moment," and quotes Roosevelt's reply to Taft on July 31st: "Your conversation with Count Katsura absolutely correct in every respect. Wish you would state to Katsura that I confirm every word you have said." [11] But Pringle does not, although Dennett does, quote Taft's apologetic explanation with which he closed the cable to Root: "Prime Minister quite anxious for interview. If I have spoken too freely or inaccurately or unwisely I know you can and will correct it. Do not want to butt in but under the circumstances difficult to avoid statement and so told the truth as I believe it." [12] While there is no question about the interview or Roosevelt's endorsement of it, it seems quite clear that the declaration was not made in pursuance of any previous instructions from the Presi-

[10] Despatch No. 293 of August 1, 1905 from Tokio, Archives of the Department of State.
[11] Pringle, *Theodore Roosevelt*, p. 384.
[12] Taft Papers, Library of Congress.

dent. Root was on his way to his vacation in Labrador and Newfoundland and at the time knew nothing of Taft's cable or of Roosevelt's
reply.

In any case, Taft's conversation with Roosevelt's confirmation lined
up the Japanese-American policy which Root inherited. In so far as
Korea was concerned, the cards were played and Root could not have
saved her from Japanese absorption except by persuading Roosevelt to
repudiate his promise to Japan that she should have Korea as part of
the peace settlement; [13] Japan's "paramount interests" in Korea were
recognized in Article II of the Treaty of Portsmouth. On November
9th, 1905, the Japanese Legation in Washington confidentially informed Roosevelt that they had decided to take charge of Korea's foreign relations [14] and on the 16th, with Japanese armed guards around
his palace, the Korean Emperor finally signed Japan's terms. A week
later, after a conversation with the Japanese Minister, and as a friendly
gesture to Japan, Root instructed our Legation at Seoul that it was to
withdraw from Korea since thereafter Japan was to be the medium
for conducting the foreign relations of Korea. The Korean Legation in
Washington transferred its archives to that of Japan and Korea passed
out of the family of nations. When the former Korean Minister to
France called at the State Department unofficially on December 11th
to make known his opinion that Japan had extorted the treaty from
Korea by force and to request the aid of the United States, he could
get nothing but a refusal. It was true that our treaty of May 19th,
1883 with Korea had provided, with ironically reciprocal obligations,
that "If other powers deal unjustly or oppressively with either government, the other will exert their good offices . . . to bring about an
amicable arrangement." But times had changed and the Korean treaties of February 23rd and August 22nd, 1904, with Japan, were invoked
to show that "Korea gave to Japan such extensive control over her
affairs and put herself so completely under the protection of the
Government of Japan as to render completely impossible the application of the provisions of the treaty with the United States. . . ." [15] It
would have been noble to try to snatch Korea from the lion's mouth
but it was not practical politics or practical diplomacy; Root was a very

[13] Pringle, op. cit., p. 383.
[14] Archives of the Department of State.
[15] Departmental Memorandum, December 18, 1905, ibid.

practical man. Moreover, in such matters, his views were what is called "imperialistic." On February 26th, 1916, he wrote to Senator Lodge: ". . . it was better for the people of Korea, who were not governing themselves, to be incorporated in the liberal and progressive constitutional Empire of Japan than to remain the puppets of their absurd, old opera bouffe emperor." He came to feel differently about the government of Japan in 1931.

Before Root entered the State Department, the anti-Japanese agitation was already full-fledged in California. The problem of oriental immigration was at the base of it. At the time of the Burlingame treaty of 1868 with China, cheap coolie labor was desired in the United States for the construction of the transcontinental railroads and that treaty encouraged Chinese immigration. The influx of Chinese, however, soon raised disturbing economic and social problems which were partly met by the treaty of 1880. Since the migration was not checked, Congress proceeded, in disregard of treaty obligations, to suspend the admission of all Chinese laborers. China grudgingly acquiesced in the situation by the treaty of 1894 and in 1904 Congress made the ban permanent. Meanwhile, the increase in arrivals of Japanese laborers began to arouse additional concern in California. "The real question in California with which we have to deal is undoubtedly this question of labor competition," Root told the Japanese Ambassador.

Our laborers on the Pacific coast find in the Japanese laborers who have come to this country, not merely a degree of physical vitality, of industry and adaptability for the various occupations in which they are engaged which makes the Japanese laborer a formidable competitor, but also a degree of economy and frugality in living which makes the Japanese laborer practically certain to drive out the American laborer if admitted to competition. The American laborer, therefore, naturally wishes to prevent competition. It might be more appropriate to say that the basis of that opposition is an admission of the Japanese laborers superiority than to say that it is an assertion of the Japanese laborers inferiority. The attempt to exclude Japanese from the ordinary public schools in San Francisco, and also the boycotting of the restaurants, and the assaults upon Japanese in the streets both of which I am glad to believe have now ceased are but symptoms of this undelying [sic] opposition to a successful labor competition.

In aid of this opposition the labor organizations have sought to create and stir up race antagonism. This is an expedient which has been used under similar circumstances countless times in many countries where laborers have been threatened by the competition of foreign labor. . . .[16]

Root on another occasion explained this situation to the Chinese Minister who inquired, "Then you would exclude us for our virtues?" "Exactly so," Root told him.[17]

In November, 1904, the American Federation of Labor's annual convention, meeting in San Francisco, favored applying the Chinese Exclusion Laws to the Japanese. On February 23rd, 1905, the San Francisco *Chronicle* published a nine column article on the perils of Japanese immigration. The article bore fruit almost at once in an anti-Japanese resolution passed unanimously by both houses of the California legislature. March 10th, 1905, the Labor Council of San Francisco, led by Olaf Tveitmoe, a laborer of Swedish extraction who had served a prison term for forgery, formed the California Exclusion League which became an active body.[18] In April, 1905, there had been tentative moves looking toward the segregation of Japanese children in the San Francisco schools. Although the Japanese Government and Japanese Red Cross contributed more than all the other foreign nations combined for the relief of the sufferers from the San Francisco earthquake in April, 1906, the anti-Japanese feeling and activity grew constantly in intensity. In searching for new homes after the great fire, the Japanese invaded "white" districts. There were boycotts of Japanese stores and restaurants, assaults on individuals, window smashings and other outbreaks of hoodlumism. Roosevelt was greatly irritated. He admired the vigor and vitality of the Japanese people and had a healthy respect for their fighting qualities.[19] He was insistent that the American fleet should be built up and kept up as a safeguard against them, but got impatient with the Californians who made trouble between the two countries. Root seems to have had more understanding of the Cali-

---

[16] Root to Ambassador Aoki, quoted in Root to Wright, January 16, 1907, Archives of the Department of State.
[17] Root to the author, September 6, 1930.
[18] Buell, "The Development of the Anti-Japanese Agitation in the United States," *Political Science Quarterly*, December 1922, p. 605.
[19] Dennett, *op. cit.*, p. 161; Bailey, *Theodore Roosevelt and the Japanese-American Crises*, p. 91.

fornian point of view, but not much less annoyance at their methods. Root probably again spoke for himself when he said that Roosevelt "sympathized fully with the insistence of the people of our Pacific coast States that their territory should not be taken away from them through peaceful invasion by a multitude of foreign laborers whose habits of life and industry were such that Americans could not compete with them in production. . . ." [20] Quite naturally, Root's interest was in keeping the United States out of trouble with Japan. In his mind the national concern was paramount to the local feeling in California. The problem was to find a solution which the Japanese Government would accept and which would make reasonable concessions to the just complaints of the Californians. The troubles came to a head with the passage on October 11th, 1906, of an order of the San Francisco Board of Education providing for the segregation of the Japanese children in the public schools. Japanese feelings were of course deeply hurt; it was an humiliating blow to a national pride which was at its crest. The blow was not softened by the fact that separate schools for the Chinese already existed in San Francisco; the Japanese were feeling and asserting a superiority over other Asiatic peoples.

Root, working closely with Roosevelt, tried to pour oil on the troubled waters. He telegraphed Luke Wright, the American Ambassador in Tokio, that the whole trouble was so much a local affair that the federal government knew nothing about it until they received reports of the reaction in Japan.[21] Wright was to explain this fact to the Japanese Government and to assure them that the United States Government would not stand for any discrimination. San Franciscans, indeed, scarcely noticed the order of the School Board because they were absorbed in the Heney-Burns investigation of their municipal administration, which, four weeks later, led to the indictment of "boss" Ruef and Mayor Schmitz for bribery and embezzlement.[22] October 25th, the Japanese Government made its formal protest against the "stigma and odium" of the segregation order.[23] They were reassured by Root's cable to Wright which was published in Tokio and by Roosevelt's statement on the 26th that Secretary of Commerce and

[20] Root, "Roosevelt's Conduct of Foreign Affairs," Foreword to Vol. XVIII, The Works of Theodore Roosevelt (Memorial Edition, 1925), p. xix.
[21] Root to Wright, October 23, 1906, Archives of the Department of State.
[22] Buell, loc. cit., p. 623.
[23] Archives of the Department of State.

Labor Metcalf was being sent to California, his native state, to investigate the situation. Root brought the matter up in a Cabinet meeting where the President insisted it was a matter of grave national concern.[24] The gravity with which Root and Roosevelt viewed the situation is indicated by the confidential memorandum which Root prepared on Roosevelt's direction for Secretary Metcalf as he was leaving for the west coast. Root stressed the proud and sensitive nature of the Japanese people. He believed that Japan was efficiently equipped for war while the United States was not; the United States would continue to be at a distinct disadvantage until the Panama Canal was completed. He appreciated the fact that there was much resentment in Japan over the terms of the peace treaty with Russia by which the Japanese felt they had been deprived of the legitimate fruits of victory. Root went on to say that Japanese hostility against us "would result in enormous injury, if not the entire destruction of our trade in the Orient. . . . What will be the effect upon the trade and the prosperity of San Francisco and the Pacific Coast?" The exclusion of Japanese children from the schools and the boycotting of Japanese restaurants on the sole ground that they were Japanese, "constitute a clear violation of our treaty with Japan," and even if it were not, it was "intrinsically unfair and indefensible." "The San Francisco attitude towards them is an exhibition of the same provincial and uninstructed narrowness and prejudice which the Japanese abandoned when Commodore Perry convinced them of its folly. . . . The Government of the United States can not and will not submit to being forced into an unjust quarrel . . . by the action of a few ignorant, narrowminded and prejudiced men who wish to monopolize for themselves the labor market of San Francisco. The entire power of the Federal Government within the limits of the Constitution will be used and used promptly and vigorously to enforce observance of treaties which under the Constitution are the supreme law of the land, and to secure decent treatment for the people of a great and friendly power within the territory of the United States." [25]

Roosevelt was about to leave for an inspection trip in Panama. On October 29th, before leaving, he wrote a formal order to the Secretary of State:

[24] Strauss, *Under Four Administrations*, p. 217.
[25] Archives of the Department of State.

During my absence in Panama I direct you if necessary to use the armed forces of the United States to protect the Japanese in any portion of this country if they are menaced by mobs or jeoparded in the rights guaranteed them under our solemn treaty obligations.[26]

His private correspondence is filled with anxiety over the whole situation.[27]

Meanwhile, the judicial process was set in motion to protect the treaty rights of the Japanese. Root corresponded at length with the Attorney General, and United States District Attorney Devlin in San Francisco assumed an active role. As soon as Secretary Metcalf reached San Francisco, he had a special conference with the justices of the California Supreme Court who were quite willing to co-operate by entertaining an agreed case which would be decided by them on the day of its submission.[28] But favorable court action seemed to be dependent upon the inclusion in the Japanese treaty of a "most favored nation" clause—a standard provision which extends to the nationals of one treaty country the privileges accorded to any other nation which has a treaty covering the same subjects. Metcalf and the United States Attorney were unable to discover such a clause in the Japanese treaty, and the former telegraphed Root to advise them. Root was absent from Washington, but Adee wrote a memorandum for Bacon showing that such a clause existed in Article one; he suggested that the matter should await Root's return, which it did despite the anxious messages from Metcalf. It was not until November 13th, after Devlin had also written the Attorney General, that Root sent the latter a full argument on the subject, sustaining the right of the Japanese to schooling on equal terms with other aliens, on the theory that educational privileges were among the "rights of residence" guaranteed to the Japanese on the most favored nation principle.[29] An agreed statement of facts for the test case was finally drawn up and Root passed upon it.[30] He also urged the Attorney General to see to it that the case was submitted in such a way as to permit an appeal on writ of error to the Supreme Court of the United States.[31]

[26] Roosevelt Papers, Library of Congress.
[27] See Bailey, op. cit., pp. 80 ff.
[28] Metcalf to Roosevelt, November 2, 1906, Archives of the Department of State.
[29] Archives of the Department of State.
[30] Root to the Acting Attorney General, December 20, 1906, ibid.
[31] Root to the Attorney General, December 24, 1906, ibid.

In the meantime, Roosevelt, in his Message of December 3rd, 1906, had devoted a good deal of attention to the whole Japanese situation, as he had promised Baron Kaneko he would.[32] He urged the passage of a law which would permit their naturalization. He called also for legislation which would enable the President to enforce the rights of aliens under treaties. Referring specifically to the exclusion of Japanese children from the schools, he called it a "wicked absurdity." [33] This Message, which stressed the solidity of the friendship between Japan and the United States, had a very soothing effect in Japan where it was widely printed in the press, but it naturally stirred up the Californians.[34]

On January 30th, 1907, Roosevelt conferred with the entire California delegation in Congress, Root and Metcalf being also present. The Californians were induced to back the Administration, which they did by telegraphing the school authorities in San Francisco and Governor Gillett, urging that no anti-Japanese steps be taken pending negotiations, and extending an invitation from the President to the Superintendent of Schools and the President of the Board of Education to come to Washington for a conference. The California State Senate had just passed an anti-Japanese resolution and Roosevelt was becoming convinced that the feeling on the Pacific coast was a fact, no matter how disagreeable, which he had to face. It appears that he failed to understand that Ruef's corrupt control in San Francisco was a stench in the nostrils of most Californians and that Ruef was cleverly attempting to win some sympathy by posing as the champion of the state against federal interference. The two school officials were quite ready to accept the President's invitation but Mayor Schmitz of San Francisco apparently saw a chance to get a little more glory for himself which might have the desirable result of easing off the prosecution in pressing the five indictments for bribery and embezzlement which the grand jury had returned against him.[35] The Board of Education was still under his thumb and an exchange of telegrams with Washington finally resulted in an invitation from Roosevelt to the entire board and the mayor. Had the city of San Francisco not been under the con-

<hr>

[32] Roosevelt to Kaneko, October 26, 1906, Roosevelt Papers, Library of Congress. Quoted in Bailey, op. cit., p. 81.
[33] Foreign Relations of the United States, 1906, Part I, pp. xl ff.
[34] Bailey, op. cit., p. 94.
[35] Ibid., pp. 124 ff.

trol of the corrupt Ruef-Schmitz administration at this period, it is possible that the chain of events would have been different [36] but the basic issue would have been the same.

The party arrived in Washington on February 8th, 1907, in the midst of another violent war scare in the press which was stimulated by a belligerent speech from Senator Perkins of California. Root and Roosevelt immediately began a series of conferences with the visitors from California. It was impressed upon them that their problem was not a local one but one that involved the whole country, with peace and war hanging in the balance. They were also told of the negotiations which were already under way for an agreement with Japan relative to the limiting of immigration. The strong argument was that the federal government would see to it that immigration was restricted if the San Franciscans would eliminate the sore spot of discrimination in the schools.[37] Root had cabled Ambassador Wright on January 16th:

> If we can represent to California labor leaders that their action stands in the way of international agreement to relieve them from pressure of labor competition, I think we can get settlement of school question.[38]

At all the conferences, Root sat at the President's left with a pencil in his hand. When the President got excited and began to threaten, Root's pencil would click on the big mahogany table and there would be an immediate halt in Roosevelt's vehemence.[39] They were all sworn to secrecy and Root, with his usual light touch, suggested that they all become charter members of the "Clam Club." The compromise formula upon which they agreed was that all alien pupils would be permitted to attend the schools if they knew English and fitted into the age limits of the various grades. Children who could not meet these tests were to be segregated in special schools. By making the qualifications applicable equally to all aliens, the obnoxious discrimination against the Japanese was removed. The Californians "understood and went home and behaved themselves admirably," although one of them caused embarrassment by talking too freely to a news-

[36] Buell, loc. cit., p. 637.
[37] Roosevelt, Autobiography, p. 380. Root to the author, July 26, 1934.
[38] Archives of the Department of State. Quoted in Bailey, op. cit., p. 141.
[39] G. G. Weigle in San Francisco Examiner, February 15, 1925.

paper correspondent. Years later, when Root stopped at the Fairmont Hotel in San Francisco, they called upon him: "They exhibited no clammish propensities then. They were a nice lot of fellows. I liked them." [40]

"The subject of the exclusion of laborers is acquiring a new interest in my mind," Root wrote Mr. Justice Holmes on March 6th, 1907:

> The struggle of the laborer to protect himself against the labor competition of an alien race, which he is unable to meet successfully, is to be classified with the struggle of the Boers to protect themselves against the political encroachment and predominance of the more alert outlanders, and with an effort which is now going on in Haiti on the part of the citizens of the Black Republic to protect themselves against the business competition of foreign traders whom they are at this moment trying to exclude. The whole subject of peaceful invasion by which the people of a country may have their country taken away from them, and the analogy and contrast between the swarming of peaceful immigration and business enterprise and the popular invasions by force of arms in former times, such, for instance, as those overrunning the Roman Empire, are most interesting. [41]

To fulfill their promises to the Californians, Roosevelt and Root were devoting themselves to attempts to solve the immigration problem. It would, of course, have been possible for the United States to settle the domestic problem by passing an exclusion law; Japan never questioned the principle of international law that every state is free to regulate immigration as it sees fit. This right was recognized in the treaty of 1894 between the United States and Japan. The trouble was that on top of the discriminatory measures in California, any exclusion law would have been so obviously aimed at the Japanese that international ill-feeling would have been intensified. The time had passed when such a law could have been passed with some face-saving device which would have enabled the Japanese Government to acquiesce in it. The agitation of relatively small groups in California was largely responsible for making that solution bad diplomacy for an administration which had a wholly justifiable though actually erroneous

[40] Root to the author, July 26, 1934.
[41] Archives of the Department of State.

conviction regarding Japanese power and war-like propensities. It was good diplomacy to attempt to secure limitation by agreement.

By a law of 1896, reenacted in 1901, Japan had forbidden its nationals to emigrate without special permission. In 1900, the Japanese Government had voluntarily assumed the obligation to refrain from issuing passports to Japanese laborers bound for the mainland of the United States. It was therefore in Secretary Hay's time that Japanese immigration was first limited by a "Gentlemen's Agreement." [42] This first attempt failed because passports were issued by local Japanese officials who could be influenced by companies promoting emigration and because there was no limitation on passports for Hawaii whence the companies brought the laborers to the mainland. One of the great difficulties which Roosevelt and Root had to overcome was the fact that Hawaiian interests favored Japanese immigration as much as Californian interests opposed it. The Japanese had poured into Hawaii and the American business men there were emphatic in asserting that their businesses, especially sugar, would be ruined if Japanese immigration were cut off. Root and Roosevelt apparently had no objection to maintaining a reasonable supply of Japanese labor in the islands, although Roosevelt had been worried about their increasing numbers.[43] The trouble was that Hawaii was being used as a stepping stone to the mainland and, under the existing law, the federal government could not prevent the immigrants from passing from one part of American territory to another. To meet that situation, Roosevelt and Root proceeded to push through Congress an amendment to the then pending immigration bill. The amendment gave the President power to exclude from the continental United States any aliens who carried passports issued for travel to the islands or to Canada or Mexico. Such a law had been suggested by Ambassador Wright in his despatch of December 26th, 1906.[44] Root had been careful to explain in advance to the Japanese Government the purpose of this legislation and had assured its cordial reception in that quarter.[45] Root had also explained the effect of the provision to Senator Lodge when he sent him a draft of it on February 11th:

[42] Bailey, op. cit., Chapter I.
[43] Ibid., p. 7.
[44] Archives of the Department of State.
[45] Root to Ambassador Aoki, quoted in Root to Wright, January 16, 1907, ibid.

You will perceive that from the Japanese point of view all that the President will be doing under such a provision will be to enforce the limitations that Japan herself puts into her passports, while, from our point of view, the provision will enable the President to keep Japanese laborers out unless Japan undertakes to force them upon us directly, which she is apparently far from wishing to do. Indeed, the fact that the Japanese laborers are coming indirectly by way of Hawaii and Mexico and Vancouver shows that they are unable to get direct passports to the United States.[46]

The amendment of course did not specifically mention Japanese laborers but no one was deceived as to its object. The bill with its amendment passed on February 18th, 1907, and the road was further cleared for definitive arrangements with Japan. Root followed up in a letter to Senator Lodge on February 23rd:

I enclose the proposed clause for a small appropriation to enable the President to enforce the Japanese proviso of the immigration act. The proviso is described in the same terms which are used in the final clause of the act.

You will perceive that the terms used in the clause as I have drafted it construe the grant of power to the President as mandatory, something which he is bound to do if he finds the described conditions exist, and not as something which he is merely to do or not as he pleases. I think it is well worth while to get this clear legislative construction for the purpose of meeting some of the arguments that were made against the provision during the passage of the bill. I have no doubt of the construction of the original statute, but if Congress clearly says what the construction is, nobody else can have any doubt. With this view the precise language of the proposed clause is of importance.

It was not only the Hawaiian sugar interests, however, which favored Japanese immigration. The American railroad companies, by advertisement and personal agents, solicited the arrival of Japanese laborers in the United States. March 26th, 1906, James J. Hill, President of the Great Northern Railroad Company, wrote to Ambassador Takahira that they were already employing over 1200 Japanese laborers and could use three to five thousand more on the Great Northern

[46] Archives of the Department of State.

and Northern Pacific. The friendly attitude of cooperation between the Japanese and United States Governments is indicated by the fact that the Japanese chargé replied to Hill that they were doing everything possible to limit the immigration of their laborers in the interest of better relations between the two countries.[47] But the railroads continued to advertise in the newspapers of California and Hawaii and their agents continued to point out to prospective immigrants how easy it was to get from Hawaii to the mainland. Even the large California fruit growers protested against legislation which would exclude Japanese labor. Those who blame the Japanese Government for not restricting the flow of emigrants must realize the share of the blame borne by these American interests. The Japanese Government also had its analogous problems in seeking to control the agencies which were drumming up immigrants and shipping them off to the United States, leaguing with steamship lines and lodging houses to keep up a business which they found highly profitable and which operated in total disregard of private or public welfare. Both governments labored incessantly and with a sincere determination to remove this impediment to friendly relations. The feeling on the Pacific coast and the attitude of American labor were far more potent influences with the Roosevelt Administration than the demands of big business for cheap labor.

Root explained his tactics in a letter to Mr. Justice Holmes on March 6th, 1907, amplifying a conversation which they had had on the previous evening:

> You will perceive that I was trying to get Japan herself to propose the exclusion of laborers, as the course least likely to create bitter feeling among the mass of Japanese against this country and with that purpose I treated the subject as a matter of Japanese policy, putting fully as much stress on some expressions of theirs as they would bear. Japan would undoubtedly have taken the course of herself proposing the exclusion as soon as the insulting assertion of inferiority involved in the San Francisco school resolution was removed, had it not been that in attempting to get that removed we were obliged to explain the situation to the official representatives of California here, in confidence, with the result that some of them immediately rushed off to the news-

[47] Memorandum of Secretary of Commerce and Labor Oscar S. Strauss, January 4, 1907, *ibid.*

papers and published the whole affair with much exaggeration and distortion.

As the matter stands now, we have got the objectionable School Board resolution rescinded, or an agreement to rescind it, and we have got authority from Congress to do the thing that Japan suggested to us; that is, enforce the limitations of her passports against laborers coming from Hawaii to the mainland; and we are in a position to go on and negotiate a treaty when the excitement has died out a little more, if a treaty is found to be necessary. The two Governments can now, acting together, completely regulate immigration, and they appear to be in entire harmony on that subject.[48]

Although Professor Bailey, seems to find the details of the conclusion of the Gentlemen's Agreement shrouded in mystery,[49] the process of the negotiations is perfectly clear. The Gentlemen's Agreement is not embodied in any one formal document, but the policy which goes by that name was worked out in a series of exchanges of messages. The Japanese Government originally rejected the idea of a treaty for the limitation of the immigration of laborers because, for obvious reasons, it would be necessary to draft such a treaty in reciprocal terms; Japanese opinion, fully aware that no American laborers were entering Japan, would not accept a solution so one sided in fact.[50] The Japanese Government, however, saw no great difficulty in arriving at some informal arrangement whereby the immigration of coolie labor would be stopped.[51] When this suggestion reached Root, he proposed to Ambassador Aoki:

. . . a new treaty providing for exclusion of laborers and for most favored nation treatment in schools. . . . [Root seems to have been bothered lest the courts decline to follow his interpretation of the old treaty.] We think it desirable that this should be proposed by Japanese Government rather than by ourselves but are willing to propose it if they prefer. Without some such arrangement we can see no escape from increased excitement and condi-

[48] Archives of the Department of State.
[49] Bailey, op. cit., p. 166. The "essential terms and practice" of the Gentlemen's Agreement were summarized by the Japanese Ambassador, Hanihara, in his note to Secretary of State Hughes on April 10, 1924; Hearings before the Committee on Immigration, United States Senate, 68th Cong., 1st Sess., on S. 2576. March 11, 12, 13 and 15, 1924, p. 167.
[50] Ambassador Wright to Root, January 23, 1907, Archives of the Department of State.
[51] Wright to Root, February 1, 1907, ibid.

tions growing worse rather than better, to an extent making position of all Japanese on Pacific Coast quite intolerable in ways that no Government can control directly. One result of these conditions would undoubtedly be a statute excluding Japanese laborers. This action is permissible under the treaty of 1894, but it would be most unfortunate if there is to be exclusion, not to have it by mutual consent.[52]

It was this plan which had been communicated confidentially to the "Clam Club" and which some of its members had unclammishly given to the press.

The publication of these stories in Japan aroused great opposition because the Japanese people believed they already had most favored nation privileges in regard to schooling. The Japanese Foreign Minister accordingly countered with a suggestion that exclusion of laborers be granted in exchange for naturalization of Japanese in the United States.[53] Root replied with the argument that the existing treaty probably would not be violated if California provided separate schools for the Japanese and that it was this possibility which could be eliminated by a new treaty. "It is wholly useless to discuss the subject of naturalization at the present time. If right exists under the act of June twenty-ninth nineteen hundred six discussion is unnecessary. If not it is clear that no statute could be passed or treaty ratified now extending Japanese rights beyond the limits of their contention regarding the schools." [54] On the same day, the Japanese Foreign Minister informed Wright that the Japanese Cabinet approved the treaty proposal which he had informally advanced, bargaining exclusion against naturalization.[55] On February 12th, Wright cabled that he had had a confidential chat with Denison, the American who long served with great distinction as adviser to the Japanese Foreign Office. Denison suggested that in lieu of the naturalization concession, Japanese opinion might be satisfied by an agreement on the part of the United States to relinquish its commercial treaty rights in order to enable Japan to conclude a customs union with Korea, permitting free trade between the two countries.[56] This suggestion "favorably impressed" Roose-

---

[52] Root to Wright, February 1, 1907, *ibid.*
[53] Wright to Root, February 4, 1907, *ibid.*
[54] Root to Wright, February 6, 1907, *ibid.*
[55] Wright to Root, February 6, 1907, *ibid.*
[56] *Ibid.*

velt.[57] On February 19th, Root informed Wright of the revocation of the School Board order and the passage of the new immigration law giving the President power to control the influx of Japanese from Hawaii. "Express to the Government of Japan informally our hope that she will withhold issue of passports for United States mainland to laborers skilled and unskilled and our wish to proceed with negotiations for treaty." [58] The Japanese Foreign Minister, Hayashi, promised to send Wright a note, giving such assurance regarding passports for the mainland.[59] The promised note was repeated by cable from Wright to Root on the 24th:

> The Imperial Government in response to the hope expressed in the telegram from the Honorable the Secretary of State a paraphrase of which was handed to Viscount Hayashi by his Excellency Mr. Wright on the twentieth February beg to state that they have no intention of cancelling or modifying the order now in force under which no passports are granted to either skilled or unskilled Japanese laborers for the mainland of the United States other than settled agriculturists, farmers owning or having an interest or share in their produce or crops. The Imperial Government confidently believe that a strict adhesion on their part to the foregoing order coupled with the continuation of the existing practice of inserting in all labor passports the destination of the laborers will be sufficient to make the new legislation of the United States more satisfactorily [sic] and obviate the necessity of adopting additional measures. If on the contrary that belief should not be realized the Imperial Government will be prepared to consider with the United States the question of a new treaty.[60]

Nearly two months later, on April 17th, Root instructed Wright that the exception of the agricultural class would cause difficulty and that "we are satisfied it is very desirable to go on with the making of the treaty providing for the exclusion of laborers." [61] Viscount Hayashi, however, "greatly feared the effect of such negotiations at this time." He agreed with Root that the excitement over the school mat-

[57] Root to Wright, February 14, 1907, *ibid.*
[58] *Ibid.*
[59] Wright to Root, February 21, 1907, *ibid.*
[60] *Ibid.*
[61] *Ibid.*

ter had subsided but "feared that to reopen the matter now would be like applying match to powder." Wright was convinced that this attitude was due to the fact that the Japanese cabinet was not at all firm politically and expected a hard fight in the next elections. It was already being criticised for lack of aggressiveness in handling the San Francisco school problem, and the voluntary negotiation of a treaty which was clearly designed to benefit the United States would offer more ammunition to their political opponents.[62] At this point the negotiations were interrupted by a new outburst in California and the Gentlemen's Agreement was not concluded until some five months later.

The new troubles were merely further indications of a condition. The Californians were still dissatisfied. Many of them who had no part in the efforts of Ruef and Mayor Schmitz to advertise themselves, were incensed at federal interference in what they considered purely state affairs. Such local feeling is by no means uncommon in the United States. The California Assembly on February 28th passed a bill limiting land ownership by Japanese and Chinese and on March 6th a bill was reported in the California Senate to exclude from the schools in the same grades with white children, Japanese over ten years of age.[63] March 10th, Roosevelt wrote Root to come in to see him about the threatened action of the California Legislature:

> I am convinced that it has been a mistake on our part not to take open action before this. Perhaps an open letter from me to Governor Gillette will accomplish the result. We can communicate by telegraph if necessary. If we let things drift we may get in a very bad situation. Of course we can always refuse to restrain the Japanese immigration; but while this will treat the San Franciscans just as they deserve, it will not solve the situation but on the contrary will make it worse. We should not longer delay. If necessary Metcalf and Flint can be brought in to talk with us.

Root at first thought it would cause "less public fuss" if they did not meet until the next day, but later on the same day he wrote that he would come that evening after all. He wrote a telegram to Mayor Schmitz and submitted it to Roosevelt. "I don't like to have you tele-

---

[62] Wright to Root, May 15, 1907, *ibid.*
[63] Bailey, *op. cit.*, p. 169.

graph him but he ought to be stirred up for he practically guaranteed the legislature. Did you ever see such idiots?" [64] Root's telegram read:

Legislative action reported in morning papers appears to be repudiation of arrangement made here. Is this understood and intended. It will probably deprive recent exclusion legislation of Congress of all effect and defeat efforts of National Government to secure exclusion of Japanese laborers by friendly agreement which has seemed certain to be accomplished. If object of California legislature is to bring about such exclusion it is taking the surest way to defeat its own object. I sincerely hope the legislation will not proceed further.[65]

That evening he and Roosevelt drafted a letter from the President to Governor Gillett which was followed by a series of letters which show marks of Root's aid in drafting. Schmitz replied to Root that "Nothing further will disturb peaceful carrying out of our arrangements. Command me further." [66] Governor Gillett also fell in line and another crisis was passed. On March 13th, the Board of Education rescinded the troublesome discriminatory order and on the following day Roosevelt ordered the test case dismissed and by executive order put into effect the regulations contemplated by the amendment to the immigration bill.[67]

The next complication began with a mob attack on a Japanese restaurant and bath house in San Francisco on May 20th, 1907, the police affording no adequate protection. The Japanese press was aroused although Root assured Wright that these were not anti-Japanese outbreaks but merely disorders incident to the street railway strike in San Francisco. Nevertheless, on May 25th, 1907, Root, on the President's orders, sent a vigorous telegram to Governor Gillett, calling his attention to the reports and to the protests of the Japanese Consul General. He called upon the California authorities strictly to enforce and protect the treaty rights of the Japanese, veiling a threat of federal action in assurances of a conviction that the local authorities would take adequate steps.[68] Roosevelt "arranged to have plenty

---

[64] Root to Roosevelt, March 10, 1907.
[65] Archives of the Department of State.
[66] Ibid.
[67] Bailey, op. cit., p. 176.
[68] Archives of the Department of State.

of troops in the neighborhood." [69]

As usual, Root was able to keep his relations with Aoki on a friendly and confidential basis. June 7th, 1907, he wrote to Roosevelt:

> The enclosed copy of a letter just received from Aoki will show you that so far as the two governments go this San Francisco affair is getting on all right as an ordinary diplomatic affair about which there is no occasion to get excited. All the trouble is being made by the leprous Vampires who are eager to involve their country in war in order to sell a few more newspapers. [70]

One detail designed to promote this friendly spirit was the fact that Root had the Attorney General instruct United States Attorney Devlin to assist the Japanese authorities in their damage suit against the city. The suit was eventually compromised through Devlin's efforts, for the mutually satisfactory sum of $450. [71]

Despite Root's reassuring message to the President, the opposition leaders in Japan began openly to call for war, probably more as a political move to harass the party in power than because of any really deep-seated hostility to the United States. [72] The Californians supplied them with ammunition; late in June the San Francisco Board of Police Commissioners refused licenses to six Japanese employment bureaus. Roosevelt wrote to Root on July 2nd in great exasperation: "I see that a new San Francisco fool has cropped up to add to our difficulties with the Japanese." Root was trying to mend his health in Clinton and Roosevelt wrote him there on July 13th:

> I am more concerned over this Japanese situation than almost any other. Thank heaven we have the navy in good shape. It is high time, however, that it should go on a cruise around the world.

He was equally indignant with the yellow press, which kept insulting the Japanese, and with the members of Congress who followed the same course but voted against Roosevelt's bills for increasing the navy. Root replied on the 21st:

> . . . What I feel & think about it is not fit to write. Apparently nothing will disturb the smug satisfaction with which San Fran-

[69] Roosevelt to Henry White, June 15, 1907, quoted by Bailey, op. cit., p. 199.
[70] Roosevelt Papers, Library of Congress.
[71] Bailey, op. cit., p. 200 and Archives of the Department of State.
[72] Bailey, op. cit., pp. 201 ff.

cisco officials pursue a policy of insult and irritation sure to land us in war, except some explicit official statement pointing out the inevitable result of their conduct. Probably that would not. . . .[73]

Root reported also that Ambassador Tower in Germany confirmed the rumors that the European foreign offices were convinced that Japan and the United States would soon be at war. Roosevelt replied two days later:

In France, England and Germany the best information is that we shall have war with Japan and that we shall be beaten. My own judgment is that the only thing that will prevent war is the Japanese feeling that we shall not be beaten, and this feeling we can only excite by keeping and making our navy efficient in the highest degree.[74]

Roosevelt's determination to send the fleet around the world was partly inspired by the Japanese crisis, but it was influenced also by his long-standing idea that a practice cruise was necessary and that while peace prevailed, the navy should acquire experience in moving from the Atlantic to the Pacific. The cruise might have aroused the Japanese jingoes but as a matter of fact they took it very calmly and this venture of Roosevelt's turned out to be a great success.

It was a bad summer for Root with his attempts at recuperation interrupted by the Japanese and other worries. On August 23rd, Roosevelt sent Lodge "a very rough draft of a memorandum relating to Japan which I have thought of putting into my annual message or of using in some way in connection with Japan. Root has been so under the weather this summer that it has not been possible for me to consult with him in any of these matters." [75] Roosevelt may have feared that he was to renew with Root his experiences with Hay as a more or less chronic invalid Secretary of State. But Root never wrote plaintive letters about his health. On September 25th, he wrote to Roosevelt just before leaving on his trip to Mexico:

. . . I have had a perfect nightmare of a summer and my poor brother's condition which had many distressing features & my

[73] Roosevelt Papers, Library of Congress.
[74] Ibid. American naval opinion did not share the view that Japan was ready for war; see statements quoted in Tupper and McReynolds, Japan in American Public Opinion, p. 43.
[75] Roosevelt-Lodge Correspondence, Vol. II, p. 278.

own entirely new experience in the way of health. However it is over & I am in good condition & ready for the next round. . . .

I find many things amusing . . . the fix the British press is in over the Vancouver [anti-Japanese] riots. I think Loeb must have sent some one there to make the demonstration & relieve our Japanese situation. It is not logical but it is certain that the strain is off. I had a talk with Aoki the other day & without a word being said the atmosphere was different. The Attorney General by my request has instructed the District Attorney in San Francisco to explain to the new [city] Government [which had come in as a result of the elections] the true bearing of the license refusal & urge the granting of licenses & my telling Aoki that made him happy.[76]

As a matter of fact, despite Root's poor health, Roosevelt had written him frequently during the summer, especially about the Japanese troubles. He kept asking Root what to do about the license matter and reminded him that he had plenty of troops ready in case the local authorities could not put down any further riots.[77] He awaited Root's advice on the advisability of Taft's stopping off in Japan.[78] He wanted his view on a suggestion for sending extra mortars to fortify the Philippines.[79] On August 2nd, he sent him the draft of a speech he was to make at Provincetown with a request for its very early return. This letter finally brought a reply from Root on the 8th which began: "I don't think my intellectuals are worth much at present but I have been over . . . the speech & return it."

. . . We can talk the Japanese situation over much better than we can write about it. On the whole I am convinced that our European friends are over excited. I think the tendency is towards war—not now but in a few years. But much can be done to check or divert the tendency.[80]

On August 13th, Root went to Oyster Bay where the Japanese situation was thoroughly discussed with Secretary of War Taft and George Meyer, the Postmaster General. Meyer wrote in his diary:

[76] Roosevelt Papers, Library of Congress.
[77] Roosevelt to Root, July 26, 1907.
[78] Ibid., July 29, 1907.
[79] Ibid., July 31, 1907.
[80] Roosevelt Papers, Library of Congress.

The Japanese situation was thoroughly canvassed. Japan, it is believed, has made some arrangement with Colombia as a base, in case of war with us. Root thinks we must from now on show a courteous but firm attitude to Japan, or else she will misunderstand and think that we are afraid of her. . . . The President reported that Sternburg [the German Ambassador] had been to see him and announced that the Emperor authorized him to say that in case of trouble with Japan, they (Germany) would furnish us with a base of supplies.[81]

After Root returned to Washington, Meyer had a talk with him on September 22nd:

He said he felt that the President at one time this summer really considered a Japanese attack imminent or liable. He [Root] had not anticipated one, for the following reasons: their financial condition and their desire not to be considered barbaric in the eyes of Western civilization if they should commence war without a proper pretext or one that would justify them in the eyes of Europe and England. If, later, that should be found before the Canal was completed, their first act after taking Hawaii, which would not be difficult, would be to seize the Canal and then offer to build, or complete it rather, as an international canal, which would find approval with Europe and demolish the Monroe Doctrine. Japan's advances to Colombia and the appointment of a minister point to the idea of a possible base of supplies in case of need.[82]

Root devoted himself to his task of checking or diverting the tendency toward war. At the Oyster Bay conference on August 13th, it was agreed that Taft should again visit Japan on his way to the Philippines but should not initiate any conversations unless the Japanese wanted them.[83] Taft arrived there on September 28th and was impressed with a reception which was in some ways more remarkable than that which greeted him two years before—"not because there was so much popular demonstration, but because there was an evident desire on the part of the Japanese Government to indicate that they had no desire for war." [84] The Japanese officials were quite ready to talk

[81] Howe, George von Lengerke Meyer, p. 365.
[82] Ibid., p. 370.
[83] Taft to Charles P. Taft, August 18, 1907, Taft Papers, Library of Congress.
[84] Taft to Charles P. Taft, October 10, 1907, ibid.

and Taft reported his conversation on October 18th in a lengthy cable which cost over $1000, explaining rather apologetically that he waited several days before sending it because the direct cable had been broken and if he had sent it at once it would have cost $3400. Taft talked first with Count Hayashi, the Foreign Minister, and later with Count Saionji, the Premier. In answer to Count Hayashi's question, Taft said there was nothing in the rumor that we would sell the Philippine Islands. On the subject of immigration, Hayashi stated that the Japanese people in general had little interest in the question but Taft reported that there were business interests concerned with supplying coolie labor and that these interests had political influence. Taft was convinced that a treaty for the control of immigration was impossible at the time but that the Japanese Government was quite ready to restrict the flow of immigrants by administrative action. He was also sure that "Japanese government is most anxious to avoid war; they are in no financial condition to undertake it." He believed they were determined to dominate China and that the Chinese were looking more and more to the United States "as the only country that is really unselfish in the matter of obtaining territory and monopolies." He pointed out that Japan was having in Canada also the same sort of immigration problem with her ally, England, and that this made her doubly anxious to introduce an effective system of control.[85]

It was this report which finally convinced Root and Roosevelt that a treaty was out of the question, and Root proceeded with his negotiations, in the "courteous but firm" manner which he had told the President was now necessary. The first step was an instruction of November 9th, 1907, to O'Brien who had succeeded Wright as Ambassador to Tokio. Root built up his case as if he were making notes for argument in court. The Ambassador was told to warn the Japanese Foreign Minister that "it is quite certain that an attempt will be made in the impending session of Congress to obtain exclusion legislation under the provision of the closing paragraph of Article II of our treaty with Japan whereby is reserved to each country the right of legislation concerning the immigration of laborers from the other country." This attempt would be supported by three considerations. First, the influx of Japanese laborers which differed wholly from "that usual and casual travel and residence contemplated in the treaty" and

[85] Archives of the Department of State.

which was injurious to the American workmen. Second, the fact that Japan herself had recognized the exclusion principle by barring Chinese and other foreign labor; Root had carefully compiled the data on this point many months before. Third, the general provisions of the immigration law of 1907 barred contract laborers from all countries of the world and this provision was clearly violated by the Japanese immigration companies. Root believed that the pressure for legislation could be forestalled only by demonstrating the effectiveness of the voluntary restrictions enforced by the power which the President was given under the amendment to the immigration law to exclude Japanese coming from Hawaii. Unless Japan could reverse the existing trend which showed over twelve thousand Japanese arrivals in the United States within the last twelve months—nearly double the number during the preceding year—the legislation was certain to be passed.[86] Three days later, Root sent a copy of this instruction to Ambassador Aoki in Washington, enclosing a compilation of statistics on Japanese arrivals.[87]

On November 18th, Root sent O'Brien a further telegraphic instruction in which he pointed out again that the Japanese measures had not succeeded but added that since it was understood that the Japanese Government was

> averse at this time to making the matter of immigration the subject of further conventional agreement, although discouraged by the complete failure of the administrative measures hitherto taken, still, in deference to the attitude of the Japanese Government and believing that there is no real divergency of policy in the premises, this Government invites Japan to join in fresh efforts adequately to meet the situation. . . .[88]

This instruction may properly be considered the first part of the Gentlemen's Agreement. O'Brien, however, misconstrued his instructions and urged the conclusion of a treaty because he had been told by a Canadian Commissioner who was then in Tokio that a similar informal arrangement with Canada had not been successful.[89]

On the 22nd, Root sent another specific instruction:

[86] *Ibid.*
[87] *Ibid.*
[88] *Ibid.*
[89] O'Brien to Root, November 20, 1907, *ibid.*

Refrain from any further suggestion of treaty. . . . Maintain hereafter an attitude of entire indifference whether the adoption of such regulations [as specified in his former instruction] by Japan is or is not accompanied by a further treaty.

He told the Ambassador to stress the fact that the desire for effective regulation was by no means inspired by anti-Japanese feeling but was "purely an economic question" of labor competition, precisely similar to that which Japan's ally, England, was experiencing in British Columbia, New Zealand and Australia. The British Empire analogy was pointed because of the Vancouver riots on September 7th, 1907, where a huge mob, irritated by the veto of a provincial exclusion bill, had attacked Orientals and damaged their property. The United States had felt the more free to press for this action on the part of the Japanese Government "because we have understood from the beginning that it was the policy of Japan to turn the direction of Japanese emigration rather towards the continent of Asia than towards America, so that for different reasons both countries have from the beginning desired to accomplish the same result." [90] O'Brien immediately acted as instructed and received a most favorable reception.[91]

The Japanese Government seems to have been sincere in its effort to make this policy successful. "Of course," Root wrote Roosevelt on August 1st, 1908,

performance is the only real test of sincerity. I think, however, that we must not be too extreme in our expectations of perfection in the working of a new system of repression on the part of the Japanese—a system in which, however good the faith of the Government may be, they cannot, in the nature of things, have the really hearty cooperation and sympathy of the great body of Japanese officials. Naturally a little time must be necessary to make such a system work satisfactorily. We ourselves have had many illustrations of the difficulty of doing things through unwilling subordinates. Time and patience and persistency will doubtless be necessary, but I am sure that the subject is being dealt with in the right spirit and in the right way, and that if what is now being done does not obviate further legislation on our part, it will create a situation where there can be further legis-

[90] Ibid.
[91] O'Brien to Root, November 27, 1907, ibid.

lation with infinitely less offence to Japan than would have been
the case a short time ago.[92]

Root's nature was admirably adapted to a policy of patience and he
constantly resisted suggestions from Roosevelt and some from Huntington Wilson that he should stiffen his tone to the Japanese Government. Slowly, very slowly, the statistics, anxiously scanned month
after month by the President and Root, began to show improvement.
When a new government took office in Japan in July, 1908, it promptly
gave assurances that the policy of regulation and restriction would be
continued. In the following month, when its attention was directed
to the practice of importing "picture brides," it immediately sought
to control this new situation, although its efforts were not wholly effective. In January, 1908, the Japanese arrivals in the continental United
States were only 495, as against 1359 in January, 1907. Two weeks before Root left the State Department, it was reported that in December,
1908, only 126 Japanese arrived on the mainland and of these, 62 were
returning residents and relatives. In the same month, 812 Japanese left
the United States for Japan and 195 left Hawaii, as compared with 174
arrivals, of whom 151 were in the relative or returning resident classes.
There was smuggling of aliens across the Canadian and Mexican bor-
ders and there were cases of Japanese who secured passports from the
Japanese officials through fraudulent representations, but the real weakness of the Gentlemen's Agreement lay in the breadth of the exceptions
which were permitted. The United States agreed that Japan might issue
passports to former residents, to parents, wives or children of residents
and to those who already had agricultural interests in the United
States.[93] Roosevelt and Root apparently thought that the situation
would be met if merely coolie labor were excluded, although Root had
at first objected to the exception in favor of agriculturists. Apparently
the agreement did check the influx of coolie laborers, but even the moderate increase of the Japanese population of the United States which
was permitted through the admission of other classes and increased by

[92] Roosevelt Papers, Library of Congress.
[93] *Report of United States Secretary of Commerce and Labor*, 1908, p. 14. *The Four-
teenth Census of the United States Taken in the Year 1920*, Vol. III, pp. 15 and 106,
shows that the Japanese population of the United States increased from some 24,000
in 1900, to 72,000 in 1910 and 111,000 in 1920. During the same period the Chinese
population decreased from nearly 90,000 in 1900, to 62,639 in 1920. The relative figures
for California are similar but even more striking.

the number of American-born Japanese, kept the issue alive and the people on the Pacific coast dissatisfied because the Japanese continued to acquire the choicest agricultural lands and to best native American competitors by "under-living" them.

In retrospect, it seems curious that the American Government was apparently not aware of the experience which the Australians had had in dealing with Japanese immigration, although the diplomatic correspondence had been published fully.[94] That experience was instructive; it revealed the difficulties and frictions resulting from attempts to operate under a Gentlemen's Agreement which was basically similar to that which Root later negotiated with the Japanese Government. It also cast interesting sidelights on the point of view of the Japanese Government and demonstrated that exclusion through the application of a language test could be enforced without straining relations too much.[95] The Australian agreement further revealed the fact that Japan was quite willing to have "exempt" classes of Japanese limited to merchants, tourists and students. If the United States had also insisted on Japan's limiting the issue of passports to these three classes, the American settlement might well have proved to be an acceptable and final one. The Dominion of Canada also had a Gentlemen's Agreement, made at the same period, which limited the number of passports to be issued by the Japanese Government to four hundred a year. In 1924, the year in which the American Congress refused to apply the quota system to Japan, that country agreed with Canada to limit the passports to only one hundred and fifty a year. It must be recalled that the British Dominions carried on their negotiations largely through the British Foreign Office which was in a most advantageous bargaining position when dealing with Japan because of the conclusion of the Anglo-Japanese Alliance on January 30th, 1902. The position of the United States was further complicated by the aggressively independent attitude of the Californians, who naturally sought to protect their interests and who distrusted the Japanese Government. Yet the Canadian Government had much the same trouble in British Columbia. In January, 1908, Sir Wilfrid Laurier, the Canadian premier, sent

[94] See especially Queensland *Parliamentary Papers* (1899) A.5; *ibid.* (1901) A.56; Commonwealth of Australia *Parliamentary Papers* No. 41 (1901); A.15 (1901); No. 2 (1901); No. 61 (1905).
[95] The subject is fully analyzed in an unpublished manuscript by Dr. E. Cyril Wynne under the title, "The White Australia Policy and Japan, 1896–1905."

MacKenzie King, then Commissioner of Labor, to Washington to talk with Roosevelt and Root about the general immigration problem. Root, then in the midst of his rapprochements with Canada, told the American Embassy in London that it was hoped the British and American Governments would work together for "a judicious and effective treatment of this subject by Japan." [96] In a personal letter to Roosevelt, King Edward on March 5th, 1908, assured the President of his confidence in Anglo-American cooperation and in the successful functioning of the British agreements with Japan regarding immigration.[97] But the British Ambassador in Tokio rejected the overtures of his American colleague, fearing lest joint British-American action should "have a bad effect with the Japanese." [98] Roosevelt wrote Laurier expressing great appreciation at the frank exchange of information resulting from MacKenzie King's visit,[99] but it is not clear whether King disclosed to the Americans the documentary evidence which he had discovered in Vancouver of the Japanese Government's complicity in the evasions of its assurances that it would restrict the immigration of its subjects.[100] In any event, there is no evidence that Root distrusted the Japanese Government, although perhaps Roosevelt, and certainly many Californians, did so. It seems probable that after King's visit to Washington and London, the British Government used its influence with Tokio to urge that the Gentlemen's Agreements with the United States and with the British Dominions be faithfully performed.

Although Root constantly kept the Governor of California informed regarding the progress of the negotiations with Japan and the results of the agreement, the whole matter received insufficient publicity and probably the people on the West Coast were not fully aware of what the federal government was accomplishing. Had the Gentlemen's Agreement been publicly presented to them as the equivalent of a treaty providing for the exclusion of laborers, the popular reaction might have been different. Root had always been careful to inspire news-

[96] Root to John R. Carter, February 6, 1908.
[97] Bishop, Theodore Roosevelt and His Time, Vol. II, p. 269.
[98] Gooch and Temperley, British Documents on the Origins of the War, Vol. VIII, pp. 457–458.
[99] February 1, 1908, Roosevelt Papers, Library of Congress.
[100] Based on information from the Laurier Papers in the Canadian Archives in Ottawa, contained in J. M. Callahan to Root, June 10, 1935, and Callahan to the author, May 19, 1938; cf. Callahan, American Foreign Policy in Canadian Relations (1937), p. 497.

paper publicity by letters to his many newspaper friends in regard to many matters in both the War and State Departments. The reason for his not doing so in this instance was probably the fact that the statistics for a long time were not sufficiently spectacular to warrant a press campaign. Moreover, the process was such a gradual one that there was no specific event which could be heralded in the papers.

Upon signing a commercial treaty with the United States on February 21st, 1911, the Japanese Government formally declared its intention to maintain the control of immigration.[101] Japanese exclusion continued to be a political issue in California through the unhappy days of May, 1924, when Congress committed "one of the most unpardonable sins in the conduct of foreign affairs—acting in a moment of irritation." [102] Stirred by the unfortunate phrase "grave consequences" in a note from Japanese Ambassador Hanihara to Secretary of State Hughes and aided by Senator Lodge who had once been a tower of strength in supporting Roosevelt against the passage of a similar law, the Senate passed the exclusion law which is still in effect and which, in Root's opinion, totally reversed the friendly trend of relations between Japan and the United States. "I think it very unfortunate," Root wrote to Wallace M. Alexander on June 9th, 1924, "and of course, it is a little more unfortunate for the Pacific coast than for any other part of the country." But California labor, veterans and other groups—not including the chambers of commerce—think differently and were pleased that, as they thought, Japan's bluff had been called.[103] It may be noted that even the law of 1924 admits students, merchants and tourists, the three classes exempted under the Australian Gentlemen's Agreement. These later stages of Japanese-American relations can not be discussed in detail here but one may note in passing that in 1935 a dispute regarding the way in which Japanese cotton cloth was flooding American markets was adjusted by a "gentlemen's agreement," under which Japan restricted exports of cotton cloth to the United States.[104]

[101] Foreign Relations of the United States, 1911, p. 319.
[102] Root to the author, September 6, 1930.
[103] Cf. V. S. McClatchy to Root, May 24, 1921.
[104] Department of State Press Release, December 28, 1935, p. 581.

CHAPTER XXVIII

"A quiet, firm maintenance of our position."

THE Gentlemen's Agreement described in the last chapter would have been impossible in an atmosphere of unfriendliness between the two governments. Root was fully aware of this and took other steps to consolidate friendly relations. Despite the continuous howls of the jingo press and the dismal prophesies of experts and European foreign offices, neither government was anxious for war, although both Roosevelt and Root in 1907 considered it a very real and dangerous possibility. "I have always felt confident," Root wrote to Ambassador Whitelaw Reid on September 3rd, 1908,

> that the Japanese Government wishes to keep on friendly terms with the United States. . . . I am sure that they have not been trying to pick a quarrel with us and that no person of intelligence would do many of the things that they have done if he wanted to quarrel. I did think a year and a half ago that there were forces at work here which might bring the two nations into conflict at some time in the future. I think those forces have been very materially checked, but they may become active again. In the meantime, however, I think both Governments and most leaders of opinion in both countries are sincerely desirous of peace for a variety of reasons. Both Governments are certainly doing everything they can to make the conditions favorable for peace. . . .

The principal instrument in these further steps was the Root-Takahira Agreement of November 30th, 1908. It is not clear whether the inspiration for this move came from Roosevelt, from Root, or from the Japanese Ambassador Aoki; it seems probable that the last deserves the credit. On October 25th, 1907, four weeks after Taft's second visit to Tokio, Aoki had lunch alone with President Roosevelt. On his own personal responsibility, he outlined a "declaration of friendly intention" by the United States and Japan.[1] Roosevelt opened

---

[1] Undated departmental memorandum by Willard Straight, written about November 11, 1908 and Despatch No. 34, November 3, 1907 with enclosures, Archives of the Department of State, give the whole course of these negotiations.

the conversation by saying that he understood the Ambassador had some idea to meet the current situation in which rumors of unfriendliness were receiving wide currency. Aoki said that his idea was that a solemn mutual declaration could be made in terms sufficiently explicit to inspire public confidence. He suggested that such a declaration should dissipate the foolish idea that either country sought an exclusive control of the Pacific, that there should be an expression of mutual respect for the territorial rights of each other and a reiteration of the principle of the integrity of China and the Open Door. Roosevelt was in hearty agreement, but the Japanese Foreign Office promptly squelched the Ambassador. The Foreign Minister said there was no question about Japan's concurrence in the policies outlined but that the public declaration of these principles was wholly uncalled for and ill-advised, because it would lend unfounded support to the prevalent popular idea that a grave situation did exist and was being met in this way. Ambassador Aoki was shortly thereafter recalled and Takahira was sent back to Washington in his place.

It was at a dinner given by one of these ambassadors that Root mastered a minor difficulty in international relations. As the guest of honor, he took out to dinner the wife of the Japanese Ambassador. "I soon discovered she could speak no English and I knew I could not say a word in Japanese. After we got settled at the table, it of course needed the starting word of a hostess to begin everyone talking, and she could not do it. I thought about it for a few minutes and then I realized that it didn't make any difference what I said as long as I gave the appearance of talking. So I started speaking Japanese, thirty to the second, talking and laughing as hard as I could. It was instantly catching as I had thought and everyone started talking. She talked and laughed too, and seemed to understand what I was trying to do." [2]

The next step in the inter-governmental negotiations came a year later when a new cabinet was in power in Japan with Baron Komura in the Foreign Office and Count Katsura, who had had the conversations with Taft, as Prime Minister. Whether or not the matter was first discussed informally by Root and Takahira, who were on terms of very friendly intimacy, does not appear, but on October 26th, 1908, the latter handed to the President a proposed form of declaration very

[2] Mr. Root to Mrs. Edward W. Root, February, 1936.

similar to that which Aoki had suggested. This time it had the approval and authorization of the Japanese Government. After a conversation with Root, Takahira transmitted the same form of declaration to him on November 7th. In regard to the first point raised in Takahira's draft, Root suggested in a note of November 11th that:

> The fact of asserting a firm resolve to preserve intact our own territorial possessions might be regarded as indicating the existence of some question on that subject which, of course, has never existed and there is in our case a possibility of misunderstanding which I am desirous to avoid. Many of our people are desirous that at some time in the future more or less complete autonomy shall be given to the Philippines. A declaration of our firm resolve to preserve intact our possession of the Philippines might be construed as a declaration negativing that contingency. I hardly think that the value of such a declaration would be great enough to counter-balance such a possibility of misunderstanding.[3]

Root therefore suggested as a substitute:

> They are accordingly firmly resolved scrupulously to respect the territorial possessions belonging to each other.

This was the phrasing used in the final text of the agreement, except that the word "scrupulously" was replaced by "reciprocally."[4]

The second point in Takahira's draft was designed to cover China and the Open Door policy which it had been Hay's chief interest and triumph to promote and to which Japan had lent apparent support in her recent treaties with England, France and Russia. Willard Straight, who, after extended experience in the Far East, was then the American Consul General in Mukden, promptly called attention to the fact that the draft omitted any reference to the "territorial integrity" of China which had been mentioned in Japan's other three treaties. Straight warned that the United States "which originally enunciated the policy of the 'Open Door,' is so far definitely committed . . . to the support of the *territorial integrity and administrative entity* of China that subscription to a declaration which did not confirm its former expressions would be a severe blow to American prestige in the

---

[3] Archives of the Department of State.
[4] *Foreign Relations of the United States*, 1908, p. 510.

Orient, a prestige attained largely by adherence to this very principle, and our consent to the omission thereof would be interpreted as a sign of weakness and surrender on the part of this Government." Straight was suspicious of Japanese activity in Manchuria and Korea and undoubtedly believed that Japan had intentionally omitted the words to which he called attention. Root accordingly suggested to Takahira that there be added to his wording: "and to exercise their influence to maintain the territorial integrity and administrative entity of China, in accordance with the policy frequently declared by both of them." He wrote the Ambassador that he was "inclined to think that without some such clause both countries might be regarded as having abandoned that position, which, of course, neither of us wishes to do."

On November 14th, 1908, Takahira reported to Root his government's reactions to the suggested changes. The first point caused no difficulty although the slight verbal change already noted was suggested. On the second point, the Japanese Government found the situation largely changed so that the insertion of the suggested clause was unnecessary and might affect the susceptibilities of the Chinese. After some further exchange of notes and conversations, Root and Takahira agreed upon the final text which stated a determination "to preserve the common interests of all powers in China by supporting by all pacific means at their disposal the independence and integrity of China and the principle of equal opportunity for commerce and industry of all nations in that Empire. . . ." The omission of the word "territorial" before "integrity of China" has been considered by some writers to reflect a concession to Japan, but the text is actually more favorable to China without the qualifying adjective, and its omission apparently was not suggested by Japan.

Willard Straight was exceedingly dubious about the advisability of making any joint declaration of this sort. To appreciate Straight's opposition, it must be borne in mind that he was deep in his plans for securing a large American loan for railroad construction as an offset to Japanese influence. He objected especially to another phrase in the agreement which referred to the maintenance of the status quo; this phrase he thought tended to favor the Japanese position at the expense of China and the United States.[5] He believed that the two countries were already agreed upon the basic policies and that nothing

[5] Croly, *Willard Straight*, Chap. VIII.

would be added by stating them in this way. "The effect of such an exchange of views upon our relations with other powers might, moreover, be unfortunate. . . . Our present position in the Far East is particularly satisfactory. We have the confidence of China. Germany is anxious to cooperate with us, and other powers respect our beneficent influence in Far Eastern affairs." Such a declaration would offend Germany by isolating her as the only power which had no such understanding with Japan. Furthermore, the Japanese agreements with the English, French and Russians, "instead of guaranteeing more firmly the 'Open Door' and the integrity of China, constitute a recognition of special spheres of influence which have been acquired at China's expense, the very eventuality which Secretary Hay in formulating his policy endeavored to prevent." England had exchanged a guarantee against a Russian advance in India for Japan's free hand in Korea; France had removed her apprehensions about the Japanese designs on Indo-China and had given Japan access to the French money markets and the confirmation of Japan's rights and interests in several quarters; Russia had undoubtedly agreed secretly with Japan to divide Manchuria into northern and southern spheres of influence under their respective domination. Straight was sure that China would regard the proposed Japanese-American declaration as being similarly hostile to her interest. A similar point of view in regard to Chinese interests was expressed by Ambassador O'Brien in a despatch from Tokio on November 4th, although he favored some such agreement with Japan.[6]

Straight was correct about the Chinese reaction. On November 21st, Root sent the text of the declaration which had not yet been made public, to Minister Rockhill in Peking, telling him to show it confidentially to the Chinese Government.

The Imperial Chinese Government will appreciate the fact that this action of the United States is the logical fruit of our traditional and frequently enunciated policy of friendly interest in and concern regarding the welfare of the Chinese Empire and has been prompted by our desire to reaffirm that policy by gaining a renewed definite and particular assurance of adherence thereto.

The Department feels that such a declaration should be pe-

[6] Archives of the Department of State.

culiarly satisfactory to the Imperial Chinese Government at this time and I rely upon you to insure its most beneficial effects.[7]

When Rockhill showed the text to the Chinese viceroy Yuan Shih-k'ai, he was surprised to be met "with considerable disappointment and some irritation." Perhaps Yuan would have been more appreciative had he known that the American Secretary of State was accustomed to be called by the viceroy's name. Root had badly injured his knee slipping on a carriage step during a tour of political speeches in Ohio and had referred to his accident as the reason for declining a dinner invitation from Madame Jusserand, the wife of his very good friend, the French Ambassador. There was current a story that shortly before, that amazing old lady, the Dowager Empress of China, had summoned Yuan Shih-k'ai to the imperial presence for the purpose, he anticipated, of cutting off his head as a slight indication of her displeasure at something he had done. The Premier respectfully declined the invitation on the ground of a rheumatic knee which prevented his traveling. Ever after, Mr. Root was known in the Jusserand household and in their informal correspondence as "Root-Shih-k'ai."

But his Chinese Excellency knew nothing of all this pseudonymous affinity and asked Rockhill whether the notes would be exchanged between the Japanese and American Governments if the Chinese Government objected. Rockhill was sure that they would be but could not imagine any objection. The fact of the matter seemed to be that the Chinese Government had hoped to conclude with the United States some sort of direct agreement which would have recognized and guaranteed their integrity in a manner more pleasing to China's amour propre. They were also anxious to secure the American loan which Straight hoped to arrange. T'ang Shao-yi, Governor of Shengking and one of the most powerful figures in Manchuria, had been designated by the Chinese Government as a special ambassador ostensibly to thank the United States for remitting a share of the Boxer Indemnity Fund, but actually, the diplomatic corps in Peking believed, "in the hope of negotiating some arrangement by which the aggressive policy of Japan in China, and especially in Manchuria, may be counteracted if not arrested." [8] Yuan Shih-k'ai, without revealing the existence of

[7] *Ibid.*
[8] Rockhill to Root, December 3, 1908, *ibid.*

his instructions to T'ang, gave away his hand by complaining that the United States had suddenly decided upon this arrangement with Japan without awaiting the arrival of the special Chinese ambassador; if they had waited, "the United States' desire to strengthen the status quo in China could have been more effectually accomplished than by the present plan." He hinted that the Japanese had rushed through the agreement in order to forestall T'ang's mission.[9] However, on the following day Yuan sent word that upon a reexamination of the text of the proposed exchange of views between the United States and Japan, they were entirely satisfied with it and their first misapprehensions had been entirely dissipated.

The history of the various proposals which finally culminated in the Root-Takahira agreement, as already outlined, indicates that on the part of the United States at least, Yuan Shih-k'ai's suspicions in regard to the timing of it were quite unfounded. In view of the Chinese attitude, however, Root finally agreed, as a polite gesture, to hold up the actual signing of the notes until T'ang arrived in Washington on November 30th. Root showed him the text at noon and the formal signature took place at four o'clock that afternoon.[10] When T'ang Shao-yi had an interview of several hours with Root on December 9th, he remarked that the Chinese translation of the notes was unsatisfactory and that he had sent a better one to Peking; he was sure that his government "would be very much pleased by the transaction." [11] But he made no specific proposal for an agreement with the United States on this general subject; it was too late.

The Chinese, who are accustomed to look philosophically further to the future than even Root was, necessarily accepted the situation with as good grace as possible. They might have been happier had they believed in the interpretation which Root, in retrospect, put on his agreement:

> My arrangements . . . negatived the special interests of Japan in China. My idea was that both the United States and Japan had rights and interests in China—there was more interest and more occasion for exercise of rights on the part of Japan, but they

[9] Archives of the Department of State.
[10] Croly, op. cit., p. 274.
[11] Archives of the Department of State.

were the same rights as ours though vastly more important for them than for us.[12]

The Lansing-Ishii Agreement of 1917, on the contrary, proceeded on the basis of recognizing Japan's special interest in China, although Lansing stated that if Ishii "when he spoke of 'special interest' meant 'paramount interest,'" Lansing "could not discuss the matter further with him."[13]

Straight had correctly foreseen the Chinese situation, but he was wrong about the reception of the news in European capitals. The Anglo-Japanese agreements had been confidentially communicated to Washington and other capitals prior to publication, and Root followed the same practice, sending the text of his agreement to London, Paris, St. Petersburg and Berlin on November 22nd. In writing to our ambassadors in the first three cities, Root took pains to point out that this understanding between Japan and the United States was very similar to the agreements which those countries had concluded. To the embassy in Berlin he wrote:

. . . the United States is glad to feel that the present declaration expresses the entire harmony between the attitude of the United States and those basic principles of Far Eastern policy which the Imperial German Government embodied in the Anglo-German agreement of October nineteen-hundred, and has also declared in hearty accord with the United States on various other occasions.[14]

The European reception was all that could be desired. Sir Edward Grey said in conversation with Ambassador Reid "that if they had been asked to name what news would be most welcome from the Far East, he could scarcely have thought of anything better than this agreement."[15] The London *Times* of November 30th rejoiced at this bringing together of England's "allies" and "kinsfolk." According to the London *Morning Post* the "New Agreement with Japan postpones indefinitely the once much-talked-of struggle for the mastery of

[12] Root to the author, September 13, 1932. For a contrary interpretation, see Morse and McNair, *Far Eastern Relations*, pp. 535–536.
[13] *War Memoirs of Robert Lansing*, p. 296. Cf. *Foreign Relations of the United States*, 1922, Vol. II, pp. 591 ff.
[14] Archives of the Department of State.
[15] Reid to Root, November 30, 1908, ibid.

the Pacific." Ambassador Hill reported from Berlin not only a warm official welcome for the news but also that "the effect of this agreement upon the public mind is as marked as it is salutary." [16] Henry White wrote to Root personally from the Paris Embassy on January 8th, 1909:

> I omitted in my last letter to mention how general is the appreciation and approval not only in this country but throughout Europe of your latest achievement: the agreement with Japan, which has at last brought about a conviction that there will be no war, at all events for a goodly number of years to come, between that country and ours. It has consequently brought about a feeling of security in that direction which has not existed for a long time. The President, the Prime Minister and Pichon the Foreign Minister, particularly the latter, have all spoken to me in most flattering terms on the subject, my Japanese colleague professes to be rapturously happy over it and in England, where there has been great anxiety of late lest their Treaty of Alliance with Japan should bring them unwillingly into conflict with us, the relief is intense.

The opinion in the United States and in Japan was also favorable and Root was showered with congratulations on his achievement— which he did not originate but which he did carry through in an atmosphere which he did much to create. Ambassador Bryce considered the agreement of great importance as marking a period in the Pacific policy of the United States and as silencing "the last echoes of the war cries of last year." [17] Roosevelt was inclined to believe that everything was due to the cruise of the fleet which had an overwhelmingly successful reception in Japan when it arrived at Yokohama on October 18th, 1908, eight days before Takahira submitted his first draft to the President. Like most things of that kind, the friendliness which made the agreement possible was due to no one incident but to a line of conduct followed over a period of time, coupled with many intangibles which it is impossible to weigh. The signature of an arbitration treaty between Japan and the United States on May 5th, 1908, was one other helpful detail; Taft's visit in 1907 was another. But

[16] Despatch No. 162, December 9, 1908, *ibid.*
[17] Mr. Bryce to Sir Edward Grey, December 1, 1908, Gooch and Temperley, *British Documents on the Origins of the War*, Vol. VIII, p. 464.

from China came the wail of the *Chung Ying Ta T'ung Jih Pao* of Peking which wondered how the Japanese would rage if China and any other power agreed to protect the independence and integrity of Japan!

Root never forgot the Senate; he wrote to Senator Cullom, Chairman of the Committee on Foreign Relations, on December 8th, 1908, that he thought "it would be useful for me to have a talk with the Committe on the subject [of the agreement with Japan], and if the members of the Committee agree in that view I should be glad of an opportunity to come before the Committee." [18] Cullom invited him to come, and Root went. Rather unusually, Roosevelt checked Root on the form of the message transmitting the notes to the Senate. Root had ordered the message drafted and it had gone to the President for signature, concluding with the phrase "for any expression of views which that body [the Senate] may see fit to make." Roosevelt returned it with a note scribbled in the corner:

Dear Elihu:
    Why invite the expression of views with which we may not agree?
                    T.R.

Root struck out the phrase.

Roosevelt and Root might well have hoped that the short remainder of the former's administration would be free from troubles with Japan. But in January, 1909, the California Legislature again started to make trouble for the federal government. A bill against alien land holdings by aliens was reported to the California Assembly on January 15th. Roosevelt immediately enlisted the aid of Governor Gillett who cooperated heartily and efficiently.[19] On January 25th, Root prepared a memorandum for the President regarding the land bills and on the same day wired Governor Gillett that such a bill was not objectionable if it applied to all aliens; many states already had such legislation. Another anti-Japanese school bill was also introduced but was not passed; the legislation was held up through the efforts of the Governor, Speaker Stanton and Grove L. Johnson, the all-powerful leader of the State Senate, who was strongly in favor of the bills but too loyal a Repub-

---

[18] Archives of the Department of State.
[19] Bailey, *Theodore Roosevelt and the Japanese-American Crisis*, Chap. XIII.

lican to resist appeals from the Administration in Washington. As an international issue the flurry amounted to nothing and Root was able to leave the State Department on January 27th, 1909, with the feeling that all was well in our relations with Japan.

Intimacy with Japan did not by any means necessarily imply cordial relations with China. China was beginning to consider her Oriental neighbor as the dangerous successor to the European powers who had gobbled up choice locations, imposed a system of extraterritorial rights, limited her financial autonomy and concluded with each other agreements to maintain Chinese "integrity," which seemed to mean the privilege of not being further dissected unless all had equal slices. Root seems to have shared Roosevelt's admiration and respect for the efficient and aggressive Japanese and Roosevelt's irritation at the pacific Chinese. Roosevelt's attitude verged on contempt; Root's did not. His first experience with them had been in the distressing days of the Boxer Rebellion when he had worked side by side with John Hay. Root's attitude seems to have had in it a shade of paternalism, desirous of being kindly but annoyed at childish misbehaviors. But Root had an appreciation of the background of the Chinese and the individual ability of many of their statesmen.

Root viewed the Japanese problem in California "against the background of the abuses of the Chinese on the Pacific Coast."

There was dreadful treatment of the Chinese in California. Many were turned back at the ports destitute and many died on the way back. I had the situation looked into shortly after I became Secretary and was satisfied there was serious mistreatment parallel to our mistreatment of the negroes and Indians, the latter being one of the worst of our national misdeeds for which we wonder whether we will not some day have to make retribution. The people on the Pacific Coast rightly objected to losing their lands by the peaceful invasion of the Asiatics. The laws shaped to deal with individual cases were not adequate to solve the whole problem. It was necessary to go back to the fundamental right of the state to say who shall enter its territory. The old adjustments of nations under international law in the international society were not adequate to this influx of swarms of aliens. Changes in law were too slow—too slow for the people interested in this matter and, as a result, Chinese were arrested when they landed. There was collusion between our consuls and the Chinese officials who were giving fraudulent certificates and visas. I had a very interesting talk with Chentung Liang-Cheng, the Chinese minister, a very intelligent and perspicacious man. I said I would fix the consular situation if he would have the Chinese officials controlled; this was the only way to stop the abuses—the poor devils came along thinking everything was all right but they were misled and deceived. I went to work and cleaned up the consulates and the abuses stopped.[20]

It is interesting to note the comparable experience of the Australian Government. In negotiating the Gentlemen's Agreement with Japan which has been mentioned in the last chapter, the Department of External Affairs of Australia called the Japanese Government's attention to the danger of abuse of passports, illustrated by the fact that "certain persons recently gained admission to Australia on exemption certificates furnished to holders of passports from the Chinese Government. Those passports had been issued by the Viceroy of Canton to Chinese gentlemen of rank, and had been duly viséd by the British Consul-General, but when presented in Australia it was found that the holders were merely working men to whom the passports had been transferred." [21]

One of the obstacles which Root met in endeavoring to adjust relations with China was the widespread Chinese boycott of American goods. It was another of the issues inherited by Root in which the policy of the United States was already formed. The boycott began in the spring of 1905 as a protest against the rumored intention of the United States to force China to sign an unfavorable treaty regarding the exclusion of Chinese laborers. The agitation was prompted by the Chinese merchant guilds in order to force the United States to amend the exclusion laws in favor of the Chinese.[22] In many quarters in the United States it was believed that the boycott was instigated by Japanese agents in order to injure American commerce.[23] Although the viceroy, Yuan Shih-k'ai, took steps to suppress the boycott before it should assume alarming proportions as a general anti-foreign demon-

[20] Root to the author, September 6, 1930.
[21] Atlee Hunt to K. Iwasaki, Acting Consul-General for Japan, April 16, 1904, *Parliamentary Papers*, Cmd. No. 61, –F. 12087—1905.
[22] Minister Rockhill to the Secretary of State, July 6, 1905, *Foreign Relations of the United States*, 1905, p. 205.
[23] Latané, "Our Relations with Japan," *American Political Science Review*, 1914, p. 592.

stration, the Chinese Government on the whole was secretly disposed to approve of it as a means for coercing the American Government.[24] On August 4th, 1905, Rockhill inquired whether he could inform the Chinese Government that "under provision Article 15th, our treaty 1858, we will hold it responsible for any losses sustained by our trade for its failure to stop present organized movement interfering therewith." [25] When this telegram reached the Department, Root was off on his Newfoundland trip and Adee consulted the President, who told him to instruct Rockhill to make that representation and "to use strong language." [26] Although the boycott in its most vigorous form was confined largely to Canton and Shanghai, and although the Chinese officials began to take some steps to check it, protests from American business interests were piling in on the State Department by the time Root took up his duties in September. The United States was already committed to the position that the Chinese Government was bound by the Sino-American commercial treaty to suppress the movement, but Root gave a new slant to the situation. The San Francisco Merchants Exchange had sent a protest to Roosevelt who asked Root to look over the reply he had drafted. Replying to the President on November 24th, 1905, Root suggested the addition of a final paragraph which read as follows:

You say in your letter that unless strong steps are taken to stop the boycott, American trade will be put back many years, and that the merchants of San Francisco feel that their interests will be jeopardized. I wish you to feel that I appreciate this, and that I am keenly alive to the apprehensions you express; but I wish you also to feel that I have done everything in my power to stop the boycott, and that the State Department has done everything in its power. Anything further must be done by your own representatives in the Senate and House, by way of making such changes in the exclusion law as to prevent the injustice and humiliation to which the Chinese who do not belong to the coolie class have been subjected in coming to this country. If you and all the other American merchants who are injured by the boycott

[24] Rockhill to the Secretary of State, August 4, 1905, Archives of the Department of State.
[25] *Ibid.*
[26] *Ibid.*

will urge your representatives in Congress to do away with the cause of the boycott, you will probably succeed.[27]

This position of justifying the action of the Chinese was officially reiterated by Roosevelt in his message of December 5th, 1905. He pointed out that the Chinese Government agreed with the United States in regard to the exclusion of coolie labor but "in the effort to carry out the policy of excluding Chinese laborers, Chinese coolies, grave injustice and wrong have been done by this nation to the people of China" by our failure to discriminate between the laborers and the professional classes and merchants who were being excluded with equal rigor. "The main factor in producing this boycott has been the resentment felt by the students and business people of China, by all the Chinese leaders, against the harshness of our law toward educated Chinamen of the professional and business classes." [28] It was an honest and creditable admission of fault, but it did not make it any easier to induce the Chinese Government to suppress the anti-American activities. Sir Chentung Liang Cheng, the Chinese minister in Washington, did not fail to avail himself of the advantage which this opening gave to him. In a brilliant note of November 28th, he replied to a protest which Root had written to him on the 14th. He failed to see how the Chinese Government could compel its subjects to buy American cotton cloth and kerosene if they preferred goods of other origin. He thought it scarcely surprising that there should be anti-foreign feeling in China in view of the way his country had been plundered by the Western powers, although he was happy to recall that the United States had not participated in these actions. He cited an opinion of Attorney General Knox on February 11th, 1902, in which Knox declared that "The Chinese exclusion laws are necessarily rigorous, and of the highest degree of technicality, and do not permit the imposition of maxims of equity, which commend and command judicial authorities to search with scrupulous care for a way to do justice when the technicalities of the law present obstructions." He recalled the anti-Chinese riots in Rock Springs, Tacoma, and California, and asserted that more Chinese had been killed in the United States than Americans in China during the past twenty years and that the Chinese record of punishment of offenders and payment of indemnities was much

[27] Roosevelt Papers, Library of Congress.
[28] *Foreign Relations of the United States*, 1905, pp. xlix–l.

better.[29] The Minister was on firm ground and was playing his hand adroitly. Root did not answer at once but on February 14th, 1906, he sent the Minister a very stiff note protesting against a proclamation alleged to have been issued by the Chinese Consul General in San Francisco in pursuance of instructions from his Government.[30] The proclamation stated that the Chinese Government had never prohibited or obstructed the boycott which was a protest against the American exclusion laws. Root declared that this position was directly contrary to the assurances given by the Chinese Government; he demanded that the proclamation be revoked or disavowed and that the Consul-General be properly disciplined.[31] Sir Chentung Liang Cheng replied on the 24th with another epistle of suave brilliancy which one can not read at a dispassionate distance without exclaiming "Touché!" He disavowed any knowledge of the proclamation but agreed to investigate.

> I might content myself with the foregoing reply, but for the peculiar tenor of your note. It is a grave act to convey to a friendly power an intimation of duplicity on its part, and this is seldom done except upon most conclusive evidence and under serious provocation. It is a deep grief to me that even a suspicion of such conduct is entertained by one whose acts have been marked by such cordial good will to my country, and whose intercourse with me has been characterized by such great friendship and sincerity. To one who has attained such high eminence in his profession and has devoted his life to a study of the force and value of evidence, it may seem almost impertinent in me to suggest that his own Department should contain facts which would vindicate my Government from the heinous offense implied in your note.[32]

He took the position that his Government had never promised to suppress the boycott and referred to the fact that he had received no answer to his note of November 28th. He quoted from President Roosevelt's Message to Congress and gave assurances that his Government had taken steps to prevent violence and injury to foreigners.

Root had not made the blunder which the Minister imputed to him; Rockhill's despatches justified the view which Root had taken

[29] Archives of the Department of State.
[30] Printed in *Foreign Relations of the United States, 1905*, p. 210.
[31] Archives of the Department of State.
[32] *Ibid*.

regarding the position of the Chinese Government. It is quite probable that the Minister was not fully posted in regard to the negotiations in Peking and it is certain that the Chinese Government's assurances were rather evasively phrased. The Minister's note undoubtedly inspired Root's telegraphic instruction to Rockhill on February 26th in which he said it was "imperatively necessary that this Government should understand the true attitude of the Chinese Government towards the United States and towards Americans pursuing their lawful business and callings in China under the protection of treaty rights and international law." Despite the increasingly alarming reports of injuries to Americans in China "the Imperial Government appears to be inert, apparently forgetful of the lessons of the Boxer Rebellion." A series of specific propositions were set forth which the President directed Rockhill to bring to the attention of the Chinese Government. To all these propositions, the Chinese Government gave satisfactory replies.

On May 28th Root made full reply to Sir Chentung Liang Cheng's notes of November 28th and February 24th and to a further note of April 17th in which the authenticity of the Consul-General's proclamation had been avowed. No lawyer, and especially no brilliant trial lawyer like Root, could have refrained from making a studied rebuttal. As an example of the art of debate, this correspondence is a marvelous exhibition. As to the boycott, Root said, "If it had been possible to regard this movement as being merely a matter of private enterprise, I should not now be troubling you with this correspondence." It seemed clear, however, that the Chinese Government sympathized with it and supported it and this view was confirmed by the Minister's own statements. The assurances received from the Chinese Government were not consistent with this fact and several passages from the Minister's notes revealed the same inconsistency. In writing his note of February 14th, Root had felt sure that the San Francisco proclamation would be disavowed. "That this has proved not to be the case is a matter of grave concern on the part of the Government of the United States." That government would insist on the responsibility of the Chinese Government for all "the damages which have been inflicted upon American merchants by this organized interference and destruction of their trade by officers of the Chinese Government." Root shrewdly turned back the thrust based upon the quotation from the President's Message by asserting that Roosevelt had "stated the case for the Chinese Government with an urgency which you yourself have never surpassed, and with a frankness and a friendliness which absolutely excluded all thought of diplomatic disputation or of any negotiation in which the one party was seeking to get the better of the other." The President had followed up his Message by securing the introduction of bills in Congress which it was hoped would remedy the admitted evils but these efforts had been defeated by the effort of the Chinese Government to apply coercion through the boycott. "There is a natural tendency among men to revolt against coercion, and a natural resentment is caused by its attempted exercise. . . . If the attempt to secure a change of the law be defeated in whole or in part, the defeat will have been caused by the action of the Chinese Government itself." But the Department of State was too sincerely desirous of continuing the friendly relations with China "in the same spirit which animated my lamented predecessor, Mr. Hay, in his long and consistent effort to preserve the territorial integrity of China and to check the process of aggression from without which threatened the gradual dismemberment of the Empire . . . to be willing that any complaints of temporary grievances or mistaken official conduct on either side shall obscure the greater considerations of peace and amity for the future." Root concluded with a final thrust, pointing out that Mr. Chung, who had issued the proclamation as Consul General, had never asked or received recognition in that capacity and that Root would therefore be glad to know upon what grounds the Chinese Government conceived it to be proper to direct him so to act.[33]

It was a brilliant reply brief, but diplomatic issues are not settled in that way. Root had discharged his duty as counsel for the United States Government; the record was clear and he proceeded to get results. The whole matter was discussed in a friendly interview with the Chinese Minister on June 11th, 1906. Root pointed out that there was little chance of the passage at that session of Congress of legislation modifying the Chinese exclusion law and expressed a willingness to renew the treaty negotiations which Hay had initiated. Since the Minister had no instructions to enter upon such negotiations and since Root was about to leave on his South American trip, the matter was allowed

[33] *Ibid.*

to drop. While Root was away, the Chinese Government agreed to pay an indemnity for the most serious consequence of the anti-American feeling—the riots at Lienchou in November, 1905, when five American missionaries were killed and much American property destroyed.[34] The boycott died out and the atmosphere of friendliness created by the remission of the Boxer Indemnity took its place.

When John Hay in 1900 had sought to secure from all the powers a recognition of the Open Door doctrine, the least satisfactory reply was received from the Russian Government.[35] Then and thereafter, Russia sought to maintain a stranglehold on Manchuria. By the peace treaty of Portsmouth, Japan acquired the South Manchurian Railway from Russia together with Russia's other rights in Southern Manchuria, especially the lease of the Liao-tung peninsula. The Chinese Eastern Railway in northern Manchuria was retained by Russia. By a treaty of December, 1905, China consented to these transfers and agreed not to build a competing line parallel to the Southern Manchurian Railway. In 1907, Russia and Japan reached an understanding to respect each other's rights in the northern and southern parts of Manchuria respectively.[36] Both countries were reluctant to acknowledge the principle of the Open Door in that region.[37] Roosevelt, however, was not inclined to have any further trouble with Japan and did not press matters with them. The Manchurian ports were not reopened to international trade until the summer of 1907. Roosevelt had no such tender feelings toward Russia but it was not until 1908, after the Russo-Japanese understanding had been reached, that the United States became rather vigorous in protesting against Russian activities in the zone of the Chinese Eastern Railway.

As already pointed out, Root had acquired some familiarity with the Chinese railway situation as counsel for the American China Development Company, but he had had no previous contact with the complicated Manchurian question. The Russian Government sought to uphold the position that the railroad grant from the Chinese Gov-

---

[34] *Foreign Relations of the United States*, 1906, pp. 308 ff.

[35] Dennett, *John Hay*, p. 293.

[36] Ernest B. Price, *The Russo-Japanese Treaties of 1907–1916 Concerning Manchuria and Mongolia*, pp. 35 ff.

[37] Korff, "Russia in the Far East," *American Journal of International Law*, Vol. 17 (1923), p. 252, 272.

ernment included powers of political administration, particularly in
the city of Harbin. On April 6th, 1908, Root had an interview with
Baron Rosen, the Russian Ambassador in Washington.

> I said, I think the whole subject of the maintenance of order in
> Harbin will have to be worked out along the lines that it has been
> at Shanghai and other treaty ports, and that the authority for any
> municipal regulations and looking to the maintenance of order
> among the foreigners living at Harbin must be the authority de-
> rived from the treaties between China and the powers, and not an
> authority derived from any alleged claim to the right of political
> administration in China's grant to the Railroad Company. I said
> the two sources of power are quite different and will lead to differ-
> ent results. . . . I said, I think that the powers ought to take up
> the subject, and work it out just as it has been worked out in other
> places. . . .
> Baron Rosen said this entirely agreed with his views.[38]

Root made a lawyer's argument to the Ambassador but could hardly
have been deceived by the ready acquiescence. He kept the American
embassies in London, Berlin and Tokio fully posted on the course of
the negotiations and his line of action was mightily strengthened by
the cooperation of Sir Edward Grey. On June 19th, Root informed
our Ambassador in Tokio that the London Embassy reported that Sir
Edward had talked with the Japanese Ambassador and assured him
that the Russian claim that the "railroad concession conveys absolute
sovereignty is extreme and hoped Japanese would be cautious about
committing themselves to a claim involving such consequences to the
open door and to the territorial integrity of China." The British Foreign Secretary was about to inform the Russian Ambassador of these
views.[39] Japan would not have been unwilling to acquiesce in the establishment of a principle which might equally have been applied to her
South Manchuria Railway Zone, but the advice of her English ally
was entitled to respectful attention. On the same day, in instructing
Adee to draft a note to the Russian Ambassador on this general subject, Root summed up for Adee's information his general policy:

> The position of the United States is that it does not purpose to
> surrender treaty rights in China or to concede that its sympathy

[38] Memorandum of interview, April 6, 1908, Archives of the Department of State.
[39] Archives of the Department of State.

can be excluded from those rights or subjected to any governmental power on the part of the Chinese railway company. On the other hand we do not wish to be bumptious or disputatious or unfriendly in the assertion of our rights, or to become a protagonist in Manchuria, taking the responsibility of carrying on a vexatious controversy with Russia. A quiet, firm maintenance of our position is our true policy and in that the interests to be preserved are the future interests of the open door and there is no present interest which would justify us in exhibiting undue excitement in this quiet and firm maintenance of our position. We believe that we have the concurrence of both Germany and England, and that being so we need not fear that we are really going to lose anything.[40]

In the last days of December, 1908, Root was still urging the Russian Government to agree to settle the Harbin question through a conference of the powers, but the issue outlasted his days as Secretary of State.[41]

As contrasted with his successor, Secretary Knox, Root took very little interest in pushing individual American commercial and business interests in China although he always furthered a general policy of promoting the trade of the United States. He kept shy of involving the United States Government in any commitment regarding an international consortium loan to China. The subject was brewing while he was in the State Department, but did not develop until Knox's time. He thought it was "a great mistake to put our Government in a controversial position for the purpose of helping our bankers and traders. . . . Our form of government allows enough help to trade to make the government a participant. The result will be that a trade controversy will be a direct cause of war. It is only because of the government's detachment that they can discuss a business controversy." [42] When in 1908, special ambassador T'ang Shao-yi told Root of his plan to abolish the likin, raise the tariff, and establish a uniform currency on a gold standard with the aid of a large foreign loan, Root on December 11th instructed Willard Straight that all of these measures were in line with our policy and our treaty of 1903 with China.

[40] Ibid.
[41] Root to Baron Rosen, December 29, 1908, and Root to Ambassador Riddle, St. Petersburg, December 31, 1908, ibid. See in general Clyde, International Rivalries in Manchuria.
[42] Root to the author, September 18, 1930.

As for the negotiation of a loan, whether in the United States or in Europe, which has been mentioned as a necessary condition precedent to the carrying out of the treaty provisions above referred to, the State Department has no wish or authority to involve the United States in any obligation either legal or moral with reference to such a loan. Keeping in mind and scrupulously regarding this fact I wish you to render to Mr. T'ang, unofficially, all proper assistance by way of facilitating him in meeting such representatives of American finance and commerce as he may wish to meet for the prosecution of his mission. And to any person whom Mr. T'ang may desire to have informed of the views of this Government you are at liberty to exhibit this letter.[43]

Root submitted this instruction to Roosevelt on December 18th, saying that it seemed to him better "to have Straight acting under express instructions which will furnish a justification for anything that he may do in assisting Mr. T'ang, rather than leave it open for evil minded persons to suspect that there is something surreptitious." T'ang's mission, however, failed, due in part, Straight thought, to the political effect in China of the Root-Takahira agreement.[44]

On October 21st, 1905, Root signed an instruction to Minister Rockhill in Peking, dealing with the request of the China Investment and Construction Company of America. The instruction is taken almost verbatim from a memorandum prepared by Adee on October 3rd, but it may be taken as expressing Root's view:

The policy to be pursued by the Legation respecting the transmission of applications of American citizens or companies for privileges in China deserves and has had careful consideration. Your position that the Legation must decline to act as a medium of communication between Mr. Bash's company and the Chinese Government, and your further point that the Legation will act where ever the company can show that it is deprived of a treaty right or unfairly discriminated against, would hold good in any except Oriental countries.

It is well known that foreign concessions in China, Siam, Persia and Turkey are almost always obtained through the personal advocacy of the diplomatic representative whose fellow-citizen may be the applicant therefor. The German envoys are especially ac-

[43] Archives of the Department of State. Cf. Croly, op. cit., pp. 275 ff.
[44] Ibid., pp. 274 ff.

tive in this way. China, like the other Eastern Governments, looks upon any privilege granted to foreign citizens or corporations as a favor to their government. The position of the United States has been the opposite of this, for it expects its agents to be scrupulous in avoiding any appearance of soliciting favors for Americans or American corporations. It is not believed that this has worked to the disadvantage of our citizens to any great extent, for they have secured a number of concessions in China.[45]

This instruction admitted that from the Chinese point of view, a request from the Company forwarded by the Legation, would be considered to have official backing but pointed out that conversely the Chinese might regard a refusal to act as an official opposition to the Company's project. "On the whole I am inclined to think that there can be no great harm in your forwarding to the Chinese Foreign Office without comment any papers in relation to applications provided they be not manifestly improper."

There is nothing in Root's record as Secretary of State to justify the fears expressed in the press when he was appointed that he would favor the large corporations for which he had been counsel, except in so far as they were beneficiaries of a general trade promotion policy which by no means began or ended with Root. In the general international struggle for commercial advantage in China, he played a minor part; the succeeding policies of Taft and Knox were much more aggressive.

[45] Archives of the Department of State.

CHAPTER XXIX

"The power of our detachment"

THE story of the Moroccan conference at Algeciras from January 16th to April 3rd, 1906, was for a time shrouded in diplomatic secrecy, but the story has now been told so fully [1] that little remains to be said. It deserves no large place in a biography of Root save as another example of skillful handling of a Roosevelt policy. "In the matter of Morocco, no less than in that of the Russo-Japanese War, Roosevelt was his own State Department. . . ." [2] The conference was the result of the tangled European diplomatic situation, the jockeying of the powers for position on the north coast of Africa and the rivalry between Germany on the one hand and France and Great Britain on the other. The situation in 1905 was ugly, and Roosevelt came to believe that the exercise of his influence was necessary to avoid a general European war. He was egged on and pulled in various directions by his intimates in the Washington diplomatic corps, Speck von Sternburg, the German Ambassador, Ambassador Jusserand of France, and Spring-Rice, then Secretary of the British Embassy. Roosevelt had played his part in bringing about the Algeciras conference and involving the United States in the very thick of European politics while Hay was still Secretary of State. There was nothing for Root to do except to carry on with the details and to exercise his usual restraining influence on Roosevelt. Root was always cautious in his diplomacy, a characteristic which coupled with Roosevelt's boldness made a good combination. It is a mistake to say that Roosevelt usually acted impulsively, but he lived in the moment far more than Root whose eyes were always turned far ahead into the future.

Root was rather dubious about American participation in the con-

[1] Especially in Nevins, *Henry White*, pp. 261 ff.; Anderson, *The First Moroccan Crisis, 1904–1906;* Pringle, *Theodore Roosevelt,* pp. 387 ff.; Bishop, *Theodore Roosevelt and His Time,* Vol. I, Chaps. xxxvi–xxxvii.

[2] Pringle, *op. cit.,* p. 392. So Roosevelt stated to Carnegie, February 26, 1909, Carnegie Papers, Library of Congress.

ference. On February 27th, 1906, he wrote to Ambassador Whitelaw Reid in London: "Between White and the German Ambassador here, we are following the Algeciras Conference pretty closely, but our interests are not sufficient to justify us in taking a leading part; and while, of course, we should be very glad to contribute towards keeping the peace, we do not wish to get into a position where we will be justly charged with intermeddling or to become a party to a controversy, and we have not yet considered that there was a situation in which any move by us would be practically useful." After the conference adjourned, he wrote to General James H. Wilson on April 3rd, 1907: "Undoubtedly the fact that we had no specific interest in the controversy and did not pretend to have any enabled us to exercise a very calming influence in that affair. I fully agree with you, however, that our great interests are this side of the Atlantic." Root may have been influenced by the row which Senator Bacon of Georgia had kicked up in the Senate by the introduction on January 8th, 1906, of a resolution opposing this violation of one half of the Monroe Doctrine which foreswore meddling in European affairs. Through the efforts of Senator Lodge, the resolution was buried in the Foreign Relations Committee.[3]

The actual handling of the conference was entrusted to Henry White. "He was an excellent man for that though not the creator of great things. He had great social grace and the training of a diplomat. He knew how to manoeuvre with diplomats." [4] Pringle's assumption [5] that Roosevelt did not carefully follow the details of the negotiations at the conference is confirmed by Root.[6] But the President did step in and bring pressure on the Kaiser when White reported that such action was necessary and in several instances exercised great influence. Root drafted the official instructions to White and Gummére, the American Minister to Morocco who was detailed to assist White because of his knowledge of local conditions. Root also wrote a personal and confidential letter to White on November 28th, 1905. "You will perceive," he wrote, that the official instructions "are very general, as are our interests in Morocco."

[3] Congressional Record, 59th Cong., 1st Sess., Vol. 40, Part I, p. 792; Part II, pp. 1069 and 1081.
[4] Root to the author, September 5, 1930.
[5] Pringle, op. cit., p. 394.
[6] Root to the author, September 5, 1930.

The only really specific thing is the supplemental instruction relating to ameliorating the condition of the Jews, which appears to be dreadful. I think you may be able to accomplish something substantial and useful in this respect. If this could be done it would be very opportune, because our immense Jewish population is now naturally much excited over the cruelties in Russia, and it is very difficult for many of them to understand why our Government cannot interfere. Of course, the leading men, like Schiff, the Seligmans, and Straus, understand, but the great mass probably do not. The suffering and humiliation which the Jews in Morocco must endure under the regulations sent to us by Schiff and transmitted to you must be beyond expression. The regulations seem quite incredible at this time of the world. They are a leaf from far distant ancient history of cruel and barbaric times . . .

As to the general subject, of course we want such a treatment of conditions generally in Morocco as to increase the trade of the country. We want the people to wear more shoes, more cotton cloth, use more articles of the kind that we produce than ever before, and anything which tends, therefore, towards peaceful and prosperous conditions will be a benefit to us. Provided, however, that the door be kept open, so that there can be no discrimination against American trade. . . .

In a further handwritten letter of the same date, intended for White alone, Root epitomized the general political policy to be followed:

I have been told by someone that Gummère [sic] is strongly pro-German in Morocco matters.

This if true must not be allowed to throw us over into even apparent antagonism to the Anglo-French *entente*, or to make us a means of breaking that up. It is useful to us as well as agreeable. Keep the American end of the business on an even keel. Keep friendly with all. Help France get what she ought to have but don't take her fight on your shoulders. Help limit France where she ought to be limited but don't take that fight on your shoulders.

In the broader and really important part that the conference is to play in the politics of Europe, keep the peace and make it as difficult as possible for any one to pick a quarrel.

You are chosen because you know that broader field and have

tact, Gummère [sic] because he knows the narrower field of Morocco.

After the conference was over, Root confirmed his impression about
the tenuousness of the thread of interest which justified American
participation.

> I found that our citizens [in Morocco] were all those who had
> come over to get the cloak of American naturalization and then
> returned to take advantage of a privileged status in their native
> home. There was not one native born citizen of the United States
> there. Fifty per cent had returned within three months of nat-
> uralization. It was a tenuous thread but gave an opportunity to
> do what the Open Door did—preserve world peace because of the
> power of our detachment.[7]

The fraudulent naturalization practices to which Root referred were
common enough to be almost a joke at that time. In sending a letter of
introduction to Thomas Nelson Page who was planning a trip to Turkey, Root wrote on October 24th, 1905: "It is a pleasure to serve you. I
feel bound, however, to warn you that if you are an Armenian by birth
and have been naturalized in this country in the hope of securing protection against the consequences of returning to Turkey for the purpose of committing murder, my letter will not be effective for your
protection. The Government of Turkey has a vulgar prejudice about
such things, which we have been unable to overcome by diplomatic
methods." "Such things" were, however, partly overcome by the passage during Root's tenure of office and with his assistance, of the
naturalization law of June 13th, 1906, and the general citizenship law
of March 2nd, 1907.

When White cabled the text of the General Act in which the formal
results of the Algeciras Conference were embodied, Root instructed
him to make a reservation in behalf of the United States. The reservation, in one of Root's long sentences containing 132 words and 8
commas, disavowed any political interest in Morocco and the assumption of any responsibility for the enforcement of the provisions agreed
upon. Root's eye was still on the Senate which was disinclined to rush
its consent to ratification. On June 25th, 1906, Root wrote to Senator
Cullom, the Chairman of the Foreign Relations Committee, a letter

[7] Ibid.

which afforded public arguments for ratification but scant assistance to the student of history. His argument was that we had made treaties with Morocco in 1787 and 1836 and had then become a party to the General Convention of Madrid signed by all the great powers of Europe in 1880. The new Algeciras treaty "merely modifies and extends the provisions of the treaty of 1880 in accordance with the requirements of the present day." The United States, Root said, could not "with decency" have refused to go into a conference with the other parties to modify the treaty of 1880 and if we declined to ratify this new treaty "we will be for the first time in one hundred and twenty years, without any treaty relation with Morocco whatever. I believe that no valid objection to the treaty can be found. The reservation under which we signed it . . . was made as broad as possible. . . . The Committee will see that we have carefully avoided any entanglement in European affairs; that we have merely done what our participation in the Madrid Convention of 1880 made it incumbent upon us to do, and that a failure to ratify the Convention would put the Government of the United States in a most humiliating position in the eyes of all the rest of the civilized world, and would leave us in a most anomalous condition with reference to our previous treaties with Morocco." [8] The Senate gave its consent and the United States ratified the treaty.

Root had other experiences with the jealous rivalry of the European powers in Africa. One case involved Liberia, the black republic in which the United States had taken a special interest.[9] In December, 1905, Ernest Lyon, the American Minister Resident in Liberia, revealed in his despatches a considerable agitation regarding the aggressive designs of England and France. He feared that Liberia would be absorbed and its independence destroyed unless the United States should step in and exercise its influence.[10] Ambassador Sternburg in the previous month had tried to put the same flea in Root's ear through a private note in his great sprawly writing which put only 34 words to a large page of letter paper.[11] In 1908, the subject was again to the fore, with the German Embassy, Adee and Bacon all suggesting to Root that he should take vigorous steps to save Liberia from an Anglo-

[8] Archives of the Department of State.
[9] See Buell, *The Native Problem in Africa*, pp. 704 ff.; Bemis, *A Diplomatic History of the United States*, pp. 566 ff.
[10] Archives of the Department of State.
[11] *Ibid.*

French protectorate. Secretary Hay had met like problems by making pointed assertions of American interest in Liberian independence.[12] On June 1st, 1908, Root gave an interview to a Liberian Commission which came to the United States. They asked that the United States guarantee the integrity of their territory and assist them with expert personnel. Root was very cordial and very non-committal. He suggested to them later that their object could be better accomplished if the United States were to act in concert with the British Government and he instructed Reid in London to ascertain "the views of the British Government as to how the United States could cooperate with that Government toward promoting the welfare of Liberia." [13] Booker T. Washington, who accompanied the Liberian delegates, was persuaded that Root's view was sound. Washington wrote enthusiastically to Roosevelt that he had never really appreciated Root's tremendous ability until this interview: "He is really a remarkable man, one that the whole nation should be proud of." [14] Since the Roosevelt Administration was drawing to a close, Root advised Mr. Washington to consult with Taft regarding the desirability of sending an American commission to Liberia. The Commission was sent with Taft's approval. Root's handling of the Liberian issue was skillful but in its broad lines merely followed precedent.

A more protracted controversy involved the Congo Free State, which had come into existence under the personal sovereignty of the King of the Belgians by virtue of the General Act signed at the Congress of Berlin in 1885. The United States was not a party to that treaty but had ratified the Brussels General Act of 1890 dealing with the slave trade and other rights of the natives of Africa. The administration of the Congo was a cold-blooded exploitation of the natives, with instances of cruelty and inhuman treatment which aroused public sentiment in both the United States and Europe.

> The case of the Belgian Congo is a very conspicuous illustration of the difficulties which are created for diplomatists, the men handling foreign affairs in a democratic country, regarding matters of sentiment. The very people who are most ardent

[12] Dennis, *Adventures in American Diplomacy*, p. 439.
[13] *Ibid.*
[14] Booker T. Washington to Roosevelt, June 16, 1908, Roosevelt Papers, Library of Congress.

against entangling alliances insist most fanatically upon our doing
one hundred things a year on humanitarian grounds, which would
lead to immediate war. That attitude practically put us into the
war for Cuba. The Protestant Church and many good women were
wild to have us stop the atrocities in the Congo. The fact we were
parties to some earlier treaties gave some basis for an interest.
The same thing goes on all the time. In China, the vocal part of
the missionaries who go out to teach Christianity are the first to
holler for gunboats when the trouble which is the inevitable result
of trying to change an old religion, comes along. Many people are
still angry because we did not keep Japan from taking Korea. There
was nothing we could do except fight Japan; Congress wouldn't
have declared war and the people would have turned out the Congress that had. All we might have done was to make threats which
we could not carry out. It was the same in the Congo. People kept
piling down on the Department demanding action on the Congo.
We went the limit which wasn't far.[15]

Root was rather hard on the missionaries in China who, as a matter
of fact, have repeatedly begged the Department of State not to interpose on their behalf. But the wave of church protests which swept
over him in the Congo affair apparently left a deep impression. Not
that Root showed any sign of irritation at the time. He granted interviews to numerous delegations, rejecting suggestions from Adee that
they be turned off with polite letters. He made them feel important
by showing them in strict confidence copies of the diplomatic correspondence which he was carrying on with our European missions.
Root sympathized with their desire to stop the atrocities and was also
aware that the support of the "good people" of the country was politically useful to the Administration. He had had his experience with
many of the same people in the days when the Anti-Imperialist
League was attacking him as Secretary of War for atrocities in the
Philippines. The recollections of those days made him sympathize also
with the troubles of King Leopold of Belgium. February 20th, 1906,
he wrote to Congressman Edwin Denby: "If the United States had
happened to possess in Darkest Africa a territory seven times as large
and four times as populous as the Philippines, we, too, might find
good government difficult and come in for our share of just or unjust

[15] Root to the author, September 5, 1930.

criticism." [16] Dr. Thomas S. Barbour of the American Baptist Missionary Union and the Congo Reform Association, showed the appreciation which was typical of these groups with whom Root talked and corresponded. On November 16th, 1907, he wrote to thank Root for an interview and added, "I have spoken of you in highest terms to thousands of people all over the United States in my Congo meetings." On January 9th, 1908, Barbour sent him a memorandum expressing the views of the Congo Reform Association praising Root's policy.[17] G. Stanley Hall, President of the Association, and twelve other representatives of it wrote to Root on March 30th, 1909, expressing their warm appreciation of his "splendid service . . . to humanity."

The New York American printed lurid stories of rubber concessions in the Congo obtained from King Leopold by a syndicate which included T. F. Ryan, J. P. Morgan, J. D. Rockefeller and the Guggenheims, but there is nothing in Root's private files or in the archives of the Department of State to indicate that Root was active in promoting those interests. The initiative seems to have been taken by King Leopold who sent Count Kowalsky to the United States to enlist the aid of American capital in developing the Congo. Kowalsky saw Roosevelt and Ryan and a Ryan-Guggenheim combination put capital in a Belgian-American company which got a royal commission on November 9th, 1906. It would have been quite natural and almost a matter of routine for the Secretary of State to facilitate the negotiations under such circumstances but it does not appear that his aid was sought or needed.[18]

December 10th, 1906, Senator Lodge introduced in the Senate a resolution advocating an international inquiry of affairs in the Congo and assuring the President of the Senate's support if he cooperated in such a movement. On the same day, Root talked with the President and telegraphed Chargé Carter at the London Embassy to tell Sir Edward Grey that the President was keenly appreciative of the British Government's activities in this humanitarian cause and was eager to cooperate.[19] On January 16th, 1907, Root informed Lodge that Sir

[16] House Doc. 565, 59th Cong., 1st Sess., p. 2. Quoted by James Brown Scott in American Secretaries of State, Vol. IX, p. 209.
[17] Archives of the Department of State.
[18] See O'Conor, The Guggenheims, pp. 178–182.
[19] Sen. Doc. 147, 61st Cong., 1st Sess., p. 9.

Edward Grey thought the passage of his resolution by the Senate would have a beneficial effect; [20] the resolution was passed on February 15th.

Throughout the ensuing negotiations, Root followed the policy of stimulating Great Britain to take the lead as a signatory of the Berlin Act. On February 24th, 1908, he wrote to Dr. Barbour that "we have been pressing England pretty vigorously to take her position upon her right under the Berlin treaty, and have made as strong representations concurrently with England to the Belgian Government as it seemed to us would be useful. I do not think we could have gone further without doing more harm than good." [21] To his New York friend, John E. Parsons, he wrote more fully on April 15th, 1908:

> We have been doing everything which seemed to be possible to bring about a change of conditions. Unfortunately the United States is not a party to the Berlin Convention which gives the great powers of Europe a right of supervision over Congo affairs, so that we have the least ground for interference of any of the great powers. Nothing that could be done which seemed at all likely to do more good than hurt, has been neglected, and nothing will be omitted in the future. Of course, we cannot send an army to the Congo to take possession of the country and administer it ourselves. It is only by moral pressure that we can accomplish anything. This we have been exercising in conjunction with England, but to do it publicly would result in complete disaster by creating resentment in Belgium against foreign interference. The officers of the Congo Relief Association have been kept advised of what we have been doing. [22]

Although the Congo reform groups in the United States were opposed to the annexation of the Congo Free State by Belgium, Root saw no basis for opposition on the part of the United States Government and acquiesced in that result which was accomplished by act of the Belgian Parliament in October, 1908. In his note of January 11th, 1909, to the Belgian Minister, he contented himself with taking the position that the United States was confident that the Belgian administration of the Congo would meet every need and objection. [23]

20 Archives of the Department of State.
21 Ibid.
22 Ibid.
23 Foreign Relations of the United States, 1909, p. 400.

Root dealt also with another humanitarian problem which had confronted Hay and which the latter handled in quite a different way. The Jews had been subjected to periodic persecutions in Russia; the Jews in America have naturally responded sympathetically. In 1902, there were pogroms in Russia and Jewish leaders invoked the aid of President Roosevelt. Roosevelt seems to have been chiefly interested in winning the American Jewish vote for his re-election in 1904 and he played "the demagogue on an international scale for the sake of winning a presidential nomination. It is a pity that . . . Hay should have lent his cleverness to the support" of such projects.[24] In 1905 and 1906, the Jewish persecutions were intensified by the current revolutionary disorders. Root had a wide circle of Jewish acquaintances, though no close Jewish friends. He had made a great point of doing something for the Jews in Morocco and was anxious to do the same in Russia. There is nothing in his correspondence to indicate that he approached the subject with the levity which characterized Hay's action.[25] On November 24th, 1905, Root wrote to Arnold Kohn:

In response to your letter of November 22nd, I enclose a check for the fund now being raised for the relief of the unfortunate Jews who have been subjected to such dreadful cruelties in Russia. I do not see how any one can fail to sympathize deeply with them in their suffering, and to hope that out of the present disorder and change in that country there may come a better day of security and freedom for them. We have little power to help them; but for some of the homeless and despoiled, money may be helpful, and for some who are in despair, the knowledge that there is friendliness and sympathy in the world may be an encouragement; and the expression of abhorrence and condemnation by the civilized world for the cruelties which have been practised, may in time come to have some little restraining effect.

Hay had written notes for the purpose of giving them publicity for political effect in the United States. Root wrote for the purpose of helping the Jews in Russia; perhaps it was fortunate for Root and for the Russian Jews that Roosevelt in Root's time was not thinking of another presidential term. On June 23rd, 1906, Root wrote to the

[24] Dennett, *John Hay*, p. 401.
[25] *Ibid.*, p. 397.

President, submitting an instruction which he proposed to send to the American Ambassador in St. Petersburg:

I think it may do some good, though I do not feel sure of it. I do not know how it will be received. It may merely give offense. I am sure that to go further would do harm. I am sure also that to publish here the fact that such a despatch has been sent would do harm, and serious harm to the unfortunate people whom we desire to help. Any possible good effect must be looked for in absolutely confidential communication to the Russian Government. The publication that any communication has been made would inevitably tend to prevent the Russian Government from acting, to increase the anti-Jewish feeling and to make further massacres more probable.

On January 8th he had written in similar vein to Robert R. Hitt, Chairman of the House Committee on Foreign Affairs. Hitt had sent him copies of resolutions introduced in the House expressing sympathy for the Jews in Russia and asking for suggestions as to the advisable course of action.

These resolutions do not appear to be the exercise of any legislative power conferred upon Congress by the Constitution, but to be merely an expression of opinion upon matters which, so far as they may be the concern of this Government, form a part of the foreign relations which the Constitution requires the President to conduct upon his own responsibility, or with the advice and consent of the Senate. The resolutions could not, therefore, if adopted, be regarded as responsible official action, and I cannot conceive that their adoption would accomplish any good purpose. I am rather inclined to think that they would tend, by producing irritation and antagonism, to aggravate the dangers of the unfortunate people whom they are intended to aid.[26]

It was another case of that American sentimental interest which confronted Root in the Congo matter. His method of handling it was far from spectacular but probably more effective than a bellicose attitude which the Russian Government would of course have known would not be followed up by forceful action.

In another matter, Root took a stand which was displeasing to the

[26] Archives of the Department of State.

government of the Czar but very satisfactory to American liberals. The Russian Government sought the extradition from the United States of two Russians, Pouren and Rudovitz. Both men were charged with murder, arson and robbery; both were Russian revolutionaries and both pleaded that the acts complained of were committed in the course of revolutionary activities and were therefore "political" offenses. The extradition treaties of the United States in general, and with Russia in particular, provide that fugitives shall not be surrendered if the demanding government wishes to punish them for offenses of a political character. The Russians insisted that killing men with their wives and daughters and especially robbing them must be considered ordinary crimes and not political offenses. The cases attracted great popular interest in the United States; mass meetings were held and thousands of petitions were signed in the interest of the fugitives. It was a difficult point and a decision either way could have been supported. In the Rudovitz case, on January 26th, 1909, the day before he ceased to be Secretary of State, Root gave his opinion in a communication to the Russian Ambassador. His statement is a classic on the subject, holding that the acts of violence were inextricably connected with the revolutionary activity and that Rudovitz would not be surrendered. Presumably on the basis of this ruling in the Rudovitz case, Pouren was discharged from custody two months later.

As Roosevelt had lined up the Moroccan conference before Root became Secretary of State, so he had also lined up a second Hague peace conference. The first Hague conference had met on the call of the Czar in 1899 and had done valuable work in creating the Permanent Court of Arbitration and in drawing up conventions on the laws of war. In October, 1904, probably due to the general interest which he had developed in the Russo-Japanese War, Roosevelt made some soundings about the convocation of a second Hague conference. The Russians replied that it could not be considered during the war and the matter dropped. "Kings and such-like are fundamentally just as funny as American politicians," Roosevelt wrote from Oyster Bay to Root on September 14th, 1905: "Odell's anxiety that he and not Platt should receive the credit of certain presidential appointments in New York is not a bit more amusing than the attitude of the Czar about the Hague conference, as outlined in the following letter which was yesterday presented to me by Baron Rosen, who came out here for that purpose." The letter suggested that a favorable moment had now come for another conference at The Hague and that the Czar was sure of President Roosevelt's sympathy because of the steps which he had initiated in the preceding year.

> After he had read the letter Rosen began to hem and haw as to the steps already taken by me a year ago, and about the fact that The Hague conference was the peculiar pet project of the Czar. I finally interrupted him and said that I thought I understood what he wished, and that he could tell the Czar at once that I was delighted to have him and not me undertake the movement; that I should treat the movement as being made on his initiative, and should heartily support it. . . . As a matter of fact I am glad to be relieved from making the move on my own initiative. I should have done it if no one else had done it because I think it ought to be done; but I particularly do *not* want to appear as a professional peace advocate—a kind of sublimated being of the Godkin or Schurz variety—and it gives us a freer hand in every way to have the Czar make the movement.[27]

Root's first task in connection with the conference was to secure its postponement. It was proposed that the conference should meet in July, 1906. This date would have brought The Hague conference into conflict with the Pan American conference at Rio de Janeiro, a conflict particularly embarrasing for many of the Latin American republics who would need to use the same delegates for both conferences. Only Mexico and the United States of the western republics had been represented at the first Hague conference and the second Pan American Conference in 1901 had requested those countries to use their good offices to secure invitations for all to the next Hague gathering when it should be convened. The American republics also wished to secure the privilege of adhering to the Convention for the Pacific Settlement of International Disputes which was signed at the first conference. These negotiations were left to Root and the privileges were duly extended despite the reluctance of some of the European powers. He had told Joseph H. Choate, head of the American delegation, in his private letter of May 31st, 1907, that the Brazilians were anxious about receiving their full share of recognition in the dis-

---

[27] Root papers, quoted in part in Bishop, op. cit., Vol. I, p. 417.

tribution of honors at the conference—vice presidencies of committees and the like. "Of course the United States does not care . . .
about these so called honors. . . . I should say that we better give
them the benefit of whatever may be coming to us, so far as practicable. If we do this, we will be repaid ten times over by their appreciation provided they do not think we are discriminating in favor
of one against another. Buchanan, as you know, is charged with the
special duty of doing all he can to help the Latin Americans in this
appearance on their part as members of the world family. We have
taken a great deal of pains to get them into the conference, and I
think most of them feel grateful for it, and I think it is a good policy
to help them all we can." [28] Root probably cared more about the conflict of dates with the Rio meeting, but another conflict existed between the date suggested by Russia and the Red Cross Congress which
was to meet in Geneva in June. Oscar Straus wrote to Roosevelt on
the subject of this second conflict but Root warned the President off
from the controversy:

> I think that, having conceded the initiative to the Czar, it
> is hardly worth your while to try to drive it away from him for
> the purpose of getting personally into the first small row that
> comes up.

After considerable manoeuvring, the date was set for the summer of
1907. The postponement was in fact necessary to enable proper arrangements to be made before the conference met. "It is quite evident,"
Root wrote Joseph H. Choate on April 17th, 1906, "that we are a long
ways from being ready for the conference to meet, and Russia's proposal to have it meet early in July was quite premature. The fact is, I
suppose that the Russian statesmen had their minds so full of their
own troubles at home that they really had not been thinking about this
subject, and, being stirred up by somebody, they took a sudden spurt
without much reflection."

The point requiring the largest amount of "preparation" was the
reservation which the United States had made in accepting the Russian
program, to raise at the conference the question of the limitation of
armaments. The consideration of this subject was the alleged reason
for convoking the first conference which had adopted innocuous reso-

[28] Archives of the Department of State.

lutions relative thereto. In writing to Ambassador Reid on this question, October 24th, 1906, Root admitted that "no results can possibly be obtained without a number of failures . . . failures are necessary steps towards success, and we might as well go ahead and meet them." It was another example of Root's long-range view, a view to which it is impossible for a man to adhere if he is interested solely in the record he is making for himself.

> If you set up one idea, no matter how good it is, and make it paramount over all others, it leads to destruction. Did you ever see a man carrying an armful of oranges and drop one? He reaches to pick that one up and then another drops, and so on until he has lost them all. The important thing is to get something that will hold two oranges and then improve it until it will carry three, and then, on the basis of your experience, improve it still further until it will carry four and then five. That is the way you get on with oranges.[29]

On the question of limitation of armaments, Root assumed in his letter to Reid that "we are in agreement with Great Britain, the only difficulty being to find some practical way to accomplish what we agree it is highly desirable to accomplish. I can see no possible way except for each country to stop naval construction right where it is, limiting further construction to maintenance and replacing. . . . I do not suppose that the adoption of this could be secured, but, in my judgment, it would be a distinct gain to civilization and the peace of the world, to fix definitely the responsibility for refusal. Any power which is put in that position would necessarily be compelled by its future conduct to rebut the presumption that it means to disturb the peace of the world. . . . I think we should work together with England on this subject."

There was no doubt that Great Britain was in agreement with the United States in regard to limitation of armaments.[30] Germany suspected, with considerable justification, that "perfidious Albion" wished to use the conference to throttle German naval rivalry. Reid had reported on July 27th, 1906, that Sir Edward Grey would prefer to have the United States take the initiative in proposing this question at the

---

[29] Root to the author, March 3, 1931.
[30] Cf. Sir Edward Grey to President Roosevelt, February 12, 1907, Gooch and Temperley, *British Documents on the Origins of the War*, Vol. VIII, p. 203.

conference. Adee thought the British proposal was "embarrassing" because the United States needed to increase its fleet to protect its long coast line, the canal and the Pacific Islands; he believed it would be better to propose the "normalization" of armaments.[31] The German opposition did not appear immediately; Russia was the chief objector. Professor Martens was sent by the Russian Government on a sounding expedition through the European capitals; Ambassador Tower in Berlin was instructed to talk with him, conferring closely with Henry White in Rome. Tower's cable despatch of January 31st, 1907, was emphatic in the conclusion that the German Government would do everything in its power to prevent the subject from taking tangible form. In view of this situation, Root did not try to push too hard. On February 19th, 1907, he cabled to White:

> We understand France does not wish to get in position of appearing to put Germany in a hole; nor do we. We think Europe ought to consider seriously and discuss this subject, and we wish to occupy a position where we can propose it if there is a reasonable prospect of doing more good than harm. If, however, when the Conference meets Europe appears unwilling, we should hardly feel called upon to try to force disarmament upon her.[32]

Root also discussed in his letter to Reid the question of land armament, in terms which showed how much less complicated the problem was at that time and yet how he put his finger on a solution which was to be utilized at the World Disarmament Conference more than two decades later.

> The limitation of military armaments is more complicated, and I think less important because it really concerns only the question of the method and degree to which governments shall train their people in military exercise. It is impossible to exclude any country from considering its entire male population capable of bearing arms as a potential army, or to say that any of them shall not receive some training for national defense. The standing armies of the Continent are practically training schools through which the men of military age are passed into the reserves. The militia systems of England and the United States are less effective means of accomplishing the same purpose. One

[31] Archives of the Department of State.
[32] Ibid.

method is suited to the genius of one country and another to that of another country. It would probably be impossible to devise any system upon which comparisons could be made which would be adapted to many countries. The most feasible method of limitation that I can see is to reduce the term of enlistment in any standing army and limit re-enlistment. That would involve difficulty in working out, but it would effect a real limitation upon great standing armies.

Roosevelt's attitude on the question was rather conflicting. He supported the general idea of limitation of armaments and suggested the device, used in after years, of limiting the size of battleships. But, as he wrote Carnegie on August 5th, 1906, "We must always remember that it would be a fatal thing for the great free peoples to reduce themselves to impotence and leave the despotisms and barbarians armed." [33] July 2nd, 1907, he wrote to Root:

> . . . ever since I found out that the English Government would not consent to a reduction in the size of ships and would insist, quite properly, upon maintaining its own great naval superiority, I felt that its attitude in favor of a limitation of armaments as regards other nations would be treated as merely hypercritical [sic] and would cause damage and not good.

On April 20th, 1907, Root assembled the American delegates to The Hague conference at a meeting in the Department of State. All items on the agenda of the conference were thoroughly discussed.[34] Root first summed up the position of the powers on the disarmament issue; it appeared that Spain was willing to discuss this subject at The Hague but was lukewarm, while Germany, Austria and Russia were opposed, with Italy sitting on the fence but plainly leaning over to her German allies. The British had changed their tactics and were urging a discussion of limiting expenditures on armaments—a method later known as "budgetary limitation." Root was sure the British would raise the subject because of the pressure of public opinion in England. It would therefore be unnecessary for the American delegation to "go so far as to introduce the project and force it upon the convention, but that it should be known that we favored the project,

[33] Bishop, op. cit., Vol. II, p. 21.
[34] Full minutes were kept by James Brown Scott, Solicitor of the Department of State and Technical Adviser to the American Delegation.

and that we would discuss it favorably if introduced." After the delegates were gathered at The Hague but before the conference "really got down to work," Root wrote Roosevelt that "of course the armament question will be shelved. It can't be that Sir Edward Grey expected to do any more than satisfy English public opinion. His action doesn't square with any other view." [35] It was raised in a purely formal way by the British and formally endorsed by Choate as head of the American delegation. The Krupps and the Schneiders and the Vickers went on making the big armaments and the big dividends which got bigger and better when the inevitable war broke out just seven years later.

The United States had reserved the right to bring up one other subject which was not on the Russian program. This was the subject of the forcible collection of contract debts, commonly known as the Drago doctrine. Root had vigorously espoused the doctrine in his speech at Buenos Aires but in extending the notion to all contract debts between a government and a foreign individual, he ignored the special reasoning by which the Argentine statesman had justified his position and had confined it to the public debts of the state. The Rio Pan American Conference had adopted a resolution suggesting that the subject be considered at The Hague and Root was particularly anxious to get results which would strengthen his program of Pan American friendship. The matter was discussed at great length with the delegates of the United States at the meeting on April 20th. Root said he had avoided an advance discussion of this topic with the European governments because he feared the development of debtor and creditors blocs, but he understood the European governments were very suspicious, thinking the position of the United States to be "much more radical than it is. Undoubtedly, when the subject is discussed in detail they will be pleased to learn that the views of the Government are really so moderate." Root believed that the subject need not be brought up separately but could be interwoven with the proposals for arbitration. He anticipated the necessity for compromise and thought it might be possible to reach agreement at least on postponing the use of force until the claim was arbitrated; he had been impressed "by the largeness of the claims presented and the smallness of the awards made when passed upon by a judicial tribunal. He said

[35] July 8, 1907, Roosevelt Papers, Library of Congress.

that the system of forcible collection of debts generated speculators who live on the people of the country, who promote revolutions by advancing money for arms and ammunition, and make at times contracts with distressed governments which are seeking to avert political destruction."

In his formal instructions which were issued on May 21st, Root suggested a draft which provided that "the use of force for the collection of a contract debt . . . is not permissible until after" the claim has been arbitrated. Root unquestionably agreed fundamentally with Drago's position, but in this instance he failed to show his usual keen appreciation of the other man's point of view. Drago bitterly opposed the American proposal at The Hague on the ground that it was a direct admission of the right to use force for debt collection after arbitration had fixed the amount and other details; this was wholly contrary to his theory. Due to his objections, a different phraseology was finally adopted at The Hague in the so-called Porter Convention— named for the American delegate, General Horace Porter, who had this item in charge. The final phrasing began with an express promise not to use force for collecting contract debts and ended in a separate paragraph with the provision that this undertaking was "not applicable" when the debtor prevents arbitration or fails to carry out an award. It was a neat lawyerlike compromise but Drago and other Latin Americans were no better pleased and refused to become parties to the convention which was designed for their especial benefit. "A peculiarity of the Latin races," Root wrote in a letter to Elbert F. Baldwin on November 1st, 1907, "is that they pursue every line of thought to a strict, logical conclusion and are unwilling to stop and achieve a practical benefit as the Anglo Saxons do." Drago's fears that the Porter Convention contained little "practical benefit," found justification in an incident which happened five years later. In the summer of 1912, the State Department under Secretary Knox was interesting itself in arranging a loan for Honduras. A proposal was made to insert in the loan agreement a clause permitting the United States to intervene in case of default. This proposal was not considered feasible but the Solicitor of the State Department suggested inserting instead a clause providing for arbitration in case of default. Calling attention to the Porter Convention, he said that it "would give the Government [of the United States] just about as good a right to use force as the original" proposal for a right of intervention.[36]

As a part of Root's policy of Latin American friendship, this episode at The Hague was a failure. In the broader view of establishing a salutary international principle, the Porter Convention satisfied Root's long-view philosophy.

Not only the conventions signed and ratified, but the steps taken toward conclusions which may not reach practical and effective form for many years to come, are of value. Some of the resolutions . . . do not seem to amount to very much by themselves, but each one marks on some line of progress the farthest point to which the world is yet willing to go. They are like cable ends buoyed in mid-ocean, to be picked up hereafter by some other steamer, spliced, and continued to shore. . . . Each necessary step in the process is as useful as the final act which crowns the work and is received with public celebration.[37]

Root's chief interest, however, centered on plans for the peaceful settlement of international disputes. The first Hague Conference had set up the Permanent Court of Arbitration, which was a valuable step forward but was not what its name implies. It was in fact merely a permanent plan whereby a list or panel of names of potential arbitrators was compiled with a specified procedure for drawing names to form a tribunal when the parties to a dispute mutually agreed to do so. Root's formal instructions to the American delegates outlined the proposals which he had already discussed with them orally.

The method in which arbitration can be made more effective, so that nations may be more ready to have recourse to it voluntarily and to enter into treaties by which they bind themselves to submit to it, is indicated by observation of the weakness of the system now apparent. There can be no doubt that the principal objection to arbitration rests not upon the unwillingness of nations to submit their controversies to impartial arbitration, but upon an apprehension that the arbitrations to which they submit may not be impartial. It has been a very general practice for arbitrators to act, not as judges deciding questions of fact and law upon the record before them under a sense of judicial responsibility, but as negotiators effecting settlements of the questions

[36] Foreign Relations of the United States, 1912, p. 616.
[37] Root's prefatory note in Scott, Texts of the Peace Conferences at the Hague, 1899 and 1907.

brought before them in accordance with the traditions and usages and subject to all the considerations and influences which affect diplomatic agents. The two methods are radically different, proceed upon different standards of honorable obligation, and frequently lead to widely differing results. It very frequently happens that a nation which would be very willing to submit his differences to an impartial judicial determination is unwilling to subject them to this kind of diplomatic process. If there could be a tribunal which would pass upon questions between nations with the same impartial and impersonal judgment that the Supreme Court of the United States gives to questions arising between citizens of the different States, or between foreign citizens and the citizens of the United States, there can be no doubt that nations would be much more ready to submit their controversies to its decision than they are now to take the chances of arbitration. It should be your effort to bring about in the Second Conference a development of The Hague Tribunal into a permanent tribunal composed of judges who are judicial officers and nothing else, who are paid adequate salaries, who have no other occupation, and who will devote their entire time to the trial and decision of international causes by judicial methods and under a sense of judicial responsibility. . . .[38]

As Root and the American delegates had fully recognized in their discussions on April 20th, the crux of the matter lay in the method of selecting the judges for the proposed court. It would obviously not be feasible to have a bench large enough to include a judge from every country of the world. The problem was to find a method for choosing the judges which would satisfy all the countries. Root felt that any system of representation should take into account the principal legal systems of the world and also geographical considerations. He did not attempt to wed the delegates to any particular scheme since "It is not expedient that you should be limited by too rigid instructions . . . for such a course, if pursued generally with all the delegates, would make discussion useless and the conference a mere formality." [39]

Root—and the delegates—were hampered during the conference by Root's ill health. The files are full of frantic cables from Choate beseeching the Secretary to send instructions on numerous points which

[38] *Foreign Relations of the United States,* 1907, Part II, p. 1135.
[39] *Ibid.*

arose on all subjects of the agenda. From Clinton and from Muldoon's
sanatorium Root wrote his letters and telegrams long-hand to Adee,
fighting against his weakened physical condition and the strain caused
by his brother's last illness. "I am assiduously doing nothing," Root
wrote to Senator Lodge from Clinton on July 2nd, 1907, "and discouraging communications from the Department by neglect of them.
My brother is running along about the same with a hopeless struggle
but he seems to get pleasure from my presence." [40]

For the solution of the problem of selecting judges, a scheme was
proposed for allocations among the countries on the basis of population. Root's files contain pages of figures and calculations, showing attempts to find arithemetical satisfactions for the small states which
of course began by demanding full equality with the large states. Root
was chiefly concerned to avoid having the Latin American countries
believe that the United States was standing with the large powers of
Europe against their equal representation. When the plan based purely
on population was varied, Root told Adee to cable Choate:

> The enumeration of European powers without regard to pop-
> ulation and including Spain seems to assume superiority over
> non-European powers which would be very distasteful to South
> America. We must not on any account sacrifice our position of
> asserting the national equality of American States with the other
> powers of the earth. It is far more important to us than the whole
> court scheme. [41]

On August 16th, Adee telegraphed to Root:

> Long telegram giving new Brazilian proposition for organizing
> Arbitration Court has been chasing you at Clinton and South-
> ampton. Briefly Brazil proposes twenty-one judges, of whom fif-
> teen named for ten years by powers over ten million inhabitants
> and the other six among the rest in rotation for various terms.
> The object is obviously to let in Mexico and Brazil in the ten
> year class. I cabled briefly to Choate to prepare him for anything
> you might send him on the subject. Have just received following
> from Choate: Quote. Brazilian plan of Permanent Court indi-
> cated in your cable absolutely impossible. If insisted on it will
> wreck the whole scheme of a Court. Our first plan which you ap-

[40] Lodge Papers, Massachusetts Historical Society.
[41] Adee to Choate, August 13, 1907, Archives of the Department of State.

proved does full justice to Brazil, and the Argentine Republic will consent to nothing that does more. It places Brazil and other South American States of equal rank on like footing with each other and with European States of similar rank. Do not ask an impossibility. We are doing our utmost to secure a Court on terms of substantial equality.[42]

Despite the Root-Nabuco entente, the Brazilians were getting out of hand, perhaps because the Brazilian press was showing resentment that their country was not being treated at The Hague as one of the Great Powers. Root tried to bring them into line by cabling our Ambassador in Rio on September 3rd:

Tell Minister for Foreign Affairs emphatically: quote: From the beginning of the Hague conference the delegates of the United States have in pursuance of their instructions bent every effort to secure satisfactory representation for all our countries in the desired permanent court. The influence of the sister republics of the American hemisphere has all been thrown in this direction.

It is hardly necessary to say that any plan proposed which might be justly distasteful to Brazil could not for that reason be entirely satisfactory to the United States.

At the same time, although we of the American nations can arrange our own conferences exactly as we wish, still, at the Hague, we must all yield something to European views when consistent with our dignity and interests. Unless we did this we should have to dissociate ourselves entirely from the Hague and its progressive efforts for world-wide peace and harmony.

The proposal to require that each country shall name a permanent member of the court is equivalent to defeating the proposed court in which we are much interested not for our own special benefit but upon general public grounds. We hope Brazil will not insist upon such a position but will agree to some plan which involves no discrimination against American nations and no derogation from the sovereignty of any but proceeds upon some basis by which the selection of a reasonable number of judges may be accomplished. It would be most unfortunate if the opposition of American republics were to prevent a practical re-

[42] Archives of the Department of State.

sult for the good of mankind to which European nations equal
in population consent.[43]

Nothing then availed to bridge the gap between the great and small.
It was not until after the creation of the League of Nations that Root,
in 1920, had the satisfaction of evolving a formula which was acceptable to all and resulted in the creation of the Permanent Court of
International Justice.

Root had instructed the American delegates to promote the development of a general treaty of arbitration. He had pointed out to
them the extent to which the Senate of the United States was willing
to go in consenting to ratification of such a treaty and during the conference gave Choate more detailed instructions on the various proposals advanced. The conference tried to agree on a very limited and
perfectly innocuous list of subjects in respect of which the states might
agree to the principle of compulsory arbitration but it was unsuccessful, due in part to the determined opposition of Germany. The German delegate, Marshall von Bieberstein, Choate remarked at one of
the sessions, was devoted to the principle of arbitration, but opposed
to every practical application of it. He reminded Choate of a mortal
who "sees as in a dream a celestial apparition which excites his ardent
devotion, but when he wakes and finds her by his side he turns to
the wall, and will have nothing to do with her." [44]

The Senate of the United States had given evidence of a similar
frigidity but for different reasons. Hay had negotiated arbitration
treaties with eleven countries. All of the treaties were based on the
Anglo-French model of 1903, excepting from the obligation to arbitrate questions which "affect the vital interests, the independence, or
the honor of the two contracting States" or which "concern the interests of third parties." The practical effect of such reservations is that
whenever an important question arises a state may invoke one of them
and avoid arbitration. They were tantamount to saying that the parties
would arbitrate any question which was not really important. But
the Senate was jealous of its own prerogatives and wished to keep in
its own hands the power to decide what cases fell within the exceptions. An important and continuing factor was the fear of the southern
Senators that the President might consent to arbitrating the question

[43] Ibid.
[44] Proceedings of the Conference, Vol. II, p. 74.

of the repudiated debts of the southern states. The Senate, therefore, consented to ratification subject to the further domestic reservation that the *compromis*—the special agreement in which a specific case is stated for submission to an arbitral tribunal—must in every case be submitted to the Senate for its advice and consent; in other words, the agreement must take the form of a treaty requiring submission to the Senate under our constitutional system. Roosevelt was furious, declared that ratification of the treaties with such a reservation would be a step backward and withdrew them from the Senate. I think that this amendment makes the treaties shams," he wrote to Senator Lodge on January 6th, 1905, "and my present impression is that we had better abandon the whole business rather than give the impression of trickiness and insincerity which would be produced by solemnly promulgating a sham. The amendment, in effect, is to make any one of these so-called arbitration treaties solemnly enact that there shall be another arbitration treaty whenever the two Governments decide that there shall be one. . . . Now, as far as I am concerned, I wish either to take part in something that means something or else not to have any part in it at all." [45]

Roosevelt was perfectly correct but the popular demand for arbitration treaties continued. Root was convinced that the Senate would not recede from its position and persuaded Roosevelt to take what he could get instead of waiting for the unattainable. Root accordingly instructed the delegates to The Hague to include in their acceptance of a general arbitration treaty the form of reservation upon which the Senate insisted. After the conclusion of the conference, Root negotiated a series of twenty-five treaties on the Hay model plus the Senate reservation. John Bassett Moore has said that they have made it "in actual practice more difficult to secure international arbitration than it was in the early days of our independence." [46] This is true, but successive presidents have been unable to shake the Senate from the position of hampering control which Root conceded to it. It is very doubtful whether the Senate would have yet receded from its demands if Root had not persuaded Roosevelt to yield, but it must remain a question of opinion whether the cause of arbitration would now be further advanced if the United States had concluded no treaty on

[45] *Roosevelt-Lodge Correspondence*, Vol. II, p. 111.
[46] *International Law and Some Current Illusions*, p. 86.

the subject. Root, of course, was applying his step by step policy of promoting the "continuous process through which the progressive development of international justice and peace may be carried on." [47]

Root also favored the establishment of the International Prize Court which was proposed at The Hague. He wrote the instructions for the American delegates to the London Naval Conference of 1908–1909 which sought to frame a code of prize law for such a court to apply. On this question the predominant naval interests of Great Britain left the lead to that country. The London Conference completed its work after Root left the State Department but the Conference's code, in the form of the Declaration of London, never went into effect, due to the opposition of the British Parliament. The establishment of the International Prize Court still awaits agreement on the rules of prize law. Root was too busy in the State Department to devote himself to the mastery of topics upon which he was not required to render decisions and he never became a master of the rules of prize law. There is, however, an interesting letter which he wrote to the Secretary of the Navy on May 21st, 1906, enclosing a letter from the great American student of naval problems, Captain A. T. Mahan. Root endorsed Mahan's proposal that the General Board of the Navy reconsider the traditional American position in favor of the immunity of private property at sea. "It is quite certain that the creation of an extensive commercial marine on the part of any great commercial country amounts now, in effect, to giving hostages for peace, and that the liability of private property to seizure in time of war insures a strong and powerful class in every commercial country deeply interested in the preservation of peace." The British Government was inclined to share this point of view.[48] Moreover, Root thought, "the necessity for protecting a merchant marine is undoubtedly an important consideration, leading to the enormous increase of naval armament now in progress."

Root had warned the American delegates to the Hague Conference that "The immediate results of such a conference must always be limited to a small part of the field which the more sanguine have hoped to see covered."

[47] Instructions to the American delegates to The Hague, *Foreign Relations of the United States*, 1907, p. 1130.
[48] Gooch and Temperley, *op. cit.*, p. 198.

. . . It is important to remember that the object of the conference is agreement, and not compulsion. If such conferences are to be made occasions for trying to force nations into positions which they consider against their interests, the powers can not be expected to send representatives to them. . . . Comparison of views and frank and considerate explanation and discussion may frequently resolve doubts, obviate difficulties, and lead to real agreement upon matters which at the outset have appeared insurmountable. It is not wise, however, to carry this process to the point of irritation. After reasonable discussion, if no agreement is reached, it is better to lay the subject aside, or refer it to some future conference in the hope that intermediate consideration may dispose of the objections.[49]

He had sounded the same warning publicly in his address before the National Arbitration and Peace Congress in New York on April 15th, 1907.[50]

The American press was inclined to report that the conference was pretty much of a failure but Root did not put much "weight upon the evil consequences of defeat. . . . In a good cause a good fight bravely lost is always a victory." [51] Choate, as a matter of fact, thought the conference "was a great success" and Root was satisfied. He did not make one of his drives to enlist newspaper support but in random correspondence with various editors, he tried to persuade them to accept his point of view. Root prepared a summary of the work of the conference for the President's Annual Message of December, 1907, and took delight in sending him later a clipping from the *Advocate of Peace* which praised that part of the Message and condemned the "muddy current" of Roosevelt's advocacy of a larger army and navy. On the margin of the clipping, Root wrote in blue pencil:

> Your name which is mud.
> *I* am an angel.

[49] *Ibid.*
[50] *Addresses on International Subjects*, p. 129.
[51] Root to Nicholas Murray Butler, October 16, 1906.

CHAPTER XXX

"Great and substantial victory"

THERE was one specific case for the application of the principle of arbitration in which Root achieved what was perhaps his greatest diplomatic triumph as Secretary of State. This was the settlement of the Newfoundland fisheries dispute which had troubled and often embittered our relations with Great Britain from the very first days of independence. The New England fishermen in colonial days had been accustomed to fishing off Newfoundland shores and their interests were taken into account in negotiating the treaty of 1783 which recognized the independence of the United States. All that the American negotiators were able to obtain from the British was an agreement that the American fishermen should have the "liberty" to fish along with the British fishermen on the Newfoundland coast, plus the very important privilege of drying and curing fish on parts of the shore. After the conclusion of the War of 1812, the British insisted that the war had terminated the prior treaty and the negotiators of the peace treaty of Ghent in 1814 were unable to agree on any new stipulation. A special treaty was concluded in 1818 whereby the Americans re-secured the liberty to fish in common with British fishermen in certain specified waters and to dry and cure their fish on the coasts of Newfoundland and Labrador until those coasts became settled. The British reserved the right to enforce regulations to prevent the Americans from abusing their privileges. By the treaty in 1871, the American fishermen obtained greater privileges but in 1885 the provisions were terminated and the treaty of 1818 again controlled. The basis was never wholly satisfactory to either side and disputes over the fisheries became chronic.

When Root prefaced his assumption of the duties of Secretary of State by a vacation trip to Newfoundland, he did it with the idea that there was no other way in which he could get a thorough understanding of the real problem. With him went William Carey Sanger, who had been his assistant Secretary of War, and Root's two sons. "We have established a division of labor for the journey," Root wrote to his wife from Quebec. "I am to do the eating Sanger is to do the drinking Elihu is to be disbursing officer & pay the bills & Edward is to look after baggage." They went to Port aux Basques, then up the South Branch of the Codroy River for salmon fishing, pushing on to the Bay of Islands and thence by steamer to Battle Harbour, Labrador, which was the chief center of the fishing industry. There they stayed for ten days, eating fried fresh cod every day. Thence they steamed down the coast to Indian Harbor, Hopedale and Nain.[1]

> From talking with the people there and seeing the way the industry was carried on, I got a new appreciation of the whole controversy. It began with a time when Newfoundland was practically unsettled, when there were no large centers there, and when practically everyone interested in fishing was a stranger who came in from the sea, and who used the land merely for drying fish, taking wood and water and mending nets. At that time the jurisdiction was entirely in the hands of the British Admiral and when I was there the room in the office where fishery matters were controlled was still called the Admiral's Room.
>
> Then settlements began to spring up in Newfoundland and a class of shore fishermen developed. It is inevitable that the interest of the shore fishermen should clash with the interest of fishermen who come in by boat from the sea. There is inevitable hostility between them. The Newfoundlanders were finally given the authority to make the regulations for the fishing industry and of course they made it in the interest of their own people. For example, they prohibited Sunday fishing. This was fine for the land fishermen who could go out any day, and did not suffer from staying at home one day in the week. But for the New England fishermen who came up there with ships and crews costing money by the day, dependent upon the weather, the necessity of ceasing from fishing on Sunday was almost ruinous.[2]

Root also came to the conclusion that much of the legislation passed by the Newfoundland Parliament was inspired by the influence of the

[1] Edward W. Root to the author.
[2] Elihu Root to the author, March 19, 1934.

big Newfoundland fish companies and not by the interests of the individual Newfoundland fishermen.

Immediately after his return, Root went to see the President at Oyster Bay, Choate and Lodge going at the same time. The main purpose of the meeting was to discuss the Newfoundland fisheries.[3] "I should ever so much like to meet Lodge and Choate at Oyster Bay," Root wrote Roosevelt on September 10th, 1905, ". . . there is a hereafter about which I should like to get the views of the Senior Senator from the fishing grounds." [4] Although Hay had consulted Lodge in negotiating a reciprocity treaty with Newfoundland, he never came to a full understanding with him and failed to take Lodge's advice about consulting the Gloucester fishing interests.[5] That was the kind of mistake which Root would not have been likely to make even if he had not been warned by Hay's experience. If the settlement of the fishery question required a treaty, as it very well might, Root wanted to count on Lodge's support; he knew too much about politics to think that Lodge out of personal friendship for him could support a treaty which was not satisfactory to Massachusetts' sea-going voters.

With that meeting at Oyster Bay, Root rounded out the preparation of one of the great international cases which he was to argue for the government through diplomatic channels and later before the bar of the Permanent Court of Arbitration at The Hague. It was a sound preparation—personal experience on the spot to learn the problem; conversation with the Massachusetts senator who represented the Gloucester fishermen and who knew what concessions they might be induced to make; conversation with the former ambassador to Great Britain who could give him something of the British point of view. Later came the mastery of the huge documentary record, a task which was meat and drink for Root. There is a story that when James Bryce came to Washington as British Ambassador, his first official call on Secretary Root at the State Department was to present a detailed argument prepared in Downing Street on the subject of the fisheries. He was ushered in to the Secretary's office and started to draw from his pocket the note which he was to read. "Just one moment, Mr. Ambassador," Root said, "if I understand correctly the position of

[3] Roosevelt to Lodge, September 6 and 15, *Roosevelt-Lodge Correspondence*, Vol. II, p. 190.
[4] Roosevelt Papers, Library of Congress.
[5] Dennett, *John Hay*, pp. 424 ff.

the British Government, it is somewhat as follows." Then, pacing back and forth across the room, he proceeded to expound an argument which Bryce realized was so much better than that which his Government had framed that he knew he could never present their note. He started to speak as Root finished, but again Root interrupted: "Now, Mr. Ambassador, the American Government's answer to these contentions is as follows:" and again pacing back and forth, Root proceeded to demolish one by one the British arguments which he had so elaborately constructed. Root "was almost perfect as Secretary of State," the British Chargé, Esmé Howard, believed; "so deliberate, so careful in his choice of words that at times when he was making a public speech one wondered when the next word would fall from his lips and remained perfectly satisfied with it when it did. Never excited over any negotiation or apparently the least annoyed or resentful on account of unexpected hitches or difficulties, perfectly courteous in argument and manner, and always almost cruelly logical and uncompromisingly to the point, he was in fact a wonderful man to do business with. He and Mr. Bryce understood each other perfectly. . . ." [6]

Senator Lodge was eager to cooperate and suggested to Root in a letter of September 26th, 1905, that the best way to avoid trouble was to let one of our revenue cutters, which were frequently in those waters to help break out ice-bound vessels, remain on the fishing grounds to hold the American fishermen in check. "The trouble about sending a Government vessel to the Bay of Islands now," Root replied on the following day, "is that it would seem like assuming that there is going to be trouble and would bring it. . . . It seems to me that we ought not to assume that the British Government is going to interfere or permit its people to interfere with the peaceful exercise by our fishermen of the rights as we understand them, and that the true course is for our fishermen to go on with their business assuming that they will not be interfered with. If there is any interference so that they cannot pursue their fishing without force, they should desist, communicate with the Government at Washington, and then we will have something upon which we can proceed by representation to the Government of Great Britain." But "that means the loss of their living that winter," Lodge replied, "something which is pretty hard for poor men, as they all are, to be temperate and reasonable about."

[6] Esmé Howard, *Theatre of Life*, 1905–1936, p. 139.

He thought the United States ought not "to be left to the action of a lot of fishermen who are hardy and reckless men and who may get themselves into serious difficulty and involve the government." [7]

Within a fortnight "something upon which we can proceed" turned up. The fishermen reported to the Massachusetts congressmen that the Newfoundland Government had prohibited American fishermen from fishing on the treaty coast. On October 13th, Root wrote at once to the British Ambassador, Sir Mortimer Durand, and sent a stiff telegraphic instruction to Ambassador Reid in London. It turned out that the prohibition was issued by subordinate officials and was disavowed by the Newfoundland Government.[8] But Root did not let the matter drop. Having received an opening for diplomatic negotiation, he was determined to push the business through to a final settlement. He had conferences with Congressman Gardner from the Gloucester district, and with representatives of the fishermen. Senator Redfield Proctor of Vermont, with whom Root had become intimate in the War Department days, talked with him on the subject and suggested that he put through a reciprocity treaty with Newfoundland, following the similar efforts of Blaine and Hay; "you are the man of all others to bring it about," Proctor wrote. "You trample relentlessly on all law and precedent, and nobody calls you to account or denounces you for the tyrant you are, for you maintain such a childlike and bland demeanor." But Root was quite aware that the Newfoundland treaty plan had been anathema to Canada and Adee probably told him, as he had told Hay, that Blaine had started the negotiations to keep up the tension between those two portions of the British Empire in the hope of promoting the annexation of Newfoundland by the United States.[9] Root was simultaneously trying to settle a number of issues with the Canadian Government. He was probably also aware that the Canadian Government would be able, if antagonized, to block in London any plan for the permanent adjustment of the Newfoundland fisheries question.

The next fishing season "closed without any collision between the British and American fishermen, or the development of any such friction as was at one time anticipated." The off-season was occupied in

[7] Lodge to Root, September 29, 1905.
[8] Root to Lodge, October 23, 1905.
[9] Dennett, op. cit., p. 423.

exchanging between the State Department and the Foreign Office in London detailed legal arguments regarding American treaty rights.[10] One of Root's principal arguments was that the Newfoundland authorities had no power to prescribe regulations controlling the time and manner of the exercise of fishing rights by the American fishermen, but he suggested that it would be quite possible for the two governments to agree upon mutually satisfactory regulations.[11] This suggestion was made just before Root left on his South American trip. He hinted also that the United States might find it desirable to send a cruiser to the fishing grounds, as France had been in the habit of doing; he was afraid there might be trouble.[12] But during his absence, Adee, Bacon and Ambassador Reid in London carried on, with the result that a *modus vivendi* covering the next fishing season was agreed upon, the final notes being exchanged on October 6th, 1906, just after Root's return to Washington.[13] Despite this agreement, there were scattered cases of interferences and continued protests.

As a part of his general program, Root accepted an invitation to visit Canada in January, 1907. Earl Grey, then Governor General of Canada, had visited New York in March, 1906, and Root had welcomed him in an address at a dinner in New York given by the Pilgrims on March 31st:

> . . . The policy . . . of the United States forbids alliances with other countries, but every lawyer knows, every man of affairs knows, that the signature and the seal upon a contract is of little value unless the character and purpose of the contracting parties is sincere, and that a sincere and genuine common purpose to do the thing to which a contract relates is as efficient without the seal and the signature as it would be with them.[14]

Grey wanted Root's speech "to sink into the Canadian mind." [15]

With Mrs. Root and his daughter Edith, Root arrived in Montreal on January 18th, 1907, going on to Ottawa the following day. There was no lavish display such as the Latin Americans had showered upon him but there was a good press, a round of the usual lunches and

10 *Foreign Relations of the United States*, 1906, Part I, pp. 661 ff.
11 Note of June 30, 1906, *ibid.*, p. 685.
12 Root to the President, July 3, 1906, Archives of the Department of State.
13 *Foreign Relations of the United States*, 1906, Part I, pp. 701 ff.
14 *Miscellaneous Addresses*, p. 151.
15 Earl Grey to Joseph H. Choate, May 11, 1906, Choate Papers, Library of Congress.

dinners and much opportunity for quiet talks with Earl Grey, Lord Strathcona, the High Commissioner for Canada, Sir Wilfrid Laurier, the Prime Minister, and others. Although the main topic was the settlement of the outstanding issues between Canada and the United States, Root took advantage of the opportunity to discuss their common problem of Japanese exclusion on the west coast. Root made his principal speech at a banquet of the Canadian Club of Ottawa on January 22nd.[16] The London *Times* of January 24th printed a despatch from its Ottawa correspondent stating that "The Canadian press is unanimous in praise" of the speech, but the London *Saturday Review*, two days later, was more cynical. It said that Root "understands the emotional appeal, he knows the value of platitudes, and of a great volume of words. He can be all things to all men and he knows how to exhibit himself in the particular form that will most flatter the peculiar vanity of the people he is preaching to. And he is a diplomatist. . . . But Mr. Root was on a flapdoodle expedition, and it would be absurd to suppose he attached the smallest importance to the propositions he was pouring forth." Whether or not this comment was inspired by British jealousy of closer ties between the Dominion and the United States, its writer missed the point; Root must have attached importance to what he poured forth because he was aware that those things have importance. Not all the world is made up of cultured cynics and friendly newspaper talk can do as much good as a jingo press can do harm. If the people and press of two countries are talking peace and friendship, such talk facilitates enormously the task of the politicians and statesmen who are seeking to secure the approval of a representative assembly for the ratification of treaties.

Not the least of the Canadian resentments was that based upon the Alaskan boundary award in 1903. Root's part as a member of that tribunal had not been forgotten and Root sought to disarm suspicion by a frank reference to that old trouble in his address.

Another important event which greatly facilitated the termination of the disputes with Canada and Newfoundland was the arrival early in 1907 of James Bryce as British Ambassador to the United States. His predecessor, Sir Mortimer Durand, had been an ineffective diplomat who had never succeeded in becoming one of that intimate diplomatic group who formed a unique coterie with the President

[16] *Miscellaneous Addresses*, p. 157.

and the Secretary of State. In that group Bryce took his place. He had known and admired Roosevelt since 1901 and he formed with Root a close friendship which lasted until his death. Bryce was also a warm friend of Earl Grey and established a precedent by making a visit to Canada where he did much to overcome the long-standing feeling that the British Ambassador in Washington was accustomed to sacrifice Canadian interests in order to curry favor with the United States.[17]

The continuance of the fisheries negotiations added another burden to Root's dismal summer of 1907 when he was weighed down with his own and his brother's illness. At Clinton he drafted despatches to Ambassador Whitelaw Reid regarding another *modus vivendi* for the ensuing season, and sent the drafts on to Bacon and Adee to be put into shape and sent off. Bacon made a trip to Clinton to discuss the question with him and went on to talk with the President at Oyster Bay. Roosevelt took an active interest in this stage of the negotiations and favored going on record as proposing arbitration before the Hague Court, partly for the effect which this announcement might have on the current conference at The Hague.[18] Sir Edward Grey, however, indicated that he did not feel that the time was quite ripe for that suggestion.[19] Yet on July 16th, Reid cabled that an apparently inspired newspaper story hinted that Sir Robert Bond, the Newfoundland premier, had proposed arbitration. "Would seem, therefore, that somebody here wants impression created proposal came from them instead of us, and attaches importance to prevalence of such a view at present." [20] The proposal had, as a matter of fact, first been made orally by Reid on July 10th, on Root's instructions after Bryce had informally suggested it.[21] July 24th, Reid cabled that Sir Edward Grey had told him orally that they accepted the arbitration proposition but were anxious "that the matter should be kept secret until Newfoundland had been heard from." [22] Root displayed similar caution in keeping Congressman Gardner and the Gloucester fishing interests informed of the course of the negotiations.[23] When the principle of

---

[17] Fisher, *Lord Bryce*, Vol. II, p. 28.
[18] Bacon to Root, July 9, 1907, Archives of the Department of State.
[19] Reid to the Secretary of State, July 10, 1907, *ibid.*
[20] Archives of the Department of State, cf. Mowat, *Diplomatic Relations of Great Britain and the United States*, p. 308.
[21] Draft of enclosure for letter from Clinton, Root to Bacon, July 3, 1907, Root Papers.
[22] Root Papers.
[23] See Adee to Root, August 28, 1907, *ibid.*

arbitration had been finally agreed upon, he consulted Senator Hale of Maine and Senator Lodge and Congressman Gardner of Massachusetts regarding the appointment of counsel to represent the United States. "You understand," Root wrote Lodge on January 24th, 1908:

> what I explained to Hale, that I want to have it understood that this particular counsel is retained upon the recommendation of the fishermen of Maine and Massachusetts so that they may understand that they are being represented by a man of their choice, and so that, if there should be an adverse result, they will not think that they have been sacrificed by the indifference of outsiders.[24]

Root also invited ex-Senator John C. Spooner to act as chief counsel; "you will have competent and well informed assistants, and you will be asked to contribute nothing to the cause except the trifling and unimportant incidents of brains, eloquence, skill, wisdom, force of character and a controlling personality." [25] Another detail was the selection of the arbitrators, as to which Root had informal conferences with Bryce, and, in accordance with the usual practice, telegraphed our appropriate ministers and ambassadors to report on the views and qualifications of the various candidates suggested. Root was much pleased to have Dr. Luis Drago, the former Foreign Minister of Argentina, selected as one of the judges. Root considered his selection significant as a "recognition of South America as an active force in the affairs of the world at large. It is another step along the line of development which was signalized by the inclusion of the South American states in the second Hague Conference." [26]

There was also much work to be done in framing the precise questions which were to be submitted to the tribunal. In this, Root drew heavily on Chandler P. Anderson who was subsequently appointed American Agent in the arbitration. It was not until midnight of Sunday, January 24th, 1909, three days before Root left the State Department, that final agreement was reached at Root's home in a twelve-hour conference with Bryce, Aylesworth, the Canadian Minister of Justice, and Kent, the Minister of Justice of Newfoundland. "The excellence of

[24] Archives of the Department of State.
[25] Root to Spooner, October 26, 1907, *ibid.*
[26] Root to Epijanio Portela, April 5, 1909.

our common aim," Bryce wrote to Root in arranging this meeting, "may perhaps justify such an employment of a few minutes on Sunday. Beati pacifici." Root announced the result at his last Cabinet meeting on the 26th.[27] The formal signing of the arbitration treaty took place on Root's last day in the Department, January 27th, 1909.

If victory is merited by careful preparation, Root merited the victory in settling this problem. From his trip to the fishing grounds in 1905, to his last midnight conference, he overlooked no detail, neglected no important interest or personage. The Senate, that final arbiter of the best laid plans of Secretaries of State, on the 18th of February, 1909, gave its advice and consent to the ratification of the treaty. It was only fitting that Root should be in at the finish but he at first declined when Chandler Anderson brought him word in October, 1909, that President Taft wanted him to act as senior counsel in the arbitration. He finally acquiesced and sailed for The Hague with the rest of the American group on May 21st, 1910. On board ship he was "the life of the party." [28]

Root thought the case the most interesting one he had ever been in,[29] but it was a long, tiresome process. The briefs of the two governments with their appended documents fill eight thick volumes and the oral arguments fill four more. Root was feeling run down and was bothered by a persistent cold; buttermilk was sent over regularly from England for him. Shortly after his arrival an over-zealous official was showing him through the various rooms of the Peace Palace where the Permanent Court of Arbitration is housed through the generosity of Andrew Carnegie. Every room was explained by Root's guide in exasperating detail. Root's patience was finally exhausted as they came to the second of the court rooms: "I quite understand," he broke in, "if you want a lot of justice you go to the large court room and if you want only a little bit of justice you go to the small court room." [30] As the interminable arguments went on and on, week after week, Root became almost as bored with the lawyers as he had been with his guide. In the custom which he had for years in many situations—including Cabinet meetings—he passed little notes to the person next him who was Chandler Anderson. Lammasch, the President of the

---

[27] Howe, *George von Lengerke Meyer*, p. 414.
[28] *Life of Samuel J. Elder*, p. 276.
[29] Root to the author, March 19, 1934.
[30] Chandler P. Anderson to the author, February 28, 1934.

tribunal, was "an awfully smart old cuss." One of the lawyers "must be a good jury lawyer, for he takes immense satisfaction in being hopelessly illogical." Another lawyer was "a great ejusdem generator." During one of the American arguments in which he felt the American counsel was making some damaging admissions: "As he seems to have stated what he regards as conclusive, I breathe as freely as a cold in the head will allow." Another American argument, so detailed that Root thought it was worked out with a "microscopic lens," drove him to the relaxation of doggerel which covered the British theory that bays were to be measured by a line drawn from headland to headland.

> The Britisher is brilliant
> But he hasn't any mind
> He blunders through existence
> With his headland on behind.
>
> Many men of many minds
> Many beasts of many kinds
> Many fishes in the sea
> Tweedledum and Tweedledee
> He can do this seems to me
> Till the end of land and sea
> We means us & us means we
> He is it & it is he
> Rub your eyes and try to see
> Fiddle dum and Fiddledee
> Haw gee buck & buckhaw gee
> What queer things we mortals be!

Root's own argument began on August 2nd and lasted for six days, not counting the intervening days when the tribunal did not sit.[31] He prepared his argument with elaborate care on 194 sheets of 5 x 8 note paper, mostly in long hand. In a few places the argument is fully written out; in greater part it is merely suggested. An elaborate system of underscorings in ink, and in blue, red and brown crayon, linked various parts of the argument together in his mind and served to catch his eye as he talked—it was a system which he often used in arguing cases in court. Although the members of the tribunal frequently inter-

[31] His argument fills 430 pages in the volume of his collected papers entitled *North Atlantic Coast Fisheries Arbitration*.

rupted with questions which forced him to deviate from his outline, he came back to it with clock-like precision and the printed record shows practically no variance from the preparatory notes. It was a great argument, requiring a summation of every one of the issues and the final appeal to the court in behalf of the American views. "I tried to present the case to the tribunal from the point of view, not of an international lawyer, or of a statesman, but from the point of view of a fisherman. I thought it was really a conflict not between two governments but merely between two groups of fishermen." [32] Samuel J. Elder, one of the other American counsel, had been taking elaborate notes on the arguments throughout the case, but when Root spoke, he noted in his diary, "I was too fascinated to take notes. It seemed like getting out of an open boat in mid-ocean onto an ocean liner and being assured of getting to port." [33] The London *Times*, which printed full accounts of the entire case, commented on August 15th, 1910, regarding the closing of his argument:

> His voice to-day has been almost inaudible, but of his speech as a whole it may be confidently asserted that, so far as argument and matter go, the United States might well have been content to rely for the due presentation of their case upon it alone. It gained greatly in its impressiveness by its moderation and its very lack of the exuberance which marked some of the earlier American utterances.

The tribunal did not render its award immediately, but Root did not linger. "I have come back from a very hard summer's work pretty tired and not feeling over well," he wrote his old friend Willard Bartlett from Clinton on September 9th. It was "I think the hardest three months work I ever did in my life. . . ." [34] When the award was made public, the papers were inclined to hail it as a British victory, as it ostensibly was since the main contentions of Great Britain were upheld.[35] But the important fact was that the Gloucester Board of Trade sent its congratulations and so did Joseph H. Choate who had labored with the problem when he was Ambassador to England. He wrote on September 19th, 1910:

[32] Root to the author, March 19, 1934.
[33] Elder, *op. cit.*, p. 302.
[34] Root to Henry M. Hoyt, September 16, 1910.
[35] Cf. Callahan, *American Policy in Canadian Relations*, p. 522.

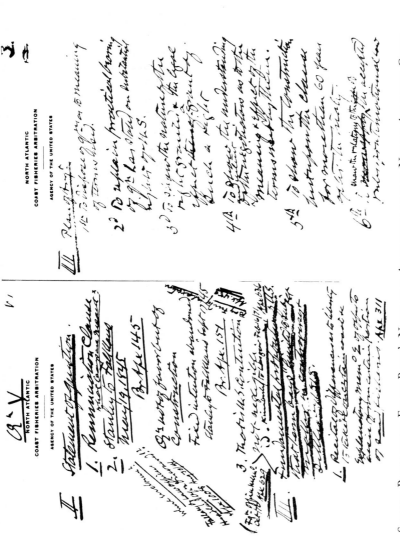

SAMPLE PAGES FROM ELIHU ROOT'S NOTES FOR ARGUMENT IN THE NORTH ATLANTIC COAST
FISHERIES ARBITRATION, AUGUST, 1910

(From the original now in the Harvard Law School Library)

I must congratulate you on what I consider your great success in the arbitration at the Hague. . . . It seems to me . . . that we got all we ought to have and that with all due respect to your associates it was your argument that did it. . . .

To which Root replied on the 21st:

We came out very well at The Hague, everything considered, and practically got substantially all that we were entitled to. There were several difficulties in the case. One was that the judges had decided it against us before the argument began. That made the fight a pretty hard and exhaustive one. After about three and half months of doing nothing else I began to feel like a monomaniac.[36]

Root explained to Willard Bartlett in his letter of September 9th that the important thing they had sought to get and had got was "not to prevent the proper regulation of the New Foundland fisheries, but to prevent New Foundland from passing laws which should go into effect without our either agreeing to them or having an opportunity to have their reasonableness passed on by someone besides the legislature of New Foundland." A great deal of fuss had been made about the Fifth Question presented to the tribunal, and decided in favor of Great Britain, regarding the measurement of territorial waters in bays, but Root told Bartlett that this question was "probably the least important practically. It has an historical interest. . . . It has not been mentioned in the diplomatic correspondence for twenty or thirty years past, and as our fishermen have all that time conformed their action to the British view, they are quite indifferent on the subject."

Taft congratulated him "on your victory before the English tribunal —a victory which at first was reported to be a defeat, but which it seems to me brings about largely all that you asked for. It is true the Court says that the local government ought not to be restricted in its police regulation, but the limitation that the police regulation shall be reasonable and the submission of that to arbitration necessarily imposes substantially all the limitation that you could have asked for. . . . I want to thank you personally for going, because I have half an impression that it was partly my personal pressure that induced

[36] The author has seen confidential data which go far toward sustaining Mr. Root's belief that one arbitrator had prepared his decision against the United States before the argument began.

you to undertake it." [37] By October 1st, Root could write to Bartlett: "The fact that we really won a great and substantial victory appears to be gradually emerging in the consciousness of American lawyers." The American papers had all gotten their news from British sources; "As a result, our American papers were placarding a British victory while our representatives at the Hague were dancing horn pipes for joy."

Root was asked to suggest the amounts proper for the compensation of the American lawyers, which he did in a letter to Secretary of State Knox on November 25th, 1910. "I cannot myself take any compensation because of my holding a salaried position under the Government." He believed that the Agent should receive $25,000 and the several counsel amounts ranging from $10,000 to $15,000. The leading British counsel received about $50,000 and two of them were honored by a peerage and a knighthood.[38] Congressman Albert Douglas of Ohio introduced in the House a concurrent resolution tendering to Root the thanks of Congress but the resolution died in Committee.

The closing word on this case may well be said by Bryce who did very much to make the agreement possible.

> It used to occur to me that we might three years ago have effected a settlement of the Fisheries question not very different from that at which the Hague Tribunal has now arrived. But our two countries would hardly have been satisfied with a settlement so made, and the example which has now been given of the utility of arbitration and of the good temper with which each nation has acquiesced in a decision which gave to neither all it claimed would have been lost. So if this is not the best of all possible worlds, it is a world in which some progress is made, as we may think when we look back on the century of bickering over these questions which we hope are closed for ever.[39]

The permanency of the settlement was secured by a treaty of July 20th, 1912 which was based on and made possible by the events of the preceding seven years.

Although the importance and pressing nature of the dispute over the Atlantic fisheries had forced Root to devote special attention to

[37] Taft to Root, September 24, 1910.
[38] New York Sun, January 11, 1911.
[39] Bryce to Root, January 8, 1911.

this problem in Canadian-American relations, he had regarded it as merely one detail in the general task of adjusting all outstanding differences with Canada. On May 3rd, 1906, he wrote an informal letter of seventeen typed foolscap pages to Sir Mortimer Durand, the British Ambassador, rehearsing sixteen different topics which should be discussed. Root recalled that a joint commission had commenced in 1898 to discuss and to settle many of these points but the failure to agree upon the Alaskan boundary dispute had led to the suspension of the sessions of the commission. Root did not propose the re-establishment of a formal commission but indicated the steps which might be taken on each of the problems, which ranged from reciprocal reduction of tariffs and regulation of fisheries to marking the boundary and facilitating the passage of goods in transit. This long letter of Root's was in reply to one which the British Ambassador wrote to him on April 26th and that letter in turn was the outcome of a discussion between Root and Earl Grey which had led to a Canadian proposal that agreement should be reached privately before formal negotiations were opened.[40]

The negotiations on all of these questions were carried on in an atmosphere of extraordinary friendliness and good will, with a minimum of wrangling. Sir Edward Grey expressed his appreciation of the attitude of Roosevelt and Root both directly and through Bryce.[41] Root was chiefly responsible for the creation of the atmosphere on the American side; the honors on the British side must be shared between Grey, Bryce and Sir Wilfrid Laurier, then Prime Minister of Canada. "Laurier was a very wise and fair-minded man and his character had a great deal to do with the fact that when the Great War came in 1914, there were no controversies left unsettled between the United States and Great Britain. . . ."[42] On the American side, the real negotiator, the man who worked out every point of detail, was Chandler P. Anderson. "His service was not as a mere assistant, but a strong coadjutor of independent thought, and a competent negotiator in his independent contacts with the representatives of other powers."[43] The complicated treaty signed on January 11th, 1909, which

[40] Cf. Callahan, op. cit., p. 495.
[41] Grey to Mrs. William Sheffield Cowles, March 1, 1909, Cowles Papers; Bryce to Root, February 1, 1909, Root Papers.
[42] Root to H. A. Powell, October 27, 1925.
[43] Root to President Hoover, November 6, 1931.

disposed of the questions arising from the use of the joint waterways of the two countries, partly by establishing a most useful Joint Commission, was the work of Anderson and George C. Gibbons who was detailed for that negotiation by Sir Wilfrid Laurier. Sir Robert Borden gave the credit for the treaty to Laurier because he sent Gibbons to Washington,[44] and the complete documentary record of the negotiations which is preserved in the Anderson Papers goes far to bear this out. On May 16th, 1910, Root wrote Gibbons that the "making of the treaty and its ratification are largely due to your personal ability and force of character. . . ." Gibbons had begun the negotiations with George Clinton representing the United States; Anderson took over in 1908 and thereafter carried the negotiations to a successful conclusion. "Mr. Root always refers to this [waterways] treaty as the 'Anderson-Gibbons Treaty' and I have always said to him that to that title should be added 'by and with the advice and consent of Secretary Root'." [45] Of course Anderson consulted Root on every step but, on the other hand, Root never failed to submit to Anderson any communication which reached the State Department and which dealt with Canadian affairs. Aside from the general arbitration treaty with Great Britain, the special treaty (not signed until 1910) for arbitrating outstanding claims and the agreements on the Newfoundland fisheries, the Root-Anderson team brought about the ratification of four treaties on issues between Canada and the United States.[46]

These negotiations with Canada are significant not only in Canadian-American history but also in the history of the British Empire. With the ability and vigor of Laurier, the broad sympathetic viewpoint of Grey, and Bryce's total lack of jealousy of his position as the sole diplomatic representative of the British Empire in the United States, events moved swiftly forward toward the day, hastened by the events of the World War, when Canada sent her own minister to Washington. Theodore Roosevelt realized that that day was approaching when he wrote to Root on May 1st, 1906, saying that the negotiations with Canada could best be handled by a special ambassador to Canada but "Of course this means a reversal of the policy that would have

[44] Sir Robert Borden to Root, August 16, 1927.
[45] Chandler P. Anderson to Charles Henry Butler, May 9, 1910, Anderson Papers.
[46] The treaties dealt with inland and coast fisheries, the delimitation of the boundary, reciprocity on conveying prisoners and salvaging wrecks, regulation of the common waterways and establishment of the Joint Commission.

to obtain were England's control of Canada absolute." [47] Root talked frankly with Bryce about the future status of Canada and it was probably with Bryce's silent approval that Root anticipated the time when Canada, as an independent member of the British Commonwealth of Nations, might take a place as a member of the Pan American Union. It was by Root's instructions that the Canadian coat of arms was included with those of the American Republics in the patio of the Pan American Building; the visitor today may mark it in the center of the north wall. He gave orders also that the bronze frieze in the Governing Board Room should include a panel depicting Champlain's negotiations with the Indians. And somewhere in storage there waits one of the special chairs for the Board Room of that building, carved with the name and coat of arms of Canada.[48]

[47] Chandler P. Anderson Papers.
[48] Root to the author, September 5, 1936, and speech of John Barrett before the Canadian Club of Toronto, New York *Times*, February 20, 1923.

CHAPTER XXXI

"The organization is defective"

IT does not make work any easier to have to use poor tools. As a whole, the American diplomatic and consular service was a poor instrument when Root entered the State Department in 1905. There were able men in both services but the system was bad. The reputation which Root had acquired in reorganizing the army led to a general belief, when his appointment as Secretary of State was announced, that he would devote most of his time to re-organizing the State Department and its foreign service. Root was immediately plunged into so many matters of international moment that the reorganization came as a secondary consideration. He reviewed the problem against the political background of the times.

A good many politicians are crooked, of course, but the great bulk of them are straight. You have to consider the standards of conduct which apply. Our whole system is based upon the creation and maintenance of political parties. Without that system you get no results whatever. We have had growing up for a great many years, since William Marcy announced the rule "to the victors belong the spoils," a rule whereby leadership in the party was maintained by giving rewards to supporters in the distribution of offices. Looking at that practice from the old mugwump standard, which was the selection of only the best man for every place, he would regard that as crooked, but it may be honest if the man is acting under a rule which he considers justified. Like all rules, they are liable to be misapplied and are liable to overturn the only principle on which sound government can be conducted, that is, a government for which a party is created. Now Roosevelt got that solved very well. Roosevelt recognized the necessity for giving consideration to party service and loyalty, in the distribution of offices, but there were certain officers to which the principle did not apply at all, like judges and the officers of the army and navy. He wouldn't listen for a minute to politicians on appointments to the Supreme Court. But he always told the politicians that if they didn't show him a man who was fitted to fill the place, he wouldn't appoint him.

I had a little illustration of the same thing in regard to the consular service. I got very much disturbed by the condition of the consular service. It had become merely a means of doing two things; one was rewarding political service and the other was to enable a man whose power in the government was worth regarding, to get rid of a competitor. If a man was making trouble, the best way to get rid of him was to get him a place as a consul—it ordinarily pleased his wife, and he could be disposed of. The important thing to do was to get the consular service out of a stagnant condition and to get some rule of action other than local political conditions. With the assistance of Lodge, I got through a bill. Before that, each consular office was by itself, without any relation to any other. The bill provided for promotions, making original appointments only in lower grades as a normal rule. At the same time I got them to provide for five inspectors, called consuls general at large. I had experience with that in the army and knew you couldn't expect a man to do the work if he was never inspected. Many consulates hadn't been seen for twelve years or more. The official reports which I got from the inspectors enabled me to drop the inefficient men; it was an official report and nobody could object. Senator Spooner came in to see me shortly after that bill was put in and said "The consulate at —— is open and that belongs to me, and I'll give you a man for it". "The devil you will," I said. I told him I'd see his state had its share of appointments and I'd consult him about those appointments; if he put up good men, his recommendations would be regarded. As soon as they found I was going to play fair they were perfectly satisfied. Under the old system, representation in appointments was divided according to votes in the last presidential election. If a state had voted for a Democrat, it got nothing. All that I threw in the waste paper basket. The Democrats really couldn't believe their states were going to get appointments but everybody accepted it as soon as they were satisfied I was going to be decent about it.

Those people are perfectly straight. A man acting under a rule that appointments belong to a Senator is just as straight as a man acting under another rule. A certain amount of fairness, honesty, integrity, is essential to success in politics. Of course, there are lots of fellows who carry the theory of maintaining the leadership and the party by distribution of spoils to an extent which practically amounts to the repudiation of the obligations of their office.[1]

The prevailing attitude toward consular appointments is illustrated by a letter which Root received from a friend in Buffalo in January, 1906: "If there are any nice berths like the Consulate at Bordeaux France, or at Buenos Ayres lying around loose, I might make an application for one. I need a rest for a while." Root declined to provide the rest cure. The system which Root worked out for handling patronage demands was most successful. It was still far from the merit system but by breaking up the tradition of political spoils, it paved the way for his further innovations. He had lists drawn up showing, on a basis of population, the proportionate share of places and amounts of consular salaries to which each state was entitled. When a Congressman or Senator called, Root would produce the list and usually—since the demanding ones were constant repeaters—could point out that his state had more places or more salaries than it was entitled to and how could he in fairness to other Senators and Congressmen throw the balance out still further? Root had been associating with politicians rather constantly for some thirty-five years; he could talk their language and usually sent the applicant away without any feeling of rancor. Root turned off one Senator who pounced down upon him very early one morning in the State Department by remarking: "Senator, you ought not to take a drink every morning before breakfast— it isn't good for you. And you ought not to get a consulate every morning before breakfast either—that isn't good for you." [2]

The rottenness of the personnel which Root found in many places was amazing. "A man may go wrong," he wrote Lodge on October 25th, 1905, "until his office becomes a disgrace to the country without the State Department hearing of it, until the humiliation and wrath of American travelers filters around through private letters, which come ultimately to the Department. The organization is defective. We must get the defect cured. . . . It is going to take money, and it is going to take affirmative legislation." But Root knew that he could not cure all the ills at once, particularly since many objectionable consuls had powerful political friends who could block general re-

[1] Root to the author, September 15, 1930.
[2] Wilbur J. Carr to the author, March 16, 1934.

forms in Congress. When President Butler of Columbia University sent him a memorandum which someone had prepared detailing some of the obnoxious cases of consular misbehavior, Root replied on December 21st, 1907:

> What the memorandum says about the consul at —— is true. I could have had the finest fight imaginable on hand by removing him, and probably have imperilled my whole consular reorganization. I shall get rid of him very soon without any fight at all, for I am about recommending that the consulate at that place be abandoned.
>
> As to the consul who gets drunk, I know very well who he is, and I have had him investigated several times with reference to this very rumor, but it has proved thus far impossible to get any evidence upon which he can be removed. If the fact exists I shall ultimately be able to prove it.

In his plans for the creation of a General Staff in the Army, Root had begun by establishing the War College through executive order. He followed a similar procedure in reorganizing the consular service. On November 10th, 1905, the President issued two executive orders which Root had drafted extending the examination system for consular appointees. The Act of August 16th, 1856, had provided for the appointment of not more than twenty-five consular "pupils" with salaries of $1000 a year or under to be appointed after evidencing their qualifications by examination "or otherwise." Even this rather innocuous provision had been short-lived, having been repealed in the following February. Subsequently, provision was made for thirteen consular clerks with salaries of $1000 a year who were to be appointed after examination and who were expected to advance later by promotion into the higher grades. But the higher grades, being political plums, were places of insecure tenure and the consular clerks preferred permanency to promotion. Thirteen consular clerks accordingly remained the only permanent members of either the consular or diplomatic service until Root became Secretary of State in 1905. Between 1865 and 1895 there were sporadic attempts to test by examination the fitness of candidates for the consular service but no serious step was taken until the latter year when President Cleveland issued an executive order on the subject. He required that any vacancy in a consulate or commercial agency which carried a salary between $1000 and $2500 a year should be filled either by transfer of some qualified person serving under the Department of State or in another position fitting him for the new duties, or by examination of persons designated by the President. During Cleveland's presidency this order was effectively administered but under McKinley and while Hay was Secretary of State, the observance of the rule was purely perfunctory. Even under Cleveland the system had never applied to the more important offices. The Root-Roosevelt orders of November 10th, 1905, covered all vacancies in consular positions which paid a salary of over $1000 a year. They provided also for the filling of all such vacancies in the ranks of secretaries of embassy or legation either by examination or by transfer or promotion from some other branch of the foreign service. Root ended the spoils system in the consular and diplomatic services. Subject to incidental and minor lapses, it has never returned.

On November 29th, Root wrote to the President:

> I would like to make a real thing of the pass examination for appointment of consuls. It has not amounted to very much hitherto. The examinations are now conducted by a purely Departmental Board, which has not been in the habit of meeting. The candidate goes into the Consular Bureau of the Department and sits down to write answers to some written questions which are handed to him, and then goes away. His papers are afterwards submitted to the different members of the Board who mark the answers to the questions on a scale of ten; a man who rates seven is passed. It has evidently come to be regarded as cruel and inhuman treatment not to pass a man. In view of the character of the examination a rejection would practically be an imputation of idiocy.

He asked that the Civil Service Commission designate a member of the examining board and this was done. On December 11th, 1905, a Board composed of the Third Assistant Secretary, Herbert Pierce, the Chief of the Consular Bureau, Wilbur J. Carr, and F. M. Riggans from the Civil Service Commission, prepared for Root a report on consular examinations, suggesting their proper scope and method of administration; the examinations of the present day do not vary widely from those recommendations. By a further executive order of June 27th, 1906, the new examination system was put into effect. The examining board reported on March 22nd, 1907, that eighteen candidates had been examined and ten passed. On July 23rd, Bacon sent Root a further report with the following comment:

> I am disappointed that only thirteen out of thirty-eight candidates have been found eligible, and having in mind what you said about the desirability of not being too radical, and of not antagonizing senators and others who have become accustomed to the old regime, I have instructed the Board of Examiners to be lenient in permitting a re-examination. In this way I hope to soothe the feelings of unsuccessful candidates without any real danger to the service.

Such reexaminations are still permitted. Root had actually stepped up the passing grade from the 70 suggested by the board to 80, but he generally refrained from interfering with the examiners. On one occasion after going over with Carr a great number of rejections, he suggested that the Board ought to keep in mind that "these are supposed to be examinations for admission to the consular service, not for exclusion from the consular service." [3]

Meanwhile Root was endeavoring to get through Congress adequate legislation for the complete reform of the service. A bill which he drafted was introduced by Senator Lodge on December 6th, 1905. Root appeared before the committees of both House and Senate, explaining the reasons for the bill's passage. As was his custom, he did not try to browbeat them into agreement but argued in so conciliatory and convincing a fashion that the committee members could scarcely find a ground for disagreeing with him. When they had real objection, Root was ready to draft substitute sections to meet the criticism. To the hearings of the House Committee on Foreign Affairs he sent Wilbur J. Carr, then Chief of the Consular Bureau and now widely known as the "Father of the Consular Service," a title which recognizes his services but does not detract from the credit due Root for taking the service out of politics and organizing it on modern lines as a permanent career. Root took the supervision of the consular service out of the hands of Huntington Wilson, the Third Assistant Secretary and placed it in Carr's hands, where it remained to the lasting benefit of the service, until 1937 when Carr went into the field as Minister to Czechoslovakia. Under Root's tutelage, Carr became equally expert in handling the committees of Congress. Congressman Edwin Denby

[3] *Ibid.*

wrote to Root on March 20th, 1906, that in the discussion of this bill, Carr "won the respect and friendship of everyone on the Committee," a judgment which Root told Carr agreed with his own observation.

Root's legislative technique included the stimulation of public opinion. In this instance he was able to enlist the support of many prominent business organizations. Both he and the President addressed a large National Consular Reform Convention which met in Washington on March 14th, 1906, and which endorsed the Lodge bill. Root's friends among the journalists were supplied with data and arguments. The bill passed on April 5th, 1906, but in emasculated form, providing merely for annual inspection of all consulates and for elimination of the old system whereby consuls were recompensed out of the consular fees they collected; thereafter all fees became the property of the government and the consuls were put on salaries. Congress had given Root a similar half loaf when he had his General Staff bills introduced; he was delayed but not defeated. On June 25th, 1906, he sent to the President a draft of an executive order extending the Civil Service merit system to the consular service, establishing a classified base for appointments and promotions and thus taking the first step to make the service a career instead of a refuge for political hacks. Root did not succeed in having further legislation passed during his term of office but his executive order worked well in practice. On December 19th, 1908, he wrote to Mr. Carr a memorandum on a further bill which had been introduced in the House and which threatened to upset that regime. Root thought the bill was "a very good illustration of the attempt by persons not familiar with administration, its requirements and its difficulties, to frame legislation for the conduct of administration. In short, the bill is crude, ill-considered, ill-informed and violates both the constitutional method of selecting consuls and the fundamental principles of good administration." [4]

Root devoted equal attention to the improvement of the diplomatic service, which was a separate branch until a consolidated foreign service was created by the passage of the Rogers Act in 1924. The executive order of November 10th, 1905, provided for promotions from men in the service on a merit basis, the examination being extended equally to apply to appointments for the junior grades. Ministers and

[4] Archives of the Department of State.

ambassadors, with a few exceptions, continued to be appointed from civil life, a condition which still exists for a large number of the diplomatic posts. George von L. Meyer, who was the Ambassador to Russia, breakfasted with Root and took a long drive with him in the fall of 1905, giving him many suggestions on the basis of his experience in the field.[5] One of the proposals for the improvement of the foreign service which he did not take up, was that a uniform should be adopted for our diplomatic representatives abroad. When Knox took over the State Department, he found in a drawer of Root's desk a dossier on this subject; there was an elaborate scheme for silk stockings and satin knee breeches, a silk coat with a red satin sash and lace frills. The proposal was annotated in Root's handwriting with an additional item: "The only suggestion I would make for the improvement of this costume is that a sprig of mistletoe be embroidered on the coat tails."

To Seth Low, Root wrote on December 24th, 1906:

> We are trying now to create a system under which there will be permanent careers by insisting upon promotions of the men who show that they have good stuff in them . . . this is a complete reversal of the former system, under which the Senators owned the places.
>
> I supposed there would be a tremendous row about the change, but I have been agreeably surprised to find comparatively few violent objections. I think we are going to maintain our position without very serious controversy throughout this Administration. I am in hopes that it will be so firmly established that it will continue. . . . The Lord only knows what will happen when another administration comes in. . . . My impression is that, while there may be some setbacks, the change in the method of dealing with the foreign service in the country will, in the main, continue and become more firmly established, just as the change in the civil service of the country has done, and I should think that the foreign service afforded a very good opportunity for a bright and capable young fellow.

Near the end of his service in the State Department, Root had the assurance that his plans would be continued for another four years under the Taft Administration but Bryan temporarily reversed the

[5] Howe, *George von Lengerke Meyer*, p. 220.

trend by rewarding "deserving Democrats."

Root encouraged Dr. Richard S. Harlan in his plans for a College of the Political Sciences at George Washington University to train students for government service and Professor Andrew Fleming West with similar plans at Princeton. He told them both that if the standard of education of applicants for the diplomatic and consular services could be raised, he would be able to raise the standards in the examinations, which he was anxious to do.[6] These trends in educational circles and in administering the examination system have continued.

Root also constantly urged the committees of Congress to increase the appropriations for the foreign services, to grant adequate allowances for rent and other expenses, and to purchase buildings for our embassies, legations and consulates. He was not very successful because Congress had then, and still has, a contemptuous indifference for the necessities of an adequate foreign service.

On the whole, Roosevelt gave Root full backing in his efforts toward reorganization, but he was not wholly free from the desire to find places for political supporters. Root warded off this pressure by making a joke of it. On November 10th, 1908, he wrote to Roosevelt:

> As to the general proposition about kicking out about half of our Ministers and Secretaries on the ground that they are perfectly good men, but of no special importance, I have to say that I have heard you accused of trying to be an Emperor, a Czar, a despot of different varieties, but this is the first time that I have observed myself any marked tendency on your part to imitate the example and breathe the spirit of the Queen in Alice in Wonderland. If you say so, off with their heads, off with everybody's head, but in their places we should *still* have perfectly good men of no special importance.[7]

On the previous August 23rd he had replied from Clinton to the President's inquiry about the desirability of appointing a minister to Abyssinia.

> I never could see anything for a minister to Abyssinia to do. When I get back I would like to look up the record made when the mission was established & then talk with you about it. I need all

[6] Root to Harlan, April 5, 1907 and March 17, 1908; Root to West, January 25, 1909.
[7] Roosevelt Papers, Library of Congress.

the money I get for use in places where it counts.

I understand that Prester John never was really there & that their only Theodore killed himself after grossly violating the constitution.

When the American minister to Persia asked for instructions regarding his joining in representations by the diplomatic corps to the Shah, urging that he compromise his dispute with the Persian Parliament, Root sent Roosevelt a note marked "Personal Confidential and foolish":

> The enclosed despatch from Jackson shows the serious results to the State Department of your yielding to your admiration for him and making him Minister to Persia purely as a matter of favor. So far as I am aware, this is the first time that the State Department has ever been called upon for instructions from Persia. We already have trouble enough. I have drafted a reply which Mr. Adee thinks too serious. I shall be glad of your instructions.[8]

The draft reply read: "Continue quarrels with missionaries as usual."

Root kept out of Roosevelt's famous row with the Bellamy Storers, although he urged him strongly not to get into a "newspaper row." [9] He agreed that Roosevelt had no other course except to dismiss Storer,[10] but "the recall was the result of the President's special personal consideration and action." [11]

With the internal reorganization of the State Department Root had less to do, the more significant changes being made under his successor, Knox. Taft had urged Root to undertake a general departmental reorganization and felt later that Root resented the fact that Knox had done what he failed to do.[12] As a matter of fact, Root was not a good administrator in the theoretical sense because he took a vast amount of the work on his own shoulders when it might have been delegated to subordinates. His delegation to Chandler P. Anderson of the work on the treaties with Canada was a striking exception. In his own case this habit did not turn out badly because he had a terrific appetite and capacity for work. Yet even his vigor-

[8] Roosevelt Papers, Library of Congress, undated.
[9] Root to Roosevelt, December 9, 1906.
[10] Root to W. M. Laffan, March 17, 1906.
[11] Root to Charlemagne Tower, March 20, 1906.
[12] William Howard Taft to Philander C. Knox, December 18, 1913; Knox Papers, Library of Congress.

ous constitution gave way for a time under the strain. He also had a capacity for distinguishing the big things from the little things. As in the War Department, he arrived early and stayed on often until seven or eight o'clock, frequently taking a batch of papers home with him under his arm. His lunches consisted of a sandwich, a couple of olives, and a bottle of Appolinaris water. March 27th, 1908, he wrote to the President a formal letter which Roosevelt forwarded to Mrs. Lodge with the comment, "This is a characteristic Rootian note":

> I acknowledge your letter of March 25th regarding Sunday work in the Department.
>
> I shall see hereafter that such work is confined strictly to the Secretary and Assistant Secretaries.
>
> Would it be deemed improper if we were to do work on Sunday regarding the affairs of the Far East where it is already Monday, and transfer our labors as Monday comes around and Sunday recedes, westward through the Near East and Europe? [13]

Root's method of handling promotions in the consular service was typical. He would send for the Chief of the Consular Bureau, who brought with him a list of persons deserving promotion on their records with a brief explanatory note on each. Root would look at the list and then ask for the dossier of each man, going through a large file of papers and asking searching questions in regard to the most minute items. He usually approved the recommendations but not without satisfying himself that they were justified. When the same official first brought his list to Root's successor, Secretary Knox, Knox glanced at the list and asked "Have you been over all these cases?" Receiving an affirmative answer, he immediately initialed the memorandum and then asked what was that great bundle of papers. It was explained that those were the dossiers of the men involved; "You have been over them carefully and are satisfied that these recommendations are borne out by the facts?" Knox would ask. When assured that this was the case, Knox let the officer know that he was being held responsible for the action taken and stated that he did not have time himself to examine the dossiers.[14] Root, on the other hand, gave these matters detailed attention because he was inaugurating a system and knew that he must be prepared to prove to disappointed Congressmen and

[13] Roosevelt Papers, Library of Congress.
[14] Wilbur J. Carr to the author, March 16, 1934.

Senators that the men who got the promotions were actually entitled to them on a merit basis.

Root, again the direct opposite of Knox, was always insistent that his staff should be scrupulous in their observance of every legal technicality. Yet when Root felt that something ought to be done, he never failed to find a way to do it, either by finding a loophole in the law or by eliminating in advance possible sources of opposition. On one occasion Root was closeted with Bacon discussing an important question of policy. The Chief Clerk came in and Root asked him sharply what he wanted. The Chief Clerk explained that there was a clerk who had served the Department for many years and who had become old and rather inefficient. He was ill and his wife had come in to carry on his work. She did it badly, but she did it until she also fell ill. Under the law, the man should have been dropped from the payroll but the couple were destitute. Root listened in his characteristic pose, tilting back in his chair, eyes fixed on the ceiling, finger tips pressed together. When the Chief Clerk finished, the Secretary got up and paced the room without speaking, looked out of the window and paced again for minutes. He then began to talk and devoted over half an hour to finding a way to keep the man on the rolls, saying "I don't give a damn what the statute says, he's got to be kept on."

He continued to be terrifying to his subordinates in the abstract, but humorous and kindly in the concrete. A young diplomat serving in the Department was in charge of the arrangements for housing the guests who were to go to Jamestown for the international exposition there. He came in to the Secretary's office in a state of great perturbation. The situation was perfectly dreadful; there was only one old hotel, very inadequate, and he didn't know how he was going to find suitable accommodations for the diplomatic corps. "Why, Mr. Secretary, the hotel is so small that I have got to put the Italian Ambassadress in the same room with the Italian Ambassador!" "Of course you can't do that," said Root. "Why not put her in the room with the French Ambassador?"

A few reforms Root did institute. He was excessively irritated by the ancient filing system in the Department under which there was no subject classification but merely great tomes in which despatches, instructions and notes were copied in "a big round hand." One needed a hand truck to assemble the papers on a question of any consequence.

He asked General Ainsworth, who had perfected the filing system in the War Department, to send him a clerk who could revise the State Department's system. Ainsworth fortunately picked David A. Salmon who is still in charge of the files subsequent to August 16th, 1906, and who has made of them a model of convenience and completeness.

Root made strenuous efforts to have the congressional committees on appropriations realize the importance of paying adequate salaries to the Department's staff and to supplement it by a sufficient number of assistants and clerks to get the work done adequately and promptly.[15] He also suggested the plan, which has been adopted, of making members of the Department's home service eligible for promotion by transfer to the foreign service.[16] He was opposed to the inauguration of the system of splitting the Department into a series of geographical divisions, perhaps because it was a pet project of his least congenial subordinate, Huntington Wilson. In March, 1908, however, he finally yielded and ordered the creation of a separate Division of Far Eastern Affairs. In this case at least, Wilson was clearly right and Root was wrong. Root finally reached that conclusion himself. Just prior to his resignation, on returning from his last appearance before the Appropriations Committee, he remarked that he was convinced that the Department had reached the point when the growth of its work and responsibilities made it necessary that it should subdivide its work into geographical areas, each in charge of a specialist, noting that beside the formally established Far Eastern Division there had grown up what was virtually a division of British and Canadian Affairs.[17] It remained for Knox, who relied greatly on Wilson, to complete this plan of organization which still obtains and has proved not only highly satisfactory but absolutely necessary in the light of the increased volume of work which now confronts the Department.

[15] See Root to Senator William B. Allison, April 4, 1906, Archives of the Department of State.
[16] Root to the Chairman of the Senate Committee on Foreign Relations, December 20, 1905, ibid.
[17] Wilbur J. Carr to the author, November 26, 1935.

CHAPTER XXXII

"Over into the field of internal politics"

A CABINET officer who had behind him a long record of loyal service to his party, who was in great demand as an effective campaign speaker, who had been offered the second place on the Republican national ticket in 1900, and who had been importuned to accept the governorship of New York in 1904, naturally could not escape constant pressure to render further political service.

The New York gubernational contest between the Republican candidate, Charles Evans Hughes, and his Democratic opponent, William Randolph Hearst, was already under way as Root was returning from his great tour of South America. On September 20th, 1906, in Panama, he received a telegram from Roosevelt saying that they were having a hard fight for the control of Congress and for the governorship of New York and urging Root to make a speech immediately after his return: "Please accept." Although weary from a continuous round of speechmaking, Root agreed. On October 4th, Herbert Parsons, chairman of the Republican County Committee in New York City, wrote asking him to agree to speak in the week of October 22nd. Root replied from Washington on the 6th:

> As I have been making speeches all summer, I do not feel much freshness and vigor, in view of making another; but I feel bound to respond to the call. The week beginning October 22nd would suit me very well. I shall not attempt to make any extensive and carefully prepared address, but just the common or garden variety of campaign speech, and I, therefore, want to have it one of several speeches made at the same meeting, rather than to have it stand alone by itself.

But very soon the political wind began to blow from a different quarter. On October 13th, Timothy L. Woodruff, Chairman of the Republican State Committee, wrote to Roosevelt that he felt it was unwise to bring national issues into the state campaign as they would be brought in if Speaker Cannon or Root should speak in New York. "Of course, it is a different thing with regard to Mr. Root because he is a New Yorker, but I am sorry that even he is going to speak in this campaign for the reason that he will necessarily have to discuss national questions and particularly for the reason that for a day or two Mr. Hughes and his campaign will be completely overshadowed." [1] On October 15th, Herbert Parsons wrote in even stronger terms to the President:

> Much as everybody admires Secretary Root, the feeling seems to be that it is unwise to have him speak here. I am responsible for his invitation to speak, and if I were to act on my personal opinion I would still favor his speaking, but almost all whose advice I have asked are against it, despite their admiration for Mr. Root and desire to hear him. The point they make is that it would give Hearst's papers the chance to ring the changes on him in regard to Ryan, his fee in the Equitable matter, & his general association with corporations. I personally, have thought that an account by him of his South American trip, with illustrations of the need for stability in government in order to assure good business conditions, and, therefore, prosperity, would appeal to even the laboring classes and overcome any of the disadvantages, but if you and he agree with the others, that it is wiser for him not to speak here, a great many people would feel relieved.[2]

By this time Root's speech had been set for November 1st at Utica in his home county of Oneida, where James Schoolcraft Sherman, a Hamilton "Sig," was having a hard fight for election to Congress. Parsons thought that even this speech would embarrass Hughes and suggested that Taft might be sent in Root's place. Root immediately wrote to Sherman to cancel the arrangements for his speech. Roosevelt wrote to Lodge on October 25th:

> . . . The New York managers are . . . continually having fits. . . . At the outset they were most nervous over the administration's taking any part in the campaign and insisted that under no circumstances should national issues be brought in; that I was to be made just as little of an issue as possible; that Taft, Moody and the other people close to me were to be kept out, but that Root was

[1] Roosevelt Papers, Library of Congress.
[2] Ibid.

to make one speech. They arranged for Root's speech; and then became horribly afraid that his corporation affiliations would enable Hearst to make a point on it, whereupon they cancelled his engagement. It has never occurred to me that he would mind it, but I find that it cut him to the quick, and I was very sorry. Of course I did not care a rap about their wish to keep me out of the campaign, as my sole concern was to elect Hughes and, as I told them, Hughes' election would be a victory for me even if they were most careful never to mention my name before election day. Root minded it very much, however.

Then they had a revulsion of feeling. At the same time that they cancelled Root's engagement Cannon came to New York . . . left the State full of the gloomiest feelings as to Hearst's probable victory. There upon about half of the local leaders wanted Root to come to the State and the other half insisted that he should not. He is to speak in Utica, in his home county, where I think he will do good. Personally, I think he would have done great good in New York City. . . .[3]

Sherman urgently pressed Root to reconsider; the Republican campaign managers became more panicky, urging Roosevelt himself to come. The President declined but again persuaded Root to go in his place. On the 24th, Root wrote to Whitelaw Reid in London:

The Lord only knows what is going to be the result in New York. Party lines are so broken up and the campaign is of such a curious character that there does not seem to be anything on which to base a forecast. There seems to be rather a disposition on the part of the State managers to fight shy of administration help, for the reason that they want to get democratic votes. I think they make a mistake, because, after all, what the President has done is the principal argument with the great body of voters against turning the country over to people of the Hearst stripe. Nevertheless, my impression is that we are coming out all right in the election.

From Clinton, Root's brother wrote to him that Sherman and Hughes would both be badly beaten and there was little use in Root's speaking at Utica. Root replied:

I was glad to get your letter of October 23rd although you seemed rather pessimistic about the political situation. I doubt

[3] *Roosevelt-Lodge Correspondence*, Vol. II, p. 252.

if you have moved about enough to get a satisfactory parallax so that you can form a very sure judgment. I have seen a good many people from the State within the past few weeks who have widely differing opinions. I have no idea what particular opinion is right. They vary all the way from 200,000 majority for Hughes to 200,-000 majority for Hearst. I feel confident that they cannot all be right. You must remember, however, that the bystander, who looks on at the course of affairs in which he is interested but in which he takes no active part, always has the tendency to think that things are going wrong.

I agreed to speak in Utica largely because I have an idea that Sherman may have a close squeak and I would like to help him. . . .

On October 30th, Root released copies of his speech to the papers, sending a personal covering letter to a few editors. Root recalled:

The first contact I had with Hearst was in the fight for Governor in 1906. (I think Hearst came in to see me once before that; he wanted something—I don't remember what it was or whether I did it; I think it must have been to ask for some letter of introduction. That was the only time I ever saw the man.) It did look as if he were going to be elected and I guess he would have been. At all events, he pays me the compliment, I understand, of saying I defeated him. It was quite accidental, too. Jim Sherman was having a hard time in his campaign for reelection to Congress, and I agreed to come up and speak for him. When the time came, the situation got so bad I decided instead of talking about Jim, I'd talk about the Governorship. I got my speech up carefully and when I had it written I took it over to the President's office, and showed it to Roosevelt. At the close of the speech I had stated Roosevelt's view of Hearst. Roosevelt took his pencil and made it a little stronger. The speech was given to the Associated Press in time for them to get it out to the coast. Of course they gave it to Hearst. Hughes and I rode up from the station in Utica to the hall in an open carriage. The news boys were running around with papers and threw into our carriage Hearst's reply to my speech. I didn't read it till afterwards. I forget what he said. I felt that I had furnished an impeachment of anything he had to say. I suppose he's been throwing mud at me ever since; I don't read his papers. He sent some men up to try to break up the meeting; we had a gay meeting. It was after that he set to work having his people try to find something on me in Cuba.[4]

Some years later one of the gang that had been sent up to Utica to break up the meeting told the story of it to Elihu Root, Jr. He said they had been sent up by the Tammany organization. When Root reached Utica, Republican supporters were buying up the issues of Hearst's *Evening Journal* as fast as they came, tearing them into shreds and making Baggs Square near the station and the streets near the Majestic Theater look as if it had been struck by a freakish and unseasonable snow storm. Across the front page spread a cartoon of "Root, the Rat" nibbling at the defenses of the common people. The gang had been told what the speech would contain and each man had been given cues on little slips of paper, with instructions to start an interruption when the cues were spoken. For example, one man had been instructed on the first reference to McKinley to get up and shout "Let McKinley rest in peace," and the others were all to roar their approval. The gang found that special badges were necessary to enable them to get on the platform so they rounded up a delegation of "farmers" who were wearing platform badges and plied them with drinks until they were able to secure from them enough badges to get most of their crowd seated. When the speech started and the first cue was reached, the holder of the appropriate slip started his interruption, but his next neighbor "socked him in the jaw. The meeting was all packed with neighbors and Hamilton College students and no one could open his mouth to interrupt without getting pushed in the face."[5]

Root's voice at first was too low to fill the theater. When he began his denunciation of Hearst one of Hearst's henchmen yelled out "It's a lie!" "Throw him out!" came the roar from all parts of the theater. Root raised his right hand, holding it extended in a dramatic gesture to quell the uproar. In a voice which carried to every corner he cried, "No, let him stay and learn!" The crowd went wild and then listened in rapt silence while Root's voice with gathering power filled the building with his great philippic.[6]

Root opened with a definition of a demagogue and pinned the label

[4] Root to the author, September 15, 1930.
[5] Elihu Root, Jr. to the author, April 11, 1934.
[6] Richard S. Sherman to the author, April 10, 1933.

on Hearst. He pointed out that Hearst always posed as the friend of the workingman and the enemy of the great corporations; skillfully he pictured Hearst as a man of enormous wealth who had created separate corporations for each of his newspapers with a holding company to control them, and cited Hughes as establishing that Hearst had juggled with these various corporations to avoid taxation. Root went directly to the corporation issue which Hearst was stressing. "Corporations are not bad in themselves, but the managers of some of them and of many of the greatest ones have used them as opportunities for wrongdoing, if not criminal wrongdoing. The thing needed is to cut out the wrongdoing and save the business. . . ." That, he claimed, was what Roosevelt had been doing with conspicuous success in the federal government, and what Hughes had been doing with equal skill and courage in the State of New York, especially in the insurance investigations. He stressed the need for a Republican Congress and a Republican endorsement in the President's own State of New York to carry on these policies. He then turned his attention to Hearst's fitness for the office of governor:

> Of his private life I shall not speak further than to say that from no community in this state does there come concerning him that testimony of lifelong neighbors and acquaintances as to his private virtues, the excellence of his morals, and the correctness of his conduct which we should like to have concerning the man who is to be made the governor of our state. . . .
> How stands Mr. Hearst's record as to political purity? Why, he comes to us covered all over with the mark of Tammany and Tammany's leader, Murphy, whom he himself has denounced as a scoundrel and a thief; he comes to us . . . nominated by his own procurement, through as shameful a deal with the boss of Tammany as ever disgraced a political history of the state—a deal under which a great body of the regularly elected delegates to the Democratic convention were unseated, and, in their absence, the nomination of Mr. Hearst was made by the solid vote of the Tammany delegation. Can hypocrisy go further than the willing beneficiary of Tammany Hall preaching political purity?

Root reviewed Hearst's record as a representative from New York in Congress. He stated that Hearst was absent from 160 out of the 185 roll calls during his term and for 442 out of the 467 days of Legislative session; "his voice was heard in that Congress in those three years but once, and that was for ten minutes in a personal explanation regarding an article in the New York *American.* . . ."

> But the worst of Mr. Hearst is that with his great wealth, with his great newspapers, with his army of paid agents, for his own selfish purposes, he has been day by day and year by year sowing the seeds of dissension and strife and hatred throughout our land; he would array labor against capital and capital against labor; poverty against wealth, and wealth against poverty, with bitter and vindictive feeling; he would destroy among the great mass of our people that kindly and friendly spirit, that consideration for the interests and the rights of others, that brotherhood of citizenship which are essential to the peaceful conduct of free popular government; . . .
>
> It is not the calm and lawful redress of wrongs which he seeks, it is the turmoil of inflamed passions and the terrorism of revengeful force; he spreads the spirit, he follows the methods and he is guided by the selfish motives of the revolutionist; and he would plunge our peaceful land into the turmoil and discord of perpetual conflict. . . .

Root quoted from the Hearst papers the epithets which he had showered upon the public men of the country, Republicans and Democrats alike; Joseph H. Choate was called "a servile lickspittle of corporations"; William Travers Jerome, a "political Croton bug"; Judge Alton B. Parker, "a cockroach, a waterbug"; Grover Cleveland, "no more or less than a living, breathing crime in breeches"; Theodore Roosevelt, one who "has sold himself to the devil and will live up to the bargain"; and so on through a long list.

> Once only has this method of incendiary abuse wrought out its natural consequence—in the murder of President McKinley. For years, by vile epithet and viler cartoons, readers of the Journal were taught to believe that McKinley was a monster in human form, whose taking-off would be a service to mankind.

Root proceeded with telling quotations from the Hearst papers:

> The bullet that pierced Goebel's chest
> Cannot be found in all the West:
> Good reason, it is speeding here
> To stretch McKinley on his bier.

This particular quotation and some others had been gathered for Root by the Washington correspondent of the New York *Herald*. They reawakened the anger manifested all over the country five years before when the same sort of charge was current against Hearst.[7] There was a long quotation listing the beneficent results in history of assassinations—that of Marat by Charlotte Corday, the murder of Caesar, Cromwell's beheading of Charles I, and others: "We invite our readers to think over this question. The time devoted to it will not be wasted." Root went on:

> What wonder that the weak and excitable brain of Csolgosz answered to such impulses as these! He never knew McKinley; he had no real or fancied wrongs of his own to avenge against McKinley or McKinley's government; he was answering to the lesson he had learned, that it was a service to mankind to rid the earth of a monster; and the foremost of the teachers of these lessons to him and his kind was and is William Randolph Hearst with his yellow journals. . . . In President Roosevelt's first message to Congress, in speaking of the assassin of McKinley, he spoke of him as inflamed "by the reckless utterances of those who, on the stump and in the public press, appeal to the dark and evil spirits of malice and greed, envy and sullen hatred. The wind is sowed by the men who preach such doctrines, and they cannot escape their share of responsibility for the whirlwind that is reaped. This applies alike to the deliberate demagogue, to the exploiter of sensationalism, and to the crude and foolish visionary who, for whatever reason, apologizes for crime or excites aimless discontent."
>
> I say, by the President's authority, that in penning these words, with the horror of President McKinley's murder fresh before him, he had Mr. Hearst specifically in mind.
>
> And I say, by his authority, that what he thought of Mr. Hearst then he thinks of Mr. Hearst now.

The speech ended and "even the ranks of Tammany could scarce forbear to cheer." Those who were present recall the dramatically forceful earnestness of those closing passages. As the people streamed out from the theater, more copies of the *Journal* were lit and carried through the streets in a torch light procession.

It was a Ciceronian effort, the most forceful and effective campaign

---

[7] Senator Spooner had suggested this line of attack in a letter of October 15, 1906, to Roosevelt, Spooner Papers, Library of Congress.

speech which Root ever delivered. The Republican state committee had passages from it reproduced on pamphlets, cards and posters; three printers were at work on the reproductions while Root was speaking and the next morning quantities were delivered to every Republican County Chairman throughout the state.[8] One and a half million copies were distributed to laborers at factories.[9] Root never received such a flood of congratulations; they came in the mails not only from New York but from Tennessee, Georgia, Ohio, California, Illinois, Virginia, Connecticut, Indiana and elsewhere. They were written by Republican leaders, by business men, by "one of the 'common people' "; by farmers, salesmen, druggists, by friends and by strangers. With them of course came the usual flood of denunciations for his "lies." Root "is a great man, and I guess everybody knows it now," Roosevelt wrote to Woodruff on November 4th.[10] "What a corker Root is, isn't he?" he exclaimed in a letter to Judge Gary on the following day.[11] Taft wrote to Root on November 10th:

> I saw a copy of your speech when I was out in the wilds of Idaho, and I cannot tell you the comfort that it gave me to read it, and how it intensified the affection and admiration that I have always had for the speaker. I can just think of your making up your mind to say the thing and do the thing that the occasion demanded. It takes a kind of moral courage, that few people have, to speak out against a moral leper with such power of mischief as he has, because he has the power of besmirching a man with a lot of ignorant but good people, whom he has gradually trained to believe everything he says. It is like shooting a skunk. It is a most unpleasant business, and yet skunks have to be shot. You selected a psychological moment, and I have no doubt that you did a great deal to prevent Hearst's election.

William E. Borah asked for a copy so that he could keep it for "even in Idaho it did us a vast amount of good. . . . I think it is one of the greatest speeches which has been delivered in this country within the last forty years. . . ." To Justice White of the Supreme Court, Root wrote on November 13th, acknowledging his congratulations:

---

[8] Timothy L. Woodruff to Root, November 1, 1906.
[9] Paul D. Cravath to Root, November 2, 1906.
[10] Roosevelt Papers, Library of Congress.
[11] *Ibid.*

It was very hard for me to make any speech at all, for my mind was full of other matters relating to our foreign affairs, and a powerful effort of detachment was necessary to get myself over into the field of internal politics. It frequently happens, however, that the things hardest to do and that we try hardest to escape from are the very things which prove to have been the most worth doing. Your commendation makes me feel that this was such a case.

To Roosevelt, Taft wrote on November 4th: "Root's speech against Hearst was a great speech, and I am delighted that he made it. It left the picture of Hearst which will be useful in all future time. He is greatly to be commended for the courage which he exhibited in the matter. Of course Hearst will now busy himself in getting up scandals and slanders against Root if he has not already begun before this letter reaches you." And in a later letter of the same date: "I observe that Hearst has come out attacking Root, but I fancy from the screams that have been emitted Root's words cut as they ought to have cut, and got under Hearst's skin." [12]

Root was perfectly well aware before he made the speech that it would involve for him the most violent denunciation of which Hearst was capable; Hearst showed that he was capable of reaching far beyond the height—or below the depth—of the quotations which Root had used in his speech. Root's old law associate, Henry L. Stimson, was distressed by the attacks which Hearst launched and wished Root to start proceedings against him. Stimson spoke to William Travers Jerome, then District Attorney of New York County, who said that though he was a Democrat, Root was his Secretary of State, and if he would say the word, Jerome would prosecute. Stimson sent Root some clippings illustrative of the Hearst attacks; he got no reply. When next he saw Root, he asked him about it. Root told him that he was at the time engaged in drafting some important treaties; he knew that if he read the clippings he would get stirred up by them and that it would distract his mind from the work which he had in hand, so he never read them.[13] He was more interested in the fact that Hughes and Sherman were elected, carrying Oneida County by over three thousand votes for the governor and over two thousand for the

[12] Taft Papers, Library of Congress.
[13] Henry L. Stimson to the author, March 10, 1934.

congressman. In Mark Sullivan's judgment, "Root's speech defeated Hearst for Governor." [14]

Throughout 1906 and 1907, Root was steadily and emphatically replying to letters from friends in many parts of the country that he was not and would not be a candidate for the Presidency. When he refused to yield to Roosevelt's arguments that he should run for Governor of New York in 1904, Root intimated to the President that he must find another standard bearer for the presidential campaign in 1908. But Roosevelt vacillated for some time between Taft and Root. It appears that Root was Roosevelt's first choice but that the President became convinced, as was Root himself, that the famous corporation lawyer would make a poor candidate. "I found that the westerners would not stand Root," he wrote to Laurence F. Abbott in 1912.[15] Yet Roosevelt tried to persuade Root that, as matters stood around 1906, the handicaps could be overcome and he could be elected; Root refused to yield.[16] As early as May 4th, 1906, Taft wrote to his wife about a long talk with Roosevelt at the White House: "He was full of the Presidency and wanted to talk about my chances. . . . He thinks I am the one to take his mantle and that now I would be nominated. He said Root had been out to talk the night before and had discussed me and my presidential chances with much detail." [17] But Roosevelt had not yet quite made up his mind. He told H. H. Kohlsaat that if he had the power of a dictator, he would make Root President and Taft Chief Justice, but as it was, "Root would make the best President, but Taft the best candidate." [18] On July 30th, 1907, he wrote at length to William Allen White, analyzing the possible candidates and his role in making a selection: ". . . of the men available for President it would seem to me that Taft comes nearer than anyone else to being just the man who ought to be President. There are some good reasons which could be advanced to show that Root would be a better President than Taft, or me, or anyone else I know. I could not express too highly my feeling for him. But at present it does not seem to me that there would be much chance of nominating or electing him, and therefore I do not consider him. . . . Hughes has been a good Governor.

[14] Our Times, Vol. III, p. 281.
[15] Abbott, Impressions of Roosevelt, p. 65.
[16] Theodore Roosevelt, Jr. to the author, November 6, 1936.
[17] Taft Papers, Library of Congress.
[18] Kohlsaat, From McKinley to Harding, p. 161.

I think he would be a good President. But he does not begin to compare with Taft, either morally, intellectually, or in knowledge of public problems." [19] Taft, however, had already made up his own mind to be the candidate.[20]

William Loeb, Roosevelt's secretary,[21] tells of a breakfast conversation with Roosevelt in January, 1908, during which Loeb suggested that Root should be the candidate; Roosevelt doubted if he could be elected, but Loeb assured him that any man he backed would win. The President authorized him to go over to the State Department and to tell Root that Roosevelt wished him to run. Loeb did so and was met by a flat refusal on the ground that he would not be a good candidate. It seems clear from the correspondence of Taft, Roosevelt and Root that Root had been definitely eliminated before 1908 and Root himself had no recollection of any such visit from Loeb.[22] James Callan O'Laughlin recalls going in 1907 or 1908 on a like mission from Roosevelt to Root with the same negative result.[23] Probably it is merely a question of dates; there is no doubt that Roosevelt would have preferred Root and the only question is when he became convinced of his unavailability.

On September 30th, 1907, as they returned from the dedication of the McKinley Memorial at Canton, Ohio, Root and James R. Garfield discussed in great detail the pros and cons of Root's becoming a candidate. Root admitted that he would like to be President, but insisted that he was too old to undertake the kind of struggle which the candidacy would involve. Root realized perfectly well the kind of attack which would be made upon him as a corporation, "Wall Street" lawyer. He was satisfied in his own mind that his attitude on the relations between government and big business would be perfectly acceptable to the people of the country, but he doubted very much whether he could, in a campaign on his own behalf, convince them of the sincerity of his views. If, he said to Garfield, he had been as young as Roosevelt was when he became Governor of New York, he would not

---

[19] Roosevelt Papers, Library of Congress.
[20] Taft to his brother Charles, March 23, 1907 and to Adolphus Busch, April 26, 1907, Taft Papers, Library of Congress.
[21] Stoddard, *As I Knew Them, from Grant to Coolidge*, pp. 322–24.
[22] Root to the author, September 2, 1935.
[23] Colonel O'Laughlin to the author, April 28, 1938.

hesitate to undertake the fight, but at his age he could not do it.[24]
Roosevelt showed that he appreciated Root's viewpoint when he analyzed the situation in talking to Oscar King Davis:

"I would rather see Elihu Root in the White House than any
other man now possible," he said. "I have told several men recently that I would walk on my hands and knees from the White
House to the Capitol to see Root made President. But I know it
cannot be done. He couldn't be elected. There is too much opposition to him on account of his corporation connections.

"But the people don't know Root. I do. I knew him when I was
Governor of New York, and I have known him here, very intimately, during the years he has been in my Cabinet. The very
thing on account of which there is so much objection to him
would make him an ideal President. He is a great lawyer. He has
always given all that he had to his clients. He has great intelligence, wonderful industry, and complete fidelity to his clients.

"What the people do not understand about him is that if he
were President they would be his clients. He would be serving the
Nation with absolute singleness of purpose, and with all that intelligence, industry, and fidelity. Nothing would be, or could be,
paramount with him to the interests of his clients. I know that,
for I have seen him repeatedly take that attitude as a Cabinet
officer.

"Root is really for the public programme that boys call the
'Roosevelt policies.' If he were to succeed me there would be no
question about their being carried out. But it can't be done. In
the first place, he couldn't be elected because of the ignorant opposition to him, and in the next place wild horses couldn't drag
him into making a public campaign. I have had awful trouble with
him to get him to make a few public speeches. He simply would
not campaign for himself." [25]

On February 23rd, 1907, Roosevelt told a group of friends at the
home of Bishop William Lawrence that Root was "without question
the greatest living statesman. I wanted him to accept the Treasury for
he has done such work in the War and State Department that he
could step into the Treasury and be perhaps one of the greatest secre-

[24] James R. Garfield to the author, April 9, 1938.
[25] Davis, Released for Publication, p. 54.

taries of the Treasury this nation had ever had. But he has deep interest and large views in connection with the State Department and he was unwilling to leave it." [26]

Having decided that Root was unavailable as a candidate for the Presidency, Roosevelt offered him a place on the Supreme Court; the story became current that Root was to be made Chief Justice, but on June 16th, 1908, Root wrote to his old friend, Judge Willard Bartlett:

> There is nothing in the story about the Chief Justiceship. The President offered me the appointment as Associate Justice to fill the vacancy to which Moody was appointed, and I told him I was too old, and I would not take it. I am inclined to think that I should say the same thing about the Chief Justiceship. I shall never have occasion to, however, because Fuller will stay indefinitely, and, as Vest said about old Senator Morrill, they will have to shoot him on the day of judgment. He will cling to the Bench with his last expiring ray of intelligence, and when that is gone he will be like our old friend Sanford, incompetent to resign or retire.

After Taft became President the rumors were revived that Root would be appointed to the bench. October 14th, 1910, Root wrote again to Bartlett: "The report about the Chief Justiceship is, I suppose, merely a newspaper guess based upon the fact that the President and I appeared to be on friendly terms the other day at Beverly. If I am any judge there is nothing more to it. If I am not any judge how can I be Chief Justice?" Joseph H. Choate urged Taft to appoint Root but Taft replied on August 25th, 1910, that "the chief objection is the appointment of a Chief Justice at sixty-five or six. I don't think this fatal, but it is an objection that has to be considered and answered." [27] Choate also wrote to Root on the same subject and Root's reply of September 21st, 1910 is similar to Taft's.

> It is very gratifying to have you feel that I ought to be Chief Justice. My own impression is that Taft would probably offer me the appointment were I not sixty-five years old, but that he will consider that he ought to appoint a younger man. I am inclined to think he is right in this. The opportunity to give the Court a Chief Justice who will have before him a long period of service

[26] Bishop William Lawrence to the author, December 26, 1936.
[27] Taft Papers, Library of Congress.

like Marshall and Tawney ought not to be sacrificed if he can find the right man. I don't see how you can do anything more and I am deeply gratified and touched, my old friend, by your doing what you have done.

Taft gave the same reason to Chandler P. Anderson at about this time,[28] although in conversation with another friend, he was impressed by the possible discomfort which would be caused to Root if he sent in his name, due to the fact that Root's corporate practice and defense of Tweed would surely be aired in the Senate in debating the confirmation.[29] Although Taft did not hold the age limit against himself when in his sixty-fourth year he accepted the Chief Justiceship, he was quite sincere in feeling that this factor weighed strongly against Root's appointment. He must also have been influenced by his general belief that only a sitting judge or at least someone with past judicial experience should be put on the Supreme Court.[30] Reading between the lines of Root's letters, one comes to the conclusion that he would have liked the Chief Justiceship but it is clear that he made not the slightest effort to further his own appointment. Moreover, at the time he doubted whether he would make a good judge in view of his life-long habit of cultivating the frame of mind of the advocate.[31] In this he was probably wrong since, more than most lawyers, he had great powers of detachment.

Meanwhile Root was immersed in the New York political situation during the summer and fall of 1908. On August 1st, he wrote to Roosevelt from Clinton that he had agreed to serve as either temporary or permanent chairman of the Republican state convention to be held at Saratoga on September 14th and 15th. "I shall probably dust the hay seed out of my hair here some time in August and get out where I can spend a day talking with the New York people, for the purpose of finding where the hurdles are placed and getting an idea of the track." The hurdles were the machine-made objections to Hughes; the track was heavy and the popular favorite was carrying a lot of weight with the opposition of the bosses. Hughes had consistently refused to "play ball" with the regular Republican organization, paying no heed to

[28] Anderson to the author, April 26, 1934; similarly Taft to Senator Crane, Butt, *Taft and Roosevelt, the Intimate Letters of Archie Butt*, Vol. II, p. 442.
[29] Dr. Henry S. Pritchett to the author, November 11, 1932.
[30] Charles D. Hilles to the author, October 19, 1933.
[31] Mrs. Henry C. Corbin to the author, December 3, 1937.

considerations of what were called party "regularity" and "loyalty." But Root decided Hughes would be the best bet at Saratoga. To be in the most advantageous position, Root went to the Convention as a delegate from Oneida County instead of from New York City; it gave him standing with the "upstaters" and the metropolitan crowd could better be left to Roosevelt. August 3rd, 1908, Roosevelt wrote to Taft that he was at his "wit's end as to whether it is absolutely necessary to nominate Hughes or whether it would be suicidal to do so." [32] Roosevelt's support would be necessary to carry the convention for Hughes. Taft, the Republican nominee for the Presidency, was also a person whose opinion counted. He, too, was for a time doubtful, but he wrote to "dear Athos" on August 15th:

> . . . I cannot but think that in New York the best course is to nominate Hughes. He may be beaten, but whether he is beaten or not, his nomination will strengthen the National ticket, not only in New York but in a good many other states. If the machine nominates somebody else, it will have a bad effect throughout the country on the National ticket. That is my deliberate judgment. I know all the objections to Hughes. I have had them stated in a letter from Herbert Parsons; but there is something about his candidacy that will arouse the country Republicans and will give a moral tinge to all the issues. I have no doubt he will get a great many Democratic votes, and that of those some Democratic votes will come to me if he be nominated.

On August 14th, William Barnes, Jr. wrote to Root that the delegates from Albany would not vote for Hughes under any circumstances.

Although by mail and by word of mouth the politicians were deluging Roosevelt with predictions of defeat if Hughes were nominated,[33] the President had made up his mind by August 24th that Hughes must be nominated, although he was "not a man I care for." [34] On September 5th, Roosevelt wrote to Root:

> As for the nomination for Governor of New York, I am convinced that Hughes ought to be renominated. But the people outside of the organization, except in distinct categories like volunteer firemen, railroad men, &c., want him renominated, and not

---

[32] Taft Papers, Library of Congress.
[33] So George J. Smith to Roosevelt, August 3, 1908; J. Sloat Fassett to Roosevelt, August 2, 1908; Elon R. Brown to Roosevelt, August 1, 1908; copies in Root Papers.
[34] Taft Papers, Library of Congress.

to renominate him would be to jeopardize in this State even the National ticket. But to renominate him is only less bad. He has wantonly and needlessly insulted the party workers, so that in my own county of Nassau I am having great difficulty in getting them to endorse him, and I can only obtain it as a personal favor to me. The fact is that Hughes is a thoroly unhealthy element in public life, for just the same reason that the professional prohibitionist is an unhealthy element in public life; but exactly as it is not wise because of indignation against a professional prohibitionist to offend honest temperance sentiment, so it is not wise because of indignation with Hughes to offend the religious and moral sentiment of the men who make up the background of the Republican party. . . .

It may be that you will want to write me a letter on the Hughes business which I shall answer, and which you can use or not at the convention just as the exigencies demand.

One week later Root submitted his convention speech to Roosevelt who was already beginning to plan his African trip: "Perhaps you may withdraw your mind from Hippopotamusses & Anthropophageusses & such like Carthagenians & glance rapidly over the enclosed. . . . Only please do not appoint any one mentioned in it to office. . . . It is not a letter of recommendation." He felt there was "a real evil" in the tendency of legislatures and conventions to "give their allegiance first to the [party] managers and second only to the voters." People were gradually being roused to the situation and it was "a dangerous condition for a clever fellow like Bryan to deal with. The Democrats are of course just as bad as the Republicans but discontent hurts only the party in power & helps the fellow with new patent remedies. . . . I have been in much doubt about the Hughes nomination . . . yet what seems to me my better judgment swings back always to the conclusion that he should be nominated." [35]

To most people Saratoga means vichy and horse-racing. Hughes' moral campaign against race-track betting somewhat dimmed the splendor of the latter distinction and perhaps made it fitting that he should triumph over the Republican machine at a convention held in that same place. Root, without much cooperation from the favored steed, filled the roles of trainer, jockey, and judge. As temporary Chair-

[35] Roosevelt Papers, Library of Congress.

man, he delivered the key-note speech which was devoted almost entirely to national questions—the record of the Roosevelt administration, the excellencies of Taft and the deficiencies of Bryan. Behind the scenes he was working quietly, talking to the "Little Bosses" in their own language, planning the strategy of the convention. He explained the situation later in a letter of November 23rd to David Jayne Hill, then American Ambassador to Germany:

Of course, I knew that the proposal of your name at Saratoga did not in any way come from you. I was present when it was made and I think I knew all about it. It was made by George Aldrich [sic] of Rochester in a meeting of party leaders at which I was present. I told them in substance that you would make a capital Governor but that I was quite certain you would not take the nomination. It was one of the incidents of a strong desire on the part of many political leaders in the State who had been ignored and offended by Governor Hughes to escape from the necessity of renominating him. Another incident in the same process was a strong effort to get me to take the nomination for Governor which was, of course, impossible, for a situation had been created in which there was nothing to do but to nominate Hughes. Anything else after our delegation had taken his name to Chicago as New York's candidate for the Presidency would have been regarded throughout the country as a turning down of Hughes, and we should have been terribly punished for it at the polls.

From Saratoga, Root exchanged telegrams with Roosevelt who was at Oyster Bay:

Very active aggressive work being done by majority of best known leaders to line up opposition to Hughes and concentrate on some other candidate. They have been urging me to take nomination which I have positively refused. A Cortelyou button has made its appearance. Several eminent Republicans not connected with organization among others Murray Butler being talked of. If they succeed in concentrating the strong feeling against Hughes in the convention will probably result in another nomination. There seems to be no leadership or organization at all of Hughes forces. I think you better send a statement of your position framed with view to be given out if found advisable although I hate to have it done. I have a telegram from Taft intended to be used. Do you think it wise to bring him into the row?

The President wired back:

> I do not think anything from Taft should be used. It might make the organization men turn against the Presidential ticket and let everything go by default. I hope you will make it clear to the organization leaders, on my behalf, and of course I am sure on your own also, that what we are doing is in no sense an attack on them and that we do not intend to sanction a general smash at them. Of course between ourselves you and I must freely admit that Hughes attitude toward many of these organization men has been unwarranted and wanton. But the very fact that we do not sympathize with attitude toward these men should make these men pay heed to us when we tell them that it is vital to their own interest, because it is vital to the interest of the Republican party, that Hughes should be renominated. . . .

He concluded with a statement of endorsement which he authorized Root to publish if or when he thought it wise to do so.

On September 14th, Frank H. Hitchcock telegraphed Root that Republican leaders from a dozen Mississippi Valley and western states believed that the failure to renominate Hughes would seriously reduce the chances of Republican success in the middle west.

Hughes was nominated and carried the state while Taft carried the nation in the November elections. "I am mighty glad we succeeded in renominating Hughes," Roosevelt wrote to Taft on September 16th. "I had to use every ounce of power I possest [sic] to bring it about; and the odd thing is that he will hate you and me more than ever, so far as such a cold-blooded creature is capable of hatred." [36] Root rarely felt so violently about people merely because he disagreed with their views; Bryan was one of the rare exceptions—Hearst was in a class by himself. Woodrow Wilson became the object of personal animosity when Root had the war fever. In the tragic break with Roosevelt which was to come four years later, he never once replied with a hard word to the flood of vilification which poured upon him from Roosevelt's pen. There is nothing in Root's correspondence to suggest that he shared Roosevelt's or Taft's dislike of Hughes. On September 24th, 1908, Root wrote to Roosevelt:

> I am glad you liked the Saratoga performance. It was most interesting. But for you there would not have been two hundred

[36] Ibid.

votes for Hughes in the convention. It was pretty hard for the
men whom he had ignored & attacked to make him governor
again when they had the power to withhold the nomination. More
than that it was the struggle of a system which with many bad
things about it nevertheless has long exhibited tremendous force
& capacity for victorious organization against the setting up of a
new standard.

I couldn't help sympathizing with the leaders who had reasoned themselves into a belief that what they were asked to do
was self destruction & that the whole Hughes boom was faked. I
think the fact of my sympathy & old acquaintance with the habits
of thought & feeling of local leaders probably enabled me to stand
pat on the general welfare without making any one mad or stirring
up the sort of a row that causes real mischief. The very discipline
that has made the Republican organization so effective & that
Hughes fails to appreciate as a governing force is what ultimately
brought about the nomination. Incidentally I have had a beastly
cold ever since I got back from Saratoga and if I cough my head
off I shall claim to have died in the service of my country.[37]

The result of the elections throughout the country equally pleased
and encouraged Root in his expressed confidence in popular government. He wrote to Ambassador Whitelaw Reid in London on November 23rd, 1908:

You will have felt in London probably even more keenly than
we have at home the satisfaction resulting from the way the election went. The prevailing feeling, here, I think, is that the American voters have shown themselves worthy of confidence by
demonstrating their ability to resist the plausible and alluring proposals and promises of Bryan and Gompers, and have followed
their own judgment based on really intelligent consideration. The
clear inference from the election returns is that the labor men and
clerks and farmers, etc., weighed Mr. Bryan in the balance with
all his fallacies and decided that he was not a safe man and rejected him. It was a vote more against Bryan than for Taft. A very
striking feature of the election was that in so many States there
was such a wide difference between the vote on the Presidency
and on the Governorship. In New York Hughes was 130,000 behind Taft. In Michigan the Republican candidate for Governor

[37] Roosevelt Papers, Library of Congress.

was 145,000 behind Taft. In Illinois the difference was, I have forgotten how many thousands, but an enormous number. In Ohio Taft had over 70,000 plurality and the Republican candidate for Governor was beaten some 20,000. In Indiana Taft had a large majority and the Republican candidate for Governor was defeated by a large majority. Generally people voted as they pleased for Governor, following a great variety of impulses, and they rejected overwhelmingly [sic], all of which shows that they cannot easily be fooled and argues well for the future.

PART VI

YEARS 1909–1915

AGE 64–70

CHAPTER XXXIII

"A leader and not a boss"

On January 26th, 1909, Roosevelt wrote to Root:

> I have once had to accept your resignation as Secretary of War. Now I have to accept it as Secretary of State. On the former occasion you retired from a great office where you had done work which no other man could have done as well, and after a few months you came back to fill a still higher office. In this higher office you have again done work which no other man could have done as well. I do not suppose that this letter can be made public, for some foolish people would think I was speaking hyperbolically, whereas I am speaking what I believe to be the literal truth, when I say that in my judgment you will be regarded as the greatest and ablest man who has ever filled the position of Secretary of State.
>
> You leave the office to go into the Senate. I do not see how you can possibly do better work in the Senate than you have done in the Cabinet, but I am sure you will do as good work.[1]

Roosevelt's convictions were often hyperbolic, but none the less sincere. On this occasion, Root's resignation did not cause the same sense of personal loss which had been caused by Root's retirement from the War Department since Roosevelt too was about to leave Washington; on the 4th of March, William Howard Taft was to take over the White House and Roosevelt was to devote his energies to the conquest of the African jungles. But that last Cabinet meeting was a sad one, like the breaking up of a happy family group. "It is a sad sort of business this closing chapters of life," Root wrote to Mrs. Lodge on leaving the meeting. It was one of the times which Theodore Roosevelt's valet may have had in mind when he wrote: "Mr. Root is known to the world as a great lawyer and is generally regarded as a man of austere manner and cold, unemotional character. And yet some of us in the White House used to call him 'Cry Baby'. This was not done

[1] Roosevelt Papers, Library of Congress.

disrespectfully or disparagingly. It was because several times we had seen him moved to tears." [2] On the evening of the 3rd of March, the Tafts dined at the White House with the Roots and a few other intimate friends. Everyone was dismally trying to make polite conversation. "Mr. Root especially was in low spirits; some of us were perfectly sure that we saw tears drop into his soup." [3]

"Taft is anxious to have me stay in the State Department," Root had written to Willard Bartlett on November 21st, "and I would rather stay here than do anything else, but there are special personal considerations which make it clear to me that I ought not to stay." The "special personal considerations" were explained in Root's letter to John L. Cadwalader on November 23rd: "Between rheumatism and the climate and the incessant and wearisome pressure of social duties I am satisfied that it [continuance in the State Department] would mean a complete breakdown of Mrs. Root's health, and that, of course, I am not willing to incur." But he accepted an alternative which kept him in public life and "made it very much easier to say no about the State Department." The alternative was election by the New York Legislature as United States Senator from New York. When Root declined Taft's invitation to continue as Secretary of State, the latter asked whom he would suggest and Root recommended Senator Philander C. Knox of Pennsylvania. Taft asked Root to approach Knox which he did, securing Knox's consent. [4]

"I quite agree with you," Root wrote to a Utica friend on January 21st, 1909, "that it would have been better for me, so far as anything like permanency of reputation is concerned, to remain at the head of the State Department, and it was with great regret that I determined not to do so. There are, however, other things in life more important than the question whether a man shall be remembered a few years more or less, and these made it necessary for me to change, so that it was really a question whether I returned to arguing cases in New York or went to the Senate." "The Senatorship," he explained in his letter to Bartlett, "involves spending so much smaller part of the time in Washington that I can do that work where I could not do the other. . . . The Senate has been much weakened recently by the loss of Hoar,

[2] Amos, *Theodore Roosevelt, Hero to His Valet*, p. 41.
[3] Alice Roosevelt Longworth, *Crowded Hours*, p. 165.
[4] Root to the author, September 15, 1930.

Platt of Connecticut [Platt of New York was no loss] Spooner, Allison, and, I am afraid after this session, Foraker, that there is eminent need of strengthening the Republican representation. I have no idea what the people in New York will work out. I have not had much confidence in the idea that all the organization men who want the place will be thrown over and a man selected who is not asking anybody to vote for him or offering any inducements." Root's statement of his attitude in November was correct, but after the decision was made, he naturally wanted to be elected and he took an active part in directing the strategy of the campaign. It was quite a different proposition in those days to secure the vote of the Legislature from what it is today under the Seventeenth Amendment to campaign for the direct votes of the electorate.

The history of his boom for the Senate is fully set out in a letter of November 21st, 1908, which he wrote to William Barnes, Jr., the Republican boss in Albany, who had written protesting against what he considered a further attempt to dictate from Washington in disregard of the regular Republican organization in New York State. Root denied that there had been any such interference.

> I could not very well help knowing the difference between academic politics and steady all-the-year-round organization work, in view of the fact that I began in politics bunching tickets and served in every capacity in the New York organization up to and including the Chairmanship of the County Committee. . . .
>
> The movement did not originate here. Neither the President nor Taft had anything to do with it. The idea started in the most natural and ordinary way in the world, in the State of New York. First, up in Oneida County where I was born and brought up and keep my active interest and live in the summer in my old home and whence I was sent as a delegate to the last State Convention, the newly elected Senator [Frederick M. Davenport] jumped into the arena immediately after the election with the announcement that he was going to propose me for Senator. He did this without any consultation whatever with me, but with the approval of the Republican organization of the County. Thereupon, the organization leader in New York City, where I have been for many years an active member of the organization, wrote to me recalling a conversation several months before in which I had declined to consider the subject, and put the question whether I would con-

sent to have my name used, and I answered substantially in the words of the public statement which I made shortly after because numerous questions began to come in from all over the State as to whether I would accept the Senatorship if elected. At the time that I made this answer to the leader of my own local organization, upon which he started in upon his campaign, the President and Taft were both urging me to remain in the State Department, and the Senatorship had never been mentioned. My decision was made without consulting either of them, or any one whomsoever, and it was in effect a decision against the course which both of them were urging. After I had answered I told the President what I had done. He asked me if I wanted him to say or do anything in the matter, and I told him I did not and he said that he should keep out of it. I believe he has. Of course, I suppose that when people go to him and talk to him about it he says something nice about me. It would be strange, in view of all our relations during the past ten years—indeed during the past twenty-five years—if he did not do so. I presume Taft does the same. I know that it would be a comfort for him to feel that I was to be in the Senate to give his administration the benefit of my very full and intimate knowledge of the executive end of the Government business.

But such expressions coming in such a way are inevitable and certainly are not open to the objection of interference. In short, I cannot see but that this business has come along in the most natural, proper and unobjectionable way imaginable, as such things ordinarily come.

As to the suddenness with which the movement was projected, the reason given for pressing me for an early answer to the question whether I would take the Senatorship if elected was that several movements had already been projected and were far advanced in securing pledges from members of the Legislature, so that the gentlemen who wanted me for Senator were entitled to have me say yes or no promptly. Nearly forty years of experience in the politics of New York made me quite certain that they were right, and I now know that they were right, for Mr. Woodruff himself called upon me within two days after I had answered and before my answer had been made public, and informed me that he considered that he already had pledges from a majority of the Republicans of the Legislature. One other prominent Republican has written me that he was about to take the field as a candidate, but that he had refrained from doing so upon learning that I had agreed to take the office if elected. Under these existing circumstances, the gentlemen who wanted to have me for Senator would certainly have been a lot of chumps to have sat down and allowed the field to be preoccupied.

On the whole, it really does seem to come down to the question whether the Republicans of New York prefer to have me for Senator or somebody else, without any extraneous reason why they should not do just as they please about it. I am glad of the opportunity of saying to you, my dear Barnes, that whatever course you take on that question will not in any way interfere with the very friendly feeling that I have long had for you or with my confidence in the sincerity and devotion to what you believe to be the best interests of the Republican party which have characterized your leadership and enabled you to achieve substantial and exceptional success.

In Oneida County, it was State Senator Davenport, a professor at Hamilton College, with George Dunham, editor of the Utica *Press*, and in New York City it was John Parsons, then a member of Congress, who pressed the proposal. To them and to others like James W. Wadsworth of Geneseo, State Senator J. Sloat Fassett of Elmira, Seth Low and Joseph H. Choate, Root wrote at first in the same vein:

I am not going to seek the office. I cannot. I do not know how. I have no such desire for it as to lead me to seek it.

On the other hand, if the people of the state of New York do really want me to represent them in the Senate because they think that I can render substantial service and should call upon me to render the service, I should not dare refuse under the existing conditions, at the risk of self disapproval all the rest of my life for failing to perform a duty of the highest obligation which lay plainly before me. I do not think it at all likely that any such call will be made because there are plenty of good men from whom the Legislature can select a Senator; but that is the way I feel about it and what I have now said is the best answer I can make to your question. . . .

Of course, doing that would mean giving up a very large income which I should be certain of making with comparative ease upon returning to the practice of law, and so far as any personal honor or eclat is to be found in the office of Senator, I should not feel like throwing away the income and the comfort and convenience and independence of private life in exchange. I do believe, however, that a man ought to spend his life doing the things that are best worth doing as they come before him. . . .

On the 12th of November, the Union League Club adopted a strong resolution in favor of Root's candidacy. On the 16th, Root issued a public statement to the effect that the Republicans in New York who were urging his election were entitled to know his position; his position was that while he did not seek the office of Senator, he would respond to the call if the Legislature thought he could render useful service in the Senate. On the 19th, the New York Republican County Committee adopted a resolution supporting Root and on the same day the Union League Club appointed a committee of thirty to promote his election. Root's principal rival was "Little Tim" Woodruff, the former Lieutenant Governor whom the machine wished to elect as a recognition of his services to the organization and because, as a machine man, he could be counted on to continue the general patronage system which Boss Platt had for so long a time used to build and strengthen the party in New York. The bosses were aware that Root knew the political game and that he appreciated the value and necessity of party organization, but he had over a long period fought the Platt machine and he could not be counted on for the same kind of cooperation which might be expected from Woodruff. "You have to speak the language of the politicos (as they are called in South America)," Root once remarked in family conversation, "you have to understand their thoughts, you have to understand what they want to get on with them. Hoover didn't, Taft didn't but McKinley did to perfection." Root might truthfully have added, "So did I." To his most active supporter, Senator Davenport, Root wrote on November 21st, showing a sympathetic understanding of the position of the Republican State Senators who were pledged to Woodruff:

> My impression is that the danger is not so much of the election of Woodruff. I do not think a majority of the Republican members of the legislature are likely to do that, but it may well be that the result of Woodruff's pressing his candidacy with the pledges that he already has may result in solving the difficulty by recourse to some other man. I think it is quite likely that several gentlemen are looking forward to the possibility of profiting by such a con-

"The Whirligig of Time"

(A cartoon in the New York *World*, March 15, 1909)

tingency. If the Syracuse people are tied up to Woodruff it might be useful for them to resolve upon going to me rather than to somebody else in case Woodruff proves to have no chance.

And again he wrote on the 30th:

The chief obstacle to a general agreement has been, not any real strength on Woodruff's part or any considerable objection personal to myself, but a feeling which has been pretty strong in a good many quarters of irritation, amounting almost to resentment, at the idea of having a Senator forced upon the members of the Legislature and the political leaders in the State from outside, as they think Hughes was forced upon them. Distinct effort was made to create the impression that my candidacy was dictated from Washington. I think that impression has been in a great measure dispelled. Its existence makes it desirable to avoid too much pressure and too much organization.

The indications now are that Woodruff will withdraw and that there will be no opposition to my election. Nevertheless, the whole thing may change in a minute. . . .

By November 24th, probably with the knowledge of Woodruff's withdrawal which was announced on the 30th, the road seemed to be clear. Root wrote to Taft: "You will perceive that the possibility of my being elected Senator seems sufficiently real for me to begin to look at the situation after the 4th of March from the legislative point of view, and to consider how we are going to stand in the two Houses with reference to working in harmony with the new Administration and agreeing upon policies and carrying them through."

Root's attitude toward campaigning for office is indicated by a letter which he wrote on December 16th, 1908, to H. W. Collingwood of *The Rural New Yorker*. Collingwood had asked him to state publicly his attitude toward the passage of a law authorizing the parcel post system under the Federal Post Office Department, a measure in which the farmers were much interested and which was being vigorously opposed by the express companies, and therefore by retiring Senator Thomas C. Platt, president of the United States Express Company. Root told Collingwood for his private information that he was in favor of the parcel post system but that he did not wish to make a public statement on the subject.

I do not want to go into a kind of civil service examination regarding my fitness for the Senate. It would be hard to put a limit on that sort of process if it were once begun, and if carried very far it would result in what I think would be the wrong way to elect a Senator. It seems to me that the way to do that is to select a man who is so well known to the people of the State that they can have confidence in his good sense to find out what their interests are and his loyalty to promote them. When men get to answering questions put to them for the purpose of determining whether the people shall favor them for office, the temptation is very strong to make the sort of answers that the people are supposed to want, and I do not think it is at all certain that the best and most honest men would come out at the top of such an examination.

In reply to a further letter from Collingwood, Root consented to having a part of his letter published in *The Rural New Yorker,* so long as it was not made to appear that he was answering a questionnaire.

On the evening of January 18th, 1909, the Republican members of the New York Assembly and Senate met in joint caucus to choose Senator Platt's successor. Senator Davenport was given the floor and proposed the name of Elihu Root. He was followed by Senator John Raines, Majority Leader in the Upper House. Raines began with a tribute to Platt which was fervid in its devotion to the old boss. His praise of Root was centered upon Root's party regularity and the fact that he had been a party worker "who does not see in party activity any disqualification for political preferment." This was generally interpreted as a dig at Governor Hughes. The nominations were at once closed and Root was unanimously declared the choice of the caucus, which, with Republican control of the Legislature, meant that his election was assured. It was confirmed by formal vote of the Legislature on the following day. There was only one notable absentee from the caucus: Senator Edgar Trueman Brackett of Saratoga, one of the three Senators who had favored Root for the same office six years before,[5] did not attend because, it was believed, he was personally favorable to Root but vehement in his denunciation of Roosevelt for trying to dictate to the party in New York.

To Raines and to Wadsworth, then Speaker of the Assembly, Root

[5] Ray B. Smith, *History of the State of New York*, Vol. IV by Roscoe C. E. Brown, p. 89.

wrote to say that he would like the privilege of addressing the New York Legislature on the subject of the relations between the state and federal governments. The speech was arranged for January 28th, 1909, and on that day Root was at Albany. He told the Legislature that he had come to Albany to talk with the men "who are leaders of opinion and of political action in the state of New York." He confessed that his long service in Washington had rather put him out of touch with New York affairs and that he was anxious to renew his old familiarity with them. He urged upon them frequent communication with him to declare their wishes. He decried the tendency to turn to the federal government constantly for help, fearing its deleterious effect upon local government.

> The tendency to vest all powers in the central government at Washington is likely to produce the decadence of the powers of the states. Now, do not misunderstand me. I am a convinced and uncompromising nationalist of the school of Alexander Hamilton.

But the powers of the federal government must be exercised within the limits established by the Constitution.

> Evidently, if the powers of the states are to be preserved and their authority is to be continued, the states must exercise their powers. The only way to maintain the powers of government is to govern.
>
> Let me say that the men who make the most noise about state rights are very apt to be the men who are the most willing and the most desirous to have the national government step in and usurp the functions of a state when there is an appropriation carried with the usurpation. . . .
>
> You cannot take power away from public bodies without having the character of those bodies deteriorate. For this reason I am opposed to the direct election of Senators, as I am opposed to the initiative and referendum, because these things are based upon the idea that the people cannot elect legislatures whom they trust.[6]

He stressed the need for cooperative action among the states for the regulation of common problems, urging the use of inter-state compacts for that purpose. It was much the same theme which he had stressed

[6] *Addresses on Government and Citizenship*, pp. 247, 251.

in a speech before the Pennsylvania Society in New York on December 12th, 1906.[7] At that time he was much misquoted and misunderstood because he had taken note of the increasing participation of the federal government in matters formerly left to the states and had warned that if the states did not remedy existing evils, public opinion would demand that the federal government do it. Similarly, in addressing the first Conference of the Governors of the States which President Roosevelt convened in Washington on May 1st, 1908, Root had pointed to the process whereby the nations of the world solved their difficulties by conferences and agreements and had suggested that the states of the Union might well follow that international example.[8] Root, of course, was not unique in the advocacy of what has become a definite trend in inter-state relationships.

After his address to the Legislature, Root conferred with many of the Republican leaders; the newspapers thought he concentrated on the machine-wing of the party and had little to do with the Hughes group. Some thought it was significant that Barnes' paper, the Albany *Evening Journal*, on January 29th editorially hailed Root as the new leader of the state and attacked Governor Hughes and his policies. Root had no idea of becoming a state boss such as Platt had been. Three years before, on December 28th, 1905, he had expressed his views in a letter to James A. Burden:

> . . . Of course, a political party, like any other organization, must have a leader; but the government of a party should be representative and republican, and not autocratic and despotic; and this I take to be the distinction between the leader and the boss. We want a leader and we do not want a boss. I suppose the difficulty is to find the right sort of man, of sufficient personal weight and recognized standing in the community, to be accepted as a leader, and who is willing to give the time and effort. It is a very laborious and engrossing occupation which few men, having the requisite qualifications, are willing to undertake. It is moreover a thankless task; for the minute any one undertakes it, however disinterested his motives and however faithful he may be to the true principals of party leadership, a lot of people will immediately accuse him of being a boss. The knowledge of this makes it difficult to get the right sort of man to take the position. . . .

[7] *Ibid.*, p. 363.
[8] *Ibid.*, p. 371.

At that time the issue was not a personal one for him. With the Senatorship it did become a personal problem. Senator Raines had posed the question in a confidential letter which he wrote to Root on January 4th, 1909, just two weeks before the Republican caucus. Raines stressed the existing dissension in the ranks of the Republican leaders throughout the state. "Today, there are a lot of good Republicans who, to a large degree, wish the best success of the Party—and also their own. They are commonly called Sub-Bosses, or Little Bosses . . . ," but there was no leader who could unite them.

It is not, perhaps, necessary that we should have what, in general terms, is recognized as a Boss; but we should have some person to act in the capacity of a Referee, if I may so term it, whose official advice, after hearing all that is to be said, should be virtually binding on all,—not perhaps, as an absolute command, but as a moral—or political force, which, perhaps is the better term to be used. Such a man must be one who is familiar with Party methods from the ground up. He must be a man of excellent judgment, and of such position in the Party as to command the confidence of those who appeal to him, or consult with him.

There is no such man active in the Organization today. Senator Platt, in his prime, occupied the nearest to such a position of any one whom I have known in politics. It was his habit to bring together and consult those who were influential in their own districts, and out of such consultation to evolve a program which usually commanded the confidence of what may be termed the Organization.

It seems to me, Mr. Root, to be up to you to occupy virtually the place of such a Referee. I believe it is vital to the continued success of the Republican Party that you should do so. I say, without any design to flatter, that I believe you have the experience and the wisdom to so adjust matters that your advice would be accepted as of the very highest value,—perhaps, indeed, as of binding force.

Root replied on January 6th he thoroughly agreed with Raines' general views.

I do not want to take on myself the burden of having to devote my life to the details of State politics, but I shall be very glad to try to exercise an influence towards good understanding, reconciliation of views, doing away with mutual suspicion and for team play on the part of the leaders of the party. I think a good deal in this way can be done without a man's making a slave of himself, and I shall try to do it. I am sure that if the political leaders in the State generally deal with the subject in the same admirable spirit which inspires your letter, very satisfactory results can be obtained.

For six years Root was to find that it was no easy task to be a leader without being a boss. He never became a dictator of that type of "invisible government" which he was to denounce before the New York Constitutional Convention in 1915, but he could not avoid being constantly enmeshed in the political squabbles of the state which he represented in Washington.

Root was rather surprised that his election went through so easily. On January 25th, 1909, he replied to a congratulatory letter from his friend, Charles R. Miller, editor of the New York *Times*:

. . . It has been indeed a most extraordinary proceeding. I had no real faith in any such thing ever happening in the State of New York and I am now studying the cause of it with much interest as a matter of political psychology. Certainly one great element was the kindly and vigorous treatment of the subject which your friendship has brought about in the Times.

It is rather a tradition of the World to regard me as a monster of iniquity. I preserve myself from all injurious effects by never reading the paper, and I doubtless receive great benefit from it, for it is necessary to have enemies and to be attacked in order not to be hated. One amusing thing about it is that on such casual inquiry as I have made from time to time I have become satisfied that the World is really sincere in its view of me and perhaps they are right. Who knows?

The *World*, which meant Joseph Pulitzer, was perfectly sincere in opposing Root. Pulitzer's instructions to his editor, Frank I. Cobb, lay down the bases for opposing Root for the Senate. There was no doubt as to Root's ability and his intellect but, the *World's* editorial was to point out with regret, this man Root was Ryan's attorney. There could be no doubt that as Senator he would be the representative of the corporations. It was too bad that a man of such capacity should be so unfit, but the greatness of his ability was the measure of his unfitness. Cobb was instructed to search Ryan's record with a fine tooth comb and play up every connection between Ryan and Root; the issue was to be whether Ryan should have a Senator.[9] What Pulitzer did not understand was what Roosevelt had pointed out to Oscar King Davis: "What the people do not understand about him [Root] is that if he were President they would be his clients." However, on the 2nd of July, 1914, the *World's* editorial declared: "The World was a vigorous opponent of Mr. Root's election to the Senate, but it is pleased to testify that none of its misgivings was ever realized, and it sincerely regrets his determination not to be a candidate for reelection."

Root's part at Saratoga in overcoming the organization's opposition to Hughes has already been described; Hughes' election by no means put an end to the opposition of the party machine. In the spring of 1909, just after Root became Senator, the "politicos" were disturbed and annoyed by the Governor's effective advocacy of a bill requiring nominations to be made directly in the primaries instead of by party conventions. On March 24th, 1909, William Barnes wrote to Root urging him not to support the direct primary bill. Barnes recalled that Root had told him in several conversations that he did not intend to enter the fight but in Barnes' opinion the active support of the bill by Senator Davenport was interpreted as reflecting Root's attitude. State Senator John Raines went further, urging Root to come out with a strong statement which would kill the bill. Root had no particular enthusiasm for Hughes' direct primary bill but he agreed with neither Barnes nor Raines. He wrote to Raines on April 13th that he did not believe that the bill actually proposed would accomplish its object "of securing more effective representation of the rank and file of the Party in the making of nominations." He did feel that the people of the state had become convinced that they were not having a "fair chance to control their own affairs" and whether this conviction was or was not justified, it would be translated into political action under the leadership of Hughes and the Republican organization would be defeated if it stood in opposition to the bill. "Of course anyone who has studied the subject must realize that no form of procedure, no arrangement of machinery for bringing about nominations can be effective in securing popular control unless the people are willing to come to the primaries and vote, and that the fundamental difficulty is in the unwillingness

[9] Memoranda for Mr. Cobb from Mr. Pulitzer, November 9 and 10, 1908; Pulitzer Papers, Library of Congress.

of people to take the trouble to attend themselves to their own political affairs." Root pointed out also that organization would always prevail over disorganized individual preferences in nominating and electing and that the bill really constituted no threat to the Republican organization. He advised that a thorough study be made of the operation of direct primaries in other states and that the Republican organization get behind a really workable bill. Root stated in this and in other letters that he was too busy with his duties as Senator, which he had just assumed, to attempt to make the necessary study himself and to draft a proper bill. Some men might have answered Raines and Barnes with a little sermon on the People and their Rights. Such sermons often give the writer great satisfaction and the receiver great disgust. Root preferred to try to persuade them by talking their own language. In the Republican Convention at Saratoga in the preceding summer, he had said that he thought direct primaries might improve the really representative character of the State Legislature and at a Republican dinner in Albany on February 25th, he had urged the party to make itself more truly representative of its rank and file. In 1915, he wrote to William C. Church that he had "long regarded the direct primary in its present form as merely a phase of change in political machinery resulting from a desire of the people of the country to get away from a bad old system. I do not think the primary is a *terminus ad quem*. I think it is merely a stopping place through which the voters are passing on their way to some system which will be developed without the manifest evils of the primary and also without some of the serious abuses of the previous system." His underlying political philosophy was always that which he expressed in a letter to Charles A. Bowen in 1911: "What a great self-governing people really requires is, not to find devices by which its members may evade the performance of their duty, but the individual sense of responsibility and the public spirit to lead them to perform their duty." From his earliest days in New York, Root had shown that he had this sense and this spirit. For the achievement of the distant goal, Root was willing to wait and meanwhile he was opposed to the mechanical remedies which were proposed by the impatient or by those who sought a popular rallying cry.

By December, 1909, the New York situation had centered around the attempt of some of the New York City Republicans, identified with the "federal crowd," to oust former Governor Timothy Woodruff from the Chairmanship of the State Committee and to break the power of the up-state bosses. As part of the movement, Senator Hinman of Albany was being groomed as Republican leader in the State Senate. On December 21st, Root wrote to Clarence O. Parker of Norwich, New York, that while he had a high opinion of Hinman, he did not think that this was a matter in which he should interfere.

> . . . In the first place, I am much opposed to having our Legislature, or either branch of it, run from the outside. I think our people ought to elect men who are competent to form their own judgments and vote in accordance with them, and not to follow anybody's dictation. The leadership of the majority in the New York Senate is not a matter of appointment or election, but rather of natural selection. . . . Every step which proceeds on the theory that the State Senators and Assemblymen ought to be considered responsible to a Senator of the United States, or a Governor, or a Party leader instead of being responsible to their own constituents, is a step in the wrong direction and tends towards the emasculation of our State Government.

But the pressure on Root was strong. Lloyd C. Griscom, newly elected Chairman of the New York County Republican Committee, wrote to President Taft on February 13th, 1910, hoping that Root, as Governor Hughes had suggested, would take hold and help them to oust Timothy Woodruff as Chairman and to put Otto Bannard in his place. Griscom was confident that Root could put it through if he would and that this would end the old corrupt alliance between business and the Republican machine in New York. Root had known Griscom favorably as a member of the diplomatic service; he was glad to talk the situation over with him the next time he came over to New York. Senator Davenport had written urgently to Root asserting that the situation in the Legislature and in the party generally was very serious. He anticipated disclosures of the old corrupt relations between business and politics and reported that the Governor was ready to take drastic action if necessary. But both Davenport and Hughes believed that Root was in a more advantageous position to get results. "There are no antagonisms to you. All within the party in this state trust and respect you. Your suggestions would be received with less friction than the suggestions of any other man. . . . Perhaps you have no idea how many within the party are looking to you for guidance." There were three urgent questions: the choice of the next United States Senator from New York; a change in the state Republican chairmanship; and the fate of the direct primary bill. "The divisive effect of bitter discussion over these three subjects can be greatly modified or very largely prevented if you could see your way clear to confer soon with a group of the leaders and throw the great weight of your personality and your public interest, for the time being, into this channel."

Root finally acted and threw a bombshell into the Republican caucus which met at Albany on March 8th. On that date, he sent a telegram to Senator Davenport urging that Hinman be chosen as the Republican leader "as the only course which will . . . correctly exhibit the real relation of the party as a whole to the principles and policies for which Governor Hughes stands and will rightly represent the wishes of the voters of the party." The papers printed the telegram and were agog with the news. Hughes stated publicly that he agreed with Root. It was well known that Woodruff had rallied his forces in favor of Senator Cobb and against Hinman. Hinman had been chief sponsor of the direct primary bill and was anathema to the bosses. On the 10th, Root wired Woodruff explaining why he had not been able to talk with him before telegraphing Davenport and urging him to support Hinman. There were the usual outcries against dictation from Washington and the Woodruff forces carried the caucus, choosing Cobb as President pro tem and Republican floor leader.

The federal group tried again. They had already failed in one other attempt; on March 2nd, 1910, Taft had sent Root a letter from Woodruff declining a suggested appointment to a diplomatic post. Taft had definitely thrown in his weight with Griscom and Bannard.[10] Sunday, March 13th, Root was in New York to see Woodruff. Among Root's papers is a draft of a letter dated March 15th, referring to "the undersigned members of the Republican State Committee." With flowery appreciation of Woodruff's great services to the party, the letter most tactfully suggests that he probably wishes to resign at once for the good of the party. The letter was never sent but there is no doubt that it expresses the gist of Root's mission. The Administration had foolishly let it be known in advance that that was the purpose of his visit. Barnes, despite his admiration for Root, had as his primary concern the task of holding together his state organization of which "Little

10 Cf. Taft to Root, September 24, 1910.

"Two's a Crowd"
(A cartoon in the New York *World*, March 15, 1910)

Tim" Woodruff was an essential cog. But Woodruff, in force of character and personality, was a weak cog and had to be strengthened for an encounter with a man like Root. Barnes and Woodruff met in Colonel Lafayette Gleason's office to rehearse. Barnes explained to Woodruff that he must begin with a direct attack, telling Root that he had no business to come over to New York on such an errand; that Root could do as he pleased as a Senator in Washington but that Woodruff was running the show in New York. Timorous Tim demurred that he could not possibly do that, but Barnes insisted. Woodruff began to say his piece in a mild and gentle way when Barnes broke in and said that would not do at all. Like a dramatic coach, he showed Woodruff how he must run up to Root and shout at him, "You have no business to come over to New York on such an errand!" For two hours Woodruff was rehearsed until Barnes declared him ready. The next day Root met Woodruff who played his part to perfection, taking Root so much by surprise that the ouster was not accomplished and Root went back to Washington.[11] Woodruff wrote to George W. Aldridge on March 14th; his letter can be summarized in the famous war cry of Stalky and Company, "I gloat!" [12]

On March 17th, Woodruff wrote to Root that since nothing had been settled at their conference, he wondered what conclusions Root had reached since it was clear that there must be a "working basis" between them. Root replied with a long letter two days later. On the question of the State Chairmanship, Root said that he gathered the general opinion was that nothing should be done before the organization of the new Committee in the following September. "There seemed no doubt that such a change would be made if the Administration chose to use its power and patronage to bring it about; but I certainly should not wish such a course to be followed." He discussed at length the current investigation of the bribery charges against State Senator Allds which he believed reflected a general interest in support of Governor Hughes' demands that something be done to clean up the political corruption in the state. He regretted that the opportunity had not been seized to elect Senator Hinman leader of the Senate. There still remained the chance to get back of a direct primary law.

[11] From information given to the author by Colonel Gleason, April 10, 1935. A circumstantial account of the interview appears in the New York *Times*, March 15, 1910.
[12] George W. Aldridge Papers, Rochester Historical Library.

For my own part, I still think, as I said at the Saratoga Convention last summer, the representation in the Legislature would be
improved and the confidence of the voters increased by a method
of nomination which makes the members of the Legislature more
directly responsible to the voters and less responsible to the managers of the political machinery. . . . There certainly ought to be
some method to enable the voters of the party to fix responsibility
much more promptly and readily than they can now upon officers of the party who use their positions for their own personal
benefit and either sell their votes or trade them for personal advantages to themselves.

Root urged also the passage of the bill pending at Albany which would
put the telegraph and telephone companies under the Public Utilities
Commission. "I see no reason why those companies should not be
under the same regulative control that railroads are under."

Woodruff wrote back on March 28th, assuring Root that he agreed
with him on all these points, that his conscience was perfectly clear
and that he would not resign under pressure. But he was kept on edge
by the report that Taft had told William Loeb to try to induce him
to resign.[18]

On the 25th, Root had written to Hughes, expressing his opinion
that they would have a very hard time in saving the state for the
Republican Party in the fall. "Some people think that my telegram to
Davenport was a mistake. I do not think so. The situation was one
which could not be dealt with by ordinary private conversation. It may
be that the startling effect of the telegram, followed by your public
statement, will prove to have called a halt on the program [of the
bosses]. If not, it is better for the state and the Republican party in it
to have just as much of that party dissociated in the public mind from
the program as possible." Hughes replied expressing his gratification
for Root's help which had had a "very salutary effect."

"I have been going around for several years now," Root wrote to
William Allen White on October 8th, 1910, "like Old Noah telling the
men who run the New York machine or machines that this is no
ordinary shower, but a flood, and that they would better hurry up and
get into the Ark. They simply can't believe it. . . . I think the im-

    18 W. L. Ward to Vice President Sherman, March 30, 1910, James S. Sherman Papers,
New York Public Library.

portant thing is to strengthen our state legislatures, and as a first step towards that I favor the direct nomination of legislative candidates. . . . The abuses of political machine control have been so grave and have been so long endured with slowly growing indignation that it is hardly possible for the people of the country to break away from the machine and not go a little too far in the other direction."

CHAPTER XXXIV

"Taft is big and good natured"

WHEN Taft took over the White House from Roosevelt, he took over also, to a considerable extent, the presidential habit of reliance on Root. Archie Butt believed that Root was Taft's "closest adviser" with the possible exception of Attorney General Wickersham,[1] but Taft was not as "advisable" a man as Roosevelt. In a letter to Mrs. Taft on June 26th, 1910, the President mentioned several Senators who had been particularly helpful to him; Root's name is not among them.[2] Despite his jovial and easy-going nature, Taft had moments of petulance. Root's puns and repartee, which delighted Roosevelt, tended at times to annoy Taft.[3] He and Root were intimate friends and, in the later years when both had escaped from the turmoil of active politics, devoted friends. During the decade from 1909 to 1919, there were little disagreements and small frictions, of which echoes are to be found scattered through Taft's correspondence. Root was never jealous of anyone but Taft was somewhat jealous of Root. The feeling may have started when Taft took over the War Department and heard his predecessor constantly quoted and eulogized by enthusiastic army officers. When Root reentered the Cabinet in 1905, however, he wrote General Corbin that he was determined to avoid mixing in army matters "except that I may here and there be of some use in helping Taft." Root did not wholly sympathize with the foreign policy of Taft and his Secretary of State Knox, and Taft felt aggrieved at his lack of support. Root privately felt that the intervention in Cuba in 1906 might have been avoided by skillful handling; Taft felt he had been instrumental in mending a bad situation which Root had created.[4] There were other points on which Root as Senator disagreed with the Taft administra-

---

[1] Butt, *Taft and Roosevelt, the Intimate Letters of Archie Butt*, Vol. I, p. 228.
[2] Taft Papers, Library of Congress.
[3] Taft to Mrs. Taft, April 3, 1904, *ibid.*
[4] Taft to Philander C. Knox, December 18, 1913, Knox Papers, Library of Congress.

tion, but these may be noted in later chapters which describe Root's legislative career. Throughout, "Will" and "Elihu," "Porthos" and "Athos" corresponded on intimate terms. Perhaps the friendship seems less deep because it contrasts with the warmth of the relationship between Root and Roosevelt. During his first presidential campaign in the summer of 1908, Taft had submitted to Roosevelt the draft of a letter which he intended to make public regarding his religious affiliations. On August 21st, he sent it also to Root saying that Roosevelt had urged him to "Go over every word of it before you make it public, and if possible, submit it to that ever present help in time of trouble, the beloved Root." The adjective was characteristic of Roosevelt and his feeling for Root; Taft would never have written it, even after 1912, when Roosevelt turned from affectionate praise to denunciation and abuse of Root because Root was loyal to Taft.

In the spring of 1909, Roosevelt was in Africa, Taft was in the White House, Root in the Senate. The miles of ocean and land which separated the dominant figure from his two former Cabinet officers were prophetic of the tragic breach which was soon to divide them politically and spiritually. There were not as yet sufficient signs to enable the most prophetic to foretell what was in store. There was some little correspondence between Roosevelt and Root and the old type of jocular messages went back and forth through Henry Cabot Lodge who wrote on June 21st, 1909, to Roosevelt:

> I was also much interested in your brief account of your hunting and I am glad to know that you have had such good fortune. . . . I accepted all the newspaper reports about the game you had killed with blind faith, and declined to doubt any of it. . . . Did I tell you Root's comment on the first despatch? He said: "Of course Theodore shot three lions with one bullet and Kermit shot one lion with three bullets." I detect in this remark a tendency to doubt which I do not wholly approve.

To which Roosevelt replied on July 26th:

> Tell Root that I don't at all like his hardened skepticism about the lions. If this kind of thing goes on, I shall have to head an insurrection to put Tom Platt back in Root's seat when the latter's term expires. . . .[5]

[5] *Roosevelt-Lodge Correspondence*, Vol. II, pp. 337 and 341.

There was as yet no breach with Taft. From Juja Farm, Nairobi, Roosevelt wrote to Root on May 17th, 1909: "Give my warm regards to the President when you see him. From all I can gather, he seems to have been doing excellently. Of course, he will have his little worries and bothers, but that simply is what has to be expected." To which Roosevelt added characteristically in his own hand, "It is all right!" By April 27th, 1910, Roosevelt was in the midst of his grand tour of Europe, lecturing the British on their imperial duties to civilization, reviewing the German army with the Kaiser, quarreling with the Pope, fêted and feasted everywhere. From Paris on that date he wrote to Root:

> I really think you ought to try to see me for a moment while abroad. People complain that I see Pinchot. So I do see him and am very glad to. They also complain that I don't see men representing the other side. Now there is not anyone, bar Cabot, whom I am so anxious to see as you, and if it can only be a day at some place where I can see you, I hope you will try to arrange it.

Here were signposts of trouble, but not as yet any active hostility on Roosevelt's part. Root was a member of the Senate Committee which investigated the famous Ballinger-Pinchot controversy. Gifford Pinchot had been one of Roosevelt's chief aids in the program of conservation which was very dear to the President's heart. Taft, on taking office, in the course of making up his own Cabinet—to which Roosevelt offered not the slightest objection—appointed Richard A. Ballinger as Secretary of the Interior in place of James R. Garfield who, in that post under Roosevelt, had led the conservation work. Ballinger was presumably a Roosevelt-Garfield man, having been the head of the General Land Office under Garfield. Louis R. Glavis, a young man in a subordinate place in the Interior Department, came to Taft with a letter of introduction from Pinchot, charging that Ballinger was improperly transferring part of the public domain to a syndicate headed by members of the Guggenheim family. Taft sent the charges to Ballinger who denied them *in toto* and in detail. Pinchot, then Chief Forester, jumped into the fray and capped the climax by writing an open letter to Senator Dolliver defending his own acts and those of Glavis. Taft knew that Pinchot's dismissal would be highly displeasing to Roosevelt and he was reluctant to act, but Root, whom he consulted, advised him "There is only one thing for you to do now, and that you must do at once." [6] The entire Cabinet concurred in this decision that the President could not ignore an attempt by a subordinate to appeal to Congress in order to block or influence the President's action in his own field. Roosevelt himself would not have hesitated an instant to take the same course. Pinchot rushed overseas to pour out his heart to Roosevelt on the White Nile, but Roosevelt wrote to Lodge in April, 1910, that he was not yet sure Taft could have followed any other course. [7] Roosevelt's friends and followers were not so forbearing and the case assumed the dimensions of a public scandal. Root was appointed a member of the Senate Committee which by a Republican majority upheld Ballinger and therefore President Taft, while the Progressive and Democratic minority held otherwise. Six months later, on March 7th, 1911, Ballinger resigned and Taft accepted his resignation, as the New York *Evening Post* put it, "in a blaze of indignant relief." [8]

It was not this incident which caused the breach although it added one more coal to the fire which friends of both Taft and Roosevelt were constantly fanning. Root wrote to Stimson on November 18th, 1909, that the Ballinger-Pinchot affair "is pregnant with immense evil for the Administration and the Republican Party. It is difficult for me to see how it can be averted, but I hope it may, and I shall do all I can to help in doing so." Between Root and Roosevelt there was not as yet any dimming of the old bright friendship. Apropos a plan of Andrew Carnegie's for universal disarmament, Roosevelt wrote to him on December 14th, 1909, asking him to get Root to draft what he had in mind: "Root's gift of phrasing things is unequalled—he is the ablest man I have ever met—and his name carries greater weight." And again on February 18th, 1910:

> . . . what Root champions along these lines you can guarantee I will champion also; you know how I trust him; he was *the* man of my cabinet, the man on whom I most relied, to whom I owed most, the greatest Secretary of State we have ever had, as great a cabinet officer as we ever had, save Alexander Hamilton alone. He is as sane and cool-headed as he is high minded; he neither lets

[6] Butt, *op. cit.*, Vol. I, p. 256.
[7] *Roosevelt-Lodge Correspondence*, Vol. II, p. 367.
[8] Sullivan, *Our Times*, Vol. IV, p. 396.

facts blind him to ideals, nor ideals to facts; he is the wisest and safest of advisers and staunchly loyal alike to friends and causes— and all I say I mean, and it is said with the full remembrance that on certain points he and I would hardly agree.[9]

On February 11th, Root had written Roosevelt on this subject of disarmament expressing vigorous dissent from Carnegie's suggestion that they should meet in Europe to blaze the trail: "Nothing could be worse than to give the idea of a conference or the idea of a voluntary mission or the idea that you are going to show Europe how to manage its affairs. I think there is just a hundred to one chance that you might drive into Emperor William's imagination the idea that he has a tremendous opportunity to make a great historic figure of himself by taking the lead in a peace movement off his own bat. 'If any one kin you kin.' But of course any such attempt would have to be in the most casual and incidental way with brass bands and evidences of premeditation strictly barred."

On May 21st, 1910, Root sailed from New York to argue the North Atlantic Fisheries case at The Hague. On the 28th, Roosevelt wirelessed to the ship, asking him to stop off to see him at Dorchester House in London. The *Lapland* was stopped off Dover and Root went up to London for a long talk. He gave Roosevelt a full account of the political situation in the United States and urged him to keep out of it when he got home. Roosevelt fully agreed with him and promised that he would do so.[10] From London Roosevelt wrote Taft, on June 8th, 1910, that their talk had been "altogether too short and yet very satisfactory —as a talk with Root almost always is." [11] Walking past Dorchester House on September 2nd, 1920, Root looked up at it and commented to his daughter-in-law: "It is there I had an interesting interview with Roosevelt. And if he had done as he promised me—kept out of things political—we would have been spared much of our past trouble."

By the 6th of September, Root was back in New York and Roosevelt wrote him a warm note of welcome and congratulation although Root's first task on arrival was to rush to Chicago for a meeting of what he called in his letter to Roosevelt, "the absurd Ballinger-Pinchot com-

[9] Roosevelt Papers, Library of Congress.
[10] Henry S. Pritchett to the author, November 11, 1932.
[11] Taft Papers, Library of Congress.

mittee." Roosevelt "greatly regretted Root's signing a report in which Gifford and Jim [Garfield] were bitterly censured. On the other hand, Gifford is going in with some of the extremists in Congress with the expectation of trying to form a third party if Taft is nominated. He has become completely identified with the ultra-extremists, and I can only work with him now to a very limited extent." [12] As a matter of fact, Root had written from The Hague on August 27th, 1910, to the Chairman of the Senate Committee, Senator Knute Nelson, urging the elimination of severe criticisms of Glavis and Pinchot. He felt it was important that the report should have a purely judicial and non-partisan tone.

Root's political advice to Roosevelt and Roosevelt's promise in reply, were duplicated in the exchanges between the latter and Henry Cabot Lodge. Lodge wrote on April 4th, 1910: "I read to Root the following sentence from your letter of March 1st: 'I shall say nothing about politics until I have been home long enough to know the situation.' I then added that this sentence seemed to indicate failing powers. Root replied: 'It seems almost to mark the approach of senility', and then 'Be sure to write Theodore what we say.' I wish that you could have heard him chuckle when he insisted on my giving you this message." On the following day Lodge had written again urging Roosevelt to see Root in Europe: "There is no saner wiser more loyal friend than he anywhere." [13] Root had himself written Roosevelt at length on February 11th, 1910, surveying the trials and tribulations of the Administration, evidently seeking to put in a word to prevent any breach from widening between Taft and Roosevelt:

Of course we have missed you immensely & not only your personal friends but the people of the country generally seem to find your return the most interesting thing on the horizon. The change has been a good deal like that from an automobile to a cab. Taft is big & good natured & easy going & lets things drift considerably. That is sometimes a good thing but not always. He is making a good president & will I think win his way into public confidence but he has not yet altogether arrived. I think he will. He deserves to.

[12] Roosevelt to Robert Bacon, January 2, 1911, Roosevelt Papers, Library of Congress.
[13] Lodge to Roosevelt, ibid.

Root then described the acts and policies of the administration with which Roosevelt would naturally be sympathetic and tried to explain the Ballinger-Pinchot row.

> Altogether, the Administration has anything but a smooth path. A good many of the so-called insurgents are talking Roosevelt against Taft & you will have to be pretty careful when you get here & before you become familiar with the various controversies, not to say things that may have meanings ascribed to them that you have never thought of. . . . Cabot and I have been much pleased by your recent statement in Scribners that Kermit (speaking of Warthogs) shot "a noteworthy sow". We have elected the noteworthy sow to the society of the milkfaced grub, the angleworm & the wild ass of the desert.

Root was worn out after his return from the Arbitration at The Hague but he had to set to work in the New York gubernatorial campaign. Henry L. Stimson, whom he had trained and aided since the latter graduated from law school, was the Republican nominee, strongly backed by Roosevelt. The fight had developed into a contest between Roosevelt and the bosses, Barnes, Woodruff and Sherman. Taft, constantly listening to "friends" who sought to poison his mind against Roosevelt, identified Stimson with the ex-President and was at first inclined to be lukewarm.[14] Root had been largely instrumental in inducing Stimson to accept the nomination but disliked being in the position of fighting Vice-President "Jim" Sherman to whom he was attached by Hamilton College and fraternity associations as well as by warm personal friendship. "I have been like a sore-headed bear," he wrote Taft on September 30th, 1910, "over having to go to Saratoga and vote against Jim Sherman, but there was absolutely nothing else to be done." He felt that the Republican Party in New York needed the victory of Stimson and he made his choice accordingly, fighting vigorously on Roosevelt's and Stimson's side. A year and a half later he had to make an even harder choice.

The Republican State Convention opened at Saratoga on September 28th, 1910. In the same place two years before, Root and Roosevelt had fought together against the bosses and had secured the nomination of Hughes. On this occasion they were similarly allied in the same

[14] Butt, op. cit., Vol. II, p. 550.

cause. Roosevelt presided as Temporary Chairman. The bosses were again routed and Stimson received the nomination. There was not as yet the slightest sign of a split between Roosevelt and Root although the shadows were growing deeper between the ex-President and Taft. In August, Roosevelt had made his tour through the West, preaching, particularly at Denver and at Osawatomie, Kansas, the doctrines of the "New Nationalism." "What is the New Nationalism?" asked Root in a letter to Willard Bartlett on October 1st. "I don't know. If it means having the Federal Government do the things which it can do better than the states and which are within the limits of its present constitutional power, I am for it. If it means more than that, I am against it." Root wrote to Taft on the same subject, October 14th:

> I have been looking over the Osawatomie and Denver speeches. So far as the New Nationalism goes, the only real objection I see to it is calling it "new." He really proposes nothing more than we learned in the law school as being a matter of course. I think, however, that at Denver, in speaking of the Courts, he said more than he really meant. I don't care so much about his grumbling at the decisions of the Court. We all do that. . . . The question as to how and when and in what words a man expresses such an opinion about a decision of the Court depends very much on temperament and training. I don't suppose it would occur to you or me to select the Colorado Legislature as the recipient of our confidences upon such a subject.
>
> In speaking at Denver of the judicial power, Theodore used the expression, "Unfortunately, probably inevitably, the courts occupy a position of importance in our government such as they occupy in no other government, because, instead of dealing only with the rights of one man face to face with his fellow men, as is the case with other governments, they here pass upon the fundamental governmental rights of the people as exercised through their legislative and executive officers." I shall be curious to know whether he really meant that he would, if he could, deprive the Courts of the power to pass upon the constitutionality of laws. Of course I have always considered that the most valuable contribution of America to political science. I don't suppose he really did mean it, but was rather using an argumentative expression.

Taft agreed in general with Root's views. "The difficulty about the speeches is their tone, and the conditions under which they are de-

livered. . . . I am the last one to withhold criticism from Supreme
Court decisions, and in the two that Roosevelt selected for his criticism
I fully agree with him. . . . The whole difficulty about the business
is that there is throughout the West, and especially in the Insurgent
ranks, to which Theodore was appealing, a bitterness of feeling against
the Federal Courts that this attitude of his was calculated to stir up,
and the regret which he expressed that courts had the power to set
aside statutes was an attack upon our system at the very point where
I think it is the strongest." Taft added an expression of his willingness
to help with the Stimson campaign in any way he could. In September,
Root expressed in a letter to Charles H. Duell his disgust at the bicker-
ings in the Party; "it seems to me . . . that nothing but a good,
thorough, wholesome licking will do the party any good."

On the same day that Taft wrote his letter, October 15th, Root summarized his view of the situation in a letter to Charles E. Magoon:

> The Wall Street people are of course wild against Roosevelt, and
> a good many of the big business people outside of Wall Street
> take the same view. That is the way a large proportion of my old
> friends in New York feel. It may be that this feeling combined
> with the general tendency towards a change which was in full
> swing throughout the state before the Saratoga Convention, and
> which was exhibited in Vermont and Maine, will defeat Stim-
> son. On the other hand, it is a pretty fair general bet that neither
> the country nor the state at large will be in sympathy with Wall
> Street on any proposition. The important question is, how will
> the farmers, small shop keepers, the laborers, the East Side vote?
> That is something no fellow can find out yet.

Root did not in September think that Taft and Roosevelt were very
far apart in their views. "The difference between them," he wrote to
Edward N. Smith, "is the natural difference between a man of a reflec-
tive cast of mind with the training of a lawyer and a judge, and a man
of intense activity who has led a life of physical and literary adventure."

Taft asked Root to intercede with Roosevelt to make one speech in
Ohio and Root did so in a jollying letter of October 19th. He pointed
out that Roosevelt was "speaking in a lot of States where your speeches
help the men who have attacked Taft. Beveridge, in Indiana, Cummins,
in Iowa, Bristow, in Kansas, La Follette, in Wisconsin, and Clapp, in
Minnesota, are all drawing strength from you. Ohio is the most impor-

tant state where you can help Taft's friends, and it has this great advantage—the Republicans there are all together for once. Garfield is
to stump the state for the Republican ticket and your old friends and
the old friends of Hanna and the old friends of Foraker are all pulling
together. A speech by you in Cleveland would wake up the old Western
reserve and it would be a service to the Republican party as a whole
without a shade of factionalism. Taft did help very materially in the
Saratoga Convention, and your help in Ohio would be generally regarded as a fair and manly thing. I think it would be a good thing for
you, and I think it would be a good thing for the party, and I think
it would be a good thing in this campaign in New York."

Roosevelt declined for a number of reasons. He had already spoken
at the request of the Ohio group in Columbus; if he spoke again outside of New York State he would have to go over and help in New
Jersey. In his reply to Root on October 21st, 1910, he revealed his full
position at that moment:

> . . . As for what you say about the President having helped
> here in New York, I can only say that I went into the fight at all
> simply at the earnest request of the Taft men—Griscom and Ban-
> nard, for instance—and the need for the fight arose purely because
> Sherman, Ward and Woodruff, from their interview with Taft,
> gave the impression that he was with them, was pleased to have
> them continue in control, and would at least indirectly support
> them. As you yourself know, I did my best to get the strongest
> Taft man (Bannard) to accept the nomination for Governor. I
> spoke this year in Missouri, Nebraska, South Dakota and [sic]
> Dakota for the Senators and Congressmen who have supported
> Taft, just as I did in Kansas, Iowa, Minnesota and Indiana for
> those who on some one point left him—just as I think I would
> have done in their places. In other words, I have been cordially
> helping the election of a Republican Congress, having split defi-
> nitely with the Insurgents, including good Gifford Pinchot, on
> this point; for though I am bitterly disappointed with Taft, and
> consider much of his course absolutely inexplicable, I have felt
> that as in so many other cases I had to make the best of conditions
> as they actually were and do the best I possibly could to carry
> Congress and to carry the State of New York, with the entire
> understanding on my part that victory in either means the im-
> mense strengthening of Taft. In New York State I deliberately

went in to put the close supporters of Taft in control of the Republican machinery, and have done and am now doing my best to elect a man whom, I assume, is a Taft man; because I felt that the one clear duty of a decent citizen was to try to put the Republican Party on a straight basis and now to try to put that party in power in the State instead of turning the State over to Murphy of Tammany Hall, acting as the agent, ally and master of crooked finance.

I am perfectly willing to tell you in detail and in full just exactly what I think about Taft, and about the situation in the republican Party, whenever you care to hear it. I have never had a more unpleasant summer. The sordid business of most of the so-called Regulars, who now regard themselves as especially the Taft men, and the wild irresponsible folly of the ultra-Insurgents, make a situation which is very unpleasant. From a variety of causes, the men who are both sane and progressive, the men who make up the strength of the party, have been left so at sea during these months in which Taft has put himself in commission in the hands of Aldrich, Cannon, Ballinger and Wickersham, that they have themselves tended to become either sordid on the one hand, or wild on the other. I do not see how I could as a decent citizen have avoided taking the stand I have taken this year, and striving to re-unite the party and to help the Republicans retain control of Congress and of the State of New York, while at the same time endeavoring to see that this control within the party was in the hands of sensible and honorable men who were progressives and not of a bourbon reactionary type. But as far as my personal inclinations were concerned, my personal pleasure and comfort, I should infinitely have preferred to keep wholly out of politics. I need hardly say that I never made a speech or took an action save in response to the earnest and repeated requests of men many of whom I well knew, in spite of their anxiety to use me at the moment, were exceedingly anxious to limit that use to before elections with the understanding that I should have no say afterwards. In Ohio the platform and candidate were arranged deliberately on the theory that the progressives, the men whom I stand with, were not to be given any share whatever in directing the party policy before the nomination or after the election; that their share was to be limited to supporting the ticket between the time of the nomination and the election. This is the naked proposition as regards my going to Ohio. It has been the steady and consistent position of the Administration, that is, of Taft, and of almost all those who have been high in power since within forty-eight hours of his election nearly two years ago. I am not at all sure that it was not a wise position, but it is out of the question to accept its advantages without its disadvantages. I have on every occasion this year praised everything I conscientiously could of both Taft and the Congress, and I have never said a word in condemnation of either, strongly though I have felt. Very possibly circumstances will be such that I shall support Taft for the Presidency next time; but this is not a point now necessary for decision, and if I do support him it will be under no illusion and simply as being the best thing that the conditions permit. I assume that you are his cordial supporter, just as I suppose Cabot either is or will be, and I write to you exactly as I should write to Cabot. The sum of the matter is that while I shall conscientious [sic] do my best to help what I regard as on the whole the preferable of two policies or two parties under any circumstances, yet that it is simple folly to expect support from me as a right in an election when all possible care is taken to show that I am not in any real sense to be consulted or considered before the nomination or after the election.

Roosevelt had already a strong, and to some extent justifiable, sense of grievance against Taft but was at the same time equally irritated with the Progressives. He still felt strongly the pull of party loyalty. On July 11th, 1910, he had written to Nicholas Longworth, his son-in-law, "Of course you must stand straight by Taft and the administration. . . . But in standing straight for the President, do keep yourself clear to stand for progressive policies." [15] Longworth, Lodge and Root were a strong trio who constantly sought to keep Taft and Roosevelt together while a host of others were pouring whispers into the ears of both the principals. Longworth pointed out to Roosevelt that it was Mrs. Taft who was jealous of the ex-president but that Taft himself was all right. Joseph B. Bishop, on the other hand, kept up a flood of correspondence from the fall of 1910 on, denouncing Taft. There were moments when he expressed sorrow for his mental and moral flabbiness but in general his tone was one of anger. To his friend, Arthur Lee, Roosevelt wrote on September 16th, 1910, that "Taft is a kindly

[15] Roosevelt Papers, Library of Congress.

well-meaning man . . . but he has no instinct of leadership. . . . I
do not believe he has been a bad President, and I am sure he has been
a thoroughly well-meaning and upright President." He thought at the
moment that Taft could be re-nominated "by the aid of pocket-
borough delegates of the South, and the big monied interests of the
conservative East" but that he would be beaten by the Democrats.
"From the Alleghenies West, in spite of certain spots of reaction the
general sentiment is overwhelmingly for me, but throughout the
Northeast there is much real hostility to me, or at least much real
uneasy dislike and distrust of me." The Democrats "will probably win
overwhelmingly. This will also probably mean defeat for whoever is
nominated in 1912, and therefore for every reason I most earnestly
hope to retain sufficient control to make Taft's nomination inevitable."
On November 11th, 1910, he again told Lee: "Taft is a well-meaning,
good natured man . . . but not a leader and no more fit than Root,
our very ablest man, to meet and grapple with the new conditions."
But by May 14th, 1912, he wrote, "Taft is not merely a fool, but he
is a good bit of a blackguard." [16] The mercury was flying up and down,
making it easy for later commentators to pick upon particular phrases
and expressions from time to time as dating the final breach between
Taft and Roosevelt. It was obviously a slow process, and not by any
means a steady one.

On October 28th, 1910, Root delivered at the Manhattan Casino in
New York an address which was his principal public contribution to
the gubernatorial campaign. He was convinced that it was necessary
to try to take people away from the side issues of Taft and Roosevelt
and to concentrate on the direct issue in New York State. He again
took upon himself the task which he had discharged in his speech to
the Union League Club on February 3rd, 1904, when he had sought
to convince Wall Street that Roosevelt was "safe." He had in 1910
the additional burden of proving that Taft was also an excellent man
and President. Root made no attempt to dodge the issue. He began
at once by commenting on the feeling of many people that their vote
in the State campaign must be a vote for or against Roosevelt. He
ventured the guess that if there were a vote upon that issue, New York
would cast a large affirmative vote for the ex-President but "there is
no such issue before the people of this state." Root denied also that the

16 Ibid.

issue was to decide then upon the renomination of Taft in 1912. He declared that votes for the Republican Party in that New York campaign would strengthen the Republican Party and therefore the administration. Roosevelt, he said, was well aware that the strenuous efforts he was making in behalf of the Republican ticket in New York and elsewhere "are services in aid of the Taft administration and tend towards the renomination of Mr. Taft in 1912." Root suggested that some people thought they should vote on the basis of current attacks upon the courts and "something called New Nationalism. . . . There is a very old American saying that when a litigant does not like a decision it is his privilege to go down to the tavern and swear at the Court. Everybody grumbles about decisions that he does not like, and Mr. Roosevelt appears to have done so out loud and in public, according to his temperament and habits. But . . . the idea that Mr. Roosevelt contemplates an attack upon our judicial system or that that system is in danger from him or from anyone else is purely fanciful and devised for campaign purposes only." Root affirmed his own belief in our judicial system and then turned to the New Nationalism in which he found nothing new, nothing "that was not taught in my class in the law school forty odd years ago." At the Saratoga Convention, Roosevelt drew his strength from the fact that he was fighting on the right side of an issue in New York on which the majority of the people lined up with him against the bosses. "The issue was a revolt against the tyranny of party machines and party machinery. It was a part of that great rebellion which has been going on all over the Union and in so many states has led to new political methods of varying merit—Direct Primaries; Direct Election of Senators; the Initiative and Referendum and Recall—all devices to enable voters to have their way notwithstanding political machines, and to deprive the professional politician of the opportunity to barter and trade for his own purposes, with the power to manipulate and control conventions and delegations and to confer nominations and appointments to office as his stock in trade." Hughes and Stimson and Roosevelt were all lined up in this movement against the machine. The rest of the speech was an analysis of some of the local issues and a comparison of Stimson's record with that of his Democratic opponent, Dix.

The suggestion that Roosevelt's attack upon the courts was merely the usual angry outburst of a disappointed litigant was hardly calculated to soothe the Colonel. It was the kind of remark which Root could, and often did, make to Roosevelt personally, but it was perhaps not well chosen in a public speech. Root probably felt that the important issue at the moment was to win New York City to Stimson's support and he never dreamt at this time that there could be a breach between himself and "Theodore."

Root did not succeed in convincing everybody that a vote for Stimson was not necessarily a vote for Roosevelt, but Dix's victory at the polls in November by over 50,000 votes was merely a part of the general reaction against the Republicans. "We got a good, sound thrashing," Root wrote to Ambassador Hill on January 29th, 1911, "and I am bound to say that we had earned it. The only question is whether there was enough of it to beat sense into the party and enable us to retrieve the situation in the coming Presidential election." Roosevelt had indeed been defeated; "his man" Stimson in New York, and Harding, whom he had endorsed in Ohio, were defeated; Woodrow Wilson became Governor of New Jersey. "The bright spot," he wrote to Lodge, ". . . is that I think it will put a stop to the talk about my being nominated in 1912, which was beginning to make me very uneasy." [17] In New York, Roosevelt's fight against the machine was so excessively unsuccessful that Barnes, the arch prototype of the machine, was elected Chairman of the Republican State Committee. Root as usual made the best of an existing situation. On January 29th, 1911, he wrote to Lloyd Griscom, New York County Chairman:

> The election of Barnes was a natural result of two things. First, the fact that the people of the state, including a great many who had been making the most noise in condemnation of the old party management in the state, allowed a red herring to be drawn across the trail in the last election and failed to support the men who had brought about a change in management. Of course if a movement of that kind is begun and the people of the state don't care enough about it to support it, it must fail. The second circumstance, which was really a sequence of the first, was the absence of any affirmative movement for any particular man representing the party as distinct from the Old Guard. The plain fact was that no man possessing the requisite qualifications was willing to make the requisite sacrifice. Under these circumstances

[17] Pringle, *Theodore Roosevelt*, p. 539.

the election of Barnes was a natural result. He is a very able, strong man, and while I don't believe that the Republican party in the State of New York can be run in the way in which he runs the politics of Albany County, it is quite probable that he is intelligent enough to see that himself. I think the chances are that, while his election will hurt us seriously in some quarters, he will make a very efficient Chairman, and the plain course for us all to follow is to turn in and help make the administration of the party machine as successful as possible.

Root continued to work along with Barnes as he advised Griscom to do. He subsequently urged Barnes to consult with Stimson and to cooperate with all the leaders of the party. It was very much the same underlying political philosophy which Roosevelt expressed in a letter to his son Kermit on January 27th, 1915:

> All my life in politics, I have striven . . . to make the necessary working compromise between what you would like to do and what you have to do, between the ideal and the practical. If a man does not have an ideal and try to live up to it, then he becomes a mean, base and sordid creature, no matter how successful. If, on the other hand, he does not work practically, with the knowledge that he is in the world of actual man and must get results, he becomes a worthless head-in-the-air creature, a nuisance to himself and to everybody else.[18]

Through 1911 the breach continued to widen between Roosevelt and Taft although it was Taft who seems to have first become convinced that their relations had reached the breaking point. Without the feelings of bitterness, Roosevelt was almost equally at outs with some of his more progressive following. On November 28th, 1910, he wrote to William Kent in California who had reproached him for his support of Stimson and Taft. Roosevelt, very much on the defensive, asserted that the New York platform had been screwed up "to as high a pitch of radicalism as was possible. Among all the people who are prominent here, Harry Stimson is the only man who is anywhere near as radical as I am, the only man, for instance, who approved my Osawatomie speech." As for his support of Taft, what he had said in New York was exactly what he had said throughout the country. "Gifford Pinchot objected . . . because I used the word 'upright' in

[18] Roosevelt Papers, Library of Congress.

describing Taft, but personally I think it absurd to say that Taft is not upright—just as I think it absurd for Taft's friends to do as they do and complain that although I acknowledge him to be upright, I nevertheless think that he lacks the gift of leadership, is too easily influenced by the men around him, and does not really grasp progressive principals." [19]

In January, 1911, the National Progressive Republican League was formed with Senator Jonathan Bourne, Jr. of Oregon as Chairman and with perhaps more than half an eye to the nomination of Senator La Follette as the Republican nominee in 1912. But Roosevelt declined to be listed as among the League's sponsors. On January 3rd, 1911, he wrote to La Follette a cautious letter, agreeing in principle with all of the League's platform but suggesting in language which would have been characteristic of Root, that one could not move too fast but must wait for people to catch up to the advanced outposts of progressive policies. Through the pages of the *Outlook* Roosevelt continued to speak well of the Wisconsin and Oregon experiments, perhaps encouraging La Follette to believe that he had Roosevelt's support, but not going to the point of full endorsement. [20] There was soon to be a chasm separating Roosevelt from La Follette as widely as from Taft. On December 13th, 1911, Roosevelt wrote to Bishop that he doubted whether La Follette could be nominated or elected. "I am a little uncomfortable as to how he would stand from the larger viewpoint." [21] La Follette was convinced that Roosevelt grossly betrayed him and his progressive principles at the Convention in the following June. [22] Roosevelt on November 26th, 1912, wrote to Hiram Johnson: "La Follette was the most contemptible and least conscientious of all our foes. We should at once make it plain that we regard him as the most efficient ally of the reactionaries and the powers of privilege." [23] It looked as if everyone were out of step except the Colonel.

Through the fall of 1911, Root continued to feel that the Republican Party was headed for defeat. But there was not yet any suggestion that the point had been reached at which men like Root would have to choose between loyalty to Taft and loyalty to Roosevelt. September

[19] *Ibid.*
[20] Pringle, *op. cit.*, pp. 547–550; 553–554.
[21] Roosevelt Papers, Library of Congress.
[22] La Follette, *Autobiography*, p. 650.
[23] Roosevelt Papers, Library of Congress.

29th, 1911, Theodore Roosevelt, Jr. wrote to his father: "During the presidential campaign I shall let it be known that I am for Taft but I shall not fight his battle at all." This was in reply to a letter from his father which had expressed the hope that he would feel that he could support Taft and that he would not follow his inclination to support Wilson. "I do not pretend," Roosevelt Senior wrote on September 22nd, "to say that I like Taft, or approve of him, or enjoy supporting him; but my disappointment in him must not blind me to the fact that he is a better President than either Harrison or McKinley; and I believe that Taft, plus the Republican Party, would do better than the Democrats could do." [24]

On January 16th, 1912, Roosevelt wrote at long length to Frank Munsey outlining his position and answering Munsey's argument that Roosevelt should come out and make a public statement regarding his candidacy. In brief, his position was that he would serve if the country demanded him and needed him but that he was not seeking the nomination and would not do so. He sent a copy of this letter to Root and Root replied after long thought on February 12th, 1912.

My dear Theodore:
I have read and reread your letter to Munsey and thought much about it. . . .
I am satisfied that your position is a sound one. You certainly have a right to say, as you do, "I am not and shall not be a candidate," and at the same time to refuse to say what you would do in the future event of a nomination being offered to you by persons having authority to make the offer.
In case of that future event there might be many circumstances and conditions which would materially affect your judgment, but which no one can foretell now, and no one has a right to insist upon your telling him now what your action would be under those unknown conditions.
My only trouble about your position lies in the question whether you can possibly stick to it. It is going to be very difficult, especially difficult because of your temperament; because of the urgent need of your nature for prompt decision and action which must make an attitude like this for you a condition of unstable equilibrium against which your whole nature will frequently cry out and urge you to end it. No thirsty sinner ever took a pledge

[24] *Ibid.*

which was harder for him to keep than it will be for you to maintain this position. Another difficulty would be that among those who seek you to discuss the presidential situation there will inevitably be a great preponderance of men who for various reasons are anxious to get you to abandon your position and to make a public statement that you will accept a nomination. Many of them will be friends whom you trust and with whom you sympathize. It is not in the nature of anybody unless he is a stick or a stone to avoid being affected by such a succession of importunities and arguments as will come to you from that side of the question. In the meantime you will not be in the way of seeing or hearing from very many of your friends who are really thinking from your point of view or whose approval of your attitude may serve to confirm your own judgment. I am stating these difficulties because I not only approve your determination but I think it would be disastrous to depart from it.

The first step of departure would be easy, but certain inevitable consequences would ensue and further steps would become absolutely necessary. If you were to say, "I will not under any circumstances take a nomination," that would of course settle the matter. I assume, however, that if you depart from your present position it will be on the other side by saying in effect that if a nomination comes to you in the right way you will accept it. The moment you say that, you are a candidate. Your two present propositions must stand or fall together. No one can say that he will take a nomination under any circumstances and not thereby become a candidate for that nomination. It would be worse than useless for you to continue to say you were not a candidate when you had also said the thing which would contradict your assertion by making you a candidate. Nor could you say that you are not an active candidate. Your statement that you would take a nomination would be authority from you to every one who wants you to be President to proceed with an active campaign to bring about a nomination, and their activity would be your activity. Nor could you refrain from helping them in your activity. You would be bound to help them. They would have a right to demand it, and they would demand it, and you could not help responding to their demand.

I see no resting place between your present position and an active contest between yourself and Taft for the nomination. If after that contest you should be nominated by even the barest majority of the convention you would have to take the nomination. You could not refuse it because of the absence of conditions which you have fixed in your own mind as material to determine whether you would take a nomination or not. Those conditions would disappear no matter how fully you might have expressed them. You could not insist upon them. There would no longer be any question of a great demand by the people of the country upon you to render great public service to which you yield against your own personal wish because your country has called upon you. You will have been nominated because you will have had the votes of delegates secured some by one means and some by other means, and altogether enough to make a majority of the convention. You would be in the position of any other man who has gone in for the presidency and has succeeded in getting the nomination. On the other hand, if Taft should be nominated you would be in the position of having tried to get the nomination and having failed. In either case I am satisfied no Republican candidate would be elected. I can see how Taft can be elected if the present breaches in the party are not widened farther and the sober judgment of a majority is that he has earned a renomination and that the party can stand upon the record of his administration. I can see how you could be elected if, without any active campaign by you in your behalf or by your authority to take the nomination away from Taft, the party turns to you and makes a demand upon you for renewed service to the country. But after such a contest as would ensue upon your making a declaration that would make you a candidate. I see no hope for the party whatever in the coming election. It may be that neither of you could be elected under any circumstances, for I am afraid that the feeling which led to such disastrous results in 1910 is not yet spent, and that we shall feel its effects again in November. At all events, it seems to me that those who ask you to make a declaration are asking you to put yourself in the position of trying to get the presidency and to incur the considerable probability of being defeated for the nomination, or, if successful in that, of being defeated in the election, and that the consequences to your future, to your power of leadership in the interests of the causes which you have at heart, and to your position in history, would be so injurious that no friend and no number of friends have any right to ask such a sacrifice.

You may have to make the sacrifice of taking the nomination if it comes to you unsought upon the general and genuine demand of your party. But the element of self-devotion which would crown with honor even defeat under such a demand would, to the general apprehension at least, disappear utterly the moment that you took the position of a candidate by or for whom the nomination was sought.

All of this I am afraid is very sententious and didactic, but you will see that it is inflicted upon you because my reflection upon your letter has satisfied me not only that you are right but that you have taken the only position in which it is possible for you to resist the force of gravitation which would draw you gradually down hill into the character of a common or garden candidate for the presidency, with the probability of defeat. I hope you will sit tight, although your position must be very much like mine when Luzon saw the cow with the gunny sack on.

Please give my love to dear Mrs. Roosevelt and Ethel, and believe me always,

Faithfully and affectionately yours,
Elihu Root

It was already too late. On January 18th and 20th, Roosevelt conferred with various of his supporters and reached the decision that it would be well for him to receive a letter from nine governors asking him to declare himself. Roosevelt began to draft his reply before the Governors had been lined up to extend the invitation.[25] On the 18th, Roosevelt wrote to Governors Osborne of Michigan, Glassrock of West Virginia and Hadley of Missouri, answering their letters and suggesting that a group of governors write him a letter along lines which he indicated, asking him to respond to the popular demand. "The letter to me might simply briefly state the writer's belief that the people of his State, or their States, desire to have me run for the Presidency, and to know whether in such a case I would refuse the nomination. I want to make it very clear that I am honestly desirous of considering the matter solely from the standpoint of the public interest, and not in the least from my own standpoint; that I am not seeking and shall not seek the nomination, but that of course if it is the sincere judgment of men having the right to know and express the wishes of the plain people that the people as a whole desire me, not for my sake, but for

[25] Howland, *Theodore Roosevelt and His Times*, pp. 204 ff.

their sake, to undertake the job, I would feel in honor bound to do so." [26]

There is no evidence available to indicate that Root was aware of this manoeuvre back of the letter of the nine governors which was dated February 9th, 1912, when he received Roosevelt's letter of February 14th:

Dear Elihu:

I thank you for your long letter, and I genuinely appreciate it. In the month that has passed since I wrote my letter to Munsey, things have moved fast. I do not believe it is possible for me now to refrain from speaking publicly. I cannot treat the request of nine Governors as I have treated mere private requests. Moreover, the action of the supporters of the President, including both his real supporters and the supporters who wish him nominated with every intention of trying to beat him when nominated, is I think at last beginning to produce in the public mind the belief that there is a certain furtiveness in my position. I am inclined to think, therefore, that the time has come when I must speak, and simply say in public very briefly what I have already said in private. I appreciate the force of all your arguments, and you yourself cannot feel as strongly as I do the disadvantages of my position from my own personal standpoint. But the arguments on the other side are even stronger. As far as I am able to judge of my motives, I am looking at this purely from the standpoint of the interests of the people as a whole, from the standpoint of those who believe in the causes which I champion, which three years ago I had every reason to believe the President ardently championed, and which most reluctantly I have come to believe he either does not understand at all, or else is hostile to.

Give my love to Mrs. Root,
Ever yours,
Theodore Roosevelt

On January 26th, Root had written positively to Ambassador R. C. Kerens at Vienna that Roosevelt "is not a candidate and I do not think he intends to be . . . but words are flying through the air in vast quantities, both spoken and written, and there seems to be some ground for hope that many editors, reporters, and magazine writers

[26] Roosevelt Papers, Library of Congress.

will presently die of hysterics over the presidential situation."

It was on February 12th that Taft had really dealt the first open blow in a speech which branded as "political emotionalists or neurotics" those who advocated the so-called "progressive policies of the referendum and the recall." February 21st, on his way to speak at Columbus, Roosevelt coined his famous phrase "My hat is in the ring." [27] That speech itself made it quite impossible for men like Root with their staunch conservatism and firm adherence to our judicial system to support him for the presidency. "I am an old tree and am beyond the limit of successful transplanting," Root said to Robert Bacon in a letter of September 11th, 1912. Roosevelt declared in favor of applying the recall to judicial officers, and much worse, to permit the voters to recall any judicial decision which they felt was in defiance of justice. Even a progressive like Senator Borah declared that the recall of judicial decisions was "bosh," [28] and men like Lodge, devoted as they were to Roosevelt, could not hide their strenuous disagreement with such a proposal. February 24th, Roosevelt replied to the inspired letter of the Governors: "I will accept the nomination for President if it is tendered to me, and I will adhere to that decision until the convention has expressed its preference."

[27] Pringle, *op. cit.*, p. 556.
[28] *Ibid.*, p. 558.

CHAPTER XXXV

"Roosevelt was the Bull Moose movement"

THE lines were drawn but Roosevelt had not yet reached the point of venting his wrath upon the Taft supporters. To his sister, Mrs. Cowles, he wrote on March 1st, 1912: "I told Nick [Longworth] and the others that they must continue of course to be for Taft, as they were already pledged." [1] Two days later, Mrs. Lodge wrote to Mrs. Cowles: "As to Theodore I feel sorry that things have come round as they have. . . . It is hard for Nick & Cabot & Mr. Root but it is not worth while to worry about yet. . . . He has written a most affectionate letter to Cabot, upon whom he looks with fond and amused contempt, but in their personal relations there will never be any change. The situation has told upon them all, Nick & Gussy [Gardner], Cabot and Mr. Root, and each has done what he thought to be right I am sure." [2]

Root's attitude toward Roosevelt was fond but more sorrowing than amused. He was fully committed to Taft and no question of deserting the President for his old chief and much closer friend entered his mind. It is hard to guess what stand he would have taken had Roosevelt declared his candidacy before Root was committed to Taft. Had Roosevelt still relied on Root, the fatal Columbus speech would probably never have been delivered in the form which it did take. Years before, when Root was Roosevelt's Secretary of State, a small group of intimate friends were dining at the White House. The Circuit Court of Appeals in Chicago had just invalidated the fine of $29,000,000 which Judge Landis had imposed on the Standard Oil Company. Roosevelt had been infuriated by the decision and became greatly excited as he discussed it at the dinner table. With fist clenched in the air, he shouted: "If I weren't President of the United States I would say that for a judge to hand down a decision like that was a . . . ." Root broke in: "What you were going to say—if you weren't President

[1] Cowles Papers.
[2] *Ibid.*

of the United States—but what you are not going to say—because you
are President of the United States—was that for any judge to hand
down such a decision was a God damned outrage—but you are not
going to say it." Roosevelt's fist was still poised in the air as Root spoke.
It came down with a thump on the table: "You're right and I guess
I won't say it." [3] It was one among many cases where Root held Roosevelt in check. Now Root remained committed to his party and his
allegiance to the Administration; it was Roosevelt who had gone off
and deserted. Root wrote to Edward S. Martin on March 9th, 1912:

> . . . I have been feeling very sad about his [Roosevelt's] new de-
> parture. I am very fond of him personally and I think we all owe
> him a debt of gratitude for the very great good that he has accom-
> plished. I have an immense admiration for him. I think that,
> rightly directed, his tremendous personality would be a great na-
> tional asset. All these things combined fill me with regret over
> what he is doing now. He is essentially a fighter and when he gets
> into a fight he is completely dominated by the desire to destroy
> his adversary. He instinctively lays hold of every weapon which
> can be used for that end. Accordingly he is saying a lot of things
> and taking a lot of positions which are inspired by the desire to
> win. I have no doubt he thinks he believes what he says, but he
> doesn't. He has merely picked up certain popular ideas which
> were at hand as one might pick up a poker or chair with which to
> strike.

On the same day he poured out his feelings to Robert Bacon, then the
American Ambassador in Paris, at that time and ever afterward a devoted friend and admirer of both Root and Roosevelt:

> Roosevelt's candidacy is widening the breach in the Republican
> party to such a degree that I can see little hope of electing any-
> body. Theodore has gone off upon a perfectly wild program, most
> of which he does not really believe in, although of course at this
> moment he thinks he does. He has a tremendous following of
> Populists and Socialists in both parties and all the advantage of
> the dissatisfaction and dislike for the rich and successful, and he
> is stimulating that element with all his extraordinary skill. His
> course has had the effect of throwing Taft into high relief in the
> public mind as the representative of conservative constitutional-

[3] James R. Sheffield to the author, October 6, 1933.

ism. I don't think Roosevelt will succeed in getting the nomination. He will, however, succeed in so damaging Taft that he can't be elected. If Roosevelt should be nominated he could not possibly be elected. Of course Lodge, George Meyer, Stimson, and myself, who cannot possibly go with Roosevelt in his new departure, have been feeling very gloomy over the situation. . . . Altogether I shall be glad to get up on to the farm at Clinton under the protection of a force of accomplished liars who will say that I am not at home. In the meantime, however, I wish to fall upon your neck and weep. I wish to walk up and down in your congenial and unrestraining presence and curse and swear and say things which I would not have repeated for the world. . . .

Taft began to strike at Roosevelt personally although he said it wrenched his soul and it undoubtedly did. Speaking in New England on April 25th, he denied Roosevelt's charges that he was leagued with the bosses and that Roosevelt was against them. "I am here to reply to an old and true friend. . . . I do not want to fight Theodore Roosevelt, but sometimes a man in a corner fights. I am going to fight." [4] He became not effective but pathetic in his fighting; the President of the United State in May damned himself by his metaphor: "Even a rat in a corner will fight." August 26th, 1912, after the Convention, Taft was trying to be philosophical, but it is doubtful whether he had succeeded as much as is suggested by a letter of that date: "I have not any feeling of enmity against Roosevelt or any feeling of hatred. . . . I look upon him as I look upon a freak almost in the Zoological Garden, a kind of animal not often found." [5] Roosevelt, as was his wont, spared no denunciation of his opponent. Root, as was also his wont, never uttered a public word against Roosevelt personally. At the Republican State Convention in Rochester on April 10th, 1912, Root vigorously supported the plank which stood out against the recall of judicial decisions; for him the judicial system of the country was the mainstay of democratic government. To substitute in that respect the rule of the mob, meant the end of our whole constitutional system of government. He minced no words in denouncing the Rooseveltian idea, but the name of Roosevelt did not pass his lips. June 7th, as the opening day of the National Convention approached, Root replied to

[4] Quoted in Pringle, *Theodore Roosevelt*, p. 560.
[5] Taft Papers, Library of Congress.

a letter from C. N. Bouvé asking whether Root had any objection to their using in a publicity pamphlet Roosevelt's statement, supposed to have been written on a fly leaf of a book he had given to Root years before, that Root was the ablest man he had ever known. "I am ever so much obliged for your kind suggestion," wrote Root, "but I would rather not use what Roosevelt said under such circumstances against him."

It was a hard position during the campaign. Taft and many of the party leaders were urging Root to speak, there and everywhere. May 15th, 1912, Root explained his position to Taft in a letter subscribed "faithfully and affectionately":

> I had intended to have a talk with you about the suggestion of my going to Ohio to speak but something always interfered, so that I have found no opportunity to bring the subject up, and I write now because I would not care to have you feel that I have been unmindful of the suggestion. I thought about it a great deal and came to the conclusion that I was not at liberty to make speeches upon the issues into which this Primary campaign has drifted. So far as concern exposition and argument against the constitutional views announced in the Columbus speech and insistence upon the vital and destructive nature of those views, and so far as opinion and public declaration that I consider you to be entitled to a renomination to the Presidency and that I am in favor of your nomination, and so far as using all my influence as Senator or otherwise to secure the adherence of my State to that view, I have had no doubt or difficulty, because in all those matters I had a duty to perform and no one could justly condemn me for performing it honestly and sincerely. When, however, we come to questions as between the two administrations, and questions of Theodore's personal right or wrong conduct during his administration, and comparisons between his course and yours, the fact cannot be ignored that I was a member of his administration, bearing the most high confidential relations, cognizant of his acts and the reasons for them, consulted about them, and with a knowledge of them derived from him under the highest obligations of confidence and loyalty, I could not enter upon a discussion of the matters to which I bore such a relation in an adverse attitude towards him without being subject, and I think justly subject, to the charge of betraying confidence and disloyalty. Nor

could I discuss him personally nor contrast you with him in public discussion without involving the knowledge which I obtained
in this way and using against him the qualifications for the discussion which I obtained through his trust in me. I have no question that you are justified in attacking him in your own defense,
because he attacked you, but he has not attacked me. He has never
said a word so far as I know, certainly in public, regarding me
which was not kindly and laudatory. There has been nothing to
relieve me from my obligation, and I feel that if I were to take
part in a public attack upon his administration or upon his qualities as exhibited in his public career, I should be subject to universal condemnation in which I should be forced myself to join.
This, of course, makes no difference whatever in my attitude
towards the nomination or in the firmness of my adherence to
your candidacy or in the distinctness and certainty of my declaration of my position in favor of that candidacy. It merely affects
the kind of service which I feel at liberty to render and leads me
to the conclusion that I cannot be of any use whatever in Ohio.
I hope you will pull through. I believe you will. I think it would
be a great misfortune if you should not. There is another circum-
stance which makes this conclusion of less importance. It is that
I am too old and running too close to the edge of that line which
separates health from a complete breakdown to be of any real
service in such a campaign as this. My fighting days are over, and
as I look about upon the political conditions of our country I feel
that the time cannot come too soon for me to step aside and let a
younger generation work out in their own way the new ideas
which seem inseparable from turmoil and strife. I cannot tell you,
old friend, how deeply I sympathize with you or how strongly I
desire and hope for your success. . . .

After the passage of many years, Root reflected on that tangled
period in which among the principal figures he was one of the few who
showed no personal bitterness and whose dominant feeling was one of
sadness:

"There was then and there is now and has been for a century a feeling reaching the point of bitterness between the agricultural and the
great manufacturing interests. It was that which put Andrew Jackson
in the White House. It is the revulsion of the hay seed, the rude
pioneer farmer in cowhide boots against the patent leathers; the sophis-

ticated against the unsophisticated; the resentment of the crude against the claims to superiority of the cultured. Andrew Jackson was the extreme representation of the crude against the Bostonian. It was the same thing in Greenback times—a desire to wipe out wealth gained in commerce because of the envy of the farmer who lived in comparative poverty.

"La Follette led the group for quite a while with considerable help from Dolliver. Roosevelt joined the 'one gallused' fellows, as he called them, and joined in the same protests of the laborers in the east against the employers, and the farmers against the manufacturers. There was no Bull Moose movement except that. Roosevelt's personality was the only unifying force. Protests due to many different specific causes rallied around him all who had to live economically and looked with dislike on the rich with their luxurious automobiles and yachts. That feeling always exists. The Bull Moose movement meant nothing but Roosevelt drawing to himself these ever present protests. Roosevelt was sympathetic and liked people generally. As a student and reader of history he had come to feel for the fellow who was being crowded down by the rich. The fight for federal control of railroad rates was an attempt to force absolute control of the railroads which could make or break a town or a man. The theoretical remedies through the courts were useless. Half a dozen men could use up their moderate fortunes fighting the case through the courts and the railroad would hardly notice it. Roosevelt adopted that side and made a strong and generally valuable contest on that.

"Roosevelt had nothing to go on except he was so darn mad at Taft. I didn't blame him for being mad at Taft but I did blame him for elevating a minor source of annoyance into a major motive. Taft had the Attorney General, Wickersham, bring suit against the Tennessee Coal and Iron Company charging illegal combination in restraint of trade. In the bill it was charged that they had deceived Roosevelt who had permitted the combination. In 1907, they came to see Roosevelt and explained the whole matter and asked if the government objected to the combination. Roosevelt went over it with the Attorney General and consulted me. We decided that there was no basis for objection. Then without a word to Roosevelt, Taft's Administration started suit, charging that their action was illegal and that Roosevelt had been deceived. Anyone would be mad. Taft himself never looked at the bill, leaving it all to the Attorney General, so it was a sin of omission rather than of commission, which mitigates it. Wickersham handled it as he would have handled any case in his own office without considering the political relations between Taft and Roosevelt. Roosevelt was so mad it dethroned his judgment.

"Roosevelt was the Bull Moose movement. Roosevelt could perfectly well have been reelected President if he hadn't deferred so long and said he wasn't and would not be a candidate. He made his fight on an issue which it is difficult for me to understand. Things the Bull Moose party claimed differentiated them from the regular Republicans were not the things which Roosevelt ever paid much attention to. When Taft was nominated and was preparing his acceptance letter, he and I went to Oyster Bay and went over it paragraph by paragraph; there were no changes of much importance. Roosevelt was satisfied with the program which Taft thus laid out and Taft went along and carried out that paper and Roosevelt's objection really was that he didn't do it as well as he ought to have done. The old minister never thinks the new one preaches as well as he did. It is a standard cynical comment on human nature. Taft was not an executive but a judge; Taft wanted to hear both sides and then reflect. Roosevelt wanted to hear and then jump. I have never been able to accept the argument that the different effectiveness of the two administrations was the basis for Roosevelt's action. The real reason was he was so damn mad. Combativeness was his essential characteristic. When he came to bolt the Convention, he created an entirely new set of issues." [6]

Root did not really seem to appreciate or to understand the progressive movement which was much wider and deeper than the Progressive Party of Bourne and La Follette or the Bull Moose Party of Theodore Roosevelt. He went along whole-heartedly with Roosevelt in believing that there were evils in the practices of big business and that those practices had to be corrected by governmental action. He was well aware of the political importance of labor and quite agreed that labor should be treated more fairly. What he did not have was the passionate sense of grievance, the conviction that the American social order was manifestly unjust, which inspired some of the popular leaders. The farmers of the middle west had grievances much more real than jealousy of the rich; it was largely the failure of men like Root to under-

[6] Root to the author, September 13, 1930.

stand their legitimate complaints against such things as tariffs and unjust railroad rates which gave strength to the progressive movement in
1912 and to the "new deal" movement twenty years later.

Taft, like Root, had begun the fight against Roosevelt with a feeling of sorrow. On March 5th, 1912, he wrote to Charles F. Brooker:

> The campaign is a very hard and sad one for me. Considering
> my close relations with Colonel Roosevelt, my admiration for
> him as a man, my gratitude to him as one who made me Presi-
> dent, and my appreciation of him as a chief with whom every re-
> lation was most delightful, it is hard for me now to be in opposi-
> tion to him and feel that he is in bitter opposition to me. I do not
> mean to lend myself, in any way, to a personal controversy with
> him, but of course it will be impossible to keep our respective fol-
> lowers from using language that will irritate and embitter.[7]

Similarly, on March 12th, he wrote to William B. McKinley that the
Cabinet agreed that bitter personalities should be kept out of the
campaign and that the Republican publicity should not be allowed
to drift into personal recriminations. By April 3rd, he wrote to Miss
Mabel Boardman: "I agree with you that the time has come when it
is necessary for me to speak out in my own defense. I shall do so
sorrowfully. I dislike to speak with directness against Theodore Roosevelt, but I can not longer refrain from refuting his false accusations." [8]
On May 29th, when it had been determined that Root would be
Temporary Chairman of the Convention, Taft assured William Barnes
that he need have no concern about Root's speech. "I am glad Roosevelt opposed him, because Root is a man who would rather avoid a
fight if he can; but when he is put to the issue he will fight as long as
anybody; and that is what they have done to him now." [9]

If Root had not had that almost religious and fanatical devotion to
duty in the party cause, he would have stayed out of the fight as Lodge
managed to do. He could not support Roosevelt politically after the
Colonel came out for the recall of judicial decisions in his Columbus
speech. Had Roosevelt been willing, he could still have been his warm
personal friend. To Root, Roosevelt was something like a wayward
son, against whom he had to take his stand but for whom affection

[7] Taft Papers, Library of Congress.
[8] Ibid.
[9] Ibid.

could not be displaced. Taft, of course, had his personal fortunes involved in the contest. Root had no political ambitions; what he desired most was to be relieved from the burden of public affairs and get back to his place at Clinton. He was feeling tired, was not well. May 11th, 1912, he wrote to George E. Dunham, his old friend and editor of the Utica *Press*, who again was seeking to induce him to consider suggestions that he might be a compromise candidate; Root did not think there was any practical chance for any third candidate; he was sure that he was not eligible and positive that he did not wish the position. He had made his decision on the presidency in 1904 and had not changed his mind. "I shall be seventy years old within a few days of the expiration of my term of office as Senator. It is my intention then to retire from official life, to declare my independence of all constituencies and superior officers except Mrs. Root, to devote myself to amassing a fortune on the farm at Clinton, with just enough incidental intellectual occupation, undertaken at my own option, to ward off softening of the brain. This may be what John Ingalls would have called an 'iridescent dream' but it looks good to me and it is what I am a candidate for." It remained only an "iridescent dream" for more than a decade after he left the Senate.

Root agreed to act as Temporary Chairman of the Convention "not because I was desirous of the distinction, but because a difficult and embarrassing duty seemed to be presented and I was not willing to flunk it." So he told Harry S. New in a letter of May 22nd, offering at the same time to withdraw if the National Committee thought it best, as he assumed they would if it appeared that Roosevelt was certain to be nominated. "I wish I had not been asked to be temporary chairman of the Convention," Root wrote to his wife on May 27th: "but it is all right. If I am elected as to which I am indifferent the kind of speech which I shall have to make will not be at all inconsistent with my letter to the President." He had in mind his letter of May 15th in which he had explained to Taft his unwillingness to discuss Roosevelt personally. But New insisted that Root was their choice and at Barnes' request, Root issued a public statement saying that he would not withdraw because of the opposition of the Roosevelt forces. Root's oldest son recalled a long talk with his father in regard to this decision. His father foresaw clearly that the Convention would be productive of a terrific row and that bitter recriminations would be his lot if he presided over it. He hated to become involved at all in a fight between his two friends, but the only consideration which weighed in his discussion with his son was whether it was his duty to preside. They both finally came to the conclusion that it was his duty.[10]

The Rooseveltians still seemed to be undecided about opposing Root. On June 1st, Roosevelt issued a statement saying that a group of his supporters had advised him that they felt "that no issue should be made about the temporary chairmanship." Two days later he came out flatly against the man who had presided as Chairman of the 1904 Convention at which Roosevelt himself was nominated: "In the past, Mr. Root has rendered distinguished service as Secretary of State and Secretary of War. But in this contest, Mr. Root had ranged himself against the men who stand for progressive principles. . . . He stands as the representative of the men and policies of reaction. He is put forward by the bosses and the representatives of special privileges. What has recently come to my knowledge makes it clear that it is a question of the absolute duty of every progressive Republican to oppose the selection as temporary chairman at Chicago of any man put forward in the interests of the supporters of Mr. Taft in this contest." [11] The recent knowledge of Roosevelt was the fact that Barnes, as head of the New York State Republican organization, had telegraphed appeals to the New York delegates-elect to support Root.[12] The issue was now fixed and Roosevelt's success or failure at Chicago would be determined by the fight on Root as Temporary Chairman. The result of that ballot would show whether Roosevelt or Taft forces were to control the Convention.

It would require a separate volume to analyze and to pass judgment on the charges of fraud and robbery which the Roosevelt forces hurled at the Taft group as a result of the Chicago Convention. Twenty years after the event those who had some part in it on one side or the other seemed to view it still with the same convictions which became settled in their minds at the time. To the Roosevelt followers it was clear as crystal that Taft stole the nomination; in the view of the Taft "regulars," the Convention was run according to rule and in the same manner as all other conventions. They do not imply that it was there-

[10] Elihu Root, Jr. to the author, September 22, 1937.
[11] Philadelphia North American, June 4, 1912.
[12] Rosewater, Back Stage in 1912, p. 143.

fore a shining example of political purity but, on the other hand, they were not willing to concede that all the Progressives were spotless angels. Root had no part in the preliminary determinations which really decided the result before he took the gavel as Temporary Chairman, although his rulings in the chair confirmed the result. "I was relieved & somewhat surprised," he wrote to Mrs. Lodge after the convention, "to find how lacking in any substantial foundation was all the talk about stealing delegates. Most of the cases seemed to me quite clear & the others of such a character that honest men might fairly differ in their conclusions." [13]

Roosevelt had decided that the best method by which he could secure delegates to the Convention was the use of the preferential primary in which the voters have an opportunity to express, in their election of delegates, a choice between the rival candidates for the nomination. He was at some disadvantage due to his late entry into the field. Particularly in California, the question arose whether state law could override the rules of the national party conventions. So far as the Republican Party were concerned, they had fought out and adopted the rule that delegates to the Convention must be elected in such a way that the Republican electors of each congressional district might have an opportunity to select the delegates from that district. Only the delegates at large represented the state as a whole. It was on this basis that the National Committee, at a meeting held in December, 1911, issued the call for the Convention. Not a single member of the Committee raised any objection; [14] Roosevelt had not yet decided to be a candidate. The National Committee had been selected at the 1908 Convention which was controlled by Roosevelt; it has always been the rule that this Committee should issue the call for the next convention, make the arrangements and hear contests for the purpose of drawing up a temporary roll of delegates to be presented to the Convention. In retrospect, this was Root's view of the situation:

"Roosevelt's main complaint was that the Convention was crooked. That was merely turning to his particular case the general popular feeling that politicians are crooked. I do not know how far that is justified but it was no more so for that Convention than in general. The Convention was run just as the 1904 Convention was run when Roosevelt

[13] Lodge Papers, Massachusetts Historical Society.
[14] Rosewater, op. cit., p. 36.

was nominated. I presided at both. The rules of proceedings were well established. There are always contests over the seating of delegates. Those contests go to a Committee on Contested Seats with a member-ship representative of all sections of the country. Its proceedings are of a rudimentary judicial character; it is impossible to summon witnesses in the time available and you must act on the basis of statements. The people on this Committee were the same people whom Roosevelt had dealt with and through whom he had controlled the party. So far as I could see, the decisions of the Committee were correct although I had nothing to do with them personally. The only things that appeared to me to be violations were in favor of Roosevelt. In 1880, when Hoar was chairman of the Republican Convention, there was a long and able discussion of the rules under which the Republican Conventions should be carried on; it was the unit rule against the representative rule. The former was the Democratic rule and the latter was at that time adopted by the Republicans. The rule was that no Congressional District might be deprived of its separate representation in the Convention. The same rule was followed in 1904 and in 1912. The chief outcry arose over the California case. In California, Hiram Johnson, who was in political control, had the Legislature pass a law saying delegates to national party conventions should be elected by the entire state. This was directly con-trary to the rules of the Republican Party. The state had no business to pass such a law.[15] The delegates came and two of them were able to show that they had a large majority of the voters in their own Con-gressional Districts and they were the only two who were legally quali-fied to take their seats. The others could not show that they were the choices of their particular districts. It was perfectly clear to me that they were the only two men who were entitled to be seated. The Com-mittee seated these two and all the others who were Roosevelt men. The greatest outcry was against seating these two men who were the only ones entitled to seats; thereupon Roosevelt made a great noise about crooked politics. The state of New York was overwhelmingly for Taft but sixteen districts were for Roosevelt and had their repre-sentatives.

"I don't know whether that is the best rule but it was the rule under which they were elected even though there may be a better rule. It

[15] Academic opinion in general agrees that state law can not bind national party con-ventions; cf. e. g., Merriam and Overacker, *Primary Elections* (1928), p. 186.

was said, and I think it may be true, that when people sent Roosevelt a list of cases which they thought were wrong, and Roosevelt asked how that would affect the result, they said it still left a majority for Taft; Roosevelt told them to put in more contests.

"As a rule the decisions are made in advance except for a fringe of trading delegations. Delegates from the important states are elected in separate localities and frequently reflect the feelings of the voters regarding particular candidates. Frequently they reflect the willingness of the voters to be guided by the judgment of some individual. It depends upon the degree to which the party organization has been carried. The head of the delegation is expected to represent the view of the delegation reached by discussion among them. If no unanimous conclusion is reached, the chairman states the view of so many delegates and asks that the delegation be polled. The system affords little opportunity for individual preferences. I knew who would be chosen before the Convention met both in 1904 and 1912. I took little interest in the Conventions after I left the Senate and I do not know whether Harding was agreed upon in advance in 1920. I agreed to preside in 1912 before Roosevelt became a candidate and I did it as rather a routine discharge of my duty as a Senator.[16] When Roosevelt announced his candidacy I was already committed to Taft. Roosevelt had written to me that he would not be a candidate. I would probably have taken the same position anyhow after Roosevelt came out for judicial recall in his Columbus speech since I am absolutely opposed to that proposal. It would change the whole constitutional basis of our government. I could not have been for Roosevelt in the face of that. Roosevelt didn't care much for rules of law." [17]

Root's reference to the manner in which the Roosevelt contests were decided upon was probably based on information from Dr. Nicholas Murray Butler who has told the story in *Scribner's* magazine for February, 1936. In April, 1913, Dr. Butler found himself on the train to Boston next to Governor Hadley, Roosevelt's floor leader at the convention. Dr. Butler asked, now that it was all over, whether Hadley would not explain to him why they had contested 74 seats rather than 174 or 274. "I will tell you," Hadley replied. "After the

[16] Mr. Root evidently had in mind an early agreement to act as Chairman and not the conflict which went on in his mind in the spring of 1912.
[17] Root to the author, September 13, 1930.

National Committee had heard the various contests and reached their conclusions, Borah, Frank Kellogg and I decided that in twenty-four cases we had been literally defrauded of our representation. We recognized that we had a very strong case in respect to other contests, but that there were debatable questions, every one of which, however, had been decided against us. There remained twenty-four contests in which we felt that we had been outraged and that injustice had plainly been done. So we three went to Colonel Roosevelt and told him this fact. We said we were going to contest these twenty-four seats on the floor of the Convention. On hearing this statement, Colonel Roosevelt cried with great vehemence: 'Twenty-four seats! Twenty-four! What is the use of contesting twenty-four? You must contest seventy-four if you expect to get anywhere.' So we raised the number to seventy-four."

On June 6th, the National Committee met in Chicago to hear the contests. Root did not come into this picture; he was still in Washington and had no part, formal or informal, in the proceedings. In the southern states, it is notorious that the Administration, through its power of patronage, has an advantage which it is practically impossible to overcome. The election of the southern delegates is notoriously tainted with fraud and corruption and they are commonly regarded as bargaining groups at the Convention, perhaps already "secured" by one candidate or another, but probably open to "persuasion," judiciously applied. In 1908, it was Roosevelt who rejected a proposal designed to eliminate corruption in the south and to cut down the control which the President in office has over these delegates chosen almost entirely from among office-holders. To one who attempts to plow through the record, it appears that in most of the contests in the South and elsewhere, the advocates of the one side or the other must have lied prodigiously. To one not involved in the actual controversy, it seems unreasonable to suppose that all the lying was done by the Taft men. One finds a morass of flatly contradictory statements of fact, frequently supported by directly opposing affidavits. La Follette concludes "that neither Taft nor Roosevelt had a majority of honestly or regularly elected delegates. This the managers upon both sides well understood. Each candidate was trying to seat a sufficient number of fraudulently credentialed delegates, added to those regularly chosen to support him, to secure control of the Convention and steam-roll the nomination." [18] To say that there was no fraud in electing delegates to the Convention of 1912 would be clearly untrue; some indications of it are plain on the record. To say that this was the first time fraud had entered into the election of delegates to a national Republican Convention would be equally untrue. It is rather interesting to note a letter which Taft wrote to Charles Nagel on June 16th, 1908, as the Roosevelt-controlled Convention at which Taft was nominated was beginning to get under way:

> I hope that everything is going smoothly in Chicago, so that the nomination will come out right. I do not feel certain, however, until the thing is done. The allies have been exceedingly venomous and have resorted to methods that I do not feel ought to commend themselves to decent politicians. They first set up 200 fake contests and then when the committee turned them down, as it had to, they charged unfair methods on the part of the committee.[19]

So Walter L. Houser, La Follette's manager, declared during the 1912 Convention: "For years ago, when Roosevelt and Taft were running things together, the same tactics were employed then as are being brought into play this year." [20]

It is unquestionably true that Roosevelt was the choice of a majority of the people. This fact was revealed in the primaries and in the November election when he polled over 600,000 more votes than Taft although the country at large swept Wilson and the Democrats into power. The conclusion from that fact is not necessarily that Taft's nomination was fraudulent; it is rather that under the standing rules and organization of the Republican National Convention, the will of the majority could not prevail. "Of course," Root wrote to S. C. Eastman on August 24th, 1912, "when anyone seeks a nomination from a voluntary organization like a national party he must seek it in accordance with existing rules, but he has no right to expect that a special rule be made for him." La Follette's conclusion is that even on the showing of the Roosevelt people themselves, Roosevelt never had a

[18] La Follette, Autobiography, p. 669.
[19] Taft Papers, Library of Congress.
[20] Rosewater, op. cit., p. 171.

majority in the Convention and that even if credence be given to their charge of fraud, the result would not have been changed. *La Follette's Weekly Magazine* engaged Gilbert E. Roe of New York City to analyze all the proceedings bearing upon the seating of delegates. Five hundred and forty votes were necessary to a majority. On the final vote for the nominee, Taft had five hundred and sixty-one; Roosevelt had one hundred and seven with three hundred and forty-four presumable Roosevelt delegates not voting, which makes four hundred and fifty-one. To this Roe added for good measure six absentees, the two Hughes votes and the seven Idaho delegates who voted with the Iowa delegation for Cummins, leaving undistributed as between Taft and Roosevelt only the ten Iowa votes for Cummins and the forty-one for La Follette; there were no contests in regard to any of these. These fifteen additional votes credited to Roosevelt bring his total to four hundred and sixty-six or seventy-four short of a majority; Roosevelt finally challenged seventy-four of the Taft delegates. Before the National Committee, the Roosevelt forces challenged two hundred and forty-eight seats. Of these, thirty-six Taft delegates were seated by unanimous vote of the National Committee after a roll call; twenty-six were seated by *viva voce* vote without any request for a roll call and fourteen Roosevelt delegates withdrew their contests when their cases were called. Nineteen of the contested seats were decided in favor of Roosevelt. That leaves only sixty-five of all the two hundred and forty-eight contested seats as to which there was any substantial dispute between the Roosevelt and Taft members of the National Committee. According to Roe's investigation, the Roosevelt minority report which contested seventy-two seats had attached to it the original pencil memorandum showing only sixty-six delegates marked for contest, the number being subsequently raised to seventy-two. It may be noted that some confusion results from the fact that the Hadley motion regarding the contests called for unseating *seventy-four* Taft delegates and for seating *seventy-two* Roosevelt delegates in their places; in the Seventh District of Texas, four Taft delegates were challenged, but only two Roosevelt substitutes proposed. Roe concluded on an analysis of all the evidence that in a maximum of only forty-nine cases before the National Committee could it be fairly said that there was reasonable basis at all for the Roosevelt claims. Adding this number to the four hundred and sixty-six credited to Roosevelt, he was still short of a majority.[21] Whether or not this analysis be accepted, there is no question that in one hundred and sixty-four cases contested before the National Committee, the Roosevelt committeemen agreed upon the decision in favor of Taft. It is impossible to avoid the conclusion that these cases were contested solely for popular effect to give the impression that Taft had far less than a majority of the delegates.

No one who agrees with either side on any of these points dealing with the 1912 Convention will be admitted to be impartial by the adherents of the other side; certainly ardent Rooseveltians would not acknowledge that an admittedly friendly biographer of Elihu Root could be impartial. It may be well, however, to emphasize again that Root had no part in the determination of the original contests as a result of which the temporary roll of the Convention was drawn up; his part was played a little later.

Root left New York for Chicago on the night of June 14th. Taft told Hilles on June 12th that "Root has a cold and does not feel very bright." [22] Henry L. Stimson, then Secretary of War in Taft's Cabinet, dropped in to see him as he was packing up. Root was very blue and down at the mouth; he remarked that it was a hard thing to go to fight against a candidate that you did not want to fight against.[23] It was of course clear that that was his task since Roosevelt had come out against him as Temporary Chairman. There seems to have been no communication between Root and Roosevelt during several weeks before the Convention opened. Root arrived in Chicago one day before Roosevelt arrived and three days before the Convention opened on June 18th. The usual formality in opening the Convention is for the Chairman of the Republican National Committee to call the Convention to order and to suggest the name of the Temporary Chairman selected by the National Committee. The recommendation is usually accepted *pro forma*, the Temporary Chairman delivers a speech extolling the virtues of the party, the committees of the Convention are selected, bring in their reports and the Permanent Chairman is then elected. On this occasion it fell to the lot of Victor Rosewater, editor of the Omaha Bee, to start the ball rolling. He was a little

[21] La Follette, op. cit., pp. 659 ff.
[22] Taft Papers, Library of Congress.
[23] Colonel Henry L. Stimson to the author, March 10, 1934; Diary of Henry L. Stimson, 1911–1913, pp. 83 and 87.

man with a little voice. His memoirs of the Convention, published in 1932, are full of frank admissions of his inexperience in such situations, his physical handicaps and a great deal of earnest determination to stand his ground. He was a Taft man but made it a point to arrange in advance with Governor Hadley of Missouri, as leader of the Roosevelt forces, to permit what was already the opposition party to have time to present its case.

Governor Hadley was recognized by Rosewater in spite of the fact that he was prepared to sustain a point of order made by James E. Watson of Indiana, as leader of the Taft forces, that no business was in order until the Convention was organized. Hadley immediately posed the basic issue which was whether the National Committee had the power to prepare a temporary roll of delegates which could be changed by the Convention only upon the report of its Credentials Committee. Hadley insisted that no business could be transacted until it had passed upon the charges of fraud made against some of the delegates on the roll. He moved to substitute for seventy-four of the delegates on the temporary roll the names of the seventy-two men whom the Roosevelt followers insisted were the properly qualified delegates. The issue was whether the delegates whose names appeared on the temporary roll should vote on Hadley's motion, or whether the names on Hadley's list should be given a vote, or whether all the contested delegates should be barred from voting until the contests were decided. The practical situation was that the barring of the votes of these contested delegates would destroy the Taft majority and enable the Roosevelt forces to organize the Convention, electing their own candidate for temporary chairman, Governor Francis E. McGovern of Wisconsin. McGovern had been elected from Wisconsin as a La Follette delegate. His selection as the Roosevelt candidate was vigorously opposed by La Follette and formally repudiated from the platform of the Convention by the latter's manager.[24] Rosewater, with the advice of the parliamentarians appointed to advise the chair, ruled against Hadley on the ground that until the Convention was "organized" by the election of a temporary chairman, the meeting was not a convention authorized to transact business but merely an assemblage of those who, under the rules, were entitled to organize a convention. The vote was taken, showing 558 for Root and 501 for McGovern.

[24] La Follette, op. cit., pp. 647 ff.

Root took the chair amid the yells from the Pennsylvania delegates that he was a receiver of stolen goods. Colonel Gleason, Secretary of the National Committee, suggested to Root that he postpone his speech until the next day; Root, who had been suffering from an attack of dysentery, was feeling sick and weak. He refused to delay and delivered his address.[25] Except for its opening plea for unity and loyalty to the party, it was mainly the usual defense of Republican principles and administration. It was cleverly put, however, to link in one flowing whole the policies and acts of the McKinley, Roosevelt and Taft Administrations. Some papers, including the New York World, hailed it as a brilliant defense of the American constitutional system.

During the ensuing days, Root regained his physical strength. He was the dominant force in the Convention. There was no weakness in his body or voice or spirit. One can admire the technique of an artist even when one is positively repelled by the picture. Even ardent Roosevelt men admitted that probably no man in the country could have handled that convention as Root did. It is doubtful if any presiding officer ever had a harder task or ever discharged it better. It may have been in a bad cause, but it was a superlative performance. There were breaches of order, many of them, but Root restored order by sheer force of character. On one occasion, Root, pointing with the handle of his gavel at an obstreperous Pennsylvania delegate, shouted above the din: "I do not know whether you want to hear what is being said upon this serious and important subject, but I know this, that if the gentleman sitting upon the other side of that aisle (indicating) does not cease his disorderly conduct, delegate or no delegate, the Sergeant-at-Arms will have him removed from the hall." [26] From the back of the platform, Senator Boies Penrose of Pennsylvania was heard to remark, "Hear how rough he talks to the Mayor of McKeesport!" [27] The most popular slogan was "steam-roller," descriptive of the implacable working of the organization, riding down all who stood in its path. From ruling to ruling, a man in the gallery emitted a whistle which was an excellent imitation and which brought uproars of applause and laughter. It was near the middle of the convention when P. W. Howard of Mississippi rose to a point of order.

[25] Lafayette Gleason to the author, April 10, 1935.
[26] Proceedings, p. 135.
[27] Nicholas Murray Butler in Scribner's magazine, February, 1936, p. 80.

The Temporary Chairman (Mr. Root):—The gentleman will state his point of order.

Mr. Howard of Mississippi:—The point of order is that the steam roller is exceeding the speed limit.

The Temporary Chairman:—The chair is ready to rule upon the point of order. The point of order is sustained. The justification is that we have some hope of getting home for Sunday.

Root made a ruling on essentially the same point which had confronted Rosewater. The point was again raised by Governor Hadley and involved the right of contested delegates to vote upon Hadley's motion to substitute his list of delegates for the temporary list drawn up by the National Committee. According to Root, "No man can be permitted to vote upon the question of his own right to a seat in the Convention, but the rule does not disqualify any delegate whose name is upon the roll from voting upon the contest of any other man's right, or from participating in the ordinary business of the Convention so long as he holds his seat. Otherwise, any minority could secure control of a deliberative body by grouping a sufficient number of their opponents in one motion, and by thus disqualifying them turn the minority into a majority without any decision upon the merits of the motion." He quoted precedents from the House of Representatives whose rules were followed by Republican Conventions and concluded: "To hold that a member whose seat is contested may take no part in the proceedings of this body would lead to the conclusion that if every seat were contested, as it surely would be if such a rule were adopted, there could be no Convention at all, as nobody would be entitled to participate." [28] Root was unquestionably sound on the precedents and the logic, but of course the practical result was that Taft controlled the Convention. It is quite likely that he could have made a plausible ruling to the effect that the delegates whose seats were contested could not vote until the contests had been decided; that would have given the nomination to Roosevelt. As a result of the ruling he did make, the Rooseveltians accused him of stealing the Convention. Had he ruled otherwise, the Taftites could equally well have accused him of stealing it for Roosevelt. McGovern declared after the Convention that if he had been elected Temporary Chairman he would have un-seated the seventy-two

[28] Proceedings, p. 160.

contested delegates. "In other words," La Follette writes in his Auto-biography, "he confesses that he would have done even more unjusti-fiable 'steam-rolling' as chairman in Roosevelt's interest than he says was done by the Convention in Taft's interest. Such a decision as this, had it been rendered, would have violated the precedents of every na-tional convention ever held, and arbitrarily and wrongfully have nomi-nated Roosevelt as the Republican candidate." [29] Subsequently, Root himself had no doubt that his ruling was correct although he believed that a change should be made in the method of determining contests. But under the rules as they existed in 1912, no other result was possi-ble.[30] In the spring of 1913, Root took a leading part in advocating two changes in the rules of the national Republican conventions; one was designed to eliminate the excessive southern representation and the other to permit the Republicans of each state to elect their delegates in their own way. In line with his suggestion, the Republican National Committee voted to change the rules to allow representation accord-ing to state laws and their resolution being approved by a majority vote in State Conventions, became the established rule of the Republican party after February 1st, 1915.

Two others among Root's rulings have aroused the greatest storm of criticism. The first, upon the California cases, had had a preliminary determination before he took the chair and has already been discussed. One should add, however, to Root's views as briefly summarized in the conversation which has been quoted, the contention of the Hiram Johnson group that, according to the certificates of state and city of-ficials, it was impossible to estimate the votes in the district which gave two delegates to Taft because there were new limits to the district which did not coincide with the old precincts on the basis of which the vote was cast.

The other ruling of Root's which aroused the greatest condemnation arose in connection with a poll of the Massachusetts delegation on the actual vote for the nominee. Henry J. Allen of Kansas had read a state-ment by Roosevelt in which Roosevelt declared that the Convention was organized by fraud; "This action makes the Convention in no proper sense any longer a Republican Convention representing the real

[29] La Follette, op. cit., p. 652.
[30] Root to S. C. Eastman, August 24, 1912.

Republican party. Therefore, I hope the men elected as Roosevelt delegates will now decline to vote on any matter before the Convention." [31] Thereafter the Roosevelt delegates followed that procedure. Where the delegates did not respond and in some cases where they replied, "Present but not voting," the alternates were called. That procedure had been followed in the vote on the adoption of the platform and no objection had been raised.[32] In the final vote on the nominee, when two delegates at large, who were Roosevelt men, answered "Present but not voting," there was a demand that the alternates be called. There was a curious situation in the Massachusetts delegation in that the eight delegates at large were all Roosevelt men but two of the alternates were Taft men. Root ruled that in these cases the alternates could vote, thus adding two votes to Taft's final total. Since Taft had a margin of twenty-one votes, these two made no essential difference but the ruling raised a great storm. Root afterwards was fully convinced in his own mind that his ruling was correct. On July 1st, 1912, he replied to an inquiry on the matter from E. P. White of Buffalo. Root asserted that every delegate was under a duty to vote and that he had no option to abstain. He cited the rules of the House of Representatives and the Senate which flatly state the duty to vote unless excused for special reasons of personal interest. "The case presented in the recent convention, however," Root continued, "was not merely the refusal of a delegate to perform the particular duty of voting upon the roll call for President. A formal announcement had been made by Mr. Allen of Kansas in behalf of these delegates, among others, that they refused to participate any further in the proceedings of the convention. This announcement stated the conclusion reached by concerted action on the part of the body of delegates, several hundred in number, in whose behalf the statement was made. It was with the avowed intent of placing the delegates in a position where they would not be bound by any action of the convention. It was a clear abdication of any further representation in that convention of the constituents by whom they had been elected. The refusal to vote in the particular case was but a confirmation of this declaration made in the delegates' behalf. Under these circumstances the constituencies were no longer represented by delegates in the convention, and, having regard to the truth and substance of things, I think

[31] *Proceedings*, p. 333.
[32] *Ibid.*, p. 371 and Rosewater, *op. cit.*, p. 193.

they were as much entitled to be represented by the alternates they had elected as if the persons who had formerly represented them had physically departed from the convention hall instead of remaining as spectators of the proceedings."

To other correspondents, Root explained that he had ruled in the Massachusetts case and not in other cases because that was the only case in which a ruling was asked for and accordingly the only one in regard to which the chair had to make a ruling. Root admitted, however, that it was a case of first impression.[33] One may well venture the guess that the ruling was demanded here because of the curious line-up of the Massachusetts delegates and alternates but there is no suggestion of collusion between Root and the Massachusetts alternate who demanded the ruling. Under ordinary circumstances, a mere quarrel about a parliamentary ruling would have amounted to little; in this Convention, due to the personality of Roosevelt, all of these incidents were cumulative and were seized upon to sustain the charges of fraud and theft and to justify the Bull Moose bolt.

August 1st, 1912, Root was in Washington as chairman of the committee to notify Mr. Taft of his nomination. His speech of notification was very brief but he took occasion to remark that the contests were decided according to the rules which had governed the Republican party for forty years. "Your title to the nomination is as clear and unimpeachable as the title of any candidate of any party since political conventions began."

By this time, when the papers were filled with Roosevelt's charges of theft and fraud and dishonesty and the political atmosphere was raised to the boiling point, Taft had lost his poise and could not understand Root's position. July 16th, he wrote to Mrs. Taft: "Senator Root . . . runs away from authentication and verification of the statement as chairman of the convention. He is very timid in certain ways, and sometimes makes you feel that he is afraid to get out into the open in his controversy with Roosevelt. He has gone so far now that I would think he would cut his bridges behind him and go as far as he can for the cause which he really believes in." [34] This was a total misconception of Root and his position. Root had no controversy with Roosevelt, but only with Roosevelt's policies at the moment. For the man he still felt

[33] Root to E. P. White, July 1, 1912.
[34] Taft Papers, Library of Congress.

an affection which then and for many years was probably greater than that which he felt for any other man. He liked Taft and their relations were cordial but there was never between them the depth of feeling which Root had for "Theodore." In veritable anguish of soul after the Convention, he burst out to an intimate friend: "I care more for one button on Theodore Roosevelt's waistcoat than for Taft's whole body."

In the *Outlook* of July 6th, Roosevelt's editorial had referred to Root in connection with his Massachusetts ruling as a "modern Autolycus, the 'snapper-up of unconsidered trifles'." On July 13th, he wrote in the same columns that those two Massachusetts votes "were publicly raped at the last moment from Massachusetts." In a long article in the issue of July 20th, he analyzed the Convention with ever recurrent charges of fraud linked to Root's name. He took up Root's general ruling about the preliminary votes of the contested delegates: "From the standpoint of that kind of pure legalism which is not merely divorced from justice but which is invariably resorted to by those who desire to do injustice, such a ruling could be both defended and attacked." Root's opinion "was substantially the same kind of opinion as those opinions given by great corporation lawyers to great corporations when the corporation is bent upon doing what the law is designed to forbid, but wishes by the purchase of legal ingenuity to escape paying the penalty which might attend technical violations of the law." Some of the actions of Taft and his supporters "could probably be defended as not technically dishonest, but . . . nevertheless are utterly incompatible with any proper standard of public morality." They were cruel thrusts at an old friend and Root felt them. Roosevelt, given his temperament, in the agony of defeat, was bitter against the man. He was at Armageddon "and we battle for the Lord." He *had* to believe that the nomination was stolen from him; he *had* to believe that Root was guilty. That was the way in which his mind always worked. On April 21st, 1910, he had written to Dr. Alexander Lambert about the storm of which he was then the center as the result of his quarrel with the Vatican: ". . . really I don't see how there is room for the slightest difference of opinion. I acted in the only possible way that anyone could act, and in my judgment no man is a good American who fails heartily to support me for it." [35]

Root knew his Roosevelt, but this was the first time in thirty years of

[35] Roosevelt Papers, Library of Congress.

association that the lightning of Roosevelt's wrath had struck upon Root's head; over and over again, Root's calmness, his wit, often his scorching sarcasm, had proved an effective lightning rod. His mind must have run back to those days in 1898 when he used that same "legal ingenuity" to defend Roosevelt from the charge of tax evasion and made it possible for him to be Governor of New York. Perhaps he recalled the hard labor he had devoted to justifying Roosevelt's "taking" of Panama. Perhaps he was mindful of many a conversation with "Theodore" about just such matters as these and of Roosevelt's tributes to him for fidelity to his clients. To James T. Williams, Jr. of the Boston *Evening Transcript*, who had recalled one of those early tributes, he wrote on December 20th, 1912:

> Of course what Roosevelt said about me in 1902 and what he is now saying are quite inconsistent. In each case his words expressed a state of feeling rather than a sober judgment. When I was with him he felt superlatively one way; now that I am against him he feels superlatively the other way. I think he has been about equally wrong in both his utterances.

Even after two years of estrangement following Roosevelt's searing attacks on Root, the latter wrote to Arthur Wallace Dunn on August 12th, 1914:

> The little article which you sent me is very nice and I am very much obliged to you. I see nothing in it to object to except a single paragraph about Mr. Roosevelt. I don't want that published. I have felt that the relations between Roosevelt and myself have been such that any controversy between us would necessarily degenerate into the kind of recrimination and exposure of confidences which accompany a divorce suit, with a loss of personal dignity to both. Accordingly I have carefully refrained from saying anything at all about him personally. I don't want to do so now. I return the paper which you sent with the paragraph to which I refer, on page 4, crossed out in blue pencil.

Roosevelt's acute feelings, however, lasted. April 1st, 1913, he wrote to Winthrop Chanler: "I feel very strongly against Root, because Root took part in as downright a bit of theft and swindling as ever was perpetrated by any Tammany ballot box stuffer, and I shall never forgive the men who were the leaders in that swindling." [36] He did forgive eventually, at least on the surface, but it took many years.

Among the many friendly letters Root received after the Convention, he valued most one written on June 24th, 1912, by Chief Justice White who could not resist expressing his "admiration for and appreciation of your services in Chicago. To an outsider it seemed we were possibly near a great crisis. The dignity, intelligence, the firmness, the patriotism so well, so superbly manifested by you in the discharge of your duty was at once felt all over the country and begot hope and confidence! You have rendered another great public service for which every self respecting American owes you a debt of gratitude. . . ." At a dinner party in Washington a few weeks after the Convention, Root sat and talked with the daughter of General Sheridan. He began to discuss the Convention and the tragic breach, talking aloud from his mind, but oblivious to his partner. There was nothing of self justification in what he said nor any indication of a call for excuses; there was nothing of bitterness, but only sadness that his close friend could have so turned against him.[37]

Root squared his shoulders and let his casual acquaintances continue to have opportunities to think of him as a man of ice and iron. He did not let himself go even to poor "Bob" Bacon who was sick at heart: "It distresses me, my dear Bob, to have you so distressed, and I personally have much regret, but I am saved the pain of doubt, for I have not for an instant the slightest question as to what my course ought to be and must be." [38] "We had a great & strenuous time at Chicago," he wrote Mrs. Lodge on June 28th, "& I am sure we did the right thing. For me the joy of conflict was clouded by regret & sorrow but never for an instant by any doubt."

[36] *Ibid.*
[37] Miss Mary Sheridan to the author, March 26, 1934.
[38] Root to Bacon, July 8, 1912.

CHAPTER XXXVI

"The most unsatisfactory way of doing things"

IT cannot be said that Elihu Root was a great Senator. His prestige, his dominant personality and his power of lucid exposition and argument were often potent factors in debate. Frequently he contributed to a proposal his extraordinary skill in drafting, a skill which included the ability to find a formula on which agreement could be reached, and a masterful use of words. On the whole, however, his powers were directed to supporting or opposing measures which others originated. Perhaps it was because the office never challenged him. "The Senate does such little things in such a little way," he is said to have remarked. "We are an awfully soggy incompetent lot of old duffers in the Senate," he wrote to his wife in the summer of 1912. There was a contemptuous sting in the wit with which he answered the question whether he thought that Congress was a mirror of public opinion: "Congress is not a mirror of anything because it never reflects." "The best way to conceal a fact," he once said, "is to get it published in a Congressional document." Perhaps after the relative freedom which he enjoyed as head of a department, he found the Senate too hampering, too difficult a place in which to get things accomplished. But there was more than feelings of that kind. In his first four years he found himself in the position of being under an obligation to support an Administration with whose policies and actions he was not always in sympathy. It would have been human if he had at times thought to himself that such and such a matter could have been handled more wisely or more adroitly had he yielded to the urgings of Roosevelt and taken on his own shoulders the presidential mantle. His fourth year was clouded and saddened by the breach with Roosevelt and then for two years he found himself a minority Senator, arguing futilely against the proposals of President Wilson's Democratic majority. In his last eight months his strong feelings about the World War absorbed his mind. Nor was he, after passing the age of sixty-five, as strong and active as he had been when he first took public office. The strain of long years of always pressing work and heavy responsibility, had told even on his rugged constitution. The long summer sessions were particularly trying: "Thank heaven there will be only one more summer of servitude," he wrote to his wife on the Fourth of July, 1913.

He himself was somewhat dubious about his capacity to be an effective Senator. "If I go to the Senate," he wrote Joseph H. Choate on January 18th, 1909, "the little experience of the Constitutional Convention [of 1894] is likely to prove quite useful. I have really become quite an expert in the affairs of our Government and my knowledge of them from the executive side will probably help a good deal. Nevertheless, I am getting to be a pretty old dog to learn new tricks, and I do not think that lawyers whose habits have become fixed at the Bar ordinarily make very successful legislators." Perhaps this was because, as Edmund Burke pointed out, training in the law, although it quickens and invigorates the understanding, "is not apt, except in persons very happily born, to open and liberalize the mind in the same proportion." Yet Root pointed out in his Commencement address at the Yale Law School in 1909, that lawyers usually develop a peculiar adaptability to the requirements of public office.[1] This is true regarding adaptability to duties and to a certain extent to new substance. It is more difficult for a man to shift from the executive to the legislative branch of government; there is a wide difference in function and in point of view which makes for a natural separation of powers. Roosevelt remarked to the Cabinet on January 19th, 1909, that a Congressman commented to him on the fact that Knox was going out of the Senate into the State Department and Root out of the Department into the Senate, and suggested that their minds and sympathies would similarly change. "I told him," said the President, "that within six months that might be the case as to Knox, but that if I knew anything, it would not apply to Root."[2] In the Cabinet Root had shown rare skill in handling Congress but he never lost the Cabinet officer's disgust at the pettiness and inefficiency of Congress which constantly holds up good bills for bad reasons. "Almost every Senator is more desirous of preventing something from passing than he is of getting anything passed," he said on

[1] Addresses on Government and Citizenship, p. 415.
[2] Howe, George von Lengerke Meyer, p. 414.

one occasion.[3] At the same time, he had the faculty of seeing the other man's point of view and he therefore appreciated such idiosyncrasies of the legislative branch as the Senate's stubborn insistence upon retaining its share of control over foreign relations.

Root's role as a senator might be viewed against the background of the two administrations under which he served, but in general he did not play a decisive part in determining the policies or achievements of either Taft or Wilson. With a few exceptions, the course of events would not have been changed had Root not been in the Senate whereas Root's contributions as Secretary of War and as Secretary of State are an essential part of American history from 1899 to 1909. Aside from the political events already described, his six years in the Senate deserve to be examined, therefore, more for the light which they throw upon his own point of view and character, and the measures with which he dealt may accordingly be considered according to subject matter rather than in historical sequence.

A new Senator usually goes through a period of apprenticeship, a freshman interlude in which he speaks not and serves not on important committees. Root's position in two Cabinets gave him a right to more recognition; his place in the Republican Party promoted the acknowledgment of this right and his close acquaintance with many members of the Senate made them ready and willing to make a place for him at once. Knox had written to a mutual friend in December that he had impressed upon his colleagues the desirability and necessity of making full use of Root's experience and abilities by putting him on the proper committees. Lodge was a powerful figure and warm friend and he wrote to Roosevelt on April 29th, 1909, that it was "a great joy and comfort" to have Root in the Senate.[4] The result was that Root could write to his daughter Edith on April 3rd, 1909: "My committees are: Foreign Relations, Public Expenditures, Library, Expenditures in the Department of State, of which I am Chairman, Revolutionary Claims, Canadian Relations and Coast Defense. The first three are of some importance, and if you have any Revolutionary Claims to put in I shall be glad to take care of them." These committee assignments he

---

[3] Root to General Grenville M. Dodge, January 22, 1903, Dodge Papers, Library of Congress; quoted in Stephenson, Nelson W. Aldrich, p. 209.

[4] Roosevelt-Lodge Correspondence, Vol. II, p. 335.

held for the first two years; for the last four years he was on the important Judiciary Committee for which he expressed a preference, and he substituted other minor committees for those dealing with expenditures.

Root had also the advantage of his intimate friendship with the presiding officer of the Senate, Vice-President "Sunny Jim" Sherman. On one occasion when Senator Beveridge was holding forth in one of those long, dull speeches which so often empty the Senate chamber, Root was conversing audibly with Senator Bacon of Georgia in the back of the room. The Vice President, in the chair, rapped his gavel and shook his head at them; there was no result and he repeated his gesture of admonition. Root scribbled a note and sent it to the chair by a page: "If the presiding officer means I am to keep quiet, I yield to his superior authority; if he means I am to listen to that damn bore, he can go to hell." [5]

It was an error on Root's part during the first major debate in which he took part to give voice to the new Senator's usual disgust with the Senate's long-winded and inefficient proceedings. It was in the discussion of the Payne-Aldrich Tariff bill, on May 14th, 1909, that he remonstrated:

> I undertake to say, sir, that in my very humble individual judgment, and I believe in the judgment of the Senate and . . . in the judgment of the people of the United States, it would be much better for the business that we have to perform if we should all confine ourselves to simple, plain, direct business statements . . . and refrain from declamation, refrain from general discussion for home consumption, and utilize our time in the transaction of business. [6]

Senator Money of Mississippi took him to task and the newspaper men made a good story out of Root's being "disciplined." ". . . My distinguished friend from New York [Mr. Root]," said Senator Money, "has delivered the Senate a lecture on how it should conduct its business and how individual Senators should conduct themselves. When he has got fairly warm in his seat and has learned a little more about the Senate he will not indulge himself in any lectures on this subject

[5] Richard S. Sherman to the author, June 14, 1931.
[6] Congressional Record, 61st Cong., 1st Sess., Vol. 44, p. 2043.

(laughter), for two reasons: First, because they are utterly ineffectual curtain lectures, and they are generally the outcome of a brand-new Member; and, in the next place, they are utterly unnecessary. He will understand, also, that the most unfortunate thing that has happened to the Senate is having a new Senator come in here to do things on 'business methods.' I hope that here business will be dropped and 'business methods' also. In this bill I fear there has been too much of business methods." [7]

The "business methods" to which Senator Money objected and which Root advocated were, as a matter of fact, the tactics of Senator Aldrich in driving through the tariff bill without giving its opponents adequate opportunity for debate. A few years later, when Root was in the Republican minority, he objected to like tactics on the part of the Democratic leaders and learned the value of the filibuster. Aside from the merits of any particular bill, however, Root did feel strongly about the inefficient procedure of the Senate and spoke on this subject two years later with more assurance and effect when a resolution was introduced for changing the procedure. He observed that the Senate "has gradually fallen into bad habits . . . substituting mere wrangling for serious debate." [8]

During his first four years as Senator, Root naturally gave general support to the Taft policies. Elbert F. Baldwin of the *Outlook* wrote to him on June 29th, 1909, to ask if they would be correct in describing him, as the *Journal of Commerce* did, as the "chief exponent of the Taft policies on the floor of the Senate." Root replied on the following day:

I should not like to describe myself as the "chief exponent" of Mr. Taft's policies on the floor of the Senate. I am rather too young a Senator to be a "chief" anything in that body, and I have no doubt that if the President were compelled to make the kind of choice which is implied in the use of a superlative he would go to some more experienced legislator. Of course, long association and friendship and habits of consultation between the President [sic] result almost inevitably in our discussing the question of policies and in my supporting, in the Senate, measures and views about which I have already been consulted. Added to this is a

[7] *Ibid.*, p. 2045.
[8] *Congressional Record*, 62nd Cong., 1st Sess., Vol. 47, p. 2921.

very strong desire on my part to make President Taft's administration successful, both on grounds of personal friendship, and
party and public interest. I think the Journal of Commerce's description is fair enough except for the "chief" part.

Taft did consult him frequently and Root always volunteered suggestions when he thought it advisable, but he was well aware that the
irritation and enmity of his fellow senators would be aroused if he set
himself up as the President's spokesman and the one closest to the
White House.[9] For himself, he cared little about capitalizing his friendship with the President. Unlike Lodge and most of the other Senators,
he was wholly unconcerned about building up a personal machine for
his own support. Questions of patronage bored him although he recognized his obligation to deal with them, as he had stated to the New
York legislators in accepting the Senatorship. In general he was content to heed suggestions from men like Herbert Parsons or William
Barnes or to endorse to the White House recommendations made by
the congressmen from New York, taking an active part only where
there was a quarrel between various factions in the state. On occasion
he advanced the claims of persons whom he knew well. His theory in
such cases is explained in a letter which he wrote on January 9th, 1909,
to Governor Hughes in reply to the latter's explanation why he did
not appoint a certain man whom Root had endorsed. It was the same
point of view which Root had expressed in his Cabinet days to his
brother Oren, namely, that a man was entitled to have the good opinion of his friends and neighbors brought to the attention of appointing
officers.

The people who respond to such a call to testify about the candidate, however, have only one candidate in mind and their statements are positive and not comparative. The only one who can
take a comparative view of different candidates is the appointing
power, and to question the correctness of the appointing officer's
judgment upon such a comparison upon a knowledge of only one
of the many candidates whom he has to compare would be absurd.
I think that the tendency to be angry with an appointing officer because he does not make the particular appointment that
one has recommended results entirely from the other view of the
subject, which is, that appointments are to be made because

[9] Charles D. Hilles to the author, October 19, 1933.

somebody wants them, and not upon their merits at all. If that view is accepted, of course, a failure to make an appointment that is wanted is naturally regarded as very disobliging. It is needless for me to say that I do not take that view. . . .

It was a similar point of view which inspired a letter he wrote to Taft on June 20th, 1908, shortly after the convention at which Taft was nominated. Taft had written him about the trouble he was having in choosing a chairman of the Republican National Committee; Root replied:

I am troubled by something you said about claims of friendship and past service in the choice of Chairman. There is no reality in the friendship that presses such claims. Such considerations should have no weight. The time has not come for distributing honors, or for gratifying your friends' wishes or even your own wishes. You are simply leading in a hard and doubtful fight, and it is your duty to the party which has nominated you to select the most efficient instrument possible in order to win, no matter what disappointment you may cause or how much you may dislike to cause it. Any true friend of yours will recognize this. . . .

In October, 1910, Root wrote to President Taft about the difficult political situation in Oneida County with the Sherman forces fighting Stimson and Davenport. He reported that a number of the postmasters who controlled the local organizations felt that they owed their appointments to Sherman and were helping him. "Now I don't demand that any postmaster shall use his position or influence politically, or that any man shall act against his convictions; but when a man has been appointed postmaster as a Republican, and has taken control of the Republican politics of his town, I do object to his using the power and influence which is thus put in his hands against the Republican ticket, and I shall never consent to the reappointment of a man who does that, nor I assume, would you reappoint such a man. . . . I should be glad to see every blooming office holder let politics entirely alone, but if they are going to be permitted to take part and to have political power because they hold office, they certainly should not use that power against the party that gave it to them." Taft replied expressing full agreement and saying that he would follow Root's suggestions to remedy the situation. Root's continuing attitude on the subject of patronage is apparent from a few bits of his correspondence:

To Secretary of the Treasury Mac Veagh, June 10th, 1911:

Far be it from me to interfere with a transfer in the service which involves no appointment of any New Yorker to office. Inasmuch as there seems to be no New Yorker available for scientific melting and refining, the less I have to do with the Assay Office the better. It is too near Wall Street. It burns incense before the money power. Its acid fumes asphyxiate the free and the brave.

To "Jim" Sherman, November 11th, 1911:

If you have a man for Marshal he ought to demonstrate his ability to conduct the Marshal's business successfully. How would it do for us each to designate a man whom we wish to have arrested and hung and see how he does it? Incidentally, what is his name? I will never give my consent to the appointment as United States Marshal in any district of New York, of a man who is unwilling to reveal his name! . . .

From President Taft, August 20th, 1912:

I am greatly amused that you should be in the dark about the appointment of an appraiser in New York when everybody else connected with it—opposed to it and in favor of it—was fully advised.

Originally there was a perfect candidate selected by the Secretary of the Treasury—one who had all that fitness for the place that makes a true reformer feel that he has made a find—but Mr. William Barnes Jr., and Mr. Samuel Koenig, with a knowledge of practical politics, read the Secretary a lecture and me a lecture on the subject of the recognition of the organization; and so after conferring with Secretary Stimson we mildly yielded to the lesson in politics which these masters taught us.

The truth is you are not anything but a fly on the wheel. Your only business is to secure the confirmation of a man whom statesmen have selected.

I hope you got my box of cigars, and that it, with its contents, have reconciled you to this impertinence, Oh Athos!

Faithfully yours,
Porthos [10]

[10] Taft Papers, Library of Congress.

Root's most active period in patronage matters was in the early days of his senatorship when the Taft Administration was coming in and many appointments had to be made. Thereafter his interest steadily diminished. On army promotions and consular appointments he adhered to the position which he had taken in the War and State Departments. He also consistently refused to be a party to any move which would introduce political influence into the courts. In the spring of 1912 he was gathering support for a state bill which originated in the New York State Bar Association and which provided for putting the names of judicial candidates in a separate column and not in any party column. He persuaded the Republican State Convention in that year to endorse that plan. To Ansley Wilcox of Buffalo he wrote on October 4th, 1912, that the Progressives had opposed adoption of that plank: "This is a queer world. Here we have been striving for years to get the judges out of politics. We were under the impression that we were urging a reform. . . . Lo, there arise new prophets who preach a counter reform consisting of putting judges into politics and putting politics into judges. . . . It is evident, my dear Wilcox, that you are an accursed reactionary, an enemy of reform, and a foe to the rule of the people."

Root's refusals to back particular candidates were always politely framed, appealing to the reason of the person asking the favor—the same procedure which he had first developed when bombarded by similar requests in the War Department. He had a series of stock excuses; he could not interfere with his successors' conduct of their positions in the War and State Departments; he could not intervene between Republican factions in New York (although at times he did in order to restore party unity); and, after the Democratic administration came in on March 4th, 1913, it was useless for him as a senator in the opposition party to make any recommendations. On April 8th, 1913, he replied to Senator John D. Works who asked his help to prevent the discharge of one of the pages in the Senate: "I have . . . little knowledge and no skill regarding matters of patronage."

Root was sworn in on March 4th, 1909, and became the junior senator from New York with the veteran Chauncey M. Depew as his colleague and senior from the Empire State in the Sixty-first Congress. After Depew's retirement in 1911, Root wrote to him: "Your account of the Garden of Eden in which you live by reason of meritorious age is so attractive that I shall hustle to get into it." [11] Root found the Republicans in full control with a majority of 61 to 32 in the Senate and 219 to 172 in the House. After the two formal days of the opening session, they were reconvened in extra session on March 15th to "give immediate consideration to the revision of the Dingley Tariff Act," as President Taft told them in his message of the following day and as the Republican platform on which Taft was elected had proposed.

Root had strongly urged upon Roosevelt in a letter of November 16th, 1904, the necessity for the Republican Party's taking a stand for tariff revision, though he adhered to the Republican slogan that tariffs "should be revised by friends of the protective system." Root reported that he had found in talking with people in all sections of the country that there was "a widespread conviction that in many respects the present tariff is too high."

> This conviction is being constantly strengthened by the manufacturers themselves, who do not hesitate to say in private conversation that the present rates of duty are wholly unnecessary to protect their respective industries; many men in the steel industry, in the glass industry, in the shoe industry, and in many others have made these statements in my hearing. An impression circulated in that way gradually permeates the entire mind of the people. There is also a strong impression that the sale of American manufactured products abroad at prices much lower than the home prices has reached an extent which cannot be explained on the theory that it is merely accidental or incidental or occasional, or is simply a disposition of a surplus. There is also an impression, which is undeniably gaining ground, that in many directions the excessive duties enable combinations of great manufacturers to exact higher prices than are reasonable in view of cost and risk of production.
>
> These views are not likely to disappear of themselves; they are likely to grow stronger and more widespread, and if four years from now we undertake to say over again what we have been saying this year, it seems quite certain that the people of the country will conclude that Mr. Cleveland was right in saying, as he has said in substance, that it is useless to talk about the tariff being revised by the friends of protection because the friends of protection never will revise it. We would then have a perfectly false is-

[11] Chauncey M. Depew Papers.

sue, in which the principle of protection would stand a strong chance of being borne down not upon its own merits, but upon the demerits of certain unfair and perverted applications of the principle. Nothing could be more unfortunate for our protective system. We would go into such a campaign, moreover, not with the record of efficiency and competency upon which we have stood this year, but with a record of irresolution and incapacity to deal with a great and vital governmental question.

But Roosevelt dodged the issue. He had made vague reference to it in a speech at Minneapolis on April 4th, 1903, by using part of a speech by Root. He told Root frankly that he did not intend to get caught in the meshes of a tariff row.[12] Throughout his second term, with more political skill than courage, Roosevelt listened to the voice of "Uncle Joe" Cannon, the Speaker of the House, whose practical political philosophy was summarized in the queries: "Whence comes this so-called demand for tariff tinkering? Aren't all our fellows happy?" [13]

In discussing the development of trade with South America, Root, in his address before the Trans-Mississippi Commercial Congress at Kansas City on November 20th, 1906, had come out flatly in favor of a maximum and minimum tariff.[14]

> A single straight-out tariff was all very well in the world of single straight-out tariffs; but we have passed on, during the course of years, into a world for the most part of maximum and minimum tariffs, and with our single-rate tariff we are left with very little opportunity to reciprocate good treatment from other countries in their tariffs and very little opportunity to defend ourselves against bad treatment.

This principle was favored in the Republican platform of 1908 and Root had an opportunity to support it in the debates, drawing on his experience as Secretary of State to suggest the phraseology best adapted to facilitating its application in practical diplomacy.[15] He urged that maximum rates be set with power to reduce them as a reward for countries which removed discriminations against the United States. Congress took the opposite road, establishing minimum rates with

---

[12] Root to the author, December 20, 1936.
[13] Pringle, *Theodore Roosevelt*, p. 414. Cf. Busbey, *Uncle Joe Cannon*, p. 207.
[14] *Latin American Addresses*, p. 277.
[15] *Congressional Record*, 61st Cong., 1st Sess., Vol. 44, pp. 4093–4.

power to apply a maximum as a punishment for countries which discriminated against us. In discussing the practical effect of administrative features of the act and the need for keeping down the tariff on precious stones to discourage the easy smuggling of them, Root also drew on his experience of over twenty-five years before when, as District Attorney in New York, he prosecuted infractions of the customs law.

Legislative tariff-making in the United States is efficient only in the sense that it affords abundant opportunity for politicians to juggle with particular rates and schedules in such a way as to curry favor with their constituents. Root always thought it was "the most unsatisfactory way of doing things I ever saw. It is the same position you get in sometimes in the trial of a case. You feel that a witness is holding back something, that something is wrong, but you haven't enough knowledge of the background to put your finger on it. When the manufacturers came down for the tariff hearings, I didn't have enough knowledge of their business to be able to cross examine them intelligently. No one there could be in a position to, or if he was, he probably didn't want to use his knowledge in that way." [16]

On June 4th, 1926, he replied to a letter from Robert S. Brookings about the debate on the tariff then current: "The courageous assault on the wool schedule appeals to my sense of humor, as I have been through the making of one tariff on wool and I know of no controversies so fatal to true Christian spirit except those about religion. Undoubtedly some faction of the wool manufacturers of America will presently prove to their entire satisfaction that you murdered your grandmother and that Mr. Smith is the regular bootlegger of the carded wool manufacturers. I regard him as a reincarnation of the early martyrs. He will probably be burned at the stake, but it will be worth while, for it really is a useful thing to have the tariff on wool studied thoroughly and impartially by somebody who is not obliged to count up the votes necessary to passing a tariff bill."

Root was heartily in favor of the provision in the Payne-Aldrich tariff bill which provided for the establishment of a tariff board to advise the President. Indeed, he drafted the sentence in President Taft's Message which had stressed the need for putting the method of tariff revision out of the old slough of log-rolling onto a basis of facts scientifically

[16] Root to the author, September 17, 1931.

ascertained.[17] This was one of the few redeeming features of the Payne-Aldrich tariff which was an outstanding factor in weakening the Taft Administration at its outset. The fight in the Senate early developed into a struggle between the stand-pat Republicans led by Nelson W. Aldrich of Rhode Island and the progressive Republican group which included men like La Follette of Wisconsin, Dolliver and Cummins of Iowa, Beveridge of Indiana and Bristow of Kansas. It was this tariff fight which first brought the Progressive group together.[18] Taft's eventual alignment with the former group was one of the factors contributing to his later breach with Roosevelt.

The bill, as required by the Constitution, originated in the House under the hands of Congressman Sereno E. Payne of New York as Chairman of the Ways and Means Committee. With their well-organized majority under the strong and skillful hand of the Speaker, Uncle Joe Cannon, the bill went smoothly through the House and was passed on April 9th by a vote of 217 to 161. In the Senate, Aldrich reported out of the Finance Committee an amended bill which completely reversed the slightly downward trend of the House bill and substituted rates which registered some six hundred increases over it. The standpatters like Hale of Maine, blandly insisted that the Republican platform had declared merely for revision and not for revision downward. But Taft during the campaign had clearly come out for a reduction in rates and of these promises the insurgent Republicans made full use.[19] Root in general stood with the regulars, defended Aldrich and his committee against the assaults of the Progressives and voted with the former on most of the schedules. Out of the 128 roll calls on the tariff bill, he voted against Aldrich seven times, with him 104 times and did not vote eighteen times.

Early in the debates he was guilty of some highly technical hairsplitting arguments which did not impress the Senate and were not much to his credit. But as the debate developed, he showed his mental powers and the result of a life-long habit of work, by mastering the facts and statistics bearing upon particular schedules in which he was interested. The bill had been put into the Senate without any explanatory or supporting statement by Aldrich's Committee, and Aldrich, in

[17] Diary of Henry L. Stimson, entries of 1911–1913.
[18] La Follette, Autobiography, p. 436.
[19] Sullivan, Our Times, Vol. IV, p. 364–365.

an attempt to drive the bill through, forced the Senate to sit from ten in the morning to eleven at night, day after day through the grueling heat of the Washington summer. The Progressives met the challenge by working far into the small hours of the morning, arming themselves with arguments which Aldrich, despite his great skill in tariff-making, was powerless to meet. Root was equally industrious; his arguments revealed a familiarity with the industry or business involved in particular schedules which made him invulnerable to attack. The interests which he sought to protect were naturally those of his New York constituents and among them in many instances, as Senator Elkins of Ohio remarked, "one could not fail to detect, running like a silver thread through the woof of his argument, the importers' interest." [20] This was perhaps most obviously true in the prolonged debate in which Root opposed the desire of the California citrus fruit growers to increase the duties on lemons which, Root remarked, "contribute very largely to innocent and healthful enjoyment among the people of my state, and pass by delivery, being an important means of expression." [21] In two instances he supported larger interests with which he was peculiarly well acquainted, as when he made a strong plea in behalf of our obligation to the Philippines which he thought would be violated by the proposed duty on Philippine cigars, although in this he opposed the views of the New York cigar manufacturers. In this instance, Root and La Follette were in accord. Again he argued the case of Cuba in objecting to the proposed duty on pineapples; he was thanked for this argument in a resolution adopted by the Cuban Senate. His broader interest was also indicated by his arguments, which won some converts, in favor of the free admission of works of art, which, he pointed out, in so many cases find their way at last into the museums and there serve the cultural interests of all the people. He again spoke in favor of free entry of books and works of art when the Underwood tariff was being debated in 1913. In two instances he received informal personal appeals from the ambassadors of France and Germany to avoid serious injury to their trade. In a letter of July 22nd, 1909, to Chairman Payne of the House Ways and Means Committee, he urged the adoption of two changes which were proposed by the Conference Committee and which, Root thought, might lessen the chances of retaliatory tariffs in

[20] *Congressional Record*, 61st Cong., 1st Sess., Vol. 44, p. 3389.
[21] *Ibid.*, p. 2561.

Europe and of a tariff war.

Root's skill was welcome to Aldrich in some tight corners although the former declined to get involved in the debate on schedules which did not concern New York or some general interest which appealed to him. Senator Rayner (Democrat) of Maryland, in a speech brilliant with sarcasm, described Root's situation in the mighty citadel of protection. He told how La Follette had launched an attack on Senator Aldrich of Rhode Island.

> The great ex-Secretary of State, whose presence is an honor to this body and who has filled with such high distinction every service into which his country has called him, was figuring and writing. The Senator seems to be always figuring and writing. The Senator from Rhode Island was looking toward him. Now, it must be understood that the Senator from New York is not within the citadel. He has a little citadel of his own, and between his citadel and the main stronghold, upon the upper floor of which his client, the Senator from Rhode Island, is located, there is a wireless system of telegraphy, and whenever the Senator from Rhode Island is in imminent danger and peril there comes a hieroglyphic message from the Senator from New York—"Hold the fort, for I am coming." [22]

Although Root found the whole legislative process on the tariff unsatisfactory, he did not feel that the bill was entirely bad. In general, he acquiesced in and defended the Aldrich bill, without attempting to fight for the reductions to which the party was pledged and in which he believed. On April 3rd, 1909, he wrote to Ambassador Whitelaw Reid: "We are having a dreadful time now about the tariff. Publication of the Payne bill woke up all the producers of the country and a bigger army than Henry Watson ever dreamed of moved immediately on Washington to insist on full protection and an increase of duty for their own products and heroic reduction upon the products of every one else, while all the importers and the foreign representatives here are on the verge of insanity over the increases that are included in the bill. . . ." And again on May 29th: "We are having a very tedious and dreadful time here over the tariff. . . . It will not be as low on many of the schedules as I should like to see it, and I think there could be a good many more reductions made without substantial

[22] *Ibid.*, p. 2579.

injury, but the Committees do not think so and if we are to have any tariff bill at all the conclusions of the Committees must, I suppose, be followed in the main. The great obstacle to securing reductions arises from the fact that most of the men who are earnestly advocating them are as earnestly insisting upon retaining or increasing the Dingley duties on the products in which their own states are interested. A few days ago the senators from the Northern Middle west voted for free lumber, and not only a majority of the Republicans but a majority of the Democrats in the Senate voted against it. Today the Democrats voted with the New York senators against increasing the duty on Barley, but substantially all the senators from the Northern Middle west voted in favor of it, and so it goes. Still I think the result will be a pretty fair bill."

The bill was finally passed by the Senate on July 8th, 1909, by a vote of 45 to 34; Root would have voted "yea," but was paired. It went into the usual conference committee of the two houses and at last Taft got into action. He had been sitting on the fence, trying to keep on good terms with both the progressives and the standpatters, but he was ill at ease. He wrote to Mrs. Taft on the day of the Senate vote: "Root thinks Aldrich will make a good bill on the tariff but I dont know. If I had more technical knowledge I should feel more confident. However, I shall have to struggle along with the assistance of such experts as I can find." [23] It was not until the bill had gone to conference that he made any determined effort and then his stand was confined to a few items such as the rates on lumber and gloves. He made futile attempts to attack the most reprehensible schedule of all, Schedule K, which dealt with wool. When the conferees finally agreed on the minutiae he smiled happily at his victory.[24] It was an empty victory; the country in general thought the bill a repudiation of campaign promises for revision downward and took their revenge by destroying the Republican majorities in Congress in the election of 1910. As a matter of fact, the increases in the tariff were not great but neither were the decreases; it brought about no essential change.[25]

In the tariff discussions of subsequent years, Root "passed the buck" to the electorate. On August 14th, 1911, he wrote to a constituent that he sympathized with his views about the tariff but the condition of

[23] Taft Papers, Library of Congress.
[24] Butt, Taft and Roosevelt, The Intimate Letters of Archie Butt, Vol. I, p. 163–164.
[25] Taussig, Tariff History of the United States, p. 407.

things in Congress was "the legitimate and logical consequence of the action of the people at the last elections which put the House of Representatives and practically, the Senate in the control of the Democratic Party . . . nothing but the President's veto power stands between the country and a complete repudiation of the protective system in favor of a tariff for revenue only." Then the people threw out the Republican control entirely and put President Wilson in the White House. On July 21st, 1913, Root wrote to another constituent interested in a protective duty on carpets: "Your trouble in securing a just measure of protection for your product resulted primarily from the fact that by the last election the power was put into the hands of the Democratic party to make a tariff under a platform which declared in the most positive terms hostility to the protective system. The Democratic party has accordingly framed a tariff which was not intended to be protective, and no appeal to them to protect any industry has really been of any avail. . . . Such discussion as there may be in the Senate will be designed to point out to the people of the country the defects and errors of the bill, but it is perfectly understood that it will have no effect whatever upon the action of the Senate." He seems to have been rather amused by the troubles of the Democratic leaders, writing to Mrs. Root that "some of their Senators who come from States with protected industries . . . are between the devil & the deep sea. Wilson being the devil who will roast them if they don't vote for the bill and the deep sea being their constituents who will drown them if they do vote for it." The Underwood Tariff of 1913 was duly passed by an almost complete party division with substantial but not devastating reductions.

Root stated his views about the propriety of representations by interested persons regarding tariff and other bills in his testimony before a subcommittee of the Senate Judiciary Committee investigating lobbies in June, 1913; the hearings were the result of President Wilson's desire to investigate particularly the sugar lobby. Root stated that he knew of nothing in Washington that he would call a lobby and that he had never had anyone improperly try to influence his vote. He described the people who had come to see him on the tariff bill and the nature of their conversations. "My feeling has always been," he told the Committee, "that the people of my state are entitled to come and tell me how any piece of legislation which is proposed affects their business and I think it is my duty to listen to them, and I do not think they are subject to be stigmatized as lobbyists when they do it . . . certainly it is my duty to listen to them, and if it is my duty to listen to them there is nothing wrong in their coming."

Just as Taft's insistence upon the passage of a tariff law had kept Root and his fellow senators in Washington through the summer months of 1909, so the President's insistence upon the conclusion of a reciprocity agreement with Canada kept them there again in the summer of 1911. On January 7th, 1911, Knox's negotiations resulted in the signing of a reciprocity agreement which placed more than one hundred articles on the free list and reduced the tariff on some four hundred more. Although Taft had hoped that this measure would appeal to the insurgent group, there was an immediate and loud opposition from the agricultural sections of the country, including the northwest, and with that opposition the insurgents fell in line. Agricultural interests in the east were similarly opposed but the industrial sections were favorable to a measure which promised wider markets for their products. Under strict control, the House, on February 14th, passed the bill designed to make the agreement effective, but despite Taft's efforts, the Senate took no action before the close of the session on March 4th. Before the adjournment, Senator Smoot urged upon Taft the political expediency of letting the question be raised and defeated at that session. Taft was adamant, insisting on his principle and refusing to sacrifice it for political expediency. Root agreed with Smoot that a vote forced before adjournment would not be a vote on the merits but that many Senators would vote merely to avoid being called in an extra session.[26] Taft proceeded to carry out his threat and called the new congress in special session on April 4th.

Root's first move on this question was to introduce in the Senate Finance Committee an amendment which was widely misunderstood and which called down upon his head the indignant wrath of most of the newspapers of the country. The House had amended the original bill so as to make a special provision for the free admission of wood pulp and cheap paper known as newsprint, regardless of any reciprocal concessions being made by Canada. Root's amendment would have made the bill reconform to the reciprocity agreement by making the concession on these articles dependent upon like concessions from

[26] Undated memorandum of conversation in Taft Papers, Library of Congress.

"In the Deep Grass"

(A cartoon in the New York *Herald*, May 27, 1911)

Canada. As Root warned the Senate, the concession thus given Canada without reciprocity would let in pulp and paper from other countries on the basis of the most-favored-nation clause in our commercial treaties. This prophecy was fulfilled within six months.[27] The newspapers, however, reported that he was opposed to the whole reciprocity agreement and was trying to kill it by amendments. "The newspapers are so crazy about getting cheaper paper," Root wrote to Henry L. Stimson on February 23rd, 1911, "that they can't report anything about this measure correctly." If his amendment were beaten in the committee, Root wrote to Robert Bacon on June 7th, "it will not be for the sake of reciprocity but through fear of the newspapers, who want not reciprocity, but free pulp and paper without any reciprocity." According to Walter Lippmann, the Philadelphia North American was one of the few papers that were not swayed by self-interest in this matter.[28] Even the President joined in opposing the Root amendment, which added strength to the newspaper charges. But Taft's opposition, as Root told Bacon, was due to his fear that any amendment, even one which he admitted brought the bill into conformity with the agreement, would injure the chance of passage of the bill as a whole. Root lost his amendment and the bill passed the Senate on July 22nd by 53 votes to 27, with twelve regular Republicans and twelve Insurgents voting with three Democrats in the minority. The section of the act relating to wood pulp and paper, was repealed by the Tariff Act of 1913.

Root's speech on the measure came on June 21st. He referred to the fact that he had been deluged with letters of opposition from the farmers of New York State and even from the pulp and paper manufacturers who did not seem to realize that he was fighting their cause against the newspapers. Root's files contain an analysis of the communications he had received on the subject, showing that while many of those in opposition were printed on form petitions, yet there was an overwhelming sentiment against the reciprocity agreement as a whole. He argued that the farming interests of the country would not suffer nearly as much as they anticipated. He caused some surprise by asserting that the protective tariff had never been of much direct benefit to the agricultural interests but went on to say that no tariff schedule

[27] The Outlook, January 13, 1912, pp. 56–57.
[28] Everybody's Magazine, Vol. 26 (1912), p. 243. Cf. "Reciprocity" of William H. Taft, written and privately published by Albert H. Walker (1912).

ought to be passed or allowed to stand merely because it favored a particular interest. He did not believe that tariffs should be made on the principle of swapping concessions from different parts of the country. He believed in the protective tariff system as of benefit to the entire country. He recognized that the elections of 1910, which had so changed the political complexion of Congress, showed that the people were dissatisfied with the Payne-Aldrich tariff and he drew from that fact the inference that there was bound to be sooner or later a general revision. He doubted whether the people in their existing mood would stand for a tariff policy which would raise the cost of their foodstuffs and he admitted in the course of questions addressed to him that there would probably be a demand for reductions in tariff which would lower the cost of clothing and other commodities. The Democratic senators who tried to heckle and corner him got little satisfaction, since Root was quite ready to admit that some schedules might be too high and should be changed. Root favored the reciprocity agreement in general because it was in line with the policy which he had sought to further when he was Secretary of State, namely, that of drawing Canada and the United States closer together. He inserted, however, an emphatic caveat against the idea that the reciprocity measure was animated by any idea of annexation which he vigorously disapproved. It was on this rock, however, that this pet measure of the Taft administration fell, because of an accidental blunder of the President himself. The Hearst papers had been favoring reciprocity and Taft wrote to Hearst after the bill passed, thanking him for his support in spreading "the gospel of reciprocity." The Hearst papers, however, had also long been known in Canada as proponents of annexation. The opponents of reciprocity in Canada immediately proceeded to make capital of Taft's endorsement of Hearst's support and on that cry defeated the agreement in Canada.[29]

Root's stand on the reciprocity question showed independence. He never minded newspaper attacks but here he withstood the opposition of the great agricultural districts of upper New York where the Republican Party found its chief strength. In his letter to Bacon, Root admitted that this was "pretty serious" and he found it "very distressing

[29] Sullivan, op. cit., Vol. IV, pp. 399–400. Cf. Callahan, American Foreign Policy in Canadian Relations, p. 528.

to have pretty nearly all of my constituents in Northern New York think I am sacrificing their interests," but he believed they exaggerated the injury which would result and in any case "a great policy ought not to be prevented by the apprehension of small injuries."

CHAPTER XXXVII

"To protect the American democracy against itself"

INVOLVED in the tariff debate of 1909 were the questions of a two per cent tax on corporate incomes and a proposal for a constitutional amendment authorizing an income tax. These measures, favored by the progressive group, were recommended by Taft in a message of June 16th, 1909. Root took an active part in drafting these proposals and was the chief exponent of the corporation tax on the floor of the Senate. His principal speech on this subject was delivered on July 1st. He opposed the passage of a provision laying a tax upon individual incomes because he believed that it was clearly unconstitutional under the prior decisions of the Supreme Court. He did not wish to have the Legislature put the Supreme Court into the position of having to yield to or to stand out against a public campaign for such a measure. His statement makes interesting reading in the light of the struggle twenty-eight years later between President Franklin D. Roosevelt and the Supreme Court:

> If they [the Supreme Court] yield, what then? Where then would be the confidence of our people in the justice of their judgment? If they refuse to yield, what then? A breach between the two parts of our Government, with popular acclaim behind the popular branch, all setting against the independence, the dignity, the respect, the sacredness of that great tribunal whose function in our system of government has made us unlike any republic that ever existed in the world.[1]

Root cited the recommendations of President Taft and stated that he fully agreed with his judgment that a corporation tax was preferable at that time to a general income tax.

> I do not care to play with words. Gentlemen may say that I am for the corporation tax to beat the income tax. I care not. I am for the corporation tax because I think it is better policy, better

[1] *Congressional Record*, 61st Cong., 1st Sess., Vol. 44, p. 4003.

patriotism, higher wisdom than the general income tax at this time and under these circumstances. I wish to beat the income tax provision because I think it is unwise, and I wish to pass the corporation tax provision because I think it is wise.

Perhaps in these remarks, Root had in mind the speech of Senator Bailey of Texas who, in discussing the personal income tax measure on May 4th, had referred to Root as earning $150,000 a year in his profession.[2]

Root, analyzing the measure in detail, reviewed the decisions of the Supreme Court and cited the experience of Great Britain with similar taxation. He was opposed to the invasion of privacy and the inconvenience which would be caused by filing in Washington all of the data relative to personal incomes, subject to the inquisitorial powers which the government officials would have to check upon the reports. On the other hand, he welcomed the fact that the corporation tax would make available to the government a great mass of information in regard to corporate activity which he believed would be of great value to Congress in future legislation. He stated that a great majority of the corporations affected were engaged in interstate commerce and that the information thus to be made available would enable Congress to legislate much more intelligently with regard to the control of interstate commerce. He pointed out also, that in making tariff laws, the pleas of business men for increased protection were based on the allegation that they needed higher tariffs to enable them to do business profitably. The information secured through the tax returns would give Congress for the first time adequate data on which to base an estimate of the soundness of such contentions. In regard to the individual income taxes, if such a bill were to be considered, he advocated lowering the exemption limit below the suggested minimum of $5,000 with a mounting scale depending upon the size of the income because he believed that those having even a small income should bear some share. He believed that earned incomes of the worker and the farmer and the professional man should not be taxed as heavily as income from invested capital wealth. He objected to the theory and to the practical result which would assess upon the East, with its accumulations of wealth, a disproportionate share of taxation which might be expended through action of Congress in parts of the country

[2] Ibid., p. 1702.

which were practically exempt from that taxation. Yet he later argued in favor of the income tax amendment to the Constitution despite the fact that the tax would bear most heavily on New York. While he was thus opposed to the personal income tax bill, he favored the passage of a resolution submitting a constitutional amendment giving the United States authority to impose such a tax because he thought "the United States ought to have the power to lay and collect an income tax. . . . I do want my country to have all the powers that any country in the world has to summon every dollar of the public wealth to its support if ever the time of sore need comes upon it. I shall vote for the income tax amendment, and I shall advocate it in my State. . . ." [3]

Root fulfilled this promise in a letter to New York State Senator Frederick M. Davenport on February 17th, 1910.[4] He regretted having to differ with Governor Hughes who had opposed the amendment in a special message to the New York Legislature on January 5th, 1910. In a covering letter of the same date, he explained that he had not discussed the economic side of the subject because he understood that Davenport would deal with that aspect. Root did deal with what had been his own argument that a very large part of the income tax would be paid by citizens of New York. "That is undoubtedly true, but there is all the more reason why our legislature should take special care to exclude every narrow and selfish motive from influence upon its action. . . ." New Yorkers would pay a large share because New York City had become the chief financial and commercial center of the country; wealth accumulated from all parts of the country was represented by those who had been drawn to live there. "We have the wealth because behind the city stands the country. We ought to be willing to share the burdens of the National Government in the same proportion in which we share its benefits." Despite this statement, Root apparently did not fully realize the sound bases in economics and equity for an income tax. He retained the idea that the advocates of the income tax were inspired by "hatred of wealth." "What these people want to do," he wrote to Mrs. Hay on April 21st, 1913, "is to take away the money of the rich, classifying as rich all who have over four thousand dollars a year, and then to pass laws distributing it among the people at home in such a way that they can get some of it." On May 2nd, 1911,

---

[3] *Ibid.*, p. 4006.
[4] Later printed as Sen. Doc. No. 398, 61st Cong., 2d Sess.

Root answered a letter from Joseph H. Choate who was a vigorous opponent of the income tax amendment: "If I had foreseen two years ago," Root wrote, "the extent to which the people in the West were going in the direction of repudiating our constitutional system of government I think I should . . . probably have said that it was better to stand pat on the constitution as it was and to defer any amendment whatever until the craze for radical changes had passed over." But he had "always thought that the National Government ought to have the power to levy an income tax for use in case of emergency" and he still believed the amendment should be approved.

Root was scornful of the lack of sense and skill shown in the drafting of the income tax law after the Sixteenth Amendment was adopted. To an old friend, Ben Johnson, who wrote complaining of its intricacies, he answered in November, 1913: "I guess you will have to go to jail. If that is the result of not understanding the Income Tax law I shall meet you there. We will have a merry, merry time, for all of our friends will be there. It will be an intellectual center, for no one understands the Income Tax law except persons who have not sufficient intelligence to understand the questions that arise under it. . . . The real trouble with the law is that it was drawn by men [i. e. the Democratic majority in Congress] who did not understand American ways of doing business."

The corporation tax speech in the Senate was Root's best effort in this his first session. It was a temperate speech, well reasoned and forceful. Its conclusion was followed by a great deal of questioning concerning the meaning of particular phrases in the corporation tax provision and its effect, with all of which Root dealt in a definitive way. The corporation tax was passed as was the proposal to amend the Constitution. President Taft commented to Archie Butt on the surprise expressed in some of the papers that Root should favor the corporation tax:

The fact is that while neither Root nor I ever got the credit for being the progressive members of the last Cabinet, we were the most progressive and the two who usually aided and abetted President Roosevelt in what were called his radical policies.[5]

[5] Butt, Taft and Roosevelt, The Intimate Letters of Archie Butt, Vol. II, p. 128.

Taft had therefore counted on Root to support this measure and "his aid had been invaluable."

If Root had been merely the tool of Wall Street, as Hearst and Pulitzer would have had people believe, he would hardly have supported the corporation tax. His mail was filled with protests from business men; they read like the protests and denunciations which came from the same sources some twenty-five years later when the policies of the New Deal were being enacted into law. The corporation tax, Root was told, would discourage private initiative and kill the profit motive. It would stifle business just recovering from the panic of 1907. It would mean a vast army of clerks prying into the business of every corporation. It was "an assault on corporate business under the guise of an excise tax." Building loan and savings associations wrote him against the bill; banks and trust companies objected; individuals and business groups protested. To most of these complaints, Root sent form replies; a few he answered in detail. The cynical may say that Root was merely wiser than the business men who protested in that he knew the corporation tax was the least of several possible evils. Such a point of view can be read into his letter of June 26th, 1909, to Charles F. Mathewson:

> I have no doubt that the Corporation provision is unpopular among all the people whom it will subject to taxation. I never knew a tax measure which was not open to that objection, nor did I ever know one which was not open to the objection also that it works inequality in some cases. In laying a tax which is not universal the line must be drawn somewhere between those who are to be subject to the tax and those who are not to be subject to the tax, and wherever the line is there will be inequalities as between those on one side and those on the other. A fact which does not seem to be generally appreciated is that a majority of the Senate is ready to vote for a general Income tax which includes a tax on corporations, a tax on inheritances treated as income, as well as a tax on individual incomes. A provision imposing such a tax is pending in the Senate and a majority of the Senate stands pledged to its support. The provisions which it contains for inquisitorial proceedings into the affairs of corporations as well as into the affairs of individuals are exceedingly drastic and injurious. If this Income tax measure is passed by the Senate it will undoubtedly be accepted by the House. It is probable that the more mod-

"INCOME TAX"

"SENATOR ROOT PLEADS FOR OUR ALREADY OVERTAXED RICH"

(A cartoon in *Life*, June 10, 1909)

erate measure which provides for a tax covering the incomes of corporations, as an excise tax, will be accepted by a majority of the Senate as a substitute for the General Income tax provision. The question is between these two, not between the Corporation tax and no tax, or between a Corporation tax and a Stamp tax. A Stamp tax would be wholly inadequate and ineffective and would receive practically no support. . . .

It may be that this legislative situation was foreseen when Root helped the Administration draft the bill, but on an examination of all the record, it appears that both Taft and Root, as the former indicated to Butt, were sincerely in favor of the measure on its merits and that these other aspects were subsequently cited by Root in defense of an Administration measure which he naturally did not wish to be a source of opposition to Taft or to the party. John A. Sleicher, editor of *Leslie's Magazine*, tried to persuade Root just after Congress adjourned to write an article on the new law. Root replied from Clinton on August 13th, 1909: "It was tedious and disgusting enough to be kept in Washington until the 6th of August by the Tariff bill without adding the burden of writing articles about it afterwards. Wild horses and teams of oxen could not draw me into writing such an article about the Corporation tax as you propose. I am building a new barn, which is much more interesting."

When Congress reconvened in regular session on December 6th, 1909, the Administration had decided that the revision of the interstate commerce and anti-trust laws should be the principal task before it. Railroad regulation had not been much discussed in the campaign of 1908, but both Roosevelt and Taft had recognized that there was need for some changes in the existing laws, beginning with the Act of 1887 which established the Interstate Commerce Commission and coming up through the Hepburn Act of 1906, which Roosevelt had forced through in the face of determined opposition from the most powerful railroad lobby in the history of the country.[6] The chief feature of the Hepburn Act had been to confer upon the Interstate Commerce Commission the first explicit grant of rate-making authority. The Act also stimulated a wave of state laws on the subject which went to such restrictive lengths that with the concurrence of the panic of 1907, a large number of railroads were forced into receiver-

[6] Ogg, *National Progress*, p. 47.

ship and others were in serious plights.

The Administration bill, tentatively drafted by Attorney General Wickersham, was laid before the House on January 7th, 1910, and before the Senate three days later. Through its sponsors in the House and Senate, it ultimately became, after drastic revision, the Mann-Elkins Act of June 18th, 1910. Although the bill was important and in some respects radical, it attracted little attention in the country and no vigorous open opposition from the railroads.[7] Root was one of the chief sponsors of the bill, although he disagreed with some of its provisions and favored a number of amendments. It was a subject with which he was very familiar. From the early days of his law practice, he had been engaged in railroad cases and for a long time had been a director and general counsel for the Hannibal and St. Jo Railroad. More recently he had been engaged in the last stages of the great Northern Securities litigation. His speech shows that he was a master of the subject; it shows that he was as usual influenced by the principle that legitimate business must not be destroyed but it does not reveal any particular tenderness for the railroad interests. There is nothing in the speech itself or in his files to show that in any sense he was arguing the case for the railroads; it was inevitable that he should be sympathetic with their difficulties which he understood so well. He was constantly interrupted by questions and at times by lengthy arguments with various Senators; it was his custom in such matters not to refuse to yield the floor to a questioner except momentarily when he wished to complete the formulation of some thought which the questioner was interrupting. It was apropos of the frequent interpellations in this speech that he remarked good naturedly, "I am well aware of the rule of the Senate that the only person not entitled to speak is the Senator who has the floor."

Root opened by quoting from both Roosevelt and Taft various statements indicating the need for some new legislation. He made a point throughout of showing that he was advocating action along the lines which Roosevelt favored, seeking constantly to dispel the impression that Taft was advocating a retrogressive measure, an impression which existed in the minds of Senators like La Follette who had many violent

[7] Dixon, "The Mann-Elkins Act," *Quarterly Journal of Economics*, Vol. 24 (1910), pp. 593 ff.

objections to the bill.[8] Root agreed with some of the positions taken by the Progressives, as for example, in advocating an amendment to the bill in order to give the shipper the right to appear by his own counsel before the courts on appeal from a decision of the Interstate Commerce Commission instead of being represented by the government in a suit against the railroad. Root agreed with the members of the Interstate Commerce Commission in favoring an increase in their powers of investigation of rate schedules. The broad principle which Root advocated was "not in having a public officer make the railroad rates for this country, but in having the railroads make the rates, subject to the supervision and control of public officers." He firmly believed in individual initiative and enterprise and felt that if the government were given the direct ratemaking power, it would be a step in the direction of government ownership, to which he was vehemently opposed. He argued in favor of the practice of permitting railroads to hold other roads under lease, asserting that the adoption of a contrary rule would be disastrous to the railroad systems of the country. Subject to a doubt as to the constitutionality of such a provision, he favored the provision of the bill giving the federal government adequate power to regulate issues of railroad stocks and bonds; he called attention to cases in which the public had been mulcted through the lack of such regulation. This part of the bill was among those which failed of adoption.

Root sailed for Europe to take part in the North Atlantic Coast Fisheries Arbitration on May 21st, 1910, and was therefore not present when the final vote on the bill was taken in the Senate on June 3rd. Nor was he present for the final vote two weeks later on the conference report. His attitude on the bill in general shows that he was eager to support the Administration and the Republican platform. Although he did not go all the way with the progressive group in the Senate, his attitude and positions were by no means wholly antagonistic to theirs. His innate conservatism often made his views identical with those of the big corporate interests and what he believed in, he advocated.

Root took a prominent part in another Administration measure which became law. This was a bill for the creation of a postal savings system; it had been endorsed in the Republican platform and had been

[8] La Follette, *Autobiography*, pp. 422 ff.

advocated for over fifty years by economists and officials of the Post Office Department. Similar systems had long been in existence in Europe. Roosevelt had recommended similar legislation but it had failed of passage. Both Root and Lodge were very much opposed to the form which the bill took as it came before the Senate. Root spoke of it in the course of a long handwritten letter to Roosevelt on February 11th, 1910. The bill, he wrote, was "having a hard time because the bankers are opposed & their special advocates especially Cummins have been able to bedevil it with amendments that make it unworkable & unconstitutional." Lodge explained to Roosevelt in a letter of September 3rd, 1910, "They converted the postal savings bank bill from what you and I desired into a scheme for wildcat banking. It was with the utmost difficulty that Root and I voted for it in order to get an opportunity of a decent bill from the House, which was what finally came to pass." [9] Root's chief objection, which he developed in an extended speech on March 4th, 1910, was that the bill as introduced provided that the money deposited in the postal savings accounts should be redeposited by the government in the local banks throughout the country. Against such a proposal Root argued first on the basis "of long experience and of anxious days and nights passed in responsible professional and official relations in every panic that has occurred, beginning with that of 1873 and ending with that of 1907." It was estimated $500,000,000 would be accumulated in these postal savings accounts; in time of panic, with runs on the banks, the depositors would of course seek to withdraw their savings. The Government would then find itself in the position of having no source from which to draw this money to pay to depositors except the banks, which were already in trouble. Root felt that the government would inevitably be forced to default and that the credit of the United States would be "dragged in the dust." The bill "instead of giving the credit of the United States to our poor, to our industrious workers," would "impose upon the United States the weakness of our defective banking system." Root accordingly introduced an amendment—parallelled by amendments introduced by other Senators—which provided that the fund, or at least some of it, would be invested in government securities which could be sold in time of panic to realize cash and check the panic. This possibility of selling its securities, Root asserted, was the only "means

[9] Roosevelt Papers, Library of Congress.

that ever has been known in our financial history always and certainly to realize the cash to meet the obligations that are imposed upon our Government." Taft endorsed Root's amendment and the bill was finally passed in reasonably satisfactory form, though again the final vote came after Root had left for The Hague.

When Root returned from the Fisheries Arbitration at The Hague in September, 1910, Congress had adjourned and he retired for a much needed rest at Clinton. Roosevelt meanwhile had returned from Europe, his split with Taft was beginning to widen, and despite the really substantial achievements of the Taft Administration, the country was aroused against the President, chiefly because of the dissatisfaction with the Tariff Act. The result was that in the November elections of 1910, the Republicans lost control of the House, which in the next Congress contained 228 Democrats and 161 Republicans and 1 Socialist. In the Senate, the Republicans still had a nominal majority of 10, but the insurgents held the balance of power and it was doubtful whether the Administration could feel secure even in the Upper House. Before this change took effect, however, the Sixty-first Congress, in the short session from December 5th, 1910, to March 4th, 1911, had some important work to do.

One part of that work was to pass on the report of a committee which had been appointed in June to investigate charges that corrupt methods or practices were used in the election of Senator William Lorimer of Illinois. The Committee on Privileges and Elections had reported that in their opinion the invalidity of Lorimer's title to a seat in the Senate had not been proved. The Chicago *Tribune* had aired the scandal and had borne the brunt of sustaining the charges against Lorimer before the Senate Committee. Roosevelt, in the preceding September, had shown his attitude and created a sensation by refusing to sit at the same table with Lorimer at the Hamilton Club dinner in Chicago.[10] Taft, judicially minded, was disturbed at this advance judgment,[11] but he later became convinced of Lorimer's guilt and persuaded Root and others to speak against the acceptance of the Senate Committee's report.[12] On February 4th, 1911, the day after Root's speech, Taft wrote to him: "It was great, one of the greatest things

[10] Pringle, *Theodore Roosevelt*, p. 541.
[11] Butt, *op. cit.*, Vol. II, p. 509.
[12] Taft to H. H. Kohlsaat, April 1, 1912, Taft Papers, Library of Congress.

you have done, and I couldn't say more— It must have been worth a good deal of the burden of work and abuse you have had at times to carry, to have felt how that audience hung on your words, and to have realized that your words were being received not as a mere speech on parade, but as a basis for judgment of your colleagues who wished to be enlightened and to do the right thing—I congratulate you from the bottom of my heart—I know the cost and the reluctance with which one goes into a discussion like this, when taking the right position makes enemies and creates uncomfortable relations, but it will be a great pleasure to look back to having done your duty and in such a masterful and magnificent way. . . . Overman said it was one of the greatest speeches he had ever heard— He said that when you finished, it seemed to him that Lorimer couldn't have a vote except the committee and that they would be glad to get out of it." Taft sent on to Root also a letter from J. H. Blount, a former judge in the Philippines who had heard Root deliver his speech. According to Blount:

> . . . It must compare favorably, in nobility of eloquence, and splendor of subdued moral fury, with any speech ever delivered in that historic chamber. To read it tomorrow may sound cold. To hear it was great. He first summed up the evidence in a quiet, deliberate, modest, masterful way, and then came the "trampling out the vintage where the grapes of wrath were stored:
> "Why, Mr. President, *before the Assembly even met*, the atmosphere of Springfield was *murky—*with the *suspicion—*of corruption." There was a pause after "murky", and another after "suspicion", which last word sounded like the hiss of a whip. And then: "Some Senators seem to treat this as the Chicago Tribune's case. The Chicago Tribune is not the custodian of the honor of the Senate of the United States. This is the case of the Senate, of the Government, of representative government throughout the world."
> The voice was not strong, but it was penetrating, & "muy sympatico", as they say in Spanish; and was vibrant with intensity of conviction and feeling. It (the speech) confirmed me in a long cherished impatience with those who think all the great men are dead.

Root did not make up his mind until he had thoroughly reviewed the testimony taken by the Committee. Lodge wrote to Roosevelt on

January 26th, 1911, that Root had told him the day before "that the Committee did not get to the bottom of the case; that they cut off all sorts of avenues of information. . . ." On February 2nd, he wrote again that Root was to speak the next day; he admitted that there was no absolute proof that Lorimer had knowledge of what was done—"only an irresistible inference." On the 6th: "Root's speech on the Lorimer case was a very great argument indeed. . . . Nothing could have been more masterly than the way in which he handled it." [13]

Root disagreed with the Senate Committee in its method of handling the investigation. He felt that they had not sought all available evidence and had let the case rest on the evidence produced by the Chicago *Tribune* as if their task were merely to see whether that newspaper could sustain its particular charges. He reviewed the testimony step by step, showing how Lee O'Neil Brown was the agent for Lorimer and how he rallied thirty of his Democratic supporters in the Illinois Legislature to vote for this candidate of the Republican Party. He showed that the direct testimony of those who admitted receiving bribes was not overcome by any contrary testimony. He showed what he described in a letter of February 11th, 1911, to H. H. Kohlsaat, as "the modern method which has superseded the old and awkward way of buying individual votes—the method of mercenary bands whose members pool their votes with a leader and receive from him distribution of what he can make out of it." He showed that there was proof of corruption in the case of seven votes at least and that the shift of these seven votes was enough to change the vote of the Legislature and to secure Lorimer's election.[14] Root did not mince words any more than he had when he denounced the corrupt gang which he helped to overthrow in Philadelphia in 1905.

Root's argument did not at the time prevail, although the resolution declaring Lorimer's election invalid was lost by only 46 votes to 40 on March 1st. But on June 2nd, 1911, the Senate adopted a resolution appointing a special committee to reexamine the Lorimer case. Eleven months later, this special committee reported in favor of Lorimer but the report of the minority holding that corrupt methods and practices had invalidated his election was adopted by the Senate by 55 votes to 28. On both votes party lines were split and the final

[13] All three letters from the Roosevelt Papers, Library of Congress.
[14] Speech reprinted in *Addresses on Government and Citizenship*, p. 291.

result was reached by a union of Democrats, regular Republicans and Progressives.

Senator Root's closing references to popular distrust of the way in which members of the United States Senate were being chosen and the necessity for reestablishing confidence, were preludes to the speech which he delivered a week later, on February 10th, 1911, opposing the resolution for a constitutional amendment which would provide for the direct election of senators. Sections 3 and 4 of Article I of the Constitution provided that the two senators from each state should be elected by state legislatures. As early as 1826, a movement for the direct popular election of senators began, but it acquired no real headway until the House of Representatives in 1893 passed a resolution for an amendment to the Constitution. The Senate at that time defeated the move but the popular pressure for it increased. By 1912, when the proposal for an amendment finally passed both Houses of Congress, twenty-nine of the states had adopted laws providing for the popular nomination of senators, with the practical effect in most cases that this nomination was equivalent to election.[15] In opposing the amendment, Root was therefore standing out against a strong current which obviously could not be stemmed. From his own State Legislature came a resolution of April 25th, 1911, endorsing the amendment; the resolution had been introduced by a young State Senator named Franklin Delano Roosevelt. Root's arguments against the proposal were various and they were put with all the vigorous effectiveness of which he was capable. Senator Bacon of Georgia, who heartily disagreed with him, thought it was "one of the most impressive and forceful" arguments that he had ever heard in the Senate.[16]

Root did not believe it "wise that the people of the United States should contract the habit of amending the Constitution."

> As Ulysses required his followers to bind him to the mast that he might not yield to the song of the siren as he sailed by, so the American democracy has bound itself to the great rules of right conduct . . . and made it practically impossible that the impulse, the prejudice, the excitement, the frenzy of the moment, shall carry our democracy into those excesses which have wrecked all our prototypes in history.

[15] Ogg, op. cit., p. 149–150.
[16] Congressional Record, 61st Cong., 3rd Sess., Vol. 46, p. 2260.

Root was always opposed to hasty and unconsidered action in all major questions of government, and he therefore approached this question with a fundamental opposition to amending any part of the Constitution except after long study and experiment. He felt that the experimental process had but begun and that a Constitutional amendment should, if necessary at all, follow and not precede the full period of experimentation. He pointed out that people had become dissatisfied with the results of the existing system but that they were merely following the usual course of snapping at the first remedy suggested without considering whether some other remedy would not be better. Root himself agreed that the existing situation was full of abuses, both because the state legislatures, through political jockeying, had shown that they could not always act efficiently and because fraud and corruption had crept into the elections by the legislatures. He had proposed an amendment to the existing federal electoral law which would have provided that if within twenty days the legislature had not been able to elect a senator by majority vote, then a plurality should suffice. For the correction of the other abuses, he believed that the proposed amendment offered no remedy. It arose from the popular belief that the state legislatures were unfaithful to their trust. The remedy for that situation was for the people to do their duty in electing state legislatures which would honestly and conscientiously perform their proper functions. "This whole proposition rests upon the postulate of the incapacity of the people of the United States to elect honest and faithful legislatures." The framers of the proposition would more accurately have stated their position had they framed their resolution to assert this incapacity and then to have proposed that the Constitution be amended to put directly in the hands of these same incompetent people the choice of United States senators. He reiterated a position which he often took, that if the people of the states did not clean house at home, our system of government would break down and the powers which the states should exercise would fall to be exercised by the federal government. The proposal for direct election of senators was "an expression of distrust for representative government" like the initiative and referendum. If you rob the state legislatures of power on the theory that they are not competent to exercise that power properly, you destroy the standards of those bodies and make them second rate, as the boards of aldermen in many of our cities had sunk to "insignificance and worthlessness, as power after power has been taken away from them" and they ceased to attract men of standing and ability. How could the people be expected to elect honest United States senators if they could not be trusted to elect honest state senators from men in their own close neighborhood?

Root stressed the fundamental notion in the Constitution that there should be a difference between the Senate and the House; that the Senate should be a body with longer tenure, less immediately responsive to every popular whim, in order that it might act as a check upon hasty and ill considered action; "the Senate was established by the Constitution to protect the American democracy against itself. . . ." He developed this argument from what were undoubtedly his own personal reactions.

> This change, sir, would prevent the Senate from having the benefit of the service of a large class of citizens who are specially qualified by character and training to render a peculiar kind of service specially needed for the purposes of the Senate, men who by lives of experience and effort have attained the respect of their fellow-citizens and who are willing to undertake the burdens of public office, but who are unwilling to seek it; men who will accept the burden as a patriotic duty, accept it doubtless with mingled feelings of satisfaction at the honor and dissatisfaction with the burden, the disturbance of life, the abuse of the press, the controversies about performance of duty, but who never would subject themselves to the disagreeable incidents, the labor, the strife, the personalities of a political campaign.

He went on to say that of course he did not deny the even greater value of the younger and more vigorous men "full of the energy of life and the willingness for strife"; but it was possible to have both and the Senate should contain "the elder statesmen." He admitted that bad men were at times sent to the Senate but when they arrived they "find their level and they find it in innocuous insignificance here."

When the final vote came on February 28th, 1911, the resolution failed to receive the necessary two-thirds, but it was reintroduced in the Sixty-second Congress. Root spoke again in the Senate on May 23rd, 1911, stressing much the same points, particularly the undesirability of experimenting through amendments to the Constitution.

"With all history strewn with the wrecks of government, with human nature still unchanged, I would hesitate long before assuming that my own judgment, or the judgment of all of us, can improve the system and framework of our government except upon experiment and demonstration by practical application." This time the Senate passed an amended resolution by the necessary two-thirds vote, although it was not until May 13th, 1912, that the House finally agreed to the Senate's position. On May 31st, 1913, thirty-six states having ratified this Seventeenth Amendment to the Constitution, it became law.

It is commonly thought that opposition to the direct election of senators was inspired by distrust of popular democratic government. In general, the line-up was between those who sought by various means to place more power directly in the hands of the people and those who opposed such policies. Root had favored one step in that process through the direct primaries but his position there was influenced by his belief that it afforded a check upon the manipulation through political machines of the party conventions. He also believed that the people of New York had been persuaded by Governor Hughes that the old system was inadequate and that the direct primary was a solution. While Root did not agree with the solution and had no alternative to propose, he thought a commission should be appointed to study the subject and evolve an intelligent substitute.[17] Root's emphasis was always on representative as distinguished from direct popular government. There is much in his argument that if the people could be trusted to elect senators directly, they could also be trusted to elect proper state legislatures. Indeed it is very doubtful whether the Seventeenth Amendment has improved the character of the United States Senate, especially with reference to the eastern industrial states where the evils of corporate control and bribery were most noticeable.[18] As Root suggested, the Amendment did not provide the remedy. His views were strengthened in retrospect.[19] If a political party is in control of a state in an election year, it can put over its choice for United States senator just as much as in the old days it could control its majority in the state legislature. Root's stand on this question was illustrative of de Tocqueville's belief that our lawyers

[17] Root to Senator John Raines, April 13, 1909
[18] Rogers, The American Senate, p. 115.
[19] Root to the author, September 5, 1930.

are "the most powerful existing security against the excesses of democracy." The same conservatism may, however, make them equally a security "against the progress of democracy." [20] "Lawyers are essentially conservative," Root told the American Bar Association in 1914. "They do not take kindly to change. They are not naturally reformers." [21] Root was undoubtedly conscious of his own feeling about entering into a campaign for the senatorship and he refused to stand for another term as United States Senator when that question came up in 1915 after the Seventeenth Amendment took effect. He could have had the nomination and the Republicans probably could have elected him in New York, as they did his successor James Wadsworth, but he would not enter upon a campaign for his own reelection.

The same fundamental theory of government was involved in Root's speech in the Senate on August 7th, 1911, on the subject of the resolution to admit Arizona to statehood. The point involved was one on which he felt deeply and in regard to which he later clashed with Roosevelt. On June 20th, 1910, Taft had approved an Act enabling the people of the territories of New Mexico and Arizona to frame constitutions in order that they might be admitted into the Union as states. The Act provided that the constitutions adopted should be submitted to the President and Congress for approval before the new states were admitted. The constitution submitted by Arizona contained a provision for the "recall" of officials; the provision was unlimited and would have included judges. This was one example of a movement which was becoming popular, especially in the West, to exercise greater popular control over all government officers by permitting a certain number of voters to petition for the officer's recall, whereupon special elections would be held in order that the people might vote for or against the continuance of the man in office. Oregon was the first to adopt such a provision in its constitution in 1908; no other state had done so at the time of Root's speech, although California was to follow suit in the same year and eight more states by 1914. In four of these ten states, the provision for recall did not apply to judicial officers. Roosevelt flirted with the idea of endorsing the recall for some time and it was not until his speech at Columbus, Ohio, in February, 1912, on "A Charter of Democracy"

[20] Rogers, loc. cit.
[21] Addresses on Government and Citizenship, p. 484.

that he came out flatly for the rather different and more extreme proposal for the "recall of judicial decisions" by popular vote.[22] Even his dear friend Lodge differed with Roosevelt on that and Taft, of course, was horrified to his very marrow.

Root, in his Senate speech which followed one by Borah to the same effect, was roused to a degree of oratorical effort which differed widely from his calm analytical discussion of the tariff, reciprocity and many other bills. He regarded the courageous independence of the judiciary as one of the cornerstones of our liberties. He stressed the fact that cases in the law courts, whether criminal or civil, frequently arouse intense popular excitement. The people are likely to judge on the basis of those items of spectacular interest which will attract the public. The public view, accordingly, is not one based upon evidence but upon passion and fragmentary bits of information. How could a judge decide cases properly with the knowledge that his decision was to be reviewed by the people acting on such a basis? "The judge is to pass upon the evidence that appears in the record, but he is to be judged upon the newspaper reports of the trial." He read from a California newspaper which stated that if the recall provision were adopted in that state, the workers would see to it that a judge who had exacted heavy bail from certain union strikers accused of illegal picketing would be the first to be removed from the bench. He read it as an illustration of the way in which the recall provision would work, a way which he felt was antagonistic to every proper concept of the administration of justice.

> I have no quarrel with the gentlemen who extol the wisdom of the people. I believe that in the long run, after mature consideration and full discussion, and when conclusions are reached under such circumstances as to exclude the interests or the prejudice or the passions of the moment, the decisions of the American people are sound and wise. But, sir, they are sound and wise because the wisdom of our fathers devised a system of government which does prevent our people from reaching their conclusions except upon mature consideration, after full discussion, and when the dictates of momentary passion or self-interest are excluded.

The "voice of an intelligent people is the voice of God" when they speak in regard to general principles of right and justice, free from a

[22] Roosevelt, Works, Vol. XVII, pp. 119–148.

direct interest in the affair of the moment, and that was the voice which had spoken in framing the general principles of our government. This provision, on the other hand, was the antithesis of such a situation; it "is not progress, it is not reform, it is degeneracy. It is a movement backward to those days of misrule and unbridled power out of which the world has been slowly progressing. . . . The American system was built upon the idea of the protection of minorities however small, to enjoy religious and political liberty."

I do not envy the men who have no sympathy with Malesherbes and De Sèze pleading for the lawful rights of Louis XVI against the dictates of the majority of the French capital in 1793.

I do not envy the men who see nothing to admire in John Adams defending the British soldiers against the protests of his neighbors and friends and countrymen, after the Boston Massacre.

Root was voicing an essential part of the creed of most members of the American Bar, a part which he stressed on many another occasion, that every man was entitled to have presented before the court his rights under the law and that the court should be unhampered in its power to decide in accordance with that law. He reemphasized his views on this same subject of the recall of judicial officers before the Republican State Convention at Rochester on April 10th, 1912, which adopted a resolution opposing the recall.[23]

Congress passed and the President vetoed on August 15th, 1911, a resolution which merely provided that the matter of recall of judicial officers should be submitted separately to the voters of Arizona. Congress at once passed a further joint resolution which was approved by the President on August 21st, making the admission of Arizona dependent upon the amendment of that article of its constitution so as to exclude the judiciary from its scope. Arizona acted accordingly and was admitted to statehood in February, 1912. Being then free of restrictions, as Root had pointed out she would be, the State of Arizona, in the following November, restored the provision to its constitution. As a matter of fact, the recall has been sparingly used and it has not gained great headway.[24]

In less spectacular ways, Root sought to further some reforms.

[23] Both speeches are reprinted in *Addresses on Government and Citizenship*, pp. 387 and 405.
[24] See Ogg, *op. cit.*, pp. 165–166.

There were many bills dealing with the federal judiciary but after the Democrats took control of Congress, Root was discouraged along this line, as along others. To Taft he wrote on June 4th, 1914: "Judicial Reform moves through the Senate with tallow legs, owing to the violent prejudice against increasing the authority of the courts or judges. I am trying to do the best I can with the Bar Association bills but I am not very sanguine." He reported favorably from a sub-committee in 1912 a proposal to amend the constitution by making the Presidential term six years, with ineligibility for reelection, but he was not disappointed when it failed to receive support because, he wrote Adelbert Moot, "we are clearly in a period of important changes in our system of government. All the new ideas are still experimental and no one can tell how they are coming out. . . . It seems rather early in the process to begin amending the Constitution. That ought to come after the experiments have been tried out, rather than as a part of them."

Root spoke also in favor of a bill which would require publicity for campaign funds. He admitted that the bill was not a perfect one, but he pointed out that they were all conscious that there had been improprieties and corruption and he considered this bill a step in the right direction; "honest men must sometimes submit . . . to inconvenience in order that adequate regulations may curb dishonest men." This was in line with the position which he had taken during the New York Constitutional Convention of 1894 in favor of restricting campaign contributions from corporations. He supported a Workmen's Compensation law for railroad employees and a bill regulating hours and conditions of work by women in the District of Columbia. Roosevelt urged him on January 20th, 1912, to support a bill establishing a Children's Bureau; Root jestingly replied: "Cabot and I are about to vote for your darling Children's Bureau bill which will probably destroy the liberties of our country." [25]

One other matter in the field of domestic legislation requires notice since it was one of the most important legislative measures which came before Congress during Root's term in the Senate. This was the Currency Bill of 1913 under which the Federal Reserve system was established. The bill's paternity has been hotly debated to such an extent that the layman in finance is readily led to the conclusion that

[25] Roosevelt Papers, Library of Congress.

it was the bastard offspring of both the Republican and Democratic parties. Senator Carter H. Glass in 1927 published "An Adventure in Constructive Finance," in which he gave the legislative history of the measure. As Chairman of the House Committee on Banking and Currency and as joint author with Senator Owen of the bill which bore their names, he speaks with authority. He also speaks with abundant irritation because Professor Seymour, in his *Intimate Papers of Colonel House,* credits the Colonel with being the "Guardian Angel of the Federal Reserve Act." Senator Glass modestly and loyally gives the credit to President Wilson, being equally sure that the Republican claim to any credit is wholly without foundation. Since Senator Glass's invective against the false "historicity" of university professors is in many respects quite convincing, it behooves another of that profession, writing on a subject about which he does not profess to have any expert knowledge, to tread cautiously and to assert at once that Senator Root should not have and never claimed to have credit for framing the Federal Reserve system. Nevertheless, he was in favor of its establishment and his powerful speech in the Senate on December 13th, 1913, apparently was instrumental in bringing about the insertion of an amendment which brought the bill more nearly into conformity with the House measure fathered by Glass. A study of the *Congressional Record* indicates that the original bill was amended fifty-seven times before reaching the Senate and three hundred and forty additional changes were made in it before it was finally enacted into law. Senator Glass, in his book, does not always focus his attention upon the exact status of the measure at the time particular criticisms were leveled against it. This seems to be true in his criticism of Root's opposition.

It is a fact that a Monetary Commission was established under a Republican Administration in 1908 with Senator Aldrich as chairman and a non-partisan membership; that this Commission proposed a bill for the revision of the banking system of the United States with a central bank of banks; that legislation along these lines was recommended to Congress by President Taft but nothing was done. The report of the Monetary Commission with their bill was referred to the Banking and Currency Committee of the House and Mr. Glass was appointed chairman of a sub-committee to devise a reserve banking scheme; he enlisted the services of Professor H. Parker Willis as ex-

"Root's Shoes"

(A cartoon in the New York *World*, July 3, 1914)

pert assistant. This was all before the elections of November, 1912, but with the advent of the Democratic Administration under President Wilson, the bill upon which Glass had been working for the reform of the currency and banking system was pressed forward. His bill differed in many important particulars from the proposals of the Monetary Commission and Senator Aldrich was much opposed to the Glass bill. From these facts, Senator Glass denies that the Monetary Commission deserves credit for the bill as finally passed. From the same facts Root affirmed in 1916 that "It is peculiarly a Wilsonian proceeding to claim all the credit of this legislation for the Democratic party. . . . The Federal Reserve Act was based directly upon the bill reported by the Monetary Commission. . . . It was the bill reported by that commission with some modifications." [26] Of course Wilson did not really invent the idea of claiming for his party credit for anything which seemed good, but Root in 1916 was feeling rather bitter about Wilson because of his policies toward Mexico and the World War. Root stressed the fact that under a Republican Administration a study was made and the first step taken to revise our admittedly bad banking system; Glass stresses the fact that when the legislation was born, there were so many fundamental changes that its Republican fathers could not and would not recognize it as their own. But Glass's expert assistant, Professor Willis, notes that as a matter of political strategy, the Aldrich bill was taken as a base in many particulars.[27]

Root quite naturally secured ammunition from New York bankers in opposing certain features of the bill. The banking community, and particularly the New York bankers, were violently opposed to the Glass bill. Senator Glass points out that they were not always consistent in their opposition, but what they lacked in consistency they made up in vigor. The Bank of North America was one of Root's first clients and for it he performed perhaps the first important legal task which he handled independently when he began practice in New York over forty years before this Senatorial period. For thirty years he was intimately connected with bankers and banking practices in New York. He never was attorney for any business or profession without

[26] Root to Aaron A. Ferris, October 25, 1916.
[27] H. Parker Willis, "The Federal Reserve Act," *American Economic Review*, Vol. IV, p. 1.

making himself familiar with the practical workings of it. While he did not rely on his own knowledge in this instance—any more than Glass did—he was in a position to understand, to sympathize with and to utilize the arguments which some of his New York friends supplied to him. A large portion of one of his speeches dealing with the panic of 1907 and its causes was written for him by Fred I. Kent, a vice president of the Bankers Trust Company, who was also helping Senator Burton and other Senators. Root told Kent that he did not fully understand all the details of his argument but he had confidence that Kent knew them and relied upon him. Root read it verbatim and when he came off the floor, said smilingly to Kent: "Did I read it right?" [28] "You may see that I have been expanding your views about inflation . . . and it has raised a devil of a hullabaloo," Root wrote to Nicholas Murray Butler on December 17th, 1913. Benjamin Strong, later a Governor of the Federal Reserve Board, also furnished Root with material to support his argument on the inflationary dangers of the bill.[29]

One of the features of the bill as it stood in the Senate was the insurance of deposits, to be adopted later under another Democratic Administration—over the opposition of Senator Glass, be it noted. Root was opposed to this proposal in 1913 and in 1933. So were the House conferees in 1913 who eliminated this provision from the bill as it passed the Senate. Root also found the Senate bill defective in its provision for adequate reserves behind the Federal Reserve bank notes which would be issued. The bill then provided for a gold reserve of 33⅓%; he proposed raising the percentage to 50, with a graduated tax on deficiencies of reserves until they fell to 33⅓% when no additional notes should be issued. *Post* or *propter hoc*, the Democratic majority in the Senate raised the reserve to 40% and included the deficiency tax; these provisions were retained in conference. It was this specific point, contained in an amendment which Root had proposed to Section 16 of the bill, to which Root particularly addressed himself in his main speech. In pressing his point—and it may be said in carrying it, although his own amendment was defeated—he dwelt at length upon the dangers of inflation and of the issue of fiat money. Root himself stated in a letter to John F. Edwards on November

[28] Kent to the author, September 23, 1937.
[29] Diary of Charles S. Hamlin, entry of March 3, 1915.

22nd, 1919, that the Democratic majority adopted amendments as a result of his speech.[30]

There were no doubt some exaggerations in his flights of oratory and there was the irresistible impulse for an old Republican to invoke the dire dangers of Bryanism, since Bryan was then Secretary of State in Wilson's Cabinet. Glass makes it clear that Bryan loyally supported the President and made no effort to revive his ancient financial "heresies," but it was not an unreasonable point for political argument. Root laid stress upon the fact that these Federal Reserve notes would be obligations of the United States and that no special governmental reserve was required to back them. Glass emphasized that this was an empty shadow yielded to conciliate one set of opinions and that because of the ample coverage required from the banks themselves in both gold and commercial paper, plus other assets, the ultimate governmental liability would not be invoked in a thousand years. Root also objected that the bill provided not an "elastic" currency but merely an "expansive" one; he advocated amendments to the bill compelling the reduction of currency at requisite periods. He admitted that under the bill the Reserve Board would have authority to contract the currency, but in view of the general human tendency to keep increasing currency issues, he thought Congress itself should provide in advance for some automatic checks. Senator Glass wrote his book praising the undoubtedly successful operation of the Federal Reserve system before the crash of 1929. In the light of the experience of that year, more experts are now inclined to agree with Root's general point of view favoring automatic checks on inflation,[31] although experience has shown that it is credit rather than currency inflation which in that case was most to be feared. Incidentally, it may be noted in passing, as an evidence of Root's intelligent appraisal of financial and business conditions, that in June of 1929, about four months before the crash in Wall Street, he sold his common stocks and invested his money in federal, state and municipal obligations, with some bonds of private companies.

[30] This was the view of the New York *Times*, December 8, 1913.

[31] *Cf.* Willford I. King, "Circulating Credit," *American Economic Review*, Vol. 10 (1920), p. 738 and C. Reinold Noyes, "Gold Inflation in the United States, 1921–1929," *ibid.*, Vol. 20 (1930), p. 181.

CHAPTER XXXVIII

"There are no politics in foreign affairs"

OBVIOUSLY a former Secretary of State would take a special interest in all international questions which came before the Congress. There were many such minor matters on which Root addressed the Senate, often for the purpose of checking that frequent tendency of Senators to barge in with some insulting resolution which may embitter our relations with foreign governments. Moreover in the Committee on Foreign Relations, Root merely continued a series of meetings and discussions which he had rather regularly carried on with its members during the four years preceding his Senatorship.

During the Taft Administration, Root was hesitant to oppose the policies which were being followed by his successor in the State Department, Philander C. Knox. Yet in regard to Latin America particularly, he was not in sympathy with that policy which bade fair to destroy all the progress which he had so carefully and laboriously made in establishing an atmosphere of friendliness on the part of the Latin Americans toward the United States. Knox was the great "dollar diplomatist"; he reawakened all of the fears and suspicions of Yankee imperialism which Root had done much to allay. "Knox was a peppery sort of fellow. He got mad very easily. He did mix into things too much. He got mad on that old pelter of a case [the Alsop claim against Chile]; that made no end of trouble. It was the real beginning of the change of feeling on the part of the South Americans. The arbitration practically decided in favor of Chile—an amount she was ready to pay. Without saying a word to anybody, Knox took it up and gave them an ultimatum—ten days. They were furious and they have never gotten over it. A big powerful country must be careful about those things. An ultimatum from a country twice as big as you are creates a lot of feeling." But Root thought many of Knox's mistakes were the result of leaving things to Huntington Wilson.[1] "Knox was

[1] Root to the author, September 15, 1930.

an awfully good fellow," Root wrote to Henry L. Stimson on September 7th, 1927, "and very able and it was a delight to have anything to do with him in any matter that came within the training and experience of an American lawyer. He was, however, absolutely antipathetic to all Spanish-American modes of thought and feeling and action, and pretty much everything he did with them was like mixing a Seidlitz powder."

Knox's successor when the Wilson Administration took over, was William Jennings Bryan for whose political views, especially on such issues as free silver, Root had had profound contempt and even bitter animosity. When he came to know the man himself, he was inclined to put him in his tolerant category of "nice fellows." On June 11th, 1913, Root wrote to his wife that he had just returned from a diplomatic reception: "I became Bryan's guide philosopher & friend & general referee as to proper conduct & we are awfully chummy—going to ride together!" Subsequent letters during that summer tell of frequent such rides, usually at seven or seven-thirty in the morning.

Root did approve the treaties which Knox negotiated with Honduras and Nicaragua in 1910 and 1911. Taft had enlisted his support and Root endeavored to secure the approval of his fellow senators but the treaties were not approved. When Bryan negotiated a somewhat similar but broader convention with Nicaragua two years later, Root again gave support, although with qualification. On July 21st, 1913, he sent to Senator Bacon, Chairman of the Committee on Foreign Relations, a memorandum which he suggested might be shown to Secretary Bryan if Bacon thought it worth while. Root said that he favored assisting the Central American countries but in making treaties of assistance "we ought to exercise great restraint, and not demand or accept from them any greater powers or authority or limitations upon their freedom of action than are absolutely necessary to secure their well being." If we accepted grants of authority which seemed to impinge upon their independence, our motives would be suspected and all Latin America would be alarmed, and if we went too far in our commitments we might find ourselves in the undesirable position of having to guarantee their debts to European countries. Root thought the provision in the treaty giving us rights to construct a canal were unobjectionable but "not of much consequence . . . because of course we do not intend to build the canal. . . ." He thought the concession of a naval station on the Gulf of Fonseca for the further defense of the Panama Canal very valuable. He opposed the enlargement of the terms of the Platt Amendment as applied to Nicaragua in this treaty. "There is no such basis in our relations with Nicaragua to justify such limitations upon sovereignty as exist in the case of Cuba, and, whatever the present Administration in Nicaragua may be willing to do, future Administrations will be certain to repudiate their action if we allow it to go beyond the point where it can be demonstrated that the real good of Nicaragua is provided for with the least possible infringement of her sovereignty." Yet he was willing to see retained in the treaty a right of intervention solely "for the maintenance of independence and a government adequate to preserve peace and order" together with the right of common defense of the proposed naval stations. The Senate, however, refused to agree to any "Platt Amendment" clause and it was omitted from the treaty signed on August 5th, 1914. With the amendments suggested by the Foreign Relations Committee of the Senate, Root voted for the favorable report on the treaty, but he was not satisfied with it. On January 7th, 1915, he wrote to Paul Fuller: "I am, however, troubled about the question whether the Nicaragua government which has made the treaty is really representative of the people of Nicaragua and whether it will be regarded in Nicaragua and in Central America as having been a free agent in making the treaty." From available information he reached the conclusion "that the present government with which we are making this treaty is really maintained in office by the presence of United States marines in Managua. . . . I should be very sorry to see the Central Americans convinced that we wish to rule them by force, for it would be the end of all our attempts to benefit them and help them along as we have been trying to do." He suggested that a fair election might be held under American supervision and that the treaty should then be submitted to the new government thus elected.[2] Fuller showed Root's letter to Secretary Bryan and Bryan sent it to President Wilson. The Secretary of State was inclined to argue that he was dealing with the actual *de facto* government and that he had no right to disregard it. He agreed with Fuller's suggestion, however, that if they could get an agreement from the

[2] This letter was read to the Senate by Senator Borah twelve years later, January 13, 1927, *Congressional Record*, 69th Cong., 2nd Sess., Vol. 68, p. 1557.

Senate to consent to ratification of the treaty, the Senate might agree at the same time to pass a resolution calling for an investigation of the representative character of the Nicaraguan Government with a view to helping the people elect another government if the situation called for such action. But he thought the Administration should not favor such a resolution unless it were part of a bargain to approve the treaty.[3] Bryan had no sense of finesse in handling the Latin Americans; he had little understanding of them. The passage of such a resolution as he suggested would have been more offensive than the ratification of the treaty in its most extreme form.

Relations with Mexico contributed particularly difficult problems during the period of Root's Senatorship. Diaz was overthrown in the revolution of 1910 which marked the first step on Mexico's path to a liberalized regime and to greater democracy, but that goal was not approached until after more than a decade of turmoil and bloody revolution. On April 20th, 1911, Root spoke for the first time on the Mexican question to register a protest against the views expressed in connection with a fiery resolution introduced by Senator Stone of Missouri as a result of riots at Agua Prieta in which two Americans were killed and eleven wounded by bullets fired across the border. The resolution proceeded on the assumption, Root said, that because American citizens had been injured in Mexico, the United States should immediately threaten war. He objected vigorously to such a departure from the normal processes of diplomacy which implied in advance that the United States was convinced that the Mexican Government was unwilling to do justice and to make compensation. The resolution was tabled. These few remarks brought an appreciative letter from one of Root's Mexican friends, Señor J. Y. Limantour, Minister of Hacienda in the Diaz Cabinet, to which Root replied on June 7th, 1911:

> . . . I have taken the deepest interest in recent affairs in Mexico and have been much distressed by the disorder which appears for the moment to check prosperity and peaceful and orderly conditions of life there. Of course I am and must be a neutral regarding the political questions and movements which are dividing your people, yet I look with great hopefulness for a speedy return to happy relations. . . . Never did a country need strong and sa-

[3] Bryan to President Wilson, January 22, 1915, Bryan Papers, Library of Congress.

gacious men more than Mexico needs them now, for you have to make a government which is free, so that the most intelligent and industrious may have equal and unrestricted opportunity, and at the same time a government that is strong, so that the turbulent elements which still remain may be repressed and compelled to respect the law. Nevertheless I mourn over the fate of General Diaz. It is one of the most pathetic and sad things that I have ever known. He was so great a man; such a true lover of Mexico; he had done such great things for his country. She owed so much to him that it is impossible to contemplate his exile with composure. The time will come again when Mexico lauds him as the greatest of her sons. I hope it will come before it is too late for him to know that his country is really not ungrateful.

Similarly the Secretary of Foreign Relations of Mexico, Manuel Calero, telegraphed Root on March 16th, 1912, to express the gratitude of the Mexican Government for Root's introduction of a resolution which was passed and which gave the President power to prevent shipments of arms and ammunition to the revolutionists. This was the first of the measures adopted by Congress for the control of the international traffic in arms and ammunition to countries disturbed by civil war or revolution.

Nothing has been found in Senator Root's papers to indicate his opinion of the unfortunate resolution adopted by the Senate on August 2nd, 1912, which declared that the United States "could not see without grave concern" the possession of a strategic harbor on the American continent by a non-American company connected with a foreign government. Lodge introduced the resolution after making much of rumors that a Japanese fishing company was about to lease land on Magdalena Bay on the west coast of Mexico. The Senate debate took place behind closed doors, but Root is recorded as voting in favor of it. Secretary Knox believed the State Department had demonstrated that the whole thing was a mare's nest and that the passage of the resolution to save Lodge's face, aroused resentment and ill-feeling in both Japan and Latin America.[4]

As the troubles of Mexico became progressively worse, President Wilson on August 27th, 1913, declared his policy of non-intervention. Root was abroad for a month that summer to receive the degree of

[4] Knox to Taft, April 28, 1914, Knox Papers, Library of Congress.

D.C.L. from Oxford University. When he landed in New York on August 24th, three days before the President's speech, he was interviewed by reporters and expressed his entire agreement with this non-intervention policy of the President.[5] Wilson wrote to him on August 25th, incidentally asking him if he had any objection to the appointment of a certain person as United States Attorney for the Northern District of New York, and continuing:

> Let me express my pleasure in your return to the country and my deep gratification that you should feel that you could reinforce my judgment with regard to the perplexing and difficult Mexican situation. The views you are reported to have expressed upon landing are exactly my own and I feel reassured by that circumstance.

Later, Root and Wilson were to be poles apart in their views regarding the proper foreign policy of the United States, but at this stage their relations were cordial and apparently marked by a considerable degree of mutual admiration. It was not much later that Root contributed so weightily to the support of Wilson in urging the repeal of the Panama Canal Tolls bill. Meanwhile the Mexican situation grew more and more serious, and Root's disapproval of Wilson's policy steadily increased. Root analyzed it in a letter to General James H. Wilson on September 8th, 1913:

> . . . The present situation of the Mexican affair seems to be that President Wilson, in advance of consulting the Senate, committed himself to a course of conduct through sending Mr. Lind to communicate with Huerta, and the reception of this communication rather closes the door to any further action by the United States until some change occurs in Mexico, unless the United States is prepared to back up its proposals by force, and this Mr. Wilson very properly repudiates. Quite without regard to our judgment upon the wisdom or unwisdom of Mr. Wilson's course, the universal feeling in Congress is that we must stand by the Administration and not present discord or controversy. It is gratifying to see that even the wildest men we have in either House agree to this view, so that we are all waiting and I think probably will wait until after the time fixed for the Mexican election. Then there may be a new departure.

[5] New York *Times*, August 25, 1913.

To General William H. Carter, then with the troops in Texas, he wrote frankly on November 6th:

> We are feeling very much troubled here about the Mexican situation and I am awfully afraid that you may have something to do beside camp out in Texas. I think the President is fully resolved not to intervene, but he may get into a situation where he can't help it. My chief trouble about intervention is not so much that I think our army, with its present strength, would have any difficulty in getting to the City of Mexico and establishing itself there, or in bringing about such an organization of Mexicans as to pacify the country, but because I think if we ever go into Mexico we shall not come out without robbing her. We shall not be honest about it. We shall take away her Northern provinces and lower California and disgrace ourselves in the estimation of all America and the rest of the world.

Two days later Taft wrote to "Athos" Root one of his long rambling letters which he opened with an expression of his pleasure at getting back "to the nomenclature that suggests others of the *dramatis personae* in some stage effects in which you and I were first walking gentlemen and d'Artignan [sic] then, as now, inclined to play all parts on the stage, as well as 'every instrument in the band'." Taft was much opposed to Wilson's policy. "Right down between us girls, just as an evidence of good faith, and not for publication, I am obliged to say that our distinguished, and I fear, at the same time, Puritan and Jesuitical President, has taken a course which only he and a gentleman like Bryan, who use the State Department for popular and election purposes, could take." He thought that Wilson, in preaching against intervention, was at the same time taking a course which could not fail to lead us into war. "Now do you suppose that in the mind of a man who plays politics every minute, quite as much as our friend d'Artignan did, and in the back of his head there is not a source of philosophic contentment that not the worst thing that could happen for his Administration is a war?" Taft, however, was inclined to think that if we went into Mexico, as appeared inevitable, to restore order, "we are entitled to compensation," in the way of drawing a "scientific frontier" which would bring Arizona down to the Gulf of California. "Bryan once told me, when he came to see me in the White House, that he hoped we might buy from Mexico, Southern

California. He has an itching for that territory." Root's letter to General Carter, however, shows that he was quite opposed to that form or to any other form of imperialistic land grabbing. Root also differed with Taft in interpreting Wilson's motives; he wrote ten days later to Edwin D. Mead of the World Peace Foundation: "I am very sure that President Wilson is sincere and positive in his intention not to resort to armed intervention in Mexico. I am not without fear that he may drift into a position where it would be very difficult for him to maintain his good intentions." Root also declined to make political capital out of a disturbed situation in our foreign relations. On January 20th, 1914, he wrote the Chairman of the Republican State Central Committee in Maryland that he would not, being a Senator and a member of the Foreign Relations Committee, make a public statement on the Mexican situation for the use of the Republican Bureau of Publicity.

Then came the Tampico incident on April 9th, 1914. A boat load of American sailors in uniform landed at a wharf in Tampico and were arrested by the Mexican authorities who represented the de facto government of Huerta. The sailors were, after a brief delay, returned to the boat. There were immediate amends in the form of disavowals by the higher authorities, regrets and apologies, discipline of the subordinate who had acted in inconsiderate haste. But the admiral of the American squadron at Tampico demanded a formal salute to the American flag. While this question was being discussed with the de facto government in Mexico City, on April 21st, the United States naval forces seized the custom house at Vera Cruz, for the alleged purpose of forcing compliance with the demand for a salute to the flag. Four marines were killed and twenty wounded. The seizure was actually ordered by President Wilson at two-thirty in the morning to prevent a German ship from landing a cargo of munitions at Vera Cruz. This fact apparently was not known at the time outside of a limited Cabinet circle.[6] On the same day, a Joint Resolution was passed in the House declaring:

> That the President of the United States is justified in the employment of the armed forces of the United States to enforce the de-

[6] Tumulty, Woodrow Wilson As I Know Him, p. 151. Baker says that Wilson told Lodge of the intended action, on April 20th, Woodrow Wilson, Life and Letters, Vol. IV, p. 325.

mands made upon Victoriano Huerta for unequivocal amends to the Government of the United States for affronts and indignities committed against this Government by General Huerta and his representatives.

The Senate, in a dramatic night session to which the news of the death of the four American marines was brought, took up the resolution. Lodge immediately introduced a substitute resolution which omitted all reference to Huerta and which closed with the statement "that the United States disclaims any hostility to the Mexican people or any purpose to make war upon Mexico." In favor of this substitute Root spoke with all the persuasiveness and dramatic force of which he was capable. According to Wilson's biographer it was "probably the ablest speech delivered." [7] Root asserted his admiration and respect for President Wilson and his confidence in his devotion to peace. But he pointed out that what they were asked to do, as a part of the Government, was to *justify* the action taken at Vera Cruz. In the House resolution, the justification was made to appear to be insistence upon amends for the insult to the flag. Root surveyed the events at Tampico and the amends already made; he reduced this "justification" to an attempt by a great and strong power to compel by force a small and weak neighbor to accept without further discussion or negotiation the exact form of salute which the United States demanded. It was the kind of question which frequently arose and which always could be handled by the normal processes of peaceful diplomacy which established the facts and then arranged the amends which were due. He referred to the fact that Secretary Bryan was then negotiating his series of conciliation treaties which provided that force should never be used until the facts were investigated.

It is intervention, technically, but it is war in its essence that we are to vote to justify tonight. How long it will continue, what its results and its incidents will be, no man can state. Men will die, men dear to us will die, because of the action that we are to approve tonight. American homes will be desolate; American women will mourn; American children will go through life fatherless, because of the action that we are to approve tonight; and when those children grow to manhood, turn back the page to learn in what cause their fathers died, are they to find that it was

[7] Baker, *op. cit.*, p. 328.

about a quarrel as to the number of guns and the form and cere-
mony of a salute, and nothing else?

But that was not the real justification for the conduct of the United
States in Root's opinion.

> Back of the incident . . . there is a great array of facts, a long,
> dreadful history . . . behind the insult to our flag by this poor,
> ignorant subordinate are years of violence and anarchy in Mexico.
> Lying behind it are hundreds of American lives sacrificed, mil-
> lions of American property destroyed, and thousands of Ameri-
> cans reduced to poverty today through the destruction of their
> property. Lying behind it is a condition of anarchy in Mexico
> which makes it impossible to secure, by diplomatic means, pro-
> tection for American life and property in that country. Lying back
> of this incident is a condition of things in Mexico which abso-
> lutely prevents the protection of American life and property ex-
> cept through respect for the American flag, the American uniform,
> the American Government. . . . The real object to be obtained
> by the course we are asked to approve is not the gratification of
> personal pride; it is not the satisfaction of an admiral or a Govern-
> ment. It is the preservation of the power of the United States to
> protect its citizens under those conditions.

For these reasons Root favored the passage of the resolution in the
form of the Lodge substitute and in that form it passed the Senate
and was agreed to by the House. To a correspondent, Root explained
the situation further in a letter of April 25th:

> . . . The President has begun military operations by the seizure
> of Vera Cruz with a definite theory of action which he stated
> to Congress. That theory is, that we can separate General Huerta
> from the great body of the Mexican people, and, while proceed-
> ing against Huerta, avoid any general war with Mexico. It is of no
> use to speculate now or to discuss whether that theory can be
> realized or not. I sincerely and earnestly hope that the President
> will prove to be right in his expectations. Time and the rapid
> course of events will very soon determine. In the meantime Con-
> gress has approved the President's course and I think we ought all
> to give him patriotic support, no matter how we may have differed
> about the policy pursued and although we may deeply deplore
> the whole business, as I do.

On the same evening, Root as President of the American Society of International Law, which he had helped James Brown Scott to found seven years before, presided at the Society's annual banquet. In a voice which shook with emotion and with tears running down his cheeks, Root pledged his loyalty to the President in his dealings with Mexico.[8] And again on the 27th, he wrote to Admiral Mahan:

. . . I am feeling very unhappy about the whole business. It seems to me that while there might have been an international justification for intervention irrespective of any question of policy on our part, the salute incident, after the disavowal and apology and explanation of the mistake and the arrest of the offenders and the discussion between the two foreign offices, did not furnish a just cause for war, certainly without much more effort towards diplomatic adjustment. It does not seem to me possible that the President can limit his liability while attacking Huerta and prevent the people of Mexico from fighting him even though he may not want to fight them so long as he invades their country and captures their cities. I sincerely desire that he may be able to do so, but I am very pessimistic about it. If we are to have a war with Mexico, as seems to me to be inevitable, I apprehend only disaster from the tentative method of beginning it instead of striking hard at the beginning. I hope, however, that I am all wrong.

When Dr. Lyman Abbott congratulated him on the stand which he had taken in the Senate, Root replied on the 29th: "It caused me great distress of spirit to determine just what I ought to do under the very extraordinary circumstances, but in reviewing it I think that what I did was right. . . ."

A month later Root was feeling still more dubious about Wilson's policy and his letters show a political bitterness against the Democrats and their domestic as well as foreign policy. To a letter from Samuel Dickson, he replied on June 3rd, 1914:

. . . I do not think that Mr. Wilson expects to invade Mexico but I believe he is engaged in what he considers a scheme of reform in the interests of the Mexican peons and that he expects this reform to be carried out by the Carranza-Villa faction, probably through something like the Irish Land Purchase Act. I apprehend that Carranza and Villa have no such conception of the

[8] Washington *Post*, April 26th, 1914.

proposed reform. Their reformatory methods appear to be to kill the owner and take the land. I cannot believe that the American government will make itself the instrument of a scheme of spoliation. I am bound to say, however, that the spirit which would dictate such a course does not differ very much from the spirit now exhibited towards the citizens of our own country who have much property and few votes.

When Wilson invited the Senate Foreign Relations Committee to the White House and told them he intended to support the Caranza-Villa faction, Root asked, "Do you think you can trust Villa, Mr. President?" "Oh yes," Wilson replied, "he's a changed man." To Root, this epitomized what he came to consider the ignorant folly of Wilson's Mexican policy.[9] In a lighter vein, but with evidently the same underlying feeling, Root wrote to his son-in-law, Captain Ulysses S. Grant, 3rd, who had been sent with the occupying force to Vera Cruz:

As I have fled from Washington to avoid the tropical heat which prevails on the thirty-ninth parallel of latitude I have been very sympathetic with our troops in Vera Cruz, but it is a great thing to be young and to have learned how to live in the tropics. I hope you will not have to stay there very much longer, although Mr. Villa seems to indicate the same disposition to eat Mr. Carranza up that Mr. Carranza exhibited as to eating Mr. Huerta up, following Mr. Huerta's example in eating Mr. Madero up because Mr. Madero had eaten Mr. Diaz up, and during these rapid changes of attitude it must be very difficult for the figures in the Mexican movie to keep their minds fixed on the subject of saluting the American flag, which was the original occasion of your going to Vera Cruz.

Even then his attitude was that the country must stand behind the President now that he had started on his course, much as Root and others distrusted the direction in which that course would lead. Root expounded his views on the Mexican situation to his fellow members on the Foreign Relations Committee at one of their meetings. A Democratic member insisted that Bryan must hear Root's view and asked if Root would tell him. Root acquiesced and Bryan came to his house. Bryan was much interested and said he wished to give Root's

[9] Root to the author, March 12, 1929.

views to President Wilson immediately, asking if Root would be available that evening. "I said I was always at the President's disposal and he said he would let me know, but I never heard anything, for when he told Wilson, he told a man who did not want to learn." [10] Root had prepared another speech on Wilson's Mexican policy which he had intended to deliver just before his term ended on March 4th, 1909; a change in the Senate program had prevented his speaking. He had intended in that speech to point out that the Administration's troubles with Mexico were largely the fault of Wilson's interfering in the internal affairs of Mexico; he had allowed his personal feelings against Huerta to influence his official conduct. [11] A great Democratic international lawyer has properly criticized Wilson on the same ground. [12]

Concurrently with the Mexican question, there developed an issue of capital importance in both the domestic and the international affairs of the United States. This was the question whether the United States was bound by the Hay-Pauncefote treaty of 1901 with Great Britain not to discriminate in favor of its own coastwise shipping by relieving it of tolls which were charged upon the shipping of all other countries through the Panama Canal. It was an issue which led Root to make the speech in the Senate which stands out as his greatest contribution during those six years. One of the most interesting aspects of his part in this controversy is that despite his strong feeling of party loyalty and his devotion to President Taft, and despite his growing irritation with President Wilson and the Democratic Party, he opposed the former and supported the latter. "There are no politics in foreign affairs according to my view," he replied to a correspondent who wrote him after his first speech in the Senate on the question of the tolls. [13] He felt very deeply on the subject since it seemed to him to attack the whole basis of the successful conduct of foreign affairs, namely faith in the pledged word of the United States. He felt deeply also because he believed he was fighting the fight of John Hay for whom he had very real affection. He was moreover defending the whole cause of arbitration and the treaties which he himself negotiated. He was dealing with a subject familiar to him for

[10] Root to the author, February 17, 1929.
[11] Diary of Chandler P. Anderson, entry of March 8, 1915.
[12] John Bassett Moore, Candor and Common Sense, p. 24.
[13] Root to Dr. A. J. Thompson, February 18, 1913.

over a decade. He told the Senate in his second speech on May 21st, 1914:

> . . . I knew something about this treaty. I knew what John Hay thought. I sat next to him in the Cabinet of President Mc-Kinley while it was negotiated, and of President Roosevelt when it was signed. I was called in with Senator Spooner to help in the framing of the Panama Treaty which makes obedience to this Hay-Pauncefote Treaty a part of the stipulations under which we get our title. I negotiated the treaty with Colombia for the settlement and the removal of the cloud upon the title to the Isthmus of Panama, and carried on the negotiations with England under which she gave her assent to the privileges that were given to Colombia in that treaty. I have had to have a full conception of what this treaty meant for now nearly thirteen years.

Especially in those negotiations with England for her assent to the Colombian treaty, Root had been most emphatic in asserting the principle of American trusteeship and in repudiating any idea that the Hay-Pauncefote treaty would ever be violated.[14]

The subject first came up in the Senate during the hot exhausting session in the summer of 1912. A bill was introduced for the opening of the Canal and for the government of the Canal Zone. The bill gave the President power to fix toll rates but prohibited him from imposing any tolls upon vessels engaged in the coasting trade of the United States. As Root stated in his first main speech on the subject, January 21st, 1913: "It is rather poverty of language than a genius for definition which leads us to call a voyage from New York to San Francisco, passing along countries thousands of miles away from our territory 'coasting trade' or to call a voyage from New York to Manila, on the other side of the world, 'coasting trade'." The term really referred merely to the special treatment of nationally monopolistic voyages between two American ports. But as Root also pointed out, when analyzing the question of discrimination, Canada had the same type of coasting trade through the Panama Canal for voyages from Montreal to Vancouver, and so for Mexico and Colombia in voyages between ports on the east and west coasts. The Hay-Pauncefote treaty provided that the Canal, when built, should, like the Suez Canal, be

[14] Root to Ambassador Bryce, January 16, 1909; copy in MS collection of Papers of Joseph H. Choate, Columbia University Library.

open to the vessels "of all nations . . . on terms of entire equality."
Those who favored the exemption for the American coasting trade,
asserted that "all nations" meant merely all foreign nations and did
not include the United States. Root took the opposite view. President
Taft wrote to his wife on July 17th, 1912, that the matter had been
discussed in the Cabinet and "We think we have that power—Mr.
Root thinks not—under the treaty." Again he wrote to her on August
15th that Secretary of State Knox, Secretary of War Stimson, Secretary of Interior Fisher and Attorney General Wickersham all agreed
that this discrimination was proper; Root was still opposed. When
the bill came before the Senate, Root moved to strike out the clause
granting an exemption to our coasting vessels. His motion was defeated without a roll call and the bill passed by 47 to 15 on August
9th, 1912; it became law on August 24th. Taft could not see what
ground Root had to stand on and thought his attitude on the subject
a "defect" in his career.[15] He thought that Hay and Choate had been
too much "saturated with the atmosphere of London society" and
that Root and Lodge had also "been affected by their stay in London
on that Alaska Boundary Commission." [16]

Great Britain had already remonstrated informally; the news of the
proposed American action was at first received in London "with amazement mingled with incredulity." [17] On December 11th, 1912, Sir Edward Grey filed a formal protest against what was considered a breach of
the treaty, suggesting at the same time that if the American government could not share their view, this was a proper subject for arbitration under the treaty of 1908—the treaty which Root had negotiated. On January 14th, 1913, in the last session under the Republican
administration, Root introduced a bill to repeal the tolls exemption;
no action was taken on it.

A few weeks later, in private conversation, Root made what was
perhaps his most important contribution to this cause. On January
31st, 1913, President-elect Wilson had come up from Princeton to
New York to attend the monthly dinner of a small dining club known
as the Round Table. Among the other members present were Henry

[15] Taft to Knox, January 27 and December 18, 1913, Knox Papers, Library of Congress.
[16] Taft to Knox, April 12, 1914, ibid.
[17] Ambassador Whitelaw Reid to Root, August 7, 1912.

White, who, as Chargé of the Embassy in London, had begun the canal treaty negotiations with Lord Salisbury; Joseph H. Choate, who as Ambassador had completed these negotiations; and Elihu Root. After dinner the conversation turned to the subject of the repeal of the tolls exemption. The three men who had first-hand knowledge of the subject, and especially Choate and Root, explained to the President-elect the reasons for their conviction that the good faith of the United States required repeal of the tolls exemption. Wilson asked a few questions and when the explanation was finished, said: "This has been an illuminating discussion. I knew very little about this subject. I think I now understand it and the principles that are involved. When the time comes for me to act, you can count upon my taking the right stand." [18]

On March 5th, 1914, despite a plank in the Democratic platform which approved the tolls repeal, President Wilson sent a strong message to Congress, saying that in his considered judgment, the discrimination then existing under the law was a violation of the treaty with Great Britain and asking for the repeal of the exemption. A bill was at once introduced in the House and passed there on March 31st. Root's principal speech came in the Senate on May 21st, 1914.

He began with the historical basis of the question, showing that throughout a long history of consideration of an isthmian canal route, the United States had always stood for equality of treatment between its own citizens and those of foreign nations. This was the basis of our treaty of 1846 with New Granada and also of the treaty of 1903 with Panama under which the United States obtained its rights of sovereignty in the Canal Zone. On this basis he answered the common argument that we were free to do what we pleased with our own territory; we had acquired rights in that territory under this specific condition akin to a trusteeship. If that principle were discarded, the whole justice of our conduct in acquiring rights in the isthmus was impugned. Here Root was actually rejustifying the course of Roosevelt in "taking" Panama, since it was on this principle of an obligation to civilization that Root, and Roosevelt himself, had justified that much criticized act. To Elbert F. Baldwin of the *Outlook*, Root wrote on June 8th, 1914:

[18] Private records of the Round Table.

. . . One great trouble with the Panama Tolls legislation is that President Taft, in a memorandum made when he signed the bill put his approval upon the ground of our exclusive right to the benefits of the canal and a complete repudiation of the position upon which President Roosevelt based the recognition of Panama and the acquisition of the Canal Zone. The main thing I have been contending for in the Tolls Repeal controversy is that we should not acquire rights upon the Isthmus upon one theory, stated by Mr. Roosevelt, and having got them, hold them on the contrary theory, stated by Mr. Taft. I have no doubt that we were both morally and legally right in what we did, but on Mr. Taft's theory of our own title to our rights, we were not morally right.

The Hay-Pauncefote treaty had incorporated by reference this obligation of the earlier treaties. But aside from this historical background, Root showed that no exception for American coasting vessels was contemplated by the negotiators of the latter treaty and that therefore no such exception could be read into its terms. Robert Lansing, then Counsellor of the State Department, and Joseph H. Choate helped him prepare his argument by collecting data for him. James Brown Scott, another former aide and then secretary of the Carnegie Endowment for International Peace, also engaged in the same task. As early as July 15th, 1912, Choate had written to him:

. . . my recollection is clear that the clause in the Treaty guaranteeing free and equal passage to the ships of all nations in peace and in war was deemed incapable of any other construction than its plain terms import—I hope that we shall not be tempted to depart from it now—

Although able arguments were made on the other side, Root's argument on this point of treaty interpretation was unimpeachable. After establishing the legal duty of the United States under this article of the treaty, Root pointed to the lack of reason for making the exemption. Our coastwise shipping was the most heavily protected part of American business and had no need of what amounted to an additional subsidy. We were not trying to help the American merchant marine as a whole, but merely to aid that part of it which less than any other needed help. Root admitted that the United States had a right to subsidize its coastwise shipping if it wished to do so, and that it could apply the receipts from the Canal tolls for that purpose. But it could not, he claimed, without violating its solemn word, accomplish that end by discriminating in favor of those ships by relieving them from the duty of paying tolls equally with the ships of other nations.

He argued also the question of arbitration which the British had suggested. He could see no alternative except to withdraw from the position taken by creating the exception, or to submit to arbitration the question of treaty interpretation involved. He argued vigorously that there was not the slightest basis for asserting that this question came within the exceptions contained in the arbitration treaty of 1908 with Great Britain—national honor, independence or vital interests. He insisted that this was merely a business question, in which the United States, by reason of its interest in the American shipping business, was following a particular line of action. Yet he showed by quoting from the debates, that it was generally understood that the necessary two-thirds vote could not be obtained in the Senate to submit this question to arbitration. With biting sarcasm, he rehearsed the cases in which the United States had sought arbitration from other countries, particularly Great Britain, as in the Alabama Claims and North Atlantic Fisheries cases—the former resulting in a British payment to the United States of some fifteen millions of dollars. "Oh, arbitration when we want it, yes; but when another country wants it, 'Never, never furl the American flag at the behest of a foreign nation'!"

> Do the American people wish their representatives to treat all the other nations that are in conventional relations with us . . . upon the theory that any question of right by them is an insult, that any accord of a right to them by us is a surrender? . . . Do they want us to be ugly and revengeful and insolent and brutal and boasting, or do they want us to be dignified and calm and considerate and reasonable in our relations with foreign countries?

He showed that Taft had favored arbitration. "President Roosevelt with all his courageous and combative nature, is in favor of arbitration." So were President Wilson and Senators Lodge and Sutherland. But since the debates had shown that the Senate would not consent to arbitration, those who favored that solution were supporting the repeal bill. "We are for this repeal first and chiefly because we cannot arbitrate it, and to refuse to arbitrate it would be discredit and dishonor for our country. Right or wrong, whatever rules or whatever exceptions may justify it, if we decide this in our favor and refuse to arbitrate we are discredited, we are dishonored, we have repudiated our principles."

There is much more meat packed into those two long arguments, much of oratorical appeal, addressed in part to the Senators and in part to the country at large. With some reluctance, Root yielded to the request of Andrew Carnegie that copies of his speeches be circulated by the Carnegie Endowment for International Peace. 741,000 copies were printed for the Endowment and distributed through the country to lists of voters including over two hundred thousand farmers, one hundred and sixty-seven thousand physicians, some hundred thousand clergymen and the same number of lawyers. This fact perhaps did more to weaken the effectiveness of Root's speech than anything else. Bainbridge Colby, as Chairman of the Committee for the Preservation of American Rights in the Panama Canal, issued a bitter attack, charging among other things that Root was acting at the behest of the transcontinental railroads who feared the competition of the shipping routes between the Atlantic and Pacific coasts. It was alleged that they had stirred up the Canadian railroads and through them had brought about the protests of the British Government. Senator Poindexter of Washington had much to say about Carnegie's ill-gotten wealth and his devotion to his native Scottish land. Root repudiated these insinuations. In private correspondence as well he asserted that he had never had a spoken or written word from railroad interests in regard to this matter. There is no paper in his files which directly or indirectly suggests that he had the interests of the railroads in mind. "So far as I have been able to observe the transcontinental railroads are entirely indifferent on the subject of tolls," he wrote to W. H. Manss on January 31st, 1913. "I have not seen, or heard, of any expression on their part one way or the other, but it is quite immaterial whether they want one thing or another." Ambassador Bryce, with whom he kept up his intimate acquaintance and confidential correspondence, assured him privately in regard to charges made by Senator O'Gorman, that the Canadian railroads had done nothing at all in the matter and that the Canadian Pacific in particular was indifferent. The reasons for Root's interest in this question and for his taking the position which he did are so obvious that the support of this charge needed much more than the wholly unsubstantiated gossip of those who opposed Root's view and favored this type of subsidy for the coastwise shipping. Of all the charges made against Root as a result of his popular reputation as the lawyer for big business, none is more completely devoid of substantiation. The railroads were opposed, and Root was opposed, but so was Wilson and so were a great many other persons who were never even thought of as being the "tools" of big business.

Back in September, 1912, Root had written to Choate: "I am feeling very badly about the Panama Canal bill. . . . The very men who are crying out most loudly against special privilege and protected interests were the loudest in their demand that this particular privilege be given to the coasting interest, which does not need it in the least. . . ." It is interesting to note that the New York Chamber of Commerce in 1913 supported Root's position although the *Marine Journal* of February 22nd, 1913, charged that this action—a reversal of their previous stand—was due to the pressure of Root, Choate, the international bankers and the European steamship companies! The Merchants Association of New York took the view opposed to Root. The New Orleans Association of Commerce and the Associated Chambers of Commerce of the Pacific Coast likewise opposed Root's position, as did a great many Irish groups who were particularly vehement about the "surrender" to England. On April 6th, 1914, Adelbert Moot of Buffalo wrote to Root that the New York State Bar Association was prevented from passing a resolution endorsing Root's stand only through the personal appeal of President Taft's brother and friends.

On June 11th, 1914, probably due largely to the power of President Wilson, the Senate passed the repeal bill by a vote of 50 to 35. It is never possible to say how much effect the speeches of individual senators influence a result of this kind, but with the split in party lines, it is fair to assume that Root's efforts contributed substantially to the final result. It was one of the few cases where, as a Senator in the minority opposition, he was able during the Wilson Administration, to be extremely effective in influencing the action of Congress.

CHAPTER XXXIX

"The value of discussions in the Senate"

IN the debate on the Panama Canal Tolls, Root had defended the principle of arbitration. He had given the principle more general support when President Taft in 1911 submitted to the Senate for its constitutional advice and consent to ratification a new type of arbitration treaty which Secretary Knox had negotiated with England and France. It will be recalled that Hay had negotiated a series of arbitration treaties embodying the sweeping reservations found in the Anglo-French treaty of 1903 which was taken as a model. Those reservations excluded all questions involving the vital interests, the independence or the national honor of either of the parties or the rights of third parties. Hay's treaties failed because he and Roosevelt were unwilling to accept the Senate amendment which required that the consent of the Senate be obtained to each particular agreement to submit any given case to an arbitral tribunal. Root had taken up the same treaties, had induced Roosevelt to yield to the Senate's demand and had signed twenty-five of them. In a speech before the Arbitration and Peace League in 1911, President Taft had boldly declared: "Personally I do not see why matters of national honor should not be referred to courts of arbitration. . . ." Sir Edward Grey, British Foreign Secretary, had commented on these remarks in Parliament, saying that if such agreements could be made, arbitration would really be an effective instrument and would enable governments to cut down on the rapidly increasing burden of armaments.[1] With this auspicious prelude, Knox, during the summer of 1911, signed treaties with the French and British Ambassadors. Abandoning the old restrictive shibboleths, the treaties provided that arbitration would be used for all international differences which were legal in their nature, the test being their justiciability by the application of the principles of law or equity. This was going far, but the treaty went on to provide

[1] See Cory, *Compulsory Arbitration*, p. 83.

for the creation of a joint commission, composed of three citizens of each country; if the parties disagreed as to the "justiciability" of a particular question, the commission would pass on that point and if all, or all but one, agreed that the question did fall within the scope of the treaty, then it would be submitted to arbitration. If merely two out of the three American commissioners decided the question was not "justiciable," it would not be arbitrated.

The treaties went as usual to the Foreign Relations Committee of the Senate; Lodge was then chairman of the Committee. Some at least of the Senators seem to have been irritated because Knox had not consulted them during the course of the negotiations.[2] Root, throughout the negotiations, had been in touch with Ambassador Bryce, partly at the suggestion of Chandler Anderson who was then Counsellor of the Department of State. Bryce thought that Root's judgment on the form the treaty should take was "better than that of the whole State Department put together." [3] But the final text did not follow Root's proposals. Bryce himself thought that Taft and Knox had erred in not explaining the treaty beforehand to the Senators "following the method so skilfully practised by Mr. Root." [4] The Committee was willing to accept the broad scope of the first article, which failed to mention national honor, vital interests and independence, because the treaty contained the provision on which Root had yielded three years before, namely the requirement that each case must be referred to the Senate for its consent before it went to arbitration. The Senate could therefore prevent submission of any dispute which it believed to be improper for submission. The other provision, giving the powers to the joint commission, they proposed to strike out entirely, because they construed the words in their rather obvious meaning of giving the majority of five commissioners power to make a decision on the point which would be binding on both governments. This provision, they believed, took away the constitutional powers of the Senate. This view was sharply attacked in a minority report from the Committee, signed by Senators Root, Cullom and Bur-

[2] Andrew Carnegie to Taft, December 15, 1912, sent by Taft to Knox, Knox Papers, Library of Congress. Also Francis B. Loomis to Nicholas Murray Butler, October 31, 1911, copy in Root Papers.
[3] Bryce to Sir Edward Grey, March 28, 1911, Gooch and Temperley British Documents on the Origins of the War, Vol. VIII, p. 558.
[4] Bryce to Sir Edward Grey, August 22, 1911, ibid., p. 596.

ton.[5] This minority report remains a document of permanent value although it has not yet shaken the Senate from its tenacious insistence upon the view which the majority, under Lodge's leadership, expressed. The report appears to have been written by Root, since a draft of it, corrected in his own hand, exists among his papers. That it was originally drafted as his individual dissent to which the other two Senators subsequently adhered, is indicated by the fact that one of the changes made by Root's pen was to substitute throughout the draft, "we" for "I." The minority report insisted that there was no delegation of power here any more than in any number of statutes where the Congress describes a class of cases and directs some executive officer to act on cases falling within such a class. Tariff acts, for example, say that a certain rate of duty shall be imposed on goods of a certain kind and it is necessarily left to the collector of customs to determine whether a particular article is within that category or some other. So here the treaty, concluded with the advice and consent of the Senate, would describe the class of cases to be arbitrated and the commissioners, if necessary, would decide whether a particular dispute fell within the class. The minority agreed that "there are some questions of national policy and conduct which no nation can submit to the decision of anyone else, just as there are some questions of personal conduct which every man must decide for himself." The minority agreed that the line between those two kinds of cases should be clearly indicated in the treaty "for nothing could be worse than to make a treaty for arbitration and then to have either party charged by the other party with violating it." To avoid any doubt on this score, the minority were willing to see included in the Senate's resolution of advice and consent an interpretative statement which would declare that the treaty did not authorize "the submission to arbitration of any question which depends upon or involves the maintenance of the traditional attitude of the United States concerning American questions, or other purely governmental policy." Root had originally written after "American questions" the words "commonly described as the Monroe Doctrine," but these words he struck out in ink. Root's plan was thus "to leave the decision of the Commission binding upon both parties, but to control the commission by interposing a construc-

[5] Sen. Doc. No. 98, 62nd Cong., 1st Sess., p. 9.

tion of the treaty which they cannot override." [6]

There was a tremendous campaign throughout the country in favor of the arbitration treaties. The peace organizations,—at that time relatively few in number—with the Carnegie Endowment for International Peace in the lead, organized meetings and distributed literature and had petitions signed in perhaps their greatest effort prior to the campaigns in favor of the World Court some fifteen years later. President Taft and Secretary Knox took many occasions to speak for the treaties; the President particularly fought hard for a cause which always was close to his heart. Root refused to take part in any public meetings or to make any speeches except in the Senate. As he told Joseph H. Choate on November 11th, 1911, other Senators would resent his drumming up popular support and pressure in favor of his minority report and, besides, as a member of the Foreign Relations Committee, he would have to "exercise a degree of caution and restraint which would make any public speech about them quite ineffective." Roosevelt was rather scornful. He was in full agreement with Lodge and objected strenuously to the idea of "allowing a commission, which as you say might consist of foreigners, to take away power which belongs both to the President and the Senate." [7] As a matter of fact, the commission could not "consist of foreigners." Roosevelt hoped that it was true that Root felt the same way. So phrased, of course, Root did, but he did not agree that the treaty was open to any such ridiculous interpretation. On September 22nd, 1911, Roosevelt wrote again to Lodge: ". . . I saw Root the other day, and he frankly admitted that he was quite as much against the treaty in its proposed form as you were, and was merely trying to break the fall for its backers. . . . If Root's amendment is adopted, the treaty in its essential feature is dead." [8] Sir Edward Grey doubted whether the treaty would be "worth accepting with Root's Declaration attached to it" and this view was shared by Ambassador Jusserand in regard to the French Treaty, but Bryce thought differently.[9] Taft was also opposed to the

[6] Root to Seth Low, November 7, 1911.

[7] Roosevelt to Lodge, August 14, 1911, *Roosevelt-Lodge Correspondence*, Vol. II, p. 406.

[8] Roosevelt to Lodge, September 22, 1911, *ibid.*, p. 409.

[9] Sir Edward Grey to Bryce, September 19 and December 19, 1911; Bryce to Grey, December 4 and December 19, 1911; Gooch and Temperley, *op. cit.*, pp. 597, 599 and 600.

Root proposal [10] but failed to understand that Root was really trying to secure ratification.[11] Roosevelt elaborated his views to Arthur Lee, in a letter of August 22nd, 1911:

> I must say I do not think much of the peace and arbitration treaty. If it were to be limited absolutely to England, well and good; but as a general model, the treaty as between the United States and Great Britain for all other powers I think would be a poor business. I do not think it will do much harm, if adopted, or be especially dangerous, simply because in any crisis I do not think it would have any effect whatever. But if we lived up to it in spirit, if we lived up to it as the apostles of peace at the moment make believe it ought to be lived up to, it would have meant that we could not have gone to war with Spain, that Cuba would now be Spanish, that we could not have started building the Panama Canal, and that the Isthmus would now belong to the Republic of Colombia, or at least not to us, and that you would not have been in Egypt; for unquestionably any neutral arbitration court would have decided against real right and justice and for technical legality against you in Egypt and the Sudan, against us about Cuba and Panama. The Chestertons and Andrew Carnegies and the like are pretty poor guides in foreign policy, not only from the standpoint of national honor and interest, but from the standpoint of world welfare.[12]

Roosevelt probably failed to understand the distinctions which were in Root's mind; at any rate his interpretation of Root's view is not borne out by Root's other correspondence. To a correspondent who wrote Root protesting against his failure to support the Taft treaties, Root replied in September, 1911: "You have been grossly misinformed." Senator Cullom, who signed with Root the minority report, wrote to him on October 27th, 1911, asking his views: "Do you still believe that the amendment introduced by you, and to which I agreed, is sufficient to protect the United States?" Root replied on November 7th:

> I have not changed my mind about the Arbitration Treaties. I think that the clause which we proposed to insert in the Resolution of Ratification amply protects us against being required to

[10] Bryce to Grey, December 4, 1911, loc. cit.
[11] Taft to Philander C. Knox, December 18, 1913, Knox Papers, Library of Congress.
[12] Roosevelt Papers, Library of Congress.

submit any question of policy to arbitration,—such, for example, as the Monroe Doctrine. Of course, it does not protect us against the arbitration of the Southern bond claims, but that I do not care about. I think those claims ought to be disposed of somehow, and unwillingness to have them arbitrated is, I think, quite inconsistent with our talk about being willing to arbitrate everything. Nor will it protect us against being called upon to arbitrate the questions arising under treaties with Oriental nations relating to the admission of their people, and their treatment after they are admitted to this country. Here again there is the inconsistency between the refusal to arbitrate and our very sweeping asseverations that we are in favor of arbitrating everything. I see no ground of principle upon which we can make this treaty and refuse to arbitrate these questions under it. A willingness to arbitrate such questions was necessarily implied in the making of the treaty. Of course the matter ought to be distinctly understood. It would be worse than useless to ratify this treaty with a misunderstanding between the parties as to what it really means. The result of that would be that some other country, considering the treaty to include more than we intend to have it include, would present a claim that the Senate would not consent to submit, and then the United States would be charged with insincerity and bad faith.

Yet Roosevelt, in a letter to Lodge of December 27th, 1911, again took much the same line: "Of course Root's amendment or supplement to the arbitration treaties takes the sting out, but yours ought to be passed too, and I should much prefer that Root had frankly put it that he was *against* the treaties as they were drawn, instead of saying that he is *for* them, but they are to be interpreted in diametrically the opposite to their real sense. . . ." [13] January 9th, 1912, he wrote Root that he hoped he would not vote for the treaties without at least his amendment. "As you know, I feel that Lodge's amendment should also be adopted, but I should regard it as a capital misfortune and a disgrace if this country ratified the unamended treaties." To which Root wrote back on January 12th: "I am as pleased as Punch over your little note about the Arbitration treaties, not because I needed it but because it is so characteristic and life-like that it seems almost like seeing you and hearing your voice. I don't think anyone really contemplates the ratification of the treaties without some resolution

[13] *Roosevelt-Lodge Correspondence*, Vol. II, p. 420.

which will protect us against being charged with bad faith when we refuse, as we certainly would refuse, to arbitrate some things that we are told the treaties are not intended to cover. Cabot has in another resolution which he has collaborated with Knox and which seems to cover the ground, although I don't like it quite as well as I do my own." And again a letter from Roosevelt on the 18th: "I guess that Cabot's amendment makes it all right, but what a preposterous farce the whole thing has been! Think of rational people being contented to get a treaty passed together with an authorized written construction of it which explains that it does not mean what it says it does! . . . Love to dear Mrs. Root. . . ."

In the final Senate debates which came on March 5th, 1912, Root argued valiantly, trying to persuade the Senate it was losing none of its powers, although he wrote to Elbert F. Baldwin on January 25th, 1912, "Personally I am not so much concerned about the powers of the Senate as I am about its duties, but I suppose they are really identical." In his letter of November 11th, 1911, to Choate, Root had said:

> Don't forget that the real difficulties to be overcome are not merely the difficulty about the Monroe Doctrine, and questions of policy. These can be disposed of by the clause in my resolution putting a construction upon the treaties, a construction which is entirely satisfactory, both to our Government and to the Governments of other countries. The great trouble is with the Southern Bond Claims, and the immigration questions. If the Southern Senators and the Pacific Coast Senators stand out, of course we cannot get a two-thirds vote.

That combination was effected and the Senate finally adopted by 46 votes to 36 a resolution offered by Senator Bacon of Georgia, which provided that the treaty did not authorize the submission to arbitration of immigration questions, rights of aliens in educational institutions, the bonds of the southern states, integrity of the territory of the several states and the Monroe Doctrine or other governmental policy. Thus they forbade arbitration of boundary questions which the United States had always considered preeminently suitable for some such solution; they cut off the possibility of any of our disputes with Japan being peacefully settled in this way and they yielded to the fears of the southerners whose state bonds were in default. Taft quite properly refused to ask France or Great Britain to accept such conditions and the treaties were tucked away to gather dust in official pigeonholes.

In his State Department days, Root had taken an active interest in the promotion of the foreign commerce of the United States, particularly with Latin America. His own experience had led him to stress the need for developing the American merchant marine. He was therefore on old familiar ground when on January 25th, 1911, he spoke in favor of the bill which dealt with the carrying of the United States mails on the seas. Root denied that this was a ship subsidy bill, although it involved payments to American ships for carrying the mails. He argued that it was merely a question of rendering efficient mail service to our merchants engaged in foreign trade. The law of 1891 had authorized the Postmaster General to award contracts to American vessels for carrying the mails and this had been done for twenty years. But it appeared that under the limitations imposed by the old law, the compensation paid, while adequate for the trade with Europe, the West Indies and the Caribbean, was insufficient to secure the service with the more distant ports of South America and Asia. The new bill provided for the necessary increase in rates subject to a maximum equivalent of the amounts received from the carriage of the ocean mails. Root therefore concluded that this was merely a question of how to expend the receipts from the ocean foreign mails so as to render efficient service. Root stressed heavily the need for developing our shipping lines to South American ports as an incidental aid to our commerce there. He believed that in some cases these mail contracts would have to be made with foreign lines but expected that the passage of the bill would stimulate the operation of American ships in the South American trade. Incidental advantages he believed would flow from stimulating commerce with South America and thus drawing closer our political ties. He called attention to the fact that unjust treatment of the Chinese had hampered our trade with China—he was mindful of the boycott with which he had to deal in the State Department—and hoped that we would be more intelligent in grasping our opportunities in Latin America. The United States needed foreign markets and this was one of the least costly and surest ways to stimulate merchants in securing them. He sought also to rally

support by pointing to the fact that dependence upon foreign shipping lines left the United States at the mercy of monopolistic com-
binations of foreign shipping lines which were even then engaged in
raising rates by agreements among themselves. Subsidized Japanese
shipping was driving our ships from the trade with the Orient.
". . . there is such a thing as the duty of a government to promote
the trade of a nation . . . it is no subject upon which to deal with
cheese-paring economy. . . ." [14] When Congress adjourned, the bill
had not been passed.

Quite different problems were raised, in Senator Root's opinion,
when three years later the Democratic Administration of President
Wilson sought to secure the passage of a ship purchase bill. The
World War was then in progress and added its complications regarding neutral and belligerent rights to a problem already full of difficulty. Far more than in the case Root had discussed, the United
States was suffering from the lack of an adequate merchant fleet. The
bill, embodying the ideas of Secretary of the Treasury McAdoo, provided for the creating of a government-owned corporation which
would build up the American Merchant Marine by purchase and construction. The purchase contemplated was that of the half million
tons of German and Austrian shipping laid up in American harbors
as a result of the World War. Root's attacks on this bill were among
the last speeches which he made, coming in January and February,
1915, just before his term expired. "Just at present we are having a
high old scrimmage in the Senate about the shipping bill," Root wrote
to Charles L. Stone on January 27th, 1915, "and instead of floating
calmly and gently out of office as becomes a man retired at the age
of seventy, I shall blow out under stress of heavy weather." He was
then a member of a rather impotent Republican minority in the
Senate, but in this instance President Wilson did not carry his point
for two years; it was not until September 7th, 1916, after Root had
returned to private life, that the ship purchase law was passed and
the United States Shipping Board was created to administer it. Root
and Lodge led the opposition in 1915 and succeeded by filibustering
in bringing about the surrender of the Democratic majority.

On January 4th, Root made his first speech which was merely a
general protest against the attempt to force the bill through the

[14] *Congressional Record*, 61st Cong., 3rd Sess., Vol. 46, pp. 1404 ff.

Senate without discussion and insisting that the opponents of the bill would discuss, to empty seats if necessary, in order that the people of the country might be aroused to its dangers. By agreement with the other leaders of the opposition, he devoted his first main speech on January 25th to the question of the right of a neutral to buy belligerent—in this case interned German—vessels and protect them by its flag. It was an argument on the applicable rules of international law in which he drew upon his experience in connection with the London Naval Conference of 1908 which had met while he was Secretary of State to codify the laws dealing with such matters. The question was whether belligerents were bound to acknowledge the neutral character of a ship transferred during war from belligerent to neutral ownership. Root pointed out that the continental European states had generally taken the position that such a transfer was void; the United States and England had maintained it was valid if it were a bona fide sale. The Declaration of London compromised with the rule that it was valid if not made "to evade the consequences to which an enemy vessel, as such, is exposed." Root declared that it was obvious that the only reason why the German owners would sell these ships was because the British control of the seas had bottled them up in American harbors. Root believed the United States could not protest if these ships were captured by the Allies after being purchased by the United States and he believed further that even though the United States acted through a government-owned corporation, it would be guilty of unneutral conduct if it carried contraband in such ships. "It is buying a quarrel, not a ship," he said. Root, as will be described in a later chapter, was vigorously "pro-Allied" in his point of view and he thought that one group favoring the bill was composed of the pro-Germans who wished to foment controversy between the United States and the Allies.[15] Official French and British opposition to the bill had been made known in Washington and Secretary Bryan urged President Wilson to announce that if the bill were passed the German ships would not be purchased. The President was unwilling to do that but apparently did have in mind using the ships on non-European trade routes.[16] When Charles Francis Adams wrote to ask Root if it were not true that the law of the sea

[15] Root to Lord Bryce, March 1, 1915.
[16] Tansill, America Goes to War, pp. 567–569.

had been torn in rags by the war, Root replied on February 4th: "The tremendous forces that are liberated by the fight for national life in Europe are bursting the mild restraints of international law in every direction. Instead of the duello, where it would be a disgrace to fire before the word, there seems to be a rough and tumble, half-horse, half alligator fight, with kicking, biting and gouging as a matter of course. Nevertheless, wherever there is international law, plainly the best way for a neutral to keep out of trouble is to observe it, and in any event neutrals better not go around looking for trouble." Manufacturers, the New York Chamber of Commerce and various shipping interests, were firm in their opposition and from some of these sources, such as the Editor of the New York *Journal of Commerce*, Root received useful data which he incorporated in his later speeches. On January 16th, 1915, Root wrote to Lawrence Godkin:

You cannot be more at a loss than I am to account for the President's strage [sic] insistence upon the Ship Purchase bill. I believe in his sincerity of purpose and high standards, and, although there have been some matters in which I have thought him seriously mistaken, I could trace the origin of what I considered mistakes to opinions which I respected. This proposal to go into the shipping business seems to be so bad internationally and economically that I am quite bewildered. The purpose apparently is to buy belligerent ships, and in that case the international situation would immediately become very grave. It is impossible to tell now whether the bill can be passed. It is understood that President Wilson insists upon it. If the Democratic majority of the Senate is willing to take the necessary steps by protracting the hours of session, sitting at night, etc., they can probably pass it. But I think even so it would necessarily be at the sacrifice of the appropriation bills and the cost of an extra session. The opponents of the bill will state their objections to it with whatever force they can command. The subject is a wide and complicated one and any adequate discussion will absorb a good deal of time. Of course in a body like the Senate, whose members for the most part are past the prime of life, the adoption of day and night sessions, which I rather anticipate, will have the effect of choking off discussion by physical and mental fatigue, and some of us are not as well able to stand up under that kind of pressure as we were twenty or thirty years ago. Nevertheless we shall do the best we can. My own idea of the value of discussions in the Senate is that their value consists very largely in their stimulating thought and discussion throughout the country upon measures of general public importance and that the responses which come from such outside discussion play a great part in determining the action which follows in the body itself. I think it is probable that if time is allowed for this process to run its ordinary course the expressions of opinion in the country would convince the Democrats in the Senate that it would be wise for their party to give more consideration to the bill than it has had. The present intention, however, seems to be not to give the country much chance to form and express an opinion. The only thing I am certain about is that the bill will not pass without a full exposure of its true character and defects upon the floor of the Senate.

The only reason which Root and Lodge could suggest for the support of the bill was the attempt of somebody to "make a great deal of money through the purchase of the imprisoned German ships," as Root wrote to Thomas J. O'Brien on February 5th. "I don't suppose the President had any such plan but I think the suggestion upon which he has acted had that origin. I think, moreover, that those suggestions are being promoted by men who wish to embroil this country on one side in the European war." Lodge was more explicit in his letter of March 1st to Roosevelt in which he asserted that certain bankers in New York, a Cabinet officer and others were engaged in a sinister plan "to make a lot of money. We have enough information to know this to be so, although it is one of those things which it is almost impossible, as you will realize, to prove." [17] Root did not believe Secretary McAdoo, who was largely responsible for the ship purchase proposal, was dishonest or corrupt but Root did think McAdoo was in a position where he was not free to disregard the wishes of men to whom he was still under heavy financial obligations.[18]

On February 4th, Root wrote to a correspondent: "The great fundamental vice in the bill is that it is a measure of state socialism which, if established, will inevitably destroy individual liberty. It is wholly unrepublican, un-American, and destructive of the principles upon which our free government has been built up and maintained." This was the chief theme of his final speech on the bill on February

[17] Roosevelt Papers, Library of Congress.
[18] Diary of Chandler P. Anderson, entry of April 15, 1915.

9th. With the growth of state socialism he saw also—it was a theme which he stressed over and again in many years before and after—the decline of the functions of the state governments and the vesting of power in the federal government. They were all small steps but

> Leg over leg the dog went to Dover; step by step, law by law, precedent by precedent, weakness by weakness, abuse by abuse, ignoring principle to-day, tomorrow and again tomorrow . . . you find that you have been going up or down, growing more free or more closely bound.

Here was a proposal which he felt would turn over to the government the transaction of the foreign commerce of the United States. Wilson insisted that the government was merely stepping in temporarily until private capital was ready to participate, but Root believed that once the government got into it, they would "continue in the shipping business unless it becomes a failure." [19] Root replied to the charges that he and the other Republicans were filibustering. He reviewed the bill's legislative history in the Senate with the vote of the Democratic caucus, taken secretly, and with its discussions undisclosed, binding the party members to the bill and binding them to reject all amendments. But a majority of the Senate was always against the bill and even with the caucus rule, the Democratic leaders lost. So they caucused again and again bound their members to a revised bill, and still the minority fought on. At one time the Senate sat continuously for fifty-five hours; cots were set up in the Senate cloak rooms; Senator Burton talked for thirteen hours at a stretch and Senator Smoot for eleven and a half hours.[20] Root pleaded for the processes of representative government which made discussion an essential and he pleaded against throwing the United States hastily and without full discussion into the midst of state socialism.

To Seth Low, who was also opposing the bill, Root wrote on February 5th: "It is still the purpose of the Administration to force through the Ship Purchase bill. They appear now to be waiting to get back some absent members and when they are back they apparently mean to proceed, with the help of one or more progressive Republicans with whom they have made a trade. We shall probably be

[19] Root to Seth Low, January 28, 1915.
[20] Baker, Woodrow Wilson, Life and Letters, Vol. V, p. 128.

driven to a renewal of the filibuster. How that will come out nobody can tell, though I think we shall succeed in preventing them from forcing the bill through. . . . I am satisfied that the bill would be abandoned but for the unwillingness of the President to admit defeat. He holds the bulk of the Democrats in the Senate in a vice through caucus action and they are standing without any regard to their personal opinions and without any regard to any argument or consideration whatever." On the other side, Wilson was registering even stronger feeling in a letter to Mrs. Toy: "I think you cannot know to what lengths men like Root and Lodge are going, who I once thought had consciences but now know have none. We must not suffer ourselves to forget or twist the truth as they do, or use their insincere and contemptible methods of fighting; but we must hit them and hit them straight in the face, and not mind if the blood comes. It is a blunt business, and lacks a certain kind of refinement, but so does all war; and this is a war to save the country from some of the worst influences that ever debauched it. Please do not read the speeches in which I use a bludgeon. I do not like to offend your taste; but I cannot fight rottenness with rosewater." [21]

It was a curious situation with the leaders on both sides convinced of the bad faith or even corruption of their opponents. Root did not impugn the personal motives of Wilson but he shared Lodge's conviction that somebody's money-making scheme was at the root of it all. Wilson thought the opposition was influenced by the selfish interests of the shipping companies. Actually Root seems to have been moved by his feeling for the Allies and his opposition to the government going into business. Wilson began by a sincere belief in the wisdom of the bill and the necessity for it, and continued with the added incentive of sustaining his leadership. Root had no expectation that his arguments, especially his legal arguments, would have any influence on President Wilson. "Wilson had no use for lawyers or law. It is a curious fact, a very curious fact, that the most successful presidents we have had for a long time are those who didn't give a damn for law." [22] The other president he had in mind was Theodore Roosevelt.

The opposition won and the bill was temporarily killed. Lodge,

[21] *Ibid.*, p. 126.
[22] Root to the author, September 13, 1931.

perhaps seeking to heal the gap between Root and Roosevelt, wrote the latter on February 22nd, praising the former's great work in organizing and supporting the opposition. The defeat of the bill was welcome news to the Allies, as Sir George Otto Trevelyan wrote happily to Root congratulating him and Lodge on their victory.

So various are the matters to which a Senator must necessarily address himself that several more chapters could be filled with a chronical of Root's activities in the Senate. He took a keen interest in the plans for celebrating the Centennial of Peace between the United States and Great Britain which would have taken place one hundred years after the signing of the Treaty of Ghent on December 24th, 1814, had not the outbreak of the World War necessitated the postponement of the project. It was the World War also which brought to naught Root's efforts to arrange for the convocation of a Third Hague Peace Conference. Following the policy of adjusting all controversies with Canada, which he had done so much to promote as Secretary of State, he busied himself in the matter of the negotiation of a treaty and the passage of legislation for the further protection of the fur seals in Behring Sea. In this work, he cooperated closely with the State Department and with his old and trusted assistant, Chandler P. Anderson, who was adding another milestone to his long record of aid in the solution of Canadian-American difficulties. Root similarly was active in finding a way through a treaty with Canada to protect migratory birds.

Root's important part when he was Secretary of War in advancing the plans for the beautification of Washington, has already been described. His interest in and influence on the solution of like problems continued through his period of service in the Senate. Most notable was the part he played in creating the National Commission of Fine Arts. President Roosevelt, without statutory authority, had appointed such a commission, but his action raised a storm of protest. Root recalled that in 1910 "Senator Depew brought in a bill for the purchase of a lot of pictures which various people wanted to sell. All such matters were referred to the Committee on Library [of which Root was a member]. I felt and we all felt that the pictures ought not to be bought but we all felt also that no one of us knew enough about the subject to be able to defend an adverse report on Depew's bill. It was a recurrent situation. I suggested that we bring in a bill for the appointment of a committee of experts to whom we could turn for advice on questions of this kind, and the result was the establishment of the Fine Arts Commission." [23]

The Act, approved by President Taft on May 17th, 1910, established a Commission of seven members to advise upon the location in the District of Columbia of monuments, statues and the like, upon designs and upon the selection of artists. The original members were all old friends of Root's, including Daniel H. Burnham, Frederick Law Olmsted, Thomas Hastings and Francis D. Millet. In reply to a letter from Millet in which he referred to the Commission as Root's "last infant," Root replied on October 20th, 1910, modestly giving credit to Senator Wetmore and adding, "I think that we can now feel that the old higgledy-piggledy way of doing things is practically at an end." On the same day, he wrote to Senator Wetmore congratulating him on the other steps which he had taken while Root was arguing the Fisheries case at The Hague: "While the lions and tigers and insurgents and stand-patters and other wild animals were howling and roaring, you seem to have gone on quietly and to have got everything that you wanted in just the right form. It really is most encouraging." Root's role in helping to create the National Commission of Fine Arts is reminiscent of his services in 1896 and 1897 when he contributed his legal services to securing the creation of the Fine Arts Federation of New York which has comparable functions in New York City.[24] In the Senate period, Root also devoted himself to the development of Rock Creek Park, the location of the Lincoln Memorial and the Grant monument and the constant care requisite to preserving the Mall from intrusions. "Untold injury," Root wrote to Theodore W. Noyes on April 1st, 1911, "is done by the mistakes that are so frequently made by people of perfectly good intentions, who, without having studied the subject comprehensively, think this, that, or the other thing would be a good thing to do. Things done in that way are usually wrong. The beauty of Washington, its superiority over other American cities, comes from the fact that it was started with a plan inspired by the genius for design in which the French have excelled all other races of men."

[23] Root to the author, October 31, 1936.
[24] Files of the Federation and Russell Sturgis, President, to Root, January 12, 1897, Root Papers.

Although it belongs back in the period when Root was Secretary of State, one final extract from a letter written by Root to President Theodore Roosevelt on May 14th, 1908, may be quoted, as indicative of the attention which he paid to even small details in the process of beautifying the capital.

Many times looking from the south windows of the White House and the State Department I have thought of suggesting to you that there should be, without any delay, planted along the north side of the railroad bridge across the Potomac a screen of fast and tall growing trees, so as to relieve that hard line which now thrusts itself out against the water of the river. Lombardy poplars would be just the thing. They could well be planted for a considerable part of the distance. The bridge is very destructive to the view which was certainly one of the most beautiful in the world. My soul is filled with mourning when I remember that I myself approved the plan of the bridge while Secretary of War.

Carolina poplars were planted as he suggested and some of them still stand.

PART VII

Elder Statesman

CHAPTER XL

"We are running a railroad with a stage-coach organization"

A NEW YORK State Constitutional Convention convened at Albany on April 6th, 1915. Elihu Root was elected president by 129 votes to 32, the split being strictly on party lines with the Democrats casting a solid vote for Morgan J. O'Brien.

The New York constitution required submitting to the voters every twenty years the question whether a constitutional convention should be held, but the moves which led to the vote on this question in April, 1914, were inspired by devious political motives. The Democrats wanted to have the vote in June, 1913, before the municipal elections in New York City, in the hope of defeating a Fusion ticket by dissension between Roosevelt and the Old Guard. Root explained in a letter to Henry L. Stimson on March 29th, 1913, that some persons thought "that by bringing on the election of candidates to the Constitutional Convention next fall, Roosevelt will be compelled to make an active canvass, and thus a rapprochement between his followers and the Republicans will be prevented." Had this strategy been successful, the Democrats might well have controlled a majority of the delegates and thus have been able to carry through a reapportionment according to their own views. The vote on the question of holding the Constitutional Convention was, however, deferred until after the Fusion victory elected Mayor Mitchell in the autumn of 1913. The question was then carried by a bare plurality of 1500 votes and even that result was tainted with fraud and was attacked in the courts. The Fusion victory, together with the effect of Governor Sulzer's impeachment, enabled the Republicans to score another victory with the Old Guard in control. The delegates included men sympathetic to some of the Progressive points of view but there was no actual Progressive representation in the Convention. As Barnes wrote to Root on April 10th, 1915, "the most noteworthy feature of it [the Convention] is the intense conservatism of most of the Republican members."

Root had been active since the tragic Convention of 1912 in movements for re-uniting the Republican Party. As early as November 18th, 1912, he had written to Murray Crane regarding the desirability of starting a quiet movement to rally the Republicans of the country to an affirmative program. On February 19th, 1913, he issued a public statement in which he advocated a special Republican convention to revise the rules under which the delegates had been chosen in 1912 and upon which he had been forced to base his rulings at the Chicago convention. Such a convention was finally held on December 17th, 1913, and the rules were revised. In New York, a series of meetings were held for the purpose of restoring harmony in the party and of agreeing on an affirmative program. The first objective of a group led by men like Henry L. Stimson and Herbert Parsons was to secure the resignation of Barnes as State Chairman. Root refused to be drawn into that conflict except as a mediator and declined to attend an "anti-Barnes" dinner arranged on May 23rd.[1] Barnes remained in his office and with a fair measure of harmony the affirmative part of the program was pushed along. Root, Barnes and eleven other New York Republican members of Congress and of the National Committee issued an invitation for a meeting of Republican leaders from all over the State at the Waldorf-Astoria on December 5th. At this meeting Root presided, advocating direct primaries, workmen's compensation laws, a drastic revision of the rules of the State Legislature, the short ballot and the executive budget. Particularly in regard to the short ballot and the executive budget, Root had been largely influenced by Henry L. Stimson who had been studying these and comparable questions ever since his campaign for the governorship in 1910, and who had been working with a number of other Republicans to develop a forward-looking program of "responsible government." Both Stimson and Root had in mind the necessity of having the Republican Party stand for principles which would meet the popular unrest to which the Progressives appealed without going the length of what they considered the unsound proposals which Roosevelt had sponsored. Stimson and his friends had carefully planned the strategy of the meeting at the Waldorf and since no one else was ready with an alternate program, the proposals which Root

[1] Root to William Barnes, May 20, 1913; C. H. Betts to Root, May 31, 1913.

listed in his opening remarks were approved by the gathering. Later, at the Constitutional Convention, Root told that body he had appointed Frederick C. Tanner chairman of the Committee on Governor and Other State Officers because he had revealed his interest in the short ballot by presenting the resolution on that subject at the Waldorf meeting.

On May 28th, 1914, a meeting of the Republican State Committee was held and it was decided to call a State Convention at Saratoga on August 18th. The same meeting appointed a Committee of Thirty under the chairmanship of Henry L. Stimson to draft a platform on Constitutional Amendments which the Republican Party might endorse as its program for the work of the ensuing Constitutional Convention. When the Republican Convention met at Saratoga in August, Root was elected Temporary Chairman and pleaded for harmony. He also outlined his views on some of the questions which he was to discuss more fully at the Constitutional Convention. The report of the Committee of Thirty was adopted with the explanation that it was not designed to regiment the views of the delegates to the Constitutional Convention but merely to record certain principles for which the party should stand. In general, the principles advocated at Saratoga were those which Root favored and those which were taken up in the Convention during the following summer. Root remained steadfastly opposed to woman suffrage but acquiesced in the Saratoga Convention's recommendation that the question be submitted as a separate proposal to the voters. He later appointed as chairman of the Committee on Suffrage a man favorable to woman suffrage and courteously entertained all requests for hearings from the suffrage advocates.

The Saratoga Convention also recommended a slate of delegates-at-large to the Constitutional Convention, the list being headed by the name of Elihu Root. Elon Brown of Watertown objected to the fact that eight of the fifteen named persons came from New York City and voted to strike out the committee's choice except for the name of Root. Root arose and moved to amend the motion by including his name also but he was smothered in a chorus of "noes" and amid great applause Brown refused to accept his amendment. Brown's principal motion was defeated. He represented the ultra-conservative up-state group of Republicans who were not in sympathy

with the program recommended by the Committee of Thirty and
adopted at Saratoga.

The presidency of the Convention could not of course be formally
determined until the delegates assembled, but with the great Republican majority of 116 to 52 Democrats, the wishes of the Republicans
were bound to prevail and it was quite understood that Root was to
be chosen President. His eminence in party circles, his intellectual
power, his past and present official positions and the fact that he had
been second in command at the Constitutional Convention of 1894,
made his choice not only inevitable but eminently suitable. Accordingly, as soon as the November elections had showed their results, he
began planning ahead, devoting as much time as he could in the
midst of his concern about the World War and while completing
his term in the Senate. "It is hard just now to keep interested in anything except the war in Europe," he wrote to Stimson on August
4th, 1914. On December 11th, 1914, he wrote at length to the
Governor-elect, Charles S. Whitman, reviewing in great detail the
legislation of the state with reference to the organization of the constitutional conventions and suggesting various bills which should be
passed in order to enable the Convention to get to work promptly
and efficiently. He rented the house of William Gorham Rice at 135
Washington Avenue in Albany, for the spring and summer of 1915
and made that his headquarters throughout the Convention period.
Mrs. Root checked all the domestic details in advance with her careful precision and came there occasionally during the late spring and
summer but did not stay throughout the period. Root did not do
much entertaining although small groups frequently dined at his
house for the purpose of conferring on the progress of the Convention's work.

After its inaugural meeting, the Convention adjourned for some
three weeks. That period was used by Root chiefly for the important
task of forming the committees in which the work of the Convention was chiefly to be done. Root decided that the Convention should
be run on non-partisan lines. The 1894 Convention had been run on
strictly party lines, had been made a party issue and carried at the
polls as such. On a non-partisan basis, Root believed, "you will have
the better constitution. On the other you will have the better chance

for its adoption by the people." [2] It may seem inconsistent with this plan that he should award all the committee chairmanships to Republicans and that the patronage of door-keepers, clerks, messengers and so on should be kept almost entirely in Republican hands. But despite a little grumbling, the Democrat leaders did not seem to think that this was unreasonable and a remarkable spirit of amity prevailed. This was partly due to the fact that many of the eminent Democratic delegates were warm personal friends of Root's; it was partly due to the fact that in the conduct of the Convention Root was scrupulously fair and on almost every issue succeeded in avoiding a split on party lines. Twelve of the thirty-three measures proposed by the Convention were adopted by unanimous vote, twelve by a vote of ten to one, two by over seven to one, two by four to one, two by three to one and only three by a vote of two to one. An analysis of the votes by parties shows that on the principal measures passed, the divisions were never along strict party lines. "I doubt if many people appreciate," Root wrote to Mark Potter on October 16th, 1915, "how hard the fight was to prevent the Convention, with its enormous Republican majority, from being turned into a party agency."

On April 7th, Root wrote to all of the 169 delegates asking them to state their preferences for committee assignments. The Judiciary Committee was the prize sought by all the lawyers but the replies are very revealing of the character of the different men. Some replied stating their eminent qualifications for this or some other committee; many wrote that they knew Root would have a hard time making assignments and that they would be perfectly content with any arrangement which would cause him the least embarrassment. Some suggested preferences but modestly doubted their preeminence over other delegates. Root became convinced that George W. Wickersham, who had been Attorney General in Taft's cabinet, was the man for the chairmanship of the Judiciary Committee. This chairmanship carried with it the floor-leadership of the Convention which Root had exercised under the presidency of Choate in 1894. State Senator Edgar T. Brackett of Saratoga, a lawyer with long experience as a political leader of the Republicans at Albany, wanted the place. He had been

[2] Root to Allston U. Sinnott, December 6, 1916.

a member of the State Senate Judiciary Committee for eleven years and Chairman for eight of the eleven years. In his letter of April 8th, replying to Root's request, he made no demands and he stated a complete willingness to abide by Root's decision, but he unquestionably wanted the appointment and he pointedly mentioned in his letter that he knew the delegates better than Root "whose work has latterly so much been outside the State." Lemuel E. Quigg, Platt's old lieutenant, wrote Root on April 10th, urging Brackett's appointment. He declared that this was a "country Convention" and that Brackett would actually be the floor leader whether he was appointed or not. No one else, he thought, had the legislative experience and the knowledge of the people of the state which Brackett had acquired. William Barnes pressed upon Root the same point of view. It would have been a good political appointment but Root was not willing to make this important selection solely on political grounds. He gladly took Barnes' advice in sounding out Brackett's second choice and made him chairman of the Legislative Organization Committee and second member on the Judiciary Committee, but Wickersham got the prize plum. Barnes and Frederick C. Tanner, Chairman of the Republican State Committee, advised Root at length and in detail about other appointments to committees and about the designation of the clerical and floor staff and in many cases Root acted on their suggestions. Barnes advised Root that among the Democrats there would be a division between the younger and older men with "Al" Smith and Wagner the vigorous leaders of the former group. Root, however, consulted the members of the older group, chiefly Delancey Nicoll, Morgan J. O'Brien and William Church Osborn. With them he held several conferences regarding the disposal of places among the Democratic members. It was, in the case of Nicoll especially, a pleasant reminder of those days twenty-eight years before when Root as Chairman of the Republican County Committee in New York had swung Republican support to Nicoll as a candidate for District Attorney. The two men were always warm friends, each endowed with a quick and sparkling wit which gave them much mutual enjoyment in each other's company.

Henry L. Stimson expressed a preference for the Committee on Finances and was made chairman of that committee. Seth Low, twice mayor of Brooklyn and once of New York, headed the Committee

ELIHU ROOT AS PRESIDENT OF THE NEW YORK CONSTITUTIONAL CON-
VENTION OF 1915

on Cities; William Barnes presided over the Committee on Legislative Powers; Frederick C. Tanner, Louis Marshall and Martin Saxe were among the other important chairmen. Colonel Gleason, the immemorial secretary of Republican conventions, told J. B. Bishop that the "federal crowd" had "built an ice house, got inside of it and froze everybody who came anywhere near them." No doubt it did make many up-state delegates "mad as fury." [3] The house at 4 Elk Street where Stimson, Parsons, Tanner, Wickersham and a number of others lived, was regularly known as the "ice house."

The assignments were made and the Convention got down to work on April 26th. Their results were to be submitted to the people in November and Root bent every effort to speed the work of the Convention. He held them rigorously to their tasks and never spared himself through those very hot summer months in Albany; even Albany was not as bad as the Washington to which he had become accustomed. When younger delegates in committee meetings thought it was time to adjourn and play a set of tennis, Root worked on, and when dinner time came would send out for sandwiches for everybody. With fierce intensity he worked at top efficiency far into the night while younger men were completely fagged out. Root also insisted that the expenses of the Convention should be held to a minimum and afford an example of economy. He personally scrutinized carefully all vouchers for expenditures, keeping the total expenditures, $45,000, under the appropriation. He followed the dissensions in every committee, made himself master of every topic and threw in the great weight of his influence to sway the result at crucial moments. He formed an unofficial steering committee out of the chairmen of all the committees and with them he constantly consulted. He never obtruded his views but he never lacked a ready way out of an impasse. Not a word was written into any proposal which Root did not study carefully.

From the very outset, Brackett put spokes in the wheels. On the 26th, there was presented a proposal framed by Root suggesting that June 1st be fixed as the last day on which constitutional amendments could be submitted to the delegates. Quigg and Brackett promptly objected and forced the question to go over. It was a small point but it was significant.

[3] Bishop to Roosevelt, November 5, 1915, Roosevelt Papers, Library of Congress.

Root had already made clear the lines upon which he thought the Convention should proceed. He did it in an address before the Academy of Political Science in New York on November 19th, 1914, and in another before the Merchants' Association of New York, March 25th, 1915. He struck the same notes in his opening address to the Convention on April 6th. He was interested in the machinery and in the principles of government. He told the Merchants' Association that our governmental machinery had not kept pace with the progress of the world: "We are running a railroad with a stage-coach organization." His proposals were not original nor daring but neither were they reactionary. He advocated the short ballot, the reorganization and consolidation of the executive departments, the adoption of an executive budget, the improvement of the judicial machinery of the state and the simplification of court procedure. In principle, his chief concern was to justify representative government against the attacks launched upon it by the advocates of direct government with their proposals for the initiative, the referendum and the recall. "I don't feel any apprehension about the people being too radical, or being too conservative," he told the Academy of Political Science. "So long as the thoughtful people of the Republic will take a real interest in questions of government, will think about them and discuss them, so long are we sure to come out right." Yet in that process of discussion, Root counted on the ability of experienced leaders like himself to guide the conclusions of the people in the way which he considered right. He remained convinced that representative government was the proper government. Had he lived a century earlier, he would undoubtedly have been an ardent advocate of the proposal which was written into the federal constitution whereby the President was to be chosen by an electoral college, although in his own day, of course, he did not advocate a return to the reality of that plan which has been retained in empty form. "We are going to keep a lot of wild stuff out of the constitution," he wrote to Taft on January 12th, 1915, "but we ought to do something affirmative and constructive to improve the present conditions." "A conservative constructive program is natural to the Republican Party," he wrote Frederick W. Hammond on December 3rd, 1915. "Pure and simple opposition belongs naturally to the Democratic Party." He told the Convention that the fundamental principle was that "responsibility and power shall always go together. Responsibility without power can never be justly enforced, and power without responsibility can never be duly controlled." In many a letter he reiterated the view that "The constitution should deal with permanent things; not with experiments and changes." He felt later that the great contribution which the Constitutional Convention made was its readaptation of the forms of representative government so that they were justified and exalted and that the popularity of what he considered mere political nostrums was considerably decreased. But his early optimistic belief in the popular interest in the work of revising the constitution was dissipated when he later observed the popular reaction at the polls. Such interest as there was stirred chiefly in professional, academic and organization circles. The bar was active, with much attention focused on a report of a Committee of Seven of the Phi Delta Phi Club, under the chairmanship of Henry W. Jessup, relative to amending the Judiciary article of the constitution.

At ten o'clock precisely in the morning, at two in the afternoon and at eight at night, Root, usually formally dressed in a cutaway coat, mounted the rostrum in the Assembly chamber and opened the sessions of the Convention. According to custom each morning session was opened with a prayer delivered by a clergyman. On the morning of May 5th, the clergyman did not appear. Root stepped to the front of the platform and to the amazement of the delegates began to pray:

"Almighty God, we pray Thee to guide our deliberations this day. Make us humble, sincere, devoted to the public service. Make us wise, considerate of the feelings and the opinions and the rights of others. Make us effective and useful for the advancement of Thy cause of peace and justice and liberty in the world. For Christ's sake, Amen."

The prayer made a deep impression. As Root explained to one inquiring clergyman: "The prayer was not previously composed nor was the occasion for making it foreseen. It was simply an expression of what was in my mind at the moment when the Convention had to be opened and the chaplain was not there." It may have had something to do with the refusal of some clergymen to follow William H. Anderson of the Anti-Saloon League who later attacked Root in his paper because of a fancied support of some provision which he deviously interpreted as an attempt to prevent temperance legislation. Root refused to reply to Anderson's open letter which he characterized in responding to an inquiry from Frederick Perkins of St. Johnsville: "The sum and substance of the letter [from Anderson] is to inform me that my character and conduct are under suspicion and that if I wish to clear myself of the suspicion I can do so by writing a letter to Mr. Anderson's newspaper. Of course no self-respecting man would pay the slightest attention to a communication of that character. Every citizen is entitled to criticize the past record of a public officer. Every citizen is entitled to call the attention of a public officer to something which that citizen thinks the officer ought to do. But no citizen is entitled to write to a public officer 'I suspect you of being a scoundrel and unless you deny that in my newspaper my suspicions will ripen into conviction.' I suppose that aspersions of this kind and possible correspondence evoked by them help to sell newspapers."

Root naturally received during the Convention a great many letters from all sorts of persons urging the adoption or defeat of this or that proposal. In most instances he sent a formal acknowledgment saying that the communication would be referred to the appropriate committee. To business and banking friends in New York he refrained from comment on the merits of pending proposals. To a man like William Jay Schieffelin, writing to him as Chairman of the Citizens Union on the question of the Home Rule Amendment, he wrote at length explaining the difficulties which the Committee on Cities was facing and urging him to support their proposal as the best which could be obtained. He readily admitted that it was not perfect but he thought it a distinct improvement and well worth supporting. To Joseph H. Choate and George McAneny he expressed full agreement with their opposition to extending civil service preference to Spanish War Veterans and volunteer firemen. When Miss May Irwin, the comedienne, wrote him in the middle of August urging some measure to check theater ticket speculation, he explained at courteous length that he would refer the matter to the Judiciary Committee, but that he feared it came too late and that in addition it seemed to be a matter for legislation rather than for a constitutional provision. "You have given me so much pleasure many times on the stage that I feel bound to pay special attention to your suggestion, and I wish that I could hold out more hope of favorable action upon it." Root always treated the leading figures of the stage with great consideration and frequently in answering appeals for aid of one kind or another expressed that same sense of obligation.

The Convention adopted thirty-three amendments out of more than eight hundred which were submitted to it. Root attached most importance to five of these. First was the Executive Reorganization, commonly referred to as the Short Ballot. In explaining the proposed amendments to the Economic Club of New York on October 25th, 1915, Root remarked that they "found that the state government had been built up from simpler times by accretion . . . until there were one hundred and fifty-two different state boards, commissions and agencies. . . ." The Convention proposed that all of these should be consolidated into seventeen departments, each with a head responsible to the Governor, very much on the cabinet system of the federal government. Such a plan made for efficiency of administration, economy of operation and responsibility of public officers. The short ballot was an incident of this proposal, the idea being to simplify the task of the voters by cutting down the number of state officers for which they were compelled to vote. It was opposed by the machine leaders who profit by having a large number of places for which they can name candidates in the primaries and who can not always persuade a governor to appoint men of their choosing. Root had originally favored including the Attorney General among the appointive officers but was persuaded by Alfred E. Smith that an officer who had to give opinions to many other state officers beside the Governor should have the independence which would result from his being elected by the people. Root was therefore not averse to a bargain struck with the Brooklyn group who agreed to support the broad proposal if the Attorney General's and Comptroller's places were left as elective offices. The Short Ballot proposal was adopted by ninety-seven to fifteen Republican votes and twenty-eight to fifteen Democratic votes, or a total of one hundred and twenty-five to thirty.

The second matter in which Root was especially interested was the adoption of the executive budget which was the chief concern and particular triumph of Henry L. Stimson. Under the existing system any member of the legislature could bring in a bill for the appropriation of money for any purpose he thought fit and the legislators were constantly beset by constituents who wanted this or that amount appropriated for their own pet projects. The Governor then had to sit down at the end of the session, figure the totals and veto where necessary. Under the executive budget plan, the Governor secures estimates in advance from all the departments and submits to the legislature a budget of estimated expenditures for the fiscal year. There can be little question on the merits which is the better system. The Executive Budget was adopted by one hundred and one Republican votes for to two against and thirty-six Democratic votes in favor to two opposed.

The City Home Rule provision was another important amendment. At that period a large part of the time of the legislature was taken up with routine matters of city administration such as the length of time of vacations for park employees, salary scales or fixing the place for an ash can dump for the Street Cleaning Department. The Amendment would have given the cities power to rule their own local affairs. Root wrote Job Hedges on August 6th that the Committee had a discussion on this proposal "which for multifariousness and discursiveness and indefinite continuance was enough to break anybody's heart. . . . Nobody is satisfied with . . . [the result] but then nobody could be satisfied with anything on that subject." One hundred and two Republicans and eighteen Democrats voted for the amendment and two Republicans and fifteen Democrats voted against it. The County Home Rule provision was adopted by an eleven to one majority with nine Republicans and two Democrats in opposition.

The Judiciary article with its provision for the reform of court procedure was one which naturally attracted Root's particular interest. In many connections he had long been preaching the need for eliminating the law's delays, for simplifying procedure, for putting an end to the type of technical practice which enabled cases to be dragged on indefinitely through numerous decisions on unsubstantial points. He made an effective speech on the subject in the Convention on August 19th, pointing out that from time immemorial "Wherever a special class of men have been entrusted with the formulation and administration of law, they tend to make it a mystery; they tend to become more and more subtle and refined in their discriminations, until ultimately they have got out of the field where they can be followed by plain, honest people's minds, and some power must be exerted to bring them back." He had on other occasions pleaded *mea culpa* to his own arraignment of the bar but he recognized at all times that an attorney in conducting a case was under a duty to give his client the benefit of all statutory rights and advantages; the evil had to be cut at the root. This Judiciary article of the proposed constitution was carried by a majority of forty-five to one.

As Root wrote to Professor William Z. Ripley on November 17th, "There was very little said upon social legislation in the proceedings of the late Constitutional Convention." Nor did Root's own interests run in this direction. He had faith that if able men were elected to public office, given an efficient governmental machinery and held to a strict responsibility, the welfare of everyone would be assured. The subject of workmen's compensation was included in the Convention's program with Root's approval and the regulation of manufacturing in tenement houses was dealt with. There was also a provision which Root vigorously supported for the regulation of public utilities by public commissions in order to prevent a return to the bad old days of "strike" bills and the famous "Black Horse Cavalry" when railroads and public service corporations had not only their paid lobbyists but also their tools in the legislature. Root, in his early days of practice at the bar, had known the system well. His effective speech on this subject occupied only nine minutes and was expressed in about eight hundred words. There is no reason to charge him with insincerity because in his later years he realized the evil of this and other systems under which he had operated and sought to remedy them. Yet that charge of insincerity or hypocrisy was raised against him, particularly as a result of his greatest speech in the Convention on the subject of "invisible government." He had forecast his views in his address as Temporary Chairman of the Republican Convention at Saratoga in the preceding year. He had said essentially the same thing in his correspondence in 1909. He had opened the attack in the Constitutional Convention on July 30th when he told the Committee on the Governor and Other State Officers that the Government of the State of New York was no more representative than that of Venezuela. On August 30th, he took the floor in behalf of the short ballot proposal and for nearly two hours he held and swayed his audience; the defeat of the opposition was assured. It was partly in answer to Quigg and Brackett that he spoke. Root showed that the short ballot had been approved by Hughes in 1910 and by James W. Wadsworth, Jr. when Speaker of the Assembly. In 1912 both the Republican and Progressive platforms declared in favor of it. The Republican support was reiterated in the meeting in New York on December 5th, 1913, and was reaffirmed over Brackett's opposition at Saratoga in August, 1914. Except that he favored the election rather than the appointment of two state officers—the Comptroller and Attorney General— Alfred E. Smith and the Democratic platform in 1914 had also endorsed the short ballot. The New York Short Ballot Organization had informed Root on June 1st of the result of their canvass of up-state newspapers, showing 86.6 per cent in favor of having all state officers except the Governor and Lieutenant Governor appointive, while only 4.76 per cent favored the other three exceptions. Of course this canvass was conducted in the Republican stronghold of the state.

Root noted that many politicians thought there was nothing wrong with the existing system under which they operated and he did not impugn their integrity but he believed that the people demanded a reform in administration. "What is the government of this state? What has it been during the forty years of my acquaintance with it? The government of the constitution? Oh no; not half the time, nor half way." He adopted the old phrase to describe the system—"invisible government." "For many years Conkling was the supreme ruler in this state; the governor did not count, the legislature did not count; comptrollers and secretaries of state and what not did not count. It was what Mr. Conkling said; and in a great outburst of public rage he was pulled down.

"Then Mr. Platt ruled the state; for nigh upon twenty years he ruled it. . . . It makes no difference what name you give, whether you call it Fenton or Conkling or Cornell or Arthur or Platt, or by the names of men now living. . . . I don't criticize the men of the invisible government. How can I? I have known them all, and among them have been some of my dearest friends. I can never forget the deep sense of indignation I felt in the abuse that was heaped upon Chester A. Arthur, whom I honored and loved, when he was attacked because he held the position of political leader. But it is all wrong. . . . I have been told forty times since this convention met that you cannot change it. We can try, can we not? I deny that we cannot change it. I repel that cynical assumption which is born of the lethargy that comes from poisoned air during all these years. . . . While millions of men are fighting and dying for their countries across the ocean . . . it is our inestimable privilege to do something here in moving our beloved state along the pathway towards better and purer government, a more pervasive morality and a more effective exercise of the powers of government which preserve the liberty of the people. . . .

"Mr. Chairman, there is a plain old house in the Oneida Hills, overlooking the valley of the Mohawk, where truth and honor dwelt in my youth. When I go back, as I am about to go, to spend my declining years, I mean to go with the feeling that I have not failed to speak and to act here in accordance with the lessons I learned there from the God of my fathers. God grant that this opportunity for service to our country and our state may not be neglected by any of the men for whom I feel so deep a friendship in this convention."

They all knew that he spoke the truth; many of them knew the system from the inside and were integral parts of it. William Barnes was there and Quigg, Platt's lieutenant, and Brackett and many others. They could sneer, as some of Theodore Roosevelt's friends sneered, because, as Root frankly admitted, he was in no position to criticize these bosses personally. But no one could say that Root himself had ever sought to take on the mantle of Platt although it would have been easy for him to yield to those who urged him to do so. In his early days in New York he had been constantly at variance with Platt and his machine and had fought the organization over and over again. He had endorsed the principle which lay behind the advocacy of the direct primary, but he had not believed in the efficacy of the means devised to achieve that end. He believed wholeheartedly in party rule but he had advocated making the party organization more representative of the party members. But he had, as he said, been devoted to Arthur and he had always worked on friendly terms with William Barnes, Roosevelt's particular *bête noir*. No one could point to an instance where Root had used his powers of patronage to feather his own nest or to strengthen his own political fences. The nearest he ever came to governing the state "invisibly" was in the days of Theodore Roosevelt's governorship when Root exercised large influence through friendship, wisdom, knowledge and sheer force of intellect. Roosevelt had for years denounced the bosses but as Governor he had worked along with Platt and not always quite

so independently as he liked to make himself believe. Roosevelt was
so mercurial and, as Root pointed out more than once, so firmly
convinced at each successive moment that he believed what he said
he believed, that it is impossible to call him a hypocrite despite the
inconsistencies of his numerous positions. Root was very different.
He did not fool himself. He was not the crusader. He took things as
he found them, used the materials ready to his hand and worked for
things which he thought worth while. Those things might be the
interests of a client who had retained his services as counsel; they
might be the success of the Republican Party in a particular election;
they might be the policies of an administration when he was a cabinet
officer. He had a great capacity for seeing the other man's point of
view. In general, personalities meant little to him. Here was his vale-
dictory, his testament. The time had come to attack the system and
he attacked, vigorously, effectively.

Root won the grateful praise of the *Jewish Daily News* for opposing the proposed literacy test for voters which was defeated at the
time but adopted separately in 1922. This was another one of the
measures upon which Brackett differed from Root and indeed on
this question Root stood with "Al" Smith, Senator Wagner and other
Democrats, against most of the staunch Republicans including Barnes,
Wickersham and Stimson. But Root believed that it was political
folly to have New York City rule the Legislature and therefore opposed, as he had in 1894, all moves to have the Convention adopt
a proposal for reapportionment. Every Democratic motion toward
that end was buried by the huge Republican majority.

There was much in the proposals adopted by the Convention which
was not sweet to the political palates of the men in the machines
of both parties. The budget system and the other measures for economy and reform of administration, including the short ballot, would
make it more difficult for them to operate as they had always operated.
The powers of invisible government were opposed to ratification.
There were long debates in the Convention as to whether the results
should be submitted as a whole or whether they should be submitted as a series of independent propositions. Herbert Parsons, as
Chairman of the Committee on Manner of Submission, telegraphed
some fifteen persons throughout the state on September 7th, inquiring whether sentiment in their districts favored submission as a whole

or separate submission of any of the amendments. The former view
finally prevailed and Root defended it later on the ground that they
were all inter-related in one scheme for the improvement of the
state government. But it was not a wise decision. Everyone who objected to any part of the whole voted against the entire proposal.
In New York City, public officials such as school teachers, court
clerks and firemen, were opposed to the home rule articles which
would prevent their getting special bills through the Legislature in
the good old way. The New York State Federation of Labor opposed
what they called "the product of aristocrats who were seeking to chain
the will of the people and substitute caste government for democracy." Perhaps Samuel Gompers' defeat as a candidate for delegate
to the Convention contributed to this point of view. Former Chief
Judge Edgar M. Cullen proved to be a powerful opponent, arguing
that the rejection of a proposed amendment to the bill of rights curb-
ing the use of military tribunals, had been due to a desire to make
such courts available for the trial of rioters, presumably in cases of
strikes. Although Root fully answered his argument, it served to
sharpen labor's opposition.[4] Up-state there was a general feeling, carefully nurtured no doubt by certain individuals, that this was a New
York City product in which their leaders and their interests had not
been given proper attention. The perennial issue of reapportionment
whereby the Democrats hoped to end the system which prevented
their numerical superiority in New York City from having its propor-
tional weight in state elections, induced Democratic opposition. They
had hoped to control the Convention and to pass a reapportionment
measure. Root had taken part in blocking it. William Lustgarten,
Chairman of the Committee on Education of the New York State
Single Tax League, responded with a word of caution on August 31st
to a proposal that the Progressive Democracy should oppose the new
constitution. "While I agree with you," he wrote Chester C. Platt,
"that not much good can come out of a convention dominated by
men of the type of Parker, O'Brien, DeLancey Nicoll, Wickersham,
Quigg and Brackett, I am not at all certain that Senator Root is not
really fighting the People's fight. While it is true that from his past
record friends of Democracy and those who have in the past always

[4] Ray B. Smith, *History of the State of New York*, Vol. IV by Roscoe C. E. Brown,
p. 264.

been found on the 'public interest' side, should not be ready to trust him, it appears that he regards the work of this Convention as his last public work and wants that to be a monument to his memory." The Progressive vote was no longer a large factor but many Progressives thought the proposed constitution a reactionary document and some saw in it an attempt of the "Federal crowd" to strengthen the Taft wing of the Republican party and to boom the presidential candidacy of Root. George W. Perkins, as National Chairman of the Progressive Party, published in the newspapers an open letter to Root stating his reasons for opposition.[5] Some said that Root's remarks praising the ability and fairmindedness of Al Smith were uttered merely to curry favor with the people. As will be apparent later in the description of Root's presidential candidacy in 1916, it is not credible that Root had any thought of using the Convention to further his political fortunes. His admiration of Al Smith persisted throughout his life. The only qualification he apparently ever made of his reported praise of Smith was when someone credited him with saying that Smith knew more about the state government than anyone else; Root admitted that he had said Smith knew a very great deal about it but he could not have said he knew more than anyone else because he didn't know how much "anyone else" knew! But Roosevelt wrote bitterly to Lodge about the way in which "the great bulk of the Republicans headed by Root have backed the Barnes theories of government," [6] and George W. Perkins still denounced Root and all his works.[7]

The constitutional proposals were complicated and only six weeks elapsed between their final submission and the vote in November. The absence of partisanship, which meant that neither party made adoption a party issue as the Republicans had done with the constitution of 1894, put no driving force behind ratification. It is the history of all constitutional amendments that they labor under a disadvantage, drawing a smaller vote and encountering the usual inertia against change. Other states had like experiences. In 1915 California defeated all nine constitutional amendments submitted at the polls. In 1914 the voters of Wisconsin defeated all ten of the amendments

---

[5] Flick, *History of the State of New York*, Vol. VII, p. 235.
[6] Roosevelt Papers, Library of Congress; published in part in *Roosevelt-Lodge Correspondence*, Vol. II, p. 458.
[7] Roosevelt Papers, Library of Congress.

submitted to them. The New York constitutional proposals were roundly defeated at the polls but for many reasons other than that which J. B. Bishop gloatingly described to Roosevelt on November 30th as a popular repudiation of the Root brand of reactionary Republicanism.

Immediate rejection, however, was not the full measure of the results. Since 1915 a large part of their work has been embodied bit by bit in the Constitution of the State of New York, due very largely to the fact that Alfred E. Smith saw their merits and took the leadership in driving them through. In 1918 the voters adopted a provision relative to the contracting of state debts which was substantially identical with the proposal of 1915. In 1919 a provision regulating eminent domain proceedings was adopted in a form similar to that proposed in 1915 although with some important changes. In that same year the voters adopted a provision for absentee voting along the lines of the principle advocated by the Convention. In the next year the people approved the Convention's plan for substituting a system of serial bonds for the old costly system of a sinking fund, and for assuring appropriations to meet carrying charges. Although changes were made in the plan, county home rule was adopted in 1921 and home rule for cities in 1923. In 1925 there were adopted plans for the reorganization of the state departments along the general lines of the 1915 proposals and for the improvement of the state judiciary system. The first of these two amendments was the result of the work of the Commission for Reorganizing the State Departments under the able chairmanship of Charles Evans Hughes; the second was a result of the Judiciary Constitutional Convention of 1921 for which a large share of the credit belongs to William D. Guthrie. In 1927, with some modification, there were approved amendments following the 1915 recommendations for increasing the pay of members of the legislature and of the governor. In 1927 the great step of adopting the executive budget was taken. There have been other points of smaller importance upon which the electorate has subsequently followed the steps of the delegates who met in Albany in the summer of 1915. That modifications were made is but natural for, as Root pointed out, most of the provisions were recognized as being imperfect results of essential compromises and each new body of persons who dealt with the same subject would undoubtedly arrive at somewhat different results.

This record of subsequent results, Root wrote to Taft on September 8th, 1926, "confirms my conviction that in public affairs every good idea if worked out and definitely recorded can be trusted to take care of itself and command acceptance in the course of time. . . . That proposed constitution was overwhelmingly defeated at the time. It is now being overwhelmingly adopted." On November 10th, 1915, just after the vote, he had prophesied to Judge Clearwater: "The main things which were put in the constitution, however, will ultimately be adopted in substance and the work that was done will prove to have been useful." In other states the results of the New York Convention attracted much attention and exerted much influence; for many years thereafter Root's files contain inquiries from delegates to constitutional conventions throughout the country asking for further light on this or that proposal. On October 18th, 1915, when the New York Republican Club under the presidency of James R. Sheffield welcomed Root at a testimonial dinner, Sheffield recalled the stirring peroration of the speech on invisible government. The newspapers reported that Root was moved almost to tears and Sheffield twitted him about it later. Root gruffly replied: "Don't be ridiculous; you know I had a bad cold."

It was a legitimate occasion for rejoicing and mutual congratulations when the delegates to the Constitutional Convention tendered Root a reunion dinner in New York on December 17th, 1926. "I think it makes but little difference," Root told them, "whether a man gives his life and his service to laying the foundation and building up the structure, or whether he is the man that floats a flag on the battlements and cries 'Victory.' " [8]

[8] In writing this chapter, the author has been greatly assisted by conversations with Delancey Nicoll, William Gorham Rice, Judge Charles B. Sears, James R. Sheffield, Alfred E. Smith, Henry L. Stimson, Frederick C. Tanner and George W. Wickersham.

CHAPTER XLI

"Swift and positive judgment"

MR. ROOT's frequently expressed distrust of contemporary biography was especially keen in regard to the writings of persons who deal with events in which they took part or of which at any rate they had contemporaneous knowledge. In such cases, he felt that personal prejudices and impressions were likely to prevent the writer from having the necessary detachment and impartiality. His favorite example was William Roscoe Thayer whose "Life and Times of Cavour" he considered brilliant, but whose treatments of Hay and Roosevelt he thought inaccurate and inadequate. As an exception, he recognized the value for future historians of recorded contemporary explanations of the actors in important affairs. As I deal with the later period of Mr. Root's life, I am quite conscious of the applicability of his stricture. On the World War, for example, I cannot escape my own personal convictions, which inevitably remain the result of personal experience and reaction.

As a college undergraduate from 1914 until my enlistment in 1917, I shared the pro-Allied convictions of Mr. Root and the majority of his friends. In France I began to share the disillusionment of many of my contemporaries. Subsequently I have become fully convinced of the essential fallacy of much of that emotional hysteria which in those war days passed for intellectual conviction. Walter Millis in his *Road to War*, despite the defects in that volume, has drawn a vivid picture of American war psychology. Borchard and Lage, in their later volume on *Neutrality for the United States*, have in more technical style analyzed the pro-Allied bias of leading American officials and their inaccurate understanding of international legal issues involved. Most recently, Charles C. Tansill, with thorough scholarship, has ably explored every detail of the subject in *America Goes to War*. Newton Baker in his *Why We Went to War* has painted the picture as his generation saw it; his little book was one with which Mr. Root heartily agreed. As the governments of Europe have published more and more of the diplomatic documents from which during the war they made known only favorable extracts, historians have reasoned learnedly and disputed hotly on the origins of the war. This book is not the place in which to re-fight those battles. Though I cannot avoid commenting on events and on Mr. Root's part in them, the principal purpose must be merely to show his attitudes and actions and the reasons for them so far as they can be deduced.

Root's contacts, his friendships, his preferences, his heritage, all inclined him to favor from the first the cause of the Allies. In Berlin in 1870, he had hoped the French would win. In the War and State Departments, he had formed the conviction that the Kaiser was a trouble-maker whose designs in the Caribbean had influenced Root in framing the Platt Amendment and in shaping the control of the finances of Santo Domingo; whose bellicose intentions had brought Europe close to war in 1905—a war averted largely by the Algeciras conference.

On April 3rd, 1909, Root had showed his estimate of Germany in writing to Andrew Carnegie, explaining how the German Foreign Office had blocked his efforts to conclude an arbitration treaty. "The fact is," he wrote, "and no well informed person can doubt it, that Germany, under her present government, is the great disturber of peace in the world. At every turn the obstacle to the establishment of arbitration agreements, to the prevention of war, to disarmament, to the limitation of armament, to all attempts to lessen the suspicion and alarm of nations toward each other, is Germany, who stands, and has persistently stood since I have been familiar with foreign affairs, against that kind of progress."

Root and his intimates received their war news from friends in England and France or, in common with most of the American people, relied on newspaper despatches which came only through British controlled cables and which were first passed by the British censor. It is a commentary rather on the irresistible force with which war passions sweep people's minds than on Root's own judgment that, in this instance, he failed to exercise that coldly critical power of analysis which so often made him outstanding as a lawyer and as a statesman. Granting the truth of what Root believed to be true on the basis of the evidence available to him, his reactions were natural, if not inevitable. The fundamental fallacy of those days was in believing all the reports from Allied sources and in doubting every word from the Central Powers. The Bryce Report on German atrocities in Belgium was particularly convincing, especially to Root who had such a warm affection and admiration for Lord Bryce. Few dispassionate persons now accept it as gospel.[1] Sir Arthur Nicolson, Permanent Undersecretary of the British Foreign Office, was one of the few responsible officials in an Allied country who was willing at the time to state his conviction that the stories of German atrocities in Belgium were grossly exaggerated.[2] In the modern war system, Bryce and his fellow-propagandists were right; they rendered to their country services even more important than could be given by those who had nothing to offer but their lives in the trenches. Root and the public generally did not know that five American newspaper correspondents with the German armies in Belgium had jointly cabled the Associated Press, "In spirit fairness we unite in declaring German atrocities groundless as far as we were able to observe. . . . We unable report single instance unprovoked reprisal. Also unable confirm rumors mistreatment prisoners or non-combatants. . . ."[3] Root and his friends could not know the revelations which were later to be made about the methods of propagandizing.[4] There was the indisputable basic fact that Germany had violated Belgian neutrality and there were crass German stupidities like the "scrap of paper" phrase,[5] but just as there had been instances of atrocities in the Philippines when Root was Secretary of War, so there will always be in every war. They are the product of war and not of the peculiar inhumanity of any people. Only "pro-Germans" uttered such thoughts as these in the war years, at least in the circles in which Root moved.

The Roots had planned to spend the summer of 1914 in Europe. On July 30th, Senator Root could still, like most Americans, write about the war in jocular vein; in a letter to his sister-in-law, Mrs. Edward H. Wales, he wrote:

[1] Cf. Tansill, *America Goes to War*, pp. 299–300.
[2] Harold Nicolson, *Portrait of a Diplomatist*, p. 310.
[3] Millis, *The Road to War*, p. 68.
[4] E. g., Squires, *British Propaganda at Home and in the United States from 1914 to 1917*; Arthur Ponsonby, *Falsehood in War-Time* (1928). Other references are collected in Tansill, *op. cit.*, p. 598, n. 47.
[5] But Bethman-Hollweg insisted that his words were distorted; Seymour, *Intimate Papers of Colonel House*, Vol. II, p. 140.

. . . When are you going to the war, and on which side are you going to fight? I want to know how to bet. We are somewhat disturbed here in our plans by the inconsiderate conduct of the great powers, who seem likely to seize all the railroad trains in Europe to carry their troops and to capture all of each other's passenger steamers. Clara [Mrs. Root] objects to being captured. I think it would be fine, as it would probably let me out of all my engagements.

At the same time he was doubtful whether his own country could be of use in the crisis. It was also on July 30th that he wrote to Miss Mabel Boardman:

I fully sympathize with the feeling expressed in your letter of July 26th about mediation. I doubt, however, if we have here any one who is sufficiently familiar with the real motives that are moving the great powers in the direction of war to make an attempt at mediation useful. I do not recall any one now remaining in office who probably understands the very complicated cross currents of policy which are grouped as constituting the Near Eastern question and who has kept track of the various grades and varieties of alliance which control the present situation. Nor does the existing feeling towards the United States appear to be favorable.

A week later he made it clear that he believed the blame for the war lay wholly with Germany. It is significant that he reached this conclusion so soon but his mind had been ready for it for many years, as his letter to Carnegie had revealed. The question of war guilt is still being debated; it is doubtful if anyone yet knows the whole truth but few reputable historians today, in the light of all the evidence published from official archives, would support the thesis current in 1914 that Kaiser Wilhelm was the sole villain. Root, like many others, was then convinced that he was. Again Sir Arthur Nicolson was practically unique in rejecting at the time the theory that Germany had provoked the war.[6] It is not possible that in August, 1914, Root knew anything of the effect of the Russian mobilization nor is there evidence that he even knew of the existence of the Anglo-French understanding. He explained his views at length in a talk with Mr. William Harrison Short at Clinton in the first week of August, 1914. Short

[6] Nicolson, *op. cit.*, p. 314.

put them in a memorandum which Root passed as accurately reflecting what he had said.

. . . The real issue of the present war is whether the German Emperor shall be the dominant power in Europe and this in its present stage can be settled only by force. For the time being, the nations of the triple entente have practically resolved themselves into an international police force for the purpose of disciplining a big, destructive, intolerable bully. . . . The Kaiser has, no doubt, intended all his life at sometime to wage a great European war. The idea of expecting from him any service for the world's peace has never been other than grotesque. He has contributed towards the preservation of the peace of Europe only as a bully may preserve the peace up to the moment when his actions become intolerable to his neighbors. . . .

If ever a war occurred in which the cause of civilization was represented by one side to the controversy, the present war furnishes an example. . . .

As Root phrased it on March 5th, 1915, to Sir George Otto Trevelyan: "Underlying all the particular reasons and occasions for the war, the principle of Anglo-Saxon liberty seems to have met the irreconcilable conception of the German State, and the two ideas are battling for control of the world."

Root went on to express in his interview with Short what was then a common point of view: "Within a few months the war will have been fought out and the stage of the controversy will have come when reason will have to be appealed to for a settlement." He was already thinking of some peace settlement which would "reconstruct the life of Europe. . . . The present duty of all friends of civilization is therefore clearly to understand and teach the lessons from the awful phenomenon of war, and to prepare for the ultimate reorganization of Europe on a basis that will prevent for the future the enormous armaments which have led to the present conflict." His constant consideration of post-war solutions will be discussed later in connection with the League of Nations.

In accordance, however, with his regular rule as a member of the Senate Committee on Foreign Relations, Root refused to have his views made public over his name. "A private citizen," he wrote to Hamilton Holt of the *Independent* on August 8th, 1914, "can often say usefully what would be unforgivable and injurious if said by a public officer. I hope . . . the American government will carefully refrain from saying or doing anything which will exclude it from the opportunity to help when the time comes to bring about the reestablishment of peaceful relations upon a new basis which will be free from the old virus."

In this hopeful anticipation that the United States might be useful in bringing about a satisfactory peace, Root's thought was paralleling President Wilson's.[7] Root as yet apparently had no thought that the United States should or would become a belligerent. Root continued his active interest in the Red Cross and on December 17th, 1914, Wilson, as President of the American Red Cross, appointed him a member of the International Relief Board. Root was an Honorary President of the Committee of Mercy for the women and children made destitute by the war. To both it and to the Belgian Relief Fund he contributed $500 in November of that year. On October 20th, he had sent another check to Senator Lodge's daughter, Mrs. Augustus P. Gardner, who was then in London for relief work. "I put it in this way because a direct contribution made to the work in any particular country might be seized upon as a departure from neutrality unless the same thing were done all around. No one can claim that there is a breach of neutrality in sending you a check for anything you choose to do, although the Lord knows that I am not at all neutral so far as you are concerned, but an active, violent and confirmed admirer, follower and partisan." Four days earlier, he had responded to an appeal from Mrs. Lodge:

> Tobacco is an Indian weed
> And 'twas the Devil sowed the seed
> But if 'twill soothe the soldiers lot
> I put five dollars in the pot.

August 26th, 1914, Root wrote to his son-in-law, Captain Grant, who was still at Vera Cruz. It is evident that it did not occur to him to question the British official documents as presenting but one side of the case:

> . . . Opinion here, and, so far as I can see, throughout the country, is overwhelmingly against the action of Germany and Austria.

[7] Cf. Baker, Woodrow Wilson, Life and Letters, Vol. V, pp. 68 ff.

The general judgment is that they have brought on this tremendous war wantonly and needlessly. My own feeling is that, although Austria took a wholly unjustifiable course towards Servia, great allowance must be made for her because of the intense feeling which must have been caused by the assassination of the heir to the throne and his wife and by the general attitude of the Servian people during the past five years regarding the annexation of Bosnia-Herzegovina. Germany, however, has no such excuse, and the official correspondence shows that, while professing to desire peace, she was backing up Austria in a course which made war inevitable. It was this, followed by the perfectly brutal and cynical violation of her own treaties and of international law with which she violated the neutrality of Belgium and inflicted the most frightful injuries upon that country without any provocation whatever that has practically determined the judgment of the entire civilized world against Germany. Yet the Germans do not see it at all.

I am sending you some sheets of the New York Times which contain in full the British White Paper containing the diplomatic correspondence. I have already received the official document, and careful comparison indicates that this print is accurate. . . .

On November 11th, 1914, he thanked Sir Gilbert Parker for sending him "the official papers relating to the war. . . . The documentary history of the war has been published very widely in the United States. . . . The effect of the publication and of the distribution of documentary evidence without any comment has really been very extraordinary. The people of the United States have made up their own minds upon the facts and no amount of argument appears to have the slightest effect upon them. Popular opinion moves along broad lines and not upon fine distinctions, and the chief ground of popular judgment here appears to rest upon the undisputed facts which exhibit the rights and wrongs of Belgium." Sir Gilbert headed a British propaganda service designed to elicit just such reactions from prominent Americans; it was not a hard task.

Root's correspondence with Lord Bryce at this period is illuminating:

Lord Bryce to Senator Root, September 10th, 1914:

. . . There are many things about which I should like to write to you, but at this moment I will mention one only. There have been suggestions made here that statements or declarations setting forth the case for the action of England in joining in this war might be sent to the U.S., signed by persons of eminence & science & literature, so as to influence U.S. opinion and counterwork the anti-British propaganda which is being carried on there.

I have doubts whether this course is desirable, or is needed, inasmuch as we hear that public opinion in the U.S. is already generally with us, and to attempt to influence it further might seem to be a needless putting of ourselves on the defensive. However I have promised to enquire the opinion of a few of those who in the U.S. are best qualified to advise, and should be grateful for your opinion, (1) as to the advisability of such a declaration, and (2) in case you do not recommend it, whether there is anything else, & what that could usefully be done from here to explain the British case & show that we should not have gone to war had not Belgium been invaded. . . .

Senator Root to Lord Bryce, September 23rd, 1914:

I have just received your letter of September tenth and I hasten to reply to your question. My impression is that you would be unwise to enter upon any argument regarding the responsibility for the present war addressed to or plainly designed to be presented to the people of the United States.

The first White Paper, containing the correspondence as far as Dispatch No. 159, has had a very wide circulation, and upon reading that the people of the country appear to have reached an amazingly swift, positive and settled judgment. I think the extraordinary rapidity of this process came to a considerable degree from the fact that it was not based upon what anybody said or upon any argument whatever, but upon consideration of the documentary evidence itself. I think the absence of argument helped the process. The conclusion reached has been much strengthened by the further paper containing Mr. Goschen's account of the "scrap of paper" conversation. That phrase is in everybody's mouth, and, taken in connection with the destruction of Louvain and the dreadful sufferings imposed upon innocent Belgium, has produced a profound impression. I cannot see that the efforts to dispel this impression and change this conclusion have produced any appreciable effect. I am inclined to think that any attempt to argue the case on your part would do more hurt than good. Of course strong, clear, fair presentations of the subject in a public way in Europe would get reported here and be very useful. Thus, the declaration in the House of Commons that this is a war against militarism has made a lodgment in almost everybody's mind. The very admirable paper signed by the British authors has had a good many readers. An address of the kind which you mention, if made to the people of Great Britain, would I think have more effect here than if it were made to the people of the United States. Of course we are all following the war with the deepest interest and have been made very unhappy by it, but I can see already the dawning of a vague hope that it means the beginning of a new era, the passing away of the old military dynasties, an immense extension of the principles of popular government, and the establishment of international relations on the basis of a peace which is something more than a military truce. Of course all such hopes are pinned upon the success of your arms.

Of course, all that I say on this subject must remain in the confidence of our personal friendship, because I am bound to make no public utterance so long as I am in the Senate which might be regarded as not strictly neutral. . . .

Lord Bryce to Senator Root, October 30th, 1914:

I hear that strenuous efforts are being made by various German & other anti-British agencies in the U.S. to work up ill feeling against Great Britain in connection with questions that have arisen regarding contrabrand & the right of search, & that the Press is being actively used for the purpose. Though I have not been able to follow the details very closely, I should like to say to you that our Government has been doing its very best to meet yours in all these matters, & has conceded not a few points on which it might, I believe have been able to press accepted doctrines of International Law more strictly than it has done. The most difficult points are still, I believe, awaiting a decision of our Prize Courts which have shown themselves so far quite fair, & anxious to avoid anything that would savour of a wish to restrict the rights of neutrals. We have shown a like feeling towards Holland & have been more considerate towards her than France has tended to be. If there is any matter in which you should think that we have gone too far I wish you would let me know, for I am sure our Foreign Office would have the greatest respect for your opinion. Perhaps you may think that some occasion may arise in which you would feel that you could say something publicly that might have a calming effect. And perhaps you know enough of our Prize Courts to be able to trust their fairness & good-will. We are most anxious, I need not say, to give no offence to the U.S. & the relations of our F.O. to your Government have been entirely cordial. It is only Press misrepresentation that I fear. . . .

Senator Root to Lord Bryce, November 21st, 1914:

About the time you were writing of it, I perceived there was danger that the men who were deprived of profits through contraband trade would stir up the Press with the effect of causing a misunderstanding as to the rights and limitations of neutral trade, and I asked the State Department to send for the newspaper correspondents and explain the subject to them and impress upon them the public duty of discouraging all sensational publications regarding incidents which arose in the course of the ordinary rules of international law upon which there is no dispute between Great Britain and the United States. They promised to do this, and I understand they have done it. I have taken steps to have prepared an accurate explanation regarding contraband and the doctrine of continuous voyages showing the precedents established by the United States and assented to by Great Britain, and citing the Supreme Court decisions in the Springbok case and the Peterhof case, and I shall look for some occasion to get this published in such a way that it will receive attention. . . . Mr. John Lane called on me a few days ago and wished me to write a preface for a book which he intends to publish containing the principal documents already printed in pamphlet form. Upon reflection I concluded that it would be unwise to do this while I continue in office, although I feel very strongly that you are fighting for the cause of liberty and peace and humanity. Among other considerations it seemed to me that for a member of the Foreign Relations Committee of the Senate to take part in presenting the Allies' case and to say what I should wish to say in such an article would cut me off from the possibility of rendering much greater services to the cause which has my entire sympathy in case of serious questions arising regarding neutral trade.

I see no indications, outside of purely German groups, of any change of American feeling. On the contrary, it seems to me to grow stronger. The fact is that the American people are radically and unalterably opposed to German militarism and its fruits as exhibited in this war, and the more fully German discussion of the subject reveals the true character of the principles and purposes which control the ruling class in Germany, the worse it is for the German side of the controversy before an American jury.

The only thing I have been afraid of is some new cause of controversy between the United States and Great Britain arising which will distract attention from the issues of the European conflict and arouse prejudice and hostile feeling. I find in the State Department the same view regarding the considerate attitude of Great Britain in the various questions which arise which you express in your letter and a fixed purpose to be considerate and reasonable on our side. . . .

In the meantime, my entire family is almost incapable of thinking about anything but the war. We go about under a sense of great misfortune. We rejoice over every Allied success and become gloomy over the reverse. . . .

It was Chandler P. Anderson who had first called Root's attention to the dangerous possibility of Anglo-American controversy over neutral rights. Anderson was then attached to the American Embassy in London and his native sympathy for the Allied cause was bound to be strengthened through association with Ambassador Page who was surely the most unneutral of all American officials. It was probably to a memorandum prepared by Anderson that Root referred in his letter to Bryce.

On November 22nd, Root wrote again to Anderson on the subject of British interference with neutral trade, saying that he had talked with people in the State Department "and they express full appreciation of the considerate treatment of the subject by Great Britain. . . . Of course the State Department is under pressure from people who find that the assertion of belligerent rights on the part of Great Britain is interfering with large profits on their part. The natural reaction of an American business man, who neither knows nor cares anything about international law, is to become very angry if any other country interferes with his making money. That has happened here and the effect has been visible in the newspapers. The natural tendency in the State Department under such pressure is to claim everything which may benefit the American exporter and thus escape the responsibility of refusing to make such claims." Root had confidence in Lansing's honesty but thought he lacked imagination and that his judgment was not reliable. He also had great confidence in Chandler Anderson and James Brown Scott who were advising Lansing on legal points; Scott became Chairman of the Neutrality Board. All three of them had been Root's assistants in the Fisheries Arbitration at The Hague, five years before. When, in the spring of 1914, Lansing's name was under consideration for the position of Counselor in the State Department, John Foster, Lansing's father-in-law, asked Root to recommend Lansing to President Wilson, which Root gladly did; Lansing was deeply appreciative. There is no evidence that Root ever came to realize that the British had violated international law in their treatment of American vessels, although in December, 1916, he regretfully noted the diminution of pro-Allied sentiment in the United States. He thought the British had bungled and that they should have sent a more effective ambassador, preferably Lord Bryce.[8] Bryce had again explained to him, in a letter of December 15th, 1914, the views of the British Government on neutral trade. Root could not have known, as the British Naval Attaché in Scandinavia, Admiral Consett, later revealed, that the British themselves were shipping to Scandinavian countries the very products which they intercepted when bound for such destinations from America.[9] He probably knew that Lansing sympathized with the Allies but he could hardly have anticipated the astonishing statement which appears in Lansing's War Memoirs that in his notes of protest to Great Britain "Everything was submerged in verbosity. It was done with deliberate purpose. It insured continuance of the controversies and left the questions unsettled, which was necessary in order to leave this country free to act and even to act illegally when it entered the war." [10] Such is the war mind and its effect upon straight-forward and honest men.

October 20th, 1914, in writing to Chandler P. Anderson at the American Embassy in London, Root had again stated his belief in "the swift and positive judgment" formed by the American people in favor of the Allied cause. "The Germans have had some very skillful men at work, trying to change the opinion, but so far as I can see they have not accomplished anything. Sometimes in trying a jury case, right in the middle of the trial a man will realize that the jury has

[8] Diary of Chandler P. Anderson, entry of December 24, 1916.
[9] Consett and Daniel, The Triumph of Unarmed Forces.
[10] Lansing, p. 128.

made up its mind and anything that follows that is of no consequence whatever." He was considering the possibility of the Carnegie Endowment, of which he was President, conducting an inquiry into the charges of German outrages, but he was not sure it would be wise. "My observation has been that for a considerable period after a fight begins, any interference at all from outsiders does more harm than good, but that, what it is the fashion to call the psychological moment is sure to arrive."

October 21st, 1914, Root was answering in a friendly and sympathetic way a letter from the Austrian jurist, Dr. Heinrich Lammasch, who had presided over the tribunal in the North Atlantic Coast Fisheries Arbitration. To him also he expressed the hope and expectation that the time would come when the United States "as a really neutral nation" might be of service in mediating for peace. At the time he was writing, the American Government was "insisting very firmly upon absolute and real neutrality . . . and I warmly approve its position in this respect."

In a letter to Elbert F. Baldwin of the *Outlook* on December 1st, 1914, Root did not advocate that the United States should protest against the invasion of Belgium but he believed that we had a right to protest because of our "direct interest in the preservation of the law of nations in favor of peace and a special interest in the preservation of that particular law which preserves the rights of neutrals." After his retirement from the Senate and especially in the Presidential campaign year of 1916, he elaborated that theme in his public addresses. Roosevelt, Robert Bacon and others began in the fall of 1914 to attack Wilson because he had not protested against the invasion of Belgium. Ray Stannard Baker's defense of Wilson's course on this point is legally sound although he does not deal with Root's actual argument.[11] To Lord Bryce, Root wrote on March 1st, 1915: "I have been doing violence to my feelings by keeping quiet all these months regarding the violation of the rights of Belgium and the way in which Germany has carried on the war, but I have felt that I could do more good by reserving whatever force I could bring to bear for practical situations of great importance which were certain to arise. . . . I am satisfied now that the course was wise, for by reason of the fact that I have complied with the President's request to observe neutrality in

[11] Baker, *op. cit.*, p. 164.

speech [Wilson had asked also for impartiality in thought] as well as in action I have been able to exercise some influence speaking from an American point of view upon both of the practical matters to which I have referred." One of these matters was the bill for the purchase of the German ships and the other the proposal to embargo shipments of arms and munitions. The proposers of this latter plan, he told Lord Bryce, were a "lot of good, well-meaning advocates of peace" who had "fallen into the trap laid by the sympathizers with Germany. . . . They illustrate the danger of sentiment without knowledge of affairs. It never seems to occur to them that freedom of trade in munitions of war is the only safeguard of a peaceful nation." To George H. Putnam, on December 11th, 1914, he had written a legal justification of the same point of view:

> . . . Such a proposition might have been debated on its merits before the beginning of the war, but to change our neutrality laws now so as to abolish a rule of action which has always existed, in such a way as to hurt one belligerent and to help the other, would clearly be itself a flagrant violation of the spirit of neutrality. I am not at all sure that it would not be such an unfriendly act as to justify not only resentment, but reprisals. I cannot believe that any such legislation is likely to be passed.

Two decades later the United States definitely embodied the arms embargo policy in its neutrality legislation.

In his great speech at the Republican Convention in Carnegie Hall on February 15th, 1916, Root vehemently attacked the Wilsonian policies toward Germany as "the policy of threatening words without deeds." Yet in a letter to Lord Bryce on March 1st, 1915, he urged him to discount any hostile expressions which might be found in the American Government's notes to Great Britain. He remarked on the large German vote in the United States and the skillful way in which it was being used by the German propagandists. (He did not think of the pro-Allied vote as being "used" by the Allied propagandists.) He told Lord Bryce how the Administration was being attacked as seeming to be for the Allies and against Germany. "Of course the effect of attacks of that kind is to create a tendency to repel the attack. . . . This should always be considered by the Allies before any hostile purpose is inferred from the action or words of our Administration." He attacked Wilson's policy when the President was seeking reelection on the slogan that "he kept us out of war" by asserting that "We have not been following the path of peace. We have been blindly stumbling along the road that continued will lead to inevitable war." But even more surely, the attitude taken by Root, Lodge, Roosevelt, Lansing, Page and others led to inevitable war and they wished that it should do so.

Root believed that the United States should have entered the war against Germany after the sinking of the Lusitania on May 7th, 1915. As already noted, he did not believe that while he was a United States Senator, he should speak out on the war issues, although Lodge felt under no such inhibition and Robert Bacon pleaded with Root to come out.[12] Roosevelt, with no official position, was one of the most vocal of the President's critics. He had felt the same way about President McKinley before he decided on war with Spain. Like Roosevelt, Root was an ardent believer in preparedness and in 1916 he was arguing strongly for universal military service. Before he left the Senate he had urged upon the leaders of the Democratic majority the introduction of a bill appropriating $200,000,000 to be spent by the President in his discretion for naval and military equipment, but they had not acted upon it.[13] After the breach of relations with Germany on February 3rd, 1917, and before the declaration of a state of war on April 6th, Root made a number of speeches urging a more vigorous policy. On April 9th, he spoke before the Republican Club in New York City; it was extemporaneous and devoid of restraint. The audience was as moved as was the speaker. Root rode home after the meeting with James R. Sheffield. After some minutes of silence, Root put his hand on Sheffield's knee and said: "We're in it, thank God, we're in it!" From then on he devoted himself heart and soul to the war, fighting partisanship and insisting on full loyalty to Wilson. He refused to be distracted by other issues and, in response to many requests, urged that all other matters should be laid aside until the war was won. He never for a moment faltered in his belief that the war must be pushed to a successful conclusion with Germany defeated absolutely and permanently crushed as a menace to the democracies of the world.

There is nothing which reveals more clearly the war spirit which

[12] Bacon to Root, October 29, 1914.
[13] Diary of Chandler P. Anderson, entry of March 8, 1915, as corrected May 15, 1915.

gripped Root's mind than his correspondence on the subject of teaching German in the public schools. On May 22nd, 1918, he replied to Lawrence A. Wilkins of the Department of Education of New York City who had asked him to present his views for use at a hearing which they were to have on this subject. "There are of course," Root wrote, "strong considerations from an educational point of view in favor of teaching German. Both for practical use and as opening the door to a very great literature such instruction may be very useful.

"I do not, however, think that under existing conditions such considerations should be deemed controlling. Our Country is engaged in a life and death struggle with the great German-speaking powers of the world, and we have suddenly come to realize that vast numbers of our population receive their ideas both as to facts and opinions exclusively or chiefly through the language of our enemies. . . . To be a strong and united nation we must be a one-language people. . . . It is of the highest importance, affecting not merely the curriculum of our schools, but their continued existence, that all the people of the United States should come to read and speak and think in the one prevailing language.

"This should be the controlling consideration. In view of it every effort should be made to promote the universal use of English, and to discourage the common use of German by any part of our population. Nothing ought to be done which will make it easier for anybody living in the United States to read and speak the German language instead of reading and speaking the English language. . . . To use the public money raised by taxation to facilitate and promote the use of German instead of the use of English seems to me on public grounds to be wholly indefensible."

The argument in favor of English is understandable—although Root had no objection to the teaching of French and Spanish—but Root went still further in replying on May 31st, 1918, to a like inquiry from Richard J. Biggs, a Commissioner of Education in Baltimore. To him Root said that he agreed that French and Spanish were the most useful foreign languages for young Americans to learn, quite apart from the war situation. But there was another aspect: "one does not intentionally introduce the young to bad company, or subject them to demoralizing influences that can be avoided. The Prussianizing of the German people has been a process of demoralization until they have become the exponents and their language the vehicle for the expression of a gross and brutal philosophy of life which involves a negation of the Christian morality of modern civilization . . . we have no right to facilitate exercise of that influence upon the youth of America." Again to Judge Joseph Buffington on September 7th, 1918, Root wrote expressing his conviction that the modern Germany differed vastly from that Germany where his brother had studied chemistry fifty years before. Prussianization, with its "organized and incessant appeal to the lower motives for more than a generation has debased the standards of life, of morals, of art, of literature" and the German nation was "living in a dream of intense egotism in which it is satisfied with principles and conduct which it would have abhorred sixty years ago. I do not think the soul of Germany is lost; but I think the Germany of Goethe, of Francis Lieber, of the liberty-loving men of 1815 and 1848, has sunk far out of sight under pride and arrogance and brutal materialism, and that only a spiritual revolution induced by a tremendous shock can restore the old Germany."

"The Boche are as cunning and tricky as they are gross and brutal," Root wrote to Edward N. Smith on February 5th, 1919. It was his constant theme in the years of the war. He shared with many Americans the belief that if Germany defeated the Allies, the Kaiser would take the British colonies, including Canada, and that we would be confronted with the German power on our northern frontier. He took frequent occasion to warn American audiences that the triumph of Germany would mean the end of the Monroe Doctrine. The notorious intercepted Zimmermann note of January 19th, 1917, suggesting to the Mexican Government an alliance between Germany, Mexico and Japan, with the offer that Mexico would recover Texas, New Mexico and Arizona, lent credence to these beliefs. It was crass stupidity for the Germans to send such a message, but in anticipation of war with the United States, it was a perfectly reasonable political manoeuvre, not differing in kind from the secret treaties of the Allies with Italy and Japan whereby those countries were offered territorial compensations for their participation in the war. In 1917, however, it was regarded as yet another example of German perfidy. On January 29th, 1918, Frank L. Polk, Assistant Secretary of State, wrote to Mr. Root asking his authority for a statement which Stanwood Menken, President of the National Security League, had told him Root had made: "that the State Department had evidence of Germany's plans to secure a part of the United States as a definite part of their policy." Root, who had in September, 1917, succeeded Joseph H. Choate as Honorary President of the League, replied with some asperity: "Mr. Menken was mistaken. I never said I knew the State Department had evidence of Germany's plans to secure a part of the United States. If I had known it, I would not have said it, for I could not have known it except confidentially. He may have had in mind something based upon the Zimmermann note, or some remark based upon the German General Staff plan which in a general way is pretty well known, but certainly would not be in the State Department."

On September 25th, 1916, Root had written to an inquirer: "You ask how to get inside information on the subject [of the attitude of the European Powers toward peace]. You can't get it. It is not to be had by you or me." But, as a matter of fact, he was throughout better informed than most people outside of government circles. Through Chandler Anderson particularly, he was the recipient of information and frequently of messages from Lansing and from Bernard Baruch, Chairman of the War Industries Board. In May, 1915, at Root's request, Chandler Anderson sent to him a complete set of the diplomatic correspondence between the United States and Germany and Great Britain.[14] Root saw Colonel House occasionally and corresponded with him. He had some contacts with Secretary of the Treasury McAdoo. Especially in the days of the Peace Conference, he was in close touch with the Senators, with State Department circles and with that indefatigable letter-writer, Henry White, a member of the American Peace Commission in Paris.

As already noted, Root set his face hard against partisanship after the United States entered the war. His ringing speech on this theme to the New York Republican Club on April 9th, 1917, elicited a grateful letter from the Secretary of State. ". . . there has been no utterance by any man," Lansing wrote to him, "which surpasses it in patriotism or in sound practical means of helpfulness to the Government.

"It is an unfortunate fact that in this time of national test there are so many men whose horizon is limited and who cannot divorce their public responsibilities from partisanship and the petty things

[14] *Ibid.*, entry of May 15, 1915; Anderson to Root, July 28, 1915, Anderson Papers.

in politics. The influence of your address upon men of this stamp throughout the country will be very great. . . ."

Theodore Roosevelt could never quite bring himself to this frame of mind, although he did his best to restrain his personal feelings about Wilson. To Lodge· he wrote on February 28th, 1917: ". . . I say nothing in public about Wilson now. . . . I wish that Root would speak up unequivocally, as he thinks. Until we broke relations with Germany I spoke plainly enough! The chatter about 'standing behind the President', when the President is nervously backing away from his duty, is sickening." [15] Superficially, at least, Root and Roosevelt were back on their old friendly basis. On March 20th, 1917, there was a great war meeting at the Union League Club; Roosevelt, Root, Hughes and Choate spoke. Later a group of them gathered in the grill room. Roosevelt, in his vehement way, was expounding his desire to go to France and appealing to each one of them for help in inducing Wilson to give him a commission. Emphatically he declared that if he went he would not expect to return but would hope to be buried in the soil of France. With mock seriousness, Root turned to him and asked him to repeat that statement; Roosevelt did so with even greater fervor. "Theodore," said Root, "if you can convince Wilson of that I am sure he will give you a commission." But Wilson never did and Roosevelt died on January 6th, 1919, under the burden of bitter disappointment.

It was at that same Union League Club meeting that Root sounded the one note which he allowed himself in the line of criticism of the President in those days; he pleaded for action. "Only one thing we will say to the party in power,—" he declared in his speech to the New York Republican Club on April 9th, 1917, "let us have a real war. Let us lose no opportunity in public or in private to urge and insist upon a vigorous and real war. There must be no dillydallying or half measures nor any giving in to peace terms until democracy is triumphant."

"I will not go to any meeting the object of which is to talk about peace," he wrote Menken on March 18th, 1918. "What we need now is concentration of the attention of the American people on war." He used all his strength preaching his doctrines of loyalty, in correspondence, in conversation and in public addresses. "It is a war be-

[15] *Roosevelt-Lodge Correspondence*, Vol. II, p. 498.

tween Odin and Christ," he cried in an address at Carnegie Hall on March 7th, 1918, before a meeting assembled to honor the Archbishop of York. From the pulpit of the Cathedral of St. John the Divine a week after the Armistice, he announced: "God Himself was on our side." "I have been a Republican all my life, but I count it as naught compared with this great issue" of winning the war through loyalty to the Administration, he told the National Security League on May 8th, 1918. He carried the same message to the New York Republican Convention at Saratoga on July 18th: "We may lose votes here and there, we may lose an office here and there; we can live without such votes and without office; but we cannot live without principles and without self-respect. This is no time for easy-going indifference. He is no true Republican who does not hate disloyalty and hold the disloyal man to be his enemy." He urged the reelection of John Purroy Mitchell as Mayor of New York in the fall of 1917, chiefly on his record as a "war mayor" whose defeat would make the enemies of our country rejoice over the failure of loyal Americanism.[16] On September 14th, 1917, he addressed a huge mass meeting in the Coliseum at Chicago whose Mayor, "Big Bill" Thompson, had consistently opposed the war. "The declaration of war between the United States and Germany completely changed the relations of all the inhabitants of this country to the subject of peace and war." Before the issue was settled by the process required under the Constitution, citizens were free to argue the merits of a war or a peace policy; they were free to favor the cause of Germany or the cause of the Allies. But now they were no longer free. "A nation which declares war and goes on discussing whether it ought to have declared war or not, is impotent, paralyzed, imbecile, and earns the contempt of mankind, and the certainty of humiliating defeat and subjection to foreign control." Having stated the legal duty, he appealed to the emotions of his hearers to do their duty with a will. He reviewed the German "atrocities"—"barbarity unequalled since the conquests of Genghis Khan. . . . It is the climax of the supreme struggle between autocracy and democracy. . . . The two systems cannot endure together in the same world."

His letter of February 16th, 1918, to Stanwood Menken also obtained much publicity. In it he argued vehemently against the talk of

16 Root to James R. Sheffield, October 18, 1917.

peace terms until Germany "has had a thorough whipping." He admitted that there had been and would be mistakes made by the government and "Sincere and constructive criticism of executive conduct is a very useful thing. But we must all be careful that neither shortcoming nor criticism tends in the slightest degree to divert or decrease the heartiness with which we all support and reinforce the President and his civil and military officers in carrying on this war."

In the congressional elections of 1918, he thought that the paramount issue should be loyalty, irrespective of party. Nothing has been found in his files to indicate that he approved the Republican policy of attacking the Administration after Wilson, on October 25th, appealed to the nation to return a Democratic majority to Congress, although Root had stressed in his speech to the Saratoga Convention the value of Republican representation in Congress. Only in districts where no question of loyalty appeared as between the two candidates, did Root think one was justified in voting on strict party lines. But he warned Menken that the Security League would make a mistake if it attacked candidates on the basis of past records—votes on preparedness or similar issues which were now past. The sole question should be the candidates' position as to the continued prosecution of the war. "There are many . . . who would be glad to come out strongly on the right side were it not for a little awkwardness arising from their former attitude. Let us make it as easy as possible for them to come. Do not let us divide the loyal forces by undertaking to punish anyone for what he did before the War. When the War is over, it may be very different."

But he could not stomach an alliance with William Randolph Hearst. On June 18th, 1918, the New York *American* published on its front page a letter from Menken to Hearst in which the former, although expressing disagreement with many of the *American's* policies, praised it and Hearst for its stand on preparedness. The National Security League ranks were torn asunder. Menken was the League's President and spoke for the organization; Root was Honorary President. He wrote on June 25th to Alton B. Parker, the Honorary Vice President, that if Menken were left in office, the League would be stamped with his endorsement of Hearst. This could be avoided only by changing the President of the League. "Unless that change is made, I do not see how anyone who is not willing to be classed among

Hearst's supporters can continue. I am not willing to be put in that category, or to take part in a campaign to teach the American people loyalty as it is exemplified by Hearst, for I think he is the most dangerous and injurious influence tending towards disloyalty and dis· union among the American people, the most powerful influence towards bringing about the kind of demoralization that will help Germany and hinder American success in the War." Menken resigned, but Root was quite willing to have him continue in a minor connection with the League. "I do not think," he wrote to George Wharton Pepper on August 8th, "the objectionable interview was the work of a hardened sinner who approved Hearst as he really is, but rather of a good-natured chucklehead who was fooled by Hearst's vehement protestations of loyalty with an absurd idea of welcoming a convert to the true faith. I think he was honestly aghast when he found what he really had done, and he certainly has abjured in the fullest possible way, and Hearst has turned on him like a cur, as he is. . . ." Root continued to be a vigorous supporter of the National Security League until after the Armistice when he felt that it adopted too broad a program which would "make the League practically an agency for universal reform, which is necessarily futile." He resigned in December, 1918, but was persuaded to reconsider; he finally withdrew in April, 1920.

Although Root practiced what he preached about whole-hearted support of the Administration during the war, he was far from satisfied and to intimate friends he revealed his disgust. He thought that Wilson was incapable of doing hard administrative work himself and that he was unwilling to delegate it. He believed also that Wilson threw on subordinates blame for things which were his own fault. The first part of this charge at least was certainly unfair. Lansing he had long known and liked personally but he had no great belief in his abilities. He thought McAdoo the one man in the Cabinet who was free from "the general paralysis of Wilsonism." [17]

Affirmatively, there was not much that Root could do aside from influencing public opinion. When President Wilson in 1917 asked him to head a mission to Russia, he felt that he had to accept as a war service; that story will be told later. For one who felt so strongly,

[17] Diary of Chandler P. Anderson, especially entries of December 30, 1917 and March 24, 1918.

it was inevitable that Root should be in the ranks of those who denounced the "pro-Germans" and pacifists. The greater part of the "men who are to-day speaking and writing and printing arguments against the war . . ." Root said in his Chicago speech of September 14th, 1917, "are at heart traitors to the United States. . . ." A month earlier he told the Union League Club in New York: "There are some newspapers published in this city every day, the editors of which deserve conviction and execution for treason." He took part in pushing the drives for the sale of Liberty Bonds and War Savings Stamps. He made at least one attempt to influence the Latin American countries to join in the war. In acknowledging the receipt of a book from an old friend in Uruguay, he took occasion on March 5th, 1918, to discuss the war; it probably would have required a conscious effort to avoid talking about it:

"I hear a great deal about wool nowadays, because Mrs. Root and our daughter Mrs. Grant who was with us when we met you in Monte Video are very busily engaged in knitting and supplying other women with the means to knit socks and helmets and sweaters and mufflers for our soldiers including a son and son-in-law who are in the army. The subject of yarns and the wool supply generally is accordingly the subject of much conversation in the family. . . .

"I wish Uruguay and the Argentine could make up their minds to formally join the list of the nations who are engaged in fighting against the domination of Germany. This is the one opportunity to act in time for the preservation of real independence by the American Republics both South and North. If Germany wins this war, we shall all be dominated by her, and her domination over other countries is practical and oppressive. When she once gets the upper hand she knows how to compel absolute obedience, and she does it in the most cruel and offensive way. That is her nature and that is her purpose. There will be no such thing as national freedom anywhere under the overlordship of Germany which is sure to come unless she is beaten now."

CHAPTER XLII

"My political career . . . drawing to a close"

BEFORE the United States had entered the war, Root had been led into acquiescing in something which in his younger days he had resolutely declined; he grudgingly permitted a group of his friends to boom him for the Presidency in 1916. His acquiescence is explicable only against the background of his feeling about the war.

On December 16th, 1913, Root had taken the floor of the Senate to make a personal statement. Three days before he had made his notable speech on the Banking and Currency bill; it had elicited from Senator Gallinger of New Hampshire a statement to the press urging that Root was the one logical candidate for the Republican Party to nominate for the Presidency in 1916. Andrew Carnegie and others were singing the same tune. Some of the Democratic senators, in rebutting Root's criticism of the pending bill, had insinuated that Root was inspired by a personal ambition to fill that role. The matter had obtained prominence in the daily press. Root repudiated the idea that he was swayed by any such personal ambition. He asked the senators to remember "that before this Administration comes to a close and the next President has been inaugurated, I shall have reached the age of seventy-two years. Before the next Administration comes to a close I shall have passed the age of seventy-six years. It is manifestly impossible that I should be the President of the United States. I could not render the service. I would not undertake it. I would not accept the nomination. I could not accept the office.

"Such suggestions are and can be merely a graphic way of expressing the feelings of friendship and approval. My political career and my public career are drawing to a close. No political ambition whatever finds its place in the horizon of my future. I look with sympathy and interest upon the younger and more vigorous men who surround me, who rightfully cherish ambitions for place and usefulness of service for our country, but I have no part in them."

There can be no question about the sincerity of this statement. He had refused far better chances to become President nearly ten years before. On December 18th, 1913, he added a postscript to a letter to Taft thanking him "for the Presidential Boom which you & Carnegie & other millionaires swing at me. I have avoided being knocked off the boat by ducking." [1] On the same day one of the seamen who had been in the crew of the *Charleston* when that warship carried Mr. Root on his South American trip in 1906, wrote that he was astonished at Senator Root's statement that he was too old to run for the Presidency: "I think Senator that you could wait many more years and still be young. Of course its been about 7 years back that you made the South American trip aboard the *Charleston* and you were certainly spry at that time." There were numerous letters with a like theme. Governor Lowden of Illinois wrote on December 23rd, 1913, suggesting that a great national crisis might arise by 1916 and that Root might be the only man to save the situation. In such circumstances, would it not be his duty to allow himself to be drafted? Root replied simply that he did not anticipate such a crisis but that it was gratifying to have his old friends feel that he might be useful in such an emergency.

In the next six months he was to resist all importunate demands of ardent admirers and party leaders that he accept another term in the Senate. His physician, Dr. Dixon, warned him against it; his inclination made him receptive to that advice. On June 3rd, 1914, he wrote at some length on the subject to his friend, George Dunham, editor of the Utica *Press*. He said that the strain of senatorial service had now become so great that he was physically unable to stand it. "I know very well that to try another term in the Senate would merely mean a break down and inability to render service and at the same time a strong probability that I should remain broken. There is another consideration: We are in a period of continual strife and turmoil. Almost everybody seems to be trying to knock somebody else down in order to climb up on his prostrate form and reach something. This is so in the government and in politics all over the country. I suppose I have passed the time of life when a man naturally enjoys that sort of thing. I certainly have passed the period of development of my own character in which I enjoy it. A large part of the fights that

[1] Taft Papers, Library of Congress.

are going on fail to interest me. Things which I thought great fun thirty or forty years ago are rather a bore now. My attitude is getting to be that of an observer rather than a participant in the scrimmage. I am satisfied that a young man who still has Donnybrook Fair in his veins can fill my official place better than I can. So I am going to get out and seek such personal freedom as the limitations of age permit, and I will not be a candidate for reelection to the Senate." It is unlikely that he would have taken a different view even if the direct election of senators had not then been required by the Seventeenth Amendment to the Constitution, but the necessity for a personal campaign, which he always abhorred, was a crowning reason for refusing to run for the office.

He was eager for the retirement which was to be long denied him. As Mr. Justice Holmes once said, "repose is not the destiny of Man." Root's next service was to be President of the New York Constitutional Convention of 1915. To that body he again expressed his determination and his hope to go back to that "plain old house in the Oneida hills . . . to spend my declining years." But the war gripped him and he could not withdraw from the demands of a host of friends and admirers who invoked his aid in causes very dear to his heart or who appealed to his strong sense of duty. He accepted a number of arduous appointments but he sought none of these things and he refused many others. Especially through 1915 and 1916 when his friends in the Republican Old Guard were pushing him for the Presidency and when his name filled the political headlines of the newspapers, he played the role not of a candidate but of a resigned and somewhat unsympathetic observer. The plain old house in the Oneida hills still seemed to him much more attractive than the White House in the Potomac valley. Such an attitude is always incomprehensible to the public, to newspaper correspondents and to politicians, and so for about a year they weighed his every act and word and judged them by the test of what a clever candidate for office should do to further his cause. By this measure most of them found him wanting, and bemoaned or rejoiced that he had lost the vigor and skills of his youth.

Throughout the duration of the Constitutional Convention, the boom of Root for president filled the newspapers. It had its ups and downs but the fact that it was in the air gave added prominence to his speeches, particularly that on "invisible government." His commanding position in the Convention made the political dopesters link the fate of the new constitution with his own fate as a presidential possibility. When it was overwhelmingly defeated by the voters of New York, they cried that Root was now out of the picture, although the generally hostile New York *World* on November 5th, 1915, declared that "Every vote for that constitution was in a way a personal tribute to Elihu Root. . . . No other man in New York could have induced nearly 400,000 citizens to vote for so bad a constitution. . . ." And they believed that if Root had been free to write his own constitution, the result would have been joyfully accepted. There were some other papers which saw Root strengthened with the Progressives as a result of his advocacy of such measures as the short ballot, and his stand against the bosses. On October 18th, 1915, at a Republican Club dinner at the Hotel Astor in New York, James R. Sheffield presided and told Root amid great applause that he could not disregard the call of the people to serve in the highest office in the nation. Root was deeply moved but his remarks were confined to a discussion of the new constitution. November 28th, 1915, the *World* reported the replies to its telegrams to the chairmen of all the Republican state committees in the country; Root was running a poor third to Hughes and Senator Cummins of Iowa. On December 18th, 1915, the *Literary Digest* published its poll of over five hundred Republican editors, senators and representatives. Root led with 279 votes as against 152 for Hughes, his nearest competitor. The wide geographical spread of his support was interesting. Of course Hughes was still on the Supreme Court bench and there were many who said that he would not and should not resign to enter a political contest.

The most determined local effort to push Root came from Minnesota where State Senator E. E. Smith, the local Republican leader, wished Root to enter his name in the primaries which came in March, 1916. Frank B. Kellogg, later United States Senator and Secretary of State, was among the Root supporters who wrote Henry L. Stimson in New York, assuring him that the State was strong for Root. On December 3rd, Frederick M. Davenport called on Stimson. Davenport, as a State Senator, had been one of Root's chief contacts in Albany and it was he who had led the movement for Root's nomination as United States Senator in 1909. The fact that in 1912 Davenport had been an ardent Progressive and had run on that ticket for the Governorship of New York in 1914, gave significance to his support at a time when the healing of the 1912 split in the Republican Party was one of the chief concerns in planning for the presidential campaign of 1916. Davenport's glowing eulogy of Mr. Root published in *Collier's* magazine for November 13th, 1915, was in demand as a precampaign document. Davenport told Stimson that he had received many letters about his article and that the general impression in the West seemed to be that Root had fought a brave fight for a reform constitution and had been beaten by the Republican and Democratic machines; his defeat was therefore a source of strength in progressive circles. Davenport felt that Root must remain as at least a potential candidate in order to preserve his leadership in the Party. He had discussed the matter with Mr. Root in Clinton and had asked with what one of Root's friends he might discuss the matter; Root had suggested that he see Stimson.

On December 7th, Root asked Stimson to lunch with him. He said that Smith had come on from Minnesota to urge him to enter his name in their state primaries; under Minnesota law, this could be done only at the candidate's own request. Root told Smith that while he would not say that he would refuse the nomination if his party in convention decided that it was his duty to run, nevertheless he did not desire the nomination and he would not become a candidate seeking the position. He told Smith that if he ran in Minnesota he would either have to be an active and aggressive candidate and place his name in nomination in every state having direct primaries or else appear as a half-hearted but avowed candidate putting up an incompetent and necessarily losing contest. He was unwilling to take either position and definitely refused Smith's proposal. Smith saw others of Root's friends who endeavored to persuade Root to change his view but he would not. To James R. Sheffield, Root indicated that he would make no commitments of any kind and that he would enter into no bargains to further his candidacy, which was but another way of turning down the Minnesota leader.

To all of his close personal friends, Root indicated his strong disinclination to accept the nomination for the Presidency. He had been so close to the Presidency for so long that it had lost its glamor and he saw in it only the strain and hard work; he wanted to go home and rest. It was only the great world crisis brought on by the war, in which his friends kept assuring him that he might be helpful, which prevented his withdrawing entirely and absolutely. He was also worried about the political situation in New York. The defeat of the constitution seemed to him the defeat of his efforts to unify the party back of a constructive, forward-looking program and he saw little hope of restoring New York to a position of power and influence in the deliberations of the next national Republican convention.

After his luncheon with Stimson, they encountered Charles Hilles, then Chairman of the National Republican Committee. To him Mr. Root repeated his point of view. Hilles reported that there was much support for Root throughout the country and that many states would fall in line if given the lead by New York. In view of Governor Whitman's apparent candidacy, which Hilles considered absurd, he thought that the New York delegation should go to the Chicago Convention uninstructed, but that someone like James Wadsworth, who had succeeded Root as Senator from New York, might come out for Root and thus indicate the position of the Empire State.

Wadsworth, on being consulted by Stimson, avowed enthusiastic support for Root, but felt that it was premature to make a statement at that time. He favored the calling of a Republican State Convention in February for the purpose of choosing four delegates at large and suggested that the question of instructions to the delegates might well be taken up at that time. This was the plan that was followed. The Convention met at Carnegie Hall on February 15th, 1916. Partly because of the insistence of Barnes, Root was slated for Temporary Chairman. It was put up to him on the ground that he alone had the ability and prestige to voice the sentiments of those who believed that Wilson had failed to represent the position of America in the great world crisis. It was a plea which Root, feeling as strongly as he did about the war, could not refuse. He prepared his speech—a scathing attack upon Wilson's policies in the Mexican and World War situations. He spent a great deal of time and labor upon it. He was tired. On the 13th he attended a conference of Republican leaders at which a first draft of a platform, prepared by Nicholas Murray Butler, was adopted with some modifications, for submission to the convention. Later he saw William Barnes and Frederick C. Tanner, Chairman of the Republican State Committee, and told them definitely that he would not himself go as a delegate to the Chicago Convention.

On the day before the New York Convention was to open, Stimson called on Root. He found him tired and pessimistic. Root told him that he had written him a letter explaining his views about the speech he was about to make. The letter is dated February 14th, 1916:

> The speech which I am going to make at the Republican State Convention tomorrow night is finished and in the hands of the Press, under release for Wednesday morning.
>
> Before it becomes a subject of public comment I would like to tell you what I anticipate as its probable effect so far as it has any effect.
>
> I think it will materially decrease any probability or possibility that the Chicago Convention will nominate me for the presidency. There is no merit implied in making the speech with this expectation, because as you know, both my judgment and my personal wishes are opposed to my own nomination.
>
> I think the views expressed will be met by a refusal of assent and by adverse criticism on the part of a considerable section of the Republican party and of the independent voters, but I think the opinions expressed will ultimately prevail among the very Republicans and Independents who begin by opposition and that the speech will contribute towards bringing about that result.
>
> I think that the good of the country requires that the main ideas which I am expressing should be expressed as a part of this political campaign, and the unsought selection of me as temporary chairman of this convention seems to require me to say these things or lose my self respect.

In the same vein Root had written to Lodge on February 11th: "I feel confident about only one result of what I shall say, and that is, that it will relieve me from any embarrassment about being called upon to run for the presidency." He told Stimson, in describing what he had written, that he wanted a few of his friends to understand in advance what his real views on the subject were so that they would not think that by any possibility he had made the speech in an attempt to get the nomination. His anticipations of the results of his speech were not unreasonable. Root was practically saying that Wilson should put us into the war when Wilson was about to run on the slogan that he kept us out of war. The German vote, which was a great political bugbear in those days, would certainly be antagonized.

Meanwhile, before the speech was delivered, the party leaders were thick in conference. The New Yorkers were split between Hughes and Root with petty fights on the side for place and position on the slate of delegates-at-large to the Convention. Mr. Root was known to be opposed to any attempt to instruct the delegates in his favor and it was the general understanding that the New York delegation would be uninstructed. But there were many who felt that the New York Convention should crystallize sentiment in favor of one candidate. With that end in view, President Butler of Columbia was proposing to introduce a resolution endorsing Root as the man who best fulfilled all the requirements for the presidential office. The Root adherents in general favored the proposal although a few feared that it would actually injure Root rather than help him since it would make it appear that the speech was a bid for the endorsement. The Hughes group were of course opposed to it. The opposition was sufficiently strong to induce the Root group to withdraw their resolution in committee and it never reached the floor of the convention.

Root's speech in fact made a great impression. Buchan calls it "in many ways the most remarkable made in any country since the outbreak of the war . . . its significance lay in the fact that for the first time a man of great eminence stated sanely and broadly the true interest of neutrals." [2] The body of delegates who would have been bored with the usual political oratory, were moved to real enthusiasm while the galleries were swept away. "No man," said Root, "should draw a pistol who dares not shoot. The government that shakes its fist first and its finger afterward falls into contempt. Our diplomacy has lost its authority and influence because we have been brave in words and irresolute in action. Men say that the words of our diplomatic notes were justified; men say that our inaction was justified; but no man can say that both our words and our inaction were wise and creditable." Even more burning was his denunciation of Wilson's Mexican policy which he properly branded as a wholly improper and totally ineffective interference in the domestic affairs of Mexico. Root's feeling against Wilson grew steadily in intensity; by November, 1916, he had come to believe that Wilson was both unscrupulous and dishonest.[3]

[2] *History of the World War*, Vol. II, p. 475.
[3] Diary of Chandler P. Anderson, entry of November 16, 1916.

Root had set a keynote for the Republican campaign; the Democrats were to be fought on the issue of foreign policy. David Lawrence reported that the Democrats welcomed the challenge; they would not have dared to raise the foreign issue but were glad the Republicans had done so. The New York *World* admired "the courage and intellectual integrity" of Root's statement but doubted whether the Republican Party would have the courage to follow him. Many papers noted that Root was preaching Roosevelt doctrine. The *New Republic* thought that Root sought to attach the Republican Party to a foreign policy "which will align the United States with the liberal European powers in the enforcement of a new code of public law." It was a reasonable deduction from his argument in favor of the right of the United States to protest against the violation of Belgium but it does not seem that Root's thought had yet gone quite so far. In general the Republican press hailed the speech while the Democratic papers attacked it with sufficient vigor to indicate that it was an important pronouncement of the opposition. Although Taft thought that Root had "injured his running qualities very decidedly by his keynote speech," [4] Root's fears of the immediate reaction were not confirmed. On the other hand, his hope that ultimately the party and the independents would rally to that cause was not fulfilled. The Republicans did keep the issue of foreign policy in the ensuing campaign, but they tried to carry water on both shoulders in order to save themselves the German vote. Wilson, on the other hand, showed courage and political sagacity in his famous telegram to a man named O'Leary who expressed the Irish anti-British view: "I would feel deeply mortified to have you or anybody like you vote for me. Since you have access to many disloyal Americans and I have not, I will ask you to convey this message to them." It was the kind of attitude which Root would probably have taken had he been the Republican nominee. As it was, Hughes spoke softly while Roosevelt thundered and the people voted for Wilson who "kept us out of war."

A small group of ardent Root supporters met frequently at lunch and dinner during the weeks following the Carnegie Hall convention. They included Cornelius N. Bliss, Jr., Otto Bannard, William Barnes, Robert Bacon, Nicholas Murray Butler, Henry P. Davison, John W. Dwight, Job Hedges, Charles D. Hilles, J. Sloat Fassett, James R.

[4] To Hilles, April 12, 1916, Taft Papers, Library of Congress.

Sheffield, George R. Shield, Henry L. Stimson and William B. Thompson. Davison was one of the prime movers and chief organizers of the group. Hilles was Chairman of the National Republican Committee and he secured through correspondence the views of Republican leaders throughout the country as to Root's acceptability as a candidate. The replies were encouraging. The group decided that it was time to launch a formal candidacy. Bannard, Davison, Hilles and Sheffield were deputized to wait upon Mr. Root in order to obtain his consent. They were not aware of a letter which Root had written to Tanner, the Republican State Chairman, on February 23rd, in which Root had strongly reiterated his view that the New York delegation should go to the national convention wholly uninstructed, adding: "For my own part I repeat what I have said to you before, that I am not a candidate for the presidential nomination and I do not wish my name presented to the Convention as a candidate."

Sheffield asked Root for an appointment; Root knew what was in the air and suggested that they were all busy and that it would be a waste of time for them to come, but Sheffield was insistent. The group called on Mr. Root in his office at 31 Nassau Street where he was continuing his practice of the law as counsel to the firm headed by his son Elihu. Sheffield was the spokesman:

"Senator, we want your permission to put you in nomination for the President of the United States."

Root replied that it was ridiculous, that he was too old, that he had said so in his speech in the Senate and he meant it and that he would not be a candidate. The delegation was of course primed with ready answers to his objections and they sounded the sure appeal that in this world crisis he was the only standard bearer behind whom the Republicans could rally to carry out the ideas which he had so eloquently phrased at Carnegie Hall. Root was emotionally aroused, speaking with that quick repetitive gesture of the forefinger and open hand which was so characteristic.

"If I were thirty years younger," he cried, "I would not consider being a candidate. I would be in France baring my chest to the German bullets."

It was rather a Rooseveltian touch of melodrama, but it was another among numerous examples of a relaxation of that iron control which gave him his reputation for coldness—a relaxation which opened

the floodgates of pent up emotions. If his friends believed the point
of view for which he stood would make the people of the country rally
to him as the representative of a policy opposed to that of Wilson, he
was willing to run. Just why Root changed his mind rather suddenly,
as he undoubtedly did, is not clear, but the reason which he gave to
his friends in response to their importunate arguments probably reflects his attitude.

The next day, Root asked Sheffield to come to see him. There was
no elation in his manner. He had the attitude of a man who has taken
on a heavy and unwelcome responsibility. He again made it clear that
he was not to be counted on for any effort in his own behalf. (His
friends never could persuade him to take any single step to further
his own candidacy.) He also told Sheffield that he counted on him to
manage the movement in such a way as not to make Root ridiculous.
He had no conviction that he could be nominated, but he thought
that if a number of delegates from New York and other states should
be instructed for him, it would make it more difficult for the Convention to be stampeded into nominating anyone without careful
consideration of the issues which he championed.[5] He told Sheffield
that if it appeared at the Convention that he would receive merely a
handful of votes from his intimate friends, he did not want his name
put in nomination. He wanted no such testimonial of personal friendship but would acquiesce if his nomination might be of real value in
the situation as it developed. Sheffield undertook to see that his wishes
were carried out.

At that time there were two possibilities, rather remote even then,
which if they had eventuated, might have made Root's nomination
conceivable. Of these two possibilities it was the second which counted
most. The first was that Hughes might announce that he would not
resign from the Supreme Court even if nominated. Hughes, in fact,
made no statement until after his nomination and with the New York
delegation split, there was no likelihood that Root could carry the
delegations of other states at the convention—except for the second
possibility, which was that Roosevelt might endorse him and that his
name could therefore be presented to the country as the united choice
of the Republican Old Guard and of the Progressives. Only the nomination of Taft with Roosevelt's backing, or the nomination of Roose-

[5] Diary of Chandler P. Anderson, entry of May 2, 1916.

velt with the backing of the Old Guard, either of which was beyond the realm of possibility, could have been more completely symbolic of a healing of the 1912 breach.

Root had labored constantly to unite the factions in his party, partly because of his ardent loyalty to the Republican Party, partly because his old feeling of affection for Theodore never died and he longed to see the old wound healed. He had not seen Roosevelt since 1912. Roosevelt was still unreconciled. On February 16th, 1915, Roosevelt wrote to John Callan O'Laughlin, one of his intimate correspondents: "You know the bitterness which I feel toward Root. But when the nation is in danger all other questions are swallowed up; and I can say quite sincerely that I wish we had him at the head of affairs now to handle this situation." [6] But this was in response to a letter from "Cal" relaying a conversation with Root in which the latter had dwelt upon Roosevelt's virtues and Wilson's defects. On March 18th, Roosevelt wrote to Joseph B. Bishop, one of his friends who continued to pour in his ears poisonous gossip about Root: "I really believe that I myself would vote for Root against Wilson or Bryan—of course when the actual time came it might be impossible for me to do so, having in memory his action at the Chicago Convention; but on genuinely patriotic grounds I feel that any man who will stand for national defense and national honor is to be preferred to the present combination." And to Gifford Pinchot on March 29th: ". . . if at this moment I had to choose I feel so strongly on foreign affairs that as a matter of prime duty I would vote to put in even a man like Root rather than continue Bryan and Wilson at the head of the government." [7] On November 27th, he wrote to Lodge that he would urge the Progressives to back Knox, though without enthusiasm, if Knox would agree to appoint Root as Secretary of State, "for while I am fairly certain the Progressives would under no circumstances support Root for President, I did not believe they would object (and I am certain they would have no right to object) to his being made Secretary of State." [8] But on December 7th he wrote again to Lodge: ". . . You must remember about Root that the leading Progressives feel that his action in the Chicago Convention was

[6] Roosevelt Papers, Library of Congress.
[7] Ibid.
[8] Roosevelt-Lodge Correspondence, Vol. II, p. 464.

morally exactly as bad as the actions for which very many Tammany and small Republican politicians who have committed election offenses are now serving or have served terms in Sing Sing. Under these circumstances you will see how very difficult it would be in any case short of a national cataclysm to get the Progressives to support him. . . ." [9] Roosevelt was annoyed at Root's and Stimson's endorsement of Wilson's preparedness program in January, 1916. He was sure they wished for Wilson's defeat, but, as he told Lodge on February 4th, "both of them would be wise to remember that it is difficult to defeat a man by agreeing with him." [10] Root had the political weakness of being fair to his opponents.

Robert Bacon was one of the men, capable of warm and unselfish devotion, who had maintained his friendship with both Roosevelt and Root. Probably sensing the fact that on the issues of foreign policy they saw eye to eye at this time, he decided to attempt a reconciliation. On March 31st, 1916, Roosevelt, Root, General Leonard Wood and Senator Henry Cabot Lodge lunched with him at his home. "All passed off well," General Wood noted in his diary, "Roosevelt cussed out Wilson as did Root and Lodge. Opinion that the country never so low in standing before. Much talk about Mexico, what they would have done had they been in power." [11] Root told Chandler Anderson, who noted it in his diary, that he had accepted Bacon's invitation because he never had any hard feeling against Roosevelt and although Roosevelt had said some hard things against him, he realized that they had been said in heat and in anger and he had always been willing to forget and forgive them. He hoped by meeting Roosevelt on a friendlier footing again that he would not only make it easier for Roosevelt to return to the Republican Party, but would make it more difficult for him to refuse to return. But nothing was said at the luncheon about politics; the talk was all on preparedness, a subject upon which they were in perfect harmony.

Roosevelt was somewhat on the defensive. He wrote to Senator Hiram Johnson on April 3rd, 1916: "As you have doubtless seen in the papers, I have seen Root. I had arranged immediately afterwards to go and report about the meeting and have it known that I went to

[9] Ibid., p. 466.
[10] Ibid., p. 476.
[11] Millis, The Road to War, p. 294.

"The Two Undertakers"

(A cartoon in the New York *World*, April 3, 1916)

report about the meeting to various Progressives at Perkins' house, including Allen of Kansas, Brown of Ohio and others, for I wanted the Progressives to understand just what I was doing. We talked only of preparedness and of the necessity from the public standpoint of doing something that would enable us to get rid of Wilson. To my great amusement Root and Lodge commented with contemptuous bitterness on Taft." [12] The last sentence may be taken *cum grano*; it does not fit the other evidence of Root's attitude although he and Taft were not at one in their views of a proper policy at that time. Roosevelt would have been keen to find such an attitude and may have magnified a chance phrase. There is nothing in Root's correspondence of the time or the recorded conversations with his friends which suggests that he had the attitude which Taft took toward him; but Taft had wholly misunderstood Root back in 1912. On February 22nd, 1916, Taft wrote to Gus Karger about Root's Carnegie Hall speech; he could see neither political wisdom nor justice in the reference to Belgium and Wilson's foreign policy. He thought it was another of Root's recent "compromises with conscience—a sop to that form of political expediency which desires to placate the ferocious Teddy." [13] Taft was assured Root had submitted the speech to Roosevelt before it was delivered but that seems clearly untrue. Root, obsessed with the war, went on following his sense of duty, misunderstood and suspected by two men, both of whom Root might have kept from the presidency if he had been the scheming politician they credited him with being.

The news of the luncheon was in all the papers on the following day; perhaps there was meaning in Roosevelt's phrase to Senator Johnson that "he had arranged . . . to . . . have it known." Root believed that George W. Perkins had taken advantage of the occasion to announce publicly all over the United States that the purpose of the luncheon was to secure the Republican nomination for Roosevelt and that Root had undertaken to support him. To counteract that report, Root had been the more willing a short time later to yield to his friends' insistence that his candidacy be formally launched. Root believed that Roosevelt would not make a bad president and that if he should be elected a great deal would depend on the men with whom

[12] Roosevelt Papers, Library of Congress.
[13] Taft Papers, Library of Congress.

he surrounded himself, because in spite of his strong personality and independent views, he had a remarkable faculty of getting at all sides of the question and adopting for his own the best advice which he could find; this was in strong contrast to the mental habits of Wilson.[14] But Root evidently did not believe that the Republicans were ready to nominate Roosevelt and he was unwilling to be put in the position which Perkins had sought to impose upon him. The tactics imputed to Perkins indeed would have had the opposite effect from what he intended, further estranging the Republicans and the Progressives. Root felt that the Democrats could be beaten only by a re-united Republican Party and that if the Democrats were not beaten it would be a national calamity.[15] The attitude of the Progressives toward Root was probably accurately reflected in the *Literary Digest* poll of Progressive members of State Legislatures published on April 29th, 1916; Hughes had 758 votes, Roosevelt 275, and Root 138.

Outsiders insisted, of course, on reading all sorts of devious political motives into the luncheon. On April 2nd, Taft, still bitter against Roosevelt, wrote to Gus Karger that it had been arranged by Bacon "with the idea of promoting Root's candidacy, whereas of course the Roosevelt lieutenants seized on it as confirming the certainty of Roosevelt's nomination. I happen to know that it was to be a secret meeting and that nobody on the Root side gave it out. . . . My own impression is that the lunch will be a nine days wonder and that it will so alarm the regular Republicans that it only makes the trend to Hughes more certain." On April 10th, he wrote to Karger again: "I don't think that Root improved his position before the public by his luncheon. Of course he was inveigled into it, and Roosevelt used the opportunity unconscionably to give the impression that Root favored him for the nomination. Bob Bacon is put in a difficult situation again, professing to be for Root and thinking perhaps he is for Root without knowing that he is really for Roosevelt. So he says that Root is his first choice and Roosevelt is his second. I agree with you that the trend, in spite of Roosevelt's efforts, is toward Hughes. He seems to be the logical solution." On April 3rd, Taft had written Charles Hilles, referring to a talk they had had on the previous day: "I suppose you will continue to 'roost on Root' for the present. Just to keep

[14] Diary of Chandler P. Anderson, entry of May 2, 1916.
[15] Partly in *ibid.*

your lines straight and to seem to yield when the pressure becomes too great. The more I think of it the more yielding Root's attitude seems to be. He has lost the snap he used to have." [16] But Taft still avowed his gratitude to Root for his services in 1912 and in May, 1916, Taft refused to make a public statement for Hughes because "Root feels keenly the desertion of old friends at this time, and especially the desertion of Parsons and Wickersham, and I don't feel called upon to declare my views and inflict an additional wound." [17]

On April 7th, 1916, the boom for Root was officially launched in a statement signed by seventy-four prominent New Yorkers drawn from all parts of the state. The list included naturally all of the small group which had been in the movement from the first; nineteen of the signers were delegates to the Chicago Convention. Joseph H. Choate was there and later came out with a strong individual endorsement. Chauncey Depew and Seth Low were included. The upstate representation was not very great and there was a strong Wall Street flavor with the names of H. P. Davison, a Morgan partner, Frederick Strauss, Isaac N. Seligman and Albert Wiggin. The statement described Root as the "ablest living American." It pointed to the critical years ahead and the need that America should be served by her best. Because of his insistence it included the statement, "While he has declined to become a candidate for even the highest political office, yet if nominated for the Presidency by the coming National Convention at Chicago his sense of public duty must compel his acceptance." It was an accurate statement.

"The ablest living American." It is not without significance that superlatives were so widely used when Root's abilities were discussed. That had been the situation in earlier years; it was the same in 1916. Taft said, "Of course Root is the best equipped man for the Presidency" [18] but he would not be a winning candidate. Roosevelt still admitted his greatness but he could not forget 1912. Even Hearst's New York *American* on September 2nd, 1915, admitted that "Mr. Root has great intellect, great ability, extraordinary competence and experience in public life . . ." but he was the "tool of Wall Street." In the private talks of the political leaders at the Convention and be-

[16] Taft Papers, Library of Congress.
[17] To Karger, May 15, 1916, *ibid.*
[18] To David Baird, March 6, 1916, *ibid.*

fore, no one questioned that Root was the ablest man. But in the system of American democracy, such high abilities are often a bar to rather than an assurance of high office, although President Butler of Columbia in nominating Root at Chicago refused to credit this slander upon democracy.

The headquarters of the Elihu Root Campaign Committee were established at the Hotel Manhattan in New York with John W. Dwight, twelve years a member of Congress, as Chairman and Charles M. Pepper as Director of Publicity. Chicago headquarters were established later. The financial end was handled by Cornelius Bliss, Jr. and James R. Sheffield. Naturally the response came chiefly from the group known as "Wall Street." There were a goodly number of checks for $1,000 and one for $5,000. Some $17,000 were returned pro rata to about thirty donors after the Convention had nominated Hughes. An ardent Root supporter of long standing, Charles H. Betts, owner-editor of the Lyons Republican, prepared a detailed analysis of the votes cast for the delegates to the Constitutional Convention in 1915, showing that Root ran very well and explaining adequately why he ran behind others in certain districts. Stimson wrote a vigorous article along the same lines in the New York Sun, answering one by George W. Wickersham which argued that Root would not make a good candidate.

Roosevelt's attitude was still undisclosed. His admirers were showering him with letters designed to give him the impression that the sentiment of the country was overwhelmingly for him. Taft, throughout, was confident that Hughes would be chosen. Among the political leaders, there was no serious belief that Root could be nominated. As William Allen White wrote to Roosevelt on May 5th, 1916: ". . . to make the fight under a man like Root is hopeless. It may be parochial, but all over the Middle West, you will find a deep abiding revulsion to Root and his type of mind among the people." [19] Roosevelt agreed and to ex-Governor Stokes of New Jersey he wrote on May 10th: "You are absolutely right. The movement to nominate Root is a movement to cut the throat of the Republican Party from ear to ear." [20] Roosevelt was sincere in his desire to have the Republicans and Progressives unite on a man to beat Wilson; on

[19] Roosevelt Papers, Library of Congress.
[20] Ibid.

Root he felt they could not unite. Hughes was the inevitable choice.

But Root's small group of friends remained hopeful. There was the natural encouragement from scattered correspondence with individuals all over the country who were enthusiastic Root supporters. There were newspapers here and there from east to west which still supported him, but there was not the kind of support which spells victory in a political convention. Boies Penrose, still master of Pennsylvania, was against Root, either because he was convinced that Root would be a poor candidate or because Penrose would not forgive, as he actually had not forgotten, Root's attack upon him in Philadephia eleven years before. He was deaf to the entreaties of Nicholas Murray Butler at Chicago who begged him for even a fraction of the votes of the Pennsylvania delegation.[21] There was only one hope: if Roosevelt would endorse Root, they could rally to him as the union of the two wings of the party.

Just before the Convention opened, Root's attitude had not changed. Senator George Sutherland, who was a delegate from Utah, talked with him before leaving for Chicago. Root told him that he did not want the nomination and thought that he was too old for it. "But suppose you are nominated?" Sutherland asked. A hard, stern look came over Root's face as he replied that he would go through with it if it killed him. Henry L. Stimson saw him in New York after the middle of May just before he moved up to Clinton for the summer. They discussed the convention in some detail and the possible developments there. Root was insistent that if Roosevelt were to run against him, or even if he would not support him, it would be the worst possible course for the Republican Party to nominate him; it would merely accentuate the old 1912 split. In that case he believed that Hughes would be the best choice provided that he would accept; he had not at that date resigned from the bench. Root was equally clear that it would be fatal to the future of the Republican Party to be bludgeoned into accepting Roosevelt as the Republican nominee when so many of the party were opposed. He believed that would be the end of party loyalty. Root was not even willing to consider running against a nominee of the Progressives in case Hughes declined the nomination and Roosevelt refused to support Root. He mentioned that, at that time, Roosevelt had resumed his old course

[21] Nicholas Murray Butler, "Across the Busy Years," *Scribner's Magazine*, March, 1936.

of sending to Root advance copies of his speeches for advice and perhaps he felt that this intimated a real reconciliation which would lead Roosevelt to support him. But he made it quite clear that his own feelings had not changed; he did not want the nomination. On June 5th, two days before the Convention opened, Root wrote Judge Laughlin of the New York Supreme Court, that the important thing was to secure a nomination which would "appeal to the country so as to make it possible to turn out the crowd that is messing up the government at Washington now. . . . I have a good deal of confidence that the men who are at Chicago will succeed in solving that question. A Republican National Convention, when it is allowed to act for itself, is usually a very wise body."

The Convention opened at Chicago on June 7th. Warren G. Harding was chosen Temporary and Permanent Chairman. There had been an early suggestion that Root should be chosen as chairman but he had absolutely refused to go to Chicago. The Progressives held a separate convention in the same city. The Progressive Convention asked for a conference and a committee was immediately appointed by the Republicans including Senator Smoot of Utah, ex-Senator Murray Crane of Massachusetts, Senator Borah of Idaho, Dr. Nicholas Murray Butler of New York, and Congressman A. R. Johnson of Ohio. The Republican conferees dined together and received the Progressive committee at 9 P. M. The Progressives in various ways expressed their belief that Roosevelt was the only possible candidate. Butler, replying for the Republicans, assured them that under no circumstances would the Republican convention nominate Mr. Roosevelt. They adjourned without being able to approach agreement on any other name. The next day the nominating speeches were made in the Republican convention. Governor Whitman of New York first nominated Hughes and Dr. Butler followed with the nomination of Root who was seconded by William P. Bynum of North Carolina and Eugene W. Britt of California. There were six other major nominees. On the first ballot, which was immediately taken, Hughes received 253½ votes. Senator John W. Weeks of Massachusetts came second with 105 and Root was a close third with 103. In the New York delegation, Root received 43 votes to 42 for Hughes; in Arkansas, Colorado, Washington and the Philippines, Root passed Hughes in a small scattering of votes and tied with him in dividing the Connecticut, New Jersey and Texas delegations. The New Jersey delegation was solid for Hughes but gave Root twelve courtesy votes on this first ballot.[22] On the second ballot, Hughes ran up to 328½, Root was second with 98½, and Weeks had dropped to sixth place. In the New York delegation one vote—that of Thomas R. Proctor, a delegate from Root's own county of Oneida—had shifted, giving the majority from the Empire State to Hughes. But Hughes still lacked nearly 170 votes of a majority and the issue was not yet closed. The Root adherents worked like Trojans, seeking to swing support to their candidate. Murray Crane was willing to turn the Massachusetts votes to Root if Roosevelt accepted him as the candidate; Crane would have agreed to almost anything which would have assured the elimination of Roosevelt himself. They were unable to move Charles B. Warren of Michigan or Smoot of Utah and Penrose's opposition has already been noted; it was not shaken by the intercession of General Atterbury, President of the Pennsylvania Railroad and a warm Root advocate. Dwight, the Root campaign manager, had an offer of the support of Georgia and some of the other southern states but he rejected it. Whether true or not, it is the standing conviction that the southern votes at Republican conventions are traded for promises of future favors. Root's supporters could not have made a trade if they had wanted to and they knew that if they accepted the southern support they would be accused of "buying" the votes.

That night the conferees from the two conventions met again and argued fruitlessly until three in the morning. But at the close of the conversations, George W. Perkins asked Nicholas Murray Butler if he would talk over Perkins' private wire to Colonel Roosevelt at Oyster Bay. After consulting with some of his colleagues, Butler agreed to do so. The group of Republicans with whom he consulted advised that he suggest to Roosevelt agreement upon Root, Knox or Fairbanks, and in that order. It was clear that if the Progressives would not unite upon one of these three, Hughes would be nominated the following morning. It was then 4 A. M. when Roosevelt got on the wire. He asked Butler if it were true that there was no possibility that the Republican nomination would turn to him. Butler assured him that it was impossible. Roosevelt then asked if Butler had any sug-

[22] David Baird, chairman of the New Jersey delegation, to W. H. Taft, June 12, 1916, Taft Papers, Library of Congress.

gestions and Butler told him what he had agreed to say. After a moment's hesitation, Roosevelt said that he was not in a position to discuss Mr. Root. He spoke well of Knox and Fairbanks but doubted if they would suit. Roosevelt in turn then suggested Leonard Wood or Lodge. Butler said that he would consult his friends and the conversation ended. Perkins told Butler that both Lodge and Wood were impossibilities and no agreement was reached. When the Republican Convention reopened in the morning, it was a foregone conclusion that Hughes would be nominated, and before the third ballot was taken, Senator Wadsworth, speaking for the New York group of Root supporters, withdrew Root's name. Hughes received 949½ of the 987 votes and in accordance with precedent, a motion was then carried to make the nomination unanimous. Roosevelt received the nomination of the Progressive Convention but refused it and came out for Hughes.

There was neither bitterness nor trace of disappointment in the letters which Root wrote after the Convention. In writing to Sheffield, for example, Root was rather in the position of thanking him and comforting him for a good fight well lost. When Sheffield saw him and told him that he heard on all sides expressions of regret that Root had not been nominated, Root replied smilingly: "I would prefer that people should regret that I had not been nominated than that they should regret that I had been nominated." To his classmate, Charles P. Arnold, on June 20th, he marveled somewhat at the lack of effect his stated unwillingness to run had had on the minds of others. "The real difficulty," at the Convention, he wrote, "which the delegates who wanted to nominate me for president found in their way was that the great party schism of 1912 could be cured only by taking someone who was not a party to the controversy. In doing this I think the Convention was wise, and although I very much regret to have Hughes leave the Bench with such a man as Wilson in the presidency to fill his place, I have strong hope for his election and great confidence in it."

Note: In preparing this chapter the following sources, in addition to those indicated in the footnotes, have been of chief value: Conversations between the author and Mr. Root; Mr. Root's papers; conversations with Cornelius N. Bliss, Nicholas Murray Butler, Frederick M. Davenport, Lafayette B. Gleason, Charles D. Hilles, Lucius Littauer, Ogden Mills, Thomas I. Parkinson, Henry S. Pritchett, James R. Sheffield, Henry L. Stimson, George Sutherland, James W. Wadsworth, George W. Wickersham; correspondence with Franklin S. Edmonds; the diaries of Chandler P. Anderson and Henry L. Stimson.

CHAPTER XLIII

"It was a grand-stand play"

A LAUNCH filled with people pulled in to the quai at Vladivostock from the old converted United States cruiser *Buffalo* which had found her own way into an anchorage at five-thirty in the morning of June 3rd, 1917. The launch was pulled up on the stretch of sloping cobbles and the party approached the flight of stone steps to the street level. At the top of the steps was a ragged group of men in dirty clothing, headed by a mechanic with a derby hat and grease-stained suit, looking as if he had just climbed out from under a car; this was the revolutionary Local Executive Committee of Vladivostock. On the edge of the group was a Russian general, obviously embarrassed.

"What do these men want?" the head of the delegation called down to the party's interpreter.

"It is our aim," replied Elihu Root, Ambassador Extraordinary of the United States of America on Special Mission to Russia, "to convey to the Russian democracy the good will of America, her sister democracy; to seek to establish closer cooperation and friendship between the two nations, and to learn what the needs of Russia are and to assist her in every way possible."

These remarks having been duly interpreted, the Committee conversed rapidly together for a few moments, talking all at once, and then called down that the party was given permission to land. Various officials appeared and extended a more formal welcome as did a committee of the soldiers and workmen of the city. The special train made up of the Czar's own coaches, resplendent with the imperial coat-of-arms, which had been kept discreetly hidden among some warehouses, now pulled up to the quai and the Root Mission started off within thirty minutes of the time they had left the deck of the *Buffalo*.

It was rather a contrast to the atmosphere in which they left the United States. Not that they had a gala departure from Seattle—it

353

was in the war days when all such official sailings were clothed in childish "secrecy," known only to newspaper men, transportation employees and anyone with sufficient curiosity to watch embarkations. Even when the Mission returned and was officially welcomed by the city of Seattle at a large luncheon with the usual speeches, the New York papers reported the event under the cryptic dateline, "A Pacific Port." But when the mission was first announced, it was hailed as an event of the very greatest importance. On April 26th, 1917, the New York *Times* said that it was admittedly "one of the most difficult diplomatic missions which the United States has ever undertaken in foreign lands. . . . In one sense the sending of Mr. Root is like pitting the best diplomatic brains which this country can provide against the machinations of German diplomacy." On May 15th, it described the purpose of the Mission as being "to save Russia to the Entente cause." The *North American Review* on June 19th declared that President Wilson had appointed Root "for the most difficult and most important position, except his own, in the world today."

The Romanovs had fallen in March in what William Henry Chamberlin describes as "one of the most leaderless, spontaneous, anonymous revolutions of all time." [1] The suddenness and completeness of the change were bewildering to the Russians themselves; small wonder that it was almost completely misunderstood abroad. The revolution was most welcome to the Wilson Administration in the United States because it removed from the Allied ranks an undisguisable autocrat whose presence had impaired the efficacy of the slogans of democracy. This joyful aspect made less impression in England and France whose governments were more directly conscious of the possible consequences of the disintegration of the Russian army, a separate peace with Germany and the release of about one hundred and fifty enemy divisions from the Eastern front, not to mention the resources which Germany could draw from a friendly Russia.

David R. Francis, the American Ambassador to Russia, urged and secured authority to be the first foreign representative to recognize the new Provisional Government headed by Prince Lvov and Professor Milyukov. Francis was a charming old gentleman with no appreciation of what was going on in Russia and without any other particular qualification for his difficult post. His reports to the State Depart-

[1] *The Russian Revolution*, Vol. I, p. 73.

"A Job for a Diplomat"

(A cartoon in the New York *Evening Post*, June 6, 1917)

ment glow with optimistic enthusiasm. To him, the great issue was whether the Russian people would adopt a constitutional monarchy or a republican form of government. The likelihood that social revolution would follow the political revolution was not envisaged by him. On April 21st, 1917, he cabled "Extreme socialist or anarchist named Lenin making violent speeches and thereby strengthening government; designedly giving him leeway and will deport opportunely." [2] Later he accepted fully the idea that Lenin was a paid German agent. North Winship, the American Counsul at Petrograd, and Maddin Summers, Consul General at Moscow, sent some illuminating despatches during April and May, but they were not received in Washington until four or five weeks later and could not have influenced the views of Wilson or Lansing at the time when the Root Mission was appointed and received its instructions. Ambassador Francis does not even seem to have appreciated the fact that from the first the Provisional Government set up by the leaders of the Duma was wholly dependent for its actual governmental power upon the Council or Soviet of Workers' and Soldiers' Deputies who exercised what little control anyone had over the army. The intellectual constitutional revolutionary ideas of men like Milyukov and the moderate parties were western ideas which they sought to transplant to Russian soil. As such, they were comprehensible to men like Francis and Sir George Buchanan, the British Ambassador. The ideas of the Bolsheviks, which were to control under Lenin's leadership after November, 1917, had been bred in exile but were distinctly Russian. The extremity of their socialism (the word "communism" was not yet in vogue) was bad enough, but even more disturbing to the Allies was their internationalism and pacifism. In all the Allied capitals, including Washington, there was a passionate desire to believe that Russia could still be counted on as an effective belligerent and all information which supported that view was most welcome. Ambassador Francis from March to November, 1917, never seems to have lost his assurance that this desirability would continue to be a reality.

Root was not an expert on Russia; his views of the revolution and the probable course of events in Russia must have been those of the State Department in April, 1917, when President Wilson inquired of him through Secretary of State Lansing whether he would be will-

[2] *Foreign Relations of the United States*, 1918, Russia, Vol. I, p. 27.

ing to head the Mission which he had decided to send. Root accepted without enthusiasm and apparently without illusions. He was seventy-two years old and had just recovered from a very severe attack of grippe. To William Howard Taft he wrote on April 30th: "You have no idea how I hate it, but it is just like our boys going into the war: there can be no question about doing it." He felt the more bound to serve because he had been such a vigorous opponent of the President and because he had so ringingly urged his fellow countrymen to support him once war had been declared. "We need no coalition government to make us loyal," he told the New York Republican Club three days after the declaration of a state of war. As matters developed, he came to the conclusion that "Wilson didn't want to accomplish anything. It was a grand-stand play. He wanted to show his sympathy for the Russian Revolution. When we delivered his message and made our speeches, he was satisfied; that's all he wanted." [3]

What induced Wilson to select Root is not clear but Secretary McAdoo had suggested and urgently pressed Root's name.[4] Organized labor was opposed to his appointment. The American socialists scoffed at the idea of sending a hide-bound conservative Wall Street lawyer to a country where the socialists had control of the government. Morris Hillquit and Victor Berger announced that the socialists in Russia would be fully informed about Mr. Root before he arrived. An attempt was made by Russian socialists from America to persuade the people in Vladivostock to prevent the mission from proceeding to Petrograd but the suggestion was defeated in the Citizens' and Soldiers' Committees which were not yet controlled by the extremists.[5] The American socialists were not appeased when Charles Edward Russell was added to the Mission as a representative of their point of view; Russell had split with the regular members of the party in endorsing American participation in the war. James Duncan, the seventy-four year old and good natured vice president of the American Federation of Labor, was also appointed, but the Federation under Samuel Gompers was as far removed from socialism as was Root himself. President Wilson had told Lansing to ask Gompers "whom we could send whom the Socialists over there would not regard as

[3] Root to the author, September 16, 1930.
[4] Senator William J. McAdoo to the author, April 28, 1938.
[5] Foreign Relations of the United States, loc. cit., p. 131.

an active opponent of Socialism." [6] As for Root, Wilson had told Lansing, "I hope that in your conference with him today you will find Mr. Root a real friend of the revolution." If so, he was to be appointed. John Hays Hammond recalls in his *Autobiography* that at the solicitation of several of Theodore Roosevelt's friends, he had asked House to suggest to Wilson that Roosevelt should head the mission. Hammond admired Root but thought Roosevelt better qualified for this task: "Indeed, I said that he [Roosevelt] would probably revive the Russian cause by personally leading its troops on the battle-field, whereas Root would talk over the head and understanding of the average Russian. House agreed with me, but when he suggested the appointment of Roosevelt, President Wilson went up in the air. . . ." [7] Lansing thought that perhaps they had made a mistake in not sending Roosevelt instead of Root, but said it had not occurred to them how useful the former would have been and that by sending him they would have avoided the issue of his request to be allowed to head a division of volunteers for France.[8] But Lansing was pleased with the choice of Root and thought that all in all it was probably the best.

An additional source of opposition was voiced by Samuel Untermyer, speaking before a great meeting of the Jewish League of American Patriots in New York City on May 3rd, 1917. "Whether rightly or wrongly, throughout Mr. Root's distinguished career he has impressed the Jews of this country with the conviction that he is utterly out of sympathy with our race and has no understanding of our problems and aspirations. Frankly, many of our people regard him as incredibly narrow and provincial in his conception of the Jew. His attitude as Secretary of State . . . and again in the Constitutional Conventions of 1894 and 1915 furnished abundant justification for this view." [9] Untermyer did not express a general Jewish viewpoint and his specific criticisms were ill-founded. Root's attitude as Secretary of State toward the suffering Jews in Morocco and Russia has been described, and it has also been noted that the *Jewish Daily News* had praised him for his stand against the literacy test in the Constitutional Convention of 1915. Wilson at first had thought of appointing a Jew as a member of the mission but for some reason abandoned the idea.

[6] Letter from Wilson to Lansing, April 19, 1917, Archives of the Department of State.
[7] *Autobiography of John Hays Hammond*, Vol. II, p. 667.
[8] Diary of Chandler P. Anderson, entry of May 28, 1917.
[9] New York *Times*, May 4, 1917.

There was a feeling among many Republicans that Wilson had appointed Root merely as a gesture to indicate non-partisanship but, as Root told Taft, "he never would have appointed me if I had not been 73 years of age." [10]

It is true that the Root Mission was foredoomed to failure but it could not have succeeded even with another chief or a different personnel. France sent Albert Thomas and England sent Arthur Henderson with no more effect upon the people of Russia. Root was not consulted as to the other members of the Mission and since his advice was not asked, he declined to volunteer suggestions. When his friend Chandler Anderson remonstrated with him on this attitude, Root said that he understood the President was reserving to himself all war appointments, however unimportant, and that he, Root, regarded himself as simply being drafted for the service.[11] He irately secured the cancellation of the appointment of a relative who had obtained a position on the Mission through the influence of friends and the fact of his relationship. Before Root was invited to serve, Wilson had already decided upon John R. Mott of Y.M.C.A. fame, Charles R. Crane, an industrialist with some experience of Russia, Cyrus H. McCormick whose Harvester Company had wide interests in Russia, and S. R. Bertron, a New York banker.[12] General Hugh L. Scott, Chief of Staff, was sent, allegedly as a compliment to the Russians, possibly to eliminate from such an important military position a man of considerable age. Rear Admiral James H. Glennon, an ordnance expert, was an excellent choice and he succeeded admirably in his contacts with the Russian naval people. Root did make one exception—he asked that Colonel T. Bentley Mott, an old friend, be detailed as his military aide. Stanley Washburn, a correspondent of real ability and wide experience, joined them at Vladivostock as secretary of the Mission. There was no one who could be called a real expert on Russia and no one but an interpreter who could speak or understand Russian.

A special Railway Commission to Russia had been appointed before the Root diplomatic Mission was organized. John F. Stevens, who had shown great ability in the early days of work on the Panama

---

[10] Taft to Bryce, January 25, 1918, Taft Papers, Library of Congress.
[11] Diary of Chandler P. Anderson, entry of May 3, 1917.
[12] Wilson to Lansing, supra.

Courtesy of Colonel Stanley Washburn

ELIHU ROOT IN THE ROOM OF CATHERINE THE GREAT IN THE WINTER
PALACE, PETROGRAD

Courtesy of Colonel Stanley Washburn

ELIHU ROOT GREETING GENERAL BRUSILOFF AT THE RAILROAD STATION,
MOGHILEV, RUSSIA

Canal, was chosen as its head. Root wrote by hand to Secretary Lansing on May 6th that he was glad to learn that the Railway Commission was being sent, but he feared confusion between the two commissions.

"It is plain that we can't have three bodies dealing with the Russian Government at the same time—the regular Embassy, the President's Mission & the R.R. Commission. The President's Mission must discuss the transportation subject with the Russian Government for that is the most important of all & if we cannot talk about that we will be discredited & of no account.

"I suggest that the R.R. Commission be attached to the President's Commission as expert advisers, make preliminary reports to it for its information & make through it any communication which seems desirable to be made to the Russian Government." [13]

Lansing's reply of May 9th must have been one of the factors which persuaded Root that Wilson did not intend his Mission to have much importance. Lansing reported that the President had explained to Mr. Bertron of the Root Mission the provinces of the respective commissioners and supposed Bertron would repeat it to Root. The President intended the Railroad Commission merely to put themselves at the disposal of Russia to give what help they could on the ground. "In view of this particular field of service the President feels that it would be unwise to make the Railroad Commission subsidiary to your commission, which is essentially political in character. This would of course not debar conferences between the two commissions if it seemed advisable, although necessity would not appear to require them except of a most informal nature." [14] As stated by Secretary Lansing in his *War Memoirs*,[15] the Root Mission had the double objective of assuring the Russians of American sympathy in their democratic experiment and of ascertaining at first hand whether Russia could be counted on to continue as a strong factor in the war.

Root made one attempt when both missions were in Russia to secure the collaboration of the Stevens Commission, but Stevens made it clear that he was authorized to run his own show and in-

[13] Archives of the Department of State.
[14] *Ibid.*
[15] P. 334.

tended to do so. He played an important part in the affairs of the Trans-Siberian and Chinese Eastern Railways on through the troubled days of 1918.

With the members of his own Mission, Root got on famously and there was no friction. They all consulted him on their own special problems and his advice was always ready and helpful.

Mrs. Root saw to it that her husband was carefully supplied for the trip with clothing of all sorts, 250 cigars especially packed in a tin box, a large package of novels and full instructions from the family physician to the Navy doctor on the *Buffalo* "describing the kind of throat trouble Mr. Root was most likely to have." Colonel Mott was a faithful friend and attendant who kept her posted about Mr. Root's health and took care that the stores included two cases of Haig and Haig and 200 gallons of Poland water "so that Mr. Root will drink what he is used to and nothing else." But Mrs. Root was naturally worried; it was to be a hard sea voyage through the north Pacific and a country in revolution is not usually selected as the safest place for visiting. Mr. Root's letters to his wife, written on the trip, are full of attempts to set at rest her fears about his health and his welfare. From Chicago, en route to Seattle, he wrote: "If I were 20 or 30 years younger I should enjoy it all. Even as I am there is no hardship to fuss about. I feel rather encouraged about making the trip within the original estimate of three months. You have so much to do that you will find that time gone before you know it."

Again he wrote from the train on May 19th, indicating his idea of the unimportance of the task he was being asked to carry out: "I shall be awfully bored in Petrograd, but only for a little while. The worst of this business is that it takes me from home & from you & I never missed you so much or loved you so much as I do now my dearest."

The voyage was uneventful for most of the Mission, although General Scott and a few of the others were victims of seasickness. The ten day trip across the Trans-Siberian Railroad passed pleasantly enough, with various officials in attendance and stops at many towns and villages where speeches were always in order and were loudly cheered by crowds ready in those days to applaud any speaker who did not actually advocate the restoration of the Czar. As Root and Mott pushed their way through the crowd and stretched their legs with a walk through one of the villages, Root remarked: "Tibby, I am a firm believer in democracy, but I do not like filth." It was a spontaneous and revealing comment. Mr. Root occupied the Czar's compartment on the imperial train. Two other members of the Mission had the compartment done in pale blue satin for the Czar's daughters.

At Petrograd they were given a warm official welcome but excited no great popular interest. The Mission was lodged in the old Winter Palace where the imperial wine cellars were put at their disposal. Root wrote optimistically to Mrs. Root on "pre-revolutionary" stationery, June 15th: "General Scott & I are in the suite once occupied by Catherine the Second whose morals, you will remember, differed from Queen Victoria's. . . . Two things are fortunate for me. One is that there is no entertainment of the ordinary dress parade kind [from which he had suffered abundantly on his tour of South America eleven years before]. Only very small luncheons & dinners. I have just come from luncheon at our Embassy where the party was only Prince Lvoff the premier, Tereschenki [sic] the minister of Foreign Affairs, Ambassador Francis & myself. That is easy & useful. The other thing is that people are a late in the morning people which suits me."

June 19th, he wrote again: "We are getting on very well with innumerable interviews with all sorts of people. This is the strangest condition of things I ever saw. There is really no governing power but moral suasion and the entire people seem to be talking at once—making up for lost time. All through the day and night they gather in hundreds of little groups and make speeches to each other in the [sic] I hope before this reaches you they will have succeeded in making an advance against the Germans. Our party is all well and very busy. We shall probably start for Moscow Thursday evening and return here for final conferences in a week or two. I enclose for Edith a memorandum I made on the train of wild flowers brought to the train in Siberia by children for sale. It is made on a score pad which was in the card table in the sitting room of the Czar's car—the room in which he abdicated—the cards and counters and cribbage boards &c &c were all there untouched."

The members of the Mission scattered and discussed their various specialities with the proper people. They all made many speeches; Root once made as many as four a day and at one gathering his was the fifteenth address. On one occasion, he addressed a meeting of a thousand or more Poles in a great hall. Washburn was beside him and sensed, as did Root, the great emotional appeal of that audience. Root abandoned his planned speech and spoke with great emotional force. Scarcely one of the audience understood English and the speech was interrupted for translation about every five minutes, yet the delivery was such that even before the translation they seemed to sense its meaning and cheered at the right moments. After the speech, Root was showered with congratulations; Washburn said nothing. That night he was standing outside Mr. Root's door as the latter was retiring.

"You haven't said anything. Wasn't it a good speech?" Root asked.

"I think it was a very indiscreet speech, sir, and if I were you I would destroy the record of it."

Root looked at him for a moment. "I wish you good night." The door closed behind him.

Washburn had charge of publicity and saw to it that no copies of the speech were given out. He had almost forgotten the incident until Root mentioned the speech as they were sitting together on the train going back to Vladivostock.

"Major," he said, "I understood you to say that there were two stenographers who took notes on that speech."

"Yes, sir."

"Suppose you ask one of them to run it off."

Root read the original while Washburn read the carbon. When Root had finished he turned to Washburn:

"We have in our hands two copies of this speech. If we destroyed the copies which we have in our hands and if the two young men destroyed the copies in their books, would it be correct to say that no record of the speech exists?"

"Yes, sir."

"See that it is done."

The speeches which were preserved are adequate statements of America's friendship for the Russian democracy and of their common aims in the war against autocracy. There were a few exhortations to the moderates and some warnings of the evil effects of allowing the "subversive" elements to induce a cessation of the war.

Mr. Mott talked with the church dignitaries, Admiral Glennon visited the Baltic and Black Sea Fleets, General Scott and Colonel Mott visited the front and made a side trip to Roumania. The whole Mission was invited to visit Roumania as well as China and Japan; Mr. Root's cabled references to the invitations suggest a desire to accept, but the State Department vetoed any extensions of the program. Their contacts were naturally largely with the officials of the government, representatives of foreign powers and American business men, and there was some rather formal contact with the representatives of the workers and the soldiers. There is no record that any member of the Mission ever met Lenin nor does it appear that they talked with many of the leaders of the Bolshevik group. Duncan spoke to labor groups about the eight-hour day and the need for three shifts in war industries, but his audience was restricted and the radicals considered organized American labor as merely a part of the capitalist system. The men in the government were in favor of continuing the war; they wanted loans from the United States and naturally they did everything in their power to convince the American Mission that they were stable and that they could be counted on as effective allies. Ambassador Francis, as has been noted, never lost his confidence in the outcome. It is therefore hardly surprising that Root and the other members of the Mission got little impression of the underlying strength of the extremists and failed to realize how essentially tenuous was the thread which held the moderates in power. Kerensky impressed them very much and it was plausible to suppose that his advent to power with the coalition which came in July, represented the extent to which the revolution was likely to swing to the left. While Francis reported with pleasure to the State Department how favorably his various speeches were received and the demonstrations which he witnessed in favor of America, Consul Winship gave a truer picture in his despatch of May 15th, received in Washington on June 20th:

"It is to be seriously noted that the socialists, who control all the workmen, at least of Petrograd, and through their absolute dominance in the Council [Soviet] of Workmens' and Soldiers' Deputies, also control the troops in this city, have so far paid practically no attention to the United States, and have passed over her entrance into the war in complete silence, and do not even mention her in their speeches and editorials. The ovations and demonstrations have all been made by the people of the middle classes [the bourgeoisie]. Neither the message of Mr. Samuel Gompers [which Francis thought very valuable] nor the proclamation of the American socialists, headed and signed by Charles Edward Russell, William Walling and Ernest Poole, were printed or commented upon in any of the dozen large and small socialist newspapers in Petrograd. The effect of these two messages on the socialist classes here has been so slight that the liberal newspapers, with the exception of the conservative *Novoe Vremya*, have not commented on the two messages. . . ." [16]

The same story could have been repeated as to the Root Mission. The Russian papers carried very little news about the Mission and practically ignored speeches by Root and the others. The Mission came to the conclusion that propaganda was the only effective means at their disposal.[17] In his cabled despatch of June 17th, Root reported to Lansing that the army was being greatly influenced by an extensive German propaganda, aided by the fraternizing of the soldiers at the front and backed by the agitation of the Bolsheviks who also favored immediate peace. "We think the people of Russia—particularly the soldiers—are going to decide whether Russia stays in the war, and we have got to get at them in some way. Communications to the Government do not reach the real difficulty. The Mission is taking steps for the immediate distribution of information which will cost about one hundred thousand dollars." They asked authority to draw this amount at once with plans for the ultimate expenditure of about five millions of dollars. "It will mean a supply of newspapers, printing and distribution of posters, leaflets and pamphlets, employment of numerous lecturers and moving pictures to go about the front." The establishment of Y.M.C.A. stations, on the model of those widely used by the British on the Western front, was warmly advocated, with provision for reading aloud to illiterate soldiers, lecture rooms, arrangements for moving pictures—"Very desirable indeed to send here immediately as many moving pictures as possible showing American preparation for war, battle ships, troops marching, factories making munitions, and other things to carry to the mind the idea that America is doing something. These poor fellows have been told that no one is really fighting except Russian soldiers, and they believe it."

[16] *Foreign Relations of the United States*, loc. cit., p. 55.
[17] See T. Bentley Mott, *Twenty Years as Military Attaché*, Chap. XX.

The British had been attempting such propaganda on a small scale but much more needed to be done. "Please say to the President that we have found here an infant class in the art of being free containing one hundred and seventy million people, and they need to be supplied with kindergarten material; they are sincere, kindly, good people, but confused and dazed."

No answer came for about ten days when Lansing replied that they were carefully considering the matter of publicity. The Mission was convinced that something should be done and done quickly; Root, Francis and Bertron personally guaranteed the sum of $30,000 to the Petrograd branch of the National City Bank for the printing and distribution of a speech of President Wilson's and one of Root's addresses. Washburn had induced the British propaganda section to finance the translating and circulation of Wilson's speech but Root was ashamed to have them do that work for the United States. On July 2nd, Bertron cabled Secretary of the Treasury McAdoo, reminding him of a conversation they had had before the Mission left Washington and urgently pressing him to put through the recommended appropriation of $100,000. On the same day, Root cabled again on the same subject: "Beg you to realize that Germany is now attacking Russia by propaganda and is spending millions, at least a million dollars monthly, to capture the minds of the Russian people. Germany expects to succeed; can be prevented only by active and immediate counter attacks by same weapons." One item of German propaganda which came to their attention was the story that the United States was in reality made up of forty-eight little kingdoms and that Root was the head of the Empire State! Raymond Robbins, testifying later before a committee of the United States Senate which was investigating Bolshevik propaganda, mentioned that the Germans reproduced in pamphlets in Russia cartoons from American papers which depicted Root as the tool of Wall Street. Robbins would not assert that these cartoons were from Hearst's New York American although he did attribute their publication to Root's earlier attack on "a very important public person." The American was not so reticent and in an editorial of March 10th, 1919, gloried in the fact that it had long been a leader in attempts to discredit Root. Robbins paid Hearst the indirect compliment of believing that these cartoons as circulated by the German agents in Russia did much to discount Root as the spokesman for democracy.[18] To Theodore Roosevelt, Robbins wrote on August 24th, 1918: "Root in revolutionary Russia was as welcome as the small pox, and occasioned as much enthusiasm as would be aroused by an Orangeman leading a popular parade in Dublin." [19]

Bertron's cable reached Washington on July 5th, but Root's of the same date was not received until the 10th, the day after the mission left for Vladivostock. The State Department's cable of July 7th stated that Bertron's cable to McAdoo had been referred by the President to the State Department. The President approved in principle of an educational publicity campaign and authorized the $30,000 already spent under the personal guaranty. The general plan was receiving "careful attention." It seems that this cable reached Petrograd after the Mission had left.

Root had not previously been at the foreign end of a diplomatic mission and probably had forgotten how frantically the delegates at The Hague Peace Conference had cabled him as Secretary of State in 1907 asking for instructions. It is by no means unusual for the diplomatic representatives in the field to tear their hair waiting for the State Department to act. Root felt that this matter was urgent; it was the one tangible thing that America could do. If it was to be done at all, it had to be done quickly. There was little that could be done in the matter of shipping supplies, because the accumulations at Vladivostock were already so great that the inadequate facilities of the Trans-Siberian Railway barely kept up with current accretions. Shortage of tonnage and the submarine campaign also made deliveries difficult even to Archangel during that port's brief open season. The Root Mission had been definitely precluded from advising on the transportation problem. There was nothing Root could do in Russia except to talk with various persons, make speeches interpreting America to the Russians and urge the State Department to act upon the plan which he vainly recommended. On July 8th, Colonel Mott and the others returned from Roumania and Root told Mott to get "the damned expedition" packed up at once. Their train for Vladivostock left Petrograd the next morning.

[18] Hearings before a Subcommittee of the Committee on the Judiciary, U. S. Senate, 65th Cong., 3d Sess., February 11 to March 10, 1919, p. 819.
[19] Roosevelt Papers, Library of Congress.

ELIHU ROOT AS CHIEF OF THE RUSSIAN MISSION, 1917, AT MOGHILEV, RUSSIA

(*Left to right*) Tereschenko, Minister of Foreign Affairs; General Brusiloff, Commander-in-chief of the Russian armies; Elihu Root; General Hugh L. Scott, Chief of Staff, U. S. A.

Root later satisfied himself that Wilson never read their despatches. "I was in doubt," he said, "as to whether to put in my report what was in the despatches, but I felt that I shouldn't make a record against the President who appointed me." Just before leaving Petrograd, he and Francis urged the extension of an emergency credit of $75,000,-000 to pay the Baltic fleet. This credit was promptly extended.

To his wife Root wrote on the day of their departure from Petrograd: "We all feel that we have accomplished far more than we dared to hope and we leave the government and the army much stronger in morale and effectiveness than when we came. . . . Life has been a pretty continuous performance for me but I have stood it well and after countless conferences and interviews and an average of about four speeches a week I have come out in rather better condition than when I left. I dare say I shall be tired when the train gets out of the station.

"I have met many very interesting people and some of them I like very much. The whole thing has been immensely interesting and when one gets to be a thousand years old it is something to be really interested."

In its final report, the Mission recommended that substantial aid in supplies and credits be furnished to the Russian Government. They stated their belief that such aid might keep the Russian army in the field and that without it there was little likelihood of its remaining even as a passive force which might hold some of the German divisions away from the Western front. They believed that the possibility was real enough and the possible gain to the Allied cause so great that it was well worth the risk. A supplementary report on an educational campaign, prepared chiefly by Stanley Washburn, was filed subsequently and was sent to the President on August 27th.[20] Washburn was finally told by Lansing that he was authorized to spend five thousand dollars on an educational campaign in Russia; it was like offering him a pail of sand to dam the Volga. After their return to Washington, they waited several days before being received by the President. Wilson was very unlike his usual dominant self; he seemed embarrassed and ill at ease. He scraped his feet and his eyes kept shifting over the floor. To one member of the Mission it seemed that the President had a sense of guilt and that he hated Root be-

[20] *Foreign Relations of the United States, loc. cit.,* p. 147.

cause he recognized Root's intellectual superiority.[21] They were impressed by Wilson's knowledge of events in Russia but his only reference to their recommendation for a propaganda campaign was to ask whether Root could come back in a week to discuss it. Mr. Root returned to Clinton, anticipating a further call, but no further call ever came. He was subsequently informed that the matter had been turned over to Creel who would be glad to discuss it with him; Root dropped it in disgust.

Although Root was never again called upon by the Administration in regard to Russian affairs, he felt constrained to take the position that he still held an official relation to the Government of the United States. He told Chandler Anderson on March 5th, 1918, that while he was of course not acting in any official capacity, everybody assumed that he was and he was more or less forced into a position of acquiescence, because the only possible reason which would have justified the President in sending him to Russia was to use him afterwards as an adviser on Russian matters. He said that any man properly qualified to be President would have sent a commission qualified to become experts on Russian affairs and would have retained them in that relation to the Administration on their return. President Wilson had not in fact consulted him or any member of the Mission since their return (although the question of the Allied intervention in Russia would have given an occasion for such consultation) but everybody else was consulting him about Russian affairs all the time. He felt sufficiently strongly on the subject to refuse to accept any employment, such as representing foreign governments and claimants, which would be inconsistent with the position of an official of the government. It was evident that he felt he had been cavalierly treated by Wilson but his animosity toward him was based on grounds that were not personal.[22] While the United States was in the war, he subordinated all objections to personalities in a whole-souled devotion to the cause of defeating Germany.

While they were in Washington, they had a long talk with Lansing as a group and Root alone had a further talk with him. Lansing records in his memoirs a memorandum which he wrote at the time.[23]

[21] Stanley Washburn to the author, June 5, 1931.
[22] Diary of Chandler P. Anderson, entries of March 5 and March 24, 1918.
[23] Lansing, op. cit., p. 337.

He reports that the members of the Mission were impressed with Kerensky's ability to carry through and to control the situation. Lansing says he was very skeptical, expecting the Russian revolution to follow the model of the French Revolution. As Labry caustically points out,[24] the analogy is bad, but Lansing is justified in preening himself upon being a better prophet than Root as to the course of events in Russia; the November revolution put Lenin's Bolshevik group in the saddle. Root thereafter frequently foretold their early destruction. Root recalled: [25] "I had information [while in Petrograd] about what Lenin was doing and I urged the Provisional Government to arrest him; any government would have arrested, tried, imprisoned and executed him. Mr. Tereshchenko, the Minister of Foreign Affairs, a young fellow, assured me he was on the verge of arresting Lenin and breaking up the whole conspiracy. He said he was only waiting for certain documents which one of his men was getting to show the complicity of Lenin and others in German propaganda. Suddenly the whole thing blew up, Lenin disappeared and the newspapers were full of it.

"The papers for the prosecution of Lenin were put in the hands of the Minister of Justice and he gave them to the newspapers and the man who was bringing the incriminating documents from Germany turned back before he crossed the border. Tereshchenko told me this. I asked Kerensky later when he came to this country and he told me the same story."

Chamberlin [26] is probably correct in saying that while "the idea of Lenin as a 'German spy' could scarcely have commanded belief even among political opponents who knew the iron fanaticism and personal incorruptibility of his character it did have a considerable, although transitory, effect among the masses, especially among the soldiers; and some of the irreconcilable anti-Bolshevik Russians cling to the idea of the Bolsheviki as German agents up to the present time." Lenin was at one with the German propagandists in his desire to bring the war to an end, but his movement was far deeper than anything inspired by foreign propaganda.

Root never lost his original attitude toward the Bolsheviks and

[24] L'Industrie Russe et la revolution, 1919, Avant Propos, esp. pp. 8–9.
[25] Root to the author, September 16, 1930.
[26] Chamberlin, op. cit., Vol. I, p. 181.

their leaders. He consistently opposed recognition by the United States of the Soviet Government, never coming to accept the view that after the triumph of Stalin over Trotsky the idea of world revolution as a primary objective had been cast aside. He favored the Allied interventions in support of the counter-revolution and felt that the United States should have gone much further in fulfilling its promise to aid the Russian people whom he regarded as enslaved by a band of wicked criminals. As late as July 14th, 1927, he wrote to Grand Duke Nicholas, to whose efforts on behalf of the Russians of the old regime he contributed liberally: "It seems to me that history, economy, science and knowledge of human nature unite in compelling the belief that the Bolshevique [sic] conspiracy of outrage is necessarily temporary in its apparent strength and in justifying a hope that we may soon join in rejoicing over the downfall of this impudent experiment in crime." Just so might one of the Grand Duke's ancestors have written ten years after the American revolution about the upstart government of the United States, which the Czar was among the last to recognize.

In 1930, liberal circles in the United States were much exercised by the publication of a letter from Root to Ralph M. Easley, Secretary of the National Civic Federation of which Root was an active supporter. Root's letter was published through a misunderstanding, but it advocated the establishment of a federal police force for ferreting out subversive conspiracies. He saw no reason why the federal government should have agents charged with locating smugglers, counterfeiters and bootleggers but should not have any force to protect the government against those who were plotting its destruction. He had no thought of advising the establishment of a secret political police, such as had existed in Czarist Russia, and had he intended his letter for publication, he would have stated his point more clearly. It was, nevertheless, another evidence of his belief in the Russian plots for world revolution.

In appraising Root's participation in the Russian Mission and his reaction to the Russian situation, it is easy in retrospect to find bases for criticism. Perhaps the only valid criticism—if it be a criticism—was that he did not show himself in this instance wiser than all those around him. He spent about three weeks in Russia where his sources of information were almost entirely those which favored and believed in the strength of the moderate parties. While they were on their way home, Kerensky had succeeded Lvov as Premier and the Bolshevik strength seemed to have been completely broken, with their leaders arrested or in hiding. General Kornilov, a strong figure who was to lead a rightist coup in late August and September, had replaced Brussilov as Commander-in-Chief. General Scott had witnessed the Russian advance on the Austrian front which began on July 1st and had been greatly impressed by this his first view of modern warfare. He had heard much of the disorganization of the troops and their abandonment of discipline but the attack had proceeded admirably, accomplishing its purpose of showing that the Russian army could still fight, even though they were driven back as soon as German divisions were brought up in support of the Austrians. The optimistic view which the Mission took was probably the inevitable view of such a group so situated at that time and it was the view of the Russian leaders with whom they were in contact. It was also the view widely held in London and Paris. Lansing's better guess must have been merely that—it could not have been a reasoned conclusion from the evidence. It must also be remembered that Root was deeply imbued with the war spirit which is the most effective instrument for elevating the emotions above the intellect.[27]

[27] In the preparation of this chapter, I have been greatly assisted by conversations with Colonel T. Bentley Mott, De Witt Clinton Poole, Michael Florinsky and Stanley Washburn.

CHAPTER XLIV

"I look for a new birth of the law of nations"

AFTER the Armistice, Root was still insistent that Germany must be punished and that Prussian autocracy must be crushed forever. "If this same business is not to be done over again," he wrote to Judge Thomas Burke on November 21st, 1918, "Germany must be made to understand that she cannot launch war upon an unsuspecting world without suffering for it. If she feels that she can do that sort of thing with impunity, there is no reason why she should not try it again. You remember what the old English Judge said:—"The Prisoner at the Bar said, 'It is very hard, my lord, to be hung for stealing a sheep.' The Judge said, 'You're not to be hung for stealing a sheep; you're to be hung that sheep may not be stolen'." But if Root had reflected instead of felt in those days, he would have realized that a whole nation can not be hung. In the spring of 1915, about a year before he retired from the Foreign Office, Sir Arthur Nicolson recorded his agreement with Bismarck's policy "not to exact conditions which will compel your former adversary to await his time of revenge." In 1917, the editor of a leading English quarterly rejected an article in which Sir Arthur pointed out that no peace would be durable "if it were thought to impose on great communities terrors which would be regarded as intolerable or humiliating and which would sow the seeds of revengeful animosity." [1] At Versailles, a punitive peace was imposed and the ground of Germany was made ready for the rise of Hitler.

One thing beside immediate and crushing victory stirred in Root's mind during the period of belligerency. In addition to punishing Germany, the peace treaty should include plans for a new organization of the world which would make it difficult for any state to wage aggressive war. He had pondered this subject in 1914 and in the two succeeding years. The climactic days of 1917 brushed it aside for a

[1] Harold Nicolson, *Portrait of a Diplomatist*, pp. 312 and 314.

time, but by the summer of 1918 it was again occupying his thoughts. On August 21st, 1914, he wrote to George H. Jones: "The time will come before very long when all the civilized world should insist that the lesson of the war shall not be ignored or forgotten, but shall be made the basis upon which the foreign relations of civilized nations shall be reestablished, free from those mistaken policies which caused the great armaments and the universal conflict." February 11th, 1915, he replied to Charles Francis Adams, who had written him that he thought we were "tending irresistibly to Tennyson's 'Parliament of man, and Federation of the World' ":

I agree with you about the tendency. It is incredible that after this war the world should go on to do precisely the same things in precisely the same way. The *bandar-log* would not be quite equal to that. To put a better scheme of things into operation, however, will involve solving difficult practical problems. My moral nature is being ruined by habitual anger at a lot of fools who think that difficulties can be solved by refusing to see them. We must have a court, that is certain; but if it is to be really a court and not a new form of arbitrary government by plot and counterplot, the court must have a law which it is bound to apply. In order that there shall be an adequate law, there must be agreement upon adequate rules of conduct. In order that the judgments of the court applying this law shall be respected, there must be sanctions for its enforcement, and here we come to the international police force. When an American thinks of that he must consider how far the United States is willing to abandon its policy against entangling alliances and interference in the affairs of Europe. Close, discriminating and instructed thought ought to deal with that subject, always remembering that the most generous sentiments are the most dangerous when the people of the country are going to stand up to them. It is going to be a business for experts who combine technical knowledge with imagination, and the abundant vocabulary of the well-meaning pacifist will not be very useful.

Root's emphasis on an international court was natural to one who lived and moved and had his being in the law. It was an old conviction of his to which he had given practical form by his instructions to the American delegates to the Second Hague Peace Conference in 1907, by engineering the establishment of the Central American

Court of Justice in that same year and by seeking to prevent the
United States from wrecking that court in 1917. It was a cause to
which he devoted himself to the time of his death. On the question
of sanctions, or the use of force to compel compliance with the decisions of such a court, he had not yet made up his mind. On April
24th, 1908, he had delivered his second annual address as President
of the American Society of International Law on the subject "The
Sanction of International Law." It was a clear statement of the proposition that no law depends for its enforcement solely upon the in-
fliction by superior power of punishment for a breach. "The force
of law is the public opinion which prescribes it." But under the influence of the World War, he told the same audience on December
28th, 1915, that "Laws to be obeyed must have sanctions behind
them; that is to say, violations of them must be followed by punishment. That punishment must be caused by power superior to the
law-breaker. . . . Many states have grown so great that there is no
power capable of imposing punishment upon them except the power
of collective civilization outside of the offending state. Any exercise
of that power must be based upon public opinion." This was a shift
in emphasis. He put forth a view which he was to stress in subsequent discussions of the subject, that the whole basic theory of international law must be changed. Under the prevailing system, breaches
of international law were regarded just as civil wrongs are regarded
in private law; only the person immediately wronged is entitled to
protest. He wished to see breaches of international law treated as in
the private field we treat breaches of criminal law—an offense against
the entire community in which everyone is interested and against
which everyone is entitled to protest. Two days later, in addressing
the Second Pan American Scientific Congress, he declared that the
changes in the world had "outstripped the growth of international
law. . . . The pressing forward of the codification of international
law is made necessary by the swift moving of events among nations.
We cannot wait for custom to lag behind the action to which the
law should be applied." He was thinking of the "crimes" of Germany and not of the international philosophy upon which he had
acted and to which he frequently referred in citing the English nursery
rhyme, "Leg over leg the dog went to Dover." "That states the
method of our true progress," he said in the Nobel Peace Prize Ad-

"How Did That Get By Us?"

(A cartoon in the New York *Herald*, December 11, 1913)

dress which he would have delivered in September, 1914, had it not been for the war. "We cannot arrive at our goal *per saltum*."

To Professor Oppenheim at Cambridge University, one of the world's great scholars in international law, he wrote on March 6th, 1915: "The more I reflect upon the possibilities of the future, approaching the subject from different angles, the more certain I become that the establishment of adequate law is the essential of every proposal for a new condition of international affairs better than the old. There can be no court without a law to guide it. Otherwise the judges would be irresponsible sovereigns. There can be no police force without the judgments of a court to enforce. Otherwise the police force would be the agent of an irresponsible majority reducing all sovereigns to vassalage and destroying national independence. At the basis of all reform, it seems to me, lies an agreement upon certain, definite, specific rules of national conduct, very general and very rudimentary at first but capable of being enlarged by continual additions. With a court to pass upon the conformity of national conduct to such rules and a tribunal of conciliation to supplement its jurisdiction with adequate power to enforce its judgments we may get away from the wretched policies and plans, intrigues and suspicions, which have brought about the present dreadful condition."

Root's correspondence with Lord Bryce has already been quoted. In it Root had referred to the need for finding some standard by which national policies could be judged. Bryce expressed his agreement in a letter of December 15th, 1914, adding that he and some of his friends had been considering plans for a post-war organization. The proposals which he then had in mind closely foreshadow the general principles on which the League of Nations was established. Root was greatly influenced by this and other statements of Bryce's thought on the subject.

It is not to be supposed that Root's was the only mind in the United States which was devoting itself to these problems of world reorganization. Through the centuries, plans for a world federation had been proposed by such diverse persons as Henry IV, the Abbé de Saint-Pierre, William Penn and Immanuel Kant. In receiving the Nobel Peace Prize in 1906, Theodore Roosevelt had advocated a "League of Peace, not only to keep the peace among themselves, but to prevent, by force if necessary, its being broken by others." In his projected Nobel Prize Address in 1914, Root had suggested that such a plan was "a counsel of perfection for which the world was not ready." In December, 1914, Colonel House had suggested to Wilson a scheme for a Pan American League and Wilson had eagerly accepted the thought.[2] On June 17th, 1915, the League to Enforce Peace was founded in Philadelphia with ex-President Taft at its head. This organization was to continue and to prove extremely influential during the next five years. It advocated a four-point program including (1) the judicial settlement of disputes by an international court; (2) all other questions to be submitted to a council of conciliation for recommendations; (3) the use of economic and military force against a state which goes to war without first submitting to one of those peaceful processes; (4) periodic conferences for the codification of international law. Senator Lodge on May 27th, 1916, at a meeting in Washington arranged by the League to Enforce Peace, had agreed that the next step to be taken was to put force behind international peace with some sort of international league. President Wilson, speaking at the same meeting, had given guarded support to the League's program. Root never affiliated himself with the League to Enforce Peace; apparently he was not ready to accept their third principle although his mind was constantly leading in that direction. He and Taft did not see eye to eye during this period and one finds some falling off in their correspondence.

On April 11th, 1918, Root lunched with Colonel House to meet the Archbishop of York. House had invited President Lowell of Harvard and William Howard Taft to join them in order that they might all discuss the League to Enforce Peace. Root apparently was led to expound his ideas at some length and House asked him to write them down later. Root procrastinated, but after repeated urgings finally wrote House on August 16th. This letter is the most elaborate statement of his views at this period and is also important because House and Wilson read it together.

Root began by reiterating his belief in the need for a universal, formal and irrevocable acceptance and declaration of the view that "an international breach of the peace is a matter which concerns every member of the Community of Nations,—a matter in which every nation has a direct interest, and to which every nation has a

[2] Seymour, *Intimate Papers of Colonel House*, Vol. I, p. 209.

right to object." (Article 11 of the Covenant of the League of Nations as finally adopted, recites: "Any war, or threat of war, whether immediately affecting any of the Members of the League or not, is hereby declared a matter of concern to the whole League. . . .") Root noted in his letter to House, and spoke of it frequently to others, that if the idea he advocated had prevailed in 1914, it would have been impossible for Germany to refuse Sir Edward Grey's suggestion for an international conference to discuss the quarrel between Austria and Serbia. He continued: "At the basis of every community lies the idea of organization to preserve the peace. . . . The Monroe Doctrine asserted a specific interest on the part of the United States in preventing certain gross breaches of the peace on the American Continent; and when President Wilson suggested an enlargement of the Monroe Doctrine to take in the whole world, his proposal carried by necessary implication the change of doctrine which I am discussing. . . . The change involves a limitation of sovereignty, making every sovereign state subject to the superior right of a community of sovereign states to have the peace preserved just as individual liberty is limited by being made subject to the superior right of the civil community to have the peace preserved. The acceptance of any such principle would be fatal to the whole Prussian theory of the state and of government. When you have got this principle accepted openly, expressly, distinctly, unequivocally by the whole civilized world, you will for the first time have a Community of Nations. . . .

"The second proposition which I made was that the public opinion of the free peoples of the world in favor of having peace preserved must have institutions through which it may receive effect. No lesson from history is clearer than this. Very strong public feeling may produce a mob which is simply destructive, or a multitude of expressions of opinion which get nowhere by themselves; but to accomplish anything affirmative some particular person must have delegated to him authority to do some particular thing in behalf of the multitude. The original form of the institutions created to give effect to popular opinion is not so important." He noted that some rudimentary institutions had already developed; the Hague Convention facilitating arbitration or submission to a commission of inquiry; the usage of the Concert of Europe in meeting in conference to consider serious exigencies. But all of these things "depend entirely upon individual national initiative. No one has any authority to invoke them in the name or interest of the Community of Nations. . . . The first and natural step . . . will be an agreement upon someone or some group whose duty it will be to speak for the whole community in calling upon any two nations who appear to be about to fight to submit their claims to the consideration (I do not now say 'decision', but consideration) of the Tribunal as it is now or may hereafter be organized, or the Commission of Enquiry, or the Conference, as the case may require. . . . Behind such a demand of course should stand also an agreement by the powers to act together in support of the demand made in their name and in dealing with the consequences of it.

"The question how far that agreement should go brings me to the third proposition which I made, and that is that no agreement in the way of a league of peace or under whatever name should be contemplated which will probably not be kept when the time comes for acting under it. Nothing can be worse in international affairs than to make agreements and break them. It would be folly, therefore, for the United States in order to preserve or enforce peace after this War is over to enter into an agreement which the people of the United States would not regard as binding upon them. I think that observation applies to making a hard and fast agreement to go to war upon the happening of some future international event beyond the control of the United States. I think that the question whether the people of the Country would stand by such an agreement made by the President and Senate would depend upon the way they looked at the event calling for their action at that future time when the event occurs,—that they would fight if at that time they were convinced that they ought to, and they would not fight if at that time they were convinced that they ought not to. It may be that an international community system may be developed hereafter which will make it possible to say 'We bind ourselves to fight upon the happening of some particular event' but I do not think that system has so far developed that it is now practicable to make such an agreement. Of course it may become so before this War is over. No-one can tell. We are certainly rather nearer to that point than we were two or three years ago. . . .''

Here was a statement, written with Root's usual clarity and logical development, which closely paralleled the League of Nations plan as it was finally set up. But it was the reservation which he expressed toward the close about blanket acceptance of commitment to future action which was disregarded when the Covenant was framed and which, more than anything else, led to its rejection by the United States. Root felt sure of his ground on this point and clung to it. In December, 1918, he knew he was here in accord with Wilson and in disagreement with Taft.[3]

House acknowledged the letter from Magnolia, Massachusetts, saying that Root's letter had arrived while President Wilson was there and that they had read it together and discussed it in detail. He thought there would be little difficulty in their reaching agreement upon some plan. He said that he had been devoting considerable thought to the subject and had reached some rather definite conclusions. House had indeed prepared for Wilson in July a first draft of a League plan and had incorporated in it, as a result of his earlier talk with Root, a provision for an international court.[4]

Almost immediately after the Armistice on November 11th, 1918, the question of the personnel of the American delegation to the Peace Conference began to be discussed in the United States. The press generally aired the view that Root would be selected. It was argued that Root's participation in the drafting of the treaty would assure Republican support in the Senate. Taft was also prominently mentioned. The choice of Root was urged upon Wilson from many quarters. Joseph Tumulty, Wilson's secretary, records that he discussed the appointment of Root with President Wilson and with Lansing and that both men were in favor of it. Secretary McAdoo urged Root's appointment.[5] Later consideration, however, convinced the President that the choice would be unwise because "the reputation which Mr. Root had gained of being rather conservative, if not reactionary, would work a prejudice toward the Peace Commission at the outset." [6] It is probable that the opposition of American labor to Root played a part in Wilson's determination [7] but those objections would not have disqualified Taft. Wilson's distrust of lawyers

[3] Diary of Henry L. Stimson, entry of December 22, 1918.
[4] Baker, Woodrow Wilson and World Settlement, Vol. I, p. 218.
[5] Senator McAdoo to the author, April 29, 1938.
[6] Tumulty, Woodrow Wilson As I Know Him, p. 337.
[7] Frank L. Polk to the author, August 30, 1935; Fleming, The United States and the League of Nations, p. 61.

undoubtedly militated against the choice of Root or of Taft, but it is hard to escape the conclusion that Wilson was unwilling to take with him any outstanding Republican leader. His appointment of Henry White, a Republican, but a career diplomat entirely removed from politics, did nothing to satisfy the opposition party's demand for recognition, even though White's friends, Roosevelt and Lodge, were delighted with his selection.

Root had no expectation that he himself would be chosen, although he would have been glad to serve and he would have served with complete loyalty to his chief. He was meticulous in his respect for the obligations of official duty and the danger would have been that he would have been so wholly loyal to the President that the Republican Senators would have been unwilling to follow his lead. But after Wilson decided to go himself, Root was doubtful whether he would have accepted an appointment had it been tendered to him.[8] In the early days of the Conference, Thomas W. Lamont, in discussing with Colonel House the organization of the American Delegation, made the inquiry as to whether House did not think it would be helpful to have at Paris a man of the wide experience and wisdom of Senator Root to advise all members of the Delegation on any questions that might come up. It was suggested that Mr. Root's relationship might be that of Counsel to the American Plenipotentiaries. Colonel House warmly favored the suggestion and recommended it by cable to President Wilson who was then in the United States. The latter, however, declined to adopt it on the ground that to make such an appointment subsequent to the initial organization of the Delegation would give to the American public the idea that the President lacked confidence in his own Delegation and had to turn to Senator Root for help,—that the move would be interpreted as a sign of weakness rather than one of strengthening the Delegation itself.[9] The relationship between Wilson and Root totally lacked that element of mutual confidence and admiration which made Roosevelt and Root so excellent a team. Root replied on November 21st, 1918, to James R. Sheffield who had written hoping for his appointment: "It seems to me that to secure a really adequate appreciation of my merits I ought to have arranged for your election to the Presidency of the United States. I think

[8] Diary of Chandler P. Anderson, entry of December 12, 1918.
[9] Thomas W. Lamont to the author, November 5, 1937.

Mr. Wilson's decision to go to Europe himself leads naturally to his selecting for the American delegates to the Peace Conference his own advisers and direct followers, which probably excludes me from the list of persons to be considered." Root believed that Lansing should head the delegation and that he should include Chandler Anderson and John Bassett Moore among his legal advisers. He thought it very unwise on several grounds for the President to go to Paris. He believed that the President should remain in this country to direct affairs; he believed it unsound to have the Chief Executive and the Secretary of State participate in the negotiations so that no questions would be referred back to Washington where they might be viewed with greater detachment; he was suspicious of Wilson's egotism, believing that his desire to be identified with the creation of a world league would lead him to go further than was then practicable and would make him overemphasize the executive side of a world organization in the expectation that he would be chosen as President of the World. He believed that Wilson was a man without convictions or moral principles and was more influenced by considerations of self-advantage than by the underlying principles upon which the American government was founded.[10]

As early as December 12th, 1918, Root had been consulted by several Senators as to their proper course of action in case the President agreed to a treaty without first consulting the Senate. He had advised them that they need have no hesitation in rejecting objectionable clauses since he anticipated that the peace treaty would be quite separate from clauses committing the Government of the United States to future policies. Even if the two parts of the treaty were combined, Root thought it would be quite feasible to ratify that part of the treaty which made the peace, with reservations as to particular clauses which the Senate might be unwilling to accept.[11] The trouble which he did not then anticipate was that the President might be unwilling to accept the Senate's reservations. Senator Lodge talked to this point in the Senate on December 21st. His speech on that day showed the influences of some of Root's ideas. Senator Knox may have been another of the Senators who consulted Root; Knox introduced in the Senate on December 3rd, the day before Wilson

[10] Diary of Chandler P. Anderson, especially entry of November 18, 1918.
[11] Ibid., entry of December 12, 1918.

sailed for Europe, a resolution suggesting that any general plan for a league of nations should be deferred until after the peace treaty was made. It is clear, however, that Root was in accord with Wilson in believing that the organization of the world for the preservation of peace was a matter of urgent importance; he would not then have agreed with Knox's idea that it should be shelved. Yet Knox's further resolution in the Senate on December 18th came closer to Root's idea that an "entente" might be formed carrying on the purposes of the Allied and Associated Powers. As the discussion of the League later became more detailed, Root was insistent that there were two separate and distinct problems to be faced. One was the liquidation of the war situation and for that he was willing that the United States should go far in committing itself. The other problem was the permanent organization of the world and that he thought should be approached slowly—"leg over leg." [12]

Root did not believe in the kind of general anticipatory criticism of Wilson in which some Senators and other persons engaged. On December 26th, 1918, he wrote to Victor F. Lawson declining to write an article on the Peace Conference for the Chicago *Daily News*. He said he did not yet know what they proposed to do at the Peace Conference "and I do not wish to embarrass or interfere with them while they are representing the Country abroad, unless I think they are attempting something which seems to me to be really injurious. This of course I do not assume."

He talked with Henry White before the latter sailed and went with him to see Roosevelt in the hospital where their former chief was coming close to the end of his career. He gave White also a copy of the letter which he had written to House in August. White wrote him from the *George Washington* on December 4th, the day the ship sailed. It was a letter of gratitude for Root's constant counsel and guidance and contained one bit of information about Wilson's attitude: "I have received further assurances since I saw you, of a satisfactory character relative to the League of Nations; i. e. that what we feared might develop in the line of making this country amenable to others and placing its troops and ships at their disposal, under certain conditions easy to be imagined, is not in the least to be apprehended on the part of my august fellow

[12] Cf. Root to Moorefield Storey, March 20, 1919.

passenger."

The text of the Covenant of the League of Nations as presented to a plenary session of the Peace Conference on February 14th, 1919, was published in the American papers on the 15th. Root went over it in detail with Colonel Stimson on the same day. His principal objection was to Article X which he thought completely abrogated the Monroe Doctrine. He thought also that there was insufficient reliance upon the establishment of international law. The next day he expressed the opinion that, with proper amendments, the document might constitute a beginning.[13] By March 9th, he thought the whole Covenant needed rewriting but his major objection was still based on the view that the United States would be compelled to abandon the freedom of action for its own protection which it had under the policy of the Monroe Doctrine.[14] Article X, which was later to be the nub of the political controversy, contained the undertaking to "preserve as against external aggression the territorial integrity and existing political independence of all States members of the League." Article XVI provided for the use of sanctions against any state which should resort to war in violation of its obligations. Root remained long in doubt upon this general subject. On December 22nd, 1918, he told Colonel Stimson that he thought there should be no specific obligation to go to war to enforce the decisions of the international court but that the parties should agree to use "all appropriate means" of enforcement. He thought the threat of economic pressure would be very effective but if force were to be used, it might come most easily and appropriately from adjacent neighbors, perhaps with an adjustment of the expenses among all the members of the League. On December 29th, he thought the specification of economic pressure to enforce decisions of the League would be unwise and that there should be merely "a covenant to unite in all measures appropriate to prevent or redress a wrong." But on March 1st, after the draft of the Covenant had been published, he saw no objection to the provision for economic pressure.[15] On March 9th, he told a small group at dinner at Chandler Anderson's home that he favored a universal international boycott as a means of compulsion against a

[13] Diary of Henry L. Stimson, entries of February 15 and 16, 1919.
[14] Diary of Chandler P. Anderson, entry of March 10, 1919.
[15] Diary of Henry L. Stimson.

nation which should refuse to submit judicial questions to arbitration or to refer for investigation and report other questions which might lead to war.[16]

In the long bitter debates on the League of Nations which were then only beginning, Root exercised large influence and always on the side of moderation. His influence was of a kind very different from that of Taft who in general appeared to the public as the great champion of the League. Taft's rallying of public support to the cause was of great importance but it proved to be as unsuccessful as Root's influence which was exerted at the fountain-head—among the Republican senators. Taft appears to have had much less influence with the key senators: Senators Lodge and Kellogg declared that he had absolutely no influence with any Republican senators.[17] At times Root had considerable influence on the public but not as much as Taft. As usual, Root brought his influence to bear not through writing articles for the magazines or newspapers, a medium which he usually shunned, but through addresses, through correspondence, some of which was made public and widely distributed, and through private letters and conversations. He was the great intellectual leader of the Republican party; Taft had the prestige which always attaches to an ex-President and his abilities were respected, but Root had the greater reputation for skilled training in international affairs and for legal acumen. And as a former Senator he had a sympathetic understanding for the Senate's point of view. He said later that the senators were defending the constitutional prerogatives of the Senate. The Senate's power in consenting to treaties and in confirming ambassadors was won with difficulty in the Constitutional Convention as a compromise between those who wished to vest full power over foreign affairs in the executive and those who wished to continue the scheme of having them handled by a committee of Congress. Root thought the League plan would practically put the Senate out of business so far as a control of foreign affairs went because the real business would be transacted at Geneva by the conversations of the foreign ministers and not in the foreign offices at home.[18] But this idea seems to have come to him later; it does not appear in any contemporaneous record.

[16] Diary of Chandler P. Anderson, entry of March 10, 1919.
[17] *Ibid.*, entry of July 30, 1919.
[18] Root to the author, September 6, 1930.

The first important part, of which there is record, which he played in the contest between Senate and President, began on March 13th, 1919. By that date President Wilson had returned to the United States and had had his unsatisfactory dinner with the Foreign Relations Committee of the Senate on February 26th. On March 3rd, the day before the end of the Congressional session, Lodge had read on the floor of the Senate the "Round Robin," ultimately signed by thirty-nine senators who declared publicly their belief that the proposal for a League of Nations was unsatisfactory in its draft form and that its perfecting should be deferred until the peace treaty had been completed. This manifesto was intended as a notice to the world and especially to the representatives of the Powers at the Peace Conference that they could not expect ratification by the United States of a treaty containing the League Covenant. This objective is clearly admitted by Senator Lodge in his book [19] and is confirmed by Senator Brandegee's contemporaneous account to Chandler Anderson which the latter recorded in his diary on March 13th. Root does not appear to have been consulted on the Round Robin. Wilson sailed back to Paris on March 5th after speaking at the Metropolitan Opera House in New York with Taft on the preceding evening.

On March 13th, Chandler Anderson came over to New York from Washington for the express purpose of consulting Mr. Root on a matter of importance. Senator Brandegee had told Anderson the day before, that Lodge had received a cable from Henry White in Paris in which White asked Lodge to cable him the exact phraseology of amendments to the Covenant which the Senate considered important. He stated that they were most anxious to meet the views of the Senate. Lodge received the cable on the 12th and consulted Senators Brandegee and Knox. Brandegee regarded it as a trap to commit the Senate and was afraid that Lodge would be ensnared. He asked Anderson if he would not go to New York to explain the matter to Mr. Root and to get him to persuade Lodge to take the same view. Senator Lodge states in his book that he also consulted Root but it is clear from Anderson's diary that Root's first reaction was that it was queer that Lodge, in view of their long and intimate friendship, had not communicated with him directly. Anderson assured him that Lodge, being in Boston, had asked Brandegee to handle the matter, which

[19] *The Senate and the League of Nations*, pp. 118 ff.

was the reason why the request for help came in that way. In his customary manner, Root walked back and forth across his study, with thought transformed into concise wording punctuating long intervals of silence. Anderson took notes and made suggestions as Root talked and then Root sent for his secretary and dictated a letter to Lodge, adding, at Anderson's request, a brief statement of his own view as to the need for amendments to the Covenant. Lodge prints the full text of Root's letter in his book already referred to. It was characteristic of Root that he dictated the letter in the first person plural, avowing it the joint work of Anderson and himself.

In general, Root agreed with Brandegee that Lodge should not accede to White's request. He advised Lodge that he should not commit himself to an unauthorized agent of the President while the President remained wholly uncommitted. "A second reason is that any views which the Senate may have, to be effective must reach the President's mind by an entirely different avenue of approach from that of information communicated by a subordinate. They should be presented not as an appeal to his judgment, but with the compelling force of expression by a co-equal power to which his judgment must yield, or his action must fail." Root thought that White must have failed to appreciate the way in which Wilson had treated the Senate. Although, as a matter of fact, it has been the exception far more than the rule for a President to consult the Senate in the course of a treaty negotiation, Root accepted the prevailing Republican senatorial point of view that Wilson should have consulted the Senate while it was in session. If he now desired the senatorial viewpoint, he should summon them in extra session. He thought White would hardly have sent the cable without consulting Wilson. "At all events, the net is spread in plain sight of the bird, and you are the bird." White's cable was sent from Paris while Wilson was still on the high seas and his letters to both Root and Lodge, written both before and after the cable, abundantly demonstrate that he had not consulted Wilson; that the newspaper reports he had of the senatorial views were not clear; and that he was sincerely desirous of helping by seeking to learn and to meet Lodge's objections. He had made the same request in a letter of March 7th to Lodge but had decided that time was important and had therefore cabled. In his letter of the 19th, after receiving Lodge's cabled reply, he explained that he had consulted no one before sending the cable. He was writing Lodge and Root constantly in an attempt to keep them confidentially posted on the developments from week to week at Paris. It is a pity that both Lodge and Root distrusted him on this occasion and failed to respond in the same confidential way. But Root's suspicions of a plot were confirmed in his own mind when he learned that other Republican senators had received similar cables from Colonel House.[20] White stated in a number of his letters that it was a great mistake to suppose that Wilson was averse to any amendments, a conclusion which later events proved to be correct at this stage. White had begged Root also for the benefit of his views on the Covenant but Root had remained silent. It was not until June 5th that he wrote White thanking him for his frequent letters and explaining that he had been very much in disagreement with American diplomatic policy at Paris and had felt it better not to write on the subject letters which "might make you unhappy; indeed, I have strongly suspected that you and Lansing and Scott were unhappy enough as it was."

Root suggested to Lodge that he reply to White in the following words which Lodge used without alteration:

"The President expressed no willingness to receive any communication from the Senate while that body was in session. If he now wishes to have amendments drafted which the Senate will consent to, the natural and necessary course is to convene the Senate in the customary way. Manifestly, I cannot now speak for the Senate, or consult its members, nor can they consult each other, nor can the President consult them while they are at their homes in forty eight States."

"You will perceive," Root added to Lodge, "that this assumes that White wishes the information for the President's benefit, which is the proper attitude for him to occupy so long as he is a member of the Commission." Lodge was about to debate the League issue with President Lowell of Harvard; Root wished him great success. "I assume that he occupies substantially the same attitude that Taft does. I think it a great mistake for Taft while he knows perfectly well that the so-called constitution [of the League] is in serious need of amendment to take a course tending to help Wilson to put it through without amendment.

"I have been studying the paper [the draft Covenant of the League]

[20] Diary of Chandler P. Anderson, entry of March 15, 1919.

and trying to dispossess my mind of the prejudice against it created by the way in which it has been presented,—a way exceedingly offensive to me. The more I study it, the more satisfied I am that it has some very useful provisions, some very bad ones, some glaring deficiencies, and that if it is not very materially amended not merely in form but in substance, the world will before very long wake up to realize that a great opportunity has been wasted in the doing of a futile thing."

Several things stand out from this letter and particularly from its ultimate paragraph; Root was striving for a fair and detached appraisal. Perhaps he was spurred on to reacquire that characteristic attitude because Henry White's letters were full of appeals to just that quality—"your impartial mind, which is accustomed to looking at international questions from a broad and world-wide point of view." On April 2nd, Root replied to a letter from John Kendrick Bangs about the League, stressing again his effort to dispossess his mind of the prejudice and resentment which Wilson's "arrogant denial of anybody's right to criticise" had aroused in him. He believed that Wilson's tactics, or apparent tactics, had given to the discussion that belligerency which Root thought was unfortunate. "It has been awfully hard for me to get out of that frame of mind myself. I think I have done so in the main." In the second place, Root's letter to Lodge shows that while he sympathized strongly with the general senatorial attitude, his chief fear was that a great opportunity for world betterment would be wasted by attempting a scheme so grandiose as to be futile. That remained his great preoccupation which was never overshadowed in his mind by personal animosities, political advantage or any other consideration.

Lodge acknowledged Root's letter with an outpouring of gratitude. His letter was full of bitterness against Wilson and echoed some of Root's ideas: that a great opportunity was being lost; that there was grave danger of entangling the United States in an agreement which this country would not live up to when it came to the test, "and that would wreck any league." Lodge wanted a long talk with Root and hoped he would analyze the problem "as you alone can, and show the public what ought to be done to accomplish as much as can practically be accomplished by a union of the nations to promote general peace and disarmament."

Root's opportunity to comply with Lodge's suggestion that he "show the public" came from another quarter almost immediately. On March 17th, 1919, Henry L. Stimson had a talk with S. R. Bertron who had been a member of Root's Russian Mission. Bertron argued that the public mind was confused, feeling that some amendments to the Covenant were needed but not knowing what those amendments should be. He thought that Root was the only man who could meet the situation by a public exposition. The next day Stimson had an appointment with Mr. Root and, on his way to Root's apartment, stopped to see Will H. Hays, Chairman of the Republican National Committee. Stimson told Hays that he thought the time had come to persuade Mr. Root to get into action. Hays had just returned from a trip throughout the West, sounding out public opinion which he believed had reached the point of agreeing on some League but not this League. He hoped Stimson would persuade Root to speak. Stimson then discussed the whole situation at length with Root. In answer to a direct question, Root said that he wanted Wilson to bring back a plan for a good League but that he did not propose to have the country yield to a League which was a little better but not good enough. Stimson suggested that since House had previously sought Root's advice on framing a plan for a League, he should cable to him or to Henry White setting forth his views. If he did that and then later set forth his views in a public address, he would forfend the criticism that he was playing politics and making suggestions too late and purely for domestic Republican purposes. Root finally agreed to this view and began to draft his statement.

The next day Stimson and Hays together called on Mr. Root. Stimson had been impressed the previous day by Root's modesty; Root had stated: "Harry, except for what you have said, this letter of Lodge's is the only indication that anybody in the United States cares for my opinion on the subject." With some men, such a remark might have been "fishing"; with Root it was genuine diffidence. Hays launched his appeal on that basis, telling Root that he was the highest authority in the country, the one man who could speak with authority on the needed amendments. He promised that his views would reach ten million readers of five thousand newspapers and that copies would be mailed personally to a million individuals. Root immediately said that if it was thought that he could help, he would do it and he proceeded to expound his point of view. Stimson's record of this conversation, compared with the final text of Root's published letter to Hays, shows almost full identity between them save for one point which will be noted later.

It was agreed that Hays should write a formal letter to Root, requesting an exposition of his views. Such a letter was written, revised by Root, and put in final form under date of March 24th, 1919. Root's reply was discussed in draft form with Hays, George Harvey and Stimson. Its last paragraph was inserted in response to a suggestion made by Hays. As published, it bore the date of March 29th. Harvey, the editor of *Harvey's Weekly* and one of the most violent of Wilson's opponents, was enthusiastic about the Root letter, telling Stimson that it would unite both wings, bringing in both the radicals and the conservatives. Hays shared his enthusiasm. Stimson, meanwhile, had talked with the secretary of Frank Polk, Acting Secretary of State. Stimson explained what Root was doing and mentioned the nature of the amendments he proposed. Polk conferred with Bertron and then sent word to Stimson that if Mr. Root would send copies to Polk's secretary and to Polk himself, who was then at White Sulphur Springs, the text of the amendments would be cabled to Paris. Root sent them on March 26th. It is not correct to assume, as many writers have done, that Root's views were solicited by the State Department. Similarly, Taft had cabled Wilson on March 18th suggesting various amendments, not at Wilson's request, but after Taft had asked Tumulty to inquire whether Wilson would care to receive his views; Wilson welcomed them.[21]

Root's letter to Hays is an admirable example of his power of clear and concise expression of logically developed thought. It is a pity that his reasons and arguments were not available in Paris along with the texts of his amendments. Tumulty's comments upon the Root amendments, for example, show that he analyzed them by themselves without their accompanying exposition and that he failed to appreciate the purpose of many of them.

Root began by stating that there was no division of American opinion upon the desirability of some international organization to preserve the peace of the world or upon the participation of the United

---

[21] Tumulty, *op. cit.*, Appendix B. The details about the preparation of the Hays letter are taken from the Diary of Henry L. Stimson, supplemented by Mr. Root's files.

States in such an organization. The question was merely one of securing the best plan. He thought that the Senate should have been asked for its views, especially since the President and Secretary of State were both actually participating in the negotiations at Paris. He stated that the chief object of the plan was to prevent future wars and that the United States, seeking no help for itself, was merely interested in contributing to that end. He noted that one class of international controversies arose from disputes about legal rights; he thought the draft Covenant was defective in not placing greater emphasis upon the development of international law. The references to arbitration he thought were feeble and while the establishment of a permanent international court was suggested, no duty was imposed to establish it or subsequently to resort to it. The first amendment he suggested was the inclusion of a provision for obligatory arbitration of carefully defined "justiciable questions," and his second amendment called for periodic conferences to develop international law. In these two amendments he was covering sins of omission rather than of commission.

He next turned his attention to those sources of international controversy which lie in the field of policy. If the United States were to set aside its traditional policy of non-interference in European affairs, it should be assured that there were sufficient affirmative reasons for doing so. He admitted that the relations between the Old World and the New had become much more intimate since the cautions of Washington and Jefferson were uttered, but the basis for their admonitions remained unaltered. The people of the United States still had no direct interest in such questions as the delimitation of frontiers in the Balkans, and the people of Europe had no direct interest in questions between Chile and Peru or between the United States and Colombia. The wisdom of the Monroe Doctrine had never been more evident. "There has, however, arisen in these days for the American people a powerful secondary interest in the affairs of Europe coming from the fact that war in Europe and the Near East threatens to involve the entire world, and the peaceable nations of Europe need outside help to put out the fire, and keep it from starting again. That help to preserve peace we ought to give, and that help we wish to give." But in giving that help, one must bear in mind that neither the United States nor any American nation was asking for similar help from Europe. (Root did not think of the Latin American Republics welcoming the League as a protection against the suspected imperialistic designs of the United States.) The United States must therefore insist upon maintaining the principle of the Monroe Doctrine and reserving its sole right to deal with such questions as immigration. The United States should not be penalized for agreeing to come to the help of Europe by being required to surrender its own peculiar interests. Accordingly he proposed as a third point a reservation safeguarding the Monroe Doctrine and modeled upon the reservation which the United States attached to its signature of the Hague Conventions in 1907 when Root was Secretary of State. It is important to note that Root did not advocate amending the Covenant by inserting a reference to the Monroe Doctrine in that instrument; he proposed to safeguard the American position by a reservation for which there was good precedent. Taft, however, had proposed and stressed the importance of an actual amendment to the Covenant on this point. Wilson, after one of his hardest battles at Paris, secured what proved to be an unsatisfactory provision in the Covenant on the Monroe Doctrine. He had become so averse to American reservations in any form that he could not favor Root's procedure.

Root's views on Article X deserve extended quotation not only because they are important in the history of the debate on the League but because they expound a wise appreciation of a situation which still exists. His underlying philosophy on this point has not been generally understood and unfortunately it was not widely shared. If it had been, the history of world organization might have been far different. To repeat, it was Article X by which the members of the League were to undertake "to respect and preserve as against external aggression the territorial integrity and existing political independence of all members of the League."

"Looking at this article as a part of a perpetual league for the preservation of peace, my first impression was that the whole article ought to be stricken out. If perpetual, it would be an attempt to preserve for all time unchanged the distribution of power and territory made in accordance with the views and exigencies of the Allies in this present juncture of affairs. It would necessarily be futile. . . . It would not only be futile; it would be mischievous. Change and growth are the law of life, and no generation can impose its will in regard to the growth of nations and the distribution of power, upon succeeding generations.

"I think, however, that this article must be considered not merely with reference to the future, but with reference to the present situation in Europe. Indeed, this whole agreement ought to be considered in that double aspect. The belligerent power of Germany, Austria, Bulgaria and Turkey has been destroyed; but that will not lead to future peace without a reconstruction of Eastern Europe and Western Asia. The vast territories of the Hohenzollerns, the Hapsburgs and the Romanoffs have lost the rulers who formerly kept the population in order, are filled with turbulent masses without stable government, unaccustomed to self-control and fighting among themselves like children of the dragon's teeth. There can be no settled peace until these masses are reduced to order. . . . [Henry White in his letters had been stressing the disturbed conditions in Germany and sounding a warning note.] The allied nations in their council must determine the lines of reconstruction. Their determinations must be enforced. They may make mistakes. Doubtless they will. But there must be decisions and decisions must be enforced.

"Under these conditions the United States cannot quit. It must go on to the performance of its duty, and the immediate aspect of Article X is an agreement to do that. I think, therefore, that Article X should be amended so that it shall hold a limited time, and thereafter any member may withdraw from it. I annex an amendment to that effect." He suggested a term of five years. As a matter of fact, Wilson's original thought had been similar to Root's. His early drafts for the Covenant embodied with the guarantee of Article X a provision for reconsideration of territorial boundaries and similar questions. He was driven from that position by the insistence of the French and of his own adviser, Dr. Hunter Miller, with the result that the Covenant finally included in Article XIX only an ineffective suggestion for such subsequent reconsideration.

Root's next point dealt with the limitation of armaments which he considered very important. He followed a proposal of M. Bourgeois of France in recommending that the permanent disarmament commission should have powers of inspection to make sure that nations really lived up to their obligations. That proposal was in advance of the thought of the time but was to be revived in subsequent years.

Finally Root suggested another amendment comparable to that which inspired his thought on Article X. He recognized that the League must begin as an alliance of the victors against the vanquished and that no permanent League of Peace could be created on that basis. "There should be provision for its revision in a calmer atmosphere and when the world is less subject to exciting and disturbing causes."

"If the amendments which I have suggested are made, I think it will be the clear duty of the United States to enter into the agreement.

"In that case," he added at the suggestion of Hays, "It would be the duty of Congress to establish by law the offices of representatives of the United States in the body of Delegates and the Executive Council, just as the offices of Ambassadors and Ministers are already provided for by law, and the new offices would be filled by appointment of the President with the advice and consent of the Senate under Article II, Section 2, of the Constitution of the United States."

Will Hays was delighted with the letter and the way in which it was received. "It is really having just the effect we hoped," he wrote on April 4th. President Lowell of Harvard, pro-League leader of the Taft school, thought it admirable. He wrote to Root on April 2nd that he had tried to make the same basic point in his debate with Lodge—that if satisfactory amendments were made, the United States should accept the Covenant. He had tried to make Lodge "rise to that point" but he had not. Lowell had some criticism for Wilson's egotism and much for the Senate's faults. "In judging my old colleagues in the Senate," Root replied, "do not forget that they really had no time to consider the subject in the closing days of the short Session, and they were boiling over with a perfectly natural rage because of Wilson's refusal to consult them and his practical denial of their right to discuss the subject at all. The offensively arrogant way in which the subject was presented here produced a very disagreeable effect upon me, and it took considerable time for me to get into the right frame of mind for a dispassionate consideration of the document."

The one point which Root had expounded privately to Stimson and Hays, but which he omitted from his letter, was his belief that the ostensible objects of the procedure in the Council of the League was "bunk" and "camouflage" because of the requirement for una-

nimity of decision. Any important nation, he said, could buy enough
votes of the little countries to prevent the achievement of unanimity.
He felt, therefore, that none of the great things claimed for the
Executive Council of the League would really be accomplished. But
he did believe that the very existence of the Council with its regular
procedure for conferences would be very important and from it would
grow the kind of safeguard of peace which all wanted to secure.

Root's proposals, like those of Taft and Hughes, received careful
consideration and partial adoption at Paris, but there was no great enthusiasm for them. Hunter Miller, legal expert of the American Delegation, whose *The Drafting of the Covenant* is the outstanding book
on the subject, notes that he showed them to Sir Robert Cecil "who
did not like them at all; he went so far as to say that he would rather
have no Covenant than have one with those amendments." But Article XIII of the Covenant had already been amended before Root's
texts reached Paris and partially met his views about the separation of
legal and political questions and emphasis on the arbitral process for
the former. The general nature of Root's thought had been known in
Paris nine days before the text of his amendments; they were set forth
in a letter to Hunter Miller from Thomas Lamont who had talked
with Root on the subject about March 10th. Miller points out that
many of the large Powers were unwilling to accept obligatory arbitration at that time and that it was certain the United States Senate
would not have done so. Root was to press on for years to achieve this
agreement, to suffer further rebuffs but to live to see most of the
world except his own country committed to that salutary proposition.
Miller also thought that no express provision was needed to enable
the League to summon periodic conferences for the codification of
international law. This was true, but the inclusion of Root's proposal
would certainly have been at least innocuous. It was not until 1930
that the League convened the First Conference for the Progressive
Codification of International Law; the movement died at least temporarily with the barren results of that first effort. As already indicated, Wilson finally secured the inclusion in the Covenant of an unsatisfactory clause covering the Monroe Doctrine; Miller disliked
Root's resort to "the stilted and obscure language" used at the time of
the Hague Conventions. Miller, in dismissing summarily Root's suggestions for a time limit in Article X and a withdrawal clause in the

same connection, missed the fundamental basis of Root's suggestion. Miller thought the matter adequately covered by the general provision for withdrawal from the League on two years' notice and the permissibility of suggesting revision of the Covenant at any time. Miller properly points out that the provision for inspection of armaments was not acceptable to the governments represented at Paris and that it still remains a desideratum for the future.[22] Root's point about immigration was indirectly taken care of by the insertion in Article XV of a provision which Taft had advocated, stating that on a domestic question the Council should not even propose recommendations for settlement. But since the text left it to the Council to determine what was a domestic question, Root was not satisfied.

Root sent a copy of his letter to Lord Bryce who was not averse to accepting all of his amendments. He agreed especially with Root's views about Article X because "The Conference is making, so far as we can learn, territorial settlements in many respects contrary to the principle of nationality, and sowing the seeds of future trouble. . . . In fact the Conference is creating for the League of Nations difficulties far beyond those which we had originally contemplated." If the United States should not come in, the League would collapse and without the League, things would be even far worse.

[22] *The Drafting of the Covenant*, Vol. I, pp. 298 ff., 377 ff., and 404.

CHAPTER XLV

"Wilson League against Americanized League"

THE revised text of the Covenant was submitted to a plenary session of the Peace Conference on April 28th, 1919. Wilson with great difficulty, great skill and great courage, had secured the insertion of the clause permitting withdrawal on two years' notice and of the recognition of the Monroe Doctrine. He believed that he had gone far enough to satisfy legitimate objections at home; he certainly had gone as far as Taft thought it necessary for him to go. The President was determined not to yield to what he believed was purely political or personal opposition. The revised text was published on April 28th and that evening Lodge had Root on the telephone. He had dictated a letter before he called, anxious to get Root's views, since Root's position was "very essential to our holding control of the Senate and of the vote in regard to the treaty. This last applies to the Democrats as well as Republicans." Lodge himself felt that very little improvement had been made; he had objections to all the amendments but he felt "as strongly as you and I both did when we talked together that the essential point is to have a majority in the Senate for necessary amendments and for handling the treaty when it is before us. To attain this object your help is vitally necessary." From that moment on through all the Senate debates, Root was in almost constant consultation or correspondence not only with Lodge but also with Brandegee, Kellogg, Lenroot, McNary and others. He never for a moment wavered from his position that the treaty should be ratified but that necessary amendments should first be made.

In June a tempest in a teapot was raised. The Senate had not been furnished with a copy of the whole peace treaty due to the fact that it had been agreed in Paris that no texts should be published until the treaty had been signed. But it was not secret, in the sense that many persons had copies of it and a number of them had brought copies back to the United States. One of these copies was brought back by Henry P. Davison, a Morgan partner who had been given it by Lamont and who sent it to Root with the request that he should not let anyone else know that he had it. Borah charged that "special interests" in New York had secured copies of the treaty; other Senators pitched in and an investigation was called for. Root wrote at length to Senator Brandegee on June 8th:

"The country is looking for leadership by the Republican Senate in a really critical emergency both internal & external. People are groping, uncertain; they are going to follow some affirmative. The President gives affirmatives. Can the Senate give any policy to follow? So long as grave questions are being sincerely discussed people will wait for the conclusion; but if they once feel that the Senate is merely quarreling about trifles instead of dealing with the great issues, the Senate will lose its audience & the President will lead. For a whole week the only thing that has struck the imagination in Senate proceedings is this squabble about the copies of the treaty which is mere piffle. There is no possible state of facts which would make it of real consequence; but I have taken pains to inquire & it is plain that the true facts will make the whole excitement a joke with the laugh on the Senate." He stated the facts of which the essence was that when the German suggestions for changes came in to the Peace Conference, it was decided to call in all copies of the treaty and not to let it be further discussed in public before a final draft was made. This was obviously, Root thought, sound policy. Root suggested that a private conference with Frank Polk at the State Department would confirm the facts as he had stated them and be sufficient to close that chapter.

Brandegee replied vigorously with much underscoring, stating in plain terms that he knew the situation in Washington and Root did not. The Senator and his group were "*Americans*" and "no international Banking Syndicate can terrify or bulldoze us!" He wrote a second letter the same day with some more veiled allusions to the firm of J. P. Morgan and warned Root that if he too were going "to bend in the middle or truckle to Wilson & Taft, God help you! I *know* what the situation is here. May be you think you know it better than I do.

"All right. If that is so—God help you!" and more of the same kind.

Root went to Washington, stayed at Lodge's home and appeared as a volunteer witness before the Senate Foreign Relations Committee

ELIHU ROOT WITH SENATOR HENRY CABOT LODGE ON HIS WAY TO TESTIFY
BEFORE THE SENATE FOREIGN RELATIONS COMMITTEE
ON THE "TREATY LEAK"

on June 11th. He had a talk with Chandler Anderson who had just returned from Paris and who confirmed his understanding about the situation; Anderson reported that people had taken first copies of the treaty as souvenirs and that when he and Davison left Paris there was certainly no restriction upon personal possession of copies. The subject was closed and Root was grateful for a letter from Murray Crane congratulating him on the way he had disposed of a troublesome issue.

The big issues remained and Root bent his efforts toward finding a solution. His second important contribution to the public record of the subject is found in his letter of June 21st, 1919, to Senator Lodge, which was given to the press. Like his letter to Hays, it was designed to do two things: first to set forth a sound constructive policy on the merits of the League issue and, second, to present that policy in such a way as to rally to his support the fluttering wings of the Republican party.[1] Root took up first the amendments which had been made in the Covenant and the extent to which they met his suggestions. Nothing had been done to meet his views about obligatory arbitration and the development of international law; he was as firmly convinced of the importance of these subjects but felt that the Senate could do nothing about them. Any suggestion covering them would mean the insertion of new matter in the Covenant which would require a reopening of the negotiation. Root did not favor that and his whole plan was based on a different theory. He suggested, however, that the Senate might well adopt an entirely separate resolution requesting the President to open negotiations for the perfecting of the system of arbitration and for the development of international law. He suggested also that when Europe had settled down again, the United States should insist upon a revision of the Covenant with the assurance that changed circumstances would permit material improvement. "Nothing has been done to limit the vast and incalculable obligation which Article 10 of the Covenant undertakes to impose upon each member of the League. . . ." The withdrawal clause left it doubtful whether the Council did not retain a veto power on the theory that the withdrawing member's obligations had not been fulfilled. The new clause on the Monroe Doctrine was "erroneous in description" and "ambiguous in meaning." The Council seemed to retain power to decide what questions are solely within the domestic jurisdiction of the

[1] Both letters are published in Men and Policies, pp. 251 and 269.

United States. These matters should be covered by action of the Senate, but "there is in the Covenant a great deal of very high value which the world ought not to lose."

Root then suggested a form of a resolution consenting to ratification which the Senate might adopt. He stated three terms or conditions: first, Article X was excluded entirely; second, the right of the United States to withdraw upon the required two years' notice was declared not to be dependent on any finding by the Council of the League; third, taking much of the language from his letter to Hays, an assertion of the maintenance of the traditional American attitude and a reservation of domestic questions. This last point was preceded by an introductory statement reciting Root's thesis that the United States did not want to interfere in Europe but was willing to respond to Europe's wish that it aid in preserving peace; he thought this very important because our negotiators at Paris seemed to have given the Europeans an idea that we had abandoned that old policy and wished to dictate solutions of European problems. Root stated that the adoption of a resolution of this type would not require reopening the negotiations since, unless another party to the treaty affirmatively objected, the treaty in so far as the United States was concerned, would stand as limited in the Senate's resolution which was to be made a part of the act of ratification. There was considerable argument on this point later but Root's position was correct. He opposed later attempts to insert in the resolution specification of the manner in which the consent of other states should be manifested. It was a point of some importance because there was criticism of reservations on the ground that they could not be accepted without reopening the whole negotiation which had closed at Paris; Root's suggested method of procedure strengthened the reservationists in supporting their line of action.

Root elaborated some of his points. Article X was "not an essential or even an appropriate part of the provisions for a league of nations to preserve peace." Wilson had called it the "heart of the Covenant"; Root considered it "an independent and indefinite alliance for the preservation of the status quo. . . . If it is necessary for the security of Western Europe that we should agree to go to the support, say, of France if attacked, let us agree to do that particular thing plainly, so that every man and woman in the country will understand the honorable obligation we are assuming. I am in favor of that. But let us not wrap up such a purpose in a vague universal obligation, under the impression that it really does not mean anything likely to happen." This was in line with his previous statement and with his later positions; it was the distinction between the American duty to carry out the liquidation of the war situation and the permanent participation in a league for peace falsely based on an alliance of the victors. White and others had impressed upon him the point that France would absolutely reject the League plan unless she were given the guarantee contained in Article X. Wilson had signed a separate treaty whereby Great Britain and the United States would have agreed to come to the aid of France in case of an unprovoked attack by Germany. Lodge says, in his book on the League of Nations,[2] that this treaty would never have had a chance of favorable consideration by the Senate, but he and other Republican leaders did agree to support it if Wilson would submit it separately. On November 3rd, 1919, Lodge wrote Root that he agreed with Root in favoring the French treaty subject to the deletion of a reference to the League Council. Root went to Washington, secured the assent of Lodge and others to this proposal and then discussed it with Lansing who was also favorable and who promised to take it up with Wilson. Nothing further was heard of it.[3]

It is interesting to note that Root's letter of June 21st to Lodge was discussed with Lodge, Knox and Brandegee in draft form which he took to Washington for that purpose.[4] Attached to the draft in Mr. Root's files are inserts written in his hand upon slips of Senate Memorandum paper. These inserts show the points which Lodge or the other Senators must have felt essential and which Root agreed to insert although he had not originally felt they needed attention. The first of these was the statement that he would be glad to see the Covenant separated from the Peace Treaty as Knox had proposed in his resolution. The next two concerned the clarification of the right of withdrawal. The third stated that if there were any doubt about his theory that silence would give assent to the reservations, it would be easy to ask the four principal powers represented in the Council

[2] *The Senate and the League of Nations*, p. 156.
[3] Root to the author, September 20, 1930 and December 21, 1933.
[4] Diary of Henry L. Stimson, entry of February 22, 1920.

whether they did in fact object.

The letter met with enthusiastic response on the part of those Republicans who sincerely desired ratification of the treaty provided that the objections which they considered vital were met. It of course did not please the "irreconcilables" who were opposed to ratification in any form. Congressman Julius Kahn of the House Military Affairs Committee wrote Root on June 24th: "In speaking to Republicans yesterday, they all agreed that you have hit upon a plan which will solve the problems that were causing them a great deal of uneasiness." In conversation, Hughes told Root that he agreed with the letter in every particular. Will Hays wrote Root on July 1st that Lodge had completed a canvass of the Republican members of the Senate with the following result: all of the forty-nine Republican senators would line up in favor of his last two reservations dealing with withdrawal, the Monroe Doctrine and domestic questions; on the other reservation dealing with Article X, forty-seven senators promised support—McCumber of North Dakota and McNary of Oregon were still doubtful on this point. Lodge was also assured that two Democratic senators, Reed and Gore, would support all three Root reservations and that possibly two more Democrats would come along. Lodge wrote confirming this poll on July 7th. He thought "the bulk of our men prefer reservations. The more I have thought of it the more satisfied I am that this is the right course to take. . . . Your letter had a very great effect as I knew it would. It brought us three or four supporters in the Senate, which is of great importance, at once."

Many have thought that Senator Lodge never actually favored ratification even with reservations; that his great and only desire was to defeat Wilson. There is persuasive evidence to support that view but his correspondence with Root does not.[5] It is not possible to say whether Root thought Lodge shared his viewpoint or whether he hoped to convert him to it. Lodge may at least have shared at this time the view which Root expressed in a letter to Adelbert Moot on July 11th. Root was sure that the adoption of the reservations would "interpose no obstacle whatever to the making of peace, unless it be that the President himself is unwilling to make peace without it [Article X], and of course in that case the responsibility would be his. I

[5] The evidence of Lodge's unqualified opposition is stressed in Fleming, *The United States and World Organization, 1920–1933* (1938), Chapters I and II.

should hardly think he would be willing to take it." July 25th, Senator Kellogg, a mild "reservationist," wrote to Chandler Anderson that most of the members of the Foreign Relations Committee were more interested in trying to beat the League than to get something constructive but that Lodge's position was the reverse.[6] In March, Breckenridge Long, analyzing the political line-up, believed Lodge would ultimately vote for the treaty, although Reed and Borah never would.[7]

In spite of the hopeful nature of Lodge's report on the effect of Root's letter, the matter was by no means settled. Taft was still opposing any reservations; Will Hays was sitting on the fence trying to draw all elements of the party together. Various individual senators kept finding new difficulties and proposing new amendments. On June 28th, the treaty was signed by the Germans and the President was reported from Paris to be opposed to any reservations on the ground that they would require the reopening of negotiations. He may have been strengthened in this view by the reported agreement on June 25th of the Lodge-Knox and Borah-Johnson groups to the effect that the other governments' acceptance of the reservations would be required. On July 10th, the day after his return from Europe, President Wilson laid the treaty before the Senate. He made no detailed comment upon the various objections which had been raised.

On July 17th, Hays informed Root confidentially that Taft had come around to the idea of reservations and had proposed the text of five. On the same day Wilson began a series of conferences with the moderate Republican senators. Taft's proposals were published on the 23rd. Root thought some of them "lacked precision" and he objected to the one on the Monroe Doctrine. He was quite ready to accept Taft's proposal, which reverted to the one Root had sent to Paris in March, that the United States should accept Article X for ten years; Taft had originally specified five years but had changed it after receiving information from French sources. But Root was afraid that such a reservation might be deemed an actual amendment to the Covenant which could not be accepted by silence under his general theory applicable to his own reservations. That was an important point, especially in view of Wilson's attitude and the reported decision

[6] Diary of Chandler P. Anderson.
[7] Long to Gordon Auchincloss, March 12, 1919, Breckinridge Long Papers, Library of Congress.

of the Foreign Relations Committee.

Root was spending the summer at Clinton as usual but he kept in touch by correspondence and by occasional trips to Washington. August 15th, Lodge besought his help in winning over Senators Kellogg and Colt who seemed uncertain. Otherwise Lodge thought that all the Republicans would vote for the reservations which Root had proposed. These reservations had now been broken up to separate the question of the Monroe Doctrine from matters of domestic policy and were spoken of as the four reservations. Lodge appealed to Root by pointing out the difficulties of his task as Republican leader: "Forty-nine men, two majority in the Senate, ranging from Borah to Colt, presents a variety of subjects to deal with and one not always easy to grasp." Root responded with canny letters to both Kellogg and Colt which were well received. Kellogg wrote him: "Your visit and your proposed reservations have done more to get the Republicans together and to clarify the situation than anything that has happened." Kellogg agreed entirely with Root about the acceptance of the reservations through silence, but many Senators shared the view upon which Lodge was insistent and which Root, at Lodge's request, had suggested in his letter, that the four principal powers should be required to state expressly their assent to the reservations. Root also took occasion in a letter to Lodge on September 10th to remark that "many friends of ratification with reservations in the Senate suspect that the extreme opponents of the Treaty are leading them along with a view not to any sort of reservation but to complete rejection. Of course, any such suspicion is liable to be very injurious. . . ." Meanwhile Chandler Anderson had also been in close contact with Lansing and with Senators Kellogg, Lodge, Brandegee and others, and had pulled a laboring oar in proposing drafts of reservations which he submitted to Mr. Root from time to time for comment. Root spotted a phrase which Anderson had taken from one of Wilson's writings and which Anderson had embodied in a preamble to his draft resolution. "Where did you get that?" Root asked. "Did you steal it from the White House, or did you pick it out of a garbage can?"

By the first part of September, much attention was attracted to the provisions of the treaty which left the Japanese in possession of Shantung instead of yielding to China's demand for its return. Senator Kellogg asked Root to draft a reservation on that point. Root complied with a mild reservation relieving the United States from any agreement with the settlement but he noted that we certainly were not going to send an army to drive out Japan any more than we had followed that course in respect of Germany whose claims Japan had taken over. If the United States insisted on deleting the Shantung settlement from the treaty, certainly Japan would not agree and neither would England or France. "It would be the height of folly for the Senate to insist upon impossible amendments to the Treaty. The amendments should be in aid of a Treaty of Peace, not destructive of it." Kellogg accepted Root's view and believed that he could rally other support for it. Later in September, Senator Edge appealed to Root for advice on several points and Root's reply won him to the view that reservations could be accepted by silent acquiescence.

In September also, Woodrow Wilson made his speaking tour of the West in an attempt to win the country to his side. He was a sick man and the inevitable breakdown came before the tour was completed. It was a tragic climax but it does not seem to have awakened any sympathy in Lodge or in Root. On September 10th, the Foreign Relations Committee made its report with a number of reservations which, Lodge told Root, had been reported for the sake of holding the ranks together but many of which would be killed on the floor of the Senate.[8] Lodge was convinced that unless strong reservations were included the treaty would be killed, but he indicated that they would ultimately concentrate on four, substantially the same as those which Root had proposed.[9] Root was especially opposed to the Johnson amendment which sought to deal with the bugaboo of the multiple votes of the British Empire; Root believed it to be quite unnecessary.[10]

Root seems to have taken little part in dealing with the reservations to Part XIII of the Treaty, the part which established the International Labor Organization. Root at first objected strongly to Part XIII, due not to any anti-labor views, but to his fear that a supernational body of considerable power was being established. He took the erroneous view that the treaty would permit individual labor representatives to hale the United States Government before a Commis-

---

[8] Diary of Henry L. Stimson, entry of September 26, 1919.
[9] Lodge to Root, September 29, 1919.
[10] Diary of Henry L. Stimson, loc. cit., and Root to Senator Edge, October 1, 1919.

sion of Inquiry.[11] As Root noted at the time, the labor covenant was but little discussed in the United States. It therefore did not symbolize the League and the United States joined the International Labor Organization in 1934 without the slightest political dither. Back in 1908 when Root was Secretary of State, Nicholas Murray Butler had proposed to him the desirability of convening an international labor conference and of planning for some kind of organization. Root had been entirely sympathetic with the idea but nothing came of it at the time.[12]

The test in the Senate came between November 7th and 19th. On the 18th, the process of voting on the individual reservations was completed, with fourteen adopted and many more defeated. In the proceedings on the following day, the thirteen Republican irreconcilables joined forty-two Democrats in voting against ratification of the treaty with the reservations; thirty-four Republicans voted in favor. The Democratic line-up against the reservations was assured by a letter from President Wilson to Senator Hitchcock asking his friends to take that course. After a vote to reconsider, an unconditional resolution for ratification was defeated by fifty-three nays to thirty-eight yeas. Congress then adjourned.

The result distressed Root. On November 12th, he had written to Senator Kellogg: "The real triumph for the Senate must be found in an acceptance by other powers of the Senate reservations. This would be the victory of established American policy speaking through the Senate, and it would condemn the President because it would show that he could have secured the terms included in the reservations if he had tried to do so or had been fit for his job. On the other hand, a failure by the other countries to accept the reservations would be both a failure of the Senate as a Treaty-making power and a vindication of the President by showing that he could not have got in the Treaty the things for which the Senate stands. Clearly, therefore, the Senate ought to make it as easy as possible for England and France and Italy and Japan to accept the reservations instead of making it as difficult as possible by putting in these requirements for an affirmative assent."

[11] Root to Albert Thomas, May 31, 1920; Diary of Henry L. Stimson, entry of June 3, 1919.
[12] Butler to Root, June 19, 1908; Root to Butler, July 30, 1908; Butler to Root, August 17, 1908.

On December 1st, he wrote to Judge George Gray: "The matter [of reaching a compromise] is much complicated by the fact that the friends of the Treaty precisely as drawn played into the hands of the irreconcilables who wished to defeat the Treaty in any and every form by maintaining a no-compromise attitude until the natural occasion for adjustment had passed and the Treaty had been rejected. At present the collapse of the President seems to leave no-one among his followers competent or willing to agree to anything. Of course, it is hardly practicable to get a modification on one side without some assurance on the other that it will be satisfactory. . . . I am much distressed by the whole business. . . ."

But Root was not prepared to give up. The new Congress convened the first Monday in December. On December 1st, Root wrote to Lodge congratulating him on his leadership: "It has been one of the greatest examples of parliamentary leadership that I have ever known or known of. I wish all the friends of the Treaty could understand that it is you who have given the Treaty its only chance for ratification,—a chance which the President in his wilful self-sufficient pride has rejected. It is evident that there will be overtures for some sort of compromise and adjustment."

Root believed it would be fortunate if there could be a face-saving modification of the reservations without sacrifice of essentials and he suggested changes which might be made. Lodge was truly grateful for the praise but impatient of the suggestions. He said they had offered Senator Hitchcock a chance to make suggested modifications before the vote and he had declined. Lodge had had to work hard to keep his forces in line and after Hitchcock's refusal could not accept any change. The treaty in his opinion "was killed by Wilson. He has been a marplot from the beginning." Lodge was getting weary of Taft and the others who were constantly asking that they make more concessions. "Why do they not put their pressure on Wilson and make him yield?" In particular, as in general, he rejected Root's suggestions. "It seems to me the next move is his [Wilson's], but I think he is incapable of making any move. I believe him to be much worse than the White House bulletins indicate." It was not a cheering prospect. But Lodge reconsidered. He says in his book [13] that he returned from the brief recess with the idea that an attempt should be made to reach an

[13] Lodge, op. cit., p. 192.

agreement; certainly his letter to Root does not confirm that point. Yet there was considerable public demand for some adjustment and a "Bi-partisan" conference of senators was convened on January 15th, 1920. For two weeks they considered the reservations agreeing to certain changes but finding it impossible to meet on others. Just what part Root played in these negotiations is not recorded, but he was in Washington just before they began and for several days while they were going on; it is unquestionable that he was consulted. One point agreed upon was his old idea that the reservations might be accepted by the other powers through silence or acquiescence instead of by an exchange of notes as specified in the Lodge reservations which the Senate had adopted on November 19th. Root would have been satisfied with the five Hitchcock reservations which Wilson, in a letter of January 28th, finally agreed to accept but it was too late then. Had the same proposal come from the Democrats even three months earlier, the treaty would probably have been ratified. Lodge reported the treaty back to the Senate and called it up for action on February 16th. Various modifications of the reservations were adopted. On March 19th, a resolution for ratification with the reservations as then adopted received forty-nine votes with thirty-five against; party lines were split on the vote, twenty-three Democrats voting or being paired in favor of ratification and twenty-three against. Lodge then moved to have the treaty returned to the President, which was passed by a vote of forty-seven to thirty-seven. Whether the responsibility rested on the President or on the Senate, the United States had refused to join the League of Nations.

On February 19th, 1920, just a month before the final vote in the Senate, Root had made an address as Chairman of the Republican State Convention in New York City. In the course of that address, he touched upon the League question, reiterating his hope that the treaty would be ratified with reservations. If the President would not "permit" that to happen, then he believed: "Immediately after the fourth of March, 1921, a Republican President should urge upon the society of nations the reform of the League Covenant, so as to make it establish the rule of public right rather than the rule of mere expediency. . . . A Congress of all nations should be called, to consider and declare what of international law still remains of binding force" and to provide for extending that law and for applying it to all justiciable disputes. This suggestion was severely criticized by both Senator Johnson and Senator Lodge, although Lodge had warmly approved an almost identical suggestion in Root's letter of June 21st, 1919. "I was trying to help them out," Root said to Colonel Stimson a little ruefully, "and now they take pleasure in parading over my prostrate form." [14]

After the treaty's defeat in the Senate, he wrote Ansley Wilcox on March 26th: "I quite agree with you that it is very desirable to have the public understand both in this Country and in Europe that the Senate's refusal to ratify the Treaty of Versailles does not mean a policy of isolation." A substantial majority of the Senate was recorded in favor of making an agreement that the United States would be "an associate with the powers who have entered into the League of Nations." On May 14th, as the Republican National Convention was drawing near, he wrote a stiff letter to Lodge:

> I hear rumors floating about that the Treaty Bitter-enders are going to force a plank into the platform or a compromise. I do not think it is quite a fair thing for them to attempt anything of the sort. They welcomed the policy of Treaty Reservations, asked for it, and urged it, at a time when they were being hammered all over the Country, and the Senate seemed in danger of being overwhelmed by a demand for some sort of a League of Nations. They have no right now to ask the Republican Party to repudiate the policy of which you became the protagonist and name saint in the Senate with their cordial cooperation. To my mind, there has been no political action during our generation which has called on public grounds for an explicit approval more imperatively than the defense by the Senate of our system of distributed powers as against President Wilson's assertion of unlimited authority. That defense rested upon the principle of reservations; and the declaration of the platform approving that policy ought to be perfectly clear and unmistakable. I hope you will not consent to shade such a declaration one hair's breadth by way of compromise. That declaration in the Republican platform is going to determine in the public mind and in history whether the work that you have been doing for the last year has been a great political achievement, a successful struggle for the maintenance of our system of government, or whether it has been a mere subterfuge

[14] Diary of Henry L. Stimson, entry of February 22, 1920.

for the purpose of defeating by indirection a Treaty which the Senate did not dare defeat directly.

But Lodge confessed in reply that he agreed with the bitter-enders in wishing to leave the future free for their President-elect. "I do not want to pledge myself to opposition to any League on March 4th or to the specific reservations that bear my name. The scene changes fast in Europe. We may need to strengthen the reservations. . . ." He hoped Root would try his hand at drafting a plank for the platform. With Lodge taking this position and with the irreconcilables trying to push him even further their way, Root must have been convinced that the Chicago Convention could not adopt the kind of plank he would have preferred, at least not without splitting the party. No record has been found of his sending a draft to Lodge, but in reply to requests from other Republican leaders, he prepared a plank. Ex-Senator Murray Crane was leading the pro-League forces at the Convention against the irreconcilable group. They reached a point in committee at which a fight on the floor of the Convention seemed inevitable, when Root's draft was produced and accepted without change.[15] It was a good piece of work in the sense that it accomplished its object of giving the two antagonistic camps a base on which they could unite; in other words, it was a perfect bit of political platform planking.[16] The Covenant was criticized but "The Republican party stands for agreement among the nations to preserve the peace of the world. We believe that such an international association must be based upon international justice and must provide methods which shall maintain the rule of public right by the development of law and the decision of impartial courts, and which shall secure instant and general international conference whenever peace shall be threatened. . . ." These were Root's old ideas to which he had held consistently but he would have much preferred at this time to see a flat statement that the Republican party favored joining the League of Nations with reservations. The Democratic platform really came closer to Root's view in favoring ratification with reservations "making clearer or more specific the obligations of the United States." But of course the Democrats played up the merits of the League and of

[15] Will H. Hays to Root, October 26, 1925; William Allen White to the author, June 29, 1938.
[16] Cf. Fleming, op. cit., pp. 33–34.

Wilson, while the Republicans played them down.

Root had been urged to go to the Convention as a delegate but had refused as early as February.[17] He knew what conventions were like and knew that he could not physically stand the strain of those long night sessions lasting until the small hours of the morning. As will be noted subsequently, he was in Europe helping to create the World Court when the Convention met. He preferred General Leonard Wood as the Republican candidate and would also have been glad to see President Nicholas Murray Butler of Columbia University nominated. "I am afraid, however," he wrote to Colonel Archibald Hopkins on May 31st, "that university presidents are rather at a discount in the public mind just at present, and that the very strength which Wood has exhibited upon the voters will lead to his destruction by a combination on the part of smaller men. I have never seen anything more idiotic in politics than the attempt to use [Senator Hiram] Johnson to beat Wood. Johnson is a very clever politician, and he has used the people who tried to use him, so that he appears to be a real danger with the pro-German vote and the Sinn Fein vote and the forces of discontent behind him. It is a dangerous thing to be too smart." Root advised privately with some of Wood's friends but wished to avoid active participation in the campaign and therefore gave no public support to any candidate. He had a high regard for Hoover's abilities also but did not believe that Senator Harding was of big enough calibre for the presidency.

Harding was nominated and in the ensuing campaign against Governor Cox, the Democratic nominee, indulged in even more vacillation on the League issue than the platform justified. On August 29th, he offered to the pro-Leaguers the statement that he was for a League of Nations which would take the best in the present organization and excise that which was bad. But on October 7th, he declared that he was seeking "not interpretation but rejection." In July and August, while Root was at The Hague working out plans for a World Court, President Lowell of Harvard, who was in London, relayed to Root reports from America which seemed to Lowell to suggest that Cox had given Harding the opportunity to come out flatly for ratification with the Lodge reservations. He begged Root to use his influence to steer Harding in that path. Root sent a confidential cable to Hays:

[17] Diary of Henry L. Stimson, entry of February 22, 1920.

"I meet many influential Americans who misinterpret our candidate's utterances as repudiating his vote for treaty with reservations, and as meaning irreconcilable opposition to any league. Unless prevented, there seems danger issue will become league against no league, instead of Wilson league unchanged against Americanized league, thus throwing into opposition many clergymen, women, and other good Republicans who strongly desire some league to preserve peace. Very serious situation may be created in Eastern States. Could not Taft's June 16th statement be supported? Consult Harding with my regards."

Hays replied that he realized the matter was of the utmost importance and that it would be attended to. A little later he cabled again to ask Root what he thought of Harding's pronouncing the League dead and proposing to transfer the "whole business" to the Hague Tribunal as a "going concern" with the usual statement that we would incorporate "all that is good and eliminating all bad from Versailles Covenant." He asked Root to cable to George Harvey care of Senator Harding. Root did so without any equivocation:

Declaration in which Hays asks opinion could not be defended. Hague Court cannot be made to cover anything but justiciable questions. Matters of State policy must be dealt with by Conference of Powers; see explanation in my letter to Hays, March 1919. Very unwise to declare League dead. That would be acceptance of issue as Wilson wishes to frame it League or no League instead of Wilson League against Americanized League. It would not be true. League has hardly begun to work, because terms of peace not yet enforced by victorious nations. Polish questions for example are properly being handled by Foreign Offices of Allies without any reference to League. They are not the League's business. In my opinion, a new deal here from beginning abandoning Versailles Treaty is impossible, and to attempt it would bring chaos, entire loss of results of war, and general disaster, involving United States. Only possible course is to keep Treaty, modifying it to meet requirements of Senate reservations and Republican platform, and probably in some other respects. The precise way in which modifications can be made best must be determined at the time in conference with the other parties. Impossible to forecast method, because conditions next March necessarily uncertain now. Central idea is that deadlock resulted from Wilson's perverse refusal to negotiate for consent of other powers to Americanization of Treaty, but that our new Administration will secure that consent. Separate declaration of peace was justified only by Wilson's refusal to act. After March 4th that will no longer be justifiable, unless other powers refuse consent to modification, which I do not anticipate. Don't allow Cox to drive you off the ground of Harding's Senate vote and our platform. Keep to the simple issue Americanization.

After his return to the United States, Root spoke at a meeting organized by the National Republican Club in New York City on October 19th. His sole subject was the League of Nations in the presidential campaign. He quoted the hopeful parts of the Republican platform and of Harding's speech of August 28th and declared that the Republican Party and candidate stood on the ground which he had advocated in his cables to Hays. If Cox were elected, he would renew the same old fight against the Senate reservations and the old deadlock would be renewed. If Harding were elected, he would re-open negotiations with the other powers for the acceptance of our reasonable reservations. Taft had been making the same plea. Both he and Root believed that if Cox were elected, since it was clear that the Republicans would still have their strength in the Senate, nothing could be done about the League.[18] Root, meanwhile, had been at work upon a statement which was eventually made public on October 15th, over the signatures of the famous "Thirty-one" leading Republicans. William H. Taft did not sign it but his brother, Henry W. Taft, did. So did President Lowell of Harvard, President Butler of Columbia, Herbert Hoover and Charles Evans Hughes. The argument was the same as that which Root advanced in his speech of October 14th. At the time, the paper caused a considerable stir, eliciting high praise and severe condemnation. It unquestionably had a great effect in turning toward Harding the votes of many sincere believers in the League. In retrospect it has been widely denounced as a disingenuous document. There is no doubt, however, that Root and other signers were convinced that their position was correct even though they may well have felt that it was making the best of a bad bargain. On October 23rd, Root wrote to Robert S. Brookings: "Before the paper signed by the 31 was prepared, Schurman and Hoover had received from Mr. Harding a most emphatic assurance that he had not changed, and

[18] Root to the author, September 6, 1930.

would not change from his speech of August 28th." Similar assurances had been given by Harding to others.[19] But on November 4th, Harding made a victory statement in which he declared that the League was dead. Whatever his deficiencies, Harding was certainly adroit at carrying water on both shoulders. The appeal of the "Thirty-one" was inspired largely by the hope that it would serve to keep Harding in line as a supporter of the League.[20]

Harding was overwhelmingly elected for reasons which Walter Lippmann admirably summarizes in his *Public Opinion:* [21] "The Republican majority was composed of men and women who thought a Republican victory would kill the League, plus those who thought it was the most practical way to procure the League, plus those who thought it the surest way offered to obtain an amended League. All these voters were inextricably entangled with their own desire or the desire of the other voters to improve business or put Labor in its place, or to punish the Democrats for going to war, or to punish them for not having gone sooner, or to get rid of Mr. Burleson, or to improve the price of wheat, or to lower taxes, or to stop Mr. Daniels from outbuilding the world, or to help Mr. Harding to do the same thing."

There is certainly nothing in the oft-repeated slogan that the election of 1920 was a referendum on the League in which the American people emphatically repudiated it.

There was a widespread belief that Harding would ask Root to be his Secretary of State. Root visited Harding in Marion, Ohio, during December, 1920, and discussed foreign policies with him in great detail, but Harding offered him no appointment. Root did not expect him to. He knew that a group of Senators, including Lodge, Knox and Brandegee, were strongly opposed to his appointment; they had just won a tremendous victory over the Executive and they intended to keep the control of foreign policy in their own hands. Lodge by this time was far away from Root's position in regard to the League, as were Knox and Brandegee, and they had a wholesome respect for Root's ability to carry through a policy to which they were opposed. Root thought the situation very similar to that which existed in

19 Fleming, op. cit., pp. 465–466.
20 Samuel McCune Lindsay to the author, December 15, 1937.
21 Pp. 195–196.

THE SENATE—"IT DOESN'T MATTER WHICH; I EXPECT TO BOSS THE FOREIGN POLICY MYSELF"

(Copyright, 1921, by N. Y. Evening Post, Inc.)

(A cartoon in the New York *Evening Post*, January 20, 1921)

Grant's time when Sumner was Chairman of the Foreign Relations Committee of the Senate.[22] Back on June 22nd, 1920, Taft had written President Lowell he thought Harding would offer Root the position. "But Root would not wish to take the place permanently and might say so; but the place would have a fascination for him if it offered him the opportunity of initiating our entry into the League and putting the matter through the Senate." [23] Taft visited Harding at Marion on December 24th, 1920, and learned that the President-elect had decided to appoint Hughes. When Taft told him that he had hoped he would take Root, Harding replied that "Root was an elder statesman in a different generation." Harding said that he planned to ask the great powers to send a commission to Washington to negotiate changes in the peace treaty and the League and declared that he would make Root the head of the American commission.[24] Taft made it clear later that he agreed with Root's diagnosis that Harding had been swayed by the opposition of members of the Senate.[25] Charles Hilles, Senator Wadsworth and all the leaders of the New York Republican organization joined in urging Harding to appoint Root and Wadsworth urged it personally upon Harding at Marion.[26] Root would probably have accepted if Harding had offered him the place, but he agreed with the political wisdom of the President-elect's decision and was pleased with the choice of Hughes.

Perhaps it was party loyalty which prevented Root and others of the "Thirty-one" from denouncing Harding's later inaction in regard to the League. They yielded too much to the hostile bloc in the Senate. So far as Root was concerned, he fell back on his patient long-range philosophy, working for the acceptance of the international court but no longer pressing for adherence to the League. In the spring of 1921, he still held to the belief that quite apart from the question of membership in the League, the United States should stand with its former allies until the war situation was fully liquidated.[27]

As the years went by and political passions in the United States

---

[22] Diary of Chandler P. Anderson, entries of January 11 and February 6–9, 1921.
[23] Taft Papers, Library of Congress.
[24] Ibid., memorandum to Mrs. Taft.
[25] Taft to Hilles, August 21, 1921, Taft Papers, Library of Congress; to the same effect, Diary of Charles S. Hamlin, Vol. 6, p. 95.
[26] Hilles to the author, November 29, 1935.
[27] Root to Colonel Bunau-Varilla, March 4, 1921.

provoked bitter recriminations against Woodrow Wilson and the League of Nations, and when the Republican Administrations adopted an attitude of discourteous aloofness from the League, Root felt ever more strongly that the American policy was wrong and discreditable. He was eager for an occasion to speak and to declare that he felt the United States had acted like a cad in repudiating its representative and then in attacking his handiwork.[28] The occasion came on December 28th, 1926, when the Woodrow Wilson Foundation made him the recipient of its award "in recognition of his services to humanity and the cause of peace through justice in helping to create the Permanent Court of International Justice." The story of his work in that cause will be told in the next chapter, but it is appropriate here to note his statement about the League of Nations. He pointed out that the United States was continuing to carry on international affairs through the old methods while Europe was operating through the new procedures of the League's machinery. "It is a very difficult thing to make a horse that trots and a horse that gallops pull evenly in the same team." What, he asked, would one expect after we had left our old friends and allies to carry on their new experiment without our expected aid? One would have expected expressions of sincere regret and of "a strong desire to do everything possible to prevent our staying out of the League from being injurious to our old friends and associates." Instead we had only harsh words and expressions of pleasure at any apparent failure of the League. And this despite the fact that "the League in the political field and the Court in the judicial field have been rendering the best service in the cause of peace known to the history of civilization—incomparably the best. . . . We have allowed insensate prejudice, camouflaged by futile phrases, to appear, but falsely appear, to represent the true heart of the American people with all its idealism, with its breadth of human sympathy, with its strong desire that our country should do its share for peace and happiness and noble life in all the world. . . . The repercussions of our domestic strife seem to have prevented the effectiveness of our noblest impulses." Root paid tribute to the fine spirit which had inspired the Woodrow Wilson Foundation to brush aside thoughts of old political opposition and to recognize identity of purpose in the pursuit of a high ideal. To carry forward that ideal, he at once donated

[28] Root in private conversation.

the award of twenty-five thousand dollars to the Council on Foreign Relations as a sustaining fund for its quarterly, *Foreign Affairs*, which has achieved the place of the most distinguished periodical in its field.[29]

In retrospect, particularly at a time when the fortunes of the League of Nations seem to have fallen to a very low depth, a survey of the difficulties which the League has faced and the obstacles by which its forward progress has been checked prove the sagacity of the two fundamental principles which Root stressed from the spring of 1918 when Colonel House first consulted him, down through the period of the Senate debates. The first was the inadvisability of asking nations to assume broad and vague general commitments for future action which, when the time came, they might be unwilling to fulfill. As he pointed out, the ill effects of a broken pledge are far more damaging than the refusal to make such a pledge. Even had the United States joined the League at the outset, who can say, for example, that the American people would have permitted their government to go further in the application of sanctions against Japan in 1931 or against Italy in 1935 than the actual members of the League were willing to go? Root's second point was that while the United States should be willing to continue its obligations as a co-belligerent by participating in the post-war pacification of Europe, no permanent league of peace could be built on the basis of an alliance of victors against the vanquished. Only recently has general opinion come to realize that the structure of the League must be reframed on the basis of a dispassionate examination of the world's problems far removed from the bitterness of the war period.

[29] His speech is reprinted in Special Supplement to *Foreign Affairs*, Vol. V, No. 2.

CHAPTER XLVI

"The World Court is now in the realm of practical politics"

ROOT's primary insistence upon the need for establishing an international court has been noted in preceding chapters. He deplored the absence of a provision in the draft Covenant imposing on the Council of the League a duty to create such a court. He had ceased to press the matter as an essential part of the Senate's reservations, however, when it became apparent that a court would be set up. In July, 1919, he had been sounded out as to whether he would accept an appointment on an international committee of jurists to frame a plan for a permanent court of international justice. Through Hunter Miller, House had sent Root a cabled message explaining that Sir Eric Drummond (later the first Secretary General of the League and then on the organization committee of the League appointed by the Peace Conference) had asked President Wilson to suggest a distinguished American lawyer to serve on such a committee. Wilson suggested Root's name and Sir Eric asked House to ascertain whether Root would be willing to serve immediately so that the plan for the court could be submitted to the first meeting of the Council of the League. Root may have thought that this was another "trap" like White's cable to Lodge and that his acceptance would make him a participant in League affairs and thus destroy his influence in the Senate debates. At the same time it revealed an encouraging intention on the part of the League to push forward the Court plan. He replied that while he appreciated the confidence implied in his selection, he did not think that it was wise for him "to entertain a proposal for such an appointment pending the action of the Senate upon the ratification of the Treaty."

On March 9th, 1920, the State Department transmitted to Root a formal invitation from Sir Eric Drummond, as Secretary General of the League of Nations, asking him to serve on the same Committee of Jurists whose appointment had been postponed. The Senate had now rejected the League Covenant and Root accepted. He sailed for Europe on June 1st aboard the *New Amsterdam*. The ten distinguished international jurists who had accepted the invitation to serve on this committee assembled at The Hague on June 16th and proceeded to elect Baron Descamps of Belgium as their Chairman and Judge Loder of Holland as vice chairman. Among the others were Lord Phillimore, a member of the British Privy Council who worked closely with Root, and Adatci, the Japanese Minister to Belgium, who remained a devoted friend of Root's through the rest of his life. Dr. James Brown Scott accompanied Mr. Root and assisted him throughout the sessions. Mrs. Root and their son Edward with his wife also went with him. There were always light moments with Mr. Root; his conversation abounded in little quips, epigrams, odd snatches of foolish verse, striking descriptive phrases, the summation of a personality in a few words:

"There is no other cereal besides oatmeal. You know I found I had been eating it for years and I gave it up because I was getting a little burr in my throat."

"You need never worry about your dignity; it's the only thing that can take care of itself."

> "The waiter dusted off the bread,
> 'It is not caviar,' he said."

"—— is a nice fellow but has a lambrequin mind."

Later Root reminisced: "I remember once at The Hague how everyone was talking at once, particularly the Latins. I have even forgotten what it was about. But after they had been at it for several moments, during which I could not understand one definite thing, they said 'Nous sommes en agrément' and then went on again. Phillimore had something to say and in the custom of the English courts, over which he had long presided as a judge, he waited in silence. He had a pencil and with it in his hand, like this, he began a very gentle 'Pardon', then another and on and on till it finally dawned on the Latins that here was one person who would not speak until they stopped. Almost all talk, all profanity, is for the satisfaction of the person who utters it. These Latins were not listening to one another, they were talking to get it off their own chests."

Root's first speech in the Committee was in support of a resolution which he offered proposing that they take as a basis for their work the acts and resolutions of the Second Hague Conference of 1907 and the plans which had been submitted by a group of five neutral powers, together with observations submitted by Germany and Austria who were·not represented on the Committee. Largely as a result of Root's instructions as Secretary of State to the American delegates to the Hague Conference in 1907, that body had drawn up a plan for a Permanent Court of Arbitral Justice. The plan had never taken effect because of a failure to agree upon the method of selecting judges—a prime difficulty which Root solved in these Committee meetings of 1920. Root wanted to show the continuity between their labors in 1920 and the progress which had been made before, and also to display appreciation of the later proposals. In substance, the Committee accepted his suggestion.

Root's solution of the impasse which blocked progress in 1907 was based upon American experience. He called attention to the compromise adopted in framing the Constitution of the United States whereby the small states were satisfied with equal representation in the Senate and the large states were satisfied with representation in the House proportioned on the size of their population. A like antagonism between the large and small nations had blocked the formation of an international court with a permanent bench; the large powers were unwilling to go into a court dominated by the small states and the small states were unwilling to have the large powers control the court. Root proposed that they take advantage of the existence of the two new bodies—the Council and Assembly of the League of Nations. The Council was dominated by the large powers and the Assembly was controlled by the small states. He suggested that these two bodies should ballot concurrently but separately on a list of nominees and that those persons receiving a majority of votes in both bodies should be declared elected. In precisely the same way, the two Houses of the Congress of the United States vote separately on bills which are before them. When the Senate and House are deadlocked, a conference committee of both houses is appointed to reach a compromise and their proposals are referred back to each house for adoption. In like manner, Root proposed a conference committee to break a deadlock between the Council and the Assembly.

In regard to nominations, he vigorously opposed the suggestion that they should be made by governments. He thought it of the utmost importance that the judges should be selected solely on the basis of eminent qualification for the office and not for political reasons. He therefore favored the plan which was ultimately adopted, whereby the national groups in the panel of the Permanent Court of Arbitration, which had been established by the First Hague Conference in 1899, should make nominations of four persons, not more than two of whom could be of their own nationality. The combined list of nominees would then be submitted to the Council and to the Assembly for balloting. In accordance with his view, it was also provided that in electing judges, consideration should be given to the need for having representation of "the main forms of civilization and the principal legal systems of the world." The whole scheme for electing judges has worked admirably and without serious friction, even since the Council of the League has been enlarged to fifteen members which has eliminated the absolute majority originally controlled by the large powers.

The other principal point for which Root argued strenuously and successfully had to do with the nature of the court's jurisdiction. Traditionally, international courts had been resorted to only when both disputing states agreed to their jurisdiction in each particular case. It has not been possible, as in the national administration of justice, for one party to hale the other into court against his will. Root believed that this new permanent international court which they were creating should have obligatory jurisdiction and he pointed to the growth of arbitration treaties as indicating that states were now willing to take that step. He was insistent, however, that governments would not accept such a plan unless they were assured that the Court would strictly confine itself to applying international law and would not, as many arbitrators had in the past, wander off into deciding cases on the basis of their individual notions of what was "just" or what would make a reasonable diplomatic adjustment. He made it clear that he was not talking in general about the nature of the judicial function but that he was concerned with the possibility of securing acceptance of obligatory jurisdiction. Although the exact wording Root favored was not adopted, the ultimate result was satisfactory to him and followed his chief aims.

Root and his English colleague collaborated in preparing and submitting to the Committee what was known as the Root-Phillimore plan. Of this plan Root was the chief architect and the plan, in turn, was the main foundation on which the Court was built. Lord Phillimore in writing to Root six years later could refer to "your and my Court of International Justice. I think we may, between ourselves at any rate, call it that; yours at any rate." As Root told the New York City Bar Association shortly after his return in the fall, he and Lord Phillimore, as representatives of the common-law system, frequently found themselves "up against a granite wall" and that he assumed the continental lawyers found themselves in similar difficulties when they tried to understand the Anglo-American point of view. But long patient effort brought about understanding and reconciliation of ideas which resulted in the final preparation of what is known as the Statute of the Permanent Court of International Justice. This Statute was transmitted to the Secretary General of the League of Nations along with several recommendations which included Root's favorite idea for proceeding with the codification of international law. The plan then ran the gauntlet of study in the Council and in the Assembly of the League where various modifications were introduced. To Root's regret, they struck out the provision for the obligatory jurisdiction of the Court because the great powers—especially Great Britain—were not ready to accept it. In its place, however, they inserted a provision in Article 36 of the Statute whereby any state may make a declaration accepting the obligatory jurisdiction of the Court on terms of reciprocity or otherwise. Root, while regretting the failure to accept the proposal for obligatory jurisdiction, appreciated the reasons for its rejection and considered the final plan satisfactory.

Both to the Committee at The Hague and to the Bar Association in New York later, Root quoted his favorite line about the dog going to Dover "leg over leg." On the latter occasion he amplified it with another homely analogy: "Every step forward has to come in contact with the ingrained habits, preconceptions, involuntary reactions of vast multitudes of people, and they have got to be treated just as a nervous horse is treated. If you go at him too fast, you get into trouble." Before Root died in 1937, the so-called "optional clause," accepting the obligatory jurisdiction of the Court, had been signed by fifty-two states, including Great Britain, France, Italy and Germany. But the United States had not even accepted the Court without this feature. "A prophet is not without honor save in his own country."

Immediately after the conclusion of the work of the Committee at The Hague, Root went to London where, on behalf of the American donors, he presented to the British people St. Gaudens' statue of Lincoln, a replica of the one in Lincoln Park, Chicago. The unveiling of the statue on July 28th in its prominent and dignified location near Westminster Abbey took place in the rain, but rain is familiar to London crowds and the occasion was not marred. The principal speeches by Root and Lloyd George, with Bryce presiding, had already been delivered in Central Hall. The English press was unreserved in its praise of Root's speech and the London *Times* reported that he drew tears from the eyes of many who heard him read passages from some of Lincoln's messages, particularly that of sympathy with the Lancashire cotton spinners.

Root took advantage of the same visit to Europe to fulfill his duties as an arbitrator. In 1913, the Governments of Great Britain, France and Spain had signed with the Portuguese Government a treaty for the arbitration of claims which the first three countries had against Portugal as a result of the expropriation of religious properties after the revolution which established the Portuguese Republic. Root was chosen as President of the arbitral tribunal of three members which was formed from the panel of the Permanent Court of Arbitration in accordance with the plan agreed upon through the Convention for Pacific Settlement of International Disputes signed at The Hague in 1907. The outbreak of the World War had prevented the tribunal from meeting in the fall of 1914 as it had planned to do and Root convened their session at The Hague in September, 1920. The other arbitrators were Jonkheer de Savornin Lohman of the Netherlands and Dr. Lardy of Switzerland. The occasion gave Root particular satisfaction because it was the first meeting of a tribunal of the Permanent Court of Arbitration to meet in the Peace Palace at The Hague. He was also pleased to participate in a demonstration that the old Permanent Court of Arbitration had survived the war and would continue to coexist with the new Permanent Court of International Justice. The tribunal rendered unanimous decisions on all of the claims presented, allowing some and disallowing others. It is interesting to note that Root, always sensible of the propriety of adjusting his own methods to those of the people with whom he was working in international affairs, conducted his official correspondence on the case in French and participated in framing a judgment which is cast in the continental rather than in the Anglo-American form. There exist also notes in his own hand written in French for remarks to be made at the public sessions of the Tribunal. He spoke French with an American accent and not fluently but he had a reasonably good understanding of it.

Root had passed his seventy-sixth birthday when Harding was inaugurated on March 4th, 1921, and had earned retirement and rest but he had no easy time in attaining it. In the summer of that year, the first elections to the bench of the World Court were under way with nominations being made by the various national groups. Five countries nominated Root but he declined to be a candidate. "I can't take the World Court place," he wrote Taft on August 21st. "Several countries have been good enough to suggest it, much to my gratification of course but it would mean living in Europe for the rest of my life & I am too old to transplant. Nor would I ask it of Mrs. Root at her age. . . ." Consideration for his wife again was sufficient to turn the scales; he mentioned her also in explaining on September 13th to his old friend Willard Bartlett why he would not accept the Court nomination. It was a sign of his affection—as it had been in a different way with Roosevelt—that he liked to tease her but never to do what she did not wish unless some consideration of public duty drove him to unwelcome action.

But there were other reasons of a less sentimental character for refusing the Court nomination. He thought he had done his part in helping to establish the Court "and there are ever so many men who will do the actual Court work better than I," he wrote in his letter to Willard Bartlett. He knew also that Harding wished him to serve on the American delegation to the forthcoming Disarmament Conference in Washington and he felt he could render more important service there. To his colleague on the World Court Committee, Lord Phillimore, he expressed much the same point of view, adding that he hoped for the election of John Bassett Moore who had been nominated by the Italian group. He "would be much more useful than I. He has an accurate mind, great learning in International Law, and practical experience in International affairs. . . ." Moore was elected and served with great distinction.

In the matter of nominations, an unfortunate situation arose in the United States. On June 2nd, Sir Eric Drummond, Secretary General of the League of Nations, had sent in due course a letter to Root and the three other members of the American group on the panel of the Permanent Court of Arbitration, asking for nominations by the American group for judges to be elected to the new Permanent Court of International Justice. In the usual way, these letters had been sent through the United States Department of State; somehow they were placed on file in the Department and not forwarded. It seems incredible that such action could have been deliberate, but the State Department at that time had adopted the practice of not replying to communications from the League; had not President Harding proclaimed its decease? Root and the other members of the American group were of course not aware that the invitation had been sent. On June 1st, Äke Hammarskjöld, who was to be the first Registrar of the Court, wrote Root that invitations to make nominations were being sent. On June 11th, Lord Phillimore wrote that he understood the invitations had been sent. During July, Root wrote to several correspondents that no invitations had yet been received by the American group. He conveyed the same information to Hammarskjöld on July 14th. July 27th, Root wrote Phillimore that he had not inquired of the State Department whether invitations had been received because he thought action could be taken under more favorable conditions if he let the matter work itself out in due course. It may be that Lord Phillimore took the hint and passed the word along, because on August 13th Drummond cabled direct to each of the four American members of the Permanent Court of Arbitration, saying that he had had no reply to his earlier communication and requesting early action. Root immediately wrote to Secretary of State Hughes who replied on the 16th enclosing the communications addressed to Root, John Bassett Moore, Judge Gray and Oscar S. Straus. He was unable to state how it had happened that they had been filed in the Department. Root at once cabled Drummond that he had now received his messages and that he was trying to gather the American group for a meeting "to determine whether under the circumstances we have authority to comply with your invitation." The circumstances were, of course, that the United States had taken no step toward joining the Court and the Administration had made no move toward collaboration with the League. Straus and Gray both objected to the suggestion that there was any reason why they should not make nominations but they were finally persuaded.

After consultations with the other members of the American group, Root wrote to John Bassett Moore, Gray and Straus on September 12th:

> After our meeting in New York on the 7th I went to Washington and had an interview with Secretary Hughes. He said that he had given the subject of our action under the invitation to nominate candidates for the Court very careful consideration. He had come to the conclusion that as we were acting under an appointment by the President and were called upon to act as members of the Court of Arbitration under that appointment it would be impossible to prevent our action from being regarded as in effect done by the government of the United States. That being so he felt bound to form and express his views upon the subject.
>
> After very full consideration he had reached the conclusion that for the American group in the old Court of Arbitration to make nominations for the new Court under the covenant of the League of Nations would involve serious risk of immediate controversy which might be very injurious to the success of the important policies the government is now pursuing, and in his view the nominations ought not to be made by us. I do not undertake to give the Secretary's words but to state as accurately as possible the substance of what he said. He explained quite fully the reasons for the conclusion which he stated, but I will not repeat them because you already understand them.
>
> Under these circumstances I suppose it is quite impracticable for us to make the nominations and I have drafted for your consideration a form of a telegram to Sir Eric Drummond based upon that view. . . .

The other members finally concurred and a telegram was sent to Drummond just as the balloting began at Geneva; the American group "Reluctantly reached the conclusion" that they were not entitled to make nominations. There is no doubt that all the members of the American group were "reluctant," and it can not be doubted that the then existing situation was the determining factor despite the legal technicality on which their action was based. Root had already agreed to serve on the American delegation to the Disarmament Con-

The Committee of Jurists Who Drew Up the Statute of the Permanent Court of International Justice at the Peace Palace in The Hague

(*Right to left*) James Brown Scott, Elihu Root, Mineichiro Adatci, Lord Phillimore

ference. He was aware that the convening of this Conference was the first attempt of the new Administration to launch some plan along the line of international cooperation and he must have been receptive to Hughes' arguments that it would be most unwise to antagonize the Senate and risk a retaliatory battle against ratification of the results of the Disarmament Conference. But the action of Root and his three colleagues can not be called political in the partisan sense; otherwise the two Democrats, Gray and Moore, would not have acquiesced so readily.

If the legal reason advanced had been a real bar, the American group would still have lacked authority to make nominations on the subsequent occasions when they were asked to do so, since the United States had still withheld ratification from the World Court treaty. But on these subsequent occasions, the American group did make their nominations. When, in the sessions of the Committee of Jurists at The Hague in 1920, Root had advocated the plan for nominations by the members of the Permanent Court of Arbitration, he did so on the ground that this scheme would eliminate political considerations from influencing the nominations; "why should governments speak in making up the list of candidates?" he asked. But he was speaking then to the question of political dictation of the choice of certain individuals and in so far as the American group has been concerned, that type of political interference has never occurred.

In 1928, when Judge Moore resigned from the bench of the World Court, Root felt that in view of the continued fight on the Court in the United States, particular care should be used in nominating his successor with a view to strengthening American popular support of the Court. Mr. Hughes, who had just retired as Secretary of State, was well selected. Upon his resignation from the World Court bench to become Chief Justice of the United States in 1930, the mantle fell upon the next Secretary of State, Frank B. Kellogg, who had also been in the Senate. By 1935, however, when Judge Kellogg resigned, the World Court had ceased to be a current political issue and Root did not feel that they were under the same necessity of selecting one who had been prominent in official life. The American group nominated Professor Manley O. Hudson of the Harvard University Law School who had made himself the outstanding authority on the Court among American scholars; he was elected to fill the balance of Kellogg's unexpired term.

The steps involving the Court which led from the summer of 1921 to the political Sargossa Sea of 1935 found Root working quietly to further American adherence to the Court which he labored so diligently and so successfully to bring into being. It was not very long after Harding's inauguration that it became apparent that the entry of the United States into the League had become a dead issue politically, despite some attempts at revival. The question of adherence to the World Court took its place. The irreconcilables were resolved not to yield an inch and with the effective support of the Hearst press, they succeeded in convincing many Americans that the advocates of American adherence to the World Court were merely trying to get the United States into the League by the "back door." They made it a point always to refer not to the "World" Court but to the "League" or "League's" Court.

On September 6th, 1921, President Harding wrote to Root that the Attorney General had told him of a talk with Root in which Root had suggested some action in connection with the World Court. Harding was inclined to think they should move more slowly in international matters until after the Disarmament Conference but he had so much confidence in Root's wisdom that he would like to have his suggestions. The nature of Root's reply does not appear in his files since he went immediately to Washington and conferred with both the President and Secretary Hughes.

On February 24th, 1923, President Harding submitted the World Court treaty to the Senate with a request for its consent to ratification subject to four conditions and understandings which were set forth in an accompanying letter from Secretary Hughes. A number of bills on the subject were introduced in the Senate but nothing was done. In April and May, Root was at the White House and it was reported that he talked with the President about the Court.

From the fall of 1923 through February, 1924, Root was ill; a stone was removed from the kidney in January and he returned home from the hospital on February 5th. June 4th, 1924, on the eve of the Republican Convention, Will Hays wrote to him that the President had asked him to request Root to draft a plank on the Court for the Republican platform. Root complied. The platforms of both the Republican and Democratic parties endorsed the Court and on December 3rd, 1924, President Coolidge again commended the subject to the favorable attention of the Senate with one additional reservation. Senator Lodge at this time was wholly opposed to the Court, considering that it was tied up with the League and that it should be wholly revamped with a new set of judges. He was bitter against John Bassett Moore for accepting an election to the bench, since he believed that no real American should have anything to do with it.[1] On April 27th, 1923, he wrote Root at length explaining his objections which were largely against what he considered the multiple votes of the British Empire, the Dominions being separate members of the League. But he summed up his opposition in the sentence which reflected a prevailing misapprehension: "The trouble with the proposed court is that it takes us into the League." Lodge had not been persuaded by Root's letter of the previous day in which Root explained to him the development of the Dominions toward independent statehood. "In general," Root wrote, "I feel sure that it is very bad policy for us to take the position of thrusting sticks into the wheels of these people while they are trying to work out their serious problems. . . ."[2] Root was interested in actualities and was convinced, as proved to be the case, that the Dominions would vote independently and not as mere echoes of the will of Downing Street. The United States could have exercised just as much influence over the votes of states like Panama and Cuba.

To some it seemed that Root himself cooled a little in the fall of 1924. There had then been proposed at Geneva what was known as the Geneva Protocol which aimed to perfect the Covenant as a means of checking resort to war. Root did not look with much favor upon the Protocol but correctly anticipated that it would not be accepted by the Great Powers. The difficulties of the European situation and the renewed Japanese insistence upon questions of immigration apparently made him feel that it might be unwise for the United States to participate in the Court at that time.[3] But if this was his view in that fall, it was a brief and temporary attitude. President Coolidge, in his Inaugural Address of March 4th, 1925, again endorsed the Court and on April 6th, he wrote to Root asking him for a memorandum on

---

[1] Diary of Chandler P. Anderson, entry of December 26, 1923.
[2] Both letters from the Lodge Papers, Massachusetts Historical Society.
[3] Diary of Chandler P. Anderson, entry of November 13, 1924.

the subject. He asked for a further memorandum on the controversial question of advisory opinions a month later, and Root's replies to these inquiries show not only a fervent desire that we should support the Court, but also a very warm and friendly feeling for the League. While showing that the Court was independent of the League, he scoffed at the thought that the other nations of the world could be persuaded to abandon the League itself. ". . . for Americans instead of striving to reduce the unavoidable injury done by our abstention from this organization, to hate it and condemn it and try to injure it, while we are not members of it, is monstrous." This was the theme he stressed in accepting the Woodrow Wilson award in 1926.

The Senate began its debate of the World Court issue on December 17th, 1925, taking as a basis the resolution of Senator Swanson, Democrat of Virginia, which embodied the Hughes-Coolidge reservations. The debates were prefaced by a further endorsement from President Coolidge in his Annual Message of December 8th. Root engaged in no barnstorming for the Court but he followed the trend of public opinion and its stimulation with closest attention through the American Foundation. This organization had been established by Edward Bok in continuation of the work of the committee which took charge of his American Peace Award. Under the efficient direction of Miss Esther Everett Lape, the American Foundation sponsored World Court Committees through many of the states and sought to bring local pressure to bear upon the various senators. Miss Lape constantly consulted Mr. Root on questions of strategy as well as on matters of substance which were raised by questioners. When, therefore, in September, 1925, George W. Wickersham wrote Root to interest him in participating in a World Court Conference in Washington for the purpose of influencing the pending Senate action, Root flatly refused on the ground that such a meeting would be a great blunder. "The gathering of distinguished gentlemen from the eastern seaboard at Washington for the perfectly plain purpose of overawing the Senate would inevitably cause resentment and give an excuse for a lot of wavering senators to vote against the Court as a personal declaration of independence. What do you suppose a senator from Kansas or Minnesota or Arizona would say if told that such a meeting as you propose shows the public opinion of the United States? He would laugh at you and would take special pains to show that he

could not be influenced in that way, by voting against it." A group
of eastern leaders did organize the National World Court Committee
which operated sporadically until 1934. At times it reached a point
of great efficiency, but through lack of funds permitting a permanent
organization, it was not able to do the same kind of consistent steady
educational work which was done by the American Foundation. Root
cooperated with this Committee also but not as intimately as he did
with the American Foundation.

The Senate, defeating a filibuster by the anti-leaguers through the
adoption of the cloture rule, consented on January 27th, 1926, to
ratification of the Court Protocol, subject to five reservations and two
"understandings." So much has been written about the Senate reservations that it seems unnecessary here to do more than recall those aspects which affected Mr. Root's part in the subsequent history of the
controversy.[4]

The fifth reservation was the one which caused trouble thereafter.
Article 14 of the Covenant of the League provides that the Court
"may also give an advisory opinion upon any dispute or question
referred to it by the Council or Assembly." The Statute contained no
provision dealing with advisory opinions, but the Court had taken
the proper view that it had authority to exercise this function. There
was at first a fear that the Court might become a secret adviser to
the political organs of the League and thus lose its purely judicial
character. This question was thrashed out in the Court itself where,
under the leadership of Judge John Bassett Moore, rules of procedure
were adopted assuring the public and judicial nature of such opinions.
Moreover, on July 23rd, 1923, the Court rendered its opinion, or
absence of opinion, in the Eastern Carelia case. This was a dispute
between Finland and Russia which the former state had referred to
the League Council and which the Council had referred to the Court
for an advisory opinion. Russia was not a member of the League and
refused to cooperate. The Court held that it could give no opinion
because it "is well established in international law that no state can,
without its consent, be compelled to submit its disputes with other
states either to mediation or to arbitration or to any other kind of

---

[4] See for example, Quincy Wright, "The United States and the Court," *International
Conciliation*, April, 1926, No. 219, and Jessup, "The United States and the World
Court," World Peace Foundation Pamphlet, Vol. XII, No. 4 (1929).

pacific settlement." Moreover, "The Court, being a court of justice, can not even in giving advisory opinions, depart from the essential rules guiding their activity as a court." But in the United States it was argued that the Court could change its rules and reverse its ruling in the Carelia case and that these points must be safeguarded. The opponents of the Court were much strengthened by receiving the support of Judge Moore who contributed to framing the fifth reservation, although his part in the matter was not at the time made public. The fifth reservation declared that the Court should not render an advisory opinion except publicly and after due notice and hearing, "nor shall it, without the consent of the United States, entertain any request for an advisory opinion touching any dispute or question in which the United States has or claims an interest." It was maintained by some that this last proviso was designed merely to put the United States on an equality with the states in the League Council, any one of which could block a request for an advisory opinion. Whether or not this was true depended upon a point of League constitutional law which had not yet been determined, namely whether such requests had to be made by a unanimous vote or whether a majority vote would suffice. Unquestionably some senators supported this reservation because they thought it might help to block American adherence; others voted for it as an innocuous concession to the opposition; some thought it really necessary to protect the United States and some may have thought with Judge Moore that it was desirable for the future welfare of the Court itself. So far as the interests of the United States were concerned, it was a tempest in a teapot because advisory opinions were admittedly not binding and the United States would have been legally and morally free to disregard such an opinion with which it did not agree. Moreover, the Court was technically free to render advisory opinions in matters concerning the interests of the United States even if the United States did not adhere to the Court Statute; the more fully we participated in the work of the Court and of the Council, the better would be our position to protect our own interests.

Root was not particularly opposed to the reservations. He explained to Lord Phillimore in a letter of July 27th, 1926, that while they might seem formidable, they were really designed merely to put the United States on a footing of equality with the League members. He argued in favor of the fifth reservation as an assurance of the perpetuation of the doctrine announced by the Court in the Eastern Carelia case.

The Senate had also inserted in its resolution an utterly stupid and wholly unjustifiable requirement that the signature of the United States to the Court Protocol should not be affixed until the reservations had been accepted by "an exchange of notes" with the other signatories, forty-seven in number. This was a clear invasion of executive prerogative with which Root had no sympathy. The President or the Secretary of State had the constitutional power to obtain the indication of assent in any way it pleased, but Secretary Kellogg was too timid to defy the Senate and President Coolidge, as Root once remarked, "did not have an international hair in his head."

The other states, having a common interest in the Senate reservations, naturally decided to confer. They would normally have done so through their routine meetings in the Council and Assembly of the League, but out of deference to American susceptibilities, they called a special conference of signatories which met in Geneva in September, 1926. It was apparent that the meaning of some of the reservations was not clear and since the United States refused to attend the conference, no official explanation was forthcoming. Secretary Kellogg declared that the reservations were "plain and unequivocal" which they obviously were not. The Conference members pored over the record of the debates in the Congressional Record and were more confused than ever. Showing great good will, they finally embodied their conclusion in what was known as the Final Act. They expressed no great concern about the first four reservations or even the first half of the fifth. But the latter part of the fifth reservation which prevented the Court from giving an opinion without the consent of the United States if that country but "claimed an interest," gave them pause. The advisory opinions of the Court were proving to be valuable and strictly judicial and the small states particularly were unwilling to see that function of the Court hampered. There was nothing to indicate how the United States would declare its interest nor how long the process would take. If Congress were not in session, would they have to wait until it reconvened? As already noted, the question of unanimity versus majority votes was still unsettled; they were not willing to give the United States a preferred position but were willing

to give it the equality which they understood it required. They therefore suggested that the opposing vote of the United States should be
given the same weight as the vote of any member of the Council
or Assembly.

The United States received information about the results of this
meeting but did nothing about it until Root again appeared on the
center of the stage.

Root was meanwhile passing through a distressing time. For several
years Mrs. Root suffered intensely from arthritis. She died on June
8th, 1928, just five months after she and Mr. Root celebrated their
golden wedding. It had been a long and devoted companionship and
during her final illness, Mr. Root was constantly with her, eagerly but
helplessly trying to make her more comfortable. His own health broke
under the strain and he had the first attacks of serious heart trouble.
For months he had to avoid even the slightest physical exertion. Yet
throughout that trying period, he could not escape the responsibilities
imposed upon him by his great abilities, his international reputation
and the constant demands of those who turned to him for the benefit
of his wisdom on affairs of public importance. Secretary of State Kellogg, for example, consulted Root while he was ill about the early
stages of the negotiations resulting in the Briand-Kellogg Pact for the
"Outlawry" of War.[5] Senator Borah, who conducted the fight in the
Senate for consent to ratification of that treaty, appealed to Root
for advice on the need for reservations. Root warmly endorsed the
treaty and emphatically declared there was no need for reservations.[6]
In response to her appeal for advice, Root wrote Mrs. Ogden Reid
that he thought her paper, the New York *Herald Tribune*, should
support the Pact.[7]

On December 14th, 1928, the Council of the League decided to
invite a committee of experts to meet in Geneva for the purpose of
considering whether in the light of seven years' experience it was desirable to make any changes in the Statute of the Court. They invited
Mr. Root to serve as a member of that committee. It meant a winter's
voyage across the Atlantic in his eighty-fifth year; it might well be that

[5] Frank B. Kellogg to Root, December 23, 1927; Diary of Chandler P. Anderson,
entry of May 14, 1928.

[6] Telegram William E. Borah to Root, January 13, 1929; telegram Root to Borah,
January 14, 1929.

[7] Elizabeth Mills Reid to Root, July 24, 1928; Root to Mrs. Reid, July 30, 1928.

MRS. ELIHU ROOT

he would not return. But he saw a chance to make a last effort to bring about American adherence to the Court and he accepted. It was decided that the present author should accompany him. When I saw him at his apartment on January 19th and asked him what his plans were after the meetings ended, he replied smilingly: "To get back alive if possible."

The Council had not originally contemplated that this committee would deal with the question of American adherence and it was in fact due to the insistence of Arthur Sweetser, American member of the League Secretariat, that the invitation was extended to Mr. Root. His acceptance was met in Geneva with amazement and delight. Immediately it began to be suggested that perhaps the American impasse could be discussed at the same time.

At Secretary of State Kellogg's suggestion, Root went to Washington on February 2nd and had long talks with the Secretary, and with several Senators, including Swanson, Walsh and Borah. To the last he wrote an ingratiating letter on January 17th:

> Now that you are through with the multilateral treaty renouncing war as an instrument of policy, I would like to go over to Washington and have a talk with you about the World Court statute. A number of the European States want to get that statute amended and a Committee of gentlemen supposed to be expert jurists has been created to study the subject and make recommendations. I have accepted a place on that Committee and shall have to go over to Geneva very soon to attend a meeting. I wish enlightenment before I go. . . .
>
> I think the concluding paragraph of your report on the multilateral treaty sufficiently saves the treaty from being involved in any confusion. You have done a fine piece of work and I congratulate you.

Root was hopeful that Borah's experience as proponent of the Briand-Kellogg Pact would make him less of an obstructionist than he had been in the past. Root already had roughly in mind the solution which he thought might be secured and he learned that in principle his idea was acceptable to all these men. President-elect Hoover sent him a cordial and confident message of farewell. Root helped Kellogg draft a note to the states who had signed the Court treaty, introducing a tone of friendliness to the League and of confidence in the possibility of American adherence. This note was sent on February 19th while Root was on the ocean and, as he planned, helped to create the cordial atmosphere which he found in Geneva.

On February 15th, 1929, his eighty-fourth birthday, he boarded the *Augustus* and started on his last international mission. No one who saw him walking vigorously around the deck in a big shaggy overcoat which his oldest son gave him as a steamer present and which he called his "woolly-bear coat," would have thought of his age or the long trying illness through which he had passed. The only indication of it was the fact that he was accompanied by Miss Emily Stewart, the trained nurse who had attended Mrs. Root through her last illness and who remained with Mr. Root until his death. She possessed a rare combination of professional skill, charm of personality and that ability to be always available and helpful but never pestering with medical care. No one could have cared for him and his household through his last eight years with greater dignity or efficiency. On the first day at sea after he had walked for a time on deck, Miss Stewart urged him to go in; he turned to me: "Do you keep a diary? Well, please note that on the first day out at 12 noon, I obeyed Miss Stewart and came in." For three days he refused to hear or speak a word about the World Court or the task ahead of him. He had brought along a large store of detective stories and he voraciously consumed his "thrillers" until his mind was completely rested and relaxed. It was a habit which he had long cultivated. He ate heartily and with discriminating taste. He selected his wines with a wide knowledge of brands and vintages and with some preference for the products of the Rhine. He enjoyed chats with a number of acquaintances aboard, especially Professor Frank Jewett Mather, Director of the Princeton University Art Museum, who reminded Root of his old friend Francis Davis Millet—"He is interested in so many interesting things." But he kept largely to his own sitting room and after the first few days worked steadily on his plan for securing an acceptance of the Senate's reservations.

The ship stopped briefly at Naples and Mr. Root took a short drive through the town but declined to visit Pompeii: "Somebody might put me in a museum as an old relic." At Genoa he was met with a show of official distinction, his car being escorted off the dock by guards in dress uniforms. Thence he went by motor to Milan and, after a brief stop, by train to Geneva. As he alighted on the platform at Geneva, Armando Mencia, a young Cuban member of the Legal Section of the Secretariat of the League, met him with outstretched arms: "Ah, Mr. Root! Welcome to Geneva!" It was a keynote played throughout his visit with no discords except as they echoed over the cables from the United States. He established himself in a comforable suite at the Hotel Beau Rivage where his windows overlooked the Quai Woodrow Wilson and the sparkling waters of Lake Leman.

Root wasted no time. On the morning of March 2nd he received a group of American newspaper men. At twelve he called on Sir Eric Drummond and spent with him an hour and a half discussing the whole situation in a most satisfying way. That afternoon he took a brief drive along the shore of the lake as far as Nyon and then returned to the hotel to rest and dine quietly. The next day was also spent quietly but March 4th was the day on which the League Council opened its session and it was a day of activity. Immediately after breakfast, Arthur Sweetser, who throughout served as an invaluable liaison officer with Sir Eric Drummond and with the press, called and had a long discussion with Mr. Root. Sweetser reported that the British reaction to his plan was entirely favorable and that he thought there would be no opposition to it in Geneva. He was fearful, as an American at Geneva chronically was in those days, lest any move seeming to come from League sources would explode the mine of senatorial suspicion in Washington. Root was inclined to belittle this danger and to refuse to truckle to the intransigeant senators. He thought that Borah, since his novel experience in taking the affirmative as the Senate leader in favor of ratification of the Briand-Kellogg Pact, had changed. (It turned out that the leopard still had his spots.) Root's refusal to take more pains to conciliate the Senate is rather surprising, but his talks with Borah and the other senators had convinced him that his plan was acceptable to them. He was more bothered about the willingness of the Council of the League and the members of the League generally to accept some of the elements of his plan and he had been at great pains to adopt forms which might prove palatable, taking as his base the "Final Act" of the 1926 Conference of Signatories. In facile retrospect, one can see that Geneva was ready to yield a little more than he asked of them in the inconsequential details which loomed so large in many senatorial minds.

On March 4th, also, Root cabled to Secretary Kellogg who was holding over under President Hoover until the new Secretary of State, Henry L. Stimson, should take office toward the end of March. He explained his plan rather fully, in so far as it related to the crucial part of the fifth reservation. His main emphasis—which he had made abundantly clear in working out his drafts on the boat—was on the need for abandoning vague generalities, with their store of potential difficulties, in favor of dealing with the concrete case. "Whenever a concrete case arises (if one ever does)," he cabled Kellogg, "common sense & practical experience will readily determine whether that particular question touches an interest of the United States . . . the discussion should therefore be shifted from the abstract & general to the concrete & specific & provision made for the solution of such a question by prompt & friendly exchange of views on that specific point." His draft accordingly provided a plan for such an exchange of views between the United States and the Council or Assembly if such a situation arose. The Senate reservations had made no provisions for such intercommunication nor had they suggested any means whereby the "interest" of the United States could be ascertained or made known. Root's cable went on to say "if an irreconcilable difference of view results, that will show such a fundamental difference regarding the proper scope of requests for advisory opinions as to make it desirable to resume the *status quo ante* by exercise of the power of withdrawal provided in Reservation IV . . . there is such an enormous preponderance of probability against such a difference arising and being insisted upon for the sake of getting an opinion on any question whatever that the arrangement is clearly worth trying out. . . ." Root said he was cabling the draft for study because it seemed to be generally acceptable in Geneva and he wanted Kellogg and the President to be prepared to act quickly if he should request authority to represent the United States in any agreement which might be made before the Council adjourned. At that moment it was not clear just what course the proceeding would take but it was ultimately decided that the Council would refer the whole matter to the Committee of Jurists and Root therefore never received any official representative authority. From first to last on this trip he was merely a private citizen, serving as an individual expert on an international committee.

On the morning of the 5th, Root had received all the American journalists and had fully expounded to them the theory of his plan, telling them they could use it without quoting him. This worried Sweetser who feared the annoyance of Council members who had not yet been consulted; one must be very careful about such punctilios in Geneva. By afternoon Root was also a little concerned; he was showing the effect of the strain of his busy days. But he was at his best in an interview that afternoon with Briand who expressed full agreement with his plan. Briand remarked as the interview drew near a close: "I quite understand; your Senate is willing to buy a ticket but they want to know for what station!" That evening Root dined with the Drummonds, returned rather late and sat down to read a detective story before going to bed.

On March 7th, he heard from Kellogg that they did not approve the idea of negotiating with the League Council as the representative of the signatory states: "We have always negotiated through individual governments. . . ." Root showed a good deal of irritation as he read this message. "Kellogg is afraid of the Senate. He has fixed on that procedure and doesn't want to change. It is ridiculously absurd. Stimson will have to change all that." Meanwhile Root's round of interviews went on, receiving Prokope and Holsti of Finland in the morning, then calling on his old friend Adatci of Japan. Rand, the American Consul, entertained him at lunch with Hugh Wilson, the American Minister to Switzerland. It is an amusing commentary on American relations with the League that this was the first occasion upon which Arthur Sweetser, American member of the Secretariat, had received such "official" notice from the American officials! That evening, Root dined in the hotel with Sir Austen Chamberlain, the British Foreign Secretary, and Sir Cecil Hurst, legal adviser to the Foreign Office and a member of the jurists' committee. It was at this meeting that agreement was reached to refer the whole matter to the committee instead of having Root bring it before the Council; Root returned in happy mood a half hour after midnight. The next day more Council members were interviewed, including the Latin American representatives. That night Root went to bed at nine-thirty, evidently tired and causing much concern to Miss Stewart; he was running a little fever. Although the fever continued the next day, he insisted upon getting up to keep an appointment with Stresemann, the German Foreign Secretary. On the table in Stresemann's room was the inevitable bottle of warm sweet champagne, but fortunately it was not offered. The conversation began a little stiffly. Stresemann remarked that he had been in New York just before the outbreak of the war—in 1914. Mr. Root replied with a smile that he had been in Berlin just before the outbreak of the war—in 1870. Thereafter they chatted amiably, Stresemann's interpreter supplying an occasional word, but the German statesman talking very good English in his loud cacophonous nasal voice, like a badly adjusted radio.

All day Sunday Root stayed in bed with a fever and troubled by an attack of rheumatism but Monday he was up and ready for the opening of the committee meeting at eleven o'clock. Scialoja, the Italian representative, a shrewd and bitingly sarcastic person, was selected as chairman, with the equally able but kindly and considerate Van Eysinga from the Netherlands as vice chairman. Whenever Root spoke in his slow deliberate way, there was absolute silence and rigid attention with every eye fixed upon him. The item of American adherence to the Court, which had just been placed on the committee's agenda by the Council, was made the first order of business. Sir Cecil Hurst presented an elaboration of Root's draft, covering some of the details which Root had not wished to include in his first proposal. Cables reached Root from Secretary Kellogg reporting that he and President Hoover approved the Root plan as did Senators Walsh, Swanson and Borah, although Walsh offered some suggestions.

On March 12th there was a private meeting of Root, Scialoja, Hurst and Politis, the Greek expert; substantial agreement on a modified form of the Hurst draft was reached. But it became apparent that Scialoja, who had represented Italy on the Council, was opposed to all advisory opinions, because, as he explained privately to Root, the Council found that the Court was too judicial and independent and they could not get the kind of advice they wanted. It was more satisfactory, from his point of view, for the Council to refer questions to a special committee of jurists on each occasion. On the other hand, the representatives of the small states, especially Raestad, the able lawyer from Norway, attached great importance to the advisory opinions and were unwilling to see the system injured even in exchange for the benefit of securing American support for the Court. It was an undercurrent of antagonism which existed throughout the meetings and which was overcome only by tactful handling.

Meanwhile discouraging cables came from Kellogg. He was becoming frightened by the welling opposition of the Hearst papers, ever ready to attack Root or the League, and by evidences of dissatisfaction among the senators. He proposed modifications which Root thought quite unsound. Root was irritated; he was aching to get back and talk plainly to Hoover about how to deal with the League. "Someday," he exclaimed, "somebody in our government has got to say something to somebody." He thought that the suggestions from Washington proposed making an unfriendly agreement while he was making a friendly agreement; he said he would take no part in making the former kind, nor approve it if anyone else did.

In the committee sessions, however, attention had shifted to the consideration of amendments to the Statute of the Court. Root held his peace while most of the other members talked and only when something which he considered of real importance arose did he take the floor. When he spoke in opposition to a measure, the chairman seemed to consider the matter settled and would remark, "All right, the next item on the agenda." On the 16th, Scialoja departed for Italy and was replaced by Van Eysinga. Before the chairman's departure, Root had a chat with him and complimented him on the way he conducted the meetings; Scialoja replied: "It's because I have said things which no other member would dare to say; because they are too well-bred, all of them."

On the 18th, the committee returned to the American question and adopted the revised draft which Root had previously agreed upon in consultation with Sir Cecil Hurst. Root was much pleased. "Well, it's done, what I came over to do." The next day saw the conclusion of the committee sessions and Miss Stewart expected that Mr. Root would spend the next day resting in bed. Instead, he called in a stenographer and for two hours dictated a statement for the press after which he went out to lunch with Van Eysinga, returning at three to talk with the Cuban and Brazilian representatives in Geneva. Then followed a few days of essential rest after which we started a leisurely motor trip through France toward Paris. At Chartres, Mr. Root received the news of the sudden death of Ambassador Herrick whose invitation to stay at the Embassy he had gladly accepted. It was a great shock to him. The next day he learned of the death of another old friend, Brander Matthews. During the period of this European trip, Bishop Brent, Lord Finley and Lord Phillimore, all old friends, died. "My little world is rapidly becoming depopulated," Root remarked, but he had reached an age where death seemed to him an inevitable and a natural thing and he took the losses stoically.

In Paris he attended Mr. Herrick's funeral. He saw with the greatest pleasure his old friends, the Jusserands. Kellogg had turned over the State Department to Stimson and was in Paris; he gave more encouraging reports about the attitude of Senator Borah and the probable outcome in the Senate. On April 9th, just after Root had finished dining quietly in his own apartment at the Hotel Crillon, Mr. Thomas Lamont, of the firm of J. P. Morgan and Co., sent up word that he would like to see him on a matter of some importance. He came up at once with Parker Gilbert, formerly Agent General of Reparations for Germany, and Owen D. Young. They were at work in the so-called Young committee which was readjusting the German reparations settlement and were evolving what came to be known as the Young Plan. Like Root at Geneva, they had received somewhat irritating instructions from Washington; in their case Washington was insisting on the absurd theory that there was no connection between Reparations and Inter-allied debts. Root advised them then as to the course which they were proposing to follow and was consulted again by Lamont after Root's return to the United States.

New York was reached on April 17th. The great trip was ended, the work was only just begun. The whole plan had to be explained to Secretary Stimson who was of course eager to do whatever he could to further the work of his old chief whom he so warmly admired. Root corresponded with senators. He talked with many private persons engaged in working for adoption of his plan but would make no public statement, written or oral; he felt that as a negotiator of the proposal he should not enter into the general public debate but should hold his fire until he appeared before the Foreign Relations Committee of the Senate, which he had agreed to do. The appearance was finally set for January 21st, 1931, nearly two years after his plan had been framed. Meanwhile it had been found acceptable by the Council and Assembly of the League, by Secretary Stimson and President Hoover, and by a very large proportion of the American press as well as by countless organizations from bar associations to farm and labor groups.

The committee room in the Senate Office Building was jammed. The session lasted for two and a half hours with people standing in the corridors hoping to catch a glimpse or a word.

In about three weeks' time, Root would be eighty-six years of age. For an hour and a half he talked without interruption, largely following a memorandum which he had prepared and put into print, but later diverging from it and amplifying it. In the latter part of the hearing, when the senators began to ply him with questions, Root began to show signs of fatigue but he did not falter. Ten years before he might have been a little quicker, a little more incisive, but there was nothing in the adverse comments of his opponents who gleefully whispered that the old man was certainly failing. His exposition was able and impressive. It is true, however, that the plan suffered from the very skill and intricacy of his drafting. It was too complicated to be clearly understood by the people at large and there were points upon which the lawyers disputed at length. Many of the most ardent supporters of the Court had difficulty in agreeing with Root's interpretation of certain points in the protocol. They did not bother about the difference because they realized that these minor shades of meaning were of little importance, and that the essential interests of the United States were amply protected against even imaginary dangers, but the opposition was strengthened by the conflict of views.

Root continued to advise in the long period which was still to elapse before the Senate acted on the Court resolution. President Hoover was very cautious and failed to press for action because this or that other matter was to the fore and he thought he could not afford to antagonize various senators. Franklin D. Roosevelt became President on a platform which still favored the Court but he too stalled for time. Finally the debate came in January, 1935. Father Coughlin, the radio priest, had been rending the air with denunciations of the Court; Hearst rallied all his forces in leading the opposition. The proponents of the Court, numerous and influential as they were, were handicapped by their respectability; they were unwilling to indulge in the kind of wildly inaccurate statement which Coughlin and Hearst unblushingly threw out in their successful effort to mislead the American public. The Administration was over-confident, refused to make minor concessions until it was too late. On the night of January 28th, the pro-Court forces were working feverishly to rally support from all over the country, counteracting the tide of Hearst's and Coughlin's inspired telegraphic appeals to the senators. It was apparent to them that if the Administration would yield on one point, enough votes might be won to carry the day. Mr. Root was again appealed to. He had already retired for the night but came out into his study in a dressing gown and at ten-thirty penned a letter to President Roosevelt urging him to change the Administration tactics. The letter was delivered to Secretary of State Hull on the morning of January 29th and was carried to the White House. There were hurried conferences with Senator Joe Robinson, leader of the Administration forces. The tactics were changed, but too late. The President exerted all of his personal influence—too late. He suffered the first great defeat which he had met except for the over-riding of his veto of the soldiers' bonus in 1934. Thirty-six senators voted against consent to ratification; fifty-two in favor; seven votes more were needed to make the necessary constitutional two-thirds.

Root gave a statement to the press: "I think the majority of the Senate which has been defeated under the two-thirds rule on the World Court issue truly represents with the President the sober judgment and the sincere conviction of the American people who hate war and wish their country to do its share toward promoting peace with justice in the world. I do not for a moment doubt that this great American majority will yet cause their will to be made effective by their government."

Still looking to the future, hopefully, confidently, but concealing a disappointment probably keener than any which had come to him in all his ninety years. He had even risked his life to bring about his country's support of the cause of law and order in the world. With a little more courage at various times in the White House, with a little more political skill in that final test, his efforts would have been crowned with victory during his lifetime. Instead there was bitter defeat. But to him, after the first blow had fallen, it meant merely a postponement. He was accustomed to looking far up into the high branches of elms which his father had set out as saplings. His own sons, or perhaps his grandsons—it did not greatly matter—would see the results of his own planting.

"STILL TURRUBLE SKEERED"

(A cartoon in the New York *Herald-Tribune*, March 27, 1929)

CHAPTER XLVII

"The Conference was the complete negation of naval policy"

THE convocation of the Conference for the Limitation of Armaments in Washington on November 11th, 1921, was in part an accidental result of the British Imperial Conference which met in London in June of that year. Arthur Meighen, the Canadian Prime Minister, was convinced that cordial Anglo-American relations were essential to the well-being of the British Empire and that the continuation of the Anglo-Japanese Alliance, which had been first concluded in 1902, provoked distrust in the United States and was inimical to his primary objective. When the Alliance was renewed in 1911 for a ten year period, the British Government took care to have it understood that it was not to be applicable against the United States. In 1920, they made this viewpoint clear to the United States.[1] This understanding, however, was not popularly known and there was a general feeling in the United States that the Anglo-Japanese Alliance was a disturbing factor in the relations of the three countries. In the late spring of 1920, there was considerable discussion in Japan of the advisability of enlarging the alliance to include the United States. It was realized that American tradition made a formal alliance impossible, but it was thought that some new international understanding might be agreed upon, merging the essence of the Anglo-Japanese Alliance, the Root-Takahira and Lansing-Ishii agreements and the Franco-Japanese agreement.[2] This suggestion, supported by the *Yomiuri*, mouth-piece of the Japanese liberals, did not produce, but accurately forecast, one of the important results of the Washington Conference.

Meighen found himself at first almost alone in the Imperial Conference, vigorously opposed by Hughes, the Prime Minister of Australia, and Massey, the Prime Minister of New Zealand.[3] Both of these

[1] *Foreign Relations of the United States*, 1920, Vol. II, pp. 680 ff.
[2] *Ibid.*, p. 684.
[3] Brebner, "Canada, the Anglo-Japanese Alliance and the Washington Conference," *Political Science Quarterly*, Vol. L (1935), p. 45.

Dominions felt strongly that the continuation of the Alliance was necessary to their future safety; the American rejection of the Versailles Treaty and of the League of Nations naturally made them distrust any suggestion of securing from the United States any valuable substitute commitment.

The political situation in the United States, however, made the moment particularly auspicious for the summoning of an important international conference. On December 14th, 1920, Senator Borah introduced a resolution urging the President to invite Great Britain and Japan to a conference for limiting naval armaments. The Senate passed the resolution on May 25th, 1921, by a vote of 74 to 0 and the House passed it on June 29th by 332 votes to 4. Secretary of State Hughes was one of the thirty-one Republicans who had signed the appeal to pro-League Republican voters to support Harding for the Presidency. He shared the view of such Republican leaders as Root and Taft, that something must be done in the way of international cooperative effort. Harding had no plan and Hughes at first had no thought more definite than that they should summon an international conference to meet in Washington. Gradually he came to accept the idea of the Borah resolution that the conference should deal with the limitation of naval armaments, but he steadfastly insisted that France and Italy should be invited to attend. President Harding approved.

Just at this time the Imperial Conference in London was reaching the climax of its discussions about the Anglo-Japanese Alliance. On July 1st, Meighen had carried his point and on July 7th, Lloyd George, the British Prime Minister, had indicated in response to a question in the House of Commons that the British Government was negotiating with the United States, Japan and China for a general conference on Far Eastern questions. Secretary Hughes had only newspaper information about this development but felt that the United States must act quickly if it were not to lose the opportunity to summon a conference under its own aegis. On July 8th, with Harding's approval, he cabled to London, Tokio, Paris and Rome asking whether an invitation to a conference in Washington on the limitation of armaments would be favorably received. His cable crossed one from Ambassador Harvey in London who reported that the British Foreign Secretary, Curzon, wished him to ascertain whether the United

States would be disposed to participate in a general conference on Far Eastern questions. For several days the wires burned between Washington and London with the final result, after some misunderstandings, that the British Government agreed to yield the initiative to Washington. The conference accordingly assembled in Washington on Armistice Day, November 11th, 1921, with an agenda which included both the limitation of armaments and Far Eastern questions.

With these preliminary *pourparlers*, Root had nothing to do. Hughes was a Secretary of State of determination and force of character. He was accustomed to reaching his own decisions. He had the same type of quick, incisive mind which Root had and the same capacity of the able lawyer to master a complicated subject and to formulate conclusions. Throughout the Conference, he was the dominant figure with Arthur Balfour, the leader of the British delegation, as his nearest rival. Not that he was domineering or that he played a lone hand; the four American delegates met frequently, beginning on October 12th, a month before the Conference opened. Every basic point was fully discussed and it is certain that all had some share in the formulation and execution of plans. Yet the major credit for the achievements of the Conference undoubtedly belongs to Hughes.

It was Hughes who had secured Root's appointment; he put the proposal to Harding most emphatically and secured ready agreement [4] although ex-President Taft, on learning that Charles Hilles had made a similar recommendation, doubted whether Harding would appoint Root.[5] President Harding, on August 17th, 1921, had already invited Root before receiving the letter from Hilles. Root promptly accepted; it had been nearly a year since he had participated in an important international conference and he was only seventy-six years of age! Hughes was to head the delegation and the other members were Senator Lodge, still Chairman of the Foreign Relations Committee of the Senate, and Senator Underwood, the ranking Democratic member of that Committee. "I am not enthusiastic about Lodge in any way but for this purpose he was indispensable," Taft wrote to Root on September 14th. "With him and Underwood any conclusion you reach will have the strongest possible support in the Senate and that is where you will need it. . . . Your appointment creates the greatest

[4] Chief Justice Hughes to the author, March 26, 1934.
[5] William Howard Taft to Hilles, August 21, 1921, Taft Papers, Library of Congress.

confidence in the United States and the world over that the President means business in this matter and is seeking a real advance. With your great familiarity with all the questions likely to be considered and with your capacity for reconciling opinions and ingenuity in devising ways and means to an end, I have great hopes that you will do something of an epochal character."

About the middle of October, Root moved to Washington, renting an apartment at the corner of 18th Street and Connecticut Avenue where he stayed until the Conference adjourned in February. To Edwin H. Blashfield he wrote in his capacity as President of the Century Club on October 29th: "I am abandoning all my New York engagements as if the 11:15 Pennsylvania train were taking me to an island in the South Pacific. During this temporary aberration, I turn over to you, as Vice President, the care of the Century. Treat the members kindly, though firmly. None of them really seeks to turn over the Constitution or even the By-laws. You will be in no danger of physical violence unless some threatening gesture on your part causes an impression that it is your purpose to assault them. Meantime they will greatly enjoy being under the presidency of an artist instead of a common or garden amateur."

The sudden course of events had made it necessary to convene the Conference before any definite plan was formulated and for some time Hughes was worried as to what they could propose. President Harding told him that something definite must be done and that he would hold him responsible. Hughes finally asked the Navy Department—using especially Theodore Roosevelt, Jr. who had followed his father's precedent by serving as Assistant Secretary of the Navy—to take as a basic assumption the idea that the American vessels then under construction, pursuant to the great naval building program which the United States had initiated, would be scrapped and that the building program would be stopped. On that basis, what would be fair equivalents for Great Britain and Japan? The equivalents worked out by the American naval advisers were steadily adhered to by the American delegation. Under the Naval Appropriation Act of August 29th, 1916, the United States had prepared to launch a huge naval building program. The necessities of the World War situation had caused a temporary abandonment, but building had been resumed in 1918 despite the destruction of German naval power. Japan had responded with a naval building program which raised her naval budget from $85,000,000 in 1917 to $245,000,000 in 1921. Great Britain, in 1920, voluntarily made the revolutionary announcement that she would henceforth be content with a one-power instead of her traditional two-power standard, that is, a navy equal to that of any other single power instead of equal to any other two navies.[6] If the American naval program had been carried out, Great Britain would have been forced to increase her construction also if she were to maintain actual parity with the new American fleet. A naval building race was definitely in sight, with the advantage on the side of the United States from the point of view of ability to bear the financial strain of the necessary expenditures.

At one of the first preliminary meetings of the American delegation, Root asked whether there was any likelihood that Congress would vote the necessary appropriations to continue the naval building program and the concomitant program for the fortification of the Philippines which was an essential element in American naval policy as it was then conceived. In the minds of the naval officers, the projected large navy was necessary to defend the Philippines and American "interests" in the Far East; this policy contemplated the creation in the Philippines of a naval base and fortifications equal to the huge British base at Singapore which was then under way. Senators Lodge and Underwood were emphatic in asserting that there was no possibility that Congress would appropriate the necessary funds.[7] Some at least of the naval officers had come to the same conclusion and for that reason were the more ready to acquiesce in a plan which was widely interpreted as an unfortunate surrender by the United States of a dominant position. The history of the next decade and a half, when the United States did not even build up to the treaty limits, confirmed the soundness of the view which Root and his fellow delegates held in 1921.

The American group also believed that the proposed limitation, which would make it impossible for Great Britain alone to compete with Japan, would give the British a feeling of dependence on the

[6] Buell, The Washington Conference, pp. 137 ff.
[7] Cf. Foreign Relations of the United States, 1922, Vol. I, pp. 74–75.

American fleet. This feeling would facilitate the abandonment of the Anglo-Japanese Alliance.[8] Apparently the American Government was not then fully informed about Meighen's victory in the Imperial Conference.

Root also suggested at one of the early meetings of the American delegates, that it would be futile for the Conference to propose naval ratios based on national needs. It was not possible for one power or any group of powers to agree upon the size of navy which another power "needed." He insisted, therefore, that the basis of limitation must be the actual existing strength of the navies. He felt later that much misunderstanding had been caused by referring to the "5-5-3 ratio" established by the treaties signed at the Conference; they were not "ratios" in any proper sense, but statements of existing fact, based upon the preliminary point that the United States would stop in its tracks and scrap a number of capital ships already under construction. It seems that Secretary Hughes had independently reached the same conclusion and there was no difficulty in uniting the American delegation on this basis; President Harding readily acquiesced. Hughes' dramatic revelation of this startling American offer at the opening session of the Conference is familiar history.

Root's duties at the Conference were fairly onerous. He attended all the plenary sessions and the meetings of the Committee on Limitation of Armaments and of the Committee on Pacific and Far Eastern Questions. He presided as chairman over the three meetings of the Subcommittee of Five on Drafting; over the nine meetings of the Subcommittee of Nine on Drafting; and over the three meetings of the Subcommittee of Delegates on the Chinese Eastern Railway. These were his formal appointments; as is always true on such occasions, the really hard labor was done between meetings, often to a late hour in the night.

Although, as will be shown later, Root might be described as having a general pro-Japanese point of view, he found the early attitude of the Japanese toward Secretary Hughes' proposals, decidedly annoying. They began to talk about how large a navy they needed, thus violating the fundamentals of the American plan. Root was inclined to believe that the Japanese, like the American Government, would in reality not be giving up very much since the money would not

[8] Diary of Chandler P. Anderson, entry of November 26, 1921.

be forthcoming to complete the building program; in the case of Japan, due to a strained financial position.[9] On November 30th, Chandler Anderson brought Fred Kent to see Root. Kent had close connections with Japanese financial interests in the United States and personal contacts with influential business men and officials in Japan. Root told Kent that there was serious danger of Japan's refusing to accept the proposed basis for naval limitation. The United States was determined not to yield and if Japan refused, the Conference would break up. In such an event, Root saw real danger of war between the United States and Japan. In any event, there would be a severe blow to Japan's trade; popular feeling in the United States, Great Britain, France and Italy, was aroused in favor of the plan for limiting the burden of armaments and popular boycotts of Japanese goods might be expected if Japan were blamed for breaking up the Conference. It was therefore time for influential people in Japan to take the matter in hand and end the existing control of the naval experts in the Japanese delegation. Kent agreed to talk to a number of prominent Japanese, including Baron Shibusawa and Mitsui, head of the great Japanese commercial house, both of whom happened to be in New York at the time. Kent, however, did not agree that the Japanese financial position was as bad as Root had been led to believe.[10]

On December 5th, Root was inclined to think that the Japanese were withholding agreement on the naval plan in order to bargain for better terms in any adjustment of their position in China. He expected them to yield on Shantung but in doing so to insist on strengthening their position in Manchuria.[11] It was not until February 1st that Chairman Hughes was able to announce simultaneously to the full conference the conclusion of the Shantung agreement between China and Japan and the agreement on the treaty for naval limitation. It is not possible to say what part Kent's inspired representations had in leading toward this final agreement.

Aside from these matters, Root appears to have had little to do with the questions of naval limitation which became matters chiefly for the technical experts, always under the control and guidance of Secretary Hughes who kept the naval experts from running away with this part

[9] *Ibid.*, entry of November 18, 1921.
[10] *Ibid.*, entry of November 30, 1921.
[11] *Ibid.*, entry of December 5, 1921.

of the agenda by making himself their equal in knowledge of the technical points involved. As Root later expressed it, "The Conference was the complete negation of naval policy." The basic governmental policy, so far as the Pacific was concerned, was to maintain friendly relations with Japan; "The first thing was to make that governmental policy our naval policy. You can't carry water on both shoulders; some of it will spill and you'll catch cold.[12] He felt later that the abortive Geneva Conference of 1927 failed because the naval experts were allowed to make naval policy the first consideration. "In one sense, the better the naval officer, the more incapable he is of judging government policy, because the postulates on which he bases his propositions are ones on which government policy has to close the door." Root appreciated the broader viewpoint of Theodore Roosevelt, Jr. at the Washington Conference. "I don't know what we should have done without you," Root wrote to him on June 29th, 1926, "for the professional naval men naturally found it very difficult to deal with the subject except in the light of their own special naval policy." In relation to the Washington Conference, the idea of the abandonment of the navy's policy of force in the Pacific came naturally to Root who, from his own days as Secretary of War during the Boxer troubles and later as Secretary of State, had always been firmly convinced that the United States would never enforce the Open Door doctrine by armed force. "It never entered the head of any President or Secretary of State or Chairman of the Committee on Foreign Relations of the Senate or Chairman of the Committee on Foreign Affairs of the House that we *would* ever send forces to China to maintain the open door," he said.[13] The misunderstanding of this American political truth has discolored much thinking and writing on the general subject of American policies in the Far East. Root was convinced that the Japanese Government knew far better than did the average American that the United States would never send its fleet to protect the open door or the integrity of China. This was another reason why the American "surrender" at the Conference was more apparent than real.[14]

One of Root's chief interests and activities at the Conference was an indirect offshoot of another aspect of the question of naval limita-

[12] Root to the author, July 6, 1931.
[13] *Ibid.*
[14] Diary of Chandler P. Anderson, entry of November 26, 1921.

tion. The British, particularly mindful of their dangerously close margin of escape from the German submarine menace during the World War, strenuously sought to secure an agreement upon the total abolition of submarines. France and Japan, with Italy concurring, were equally insistent that the submarine was a valuable and legitimate weapon of naval defense particularly for the weaker naval powers. The United States accepted the view of its naval experts that it too required submarines. It is not necessary here to go into the long arguments on this subject but it was clear from an early point in the discussions that the British thesis would fail. As soon as the public acknowledgment of this fact was reached, Root was ready with an alternate plan which he hoped would achieve the objective which the British had in mind. It was an objective with which he fully sympathized, since no British subject had a more ardent horror for the German method of submarine warfare or condemned it on grounds of law and morals more heartily than he. It must be borne in mind that the Conference was primarily a meeting of the Principal Allied and Associated Powers convening on the third anniversary of the Armistice, with the war psychology still very much to the fore. The debates abound with condemnations of the Germans and with mutual exchange of compliments among the former allies, although the latter were occasionally laid on with special unction to gloss over points of friction which had developed.

At a meeting of the Conference on December 28th, Hughes called on Root to present a resolution on submarine warfare. The general idea had not originated with Root. The agenda of the Conference had called for consideration of "Rules for control of new agencies of warfare," which had been explained in advance to contemplate aircraft, poisonous gases and submarines. As early as December 5th, Professor George Grafton Wilson, one of the technical experts on international law attached to the American delegation, was at work upon plans for a comprehensive revision of a code of maritime warfare and of neutral rights as they had been formulated in the Declaration of London of 1910. Root, on the contrary, had agreed with the French view, which was that such a comprehensive revision should be referred to a subsequent conference which would include other nations in addition to those represented at Washington. He assisted in preparing the resolutions under which a commission of experts met at The Hague later in

1922 and drafted rules on the use of radio and aircraft in time of war. Root also aided in preparing the resolution against the use of poison gas which was adopted at the Conference. Early in December, Root held the idea of a general agreement upon an international criminal code under which individuals like submarine commanders could be held personally responsible for illegal acts and could be brought to trial in any country of the world. He felt that the Peace Conference at Paris had missed a great opportunity by failing to establish this rule, although they had discussed the idea of trying the Kaiser and had actually brought about the trial of some submarine commanders by a German high court.[15] It was essentially the same idea which Root had expressed to Colonel Stimson in 1918.[16] On December 20th, 1921, Root had asked James Brown Scott, another of the technical legal advisers, to begin drafting the submarine treaty which he had in mind and had asked him to consult with Chandler P. Anderson and Fred K. Nielsen in perfecting the draft. The first draft was prepared by Scott, partly at the dictation of Root, and its later stages were developed by the other advisers in frequent consultation with Root.[17] This was the general method of operation which Root followed in all of the Conference matters with which he was particularly concerned; his reliance in matters of drafting was chiefly on Anderson and Scott who had worked with him in the past and with whom he had particularly warm and close personal relations. Major Stanley Washburn, who had been with Root on his Russian trip, and whose contacts with the Japanese had won him many Japanese friends, was of great value to Root in dealing with Far Eastern questions. Root was himself an expert draftsman, but the other duties of the Conference left him inadequate time for such work. It is clear from Mr. Anderson's diary that he carefully went over and revised successive drafts but the exact authorship of particular provisions can not be traced.

In proposing his submarine resolution to the Conference on December 28th, Root stated that his purpose was "to put into such simple form the subject which had so stirred the feelings of a great part of the civilized world that the man in the street and the man on the

15 *Ibid.*, entry of December 5, 1921.
16 Diary of Henry L. Stimson, December 22, 1918.
17 Diary of Chandler P. Anderson, entries of December 21 and 22, 1921.

farm could understand it." [18] His draft began with a statement that the signatory powers "desiring to make more effective the rules adopted by civilized nations for the protection of the lives of neutrals and non-combatants at sea in time of war," declared that the rules which followed were to be deemed an established part of international law. These rules expressed the well established doctrines that a merchant vessel must be ordered to stop for visit and search to determine its character, that it cannot be attacked unless it refuses to submit to visit and search, and that it cannot be destroyed unless the passengers and crew have first been placed in safety. In the next place, the draft announced that belligerent submarines are not under any circumstances exempt from observance of these rules and that if they could not capture a merchant vessel in conformity therewith, they must allow the merchantman to proceed unmolested. Other powers were to be invited to concur in these statements of existing law. But the resolution then went further, proposing new law. The signatories were to "recognize the practical impossibility of using submarines as commerce destroyers" without violating the rules, and they were therefore to agree to the prohibition of such use and to invite other nations to accept the same prohibition. The final proposal embodied Root's idea of the criminal code and declared that any individual who violated these rules, whether or not under orders, should be deemed to have violated the laws of war "and shall be liable to trial and punishment as if for an act of piracy." The reference to piracy was designed to invoke the well established rule of international law that pirates may be tried in any country irrespective of the usual limitations upon national jurisdiction in criminal matters. But Root's proposal would have modified the old offense of piracy, an essential part of which is the absence of any governmental authorization.

Root defended his proposal with passionate zeal. He fought off an attempt to have the whole matter passed over and referred to another conference of technical legal experts. He "declared that the members of the Committee could not justify themselves in separating without some declaration that would give voice to the humane opinion of the world upon this subject which was the most vital, the most heartfelt, the most stirring to the conscience and to the feeling of the people of all our countries of anything that occurred during the late war. He

[18] *Proceedings* of the Conference, p. 594.

felt to the depth of his heart that the man who was responsible for sinking the *Lusitania* committed an act of piracy. He knew that all his countrymen with whom he had had intercourse felt the same. . . . Those Resolutions would not down; they spoke with a voice that would continue insistently. Mr. Root said that he was not going to be buried under a committee of lawyers, and that these rules could not be buried under one. Either the Delegates assembled here must speak clearly and intelligently the voice of humanity which had sent them here, and to which they must report, or that voice would speak for itself, and speaking without them, would be their condemnation." [19]

It was clear that some of the delegates were not eager to accept the resolutions but it was impossible to resist a plea of this kind strongly supported by Senators Lodge and Underwood. Root commanded respect; on an occasion like this he was at his oratorical best. But he was not at his legal best. As he said, these resolutions "gave voice to the feeling" which the war created; they were the register of an emotion and not the conclusions of the jurist. The rules which he proposed would not have solved the problem which he had in mind. The legal core of the controversy over submarine attacks on merchant vessels is the status of the armed merchantman. Merchant vessels have a right to arm, as Root insisted,[20] but he failed to recognize that by so doing they lose their immunities as merchantmen. No final solution of the controversy over submarine warfare is possible without agreement upon the status of the armed merchantman.

The French and Japanese, in opposing the total abolition of submarines, had necessarily taken the position that they of course abhorred the German method of using submarines as commerce destroyers. It was therefore impossible for them to oppose the substance of the proposals. In the usual way of conferences, there was general discussion of meaning, acceptance in principle, and reference to the Subcommittee of Five on Drafting, over which Root presided as chairman. One gets the impression from reading the minutes of this and of other subcommittees over which Root presided at the Conference, that he showed some tendency to be a little impatient of opposition and that he was inclined to be rather dominant. Of course he ob-

---

[19] *Ibid.*, pp. 614 ff.
[20] Diary of Chandler P. Anderson, entry of January 2, 1922.

THE AMERICAN DELEGATES TO THE WASHINGTON DISARMAMENT CONFERENCE

(*Left to right*) Elihu Root, Senator Henry Cabot Lodge, Secretary of State Charles Evans Hughes, Senator Oscar W. Underwood. General Pershing is standing in the second row between Senator Lodge and Secretary Hughes

served the amenities of diplomatic practice and in due course a draft was approved with very slight changes from Root's original submission. One statement which he made in the course of the debates expresses a very sound and important principle which the ignorant often lose sight of in decrying the whole system of international law: ". . . the law had been broken by a sea Power but was still the law; it was necessary that this should be brought before the public mind. The law was not like a teacup or a pitcher which, once broken, was irretrievably ruined." [21]

The Root resolutions on submarines served to crystallize shortly after the war the sound proposition that submarines were bound by the rules of international law governing surface ships in their operations against merchant vessels. In their further implications they were of only fleeting importance. Not all of the five powers which signed the submarine treaty at Washington were willing to ratify it and the treaty accordingly never came into force. When the subject was again raised at the London Naval Conference of 1930, a new and much briefer treaty was adopted, stating that submarines were bound by the usual rules of visit and search. This treaty has now been ratified by thirty-eight states, including all the principal naval powers. Root's views on the drafting of this treaty were asked and given but did not have material effect. The Root idea for criminal sanctions did not command wide approval and was not retained. It must be recorded as an evidence of war-time zeal rather than as a monument to his ability as a jurist or statesman.

Root's part in the handling of the Far Eastern questions before the Conference is not easy to appraise. He told Major Washburn at the outset that the problem of China and Japan was the most important one before the Conference. In retrospect he dwelt upon the fact that the Japanese had recognized in him a sympathetic friend and had often come to him privately for advice. He believed that they had come to Washington anticipating that an attempt might be made to humiliate them in regard to the return of Shantung to China and in other matters. He said that the American group was very careful to dispel such suspicions and to assure Japan that we earnestly desired her friendship. They wished to make proposals which were so obviously friendly, that the liberal elements in Japan which wanted better

[21] *Proceedings of the Subcommittees*, p. 142.

international relations would be strengthened in supporting acceptance of them.[22] He believed that his handling of the immigration
and other questions while he was Secretary of State had built up an
atmosphere of friendliness and that the developments of the Washington Conference had done much to perpetuate that feeling. He felt
very bitter indeed when the Senate passed the notorious Japanese
exclusion section of the Immigration Act of 1924.

There is no question about Root's sympathy for the Japanese and
it seems clear that he felt more warmly toward them than toward the
Chinese. But the Chinese also turned to him confidentially to explain
their views before the Conference opened.[23] He was impressed by the
secret treaty between China and Russia whereby he felt that China
had clearly granted to Russia the right to build the Chinese Eastern
Railway in Manchuria for use as a strategic railway against the Japanese. He felt that Japan had great justification for her attitude toward
China and he was most sympathetic with the Japanese feeling that
the Powers had thwarted their legitimate claims time and again. He
thought that the Western Powers would have to get away from their
sentimental attitude of defending China and recognize the logic and
necessity of the position of Japan which faced a vast country at once
so disorganized and so rich in potentialities for expansion. It was because the Western Powers had not been fair to Japan, he said on the
eve of his ninetieth birthday, that the liberal groups in that country
had been forced into the background and the naval and military men
had been put in the saddle.[24] He believed that the "Twenty-one Demands," which Japan made of China in 1915, were a mark of "the
complete ascendancy for the time being of the military party." [25]
Root felt that China was continually seeking all the rights of a state
without being in a position to fulfill the responsibilities of a state. He
told the American Society of International Law on April 27th, 1922,
when he was discussing the Washington Conference, that China had
not yet become a full-fledged member of the family of nations. At the
Conference, he impressed two of the American Far Eastern experts
as too intent upon the technical legal rights involved in such complicated matters as that of the Chinese Eastern Railway, and too lit-

[22] Diary of Chandler P. Anderson, entry of November 26, 1921.
[23] Ma Soo to Root, August 15, 1921.
[24] Root to the author, February 12, 1935.
[25] Root to Elbert F. Baldwin, July 26, 1921.

tle cognizant of the underlying and controlling political forces. He showed a tendency at times to try to argue the Chinese out of court by legal technicalities in a situation where there was no judge to sustain his points and the real task was to effect a political compromise. Unlike Hughes, he did not make full use of the staff of technical experts and therefore failed to have in mind some of the developments which had become of great importance in the decade since he had controlled American foreign policies. On one occasion Root refused to yield to Hughes' plea that he take a technical expert on radio to a meeting at which that very difficult subject was to be discussed. In the subcommittee, he drafted a proposal indicating general approval of the idea of joint international action in the development of radio services in China. The official American view was opposed to such joint action which was favored by the British, French and Japanese. Root subsequently proposed an amended text, but the embarrassment caused by his original concession was not wholly obviated. He constantly played a lone hand as confidential adviser to both the Japanese and Chinese—particularly Hanihara and Koo—in their long negotiations for an adjustment of the Shantung and other delicate issues. Other members of the American group did not know what statements he was making and at times had, with much difficulty, to counteract the too sanguine hopes which Root had held out. He had learned that the Japanese feared that they might be asked to give up not only Shantung but Port Arthur as well. Port Arthur had become a national symbol in Japan and the Japanese had indicated that they could not remain in the Conference if that subject were even discussed. Root thereupon in a private conversation with Wellington Koo, the second member of the Chinese delegation, held forth at some length upon the Japanese right to hold Port Arthur. He defended the Japanese case with such vigor that Koo was quite taken aback. It is quite clear that there was conflict between Root's own private negotiations as go-between in the Sino-Japanese negotiations and the more official intermediation of other members of the American delegation, but on the basis of the available evidence it is impossible to say whether in the long run Root helped or hindered the achievement of the final results.

Root seems to have played no part in the negotiations of the Four Power Treaty which substituted for the Anglo-Japanese Alliance which it specifically terminated, a rather innocuous statement of non-aggressive design and of a willingness to confer.[26] There was subsequently quite a furore about this treaty due to the suspicion that it required the parties to use force for its fulfillment. There was also a rumor of a private understanding between Great Britain and the United States that they would cooperate against Japan. These reports were vigorously denied in official quarters and nothing has been found to suggest that they had any substance. Hughes took the position that since the supercession of the Alliance was the main object of this agreement, the initiative should be left to the British and Japanese, although he did devote himself most vigorously and successfully to the task of securing their consent to bringing in the French Government as a fourth party to the treaty.[27] This was such welcome news to the French that when Hughes told it to Viviani, the latter threw his arms around his neck and kissed him on both cheeks. Balfour had come to Hughes the night before the opening of the Conference to ask what he thought should be done about the Alliance. Balfour had carefully avoided meeting the Japanese delegates before seeing Hughes since he knew that they would immediately question him on this point and he did not know what to say. Hughes explained to Balfour, as he had previously explained to the British Ambassador, Geddes, the feeling in the United States about the Alliance. He told him also that while the United States could not enter an alliance, it would join in a declaration of principles if this declaration could be broadened by the inclusion of France.[28] When the Dutch delegates raised objections to their being omitted from this group, Root prepared a draft to cover their situation but his proposal was not found to be acceptable. The matter was later covered by an exchange of notes with the Dutch Government. The Four Power Treaty was handled in informal negotiations and did not come before the Conference or its subcommittees

[26] There does exist among the Lodge Papers, however, a paper entitled "Draft Outline of an Agreement Between the United States of America, the British Empire, France and Japan"; this paper bears a penciled notation—"Perfected draft agreed to & discussed by H.C.L. & R.—Dec—8—1921." The concluding discussions between Hughes, Balfour, Shidehara and Viviani, regarding the text of the treaty, took place on December 8 and 9: *Foreign Relations of the United States, 1922.* Vol. I, pp. 13–27. See also p. 50.

[27] Cf. *ibid.,* pp. 5 and 40.

[28] Diary of Chandler P. Anderson, entry of March 10, 1922; *Foreign Relations of the United States, 1922,* Vol. I, p. 1.

until its announcement in finished form on December 10th.

Root did have a good deal to do with the so-called Nine Power Treaty whereby the United States, Great Britain, France, Italy, Japan, Belgium, the Netherlands and Portugal, declared certain principles and policies relating to China. On November 16th, at the first meeting of the Committee on Pacific and Far Eastern questions which included the principal delegates of all the countries present, Mr. Sze, the head of the Chinese delegation, read a statement of the principles which China would like to have adopted. At the second meeting of that committee, after all the delegations had made general statements, Root commented on the several points of view and offered to draft some general principles on which they all seemed to agree.[29] In the course of his remarks, he caused some concern to the Chinese by stating that he thought they should limit themselves to dealing with China proper, leaving the territories over which China exercised suzerainty to be discussed later. It appears that he had in mind only Mongolia and Tibet [30] but the Chinese naturally suspected an intent to recognize Japan's special position in Manchuria. Mr. Koo replied that this was a matter of Chinese internal administration and that the Conference should deal with the Chinese Republic as such without attempting to distinguish between any various sections. Mr. Root was apparently not convinced but when he brought in his four propositions the next day, he stated that the word "China" had always been used in the past and that it seemed undesirable to introduce any variation.

These principles were drafted by Root himself, although they were later discussed with others.[31] They constitute a restatement or readaptation of Hay's Open Door doctrine, the Root-Takahira agreement and similar agreements. His fourth point repeats verbatim part of the language of the proposal which Secretary Lansing discussed with Ambassador Ishii in 1917 and which appears to have been included in the secret protocol to the published Lansing-Ishii Agreement.[32] The inclusion of Lansing's wording was the result of a direct suggestion to

[29] *Proceedings*, p. 882.
[30] Diary of Chandler P. Anderson, entry of November 18, 1921.
[31] *Ibid.*, entry of November 20, 1921.
[32] See *War Memoirs of Robert Lansing*, pp. 298 ff. and Bemis, *A Diplomatic History of the United States*, pp. 683 and 695.

Root from Hughes who called his attention to this theretofore secret article.[33] Since the Root proposals as thus hastily drafted were embodied in the Nine Power Treaty with only minor modifications, they may well be reproduced here:

It is the firm intention of the Powers attending this Conference:

(1) To respect the sovereignty, the independence, and the territorial and administrative integrity of China.

(2) To provide the fullest and most unembarrassed opportunity to China to develop and maintain for herself an effective and stable Government, overcoming the difficulties incident to the change from the old and long-continued imperial form of Government.

(3) To safeguard for the world, so far as it is within our power, the principle of equal opportunity for the commerce and industry of all nations throughout the territory of China.

(4) To refrain from taking advantage of the present conditions in order to seek special rights or privileges which would abridge the rights of the subjects or citizens of friendly States and from countenancing action inimical to the security of such States.[34]

In regard to paragraph (4), it may be noted that "the present conditions" which Lansing had in mind were those obtaining during the World War. In Root's use of Lansing's words, they appeared to refer to the disturbed conditions in China attendant upon the change from an empire into a republic. In the final text of the Nine Power Treaty, the word "present" before "conditions" is omitted. One other change which Root's draft makes in the Lansing proposal, is the addition of the words "and from countenancing action inimical to the security of those states." The exact significance of this phrase has not been made apparent.

Professor W. W. Willoughby, who served as Technical Expert to the Chinese delegation at the Conference, points out that this fourth paragraph was essentially a new proposition upon which the Powers were asked to commit themselves and that for this additional safeguard "China owes a debt of gratitude to the American Govern-

[33] Chief Justice Hughes to the author, March 26, 1924; *Foreign Relations of the United States*, 1922, Vol. I, p. 279 n.
[34] *Proceedings*, p. 890.

ment." [35] So far as the debt is owed to an individual, Mr. Hughes rather than Mr. Root must be the individual creditor, since the latter was in this case merely the formulator of language and not the originator of policy. Yet this seems to be the chief instance during the Conference where Root's experience and drafting skill showed to the best advantage. He presided efficiently over the subcommittee of delegates charged with the question of the Chinese Eastern Railway and at the first session delivered a summary of the legal situation which was clear and able but probably too technical in its viewpoint to be of great help in reaching a solution. In the meetings of the American delegation before the Conference opened, this subject had been assigned to his special charge. In the subsequent discussions, he insisted upon China's duty to afford adequate protection and her actual inability to do so. This was but another example of his rather stern attitude toward the Chinese.

Root had a strong feeling of affection for the French and was particularly fond of Ambassador Jusserand who was a member of the French delegation but somewhat slighted by his colleagues. Root was saddened by the ineptness of the French policy at the Conference. Root felt that the preliminary American gesture offering to make a great sacrifice of its unquestionably advantageous naval position, had set a tone and spirit for the Conference which the French wholly failed to comprehend. They were prepared for the usual bargaining give-and-take method of diplomacy and demanded much that they never expected to get or really wanted to have. Basically he felt there was real merit in the French position. As a contribution to the common cause in the war, she had concentrated on her land forces and allowed her navy to run down. The measure of existing naval strengths adopted by the Conference was therefore unfair to her. If she had come out frankly with the statement that she had no wish to build capital ships during the naval holiday but that she did not wish to be put permanently in the position of a third-class naval power, her demands would have been met and she would have received the recognition of her right to build up her navy at the end of the ten year period. As it was, she took an obstructionist attitude throughout and succeeded only in appearing always to be in the wrong. When Hughes suggested 175,000 tons for France, Sarraut and Jusserand demanded

[35] Willoughby, *China at the Conference*, p. 43.

350,000, or 50,000 tons more than that allotted to Japan. Hughes told
them that the publication of such a demand would leave them not
one friend in the United States; that the stream of American philanthropy to French war orphans would cease. They were unmoved.
Briand had already returned to France but before he left he told
Hughes to cable him if any difficulty arose. Hughes did so on this occasion and Briand took personally the responsibility for accepting
175,000 tons.[36] France prevented any action being taken in regard to
land armaments and was the chief objector to the limitation of submarines. At a dinner party given to the delegates, when a member of
the French delegation entered the room, Root whispered to Lodge's
daughter, "Don't mention submarines to the little fellow; he's nervous." [37] The situation was made worse by unfortunate press reports
which were unfounded and some of which were sufficiently important
to evoke official disavowals at the sessions of the Conference. Yet, as
Buell points out,[38] these press reports were the logical result of the
French attitude. One instance which Root reported to Chandler Anderson and which the latter recorded in his diary for February 6th,
1922, was typical. Hughes and Balfour had secured the agreement of
the Chinese and Japanese that American and British experts should
sit in on their conversations regarding Shantung. The Chinese had
been anxious for this arrangement because of their fear that otherwise
unwelcome terms might be pressed upon them by the Japanese and
also because they felt that the results might better be justified in their
own country if the negotiations took place in this way. When Viviani
heard of the arrangement, he insisted that a French representative
must also sit in on the discussions since France demanded that she be
kept informed of all that went on. He delivered an ultimatum that
he would sail for France the following day unless his demand was
granted. It was explained to him that the invitation would have to
come from the Chinese and Japanese since this was not a part of the
Conference as such. In an effort to smooth over the situation, the
Americans persuaded the Chinese to consent, but the Japanese insisted that they must refer the matter to Tokio for express instructions. They were unwilling to have it appear that their negotiations

[36] Cf. *Foreign Relations of the United States*, 1922, Vol. I, pp. 130 ff.
[37] Mrs. Clarence Williams to the author, August 24, 1937.
[38] Buell, *op. cit.*, p. 234.

with the Chinese were being dictated by the Great Powers or by the Conference. They agreed to cable for instructions, Viviani was so informed, and that was the last which was ever heard of the matter.

Another example of pettiness was the French insistence just before the final plenary session, that unless the French text were given the place of honor in the parallel texts of the treaties and the word "French" put before the word "English" in the clause stating that both texts were authentic, France would refuse to sign the treaties. When Root heard of this, it was the only time that Lodge ever saw him lose his temper. "To hell with them!" Root cried. "Let the whole business go to pot—I wouldn't care." [39] Hughes was naturally provoked but acquiesced in paying what was in reality a very cheap price for harmony. [40]

"It got to be the fashion," Root remarked ten years later, "to decry the results of that Conference. People assume you haven't done anything if you haven't done everything. But observation of the progress of the European nations had made people see that the Washington Conference was the only thing that has actually been done" in securing the limitation of armaments. Subsequently he included the London Conference of 1930, the successor to the Washington Conference, as among the sole achievements in this field. The internationally minded Americans did belittle the achievements of the Conference because it limited itself to capital ships and did not end Japanese imperialism. The nationally minded attacked it as giving up American supremacy on the seas and a position of power in the Far East. The results were actually of very real importance in relation to the limitation of armaments and to the political problems of the Pacific. The fact that both groups of treaties have now gone by the board does not brand them as failures.

One cannot rank Root's contributions at the Washington Conference as among his great personal achievements. He was an influential elder statesman and at times he showed that he was still sage in counsel. He never had any egotistical pride which could have been hurt by the feeling that he was playing second fiddle to Hughes, although this was his first experience as a definite subordinate at an interna-

[39] Mrs. Clarence Williams to the author, August 24, 1937.
[40] Details on France from Chandler P. Anderson's Diary, the Diary of Henry L. Stimson, entry of February 27, 1922, and conversations between Root and the author.

tional gathering. On the Russian Mission he had been subordinate to the distant State Department but he had been head of the delegation. Root had shown when he served McKinley and Roosevelt that he could be a good subordinate; he would have been loyal and faithful to Wilson if he had been taken to Paris. He probably went too far in assuming to mediate between the Chinese and Japanese at Washington and perhaps he failed to realize completely that he no longer had the authority to speak for his country. It can not be said, however, that Secretary Hughes or President Harding made any mistake in selecting him for the delegation. He added prestige, as Taft had pointed out, and except for the political service in pushing the treaties in the Senate afterward, he was a more useful delegate than Lodge or Underwood.

It will perhaps never be possible to pass final judgment on his conception of the proper Far Eastern policy for the United States. It can be said that the policy which the United States has followed has not prevented Japan from pushing her interests in China, while at the same time it has created dangerous friction and rivalry between the United States and Japan. Had the United States followed Root's idea of cultivating friendship with Japan while insisting on respect for Chinese sovereignty, we might now find ourselves in a position of helpful friendliness with both those Asiatic powers, much to our own benefit and to theirs.

Note: The following sources in addition to those mentioned in the footnotes have been used in preparing this section on the Washington Conference: conversations with Chief Justice Charles Evans Hughes, John V. A. MacMurray, Stanley Washburn and DeWitt C. Poole; Foreign Relations of the United States for 1920, 1921 and 1922; Ichihashi, The Washington Conference and After; Council on Foreign Relations, American Foreign Relations (1928); A. Whitney Griswold, unpublished manuscript of The Far Eastern Policy of the United States.

Buell, The Washington Conference, though published so soon after the Conference, covers the ground thoroughly and deals with many matters not touched upon here.

CHAPTER XLVIII

"The bar has risen out of its interment in the individual case"

Root's active interest in law reform dates back to the end of the century when he was in his fifties and still had forty years to give to that cause. If one compares his speeches at the time of the New York Constitutional Convention of 1894 with those of the later Convention of 1915, one sees how greatly his interest in the subject had developed; the intervening years had heard a number of his vigorous speeches on the subject. When he was welcomed back to the New York Bar after his retirement from the Senate in 1915, he remarked that there had been "a radical change in the attitude of the bar. . . . The bar has risen out of its interment in the individual case, out of its concentration of interest in the success of plaintiff or defendent in the particular case, into a realization of its interest and its duty to the law. . . ." In this decade he referred back frequently to the time when he was a young practitioner and David Dudley Field was advocating the adoption of his code of procedure. It was a move in the direction of simplification to which Field devoted himself in his riper years and to which Root also turned after he passed the half century mark. Fortunately the trend is now in the direction which Root noted and the younger members of the bar concern themselves more with legal reform than was the custom in the 1860's and '70's.

Root urged his fellow lawyers to get away from the idea that the trial of cases was a game, "like a prize fight, a gladiatorial contest, that furnished the chief amusement throughout the country for the people who would flock to the court house . . . to hear two distinguished counsel lambaste each other.

"And the Judge refereed the game. . . . But now that the public has baseball and the movies, it seems unnecessary that the Government should furnish a further kind of amusement under the name of judicial proceedings" and the bar should recognize that the public is a third party in interest in the trial of every case.[1]

In this reform of procedure, Root thought that statutes should deal only with the most general aspects and that the courts should have the power to fix the rules in detail. The trouble with detailed codes of procedure, Root wrote to the Chairman of the Louisiana Bar Association on December 24th, 1920, "is that as a whole they make procedure so technical that the adroit, subtle, crafty man has an immense advantage over the honest and simple-minded man who is merely trying to get his rights." He was constantly inveighing against the piling up of the huge mass of statutory and case material and it was this feeling of his which made him take such a keen and active interest in the work of the American Law Institute, although this movement began as a result of still another aspect in which he was much concerned.

Since 1893 the American Bar Association had had a Section on Legal Education but its work was desultory. In 1913, William Howard Taft, then Professor of Law at Yale, read a paper on proper standards for admission to the Bar before a joint session of the Association of American Law Schools and the Section on Legal Education of the American Bar Association. In the same year, Dr. Henry S. Pritchett, President of the Carnegie Foundation for the Advancement of Teaching, accepted the Bar Association's invitation to make a survey of legal education comparable to one which the Foundation had just completed on medical education. Root, always close to Pritchett and to the work of the Foundation, took a keen interest in this project. In 1919, upon the urging of William Draper Lewis, Root accepted the position of chairman of a new section on Legal Education and Admissions to the Bar of the American Bar Association; he had been president of the Association three years before. In 1921, as chairman of a committee of the section, Root sent out a questionnaire to law schools, bar associations, Boards of Bar Examiners, and individual lawyers. On the basis of the replies, a report was circulated to the members of the Bar Association. In the very hot August days of 1921, Root stayed with Taft at Charles Taft's home in Cincinnati during the sessions of the Bar Association. They were the chief protagonists of the proposal for adopting minimum standards for training candidates for admission to the bar.

[1] New York *Times*, January 5, 1927.

The opposition came from two sources: one was the bar of those states where any person could practice law without examination if he were of good moral character; the other was the night law schools who alleged that they served the interests of the poor boys who could not afford to attend a full-time law school. To the President of the State Bar Association of Indiana, where the State Constitution provided that any man of good moral character could practice law, Root wrote in 1922: "If the bar is to be a learned profession, then somebody should see to it that its members become reasonably learned before they are admitted to practice, otherwise they will be practicing under false pretenses and deceiving the public. The theory of the Indiana constitution, of course, is that the bar is not to be a learned profession." "The chief faults in our administration of justice . . . ," he wrote to Dr. Willis of the University of North Dakota in 1921, "can be traced directly to the great proportion of half-educated lawyers at our Bar. They are like the clumsy apprentice who spoils good material, and makes more work than he disposes of. The right to practice law is a privilege coupled with a duty, and to secure the privilege without qualifying for the duty is to swindle the public, which ought to protect itself just as it does against quack doctors and untrained motor car drivers." Just before the Cincinnati meeting, Root answered the other objection in a letter to Robert McMurdy of Chicago: "I quite agree with what you say about young men who are poor and struggling and sacrificing, having an opportunity to fit themselves for the Bar. I do not think that the plan proposed by the committee of the section of legal education interferes at all with night schools. It was not our intention to do so. We specifically agreed that we should not do so. All that we propose to require is that if any young man does his work in a night school he should do just as much work as he does in a day school. It seems to me that is fair."

The recommendations of Root's committee were that every candidate for admission to the bar should have been graduated from a law school which met certain standards, including the requirements of two years of college prior to admission; the completion of three full years of work in law school; the possession of an adequate library and a sufficient number of full time teachers. It was also recommended that after graduation, every applicant should be examined by public authority before being admitted to the bar. It was proposed to draw up a list of approved law schools and to make the list public. After these recommendations were carried at Cincinnati, Root secured the adoption also of a proposal to call a conference of delegates of state and local bar associations. Such a conference met in Washington in February, 1922, and there Root, after a full exposition, finally carried the day with a brief speech full of dramatic appeal. Simultaneously, progress was being made with a plan, fathered by Root in 1916, for developing an integrated bar through the organization of a national conference of bar association delegates. This plan was perfected in 1936 and on the achievement of that result, the Conference of Delegates telegraphed their recognition to Root as the "founder" of the movement.

Root did not think the progress slow. "It is necessary to allow time in such things," he wrote to Clarence E. Martin in 1933. "We are intensely conservative at the Bar. That is our business. If we were not, there would not be any law. Being conservative we are like a watch dog barking at every unfamiliar step. After a time we become familiar with the step, exercise unbiased judgment, and the trouble is over."

It is impossible to measure the extent of Root's influence in these matters because it was not limited to his actual participation in meetings and committees of bar associations or in public speeches. His files show appeals from lawyers in many states of the Union in all geographical sections, asking his advice on this problem or that, whether constitutional, statutory, judicial or on private initiative. He answered such inquiries fully, giving much ripe wisdom, pungent expression and forceful argument. He had furthered another project having to do with the question of the use of expert testimony, being chairman of a committee of the American Association for the Advancement of Science which made a study of this problem and the way in which it is solved in various countries.

It was largely due to Root's influence that the Carnegie Corporation contributed the large sums necessary for the work of the American Law Institute. This Institute did not spring full fledged from anybody's brow. Its inception can be traced to the discussions of a Committee of the Association of American Law Schools. William Draper Lewis, who has been its sole director, conferred with Mr. Root in New York in March, 1922, about the desirability of a permanent organization for the constructive improvement of the law, especially the clarification and simplification of the common law. In the work of the American Law Institute which was then launched, for the first time, from all parts of the United States, leading law teachers, judges and practitioners have united in a common effort for the restatement of the law. Mr. Lewis vividly recalled the scene in Mr. Root's apartment at 998 Fifth Avenue: "After I had been talking I suppose for about fifteen minutes he put his right hand, which as usual was held against his vest, on the table. His hands . . . were the most expressive that I have ever seen. I knew him well enough to realize that he was not only interested, but that the slight movement of the hand across the table toward me meant that he wished to express his own ideas. Of course I stopped and he began to talk, how long I do not know, but before he ended he had taken the plan that I suggested, and changed it here and there out of his great experience as to what was practicable. Furthermore, as was characteristic of him when thoroughly interested, he did not stop with stating the underlying objects and the way to obtain them, but carefully went over the detailed steps which had to be taken in order to launch the organization successfully." [2]

After that time Root followed every aspect of the plans, in the large and in minute detail. They were eager to have him accept the presidency of the Institute but he knew that his strength was not equal to that task and it was his suggestion which was followed in electing George W. Wickersham. Root himself agreed to serve as Honorary President and as such on the Executive Committee. For several years he was regular in his attendance and when he was no longer able to attend, Wickersham or Lewis, on Law Institute business, were among the many callers who came to 998 Fifth Avenue to seek and to obtain advice and help. It was the experience of not a few, who arrived with a cautionary word from Miss Stewart that their visit should be brief to avoid tiring Mr. Root, that when his interest was aroused, he would keep on and on, by the half hour and the hour, talking with humor, with breadth of knowledge and of outlook, until they went away wondering if he were really around his ninetieth year. I have inquired of many who saw him in his ninety-first year up to within a very short

[2] Lewis to the author, August 30, 1937.

time of his death and I have found no one who does not independently confirm my own observation that there was no impairment of
the keenness of his intellect and the shrewd processes of his mind.
He never abandoned his exploration of a subject until he had thought
through one or more steps into the future beyond the point at which
the calculations of ordinary men stop.

Root always insisted that a lawyer must have a complete mastery of
all the essential facts bearing upon his clients' cases. He told the grad-
uating class of the Yale Law School in 1904 that in preparing for the
trial of a case, the lawyer had "to become familiar with the history
and methods of a great manufactory, the sources and cost of its raw
material, the markets for its finished product, the elements of its success or failure, the difficulties and hopes and fears and ways of thinking of its managers. Next week he may go through the same process
with a railroad company, and the next week with a banker and the
next with a merchant, or a ship owner, or a contractor, or a charitable institution, or a church." His own practice was a good illustration
of this diversity even after 1915 when he was less active but frequently
retained as counsel for important interests. Over a long period he
acted as counsel for the Guggenheims in connection with the American Smelting and Refining Company and other companies. The officers of the Smelting Company were impressed by the fact that Root
knew as much about their business as they did. This was one reason
why he was able in 1922 to deal in a masterful way with a dispute
between the management and a group of minority stockholders in
that company. In 1920 he advised members of his son's firm of Root,
Clark, Buckner and Howland on an intricate problem which arose in
connection with the estate of Marshall Field of Chicago. Root's analysis opened up a new and successful line of approach which had not
been discovered by a whole battery of eminent lawyers who had been
working on the case. In the summer of 1929, at the age of eighty-four,
he came down to New York from Clinton and expounded at a special
meeting of the Board of Directors of the United States Steel Corporation their rights and liabilities under the Sherman Anti-Trust Act
with reference to a projected purchase of the business of the Columbia
Steel Company; his mastery of the facts and the law in the case was
absolute. Probably the last legal opinion which he delivered—at the

ELIHU ROOT

(From the marble bust by James Earle Fraser in the Army War College)

age of ninety-one and just two months before his death—analyzed with great sagacity and astuteness the problems laid before him by the Massachusetts Institute of Technology in regard to their future patent policy.[3]

In the field of international law, Root was never a great scholar like John Bassett Moore. He was a skillful administrator of international affairs and with his legal skill made himself master of particular branches of the law which were involved in actual matters which came before him. An example is his classic opinion in the Rudovitz case on extradition for political offenses. In 1907, he helped James Brown Scott establish the American Society of International Law and from that date until 1924 he was its active president. He had an amazingly resourceful and ingenious mind but was not a great creative thinker. In the law and even in statecraft, one searches long to find real originality in the sense in which that term might be applied to a Darwin or an Einstein. Greatness in the legal and political fields is generally revealed by the wise adaptation of past experience. That kind of greatness Elihu Root possessed to a marked degree. He could fashion the device for the election of judges which made possible the creation of the World Court, but had he sat as a judge upon its bench he would not have been the author of brilliant dissenting opinions which are often the vehicle—as in the case of Holmes and Brandeis in Washington and Anzilotti at The Hague—for expressing views a little in advance of the current thought of the time. Root would have been more interested in bringing a majority of the court to reach a common agreement. He was a great conciliator and would have been an outstanding figure in the American Constitutional Convention of 1787 where vital compromises had to be thought out and carried to adoption.

What he said of Theodore Roosevelt might also be said of Root himself: "He did not originate great new truths, but he drove old fundamental truths into the minds and the hearts of his people so that they stuck and dominated. Old truths he insisted upon, enlarged upon, repeated over and over . . . never straining for novelty or for originality, but always driving, driving home the deep fundamental

[3] Root to Dean Vannevar Bush, December 22, 1936; Dean Bush to the author, August 16, 1937.

truths of public life, of a great self-governing democracy, the eternal truths upon which justice and liberty must depend among men." [4]

While Root was primarily the attorney, representing the interests of a client, he did have to a high degree the power of judicial detachment and this quality would have been valuable had he served on the Supreme Court of the United States. But he was not a great constructive jurist in the sense that he would have rendered notable service in the development of the law. In the law, as in other things, he was a staunch conservative. The controversy over Wilson's appointment of Louis D. Brandeis to the Supreme Court in 1916 has come to have a measure of symbolic significance as typifying the clash between so-called "liberal" and "conservative" schools of thought. Root joined with Taft and five other former presidents of the American Bar Association in protesting against the appointment, but Root's opposition was the result of careful study on the basis of which he reached the conclusion that Brandeis did not have the moral standards which Root thought a Supreme Court justice should possess.[5] Root and Taft saw eye to eye on the matter of constitutional interpretation yet Root was a great admirer of Mr. Justice Cardozo who belongs to another school. Root enjoyed a cordial friendship with Mr. Justice Holmes but probably agreed with Taft that it was unfortunate that Holmes tended to side with Brandeis on constitutional questions. Root, however, was far from believing in the immutability of the Constitution. His correspondence abounds with statements like the following from a letter to Claris Adams in September, 1912: "The increasing complexity of modern social and industrial life requires continual extensions of the police power, and extensions of the police power always necessitate limitations upon liberty of action and in the use of property. . . . Police regulations which would have been such unjustifiable limitations upon liberty and the enjoyment of property a hundred years ago as to be justly condemned under the constitution may be perfectly proper exercises of the police power now, and regulations which would be unjustifiable now may be justified by the conditions existing a hundred years hence."

In his presidential address to the Bar Association of the City of

[4] Men and Policies, p. 15.

[5] Elihu Root, Jr. to the author, June 24, 1938. Much of the opposition to Brandeis was undoubtedly based on objection to his views on social and economic problems; Baker, Woodrow Wilson, Life and Letters, Vol. VI, pp. 111 ff.

New York in 1912, Root pointed out the difficulties arising from the fact "that the new conditions incident to the extraordinary industrial development of the last half-century are continuously and progressively demanding the readjustment of the relations between great bodies of men and the establishment of new legal rights and obligations not contemplated when existing laws were passed or existing limitations upon the powers of government were prescribed in our Constitution. . . . The relations between the employer and the employed, between the owners of aggregated capital and the units of organized labor, between the small producer, the small trader, the consumer, and the great transporting and distributing agencies, all present new questions for the solution of which the old reliance upon the free action of individual wills appears quite inadequate." [6] His exposition of this point of view was such that it was used verbatim by a leading exponent of the "New Deal" in 1936, Professor Felix Frankfurter, as a description of his own outlook on socio-economic problems.[7] Yet Root was violently opposed to many of the policies of the administration of Franklin D. Roosevelt. He was always convinced of the view which he expressed in 1923 that "our country is too big to have the people of the different sections governed in their local affairs by a central authority in Washington." [8] He constantly asserted his belief in the proposition that many of the functions which were being absorbed by the federal government should be left to the governments of the several states. Had he lived through the controversy over President Franklin Roosevelt's proposal to "pack" the Supreme Court, he would unquestionably have been a vigorous opponent of that project. With some of the "New Deal" policies he was in sympathy but he felt that they were being pressed too fast. He pointed out a fundamental fallacy in President Franklin Roosevelt's program, that is, the attempt to do two inconsistent things at once—the promotion of a program of social reform and the reestablishment of business confidence and activity.[9]

Root's part in opposing the Eighteenth Amendment is illustrative of his general views on such subjects. "I never cared much for Cato," Root replied to a letter from Judge Clearwater in July, 1933.

[6] *Addresses on Government and Citizenship*, p. 448.
[7] Professor Frankfurter to the author, March 23, 1938.
[8] Root to John Van Norden, March 2, 1923.
[9] Root to the author, December 20, 1934.

"He was an egotistical cold-blooded old brute for whom I have no sympathy whatever, but I do agree heartily to the application of his famous remark to National Prohibition. It will take a long time for our country to recover from the injury done by that great and stupid error in government, but it seems as if both of us may possibly see the beginning of the recovery. It is really very fine." He had just returned to Clinton from attendance upon the New York State Repeal Ratification Convention at Albany, which, as he wrote Harry D. Yates, he enjoyed very much "largely because of its atmosphere of friendly good humor. Nobody seemed to remember that it was his duty to hate anybody else, and that made the occasion both novel and refreshing."

He had been from the outset opposed to the form and spirit, the purpose and the effect of the Eighteenth Amendment. It irked him as a lawyer that a legislative act should be written into the Constitution; it outraged his sense of good government that a sumptuary law should be given constitutional status and that a local matter should be transferred to the federal government; it infuriated him as an individual that anyone should thus attempt to regulate his personal habits. The prohibition era is close enough to this writing to make it unnecessary to recall the fanaticism of the temperance advocates and the rage of those who opposed them. Respectable persons who never drank before began drinking to show their contempt and disgust for the law. Many thought as Root did, that "the cause of temperance has been seriously set back by this ill-advised attempt to hasten temperance by compulsion." "Temperance" he said in 1930, "means moderation through self-control. When one is grown up compulsion through the law creates revulsion. You cannot make man just through the law, you cannot make man merciful through the law, you cannot make man affectionate through the law."

He had a very warm admiration for Hoover but nearly lost his faith in the Republican Party when it failed to come out flatfootedly for repeal. Hoover's phrase that prohibition was "a noble experiment" made him snort with indignation: "Prohibition is as much 'a noble experiment' as the Spanish Inquisition—it is the same idea of forcing people to conduct their lives as you want them to." Root also had the very highest opinion of James W. Wadsworth who was defeated for reelection to the United States Senate because he refused to qualify his forthright stand against prohibition. Despite his long life which is an examplar of party loyalty, Root could say in 1930: "I regard myself under no party obligations at all to support any candidate put up by the Drys of this state. Yes, I feel the same way nationally but you can't get national leaders in a position like that of the New Yorkers who repudiated Wadsworth. Hoover says he must enforce the law which is a position you can't quarrel with and you can't repudiate him for that. The repudiation of Wadsworth gave New York two Democratic Senators both from New York City. Wadsworth was the best and ablest representative of upstate New York we ever had in the Senate; a man who has made more contributions than any other man from the state. The Drys eliminated him by elevating the dry issue over all others.

"The Republicans are torn apart by the Wet and Dry issue. The religious prohibitionists are arrogant over their control. As soon as they bolted Wadsworth and put up a candidate to draw votes from him, reprisals were inevitable. You can suppress an issue like liquor for a time and kick it under the sofa but when it once comes out you can't suppress it." [10]

A year later he remarked: "I think the Republican Party needs a licking. They have kept in office by fraud, trickery and dishonest practices and statements. The only thing I would regret is that Hoover would suffer. He has been a fine president. I think he was the only man in the United States for the presidency at this time. He has done a great deal of good work and has prevented the catastrophe from being much worse. But he will be punished. He will be bitten by the very people he has tried to help." [11]

And twelve months later: "If I weren't one hundred and fifty years old and had to make a public statement, I would have a hard time defending why I am a Republican. I think they are wrong on tariffs, they are wrong on prohibition, wrong on foreign affairs. They have made into a formal policy a political squabble with Wilson over the League. Anyone with any vision should see how foolish that is."

Even many opponents of prohibition agreed that the saloon was an evil in American life which should be regulated in some way. But Root argued differently in a letter of November 22nd, 1919, to Everett

[10] Root to the author.
[11] *Ibid.*

P. Wheeler: ". . . prohibition at this time takes away the chief pleasure in life for millions of men who have never been trained to get their pleasure from art, or literature, or sports, or reform movements, and that necessarily creates an exceedingly dangerous social situation. Whether it be natural or acquired, the gregarious instinct is very deeply implanted in human nature. You and I have our clubs. Throughout the small towns in this country you find the Masonic Lodge or the Lodge of the various orders like the Odd Fellows and the Elks, and the Woodmen of the World, &c., &c., which are in the main the outcome of the club instinct. Answering the same instinct, millions of men who do the hard labor of the world have been in the habit of meeting their fellows over a glass of beer, and finding in that way the chief relaxation and comfort of very dull grey lives. This prohibition is taking away that recourse from these men just at a time when all the world is stirred up, feverish and dissatisfied. Everybody is trying to climb up over somebody else. Nobody rests content. Prohibition is taking away the comfort and increasing the discontent of a vast number of lives which really have very little to make them happy. I think it is a very material element in the serious labor situation that we now have in this country." By 1930, he agreed it was just as well the saloon should not return.

He opposed every stage of the prohibition movement from the time of the enactment of the so-called War-time Prohibition Act on November 21st, 1918. That Act, he wrote Franklin D. Locke in March, 1919, "is a fraud based upon false pretenses, and has no relation whatever to the exercise of the Constitutional power to carry on war, because the war was really over before the Act was passed. The question whether the courts can act upon this indisputable truth is exceedingly interesting." He had to admit later that the state of war technically continued after the signing of the Armistice but that did not lessen his opposition.

"It is impossible," Root wrote to Judge Bartlett on September 4th, 1918, ". . . to make even a colorable argument upon the proposition that the people of Iowa have any concern with the question what the people of New York eat and drink. The personal habits of the people of any State are entirely a domestic affair, and the insertion of a sumptuary law in the Constitution of the United States is plainly an attempt to prevent local self-government, and to enable part of the

people to exercise tyranny over another part of the people." When
the Amendment was adopted, he felt that the constitutional process
of the American government had been swept aside: "Where did the
Commander of the Lost Battalion tell the Germans to go when they
demanded his surrender? Seek there the Constitution." So he wrote
to a friend, but in unrecorded conversations there were unquestionably stronger statements unembellished by any such circumlocution.
He believed that if national prohibition were to be adopted at all,
it should have been done by submitting the question to the people
and not to the legislatures of the states. That Congress should submit it as it did, he told one correspondent in 1919, was a breach of
trust. "It is quite common to see legislative action in a democracy
controlled by some violent and vindictive minority, which is much
more certain to punish a legislator for refusing to do their will than
the great body of the public is to reward him for acting in the public
interest."

He accepted retainers from the brewing interests trying to upset
the validity of the first war-time Act and later arguing the unconstitutionality of the Eighteenth Amendment itself. He accepted no
retainer from the hard liquor interests although there is no evidence
that he shared the widespread impression that the "liquor trust" was
a menace. After he had been retained by the brewers, Attorney General A. Mitchell Palmer wrote him with great chagrin to explain that
the newspapers were wholly false in attributing to him the "cheap
witticism" that " 'Hires' Root Beer' has now been changed to "Beer
Hires Root'."

Root's view that the Eighteenth Amendment to the Constitution
was unconstitutional was not shared by many of his brethren at the
bar and he was considerably comforted when a few lawyers took the
same position. Under the theory of our constitutional practice, Root
was wrong, because the Supreme Court overruled though they did
not answer his argument, powerful and dramatic as it undoubtedly
was. An eye-witness has described the scene on March 9th, 1920, as
Root came toward the close of his argument. Root looked up at the
clock and saw that it lacked six minutes to four-thirty when the court
would rise. "It was important for the psychological situation that he
occupy those six minutes, and not permit them to be given over to
some extraneous case. Mr. Root put his glasses in his pocket, and,

drawing himself up to his full height, pointing his finger at the Chief Justice, with the whole nine Justices fixing their eyes upon him, he concluded his argument with these memorable words, which have burned themselves forever into my memory: 'If Your Honors . . . shall find a way to uphold the validity of this amendment, the government of the United States, as we have known it, will have ceased to exist. . . . Your Honors will have found a legislative authority hitherto unknown to the Constitution and untrammeled by any of its limitations. . . . In that case, Your Honors, John Marshall need never have sat upon your bench. . . .' The clock was at half past four." [12]

In brief, Root's idea was that while an amendment could confer upon Congress a new legislative power, namely the power to regulate the manufacture and sale of intoxicating liquors, the Eighteenth Amendment did not do this but sought directly by constitutional enactment to legislate upon the subject. "Neither Congress nor three-fourths of all the States nor both put together have any right to legislate within the reserved powers of a single non-consenting State." Root argued that Article Five of the Constitution used the term "amendment" as applying to something germane to a proposition contained in the constitution; "the police regulation of personal unofficial conduct is not germane to such an instrument." The people themselves could adopt any amendment they choose, even impairing such a guaranty as the freedom of religion. But the legislatures, as amending agents who might represent a minority of the people of the nation, could not do so. The argument involves a rather nice distinction and even William D. Guthrie, who was counsel with Root in arguing the National Prohibition Cases before the Supreme Court, thought that Root's argument was weak and that it should not have been pressed.[13] With Root's views as to the wisdom and desirability of the Amendment, there was of course much more wide-spread agreement, as was indicated by the extraordinary rapidity with which the Twenty-first Amendment, eliminating the Eighteenth Amendment, was finally adopted in 1933. Root followed the process of ratification by the states with the closest attention. It was the triumph

[12] Nicholas Murray Butler, address at the Odeon, St. Louis, Missouri, December 14, 1927.
[13] William D. Guthrie to the author, May 2, 1933.

of Repeal which encouraged Root again in his confidence in the American people and in the processes of democracy. It was a gratification to him that his daughter-in-law, Mrs. Edward W. Root, took a leading part in the amazingly effective work for repeal accomplished by that group familiarly known as the "Sabine Women," from the name of their leader, Mrs. Charles H. Sabin. Shortly after Repeal, Mr. Root was in the Century Club and went into the bar for a convivial glass with a fellow member. He planted his foot ostentatiously on the rail and declared, "This is a step in the right direction."

"On general principles," Root wrote to Gaspar Bacon on January 25th, 1926, "I am opposed to the amendment of a constitution. I think like Falkland that 'where it is not necessary to change, it is necessary not to change'." On both general and particular principles, Root was strongly against the proposed Child Labor Amendment to the federal constitution. His principal point was that this was a matter which ought to be regulated by the states and not by the federal government. On February 28th, 1934, he wrote his views to William D. Guthrie and his letter was published in the newspapers on March 2nd. Root pointed to the "necessary expansion of Federal control over interstate and foreign commerce, over currency and banking, over post offices and means of transportation, the unlimited control of Congress over vast expenditures of money raised by Federal taxation" which had inevitably "built up a vast Federal bureaucracy." He recognized the necessity for such measures in the emergency through which the country was passing but he was afraid of the future trend. To guard against the continuance of such emergency powers after the crisis had passed, he felt "it becomes continually of more vital importance to the maintenance of our system of government, that the authority, the dignity and the independence of action in all local affairs by our separate States shall be maintained and insisted upon. Such Constitutional amendments as this about child labor are powerful aids to this process of weakening State government, which we ought to be resolute in withstanding. . . ." Root did not question the evils of child labor but to him the fundamental principles of government in which he believed were more important than the quick removal of the evil. If public opinion could be directed to pressing for action by State governments instead of by the Federal Government, he believed that the remedy would be secured in the course of time. Some call such an attitude reactionary; others consider it the part of patient sagacity.

Organized labor in general would have classified Root as a reactionary. When he was Secretary of War they attacked his motives and his policies but it was he who was largely responsible for settling the anthracite coal strike of 1902. They were opposed to his appointment as chief of the Russian Mission in 1917 and they were influential in Wilson's decision not to appoint him a member of the Peace Commission in 1919. Yet in 1926 his was the only name in a list of one hundred prominent Americans upon whom they could agree as a man whose wisdom and justice they could trust in settling a major dispute in their own ranks.

It was a serious situation which threatened to disrupt the ranks of organized labor and which had tied up hundreds of millions of dollars' worth of building construction throughout the United States. The Bricklayers, Masons and Plasterers International Union included men whose chief work was plastering; so did the Operative Plasterers and Cement Finishers International Association, but the latter organization also included large numbers of cement and stucco workers, who were in great demand as the building industry began to turn more and more to the use of artificial stone. Both unions sought to organize locals in various communities and to compel contractors to accord them exclusive recognition. The Plasterers' Union had started as a branch of the Bricklayers' Union and, after splitting off, disputed the right of the older union to retain men permanently on its membership rolls. In 1911, the two unions reached an agreement delimiting the territory of each union and specifying that neither would invade the territory of the other. The Bricklayers, ten years later, abrogated two sections of the agreement of 1911 and appealed their case to the National Board of Jurisdictional Awards. The plasterers considered this a breach of the entire 1911 agreement and abrogated it in toto. Then came the building boom in Florida, a state which had been allocated as Bricklayers' territory. The Plasterers came flocking in and established locals in a number of cities throughout the state. Where contractors employed plasterers from one union, members of the rival union quit the job. Other unions took sides and employers sought to aid one group or the other. The dispute became nationwide;

President Coolidge made an unsuccessful effort to mediate. President William Green of the American Federation of Labor, realizing the damage which was being done to the two unions and to the general cause of organized labor, intervened and succeeded in establishing a truce by an agreement reached at Atlantic City in October, 1925. Both sides agreed to submit the dispute to impartial arbitration by a board to be composed of three persons, one appointed by each union and the third to be chosen by common agreement. Conferences were held and over one hundred names were suggested by President Green without any agreement being reached. Finally, on July 14th, 1926, both organizations accepted the name of Elihu Root. Green telegraphed to Root at Clinton and, on July 20th, came to explain what they wanted Root to do.

With the tips of his fingers pressed together, Root listened, tilting back in his modern swivel desk chair behind the old claw-foot table, with brass handles on the drawers. Behind him, between the lightly curtained windows which looked out past the leaves of the ginko tree under the high branches of a wine-glass elm across the Hamilton College campus, glass-doored sectional bookcases held some volumes on international law, the works of Lord Bryce, a set of his own collected speeches and papers, and various reference books. Over his right shoulder, another bookcase was filled largely with Hamilton College publications, family genealogies and local histories. On a stand near by, the Encyclopedia Britannica. An open fireplace was opposite him; on the walls, maps and photographs of Theodore Roosevelt, William Howard Taft, Joseph H. Choate, Lord Bryce and other old friends. In a corner some guns in cases and a pack basket bristling with saws and garden tools; he still went out with the men to trim the trees. His eighty-one years had not stooped his shoulders nor dimmed the clear, quick processes of his mind. He would inevitably have been wearing a pepper and salt suit with lapels on the vest, a soft shirt and high black shoes.

Root agreed to be the arbitrator—as a public service and without fee. In October he met the other two members of the tribunal in New York and their unanimous decision was reached on January 28th, 1927. It was communicated to the representatives of the two unions at a meeting in Root's law office at 31 Nassau Street on

February 1st. The tribunal held that the Plasterers were not justified in considering that the 1911 agreement was abrogated when the Bricklayers appealed to the National Board for Jurisdictional Awards and that they were not justified thereafter in establishing locals in Florida. But Root pointed out to them in some extemporaneous remarks as he communicated the decision, "while we have decided in the negative both the questions, we do not think either of you without fault. We consider that both parties mistook their powers; and it is plain to be seen . . . that this was the result of a change in the state of mind, a drifting away from the old kindliness and desire for harmonious action to a condition of irritation which warped and misled the judgment of both parties to this arbitration . . . the result ought to be not that either party should feel that it is entitled to walk away with bagpipes playing for it, but that each party should be led to make an honest effort to restore the old spirit in which the favorable working of the peace agreements will be possible again . . . putting the great idea which is embodied in the formal and customary address and signature of your letters—Dear Sir and Brother—Fraternally yours—putting that to the fore and answering to the kindly spirit which gave origin to those forms of communication. . . . In the broad view of the battle of labor for its fair share of the great new wealth of the world, it is a matter of slight consequence to what particular organization the locals in Florida or in New Mexico . . . belong, but it is of vast importance that the example and the infectious spirit of dislike and hatred shall not extend through the ranks of labor organizations. . . . Forgive me for preaching." Root admitted that "our labor organizations in America do many things" which he did not like, "have in the past and probably will again" but he felt that "the efficient organization of labor . . . is rendering very great and indispensable service to the maintenance of order and justice. . . ." The Plasterer, magazine of the Plasterers' Union, in its issue of April, 1927, reporting the above remarks of Root, thanked him editorially: "Mr. Root, you have dignified the labor movement, you were an inspiration and an influence. There was no anxiety on the part of the contending parties as to the justice or wisdom of your findings." They promised to show their appreciation by loyally carrying out the award. Both sides did so; there was one short period of revived hostility but again through the mediation of Green, it was

Mr. and Mrs. Elihu Root at
Clinton in 1924 with their
daughter-in-law, Mrs. Edward
W. Root, and their grandson,
John Buttrick Root

Elihu Root at Clinton in
1928 with his sons, Edward
Wales (*left*) and Elihu, Jr., and
his grandson, John Buttrick
Root

The home of Elihu Root at Clinton, New York

quickly adjusted and the American Federation of Labor's *Proceedings* for 1927 could report: "The 1911 agreement has been restored completely and the officers and members of the two organizations manifest a spirit of determination to adhere strictly" to that agreement.

CHAPTER XLIX

"Age has its compensations"

"THE labors which ensued upon my association with Mr. Carnegie begun a great many years ago," Mr. Root wrote to Mrs. Carnegie in 1925, "have played a great part in my latter life and I feel profoundly that they have played a great part in keeping me from drying up quite as much as old men are apt to do when they withdraw from the conflicts of life and think chiefly of themselves. So I consider myself not merely a trustee but a beneficiary of Mr. Carnegie's philanthropic enterprises." In his Foreword to Burton J. Hendrick's biography of the great philanthropist, Root points to a number of characteristics which, in fact, he too possessed and which may have contributed to the mutual friendship of the two men; devotion to father and mother and to the scenes and companions of childhood, for example. Within the relatively modest limits of his own income, Root, like Carnegie, was responsive to many appeals for financial assistance and those which always found a ready generosity were particularly such as were connected with some association of younger days. Relatives, old servants, the little village churches in Vernon and Paris Hill near Clinton, as well as such enterprises as the building of the Cathedral of St. John the Divine in New York and a long list of charitable and educational institutions were the steady recipients of Root's contributions. For Hamilton College he secured large gifts from Carnegie and others. When Root first appealed to Carnegie for aid to Hamilton, Carnegie responded with $100,000 "in recognition of the sacrifice you have made for the public good" as Secretary of War. When Root appealed again for the same cause six years later, he is said to have remarked jestingly, "If you think my work for peace isn't worth any more than my work for war, I am very much mistaken in you." Thereupon Carnegie gave Hamilton College $200,000 in honor of Elihu Root's services as Secretary of State. Root himself donated to the College more than a quarter of a million dollars during his lifetime and in his will he left it two hundred thousand dollars. In memory of his father, he gave the science building and endowed an annual fellowship in science. Equally significant were the small sums which showed his intimate and sympathetic knowledge of conditions and needs—now a little to purchase shrubs and trees to beautify the campus, now enough to paint a professor's house, now a contribution to help the work of a particular department when he felt the professor in charge was discouraged or hampered in his work through a lack of equipment. More often than not the beneficiary knew nothing of the source of the gift and many of Root's contributions were given indirectly so that they do not even appear on the books of the College. Root had what he describes in the Foreword to the biography of Andrew Carnegie as "a philosophy of helpfulness distinct from simple charity."

Hendrick's remark that "Carnegie had strong faith in the eventual triumph of intelligence, but had outgrown belief in sudden methods" might equally well be written of Root. Mrs. Root wrote to Mrs. Carnegie in 1925 after Mr. Root had been through a long illness, "He works all the time, and enjoys it and says when he gets to a time that he cannot work, he does not want to live." Mrs. Carnegie might have written the same to Mrs. Root. So, too, Root's birthday letter to Carnegie in 1914 might have been repeated vice versa, though with different implications: "It is a great thing to have been able to do what you have done for humanity and to be strong and active in body and mind and able to view from the height of serene age the field in which a multitude of forces set in motion by you are working for the progress of civilization."

Hendrick remarks that those who received from Mr. Carnegie presents of the famous whiskey directly from the "Queen's Vat," that is, especially distilled for Queen Victoria, were marked as having entered "the inner Carnegie circle." Root was among the beneficiaries of this type of philanthropy. "The support of my unjustifiable age by Skibo oatmeal," he wrote to Mrs. Carnegie in 1936, "entitles me to claim that I am a Carnegie subsidiary institution." His affectionate friendship for the Carnegie family was shared by Mrs. Root and extended to Mrs. Carnegie and her daughter Margaret. Root had known Mrs. Carnegie's father; when someone introduced him to her on the occasion of the dedication of the Carnegie Library in Washington, he stretched out both hands with a welcoming "Why of course I know John Whitfield's daughter!"

". . . you have always understood him [Mr. Carnegie] better than anyone else," Mrs. Carnegie wrote Root in 1932; "and have had a clearer vision of his deeply affectionate nature." She could remember her husband's talking about Mr. Root and saying "So wise! So wise!"

When Root was in the Cabinet, he and Carnegie were in frequent contact. Carnegie's associations with men prominent in the British Government were utilized by Roosevelt and Root. All three were interested in the cause of peace and particularly the advancement of that cause through the effective though undramatic progress of international arbitration. Root interested Carnegie in contributing the funds for the Pan American building in Washington and the building for the Central American Court of Justice at Cartago. He did not, however, succeed in persuading him to establish for Latin American students a fund comparable to the Rhodes Trust.

On December 14th, 1910, twenty-two persons met with Mr. Carnegie in the building of the Carnegie Institution in Washington and received from him ten million dollars of United States Steel bonds which they were to hold and administer as trustees of a Carnegie Endowment for International Peace. The idea had often been broached to Carnegie but he had rejected it for lack of practicality. The progress of the peace movement of the world along sane and practical lines began to change Carnegie's view and he was finally persuaded through President Taft's stirring appeal on March 22nd, 1910, for the arbitration even of questions of national honor. Carnegie consulted Root and others and the meeting mentioned above was the result. At this preliminary meeting Root was chosen President of the Board and he held that office until his resignation in 1925, when he was suceeded by Dr. Nicholas Murray Butler. Root, who was then in the Senate, prepared the draft of a federal charter and introduced the appropriate bill in the Senate but it did not pass. The Endowment was finally incorporated in New York in 1929. He was always intensely interested in the work of the Endowment and as President he followed its various projects with an eagle eye. At the original meeting when he and the other trustees accepted the trust, he pointed out that their work must be "thorough, practical; and it must base its action upon a careful, scientific and thorough study of the causes of war and the remedies which can be applied to the causes, rather than merely the treatment of symptoms." The long painstaking work of scholarship always was classified in his mind as "practical," and it was he who was largely responsible for the Endowment's fathering the monumental series of studies on the *Economic and Social History of the World War* which were inaugurated by John Bates Clark and ably completed by James T. Shotwell of Columbia University. Root followed the course of the work not in any perfunctory way but with keen personal interest and a strict sense of responsibility.

Root's last participation in a Carnegie meeting took place on December 14th, 1935, when the twenty-fifth anniversary of the Peace Endowment was celebrated in the library of the Carnegie home at Ninety-first Street and Fifth Avenue. Mrs. Carnegie and her daughter were there with the four survivors of the original meeting and some twenty newer appointees to the Board. Mr. Root was in his ninetieth year; they expected him to drop in for about five minutes. He stayed for over an hour and in response to a toast spoke as effectively as ever he had in his life.

The Carnegie Institution of Washington was Andrew Carnegie's chief provision for the advancement of the fields of pure science. In formulating the plans for its establishment "to encourage in the broadest and most liberal manner investigation, research and discovery and the application of knowledge to the improvement of mankind," he consulted numbers of people but particularly President Daniel Coit Gilman of The Johns Hopkins University. As the organization was originally planned in consultation with President Theodore Roosevelt, the Institution would have been a sort of public body under the control of the President and Congress. Dr. Nicholas Murray Butler of Columbia University was at the White House trying to persuade the President that such an arrangement would be most unfortunate, but Roosevelt was adamant. Finally Dr. Butler suggested that the President ask Secretary Root to come over. It was about ten o'clock in the evening and Root came rather grumpily in response to a telephone call. The project was shown to him; he ran through it quickly and looked up: "What damn fool suggested this idea?" he asked. The plan for a public body was abandoned and the Institution was set up as a private corporation under the laws of the District of Columbia, in 1902. Upon his death in 1937, Mr. Root was the sole surviving member of the original board of trustees. Through those thirty-two years he was a member of the Executive Committee, from 1903 to 1912 he was Vice Chairman of the Board, and he was Chairman from 1913 to 1937. In this close association with scientific men, Mr. Root revived the memories of his early years when he heard his father and Dr. Peters discussing scientific matters around the family table at Clinton. "I have long put a very high value," he wrote to Dr. Stewart Paton in 1932, "upon the opportunity for association in the Carnegie Institution, with scientific men earnestly engaged in actually doing scientific work. I know nothing else so useful as that to pull a man out of his ruts and push back his horizon. The people who are themselves trying to do something naturally have a sympathetic interest with all who are sincerely working, in whatever field, and this sympathy finds an understanding of human life which is missed entirely by the mere critic and the cynics which mere critics become." His interest was equally keen in all fields to which the Institute devoted its attention—atomic physics, geologic time, the significance of chromosomes or genes, astronomy or historical research. He was particularly insistent upon their keeping in mind Mr. Carnegie's strong feeling that not only must research be furthered but the results of the research must be so "interpreted and presented that they become imbedded in the thought of the people." [1] On October 29th, 1918, Root wrote to Major Henry Lee Higginson dissuading him from his intention to resign as a trustee of the Carnegie Institution. The letter actually describes Root's own attitude and the value of his own services:

> . . . A man lives a long life of active touch and experience in affairs; he acquires the respect and confidence of the community; his strength declines but his judgment ripens. As he loses his capacity for the service of youth in active exertion, he acquires capacity for a new service of discrimination and guidance between the true and false objects and methods to which the oncoming generations are to devote themselves. Thousands of vague proposals, visionary schemes, dishonest schemes, waste money and effort, come to nothing. One of the services a man can render in his old age is to give the credit acquired in a long life to the things that are honest and practical and useful; so that there shall be

[1] Report of Dr. John C. Merriam, President of the Institution, for 1937.

some leadership of effort, some guide to the abounding energy of people who want to do good in the world, and do not know quite how to direct their own energies. Without something of that kind, the cranks and ignorant enthusiasts and fakers have a fair chance to dry up the springs of benevolence with disappointed expectations. . . .

It was shortly after the establishment of the Peace Endowment that Carnegie became concerned with the problem of the disposition of the balance of his fortune which, despite his heroic generosity, still totaled $150,000,000. He turned to Root, handing him a will which he had written himself largely in his own hand. Root found that the will proposed to create a trust to which most of the money was to go on Carnegie's death. Root advised him strongly against such a plan. He told him that he could of course give him an opinion on the validity of the trust but that even that great lawyer, Samuel J. Tilden, in drawing his own will, had set up a trust which the courts held to be invalid. He therefore proposed that Carnegie should at once, during his lifetime, establish a corporation to which a moderate sum should be transferred forthwith. Such a corporation established by statute and already in existence could be made the chief beneficiary in his will. Carnegie immediately accepted the suggestion. The "moderate sum" which Root suggested as a beginning, turned out to be $25,000,000, which was increased in a short space of time to $125,-000,000. Carnegie himself composed the letters of instructions to the trustees of the Corporation which was incorporated in New York in 1911. Although Root appreciated the confidence which Carnegie placed in him personally, he remarked many years later that Carnegie had a distrust of lawyers, regarding them as people who tried to prevent him from doing what he wanted to do. Root had had an illustration of this when Carnegie had decided to take $10,000,000 from the Corporation and give it to a trust in Great Britain. Root had to point out to him very firmly that he had parted absolutely and forever with the money which he had given to the trustees of the Corporation. Carnegie characteristically solved the difficulty by going into his own pocket for another ten millions which he gave to the British Foundation.

Until the very last days of his life, Root served the Corporation assiduously and most effectively. When Mr. Carnegie, after eight years as President, retired in 1919, Root filled that position for one year, and from 1920 to the date of his death he was Chairman of the Board. Throughout the whole period scarcely any major question of policy was answered until he had expressed an opinion. He had great reason to be pleased with his part in the selection of its two other presidents— James R. Angell who served for one year, and Frederick P. Keppel who has been President since 1921. Through the Corporation, he continued to serve causes which he had helped individually, such as the American Federation of Arts, the American Law Institute, the American School for Classical Studies in Athens and the general cause of adult education and the fostering of the arts. He never accepted a trusteeship nor continued to hold it unless he felt able to devote himself to that responsibility. He stated once that the function of a board of trusteees is not to be right but to give their very best consideration to the problems before them and to keep a record of the steps by which they reach their conclusions. He could always see the inter-relation between the immediate project and the larger objective. In 1929, for example, he wrote President Keppel of the Corporation that he favored supporting an inquiry "into the problem rendered by the life of second generation Japanese in the United States for very much the same reason which leads me to favor a Mexican Art Exhibition. We need in this country to think a little more about other people, and to do that we must learn a little more about them. We are too self-centered; we lack humility; we unconsciously feel as if we stood alone in the universe. We feel under no obligation to consider the rights or interests or feelings of other peoples. This condition of things among a great and powerful people soon becomes national arrogance, and that is something which the high Gods always punish soon or late."

"One sees thousands of evils preventing the happiness and progress of mankind," he wrote to Keppel in that same year with reference to the progress of the Regional Plan for New York, "because no one comes along with intelligence and faith and courage to lead the multitude out of that particular wilderness. At the same time thousands of men who have intelligence and faith and courage are devising and proclaiming plans for human betterment and are all the time crying aloud in the wilderness where no one listens. Where the two succeed in getting hitched together, as they have here, I feel like cheering and looking for somebody to join me in violating the prohibition law."

Root was also closely associated with the work of another of Carnegie's benefactions, the Carnegie Foundation for the Advancement of Teaching. Through the twenty-four years when Henry S. Pritchett was head of that Foundation, the two men conferred together, each enjoying and benefiting from association with the other. In 1930, when Pritchett retired, Root wrote to him: "It is seventy years since I entered college . . . and my life has never been free from the powerful influence of the American college tradition. I have known personally most of the heads of American universities and colleges, and some of them very intimately for the last fifty years, and I have just finished my forty-seventh year as an active college trustee. So that I have a background, and I have been really interested in what you have been doing. I think as I review your work that you have done something for education and America which would not have been done in any other way, and which so far as my knowledge extends could not have been done by any other man." To fill out the bill of particulars, one may add that Root was chairman of the Board of Trustees of Hamilton College from 1909 until his death in 1937

His fellow trustees on several boards remarked the manner in which Elihu Root presided over such bodies. He would allow a discussion to take its course with no word from him until everyone had had his say. Often he would appear to be inattentive, writing notes on little pieces of paper. Then a moment would come when he would speak, summarizing clearly and concisely the several points of view expressed and then offering a solution of the problem which carried instant conviction, both by its intrinsic reasonableness and by the dominating force of his personality. So conclusively persuasive was he on such occasions that one fellow trustee once remarked in an awestruck way, "No single man ought to have such authority!" It was not that he was domineering, it was merely that his personality was so impressive and his logic so unanswerable.

He served so many organizations well not only because he was full of knowledge about a great variety of activities, but because he was wise and understanding and had rare capacity for conciliating conflicting points of view. Personalities are not the least of the difficulties in any human organization and Root had a genius for handling such human relations. He could quiet a controversy by the persuasive force of his logical reasoning; he could use a little flattery when the occasion called for it, or he could suddenly become coldly incisive and strike like a hammer on an anvil. On one occasion when he was presiding as President of the Board of Trustees of Hamilton College, his old friend, Hamilton B. Tompkins, who had been a freshman when he was a sophomore in college, had taken the floor and was speaking at endless length and in a manner which Root thought was not contributing to the solution of their problem. Root became more and more impatient and finally burst out, "Oh, Tommy, sit down!" "Tommy" sat. But it was a sign of intimacy when on such occasions he departed from his usual courtesy. At another time, a disagreement on methods of political procedure arose among the leaders of the National Economy League with whose anti-New Deal platform Root heartily sympathized. They brought their quarrel to Root at his apartment and there were some heated statements. Root listened for a time, tilted back in his swivel chair with finger tips pressed together. Finally he interrupted. "It is my observation," he said, "that politicians are aware that a strong minority will punish where a weak majority will not protect." He proceeded with his political philosophizing in so interesting a way that the callers "quite forgot their quarrel."

There is an ever valuable instrument for facilitating the work of any group of men and that is humor. Anyone who served with Mr. Root in meetings of almost any type can recall the flashes of wit, the turn of a phrase or the apt anecdote which put the group into good humor. It had been a very useful quality in his dealings with Theodore Roosevelt. At a meeting of the trustees of Hamilton College, they were discussing the retiring age for professors. Someone asked whether there were any members of the faculty approaching that age; Mr. Root replied, "Well, we haven't any going in the opposite direction." At the outset of another meeting, there had been informal talk about a current contest between a Utican and a citizen of Syracuse for some judicial office; Mr. George E. Dunham, editor of the Utica *Press* and clerk of the Board, who always sat next to Mr. Root, was of course ardently in favor of the Utica candidate. In the later course of the meeting there was discussion of an item in the librarian's report which referred to incunabula. Dr. Dunham passed to Mr. Root a piece of paper with the inquiry, "What does incunabula mean?" Mr. Root passed it back with an answering scribble: "It is a Greek word. It means 'to hell with Syracuse'." Mr. Root used to discuss most of the

ELIHU ROOT, PRESIDENT OF THE BOARD OF TRUSTEES OF HAMILTON
COLLEGE, WITH RUTH DRAPER, HONORARY MASTER OF ARTS, 1924

ELIHU ROOT WITH PRESIDENT FREDERICK C. FERRY OF HAMILTON
COLLEGE, IN THE ACADEMIC PROCESSION AT COMMENCEMENT

problems of the college with its president. At one time they found that the trustees would have to deal with a disagreeable matter, any solution of which was bound to arouse opposition and ill feeling. They agreed upon the action which would have to be taken. As they went into the trustees' meeting, Mr. Root asked the president if he had drafted a resolution on the subject which they had discussed. The president said that he had, whereupon Mr. Root gruffly demanded, "Give it to me, I prefer to draft that myself." The president watched as Mr. Root sat at his place and laid the draft beside him. He saw him carefully copy the president's resolution off onto another piece of paper. When that item on the agenda was reached, Root announced that he wished to offer a resolution and he proceeded to read from his own paper the exact wording of the resolution which the president had prepared. He thus took on his own shoulders the onus of disposing of an unpleasant subject. In 1925, the president of the college, Dr. Ferry, wrote to ask Mr. Root's advice as to whether he should accept an invitation to serve on the board of the Rome Custodial Institution, an establishment devoted to the care of morons. Mr. Root replied:

> This Rome business is too much like what you have to do already. You might find a higher average standard of intelligence among the pupils of the Rome School than you have at the College, but that would be only a slight relief. I am clear that if you can find any time from your college duties to do other things, you should do things as unlike as possible—go to a prize fight, bet on the races, shoot big game, read Ethel M. Dell's novels, or if those tax your mind too much, plunge into detective and mystery stories, kill salmon and catch fish, take to drink, do something or anything that is interesting, but not in the slightest degree educational and you will secure to the world the blessing of a long and useful life.

While Root admitted "that there is no man, however successful, who does not really value and appreciate words of praise from his fellow men," he found his chief satisfactions in the knowledge that he had completed a difficult task or that he had won a cause to which he devoted himself. His puritan self control and discipline of his will, coupled with a modesty which often approached diffidence, kept him alike from discouragements and from vain glorying. He saw through toadying flattery and was scornful of those who indulged in it. For

uncritical adulation in biographical sketches of himself he had, because of his reticence, distaste; because of his intellect, a pitying or
amused contempt. Yet he knew that many of his juniors as well as
numerous contemporaries admired him enormously and when the association was also one of affectionate friendship, as it frequently was,
their good opinion gave him pleasure. "I think I have always been
rather indifferent about popularity," he wrote to Andrew D. White
in 1915, "but fond of approval by competent judges. So I care very
little about newspaper comment one way or the other, but that you
should feel able to say what you did in your letter is very grateful to
me and pays for a great deal of hard work and discouragement." In
his later years he liked to recall friendly words of commendation from
men like Chief Justice White or Mr. Justice Holmes. More and more
as he grew older, he valued recognition of his devotion to things
scholarly, educational and artistic because through that devotion he
was paying tribute to old "Cube" whose memory freshened, especially
in the last decade of summers at Clinton after the death of Mrs. Root.
When the Carnegie Institution of Washington established in 1934
the "Elihu Root Lectures on the Influence of Science and Research on
Current Thought," Mr. Root expressed great depth of feeling in saying
quietly: "That would have pleased my Father." Just as it was with
the memory of his father still fresh that he tended the trees and
shrubs of Clinton, so it must have been partly at least in response to
that same boyhood stimulus that he poured out so much of himself
in serving the Metropolitan Museum of Art, the New York Public
Library, the several Carnegie boards, the Milbank Fund and a variety
of other organizations. His nature, like his father's, had permitted few
outward demonstrations of affection while his father lived, but service
to education and to the promotion of wider enjoyment of the beautiful,
were spiritual wreaths laid upon "Cube's" memory.

The general newspaper portrayal of Elihu Root as the inhumanly
cold personification of sheer intellect is most clearly seen to be false
when one knows his relations with his family and the devotion of
the many men and women who were among his friends. He was fond
of children and had an understanding of youth, partly perhaps because
he never lost a boyish love of mischief. Perhaps he illustrated Holmes'
phrase, "aging toward youth." He had great gentleness and sensitive-
ness to others in a group. To a granddaughter on her eighteenth birth-

day, Root sent a check as "an official recognition that on Saturday the 20th you cease to be a timid little girl & become a proud & haughty lady with all the rights powers & privileges thereunto appertaining, entitled to high roll, to vamp, to paint your finger nails & to make trouble generally." "From the standpoint of youth," he wrote to Chauncey Depew in 1912, "which possesses and exercises all the real wisdom of life, a man becomes old when he passes fifty, and that is all there is to it. Fifty, sixty, seventy, eighty, ninety, is just old, and there are no degrees. From a man's own standpoint, age depends upon the degree of his interest in the life of the world. When a man loses that he is old, no matter what decade he is in."

From his school and college days, Root was fond of feminine companionship and was a gay and popular member of any mixed group. In his middle years he was too busy practicing law to have much social life but throughout his life he had a genial bantering way which was most attractive. Yet no scandal ever attached to him. When he was over seventy, the gossips of Washington chuckled over a "flirtation" with a woman of his own age but the flirtation was as innocuous as those which he carried on by correspondence. To be prominent, human and not the subject of gossip in Washington, is an impossible combination. Lady Bryce was as devoted to him as was the Ambassador; Madame Jusserand and her husband would equally sign themselves with affection for him whom the former always called "Root-Shih-Kai." "Mrs. Root did not admit many to the circle of her real affection, but you were there," Mr. Root wrote Madame Jusserand after his wife's death. Mrs. Cowles, Theodore Roosevelt's sister, whose brilliance and charm made her home an informal salon for the interesting people in Washington, did not lose her fondness for Mr. Root even after the tragic breach of 1912. The wife of Root's very close friend, Robert DeForest, rarely failed to receive a mention as one of Root's "young ladies" at Miss Greene's school. To Chauncey M. Depew, then in his ninety-first year, Root wrote in acknowledgment of a telegram received on his own eightieth birthday, "I suppose you like to go off and play around in places where people think Mrs. Depew is your grand daughter. Please give my love to her and believe me always affectionately yours. . . ." To Mrs. M. Woolsey Stryker, whose daughter married his oldest son, Root wrote after Dr. Stryker's death, commending the reading of Shelley's "Hymn to Intellectual Beauty";

"Begin with the words 'The day becomes more solemn and serene' and read to the end, and then rejoice at having entered such a delightful society as that to which we belong." To Senator Lodge's daughter, he wrote in 1933: "I daresay you are right about your grand-daughter's flying, but I don't suppose that will make much difference in the interest of the world or in the happiness of life. The spirit of youth will still fly and the treasures of age will still be memories, and to these, my dear Constance, you have contributed richly and I am always Yours gratefully and affectionately. . . ." He wrote in 1926 to Mrs. Stewart Farrar Smith, the daughter of his old friend Wayne McVeagh: "I was affected to mingled tears and laughter when with your own fair hand you brought the package of sausage up to me from your favorite sausage maker near Philadelphia. I ate the sausage, gave Mrs. Root only the least little bit, and I think I could have eaten it all at once without the slightest feeling of indigestion so cheerful were its associations. Every mouthful was mingled not only with baked potatoe but with the thought here is perfect sausage brought by a perfect woman, both nobly planned. Perhaps I have told you all about this before. Never mind if I have. It is my purpose to refer to it in terms of grateful appreciation at least annually so long as you and I and sausage occupy the earth. Do not think it is my intention to get more sausage. I may have hopes, but I have no selfish purpose. I merely wish to give one specification underlying the general statement that you, dear Marguerita, are the dearest, most delightful and the most unexpected of women, and I am awfully fond of you. . . . Give my kind regards to your sailorman. . . . Mrs. Root joins me in sending love."

James R. Sheffield and Mrs. Sheffield constantly enjoyed the passages in Mr. Root's letters to the former such as: "Please give my love to Mrs. Sheffield and don't mess it up but hand it over in a respectful and sincere manner. Tell her that dear Senator Root is as well this summer as he could expect to be in view of the long time since he has seen her, and that he is not half as dear as he would like to be. . . . There is something very attractive about the account of your golf party. If I were in your camp I should ask nothing better than to have you go off and play golf with the ruffians you name while I remain and sing roundelays and play the mandolin to Mrs. Sheffield." Again he wrote to Mr. Sheffield:

Dear Jim:—

I have received a letter dated 80 Maiden Lane, New York, July 24th, 1929. The letter has no signature but the perfection of its style, the wisdom of its observations, the charm of its gentle humor, all impress me with the idea that you are the author. This impression is confirmed by the following statement which I quote from this anonymous communication:—

'If you would like a few days of rest and quiet amid pine woods and mountain air, it would, of course, give Mrs. Sheffield and me the greatest pleasure to have you come and visit us.'

This paragraph indicates that the writer and Mrs. Sheffield are together at a camp in the Adirondacks for a considerable period. I feel perfectly certain that if Mrs. Sheffield were to be found in such circumstances with any man except her husband, I should be that man. Under the painful certainty that I am not that man I can only infer that you are the man who was with Mrs. Sheffield and accordingly that you are the writer of the letter. . . . On your life I charge you to give my love to Mrs. Sheffield and tell her that if you were not there I certainly should come but I cannot bear to see you together.

Another typical letter was written in 1931 to his daughter-in-law, Mrs. Elihu Root, Jr.: "I now sincerely and truly declare and affirm that no man, woman or child has any authority or justification for writing to me any letter which may not be opened by any daughter-in-law whatsoever. So don't bother your dear soul over having opened letters intended for me. You have my full authority if any letter opened by you contains a check to forward it, if it contains a bill to pay it, if it contains an invitation to dinner, to attend and if it contains a request for an autograph, to write it."

The young daughter of one of the professors at Hamilton College wrote him in 1933 requesting an interview for publication. Root replied: "If we were in the Garden of Eden and you were to offer me an apple I should bite it without hesitation and I should insist that I had a perfect justification, but an interview—no. One of the conditions of my continued existence is refusal of interviews." Interviews he always refused but in the last decade of his life he had constantly to decline a flood of appeals and invitations. He summed up his reasons in explaining to a fellow-alumnus why he could not come to a Hamilton dinner in 1930:

> I cannot continue to exist if I attend public dinners;
> If I do not continue to exist I cannot attend public dinners;
> and there you are!

Mr. Root's relations with his family had no aloofness about them. Mrs. Root was no more a demonstrative person than he was, but all members of the family understood each other. The suppression of the outward manifestations of affection may eventually cause the source to shrivel up but with the Root family, as in others, it results rather in deepening and expanding the feeling. Mr. Root loved to tell the story of his return to New York from Washington one wintry night when the snow was so deep and so newly fallen and the moon was so bright that all the ugliness of New York was hidden as they came out from the ferry slip and entered their carriage. "How perfectly beautiful it is!" Mr. Root exclaimed. "Have you got on your heavy underwear?" was his wife's reply.

There must have been a mutual understanding that just as his absorption in the practice of law had held him fast in the early decades of their married life, so she too was absorbed in the duties of wife, mother and mistress of the household. Although the children had pleasant memories of Southampton, of playing in the sand and of sailing, it was Clinton around which the family interests centered, especially after the death of Mr. and Mrs. Wales removed the chief reason for their having a summer home in Southampton. Mr. Root's daughter, Mrs. Grant, was the first of the family to share with him the delight of tending the garden but his son Edward and his wife, who took up their residence in the house where "Cube" had lived, devoted themselves to the same enjoyment. That son in 1934 had sent his father a collection of shells which he had gathered on the west Florida beaches. Mr. Root enjoyed them as his own father had enjoyed his minerals. "They are very beautiful," he wrote. ". . . Do you think that the occupants of these shells have enjoyed their own beauty? If they have I must reconstruct my idea of the amount of happiness existing in the world. Why should they not have such enjoyment? Peacocks do . . . and where will you draw the line between a peacock and a rose colored shell fish?" The other son, Elihu Jr., who married a

ELIHU ROOT LOOKING AT THE TREES, CLINTON, 1935

daughter of President Stryker of Hamilton College, raised his roof tree also on a continuation of the family land. Both sons had a keen interest in painting and one of them liked to do with oils and brushes what his father and grandfather did with pick and shovel when they planted for effects of mass and shade and color. "Trees planted in dreams never live long," Root wrote to Richard U. Sherman in 1914, as the late Vice President's son was developing a new place between Utica and Clinton. "You better order five hundred or a thousand trees and set them out this spring and get them to growing. Mass Colorado Blue Spruce on the banks of the ravine; plant a lot of White Pine so that by and by when they grow up you will see them against the blue sky; plant Beech and Norway Maples where they will have room to grow and develop singly without interference so that you can look at them across a lawn or a meadow; put in some thickets of Sugar Maple for the autumn color; make a beginning; get things started." "In planting a picture of trees," he once said as he stood in front of his house at Clinton, "there are two things to look out for—contrasting shades of green alongside each other, and variety of outline. We say there are colors in autumn, but look at that ginko, the hemlock and the butternut together now. What variety there is!

"One of the most beautiful sights I ever saw was on a winter's day over in the pasture. I came upon a group of witch hazel with the sun shining full on their golden bloom as it stood out against the white of the snow and the blue of the sky."

As the son of a scientist, he was not content to have merely a sentimental or artistic fondness for trees. He knew them by their Latin as well as by their familiar names; he knew their needs of sun and soil. One is reminded that it has been said of George Washington that trees were his "really great love in nature." Washington wrote more than ten thousand words in his diaries from 1760 to 1788 about the planting of trees, their habits and their growth. Root, after walking back one day across his place in 1921, sat down and wrote a list of forty-three varieties of trees and shrubs which he had passed on his way. He could tell you just how many oaks or elms there were on the College campus, their location, the variety and, in most instances, their history. In his later years, he often got to sleep at night by reciting to himself lists of the trees and shrubs which one would pass in any given walk on the place. Elihu Root himself and his father before him, by planting and opening vistas, had contributed something toward the fairness of the scene which he described in a letter written in 1929 to John Finley, whose own poetic touch often roused the strong poetic feeling in Root; "The trees and the green fields, and the ever-youthful streams and the blue haze against distant hills are making this height of land a wonderful place this summer."

He liked motoring and did a great deal of it, especially in the last eight years of his life after Mrs. Root's death, since she had not enjoyed it. He habitually motored the two hundred odd miles between New York and Clinton and liked to drive at high speed. "One of the great things about motoring," he once wrote, "is that in hot weather you can make your own cool breeze by moving swiftly without having to feel sorry for the horse." He drove throughout Central and Western New York from Clinton, being especially interested in finding places of historic interest and in visiting in a few minutes the places from which his father's generation had made long excursions by horse and buggy. It was his habit in traveling familiar routes such as those between Clinton and New York or New York and Washington, to keep careful record of the time, the distance and the speed. He was fond of maps and had a real geographical sense, liking to trace river valleys and water sheds and geological formations. Not only did he never lose his interest in or his influence upon events of public importance, but he had such a variety of personal interests that he was never bored. As "Cube" had whetted the edges of his mind in his last years by relearning the Indian tongue which he picked up as a boy, so Elihu Root, out of a life which had interests further flung, kept his own mind keen by a dozen different devices. He was widely read in both literature and history and his memory was stored with poetry—Shelley and Shakespeare's sonnets, for example, and Bryant's "Water Fowl" which was a favorite of his father's.

Root's character was a mixture, as all men's characters are mixtures. In the last few decades of his long life it was hard for others to realize how close he was to the farm and to the frontier. The radicalism or progressive spirit of the frontier is somewhat paradoxically close to the conservatism of the farm. Elihu Root's grandfather had been of that generation which in a short space of years spanned the gap between the frontiersman and the farmer. The grandson retained the physical and mental alertness of the pioneer, combined with the distrust of innovations which the small farmer possesses. His inherited equipment was unusual in that the farmer's viewpoint had been filtered through a generation of genuine scientific spirit—the search for truth and its acceptance for its own sake. I have heard him scoff at professors of law and of other social sciences but never at students of natural science. To be really useful, he told the Harvard Law School alumni in 1926, they must "labor in the spirit of science, of true pure science."

From the quiet cultured atmosphere of a small academic community, he was thrust when only twenty-two years old into the welter of competitive life in New York City. His environment was the ruthlessness of American business in the period which followed the Civil War. His success was almost immediate and it was enormous. The rich and the great were his friends and acquaintances and many of them were debtors to his professional skill. His natural conservatism tended to harden into habitual conviction, but since he also possessed that rare quality, wisdom, he was not blind to defects in the system under which he lived and prospered. He did not have the instincts of a reformer or a zealot, but with slow, careful steps he patiently fostered policies which he thought were pregnant with ultimate good, rejecting in the meantime the nostrums or experiments which captivated the fancies of many of his more impetuous contemporaries. "Growth is the law of life," he wrote to James R. Sheffield in 1916, "and the perennial problem is how to hold fast to what is good and essential and at the same time substitute new growth for dead matter." The world needs its radicals and its reformers but it would be an even sorrier place were they not balanced by conservatives.

His was a pragmatic philosophy. There were always so many things to be done which could be done, he found it foolish to attempt the impossible. Yet his practicality was not opportunism. Everything he did was tested first in his mind against the needs of that moment and of the next, and the next and still on one more step into the future. When he dealt with long-range policies, he advocated much that might have seemed visionary at the time but which the future justified. One may go back to his speech at Hamilton College in 1879 when he talked on the need for changed relations between capital and labor; his pioneering steps toward a "good neighbor" policy with Latin America; his advocacy in 1920 of compulsory jurisdiction for an international court; his warning in 1905 that if the several states did not remedy evils, the federal government would do it. He was not infallible but he was very wise. He has been criticized for failing to devote his great abilities to causes which the critics think more important than those to which he did attend. Many of the critics, however, are misled by a lack of knowledge of what he did accomplish, often by indirection, as for example through his influence on Theodore Roosevelt. Although a great collection of medals and awards, and honorary degrees from thirteen American institutions and the universities of six other countries, bear testimony to expert recognition of his achievements in many fields, his popular reputation has suffered through his indifference to it. He viewed, for example, the award to him of the Nobel Peace Prize in 1913, not as a personal tribute, but as a "conservative European approval of the conduct of the American Government in colonial and foreign affairs during the administrations of McKinley and Roosevelt." [2] "The Chinese are about the only people," he remarked in another connection, "who understand how to make the heroes of peace gorgeous and striking to the imagination." [3] Root was not the originator of any new school of political or social philosophy but he was wise in advice, skilled in advocacy and successful in administration.

The myth of the Elihu Root who was cold and ruthless was the not unnatural result of his self control and his indifference to public opinion. He could be cold and ruthless but his ruthlessness was never directed toward serving his personal ends. He could set his teeth and hew to the line for the sake of a member of his family, for an institution, for a client, for the Republican Party, for a cause which had enlisted his support, but it often caused him personal suffering.

There were many who disliked him and not a few who distrusted him, but even these freely admitted his great abilities. So far as I have been able to trace through spoken and written word, this opposition can be classified among the following groups: the crusaders who resented the fact that Root did not take an active leadership in many reform movements; the liberals who call his staunch conservatism reaction; lawyers and laymen who identify Root with the type of corporate law practice and reliance on technicalities which they disapprove; those who ran up against his subtleties and thought them indications of intellectual dishonesty (and here perhaps belong some of

[2] Root to Henry L. Stimson, December 17, 1913.
[3] Root to Mark Sullivan, May 20, 1922.

the devoted followers of Colonel Roosevelt who have never lost their contemporaneous wrath over his management of the 1912 Convention); those small-minded persons who were thwarted by him in one way or another; the members of the public who knew him only through newspaper accounts, cartoons and general reputation. Most of the persons in all of these groups did not know him intimately as a man. Those who were thrown into intimate contact with him as servants, clerks, secretaries, companions, friends, colleagues, partners or co-workers, with no exception that I have been able to find, felt for him not only admiration but affection and the more intimately they knew him, the warmer was their loyalty. The extent to which one or the other group gauged the true measure of the man may perhaps be judged by the reader of these pages. As Root said in speaking of Theodore Roosevelt, "Sermons are forgotten; men are remembered. Truths are told in ten thousand volumes and pamphlets, from a thousand pulpits and rostrums. They are forgotten. For a moment they enter the mind, and in a moment they are displaced. But the perpetual lesson of a great example, inseparably united to a great truth, carries on the work of a lifetime through generations and ages to come."

"I am . . . enduring the infirmities of age with cheerfulness based upon a clear understanding that the only way to avoid them is by dying young, which I have neglected to do," Root wrote in 1929. "Age has its compensations and it is much better to enjoy them than to quarrel with the order of nature and grouch over the familiar fact that one cannot remain young forever," he wrote to an old college friend in 1933. He outlived most of his contemporaries and many of his younger friends and became philosophical about the ending of a lifetime. "I suppose," he wrote on another occasion, "that the cutting of one thread after another is a part of the process by which we ourselves let go of life." Near the end of his own life, his friend Stanley Washburn asked him whether he believed in God; Mr. Root answered that he had devoted considerable thought to the question, with the result that while, as a lawyer, he could not prove a case for the existence of a God, as an individual he firmly believed that there is a God and he had no fear of death.

Late in January, 1937, after an attack of bronchitis, pneumonia developed. With amazing vitality he rallied temporarily but complications set in and his system was too weak to resist. On February 7th,

1937, he died. One week before his ninety-second birthday, he went back for the last time to that "plain old house in the Oneida hills, overlooking the valley of the Mohawk, where truth and honor dwelt" in his youth. On February 9th, the cold rain drizzled across the campus as the simple funeral service was conducted in the College Chapel. The College choir sang and the undergraduate members of his own fraternity were the only pallbearers. They carried him along familiar campus aisles under the vaulted nave of gray, high-arching elms. By trees which he and his father had planted, overlooking the valley which they both had loved, the final words were spoken. In that peaceful place a symbol of wisdom, truth and great honor now forever dwells.

APPENDIX I

Sources and Bibliography

A MERE bibliography can not indicate adequately the sources on which this book is based and the following explanations may be helpful to those who are interested in source materials. They also afford the author a welcome opportunity to express his gratitude to many who have assisted him.

Throughout the book, unless otherwise indicated, the letters to and from Mr. Root are to be found among his papers. Those dated subsequently to the summer of 1899 when he became Secretary of War are deposited in the Manuscript Division of the Library of Congress. His office files, which are practically complete from 1867 on, are in the custody of the firm of Winthrop, Stimson, Putnam and Roberts for the period down to 1915, and of the firm of Root, Clark, Buckner and Ballantine for the subsequent years. Some personal letters are in the possession of Mr. Root's family. As explained in the Foreword, much material has been drawn from conversations with Mr. Root, recorded by the author or by Mrs. Edward W. Root. Mr. Root's principal addresses and public papers up to 1924 were collected and edited by Robert Bacon and James Brown Scott and published in eight volumes by the Harvard University Press, to which I am indebted for permission to use this valuable compilation with its important editorial notes. In Appendix II will be found a chronological list of Mr. Root's principal speeches with an indication of the places in those volumes and elsewhere in which they have been printed. I utilized also Mr. Root's collection of newspaper clippings in fifty-two volumes which are now in the possession of the New York Public Library.

In the Foreword, I have already acknowledged my debt to members of Mr. Root's family. No acknowledgment of the help which I have received from my wife would be adequate. A host of Mr. Root's friends and acquaintances have put me under obligation for their kindness in supplying details or backgrounds for particular events or attitudes and in granting me permission to publish extracts from correspondence and diaries. In this connection I wish to mention especially the courtesy of Colonel Theodore Roosevelt, Jr. and the Trustees of the Theodore Roosevelt Estate, of Mr. Robert A. Taft and of Mr. John E. Lodge for permitting me to quote extensively from the papers of President Roosevelt, President Taft and Senator Henry Cabot Lodge. While I can not mention all others, I must speak of the great help given me by Miss Emily A. Stewart who, among other things, classified and arranged the memoranda of conversations with Mr. Root; by Mr. Chandler P. Anderson and, after his death, by Mrs. Anderson; by the Misses Agnes and Maud Bartlett; by Senator Frederick M. Davenport; by Mr. Tyler Dennett; by Mr. James R. Garfield; by Mr. and Mrs. Charles S. Hamlin; by Mr. Burton J. Hendrick; by Mr. José Thomaz Nabuco; by Mr. Henry F. Pringle; by Mr. James R. Sheffield; by Colonel Henry L. Stimson; and by numerous others whose names appear in the footnotes. Helpful criticisms have been received from persons who were kind enough to read various chapters, including: Mr. Wilbur J. Carr who read Chapter XXXI; President William C. Dennis who read Chapter XXVI; Professor Michael T. Florinsky who read Chapter XLIII; Colonel Ulysses S. Grant, 3rd, who read Part III; Mr. James Hazen Hyde who read part of Chapter XXI; Chief Justice Charles Evans Hughes who read Chapter XLVII; General Frank R. McCoy who read Part III; Mr. Frederick C. Tanner who read Chapters XL and XLII; Professor Charles C. Tansill who read Chapter XIX; Colonel Stanley Washburn who read Chapters XLIII and XLVII; Under Secretary of State Sumner Welles who read Chapters XXIII, XXIV and XV; Dr. Cyril Wynne who read Chapters XXVII and XXVIII. Mr. Franklin S. Edmonds of Philadelphia, with the cooperation of Hon. James Gay Gordon, Hon. George A. Welsh and Mr. Thomas Raeburn White, gave me helpful information in connection with Chapter XXI. Professor Ernest Scott of the University of Melbourne and the staff of the American Council of the Institute of Pacific Relations supplied me with valuable material for Chapter XXVII.

All institutions and government departments with which Mr. Root was connected have been unfailing in their courtesy. I should like to mention especially in the Department of State: Mr. Wilbur J. Carr, former Assistant Secretary of State, Dr. Hunter Miller, Historical Adviser, Mr. David A. Salmon, Chief of the Division of Communications and Records, Mrs. Natalia Summers, Archivist, and Dr. Cyril

Wynne, Chief of the Division of Publication and Research; in the War Department and the Army: Major General William Crozier, Major General Hugh A. Drum and Major General George S. Simonds; in the Library of Congress: Dr. Herbert Putnam, the late Dr. James F. Jameson and Mr. Thomas P. Martin, as well as the staff of the Manuscript Division; at Hamilton College: President Frederick C. Ferry, Mr. Edward M. Coughlin, the Bursar, Professor Joseph D. Ibbotson, the former Librarian, and Mr. Lewis Francis Stieg, the present Librarian; in the various organizations established by Mr. Carnegie: Mr. Frederick P. Keppel, the President, the Trustees of the Corporation who generously assisted my work, and Mr. Robert M. Lester; Dr. John C. Merriam, President of the Institution; Dr. Henry S. Pritchett, former President of the Foundation for the Advancement of Teaching and Dr. Nicholas Murray Butler, President of the Endowment for International Peace; in the Commission of Fine Arts, Mr. Charles Moore; in the Fine Arts Federation of New York, Mr. Armistead Fitzhugh; in the New York Public Library, Mr. H. M. Lydenberg and Mr. Frank L. Polk.

Professor Allan Nevins read most of the manuscript and his help in this and many other respects has been invaluable. Mr. Harold Jonas and Mr. Sanford Schwarz read the manuscript and contributed many valuable suggestions of both a substantive and editorial nature. Mrs. Katharine McGee not only typed the entire manuscript but aided very materially by her researches and criticisms and by her efficient handling of all matters of detail.

In the actual collection, arrangement and checking of the voluminous data, I have been fortunate in securing the help of a number of very competent persons, including Messrs. Frederick E. Emmerich, E. B. Fincher, George Krauss, Norman Leonard, Oliver J. Lissitzyn, Walter Maloney, Nathan Pelcovits, Frederic C. Smedley, Walter Wittman and Mrs. Stuart W. Kellogg. Mr. David King Rothstein devoted his unusual abilities to locating and examining on my behalf numerous collections of private papers. Miss Helen M. Jackson ably bore the burdens of typing, filing and classifying in the earlier stages of the work. Mr. Cleveland Chase made available to me a collection of newspaper clippings and other materials.

I am grateful also for many courtesies of the staff of the Library of Columbia University. The ready cooperation of the publishers on all points has been most helpful.

I wish to acknowledge my appreciation of the permission granted by the following publishers to quote from the books indicated: Little Brown and Company, *The Epic of America* by James Truslow Adams; Macmillan Company, *Public Opinion* by Walter Lippmann; Charles Scribner's Sons, *Selections from the Correspondence of Theodore Roosevelt and Henry Cabot Lodge*; The Vanguard Press, *Our Cuban Colony* by Leland Hamilton Jenks. Mrs. Oscar King Davis kindly gave me permission to quote from Mr. Davis's *Released for Publication*. I am also grateful to the New York *Herald Tribune* for permission to reproduce the cartoon entitled "On the Bargain Counter" which appeared in the New York *Tribune* on September 27th, 1900, and the cartoon by Darling which appeared in the *Herald Tribune* on March 27th, 1929, and to the New York Evening *Post* for permission to use the cartoon by Cesare appearing in their issue of June 6th, 1916 and the cartoon by Haydon Jones which appeared on January 20th, 1921. *Harper's Magazine* has kindly given me permission to use the cartoon entitled "Too Busy to Talk Politics" which appeared in *Harper's Weekly* for March 31st, 1900.

SELECTED BIBLIOGRAPHY [1]

1. Collections of Private Papers

A. In the Library of Congress
   The Papers of William Jennings Bryan, Andrew Carnegie, Joseph H. Choate, Henry C. Corbin, John W. Foster, John Hay, Philander C. Knox, Breckinridge Long, William B. McKinley, John Tyler Morgan, Joseph Pulitzer, Theodore Roosevelt, Elihu Root, John C. Spooner, William Howard Taft, Benjamin F. Tracy, Henry W. Watterson.
B. In the Columbia University Library
   Ms. collection of the Papers of Joseph H. Choate
C. In the Cornell University Library
   The Papers of Andrew D. White
D. At the Massachusetts Historical Society, Boston
   The Papers of Henry Cabot Lodge
E. In the New York Public Library
   The Papers of James Schoolcraft Sherman
F. In the Rochester Historical Library
   The Papers of George W. Aldridge

[1] Only items which have proved of particular value are included here.

G. In private custody
   The Papers and Diaries of Chandler P. Anderson, the Papers of
   Willard Bartlett, Mrs. William Sheffield Cowles, Chauncey M.
   Depew, John Hay and Elihu Root; the Diaries of Charles S. Ham-
   lin and Henry L. Stimson

2. Published Materials

A. Autobiography, Biography and Letters

Abbott, Lawrence F., *Impressions of Theodore Roosevelt*, Doubleday
   Page, 1919.
   Letters of Archie Butt, Doubleday Page, 1924.
Amos, James E., *Theodore Roosevelt, Hero to His Valet*, John Day,
   1927.
Auerbach, Joseph S., *Delancey Nicoll, An Appreciation*, Harpers, 1931.
Baker, Ray Stannard, *Woodrow Wilson, Life and Letters*, 6 volumes,
   1931–1938.
Beer, Thomas, *Hanna*, Knopf, 1929.
Bemis, Samuel Flagg, ed., *The American Secretaries of State and Their
   Diplomacy*, Volumes 9 and 10, 1929.
Bishop, Joseph B., *Theodore Roosevelt and His Time*, 2 volumes,
   Scribners, 1920.
Busbey, L. White, *Uncle Joe Cannon*, Henry Holt, 1927.
Butt, Archie, *Taft and Roosevelt, The Intimate Letters of Archie
   Butt*, 2 volumes, Doubleday Doran, 1930.
Century Association, *Addresses Made in Honor of Elihu Root*, 1937.
   Joseph Hodges Choate, Memorial Addresses, 1918.
   Theodore Roosevelt, Memorial Addresses, 1919.
Croly, Herbert, *Marcus Alonzo Hanna, His Life and Works*, Mac-
   millan, 1912.
   Willard Straight, Macmillan, 1924.
Davis, Oscar King, *Released for Publication*, Houghton Mifflin, 1925.
Dennett, Tyler, *John Hay, From Poetry to Politics*, Dodd, Mead, 1934.
Depew, Chauncey, *My Memories of Eighty Years*, Scribners, 1922.
Elder, Margaret Munro, *Life of Samuel J. Elder*, Yale University Press,
   1925.
Fisher, Herbert A. L., *James Bryce*, 2 volumes, Macmillan, 1927.
Gray, Jane Loring, ed., *The Letters of Asa Gray*, Houghton Mifflin,
   1893.
Gwynn, Stephen, *The Letters and Friendships of Sir Cecil Spring Rice*,
   Houghton Mifflin, 1929.
Hagedorn, Hermann, *Leonard Wood, A Biography*, 2 volumes, Harpers,
   1931.
Hendrick, Burton J., *The Life of Andrew Carnegie*, 2 volumes, Double-
   day Doran, 1932.

The Life and Letters of Walter H. Page, 3 volumes, Doubleday Page, 1922–1925.

Holthusen, Henry F., *James W. Wadsworth, Jr., A Biographical Sketch*, Putnams, 1926.

Houston, David F., *Eight Years with Wilson's Cabinet, 1913 to 1920, With a Personal Estimate of the President*, 2 volumes, Doubleday Page, 1926.

Howard, Esme, *Theatre of Life*, Hodder and Stoughton, London, 1936.

Howe, George Frederick, *Chester A. Arthur, A Quarter-Century of Machine Politics*, Dodd, Mead, 1934.

Howe, M. A. de Wolfe, *George von Lengerke Meyer*, Dodd, Mead, 1920.

Howland, Harold, *Theodore Roosevelt and His Times*, Yale University Press, 1921.

James, Henry, *Charles W. Eliot*, 2 volumes, Houghton Mifflin, 1930.
  Richard Olney and His Public Service, Houghton Mifflin, 1923.

Kennan, George, *E. H. Harriman, A Biography*, 2 volumes, Houghton Mifflin, 1922.

La Follette, Robert M., *Autobiography*, Robert M. La Follette Company, Madison, Wisconsin, 1913.

Lansing, Robert, *War Memoirs*, Bobbs Merrill, 1935.

Lawrence, William, *My Memories of a Happy Life*, Houghton Mifflin, 1926.
  Henry Cabot Lodge, A Biographical Sketch, Houghton Mifflin, 1925.

Lodge, Henry Cabot, ed., *Selections from the Correspondence of Theodore Roosevelt and Henry Cabot Lodge, 1884–1918*, 2 volumes, Scribners, 1925.

Longworth, Alice Roosevelt, *Crowded Hours*, Scribners, 1933.

McCall, Samuel W., *The Life of Thomas Brackett Reed*, Houghton Mifflin, 1914.

McElroy, Robert, *Levi Parsons Morton*, Putnams, 1930.

Michie, Peter Smith, *The Life and Letters of Emory Upton*, Appleton, 1885.

Morgenthau, Henry, *All in a Lifetime*, Doubleday Page, 1922.

Muzzey, David S., *James G. Blaine, A Political Idol of Other Days*, Dodd, Mead, 1934.

Mott, T. Bentley, *Twenty Years as Military Attaché*, Oxford, 1937.

Nabuco, Carolina, *A Vida de Joaquim Nabuco*, Compania Editora Nacional, São Paulo, Brazil, 1929.

Nevins, Allan, *Grover Cleveland*, Dodd, Mead, 1932.
  Hamilton Fish, Dodd, Mead, 1936.
  Abram S. Hewitt, Harpers, 1935.
  Henry White, Thirty Years of American Diplomacy, Harpers, 1930.

Nicolson, Harold F., *Portrait of a Diplomatist*, Houghton Mifflin, 1930.

Olcott, Charles S., *The Life of William McKinley*, 2 volumes, Houghton Mifflin, 1916.

Palmer, Frederick, *Newton D. Baker*, Dodd, Mead, 1931.

Platt, Thomas C., *The Autobiography of Thomas Collier Platt*, edited by Louis J. Long, B. W. Dodge & Co., 1910.

Pringle, Henry F., *Theodore Roosevelt: A Biography*, Harcourt Brace, 1931.

Roosevelt, Theodore, *An Autobiography*, Scribners, 1920.

Works, National Edition, 20 volumes, Scribners, 1925.

Scott, James Brown, *Robert Bacon, Life and Letters*, Doubleday Page, 1923.

Elihu Root, in Volume 9 of *The American Secretaries of State and Their Diplomacy*, edited by Samuel Flagg Bemis, Knopf, 1929.

"Elihu Root's Services to International Law," *International Conciliation*, No. 207, February, 1925.

Seitz, Don C., *Joseph Pulitzer, His Life and Letters*, Simon & Schuster, 1924.

Seymour, Charles, *The Intimate Papers of Colonel House*, 4 volumes, Houghton Mifflin, 1926–1928.

Skelton, Oscar D., *Life and Letters of Sir Wilfrid Laurier*, 2 volumes, Century, 1922.

Smalley, George W., *Anglo-American Memories*, Putnams, 1911.

Steffens, Lincoln, *The Autobiography of Lincoln Steffens*, Harcourt Brace, 1931.

Stephenson, N. W., *Nelson W. Aldrich*, Scribners, 1930.

Stoddard, Henry L., *As I Knew Them*, Harpers, 1927.

Straus, Oscar, *Under Four Administrations: From Cleveland to Taft*, Houghton Mifflin, 1922.

Thayer, William Roscoe, *The Life and Letters of John Hay*, Houghton Mifflin, 1915.

Tumulty, Joseph P., *Woodrow Wilson As I Know Him*, Doubleday Page, 1921.

White, Andrew D., *Autobiography*, Century, 1922.

Wilson, James H., *Charles A. Dana*, Harpers, 1907.

Wister, Owen, *Roosevelt, The Story of a Friendship*, Macmillan, 1930.

B. On New York and National Political History

Adams, James Truslow, *The Epic of America*, Little Brown, 1931.

Alexander, De Alva S., *Four Famous New Yorkers*, Volume IV of his *Political History of the State of New York*, Henry Holt, 1923.

Breen, Matthew, *Thirty Years of New York Politics*, published by the author, New York, 1899.

Bryce, James, *The American Commonwealth*, with a chapter on the Tweed ring in New York by Rufus R. Wilson, 2 volumes, from the second edition, revised, The Commonwealth Publishing Company, New York, 1908.

Citizens' Union, Campaign Book, *The City for the People*, New York, 1897.

　Pamphlets: No. 2, *Clean Streets*, New York, 1897; No. 7, *Home Rule in Cities*, New York, 1897.

　The Searchlight, Volume XII, No. 4 (December 14, 1922), p. 3.

Carman, Harry J., *The Street Surface Railway Franchises of New York City*, Columbia University Press, 1919.

Dunn, Arthur Wallace, *From Harrison to Harding*, 2 volumes, Putnams, 1922.

Flick, Alexander C., *History of the State of New York*, 10 volumes, for the New York State Historical Association, Columbia University Press, 1934.

Gosnell, Harold F., *Boss Platt and His New York Machine*, University of Chicago Press, 1924.

Kohlsaat, H. H., *From McKinley to Harding*, Scribners, 1923.

Lynch, Denis Tilden, *"Boss" Tweed*, Boni Liveright, 1927.

Merriam, Charles E., and Overacker, Louise, *Primary Elections*, University of Chicago Press, 1928.

Myers, William Starr, *The Republican Party, A History*, Century, 1928.

New York State, *Revised Record of the Constitutional Convention of the State of New York, May 8th, 1894 to September 29, 1894*, 5 volumes, The Argus Company, Albany, New York, 1900.

　Revised Record of the Constitutional Convention of the State of New York, April 6th, 1915 to September 10, 1915, 4 volumes, Lyon, Albany, New York, 1916.

Oberholtzer, Ellis P., *History of the United States since the Civil War*, Volume V, 1888–1901, Macmillan, 1937.

Ogg, Frederic Austin, *National Progress*, Harpers, 1918.

Peck, Harry Thurston, *Twenty Years of the Republic, 1885–1905*, Dodd, Mead, 1906.

Republican National Convention, *Official Proceedings of the 13th Republican National Convention, held in the city of Chicago, June 21, 22, 23, 1904*, Harrison & Smith Co., Minneapolis, 1904.

　Official Report of the Proceedings of the 14th Republican National Convention, held in Chicago, Illinois, June 16, 17, 18 and 19, 1908, Columbus, Ohio, 1908.

　Official Report of the Proceedings of the 15th Republican National Convention, held in Chicago, Illinois, June 18, 19, 20, 21 and 22, 1912, Tenny Press, New York, 1912.

　Official Report of the Proceedings of the 16 Republican National Convention, held in Chicago, Illinois, June 7, 8, 9 and 10, 1916, Tenny Press, New York, 1916.

Official Report of the Proceedings of the 17th Republican National Convention, held in Chicago, Illinois, June 8, 9, 10, 11 and 12, 1920, Tenny Press, New York, 1920.

Rhodes, James Ford, *The McKinley and Roosevelt Administrations, 1897–1909*, Macmillan, 1923.

Rosewater, Victor, *Back Stage in 1912*, Dorrance and Company, Philadelphia, 1932.

Rothstein, David K., *Benjamin B. Odell*, unpublished mss.

Smith, Ray B., ed., *History of the State of New York*, 6 volumes, Syracuse Press, 1922.

Sullivan, Mark, *Our Times*, 6 volumes, Scribners, 1926–1935.

Taussig, Frank, *The Tariff History of the United States*, Putnams, 1931.

Van Pelt, Daniel, *Leslie's History of New York*, Arkell Publishing, Company, New York, 1898.

Werner, Morris R., *Tammany Hall*, Doubleday Doran, 1928.

C. On Military and Colonial Affairs

Blount, James H., *The American Occupation of the Philippines, 1898–1912*, Putnams, 1912.

Elliott, Charles Burke, *The Philippines to the End of the Military Regime*, Bobbs Merrill, 1916.

Forbes, W. Cameron, *The Philippine Islands*, 2 volumes, Houghton Mifflin, 1928.

Meneely, Alexander H., *The War Department, 1861, A Study in Mobilization and Administration*, Columbia University Press, 1928.

Spaulding, Oliver Lyman, *The United States Army in War and Peace*, Putnams, 1937.

Randolph, Carman F., *The Law and Policy of Annexation*, Longmans Green, 1901.

Thomas, David Yancey, *A History of Military Government in Newly Acquired Territory of the United States*, Columbia University Press, 1904.

United States

Senate:

Carter, Major General William Harding, *Creation of the American General Staff*, United States Senate Document, No. 119, 68th Congress, 1st Session.

Committee on the Philippines, *Hearings on Affairs in the Philippines*, 1902, United States Senate Document, No. 331, 57th Congress, 1st Session.

Upton, Emory, *The Military Policy of the United States*, United States Senate Document, No. 379, 64th Congress, 1st Session (4th edition, 1916).

War Department:

Annual Reports of the War Department, 1899 to 1903.
Willoughby, William F., Territories and Dependencies of the United States, Century, 1905.

D. On International Affairs

Abbott, J. F., Japanese Expansion and American Policies, Macmillan, 1916.
Anderson, E. N., The First Moroccan Crisis, University of Chicago Press, 1930.
Bailey, Thomas A., Theodore Roosevelt and the Japanese-American Crises, Stanford University Press, 1934.
"Theodore Roosevelt and the Alaska Boundary Settlement," 18 Canadian Historical Review (1937) 123.
Baker, Ray Stannard, Woodrow Wilson and World Settlement, 3 volumes, Doubleday Page, 1922.
Bemis, Samuel Flagg, A Diplomatic History of the United States, Henry Holt, 1936.
Borchard, Edwin M., and Lage, William P., Neutrality for the United States, Yale University Press, 1937.
Brebner, J. Bartlett, "Canada, The Anglo-Japanese Alliance and the Washington Conference," 50 Political Science Quarterly (1935) 45.
Buell, Raymond L., "Anti-Japanese Agitation in the United States," 37 Political Science Quarterly (1922) 605.
The Native Problem in Africa, Macmillan, 1928.
The Washington Conference, Appleton, 1922.
Callahan, James Morton, American Foreign Policy in Mexican Relations, Macmillan, 1932.
American Foreign Policy in Canadian Relations, Macmillan, 1937.
Chang Chung Fu, The Anglo-Japanese Alliance, Johns Hopkins University Press, 1931.
Chapman, Charles Edward, History of the Cuban Republic, Macmillan, 1927.
Clyde, Paul H., International Rivalries in Manchuria, Ohio State University Press, 1926.
Corbett, P. E., The Settlement of Canadian-American Disputes, Yale University Press, 1937.
Council on Foreign Relations, Survey of American Foreign Relations, edited by Charles P. Howland, 4 volumes, 1928–1931, Yale University Press, 1928–1931.
Dennett, Tyler, Americans in Eastern Asia, Macmillan, 1922.
Roosevelt and the Russo-Japanese War, Doubleday Page, 1925.

Dennis, A. L. P., *Adventures in American Diplomacy*, Dutton, 1928.
  The Anglo-Japanese Alliance, University of California Press, 1923.
Fitzgibbon, Russell H., *Cuba and the United States, 1900–1935*, George
  H. Banta Publishing Company, 1935.
Fleming, Denna Frank, *The United States and the League of Nations,
  1918–1920*, Putnams, 1932.
  The United States and World Organization, 1920–1933, Columbia
  University Press, 1938.
Foreign Policy Association, *Problems of the New Cuba*, Report of the
  Commission on Cuban Affairs, Foreign Policy Association, Inc.,
  1935.
Gooch, George P. and Temperley, Harold, eds., *British Documents on
  the Origins of the War*, Volume VIII, London, H. M. Stationery
  Office, 1932.
Griswold, A. Whitney, *The Far Eastern Policy of the United States*,
  Harcourt Brace, 1938.
Die Grosse Politik der Europaischen Kabinette, 1871–1914, Lepsius et
  al., eds., Berlin, Verlagsgesellschaft für Politik und Geschichte,
  1922–1927.
Hill, Howard C., *Roosevelt and the Caribbean*, University of Chicago
  Press, 1927.
Hudson, Manley O., *The Permanent Court of International Justice*,
  Macmillan, 1934.
Ichihashi, Yamato, *The Washington Conference and After*, Stanford
  University Press, 1928.
Ishii, Kikujiro, *Diplomatic Commentaries*, Johns Hopkins University
  Press, 1936.
Jenks, Leland Hamilton, *Our Cuban Colony*, Vanguard, 1928.
Latané, John H., *America as a World Power, 1897–1907*, Harpers, 1907.
  A History of American Foreign Policy, revised edition, Doubleday
  Doran, 1934.
  The United States and Latin America, Doubleday Page, 1920.
Lockmiller, David A., *Magoon in Cuba*, University of North Carolina
  Press, 1938.
Lodge, Henry Cabot, *The Senate and the League of Nations*, Scribners,
  1925.
McCain, William D., *The United States and the Republic of Panama*,
  Duke University Press, 1937.
Mathews, John M., *The Conduct of American Foreign Relations*, Cen-
  tury, 1922.
Miller, David Hunter, *The Drafting of the Covenant*, 2 volumes, Put-
  nams, 1928.
Millis, Walter, *The Martial Spirit*, Houghton Mifflin, 1931.
  The Road to War, Houghton Mifflin, 1935.
Munro, Dana G., *The Five Republics of Central America, Their Politi-*

cal and Economic Development and Their Relations with the United States, Oxford, 1918.

The United States and the Caribbean Area, World Peace Foundation, 1934.

Morse, H. B., and MacNair, H. F., Far Eastern International Relations, Houghton Mifflin, 1931.

Mowat, R. B., The Diplomatic Relations of Great Britain and the United States, Longmans Green, 1925.

Parks, E. Taylor, Colombia and the United States, 1765–1934, Duke University Press, 1935.

Perkins, Dexter, The Monroe Doctrine, 1876–1907, Johns Hopkins University Press, 1937.

Permanent Court of Arbitration, The Hague Court Reports, Great Britain, Spain and France versus Portugal In the Matter of the Expropriated Religious Properties in Portugal, Awards rendered September 2 and 4, 1920, under the Compromis signed at Lisbon on July 31, 1913, between Great Britain, Spain and France on the one hand, and Portugal on the other, Carnegie Endowment for International Peace, Division of International Law, Pamphlet No. 37, 1921.

Permanent Court of International Justice, Advisory Committee of Jurists, Procès-Verbaux of the Proceedings of the Committee, June 16th–July 24th, 1920, with Annexes, The Hague, Van Langenhuysen Brothers, 1920.

Committee of Jurists on the Statute of the Permanent Court of International Justice, Minutes of the Session held at Geneva, March 11th–19th, 1929, League of Nations Publication V. Juridical Questions 1929. V. 5.

Pooley, A. M., ed., The Secret Memoirs of Count Hayashi, Putnams, 1915.

Price, Ernest B., Russo-Japanese Treaties of 1907–1916 Concerning Manchuria and Mongolia, Johns Hopkins University Press, 1933.

Tansill, Charles Callan, America Goes to War, Little Brown, 1938.

Treat, Payson J., The Far East, revised edition, Harpers, 1935.

Tupper, Eleanor and McReynolds, George E., Japan in American Public Opinion, Macmillan, 1937.

United States

Conference on the Limitation of Armaments, Washington, November 12, 1921–February 6, 1922, Government Printing Office, 1922.

Conference on the Limitation of Armaments, Washington, November 12, 1921–February 6, 1922, Minutes of Sub-Committees, Government Printing Office, 1922.

Department of State:

Clark, J. Reuben, *Memorandum on the Monroe Doctrine*, prepared December 17, 1928, Department of State Publication, No. 37, 1930.

Papers Relating to the Foreign Relations of the United States, 1899–1922.

Proceedings in the North Atlantic Coast Fisheries Arbitration before the Permanent Court of Arbitration at The Hague under the provisions of the General Treaty of Arbitration of April 4, 1908, and the Special Agreement of January 27, 1909, between the United States of America and Great Britain, 11 volumes, Government Printing Office, 1912.

Senate:

Affairs in the Kongo, United States Senate Document, No. 147, 61st Congress, 1st Session.

Proceedings of the Alaskan Boundary Tribunal, convened at London, under the Treaty between the United States of America and Great Britain, concluded at Washington, January 24, 1903, for the settlement of questions between the two countries with respect to the boundary line between the territory of Alaska and the British Possessions in North America, 7 volumes, United States Senate Document, No. 162, 58th Congress, 2nd Session.

White, James, "Henry Cabot Lodge and the Alaska Boundary Award," 6 *Canadian Historical Review* (1925) 332.

Willoughby, Westel Woodbury, *China at the Conference*, Johns Hopkins University Press, 1922.

Wisan, Joseph E., *The Cuban Crisis As Reflected in the New York Press, 1895–1898*, Columbia University Press, 1934.

Wynne, E. Cyril, *The White Australia Policy and Japan*, unpublished mss.

E. General and Sundry

Adams, Charles F., Jr., and Henry, *Chapters of Erie and Other Essays*, James R. Osgood and Co., Boston, 1871.

Arnold, Thurman W., *The Folklore of Capitalism*, Yale University Press, 1937.

Cohen, Morris R., "The Legal Calvinism of Elihu Root," in *Law and the Social Order*, Harcourt Brace, 1933.

Dixon, F. H., "The Mann-Elkins Act," 24 *Quarterly Journal of Economics* (1910) 593.

Glass, Carter H., *An Adventure in Constructive Finance*, Doubleday Page, 1927.

Hamilton College, *Documentary History of Hamilton College*, Clinton, New York, 1922.

Life.

Literary Magazine.

Hicks, Frederick C., *High Finance in the Sixties*, Yale University Press, 1929.

Jones, Pomroy, *Annals and Recollections of Oneida County*, Rome, New York, 1851.

Josephson, Matthew, *The Robber Barons*, Harcourt Brace, 1934.

McAdam, David, ed., *History of the Bench and Bar of New York*, New York History Company, 1897.

Riegel, Robert Edgar, *The Story of the Western Railroads*, Macmillan, 1926.

Rogers, James Grafton, *American Bar Leaders*, American Bar Association, Chicago, 1932.

Rogers, Lindsay, *The American Senate*, Knopf, 1926.

Willis, H. Parker, "The Federal Reserve Act," 4 *American Economic Review* (1915) 1.

APPENDIX II

Chronological List of the Principal Public Speeches and Papers of Elihu Root

NOTE: Those speeches and papers which are included in the volumes edited by Robert Bacon and James Brown Scott and published by the Harvard University Press are cited by the indicated abbreviations:

Addresses on Government and Citizenship (1916)—Govt.
Addresses on International Subjects (1916)—International.
The Military and Colonial Policy of the United States (1916)—Mil. and Col.
Latin American and the United States (1917)—L.A.
Miscellaneous Addresses (1917)—Misc.
North Atlantic Coast Fisheries Arbitration at The Hague, Argument on behalf of the United States by Elihu Root (1917)—Fisheries Arbitration.
The United States and the War, The Mission to Russia, Political Addresses (1918)—War and Russia.
Men and Policies (1925)—Men and Policies.

The four lectures delivered at Yale University under the William Earl Dodge Foundation on May 13th, 14th, 20th and 21st, 1907, were also published separately by the Yale University Press under the title, The Citizen's Part in Government (1907).

The two Stafford Little lectures delivered at Princeton University on April 15th and 16th, 1913, were published separately by the Princeton University Press under the title Experiments in Government and the Essentials of the Constitution (1913).

His five annual reports as Secretary of War were published in a separate volume under the title, Five Years of the War Department following the War with Spain, 1899–1903, as shown in the Annual Reports of the Secretary of War (Washington, 1904).

His speeches in Russia in 1917 were published in a separate volume under the title, America's Message to the Russian People, Addresses by the Members of the Special Diplomatic Mission of the United States to Russia in the Year 1917 (Boston, Marshall Jones Company, 1918).

No complete copy exists of many speeches reported in the newspapers and so cited in footnotes throughout the book.

1879
June 25   Commencement Address at Hamilton College, Clinton, New York. Utica Morning Gazette, June 26, 1879.

1885
March 5   Remarks at a meeting of the New York University Law
                       School Alumni, New York City. Typescript.

1887
February 11   Three Views of the Partisan Activity of Public Officers.
                       A Republican View. *The Epoch*, Volume I, No. 1, p. 6.

1891
October 24   Address at a mass meeting of the New York Republican
                       Club, Cooper Union, New York City. New York *Trib-
                       une*, October 28, 1891.

1893
April 28   Our Sister Republic—Argentina. Address at a banquet
                       of the Chamber of Commerce of New York to officers of
                       foreign and United States squadrons, New York City.
                       L.A., p. 235.

In the New York Constitutional Convention [1]

1894
June 26   The Assassination of President Carnot. Remarks on a
                       resolution tendering sympathy to France. *Misc.*, p. 149.

July 17   Trial by Jury. *Govt.*, p. 121.

August 15   Address opposing suffrage for women. *Revised Record*,
                       Volume II, p. 521.

August 20   The Judiciary, address presenting to the Convention an
                       explanatory statement of the Judiciary Committee.
                       Govt., p. 125.

September 1   Sectarian Education. *Govt.*, p. 137.

September 3   The Political Use of Money. *Revised Record*, Volume
                       III, p. 877. Slightly different text in *Govt.*, p. 141.

September 21   The Civil Service. *Govt.*, p. 145.

*   *   *   *   *

December 22   Presidential Address at the 89th Annual Festival of the
                       New England Society in the City of New York, New
                       York City. *New England Society Reports*, 1894, p. 20.

---

[1] For Mr. Root's other remarks at this Constitutional Convention, see index to the
*Revised Record of the Constitutional Convention of the State of New York, May 8th,
1894 to September 29, 1894* (The Argus Company, Albany, New York, 1900).

1895

Opinions of James C. Carter, Elihu Root and others as to the unconstitutionality of the Lexow bill relating to the Police Department of New York City. Pamphlet.

December 23   Speech as Retiring President at the 90th Annual Festival of the New England Society of New York, New York City. *New England Society Reports*, 1895, p. 24.

1896
December 7   The Dutch Founders of New York. Remarks at the 61st Anniversary Dinner of the St. Nicholas Society of the City of New York. *Misc.*, p. 85.

1897
June 8   Address presenting a portrait of Justice Charles H. Van Brunt to the Appellate Division of the Supreme Court of New York in the first Department, New York City. *Misc.*, p. 245.

1898
September 27   The Eligibility of Colonel Theodore Roosevelt. Speech at the Republican State Convention in Saratoga Springs, New York. Pamphlet.

December   Address at a memorial meeting to Robert R. McBurney. *Robert R. McBurney, A Memorial* (International Y.M.C.A., New York, 1899).

1899
June 13   Address at the unveiling of a statue of President Arthur in Madison Square, New York City. *Misc.*, p. 109.

October 7   The American Soldier. Address at the Marquette Club, Chicago, Illinois. *Mil. and Col.*, p. 3.

November 29   Annual Report of the Secretary of War to the President. *Annual Reports of the War Department*, 1899, Vol. I, p. 1. Extracts printed in *Mil. and Col.*, pp. 161, 177, 189, 225 and 350.

1900
April 7   Instructions to the Philippine Commission. *Annual Reports of the War Department*, 1900, Vol. I, p. 72. *Mil. and Col.*, p. 287.

October 24   The United States and the Philippines in 1900. Address at Canton, Ohio. *Mil. and Col.*, p. 27.

1903

February 6   The Union League Club. Address at a meeting of the Club to celebrate its fortieth anniversary, New York City. *Misc.*, p. 123.

February 21   The Army War College. Address at the Laying of the Cornerstone, Washington, D. C. *Mil. and Col.*, p. 121.

March 14   The Home of the Oneidas. Address before the Society of the Sons of Oneida, New York City. *Misc.*, p. 61.

April 2   The Condition of Tariff Revision. Address delivered at a banquet of the Home Market Club, Boston, Massachusetts. Pamphlet.

April 14   The Army Medical School. Address at Graduation Exercises, Washington, D. C. *Mil. and Col.*, p. 131.

May 2   The Citizens' Army. Address at Junction City, Kansas. *Mil. and Col.*, p. 135.

May 4   The Militia Act of 1903. Address at the Fifth Annual Convention of the Interstate National Guard Association of the United States, Columbus, Ohio. *Mil. and Col.*, p. 137.

May 9   The Old and the New New York. Address at a dinner of the Lotos Club in honor of the Secretary of War, New York City. *Misc.*, p. 133.

May 26   The City of New York. Remarks at the Celebration of the 250th Anniversary of the Founding of its Municipal Government. *Misc.*, p. 129.

May 30   William Tecumseh Sherman. Address at the Unveiling of St. Gaudens' Statue of General Sherman, New York City. *Misc.*, p. 115.

December 7   Annual Report of the Secretary of War to the President. *Annual Reports of the War Department*, 1903, Vol. I, p. 1. Extracts printed in *Mil. and Col.*, pp. 306, 325, 398, 426, 431, 456, 468.

December 10 Testimony before Senate Committee on Military Affairs regarding the confirmation of Leonard Wood as Major General. *Senate Confidential Document, Executive C, 58th Congress, 2nd Session*, p. 868.

1904

January   Promotions in the Army. Extracts from Hearing before the House Committee on Military Affairs, Washington, D. C. *Mil. and Col.*, p. 479.

1904

February 3 — Tribute to Theodore Roosevelt. Address at a banquet in honor of the Secretary of War at the Union League Club, New York City. *Misc.*, p. 217.

February 22 — The Preservation of American Ideals. Washington's Birthday Address at a dinner of the Union League Club, Chicago, Illinois. *Misc.*, p. 259.

February 22 — The Ethics of the Panama Question. Address before the Union League Club, Chicago, Illinois. *International*, p. 175.

June 8 — The Object and the Opportunity of Columbia University. Address upon the conferring of the Doctorate of Law, New York City. *Misc.*, p. 75.

June 21 — External Policies in 1904. Address as Temporary Chairman of the Republican National Convention, Chicago, Illinois. *Official Proceedings of the Thirteenth Republican National Convention, 1904*, p. 47. *Mil and Col.*, p. 99.

June 27 — Some Duties of American Lawyers to American Law. Commencement Address, Yale Law School, New Haven, Connecticut. *Govt.*, p. 413.

October 22 — The Campaign of 1904. Address at Buffalo, New York. *War and Russia*, p. 185.

October 26 — Samuel Kirkland, Founder of Hamilton College. Address at the Laying of the Cornerstone of new Dartmouth Hall and the visit of the Earl of Dartmouth to Dartmouth College, Hanover, New Hampshire. *Misc.*, p. 17.

December 22 — The Monroe Doctrine. Address at the 99th Annual Festival of the New England Society of New York, New York City. *New England Society Reports, 1904*, p. 51. *Misc.*, p. 267.

1905

January 11 — Art and Architecture in America. Remarks at the Annual Dinner of the American Institute of Architects, Washington, D. C. *Misc.*, p. 189.

1906

March 31 — Canada and the United States. Address at a dinner given by the Pilgrims of the United States in honor of Earl Grey, Governor General of Canada, New York City. *Misc.*, p. 151.

1906

April 20 Benjamin Franklin. Address on presenting to France the Gold Medal authorized by Congress, Franklin Bicentennial, Philadelphia, Pennsylvania. *Misc.*, p. 141.

June 18 Instructions to the delegates of the United States to the Third International Conference of American States at Rio de Janeiro, Washington, D. C. *Foreign Relations of the United States*, 1906, Part 2, p. 1566.

South American Trip

July 17 Reply to Governor's speech at a breakfast given by the Governor, Para, Brazil. *L.A.*, p. 45.

July 22 Reply to Governor's speech at a breakfast given by the Governor, Pernambuco, Brazil. *L.A.*, p. 47.

July 24 Speech at a banquet given by the Governor, Bahia, Brazil. *L.A.*, p. 50.

July 28 Replies to speeches at a banquet given by the Minister for Foreign Affairs, Rio de Janeiro, Brazil. *L.A.*, p. 15. *Foreign Relations of the United States*, 1906, Part 1, p. 132.

July 31 Speech as Honorary President of the Third Conference of the American Republics, Rio de Janeiro, Brazil. *L.A.*, p. 6. *Foreign Relations of the United States*, 1906, Part 1, p. 127.

August 2 Reply to addresses in the Chamber of Deputies, Rio de Janeiro, Brazil. *L.A.*, p. 31.

August 4 Reply to speeches at a mass meeting of Law School students, São Paulo, Brazil. *L.A.*, p. 38.

August 4 Speech on presenting football trophy at São Paulo, Brazil. *L.A.*, p. 40.

August 7 Reply to speech of Dr. Rezenal at the Commercial Association of Santos, Brazil. *L.A.*, p. 42.

August 10 Reply at a banquet given by the Minister for Foreign Affairs, Montevideo, Uruguay. *L.A.*, p. 58. *Foreign Relations of the United States*, 1906, Part 2, p. 1426.

August 11 Reply at a banquet given by the President, Montevideo, Uruguay. *L.A.*, p. 63. *Foreign Relations of the United States*, 1906, Part 2, p. 1424.

August 12 Reply at a breakfast given by the Reception Committee, Montevideo, Uruguay. *L.A.*, p. 69.

1906

August 14	Reply at the Presidential Banquet, Buenos Ayres, Argentina. *L.A.*, p. 84. *Foreign Relations of the United States*, 1906, Part 1, p. 26.
August 16	Reply at a reception given by American and English residents, Buenos Ayres, Argentina. *L.A.*, p. 90.
August 17	Reply at a banquet at the Opera House, Buenos Ayres, Argentina. *L.A.*, p. 97. *Foreign Relations of the United States*, 1906, Part 1, p. 29.
September 1	Reply at the Government House, Santiago, Chile. *L.A.*, p. 103. *Foreign Relations of the United States*, 1906, Part 1, p. 150.
September 2	Reply at the Presidential Banquet, Santiago, Chile. *L.A.*, p. 109. *Foreign Relations of the United States*, 1906, Part 1, p. 153.
September 10	Reply at the Presidential Banquet, Lima, Peru. *L.A.*, p. 114. *Foreign Relations of the United States*, 1906, Part 2, p. 1229.
September 10	Reply at the reception given by the Municipal Council, Lima, Peru. *L.A.*, p. 129.
September 11	Reply at a banquet given by the Minister for Foreign Affairs, Lima, Peru. *L.A.*, p. 123. *Foreign Relations of the United States*, 1906, Part 2, p. 1233.
September 13	Reply at the reception given by the Senate, Lima, Peru. *L.A.*, p. 132.
September 14	Speech at installation as a member of the Faculty of the University of San Marcos, Lima, Peru. *L.A.*, p. 140.
September 21	Speech at the National Assembly, Panama. *L.A.*, p. 148. *Foreign Relations of the United States*, 1906, Part 2, p. 1200.
September 24	Reply at a breakfast given by the Minister for Foreign Affairs, Cartagena, Colombia. *L.A.*, p. 154. *Foreign Relations of the United States*, Part 1, p. 441.

* * * * *

November 1	The Demagogue in Politics. Campaign Address at Utica, New York. *War and Russia*, p. 203.
November 10	Justice George Carter-Barrett. Address at a memorial meeting of the bench and bar, New York City. *Misc.*, p. 241.

1906

November 20   How to Develop South American Commerce. Address at the Trans-Mississippi Commercial Congress, Kansas City, Missouri. *L.A.*, p. 245. *United States Senate Document* No. 211, 59th Cong., 2nd Sess.

December 2   Remarks on unveiling a memorial window to John Hay at Keneseth Israel, Philadelphia, Pennsylvania. Pamphlet.

December 12   How to Preserve the Local Self-Government of the States. Speech at a dinner of the Pennsylvania Society of New York, New York City. *Govt.*, p. 363.

1907

January   The Need of Popular Understanding of International Law. Article contributed to the first issue of the *American Journal of International Law*, p. 1. *International*, p. 3.

January 14   South American Commerce. Address at the National Convention for the Extension of the Foreign Commerce of the United States, Washington, D. C. *L.A.*, p. 269.

January 22   The Builders of Canada. Address at a banquet of the Canadian Club of Ottawa, Ottawa, Canada. *Misc.*, p. 157.

April 15   The Hague Peace Conferences. Address at the National Arbitration and Peace Congress, New York City. *International*, p. 129.

April 19   The Real Questions under the Japanese Treaty and the San Francisco School Board Resolution. Presidential Address at the First Annual Meeting of the American Society of International Law, Washington, D. C. *Proceedings of the American Society of International Law*, 1907, p. 43. *International*, p. 7.

May 13, 14, 20, 21   The Citizen's Part in Government. Four Lectures under the Dodge Foundation at Yale University, New Haven, Connecticut. *Govt.*, p. 1.

May 18   The Pan American Cause. Response to toast of the Brazilian Ambassador at a dinner in honor of visiting Brazilian naval officers, Washington, D. C. *L.A.*, p. 219.

May 31   The Second Hague Peace Conference. Instructions to the American Delegates. *Foreign Relations of the United States*, 1907, Part 2, p. 1128. *Men and Policies*, p. 295.

Mexican Trip

1907

September 28 Speech at a banquet given by the International Club, San Antonio, Texas. *L.A.*, p. 159.

September 29 Reply at a reception given by the Mexican Delegation, Nuevo Laredo, Mexico. *L.A.*, p. 162.

October 2 Reply at a banquet at the National Palace, Mexico City, Mexico. *L.A.*, p. 164. *Foreign Relations of the United States*, 1907, Part 2, p. 853.

October 3 Reply at a reception at the Municipal Palace, Mexico City, Mexico. *L.A.*, p. 167. *Foreign Relations of the United States*, 1907, Part 2, pp. 854 and 856.

October 4 Speech at a luncheon given by the American Colony, Mexico City, Mexico. *L.A.*, p. 179. *Foreign Relations of the United States*, 1907, Part 2, p. 858.

October 4 Address at the Mexican Academy of Legislation and Jurisprudence, Mexico City, Mexico. *L.A.*, p. 188. *Foreign Relations of the United States*, 1907, Part 2, p. 862.

October 5 Reply at a banquet given by the American Ambassador, Mexico City, Mexico. *L.A.*, p. 193.

October 7 Reply at a banquet given by the Minister for Foreign Affairs, Mexico City, Mexico. *L.A.*, p. 199. *Foreign Relations of the United States*, 1907, Part 2, p. 866.

October 7 Speech at a farewell supper given by Secretary Root, Mexico City, Mexico. *L.A.*, p. 202. *Foreign Relations of the United States*, 1907, Part 2, p. 868.

October 9 Reply at a banquet at the Municipal Palace, Puebla, Mexico. *L.A.*, p. 205.

October 10 Reply at a luncheon at the Cocolopan Factory, Orizaba, Vera Cruz, Mexico. *L.A.*, p. 206.

October 10 Reply to the Governor's speech, Guadalajara, Mexico. *L.A.*, p. 209. *Foreign Relations of the United States*, 1907, Part 2, p. 869.

* * * * *

December 13 Address opening the Central American Peace Conference, Washington, D. C. *L.A.*, p. 214.

December 20 Closing address at the Central American Peace Conference, Washington, D. C. *L.A.*, p. 217.

1908

April 24   The Sanction of Internationl Law. Presidential Address
at the Second Annual Meeting of the American Society
of International Law, Washington, D. C. Proceedings of
the American Society of International Law, 1908, p. 14.
International, p. 25.

May 1   Prefatory Note to Texts of the Peace Conferences at The
Hague, 1899 and 1907, by James Brown Scott (Boston,
Ginn and Co., 1908).

May 11   The Pan American Union. Address at the Laying of the
Cornerstone of the Building of the Pan American Union,
Washington, D. C. L.A., p. 228.

May 13   Address at the Conference of the Governors of the
States, Washington, D. C. Govt., p. 371.

June 15   Address to Members of the United States Delegation to
the Pan American Scientific Congress at Santiago, Washington, D. C. Pamphlet.

September 14   The Campaign of 1908. Address at the Republican State
Convention, Saratoga Springs, New York. War and Rus-
sia, p. 227.

October 28 Campaign Address at Cincinnati, Ohio. Pamphlet.

October 31 Campaign Address at Durland's Riding Academy, New
York City. Pamphlet.

November 9 Address at dedication of the Army War College, Washington, D. C. Mil. and Col., p. 127.

November 21 Instructions to the American Delegates to the Conference
at London to Formulate Rules to be Observed by the
International Prize Court. Foreign Relations of the
United States, 1909, p. 300.

December 15 Address at Memorial Meeting of the American Institute
of Architects in appreciation of Augustus St. Gaudens,
Washington, D. C. Pamphlet.

1909

January 26 Remarks on taking leave of the officials of the Department of State, Washington, D. C. Pamphlet.

January 28 Acceptance of the New York Senatorship. Address to the
New York State Legislature, Albany, New York. Govt.,
p. 247.

1909

February 26   The Causes of War. Address at a dinner of the New York Peace Society in recognition of the services of the Secretary of State to international peace, New York City. *Misc.*, p. 275.

March 18   Grover Cleveland. Memorial Address at the College of the City of New York. *Misc.*, p. 105.

April 23   The Relations between International Tribunals of Arbitration and the Jurisdiction of National Courts. Presidential Address at the Third Annual Meeting of the American Society of International Law, Washington, D. C. *Proceedings of the American Society of International Law*, 1909, p. 17. *International*, p. 33.

May 6   Address at a dinner given by Ambassador Nabuco to the Gridiron Club in honor of a Brazilian editor, Washington, D. C. *Bulletin of the International Union of the American Republics*, June, 1909, p. 1042.

May 11   Address at the Convention at which the American Federation of Arts was formed, Washington, D. C. Pamphlet.

May 31   The Lemon Schedule. Speech in the Senate. *Congressional Record*, Volume 44, p. 2569.

July 1   The Corporation Tax Amendment. Speech in the Senate. *Congressional Record*, Volume 44, p. 4002.

July 7   The Iroquois and the Struggle for America. Address at the Tercentennial Celebration of the Discovery of Lake Champlain, Plattsburg, New York. *Misc.*, p. 3.

September 9   The Great Reconciliation. Address at a reunion of Union and Confederate Soldiers, Utica, New York, *Misc.*, p. 119.

November 12   Address at the Installation of Dr. William Arnold Shanklin as President of Wesleyan University, Middletown, Connecticut. Pamphlet.

November 18   Address at the dinner of the Chamber of Commerce of the State of New York, New York City. Pamphlet.

November 23   Charles Follen McKim. Address at a Memorial Meeting, New Theatre, New York City. *Misc.*, p. 197.

November 23   Importance of Seeking Reform through State Governments. Remarks at the Tenth Annual Dinner of the National Civic Federation, New York City. *Govt.*, p. 375.

1909

December 15   Charles Follen McKim. Address at a Memorial Meeting, American Institute of Architects, Washington, D. C. *Misc.*, p. 198.

December 18   Address at the Proceedings of the Bar and Officers of the Supreme Court of the United States in memory of Rufus Wheeler Peckham, Washington, D. C. Pamphlet.

1910

February 7   Letter to Hon. Frederick M. Davenport on the income tax amendment. United States *Senate Document* No. 398, 61st Cong., 2nd Sess.

March 4   Postal Savings Banks. Speech in the Senate. *Congressional Record*, Volume 45, p. 2708.

March 30, 31
April 1   Court of Commerce Bill. Speeches in the Senate. Printed together in *Congressional Record*, Volume 45, p. 4100.

April 26   The Pan American Union. Address at Dedication of the Building, Washington, D. C. *L.A.*, p. 231.

April 28   The Basis of Protection to Citizens Residing Abroad. Presidential Address at the Fourth Annual Meeting of the American Society of International Law, Washington, D. C. *Proceedings of the American Society of International Law*, 1910, p. 16. *International*, p. 43.

August 2–15   Argument of Elihu Root on behalf of the United States of America, North Atlantic Coast Fisheries Arbitration at The Hague. *Proceedings in the North Atlantic Coast Fisheries Arbitration before the Permanent Court of Arbitration at The Hague under the provisions of the General Treaty of Arbitration of April 4, 1908, and the Special Agreement of January 27, 1909, between the United States of America and Great Britain*, Vol. XI, pp. 1927–2231 (Washington, 1912). *Fisheries Arbitration*, p. 1.

October 28   The New York State Campaign of 1910. Address at Manhattan Casino, New York City. *War and Russia*, p. 259.

November 11   John Hay. Address at the dedication of the John Hay Library, Brown University, Providence, Rhode Island. *Misc.*, p. 91.

December 10   Melville Weston Fuller. Address at the Proceedings of the Bar and Officers of the Supreme Court of the United States, Washington, D. C. *Misc.*, p. 237.

1911

June 21   The Canadian Reciprocity Agreement. Speech in the Senate. *Congressional Record*, Volume 47, p. 2370. *Misc.*, p. 163.

August 7   The Arizona Constitution and the Recall of Judges. Speech in the Senate. *Congressional Record*, Volume 47, p. 3688. *Govt.*, p. 387.

November 9   Inauguration of Elmer Brown as Chancellor of New York University, Response for Educational Foundations, New York City. *Misc.*, p. 71.

December 16   John Marshall Harlan. Address at Memorial Exercises in the United States Supreme Court. *Misc.*, p. 233.

December 19   The Treaty of 1832 with Russia: the Right of Expatriation. Speech in the Senate. *Congressional Record*, Volume 48, p. 482. *International*, p. 313.

1912

January 19   Judicial Decisions and Public Feeling. Presidential Address at the Annual Meeting of the New York State Bar Association, New York City. *Report of the New York State Bar Association*, Volume 35 (1912), p. 148. *Govt.*, p. 445.

January 20   The Independent Bar. Address at a dinner of the New York State Bar Association, New York City. *Report of the New York State Bar Association*, Volume 35 (1912), p. 515. *Govt.*, p. 463.

March 13   The Export of Arms and Munitions of War to American Countries. Speech in the Senate. *Congressional Record*, Volume 48, p. 3257. *Mil. and Col.*, p. 153.

April 10   The Recall of Judges. Remarks in the Republican State Convention, Rochester, New York. *Govt.*, p. 405.

April 25   The Real Significance of the Declaration of London. Presidential Address at the Sixth Annual Meeting of the American Society of International Law, Washington, D. C. *Proceedings of the American Society of International Law*, 1912, p. 4. *International*, p. 73.

May 7   Address at the opening of the Red Cross Conference, Washington, D. C. Pamphlet.

May 10   Francis Davis Millet. Address at the Memorial Meeting of the American Federation of Arts, Washington, D. C. *Misc.*, p. 205.

1912

June 17　　　The Centenary of Hamilton College. Historical Address at the Centennial Celebration, Clinton, New York *Misc.*, p. 23.

June 18　　　The Achievements of Republican Administrations. Address at the Republican National Convention, Chicago. *Official Proceedings of the Fifteenth Republican National Convention, 1912*, p. 88. *War and Russia*, p. 277.

August 1　　　The Renomination of President Taft. Address as Chairman of the Republican National Convention of 1912, notifying Taft of his nomination, Washington, D. C. *Official Proceedings of the Fifteenth Republican National Convention, 1912*, p. 412. *War and Russia*, p. 297.

August 14　　　The Power of the President to send United States Troops out of the Country. Speech in the Senate. *Congressional Record*, Volume 48, p. 10929. *Mil. and Col.*, p. 157.

November 21　　　The Spirit of Self Government. Address at the 144th Anniversary Banquet of the Chamber of Commerce of New York State, New York City. *Govt.*, p. 379.

November 24　　　Address at the Memorial Meeting for James S. Sherman, Republican Club of New York City. Pamphlet.

1913

January 16　　　Latin America and the United States. Denial of Honduran report of a speech by Mr. Root in the Senate. Speech in the Senate. *Congressional Record*, Volume 49, p. 1604. *International Conciliation*, Special Bulletin, January, 1913.

January 21　　　The Obligations of the United States as to the Panama Canal Tolls. Speech in the Senate. *Congressional Record*, Volume 49, p. 1818. *International*, p. 207.

January 25　　　Address at a dinner in honor of Judge John Clinton Gray, New York City. Pamphlet.

February 12　　　Statement on the Panama Canal Tolls, *Hearings before the Committee on Interoceanic Canals, United States Senate, 62nd Cong., 3rd Sess. on S. 8114, Statement of Hon. Elihu Root, February 12, 1913* (separately paged).

February 15　　　James Schoolcraft Sherman. Address at the Memorial Exercises in the Senate. *Congressional Record*, Volume 49, p. 3205. *Misc.*, p. 65.

February 15　　　Joseph G. Cannon. Address at a dinner in his honor, Washington, D. C. *Misc.*, p. 213.

1913

March 1   Address at a Memorial Service of the Senate in honor of
                 Weldon B. Heyburn. *Congressional Record*, Volume 49,
                 p. 4386.

April 3   John Pierpont Morgan. Address at the Memorial Meet-
                 ing of the Chamber of Commerce of the State of New
                 York, New York City. *Misc.*, p. 227.

April 15, 16   Experiments in Government and the Essentials of the
                 Constitution. Stafford Little Lectures at Princeton Uni-
                 versity, Princeton, New Jersey. *Govt.*, p. 77.

April 24   Francis Lieber. Presidential Address at the Seventh An-
                 nual Meeting of the American Society of International
                 Law, Washington, D. C. *Proceedings of the American
                 Society of International Law*, 1913, p. 8. *International*,
                 p. 89.

June 18   Our Sister Republic—Brazil. Address of welcome to the
                 Secretary of State for Foreign Affairs of Brazil at a ban-
                 quet of the Chamber of Commerce of the State of New
                 York, New York City. *L.A.*, p. 239.

July 20   Letter of Instructions as Chairman of the Board of Trus-
                 tees to Robert Bacon as the representative of the Car-
                 negie Endowment for International Peace to visit South
                 America in the interests of Latin American cooperation
                 with the purposes of the Endowment. *Men and Policies*,
                 p. 315.

September 23   Speech as Permanent Chairman at the Republican State
                 Convention, Carnegie Hall, New York City. Pamphlet.

December 5   Speech as Chairman of the Republican Conference at
                 the Waldorf Astoria Hotel, New York City. Pamphlet.

December 13   The Banking and Currency Bill. Speech in the Senate.
                 Congressional Record, Volume 51, p. 828. *Govt.*, p. 323.

December 16   A Personal Statement. Remarks in the Senate. *Congres-
                 sional Record*, Volume 51, p. 965. *Govt.*, p. 361.

1914

January 2   Address at the inauguration of Dr. John Finley as Presi-
                 dent of the University of the State of New York, Albany,
                 New York. Pamphlet.

February 27   Reforms in Judicial Procedure. Statement before the
                 House Judiciary Committee. *Govt.*, p. 467.

1914

April 21   The Mexican Resolution. Speech in the Senate. *Congressional Record*, Volume 51, p. 6985. *International*, p. 327.

April 22   The Real Monroe Doctrine. Presidential Address at the Eighth Annual Meeting of the American Society of International Law, Washington, D. C. *Proceedings of the American Society of International Law*, 1914, p. 6. *International*, p. 105.

April 23   Address at the Conference of Teachers of International Law, Washington, D. C. *Proceedings of the American Society of International Law*, 1914, p. 250. *International*, p. 125.

May 21   Panama Canal Tolls. Speech in the Senate. *Congressional Record*, Volume 51, p. 8942. *International*, p. 241.

June 10   Address as Honorary Chancellor of Union University, Schenectady, New York. *Misc.*, p. 45.

August 18   The Republican Party in Opposition. Address at the Republican State Convention, Saratoga Springs, New York. *Proceedings of the Republican Convention of the State of New York*, 1914, p. 49. *War and Russia*, p. 301.

September 8   Address on receiving the Nobel Peace Prize of 1912. Prepared but not delivered. *International*, p. 153.

October 13   Address at a political meeting of the Union League Club, New York City. Pamphlet.

October 20   The Layman's Criticism of the Lawyer. Address at the Annual Meeting of the American Bar Association, Washton, D. C. *Reports of the American Bar Association*, Volume XXXIX (1914), p. 386. United States Senate Document No. 612, 63rd Cong., 2nd Sess. *Govt.*, p. 479.

October 22   The Spirit Which Makes a Nation Live. Address at a dinner of the American Bar Association, Washington, D. C. *Govt.*, p. 499.

November 19   The Principles and Practice of Constitutional Revision. Address as Presiding Officer at a meeting of the Academy of Political Science, New York City. *Proceedings of the Academy of Political Science*, Volume V, p. 1. *Govt.*, p. 147.

1915

January 4   The Ship Purchase Bill. Speech in the Senate. *Congressional Record*, Volume 52, p. 908. *International*, p. 337.

1915

January 25	Second speech on the Ship Purchase Bill in the Senate. *Congressional Record*, Volume 52, p. 2208. *International*, p. 341.
February 9	Third speech on the Ship Purchase Bill in the Senate. *Congressional Record*, Volume 52, p. 3340.
March 13	The Lawyer of Today. Address before the New York County Lawyers Association, New York City. *Govt.*, p. 503.
March 25	The Business Men and the Constitutional Convention. Address before the Merchants' Association of New York, New York City. *Govt.*, p. 155.
April 1	The Origins of Law. Address before the Harvard Law School Association of New York City. Proof sheets.

At the New York State Constitutional Convention [2]

April 6	Opening Address. *Govt.*, p. 163.
June 15	Magna Charta. *Govt.*, p. 169.
August 19	On Ending the Scandal of the Law's Delay. *Govt.*, p. 177.
August 20	Impeachment. *Govt.*, p. 173.
August 23	Courts of Justice for Small Causes. *Govt.*, p. 185.
August 25	The Regulation of Public Utilities and the Decline of the "Black Horse Cavalry." *Govt.*, p. 187.
August 30	Invisible Government. *Govt.*, p. 191.
September 10	Speech on closing the Convention. *Govt.*, p. 207.

* * * * *

October 18	A Study of the Proposed Constitution. Address at a dinner given to him by the Republican Club of New York, New York City. *Govt.*, p. 213.
October 22	The Supreme Treasure of Our Country. Address upon receiving the degree of Doctor of Laws from the University of the State of New York, Albany, New York. *Misc.*, p. 81.
October 25	The New York Constitution and Representative Government. Address at the Economic Club of New York, New York City. *Govt.*, p. 227.

[2] For Mr. Root's other remarks at this Constitutional Convention, see index to *Revised Record of the Constitutional Convention of the State of New York, April 6, 1915 to September 10, 1915* (Lyon, Albany, New York, 1916).

1915

December 28   The Outlook for International Law. Presidential Address at the Ninth Annual Meeting of the American Society of International Law, Washington, D. C. *Proceedings of the American Society of International Law*, 1915, p. 2. *International*, p. 391.

December 30   Address of Welcome to the Second Pan American Scientific Congress, Washington, D. C. L.A., p. 291.

December 30   Should International Law Be Codified? Address at a joint meeting of the Subsection on International Law of the Second Pan American Scientific Congress, Washington, D. C. *Proceedings of the American Society of International Law*, 1915, p. 162. *International*, p. 405.

December 30   The Spread of International Law in the Americas. Remarks at a dinner of the Division of International Law of the Carnegie Endowment for International Peace and the Pan American Scientific Congress, Washington, D. C. *Misc.*, p. 295.

1916

January 15   Individual Liberty and the Responsibility of the Bar. Address at the Annual Dinner of the New York State Bar Association. *Report of the New York State Bar Association*, Volume 39 (1916), p. 473. *Govt.*, p. 511.

February 15   A Blundering Administration. Address as Temporary Chairman of the New York Republican State Convention, New York City. Pamphlet. Portions of his address dealing with international matters in *International*, p. 427.

February 20   Remarks at the 100th Anniversary Celebration of the Graham School, New York City. Typescript.

April 27   The Declaration of the Rights and Duties of Nations of the American Institute of International Law. Presidential Address at the Tenth Annual Meeting of the American Society of International Law, Washington, D. C. *Proceedings of the American Society of International Law*, 1916, p. 1. *International*, p. 413.

August 8   Prefatory Note to *The Philippines to the End of the Military Regime*, by Charles B. Elliott (Bobbs Merrill, 1916).

August 30   Remarks before the Judicial Section of the American Bar Association. *Reports of the American Bar Association*, Volume XLI (1916), p. 731.

1916

August 30
Public Service by the Bar. Address as President of the Annual Meeting of the American Bar Association, Chicago, Illinois. *Reports of the American Bar Association*, Volume XLI (1916), p. 355.

October 3
Opening remarks as Chairman at a Reception to the Honorable Charles Evans Hughes, Union League Club, New York City. Pamphlet.

October 5
The Campaign of 1916. Address at a public meeting held under the direction of the Republican Club of New York City at Carnegie Hall. *War and Russia*, p. 323.

December 7
The Federal Amendment; a destruction of the right of self government. Statement read at the National Anti-Suffrage Convention, Washington, D. C. Pamphlet.

December 15
The Enslavement of the Belgians. Address at a mass meeting in New York City. *War and Russia*, p. 3.

1917

January 25
America's Present Needs. Address at the Congress of Constructive Patriotism held under the auspices of the National Security League, Washington, D. C. *War and Russia*, p. 11.

March 20
America on Trial. Address before the Union League Club, New York City. *War and Russia*, p. 27.

March 22
The United States and the World Crisis. Address as Chairman of a Patriotic Mass Meeting, Madison Square Garden, New York City. *War and Russia*, p. 33.

April 9
The Duty of the Republican Party in the War. Speech before the New York Republican Club, New York City. *War and Russia*, p. 39.

April 26
The Effect of Democracy on International Law. Presidential Address at the Eleventh Annual Meeting of the American Society of International Law, Washington, D. C. *Proceedings of the American Society of International Law*, 1917, p. 2. *Misc.*, p. 281.

Mission to Russia

June 15
Address to the Council of Ministers, Petrograd. *War and Russia*, p. 98. *American Journal of International Law*, Volume XI (1917), p. 757.

*   *   *   *   *

1917

September 3   A Federated Union of the American Bar. Address at a special conference of delegates from Bar Associations, Saratoga Springs, New York. *American Bar Association Journal,* Volume 3 (1917), p. 581. *War and Russia,* p. 57.

September 4   The American Bar and the War. Speech presenting the resolutions of the American Bar Association, Saratoga Springs, New York. *Reports of the American Bar Association,* Volume XLII (1917), p. 25. *War and Russia,* p. 63.

September 6   Sympathy with Russia. Address at a banquet of the American Bar Association, Saratoga Springs, New York. *American Bar Association Journal,* Volume 3 (1917), p. 646. *War and Russia,* p. 169.

September 14   The War and Discussion. Address at a war mass meeting in the Coliseum at Chicago, Illinois. *War and Russia,* p. 65.

October 1   Japan and the United States. Address at a luncheon in honor of the Imperial Japanese Mission, New York City. *War and Russia,* p. 81.

December 20   Joseph H. Choate. Memorial at the Association of the Bar of the City of New York. *Men and Policies,* p. 17.

1918

Foreword to *The Imperial Japanese Mission, 1917; a record of the reception throughout the United States of the special mission headed by Viscount Ishii* (Carnegie Endowment for International Peace, Washington, D. C., 1918).

January 19   Joseph H. Choate. Address as presiding officer at a meeting of the Century Association, New York City. *Men and Policies,* p. 43.

February 16   Letter to the President of the National Security League, *Men and Policies,* p. 169.

March 7   Speech at a meeting in honor of the Archbishop of York, New York City. *Men and Policies,* p. 173.

April 24   Speech before the National Security League of Philadelphia. *Men and Policies,* p. 178.

May 8   Address as Chairman of the Annual Meeting of the National Security League, New York City. *Men and Policies,* p. 185.

1918

June 17   Alexander Hamilton. Address as Chairman of the Board of Trustees of Hamilton College in accepting a statue of Hamilton, Clinton, New York. *Men and Policies*, p. 76.

July 2   Public Statement for the National War Savings Committee in New York City. *Men and Policies*, p. 190.

July 18   The Duty of the Opposition Party in the War. Address before the Republican State Convention, Saratoga Springs, New York. *Men and Policies*, p. 192.

August 27   Address as presiding officer at the Conference of Bar Association Delegates, Saratoga Springs, New York. *American Bar Association Journal*, Volume 5 (1919), p. 15.

August 29   Remarks as Chairman of the Fourth Session of the Council on Legal Education of the American Bar Association. *Reports of the American Bar Association*, Volume XLIII (1918), p. 70.

October 1   Address to students of Columbia University who had joined the United States Army, New York City. Typescript.

November 17   Address at the Cathedral of St. John the Divine, New York City. New York *Times*, November 18, 1918.

1919

February 9   Theodore Roosevelt. Address as presiding officer at a meeting of the Century Association, New York City. *Men and Policies*, p. 3.

February 12   The Resumption of Individual Liberty. Speech at Lincoln's Birthday Dinner in Utica, New York. *Men and Policies*, p. 202.

February 20   James Russell Lowell. Address as Chairman at a dinner on Lowell's Centenary given by the American Academy of Arts and Letters to British and American authors, New York City. *Men and Policies*, p. 58.

March 29   Letter to Will Hays on the League of Nations. United States *Senate Document* No. 41, 66th Cong., 1st Sess. *Men and Policies*, p. 251.

April 5   Address at a dinner given by the Association of the Bar of the City of New York to Lord Reading as Ambassador to the United States. *Men and Policies*, p. 130.

1919

May 15   War Memorials. Speech at the Convention of the National Federation of Arts, Metropolitan Museum of Art, New York City. *Men and Policies*, p. 232.

June 11   Testimony at Investigation Relative to the Treaty of Peace with Germany, *Hearing before the Committee on Foreign Relations, United States Senate, 66th Congress, 1st Session, Pursuant to S. Res. 64, directing the Committee to investigate whether copies of the Peace Treaty with Germany are in the City of New York, by whom and how they were obtained, and so forth*, Part 2, p. 28.

June 21   Letter to Henry Cabot Lodge on the League of Nations. *United States Senate Document*, No. 41, 66th Cong., 1st Sess. *Men and Policies*, p. 269.

September 2   Remarks as President of the Conference of Delegates at the meeting of the American Bar Association, Boston, Massachusetts. *American Bar Association Journal*, Volume 6 (Part 1) (1920), p. 14.

September 3   Remarks at the Annual Meeting of the American Bar Association, *Reports of the American Bar Association*, Volume XLIV (1919), p. 25.

September 4   Judges and Legislatures. Remarks to the Judicial Section of the American Bar Association, Boston, Massachusetts. *American Bar Association Journal*, Volume 5 (1919), p. 676. *Men and Policies*, p. 135.

September 17   The Constitution of the United States. Address at Carnegie Hall on the Anniversary of the Signing, New York City. *Men and Policies*, p. 121.

October   *Feigenspan vs. Bodine et al*, Supreme Court of the United States, October Term, 1919, No. 788, Brief for Appellants on the Validity of the So-called Eighteenth Amendment. Pamphlet.

October 27   Address at the Rocky Mountain Club Dinner on the Anniversary of Theodore Roosevelt's Birth, New York City. *Men and Policies*, p. 11.

1920

February 17   Address on the Fiftieth Anniversary of the Association of the Bar of the City of New York. *Addresses Delivered February 17th, 1920, and Historical Sketch Prepared to Commemorate the Semi-Centenary of the Association of*

1920

the Bar of the City of New York (New York, 1920), p. 27. Men and Policies, p. 111.

February 19   The Restoration Policies of the United States. Address as Chairman of the New York Republican State Convention, New York City. Men and Policies, p. 210.

April 25   The Life and Work of Andrew Carnegie. Address at a Memorial Meeting under the direction of the Authors Club, New York City. Men and Policies, p. 49.

May 18   Address as Vice President on the Fiftieth Anniversary of the Metropolitan Museum of Art, New York City. Men and Policies, p. 105.

June 17–
July 24   The Permanent Court of International Justice. Remarks as a member of the Advisory Committee of Jurists at The Hague. See index to Procès-Verbaux of the Proceedings of the Committee, June 16th–July 24th, 1920, Advisory Committee of Jurists, Permanent Court of International Justice (The Hague, 1920). American Journal of International Law, Volume 15 (1921), p. 1. Men and Policies, p. 324.

July 28   Abraham Lincoln. Address at Parliament Square, London, presenting St. Gaudens' Statue of Lincoln to the British People. Men and Policies, p. 63.

October 19   Presidential Election of 1920. Speech at a meeting under the direction of the National Republican Club, New York City. Men and Policies, p. 277.

October 21   The Court of International Justice. Address before the Association of the Bar of the City of New York. American Bar Association Journal, Volume 6 (Part 2) (1920), p. 181. Men and Policies, p. 391.

December 7   Statement as President regarding the problems confronting the Carnegie Endowment for International Peace at the semi-annual meeting of the Board of Trustees, Washington, D. C. Reprinted from the Minutes by the Carnegie Endowment for International Peace. Pamphlet.

1921

April 27   The Conditions and Possibilities Remaining for International Law after the War. Presidential Address at the Fifteenth Annual Meeting of the American Society of

1921

International Law, Washington, D. C. *Proceedings of the American Society of International Law*, 1921, p. 1.

August 26   Democracy and Foreign Affairs. Speech at a banquet concluding the discussions of the Institute of Politics, Williamstown, Massachusetts. *Men and Policies*, p. 469.

August 31   Remarks as Chairman of the Section on Legal Education and Admissions to the Bar at the 44th Annual Meeting of the American Bar Association at Cincinnati, Ohio. *Reports of the American Bar Association*, Volume XLVI (1921), pp. 37, 39, 656.

1922

February 1   The Prohibition of Submarines and Poisonous Gases. Speech at the Fifth Plenary Session of the Conference on the Limitation of Armaments, Washington, D. C. *Conference on the Limitation of Armaments, Washington, November 12, 1921–February 6, 1922*, p. 258.[3] *Men and Policies*, p. 446.

February 23, 24   The Standard of Legal Education. Speech at the Conference of American Bar Association Delegates, Washington, D. C. *Reports of the American Bar Association*, Volume XLVII (1922), p. 485. *Men and Policies*, p. 141.

April 21   Remarks before the Board of Trustees of the Carnegie Endowment for International Peace, Washington, D. C. *Men and Policies*, p. 320.

April 22   Address as President on the 75th Anniversary of the Century Association, New York City. *Men and Policies*, p. 99.

April 27   International Law at the Washington Conference on the Limitation of Armaments. Presidential Address at the Sixteenth Annual Meeting of the American Society of International Law, Washington, D. C. *Proceedings of the American Society of International Law*, 1922, p. 1. *Men and Policies*, p. 452.

May 10   The New York Regional Plan. Remarks in behalf of a project of the Russell Sage Foundation, Engineering Society Building, New York City. *Men and Policies*, p. 238.

[3] For additional remarks of Mr. Root at the Conference, see index to that volume and of *Conference on the Limitation of Armaments, Washington, November 12, 1921–February 6, 1922, Minutes of Sub-Committees* (Washington, Government Printing Office, 1922).

1922

September 15   A Requisite for the Success of Popular Diplomacy. Article contributed to the first issue of *Foreign Affairs*. Reprinted in *Foreign Affairs*, Volume 15 (1937), No. 3. *Men and Policies*, p. 479.

September 27   Address as Temporary Chairman of the Republican State Convention at Albany, New York. Proof sheets.

November 20   The Cathedral. Address before a mass meeting of the Episcopal Diocese of New York to raise funds for the completion of the Cathedral of St. John the Divine, New York City. New York *Times*, November 21, 1922.

1923

Introduction to *Grover Cleveland, The Man and the Statesman*, by Robert M. McElroy (Harpers, 1923).

Introduction to *Robert Bacon, Life and Letters*, by James Brown Scott (Doubleday Page, 1923).

January 17   The Education of Democracy in Foreign Affairs. Speech before the Committee on Foreign Relations and National Defense of the National Civic Federation, Washington, D. C. *Men and Policies*, p. 489.

February 23   The Restatement of the Substantive Law. Address as Chairman of a Meeting of the Bench and the Bar to organize the American Law Institute, Washington, D. C. *Proceedings of the American Law Institute*, Volume I (1922), p. 48.

March 1   How to Interest Democracy in Foreign Affairs. Remarks in the Executive Committee of the Committee of One Hundred on Foreign Relations, National Civic Federation, New York City. *Men and Policies*, p. 498.

April 26   The Court of International Justice. Presidential Address at the Seventeenth Annual Meeting of the American Society of International Law, Washington, D. C. *Proceedings of the American Society of International Law*, 1923, p. 1. *Men and Policies*, p. 405.

May 18   The Permanent Court of International Justice. Address at the Union League Club, New York City. Pamphlet.

1924

October 3   Address at the Formal Opening of the School of Citizenship and Public Affairs, Syracuse University. *Bulletin of Syracuse University*, Volume XXV, No. 17a, October, 1924.

1924

October 6   Speech at the Introductory Dinner of the Hamilton-Jefferson Association, Utica, New York. Pamphlet.

October 27   Address at the Ratification Meeting and Reception to Colonel Theodore Roosevelt, Jr., Union League Club, New York City. Pamphlet.

November 10   Address as First Vice President at the Opening of the American Wing of the Metropolitan Museum of Art, New York City. *Addresses on the Occasion of the Opening of the American Wing* (The Metropolitan Museum of Art, New York, 1925).

November 20   Address at a dinner of the Advisory Council of the Milbank Memorial Fund launching a health demonstration. Pamphlet.

November 29   Remarks at a Testimonial Banquet to His Excellency Jules Jusserand, New York City. Pamphlet.

December 30   Address at a meeting in memory of Mr. August Belmont and Mr. Samuel Gompers at the National Civic Federation, New York City. Pamphlet.

1925

    Roosevelt's Conduct of Foreign Affairs. Foreword to Volume XVIII, *The Works of Theodore Roosevelt*, Memorial Edition (Scribners, 1925).

February 13   American Ideals during the Past Half Century. Speech at a dinner of the Union League Club to celebrate his 80th birthday, New York City. *International Conciliation*, No. 210, May, 1925.

April   *Steps Toward Preserving Peace*. Article in *Foreign Affairs*, Volume 3 (1925), p. 351.

May 14   Address in response to the presentation of a gold medal awarded by the National Institute of Social Sciences, New York City. *Journal of the National Institute of Social Sciences*, Volume 10, p. 1.

June 15   Address at the Alumni Luncheon of the Sigma Phi Society at Hamilton College, Clinton, New York. *Sigma Phi Flame*, September, 1925, p. 30.

September 19   Address to the Undergraduates of Hamilton College, Clinton, New York. *School and Society*, October 24, 1925, p. 1.

October 1   The Codification of International Law. Report submitted to the 23rd Conference of the Interparliamentary Union

1925

on the Development of International Law, Washington, D. C. Printed in *American Journal of International Law*, Volume 19 (1925), p. 675.

October 23   Address at a dinner of the Pilgrims of the United States in honor of Sir Robert Horne, New York City. Pamphlet.

November 10   Address at a dinner in honor of the Hon. Charles Evans Hughes, New York City. Pamphlet.

1926

Memorial in *Arguments and Addresses of Joseph Hodges Choate*, edited by Frederick C. Hicks (West Publishing Company, 1926).

Preface to *James W. Wadsworth, Jr.*, by Henry F. Holthusen (Putnams, 1926).

January 4   Speech at a dinner of the Trustees of the National Research Council of the National Academy of Sciences, New York City. Typescript.

January 28   The Citizen's Part in Government. Remarks at a meeting of the Department on Public Education of the National Civic Federation, New York City. Pamphlet.

November 9   The Search for Truth in the Field of Law. Address at the Harvard Law School Endowment Fund Dinner, New York City. Pamphlet.

December 17   Address at a Reunion Dinner of the Delegates to the New York Constitutional Convention of 1915, New York City. Pamphlet.

December 28   America and Europe. Speech in accepting the Award of the Woodrow Wilson Foundation, New York City. *Foreign Affairs*, Special Supplement, Volume V (1927), No. 2.

1927

January 15   Address as Honorary Vice President at a luncheon of the State Charities Aid Association, New York City. Pamphlet.

January 27   Opinion in the matter of the Arbitration between the Bricklayers, Masons and Plasterers International Union and the Operative Plasterers and Cement Finishers International Association, under an agreement made at Atlantic City, October 2, 1925. Pamphlet.

1927
March 4
Address at the Centennial Celebration of the Sigma Phi Society, Schenectady, New York. *Sigma Phi Flame*, March, 1927, p. 15.

1929

Foreword to *The United States and the World Court*, by Philip C. Jessup (World Peace Foundation, 1929).

October 10
Address to Institut de Droit International at its 36th meeting, Briarcliff Manor, New York. *Annuaire de l'Institut de Droit International*, Volume 35, Part 2 (1929), p. 1.

October 11
Introduction of Prime Minister Ramsay MacDonald at a dinner in his honor given by the Council on Foreign Relations, New York City. *Foreign Affairs*, Special Supplement, Volume 8 (1929), No. 1.

1930
August 22
Response at the Annual Meeting of the American Bar Association upon the presentation to him of a Medal for Conspicuous Service in the Cause of American Jurisprudence, Chicago, Illinois. *American Bar Association Journal*, Volume 16 (1930), p. 639.

November 28
Public Opinion and Foreign Policy. Address at the opening of the new building of the Council on Foreign Relations, New York City. *Foreign Affairs*, Special Supplement, Volume 9 (1930), No. 2.

1931
January 21
Memorandum for Hearing and Statement at Hearing of the Senate Committee on Foreign Relations. *Hearing before the Committee on Foreign Relations of the United States Senate, Seventy-first Congress, Third Session, Relative to Protocols Concerning Adherence of the United States to the Court of International Justice*, pp. 1 and 42.

1932

Introduction to *The Life of Andrew Carnegie*, by Burton J. Hendrick (Doubleday Doran, 1932).

1933
January 18
Remarks during the Proceedings at the Presentation of a Memorial Portrait of General Tasker H. Bliss to the Council on Foreign Relations, New York City. Pamphlet.

February
The Origin of the Restatement of the Law. Article in *Oklahoma State Bar Journal*, Volume 3 (1933), p. 308.

1933
June 27

Remarks as Honorary President at the Convention Called to Act upon the Ratification of the Amendment to the United States Constitution Providing for the Repeal of the 18th Amendment, Albany, New York. *Proceedings* of the Convention, p. 17.

1934

Foreword to *Papers on Public Credit, Commerce and Finance*, by Alexander Hamilton, edited by Samuel Mc-Kee, Jr. (Columbia University Press, 1934).

February 28

Letter to William D. Guthrie on the Child Labor Amendment to the Constitution. New York *Times*, March 2, 1934.

May 25

Remarks as Chairman at the Annual Meeting of the Board of Trustees of the Carnegie Institution of Washington, Washington, D. C. Reprinted from the Minutes of the Annual Meeting by the Executive Committee. Pamphlet.

1935
February 15

Remarks at a dinner celebrating the 70th anniversary of the University Club of New York City and the 90th birthday of Elihu Root. Broadcast to the dinner from his home, New York City. Typescript.

INDEX

Abbott, Austin, i, 92.
Abbott, Laurence F., i, 21, 386; ii, 123.
Abbott, Lyman, i, 346-347, 387; ii, 260.
Absentee voting, ii, 307.
Abyssinia, ii, 108.
Academy of Political Science, ii, 296.
Adams, Charles Francis, i, 329; ii, 279, 373.
Adams, Claris, ii, 474.
Adams, Henry, i, 453.
Adatci, Japanese Minister to Belgium, ii, 419, 439.
Adee, Alvey A., i, 381, 383-384, 454-455, 457, 477, 494, 499, 501, 505-507; ii, 11, 46, 52, 54, 60, 62, 71, 77, 87, 90.
Admission to the Bar, ii, 468-470.
Advisory opinions, ii, 431, 438, 440.
Advocate of Peace, The, ii, 82.
Africa, ii, 56.
Agadir incident, The, i, 473.
Agassiz, Louis, i, 25.
Agua Prieta riots, ii, 253.
Aguinaldo, Emilio, i, 330-332, 335, 353, 361.
Ainsworth, General F. C., i, 262; ii, 112.
"Alabama" claims, i, 140; ii, 267.
Albany Evening Journal, The, ii, 146.
Albany Law Journal, The, i, 91.
Aldrich, Senator Nelson W., i, 232; ii, 166, 209, 217-220, 246-247.
Aldrich Monetary Commission, The, ii, 246-247.
Aldridge, George W., ii, 130, 153.
Alaskan Boundary dispute, i, 389-401, 412, 421, 452; ii, 89, 97, 264.
Alexander, James W., i, 436-437.
Alexander, Wallace M., ii, 33.
Alexis, Nord, i, 557.
Algeciras Conference, The, ii, 56-60, 310.
Alger, General Russell A., i, 216, 220, 222, 250, 252, 294, 296.
Allds, Jotham P., ii, 153.
Allen, Judge, i, 89.
Allen, Charles H., i, 350, 376-377.
Allen, Henry J., ii, 199-200, 345.
Allison, William B., ii, 139.
Alsop claim, The, i, 488; ii, 250.
Alverstone, Lord, i, 394, 397-401.
Amador de Guerrero, Manuel, i, 524-525.

Amapala, Honduras, i, 504, 507.
American Academy of Arts and Letters, The, i, 280.
American Academy at Rome, The, i, 280.
American Association for the Advancement of Science, The, ii, 470.
American Baptist Missionary Union, The, ii, 63.
American Bar Association, i, 285; ii, 468-470.
American Bridge Co., i, 102.
American China Development Co., The, ii, 51.
"American City," Brazil, i, 483.
American Exporter, The, i, 491.
American Federation of Arts, The, i, 280, 282; ii, 492.
American Federation of Labor, The, i, 268; ii, 8, 356, 483, 485.
American Foundation, The, ii, 430, 431.
American Indies Co., i, 289.
American Institute of Architects, The, i, 283.
American Law Institute, The, ii, 468, 470-472, 492.
American Peace Award, The, ii, 430.
American Red Cross, The, ii, 314.
American School for Classic Studies in Athens, The, ii, 492.
American Smelting and Refining Co., The, ii, 472.
American Society of International Law, The, ii, 260, 374, 458, 473.
American Surety Co., The, i, 187.
Anderson, Chandler P., i, 456, 512; ii, 91-92, 97-98, 109, 127, 271, 284, 320, 326, 344, 358, 368, 381, 383, 385-386, 399, 403, 451, 454, 464, 508.
Anderson, Mrs. Chandler P., ii, 508.
Anderson, William H., ii, 297.
Andrews, Avery D., i, 191.
Angell, James R., ii, 492.
Anglo-French entente, The, ii, 58.
Anglo-Japanese Alliance of 1902, The, ii, 4-5, 31, 42, 445-446, 450, 459, 460.
Anthony, Susan B., i, 13.
Anthracite coal strike of 1902, The, i, 272-277; ii, 482.
Antilla, Cuba, i, 296.

Due